ANTISEMITISM

ANTISEMITISM

A HISTORICAL ENCYCLOPEDIA
OF PREJUDICE AND PERSECUTION

VOLUME 1: A–K

Richard S. Levy, Editor

A B C ⬥ C L I O

Santa Barbara, California   Denver, Colorado   Oxford, England

4-20-2006
WW
₱ 92.50

Library of Congress Cataloging-in-Publication Data is available from the Library of Congress

Antisemitism : a historical encyclopedia of prejudice and persecution /
    Richard S. Levy, editor.
        p. cm.
Includes bibliographical references and index.
ISBN 1-85109-439-3 (hardback : alk. paper) — ISBN 1-85109-444-X (ebook)
1. Antisemitism—Europe, Western—Encyclopedias. 2. Antisemitism—History—Encyclopedias.
I. Levy, Richard S. II. Title.

DS146.E8A58 2005
305.892'4'009—dc22   2005009480

06 05 04 03 02 01   10 9 8 7 6 5 4 3 2 1

This book is also available on the World Wide Web as an eBook. Visit abc-clio.com for details.

ABC-CLIO, Inc.
130 Cremona Drive, P.O. Box 1911
Santa Barbara, California 93116–1911

This book is printed on acid-free paper.
Manufactured in the United States of America

CONTENTS

Contributors and Their Entries, xiii
Introduction, xxix

ANTISEMITISM
A HISTORICAL ENCYCLOPEDIA OF PREJUDICE AND PERSECUTION

CONTRIBUTORS
AND THEIR ENTRIES

John Abbott
Purdue University Calumet
Hammond, Indiana
  Agrarian League
  Memminger, Anton (1846–1923)
  Oberammergau Passion Play
  Ratzinger, Georg (1844–1899)
  Riehl, Wilhelm Heinrich (1823–1897)

Ernst Baltrusch
*Friedrich-Meinecke-Institut, Free University
  Berlin*
Berlin, Germany
  Roman Empire
  Roman Literature

Henryk Baran
University at Albany, SUNY
Albany, New York
  Doctors' Plot (1953)
  Leskov, Nikolai Semenovich (1831–1895)
  Protocols of the Elders of Zion on Trial
  Rabbi's Speech, The
  Solzhenitsyn, Aleksandr (1918–)

Lawrence Baron
San Diego State University
San Diego, California
  Hollywood, Treatment of Antisemitism in
  Night of Broken Glass (November 1938
    Pogrom)

Boris Barth
University of Konstanz
Konstanz, Germany
  Versailles Treaty

Scott Beekman
Ohio University
Athens, Ohio
  Pelley, William Dudley (1890–1965)

Dean Phillip Bell
Spertus Institute of Jewish Studies
Chicago, Illinois
  Court Jews
  Expulsions, Late Middle Ages
  Host Desecration
  Jud Süss (Joseph ben Issachar Süsskind Op-
    penheimer), (1692–1738)
  Middle Ages, High (1096–1343)
  Middle Ages, Late (1343–1453)
  Prague Massacre (1389)
  Rindfleisch Massacre (1298)
  Shabbetai Zevi
  Sorcery/Magic
  Yellow Badge

Steven Beller
George Washington University
Washington, D.C.
  Degeneration
  Herzl, Theodor (1860–1904)
  Nordau, Max (1849–1923)
  Weininger, Otto (1880–1903)
  Zionism

Joseph W. Bendersky
Virginia Commonwealth University
Richmond, Virginia
  Armed Forces of the United States
  Moseley, George Van Horn (1874–1960)
  Patton, Gen. George (1885–1945)

Doris L. Bergen
University of Notre Dame
Notre Dame, Indiana
  Churches under Nazism
  Deutsche Christen
  Institute for the Study and Eradication of
  Jewish Influence on German Church Life

Lena Berggren
Umeå University
Umeå, Sweden
  Sweden

Katell Berthelot
National Center for Scientific Research
Aix en Provence, France
  Misanthropy

Burton J. Bledstein
University of Illinois at Chicago
Chicago, Illinois
  Norris, Frank (1870–1902)
  Passing of the Great Race (1916)
  Twain, Mark (1835–1910)

Susan R. Boettcher
University of Texas, Austin
Austin, Texas
  Entdecktes Judenthum (1700, 1711)
  Reformation (1517–1648)
  Supersessionism

Dorothee Brantz
German Historical Institute
Washington, DC
  Kosher Slaughtering

Edward Bristow
Fordham University
New York, New York
  Alliance Israélite Universelle
  White Slavery

Matthias Brosch
Independent Scholar
Hamburg, Germany
  Bayreuth Circle
  Dinter, Artur (1876–1948)
  German Racial Freedom Party
  *Handbook of the Jewish Question (Anti-
    semites' Catechism)*
  Jews and the German State, The (1861)
  Myth of the Twentieth Century, The (1930)
  Sin against the Blood (1917)
  Yellow Star

Micha Brumlik
Johann Wolfgang Goethe University
Frankfurt, Germany
  Schopenhauer, Arthur (1788–1860)

Randall L. Bytwerk
Calvin College
Grand Rapids, Michigan
  Streicher, Julius (1885–1946)
  Stürmer, Der

Vicki Caron
Cornell University
Ithaca, New York
  Alsace

Jolene Chu
Jehovah's Witness Holocaust-Era Survivors Fund
Patterson, New York
  Jehovah's Witnesses

Geoffrey Cocks
Albion College
Albion, Michigan
  Psychoanalysis

Richard I. Cohen
Hebrew University
Jerusalem, Israel
  Gobineau, Joseph Arthur de (1816–1882)
  Jew Bill (1753)
  Renan, Ernest (1822–1893)
  Toland, John (1670–1722)
  Wandering Jew

Gaby Coldewey
Humboldt University
Berlin, Germany
  LANC–National Christian Defense League

Brian Crim
University of Maryland University College
Adelphi, Maryland
  Jew Census (1916)
  Roth, Alfred (1879–1940)

Philip A. Cunningham
*Center for Christian-Jewish Learning at
  Boston College*
Chesnut Hill, Massachusetts
  Gospels

Peter R. D'Agostino
University of Illinois at Chicago
Chicago, Illinois
    Coughlin, Charles E. (1891–1979)
    Cross and the Flag, The
    Smith, Gerald L. K. (1898–1976)
    Winrod, Gerald B. (1900–1957)

Peter J. Davies
University of Huddersfield
United Kingdom
    Le Pen, Jean-Marie (1928–)

Manfred Deselaers
Center for Dialogue and Prayer in Oświęcim-
    Auschwitz
Oświęcim, Poland
    Höss, Rudolf (1901–1947)

Carol Diethe
Middlesex University
London, United Kingdom
    Förster-Nietzsche, Elisabeth (1846–1935)

Betty A. Dobratz
Iowa State University
Ames, Iowa
    White Power Movement

Hans-Jörg Döhla
University of the Saarland
Saarbrücken, Germany
    Almohad Persecution

Marc Dollinger
San Francisco State University
San Francisco, California
    African American–Jewish Relations
    Black Nationalism
    Farrakhan, Louis (1933–)
    Immigration and Naturalization Laws
    (U.S.)
    Multiculturalism
    Nation of Islam
    New Left
    Secret Relationship between Blacks and Jews,
      The
    Student Nonviolent Coordinating
      Committee (SNCC)

William Collins Donahue
Rutgers University
New Brunswick, New Jersey
    Fontane, Theodor (1819–1898)
    Garbage, the City and Death, The
    Jews' Beech, The (1842)
    Mann, Thomas (1875–1955)

Gilles Dorival
University Aix-Marseille I
Aix-en Provence, France
    Origen (ca. 185–ca. 251 or 254)

Michael Dreyer
Northwestern University
Evanston, Illinois
    Frantz, Constantin (1817–1891)

Elizabeth A. Drummond
University of Southern Mississippi
Hattiesburg, Mississippi
    Class, Heinrich (1868–1953)
    German Eastern Marches Society
    If I Were the Kaiser (1912)
    Pan-German League
    Schemann, Ludwig (1852–1938)
    Treitschke, Heinrich von (1834–1896)

Albrecht Dümling
Center for Research of Antisemitism, Technical
    University of Berlin
Berlin, Germany
    Music, Nazi Purge of Jewish Influence in

Simone Duranti
Scuola Superiore S. Anna
Pisa, Italy
    Manifesto of the Racial Scientists (1938)
    October Roundup (Rome, 1943)
    Preziosi, Giovanni (1881–1945)
    Racial Laws (Italy)

Richard K. Emmerson
Medieval Academy of America
Cambridge, Massachusetts
    Antichrist

Frank Felsenstein
Ball State University
Muncie, Indiana
    Caricature, Anti-Jewish (Early)
    Hogarth, William (1697–1764)
    Pork
    Punch
    Rowlandson, Thomas (1756–1827)

Lars Fischer
King's College London
London, United Kingdom
    Feuerbach, Ludwig (1804–1872)
    Hegel, G. W. F. (1770–1831)
    Jewish Question, The (1843)
    Léon, Abram (1918–1944)
    Mehring, Franz (1846–1919)
    Young Hegelians

Samuel Fleischacker
University of Illinois at Chicago
Chicago, Illinois
    Kant, Immanuel (1724–1804)

Saul S. Friedman
Youngstown State University
Youngstown, Iowa
    Slave Trade and the Jews

Yvonne Friedman
Bar-Ilan University
Ramat-Gan, Israel
    Peter the Venerable (ca. 1092–1156)

Sandra Gambetti
College of Staten Island, CUNY
Staten Island, New York
    Alexandrian Pogrom
    Apion
    Arch of Titus
    Bar Kochba Revolt
    Claudius (10 BCE.–54 CE)
    Diaspora Revolt (115–117 CE)
    Manetho

Evelien Gans
Netherlands Institute for War Documentation
University of Amsterdam
Amsterdam, the Netherlands
    Netherlands in the Twentieth Century

Richard S. Geehr
Bentley College
Waltham, Massachusetts
    Aryan Theater
    Kralik, Richard von (1852–1934)
    Lueger, Karl (1844–1910)
    Müller-Guttenbrunn, Adam (1852–1923)

Jay Howard Geller
University of Tulsa
Tulsa, Oklahoma
    Bubis, Ignatz (1927–1999)
    German Democratic Republic (East Germany)
    Germany, Federal Republic of (West Germany)

Alexandra Gerstner
Free University Berlin
Berlin, Germany
    German National White Collar Employees Association (1893–1934)

Simone Gigliotti
Victoria University of Wellington
Wellington, New Zealand
    Eichmann Trial
    Holocaust
    Wannsee Conference

Hermann Glaser
Technical University of Berlin
Germany
    Theater, Nazi Purge of Jewish Influence in

Elaine Rose Glickman
Independent Scholar
Houston, Texas
    Haman

Ivo Goldstein
University of Zagreb
Zagreb, Croatia
    Croatia
    Croatia, Holocaust in
    Pavelić, Ante (1889–1959)
    Ustasha

Richard J. Golsan
Texas A&M University
College Station, Texas
  Crimes against Humanity (French Trials)
  Fascist Intellectuals (French)

David G. Goodman
University of Illinois
Urbana, Illinois
  Fugu Plan
  Japan

Julie V. Gottlieb
University of Sheffield
Sheffield, United Kingdom
  British Union of Fascists
  Webster, Nesta (1876–1960)
  Women and British Fascism

Keith R. Green
University of Illinois at Chicago
Chicago, Illinois
  Steiner, Rudolf (1861–1925)
  Theosophy

Kim M. Gruenwald
Kent State University
Kent, Ohio
  Colonial America
  Stuyvesant, Peter (1592–1672)

Michael Hagemeister
European University Viadrina
Frankfurt an Order, Germany
  Liutostanskii, Ippolit (1835–1915/1918?)
  Nilus, Sergei (1862–1929)
  Pranaitis, Justinas (1861–1917)
  Protocols of the Elders of Zion

Michaela Haibl
University of Vienna
Vienna, Austria
  Doré, Gustave (1832–1883)

Murray G. Hall
University of Vienna
Vienna, Austria
  Bettauer, Hugo (1872–1925)

Rita Haub
Archivum Monacense Societatis Jesu
Munich, Germany
  Jesuit Order

Peter Hayes
Northwestern University
Evanston, Illinois
  Aryanization (Germany)
  German Big Business and Antisemitism
    (1910–1945)

Ludger Heid
University of Duisburg
Duisburg, Germany
  Ostjuden

Armin Heinen
*Historical Institute, Technical University of
  Rhineland-Westphalia*
Aachen, Germany
  Iron Guard

Jonathan M. Hess
University of North Carolina
Chapel Hill, North Carolina
  Dohm, Christian Wilhelm von
    (1751–1820)
  Fichte, J. G. (1762–1814)
  Michaelis, Johann David (1717–1791)
  State-within-a-State

Laura Higgins
University of Illinois at Chicago
Chicago, Illinois
  Jung, Carl Gustav (1875–1961)

Klaus Hödl
Center for Jewish Studies, University of Graz
Graz, Austria
  Masculinity

Christhard Hoffmann
University of Bergen
Bergen, Norway
  Berlin Movement
  Christian Social Party (Germany)
  Henrici, Ernst (1854–1915)
  Neustettin Pogrom (1881)
  Stoecker, Adolf (1835–1909)

Colin Holmes
University of Sheffield
Sheffield, United Kingdom
   Boer War (1899–1902)
   British Brothers League
   Cause of World Unrest, The
   Gwynne, H. A. (1865–1950)
   Hobson, J. A. (1858–1940)
   Webb, Beatrice (1858–1943)

Klaus Holz
Evangelisches Studienwerk e.V. Villgst
Schwerte, Germany
   Anti-Zionism in the USSR
   "Jewish" Press
   Purges, Soviet

Brian Horowitz
Tulane University
New Orleans, Lousiana
   Russia, Imperial

Gregor Hufenreuter
Free University Berlin
Berlin, Germany
   Central Association of German Citizens of
     Jewish Faith
   League against Antisemitism
   Stauff, Philipp (1876–1923)

Jack Jacobs
John Jay College, CUNY
New York, New York
   Marx, Karl (1818–1883)
   Socialists on Antisemitism

Stephan Jaeger
University of Manitoba
Winnipeg, Manitoba, Canada
   Varnhagen von Ense, Rahel Levin
     (1771–1833)

Christoph Jahr
Humboldt University
Berlin, Germany
   Pückler, Count Walter von (1860–1924)

Paul B. Jaskot
DePaul University
Chicago, Illinois
   Degenerate Art
   Eichmann, Adolf (1906–1962)
   Himmler, Heinrich (1900–1945)
   Schwarze Korps, Das

Robert D. Johnston
University of Illinois at Chicago
Chicago, Illinois
   Frank, Leo (1884–1915)
   Ku Klux Klan (1915–1941)
   Populist Movement
   Watson, Tom (1856–1922)

Jeremy Jones
Executive Council of Australian Jewry
Sydney, Australia
   Australia

Jonathan Judaken
University of Memphis
Memphis, Tennessee
   Action Française (1899–1945)
   Barrès, Maurice (1862–1923)
   Camelots du Roi (1908–1936)
   Drumont, Édouard (1844–1917)
   France (1789–1939)
   France juive, La (1886)
   Maurras, Charles (1868–1952)
   Sartre, Jean-Paul (1905–1980)
   Stavisky Affair (1933–1934)

Gema A. Junco
Florida International University
Miami, Florida
   Spain under Franco (1938–1975)

Rainer Kampling
Seminar for Catholic Theology, Free University
   Berlin
Berlin, Germany
   Adversus Iudaeos
   Capistrano, John of (1386–1456)
   Chrysostom, John (349–407)
   Deicide
   Demonstratio Adversus Iudaeos
   Dialogue with Trypho
   Iconography, Christian

Jonathan Karp
Binghamton University
Binghamton, New York
   Banker, Jewish
   Capital: Useful versus Harmful
   Coin Clipping
   Shylock

Ralph Keen
University of Iowa
Iowa City, Iowa
   Erasmus (1466–1536)
   Luther, Martin (1483–1546)
   Melanchthon, Philipp (1497–1560)
   On the Jews and Their Lies (1543)
   Reuchlin, Johann (1455–1522)

Peter Kenez
University of California, Santa Cruz
Santa Cruz, California
   Hungary, Pogroms in (1946)
   Hungary, Post-Soviet
   Jewish Anti-Fascist Committee

Emil Kerenji
University of Michigan
Ann Arbor, Michigan
   Ljotić, Dimitrije (1891–1945)

David I. Kertzer
Brown University
Providence, Rhode Island
   Civiltà Cattolica
   Mortara Affair
   Papacy, Modern

Hillel J. Kieval
Washington University
St. Louis, Missouri
   Ritual Murder (Modern)

Deeana Klepper
Boston University
Boston, Massachusetts
   Franciscan Order
   Dominican Order

John D. Klier
University College London
London, United Kingdom
   Black Hundreds

   Kishinev Pogrom (1903)
   Krushevan, Pavolaki (1860–1909)
   May Laws
   Odessa Pogroms
   Pale of Settlement
   Petliura, Symon (1879–1926)
   Pobedonostsev, Konstantin (1827–1907)
   Pogroms (Russian, 1881)
   Purishkevich, Vladimir Mitrofanovich
     (1879–1920)
   Russia, Revolution of 1905
   Russian Civil War

Christoph Knueppel
Independent Scholar
Herford, Germany
   Imperial Hammer League
   Settlement Heimland

James Kollenbroich
University of Illinois at Chicago
Chicago, Illinois
   Hirschfeld, Magnus (1868–1935)
   Homophobia

Frederic M. Kopp
Columbia College
Chicago, Illinois
   Nazi Rock

Tom Kramer
University of Sydney
Sydney, Australia
   "Blood for Trucks" (Brand-Grosz Mission)
   Horthy, Miklós (1868–1957)
   Hungary (1848–1944)
   Hungary, Holocaust in
   Jewish Council (Budapest, 1944)
   Kallay, Miklós (1887–1967)
   Numerus Clausus (Hungary)
   Szalasi, Ferenc (1897–1946)
   Tiszaeszlar Ritual Murder (1882)
   White Terror (Hungary)

Virgil I. Krapauskas
Chowan College
Murfreesboro, North Carolina
   Lithuania
   Lithuania, Holocaust in
   Lithuania, Post-Soviet

Carsten Kretschmann
Johann Wolfgang Goethe University
Frankfurt am Main, Germany
  Boniface Society for Catholic Germany
  Rohling, August (1839–1931)
  Talmud Jew, The
  Ultramontanism

Alfred Kube
Historical Museum Bremerhaven
Bremerhaven, Germany
  Göring, Hermann (1893–1946)

Lisa Moses Leff
Southwestern University
Georgetown, Texas
  Fourier, Charles (1772–1837)
  Gougenot des Mousseaux, Henri
    (1805–1876)
  Infamous Decree (1808)
  Proudhon, Pierre-Joseph (1809–1865)
  Toussenel, Alphonse (1803–1885)
  Veuillot, Louis (1813–1883)

Russel Lemmons
Jacksonville State University
Jacksonville, Alabama
  Angriff, Der
  German National People's Party
  Goebbels, Joseph (1897–1945)
  Hugenberg, Alfred (1865–1951)

Jeffrey Lesser
Emory University
Atlanta, Georgia
  Brazil

Jay Levinson
Independent Scholar
Jerusalem, Israel
  Cuba

David W. Levy
University of Oklahoma
Norman, Oklahoma
  Dewey, Melvil (1851–1931)

Richard S. Levy
University of Illinois at Chicago
Chicago, Illinois
  Ahlwardt, Hermann (1846–1914)
  Antisemites' Petition (1880–1881)
  Antisemitic Correspondence
  Antisemitic Political Parties (Germany,
    1879–1914)
  Antisemitism, Etymology of
  Anti-Zionism
  Böckel, Otto (1859–1923)
  Fritsch, Theodor (1852–1933)
  Glagau, Otto (1834–1892)
  Judaism as an Alien Phenomenon
    (1862–1863)
  Liebermann von Sonnenberg, Max
    (1848–1911)
  Marr, Wilhelm (1819–1904)
  Mirror to the Jews, A
  Our Demands on Modern Jewry
  Victory of Jewry over Germandom, The
    (1879)
  Word about Our Jews, A (1880)

David Isadore Lieberman
Brandeis University
Waltham, Massachusetts
  Evolutionary Psychology
  Herder, J. G. (1744–1803)
  Musicology and National Socialism
  Nietzsche, Friedrich (1844–1900)

Albert S. Lindemann
University of California, Santa Barbara
Santa Barbara, California
  Beilis Case (1911–1913)
  Chmielnicki Massacres (1648–1649)
  Damascus Blood Libel (1840)
  Disraeli, Benjamin (1804–1881)
  Dreyfus Affair
  Jewish Question
  Mosley, Oswald (1896–1980)
  Mussolini, Benito (1883–1945)
  Rothschilds

Jay Lockenour
Temple University
Philadelphia, Pennsylvania
  Ludendorff, Erich (1865–1937)
  Ludendorff, Mathilde (1877–1966)
  Ludendorff Publishing House

Kevin Madigan
Harvard Divinity School
Cambridge, Massachusetts
  Augustine of Hippo (354–430)
  Church Councils (Early)
  Church Fathers
  Constantine, Emperor (274–337 CE)
  Gregory the Great, Pope (590–604)
  Judensau

Ellen Martin
Johann Wolfgang Goethe University
Frankfurt/Main, Germany
  Pfefferkorn, Johannes (1468/1469–1522)

Jonathan Marwil
University of Michigan
Ann Arbor, Michigan
  Antisemitism, Accusations of
  Lindbergh, Charles (1902–1974)

David A. Meier
Dickinson State University
Dickinson, North Dakota
  Militia Movement

Gerd Mentgen
Arye Maimon Institute for the History of the Jews, University of Trier
Trier, Germany
  Crusades

Matthias Messmer
International Research and Consulting Centre
Fribourg, Switzerland
  Ukraine, Post-Soviet

Brigitte Mihok
Center for Research of Antisemitism, Technical University of Berlin
Berlin, Germany
  Antonescu, Ion (1882–1946)
  Romania, Holocaust in

Victor A. Mirelman
West Suburban Temple Har Zion
River Forest, Illinois
  Argentina
  Buenos Aires Pogroms (1910, 1919)
  Tacuara

Richard Mitten
Weissman Center for International Business, Baruch College, CUNY
New York, New York
  Austria
  Waldheim Affair
  Wiesenthal-Kreisky Controversy

Douglas Moggach
University of Ottawa
Ottawa, Ontario, Canada
  Bauer, Bruno (1809–1882)

Birgitta Mogge-Stubbe
Rheinischer Merkur
Bonn, Germany
  Dühring, Eugen (1833–1921)
  Jewish Question as a Racial, Moral, and Cultural Problem, The

Jonathan Morse
University of Hawaii at Manoa
Honolulu, Hawaii
  Belloc, Hilaire (1870–1953)
  Chesterton, G. K. (1874–1936)
  Eliot, T. S. (1888–1965)
  English Literature of the Twentieth Century
  Pound, Ezra (1885–1972)
  Wharton, Edith (1862–1937)

Gary Saul Morson
Northwestern University
Evanston, Illinois
  Dostoevsky, Fyodor (1821–1881)

Johann Baptist Müller
University of Stuttgart
Stuttgart, Germany
  Stahl, Friedrich Julius (1802–1861)

Cary Nathenson
Northwestern University
Evanston, Illinois
  Film Industry, Nazi Purge of Jewish Influence in
  Film Propaganda, Nazi

Hannah Newman
Independent Scholar
Ariel, Israel
    Aquarius, Age of
    Bailey, Alice A. (1880–1949)
    Blavatsky, Helena P. (1831–1891)
    Devi, Savitri (1905–1982)
    Invocation, The Great
    Jewish Force
    New Age
    The Plan of the Hierarchy
    Secret Doctrine, The (1888)

Sören Niemann-Findeisen
Hamburg University of Economics and Politics
Hamburg, Germany
    Wells, H. G. (1866–1946)

Donald L. Niewyk
Southern Methodist University
Dallas, Texas
    Social Democratic Party (Germany,
        1875–1933)
    Weimar

Dietrich Orlow
Boston University
Boston, Massachusetts
    National Socialist German Workers' Party
    Nazi Party Program

Steven Paulsson
University of Oxford
Oxford, United Kingdom
    Boycott of 1912 (Poland)
    Dmowski, Roman (1864–1939)
    Ghetto Benches
    Hlond, August (1881–1948)
    Jedwabne
    Kolbe, Maksymilian (1894–1941)
    Moczar, Mieczysław (1913–1986)
    National Democrats (Poland)
    Poland (1918–1989)
    Poland since 1989
    Purge of 1968 (Poland)
    Twilight of Israel, The (1932)

John T. Pawlikowski
Catholic Theological Union
Chicago, Illinois
    Pius IX, Pope (1792–1878)
    Pius XII, Pope (1876–1958)
    Vatican Council, First (1869–1870)
    Vatican Council, Second (1962–1965)

Anton Pelinka
University of Innsbruck
Innsbruck, Austria
    Vogelsang, Karl von (1818–1890)

Edward Peters
University of Pennsylvania
Philadelphia, Pennsylvania
    Innocent III (1160/61–1216)
    Inquisition
    Lateran Council, Fourth (1215)
    Raymund of Peñafort (1175/1180?–1275)
    Talmud Trials

Fritz Petrick
Historical Institute of Ernst Moritz Arndt
    University
Greifswald, Germany
    Best, Werner (1903–1989)

Larry L. Ping
Southern Utah University
Cedar City, Utah
    Debit and Credit (1855)
    Freytag, Gustav (1816–1895)

Wendy Plotkin
Arizona State University
Tempe, Arizona
    Restrictive Covenants

Michael Posluns
St. Thomas University
Fredericton, New Brunswick, Canada
    Canada

Pamela M. Potter
University of Wisconsin
Madison, Wisconsin
    Judaism in Music (1850, 1869)
    Wagner, Cosima (1837–1930)
    Wagner, Richard (1813–1883)

Alfredo Mordechai Rabello
Hebrew University
Jerusalem, Israel
   Justinian Code (Corpus Iuris Civilis)
   Theodosian Code

Benjamin Ravid
Brandeis University
Waltham, Massachusetts
   Ghetto

Ian Reifowitz
Empire State College, SUNY
Old Westbury, New York
   Bloch, Joseph Samuel (1850–1923)

Helmut Reinalter
University of Innsbruck
Innsbruck, Austria
   Freemasonry

Paul Reitter
Ohio State University
Columbus, Ohio
   Benn, Gottfried(1886–1956)
   Billroth, Theodor (1829–1894)
   Book Burning (May 10, 1933)
   George, Stefan (1868–1933)
   Lanz von Liebenfels, Jörg (1874–1954)
   List, Guido von (1848–1919)
   Mahler-Werfel, Alma (1879–1964)
   Rosenberg, Alfred (1893–1946)
   Self-Hatred, Jewish

Johannes Rogalla von Bieberstein
University of Bielefeld
Bielefeld, Germany
   Judeo-Bolshevism

Daniel Rogers
University of South Alabama
Mobile, Alabama
   Historians' Controversy
   Neo-Nazism, German

Stefan Rohrbacher
Institute for Jewish Studies, Heinrich Heine University
Düsseldorf, Germany
   Hep-Hep Riots (1819)

Susan Rosa
Northeastern Illinois University
Chicago, Illinois
   Balzac, Honoré de (1799–1850)

Emily Rose
Princeton University
Princeton, New Jersey
   Hugh of Lincoln
   Ritual Murder (Medieval)
   Simon of Trent
   Usury
   Well Poisoning
   William of Norwich (d. 1144)

Vadim Rossman
University of Texas
Austin, Texas
   Rozanov, Vasilii (1856–1919)
   Russia, Post-Soviet
   Russian Orthodox Church (ROC)

Bernd Rother
Federal Chancellor Willy Brandt Foundation
Berlin, Germany
   Auto-da-Fé
   Ferrer, Vincente (1350–1419)
   Pure Blood Laws
   Spain, Riots of 1391
   Torquemada, Tomás de (1420–1498)

Jens Rybak
University of Bielefeld
Bielefeld, Germany
   Arndt, Ernst Moritz (1769–1860)

Jeffrey L. Sammons
Yale University
New Haven, Connecticut
   Biarritz (1868)
   Heine, Heinrich (1797–1856)
   Heine Monument Controversy
   Raabe, Wilhelm (1831–1910)
   Young Germany

Karl A. Schleunes
University of North Carolina
Greensboro, North Carolina
   Boycott of Jewish Shops (Germany, 1933)
   Nazi Legal Measures against Jews (1933–1939)
   Nuremberg Laws (1935)
   Purge of the German Civil Service (1933)

Charlotte Schönbeck
Pedagogical University of Heidelberg
Heidelberg, Germany
　　Physics, "German" and "Jewish"

Ralph Schoolcraft III
Texas A&M University
College Station, Texas
　　Bardèche, Maurice (1909–1998)
　　Brasillach, Robert (1909–1945)
　　Céline, Louis-Ferdinand (1894–1961)
　　Darquier de Pellepoix, Louis (1897–1980)
　　Rebatet, Lucien (1903–1972)

Alexander Schürmann-Emanuely
Independent Scholar
Vienna, Austria
　　LICA—International League against Anti-
　　　semitism

Frederick M. Schweitzer
Manhattan College
Bronx, New York
　　Zündel, Ernst (1939–)

Alyssa Goldstein Sepinwall
California State University, San Marcos
San Marcos, California
　　Grégoire, Henri-Baptiste (1750–1831)
　　Voltaire, François-Marie-Arouet de
　　　(1694–1778)

Esther Shabot
Excelsior
Mexico City, Mexico
　　Mexico

Milton Shain
University of Cape Town
Cape Town, South Africa
　　South Africa

Amy Hill Shevitz
California State University, Northridge
Northridge, California
　　Adams, Henry Brooks (1838–1918)
　　General Orders No. 11 (1862)
　　Restricted Public Accommodations,
　　　United States
　　Seligman-Hilton Affair (1877)
　　United States

Frederick J. Simonelli
Mount St. Mary's College
Los Angeles, California
　　American Nazi Party
　　Carto, Willis (1926–)
　　Christian Identity Movement
　　Liberty Lobby
　　Rockwell, George Lincoln (1918–1967)

Helmut Walser Smith
Vanderbilt University
Nashville, Tennessee
　　Center Party
　　Konitz Ritual Murder (1900)
　　Kulturkampf
　　Xanten Ritual Murder (1891–1892)

Roderick Stackelberg
Gonzaga University
Spokane, Washington
　　Bartels, Adolf (1862–1945)
　　Chamberlain, Houston Stewart
　　　(1855–1927)
　　Förster, Bernhard (1843–1889)
　　Hentschel, Willibald (1858–1947)
　　Lagarde, Paul de (1827–1891)
　　Lange, Friedrich (1852–1917)
　　Lienhard, Friedrich (1865–1929)
　　Völkisch Movement and Ideology

Michael E. Staub
Bowling Green State University
Bowling Green, Ohio
　　Rosenberg Trial

Roni Stauber
Stephen Roth Institute, Tel Aviv University
Tel Aviv, Israel
　　Auschwitz Lie
　　Faurisson, Robert (1929–)
　　Holocaust Denial, Negationism, and Revi-
　　　sionism
　　Institute for Historical Review (IHR)
　　Irving, David (1938–)
　　Leuchter Report

Alan E. Steinweis
University of Nebraska
Lincoln, Nebraska
　　Nazi Cultural Antisemitism
　　Nazi Research on the Jewish Question

Norman A. Stillman
University of Oklahoma
Norman, Oklahoma
   Arab Antisemitic Literature
   Arab Boycott
   Arafat, Yasir (1929–2004)
   Constantine Pogrom (1934)
   Farhud (1941)
   Hamas
   Hussaini, Mufti Hajj Amin al- (1895–1974)
   Iranian Revolution
   Islam and the Jews
   Islamic Diaspora
   Islamic Fundamentalism
   Khomeini, Ayatollah (1902–1989)
   Mohammed (ca. 570–632)
   Muslim Brotherhood
   Nasser, Gamal Abdel (1918–1970)

Kenneth Stow
University of Haifa
Haifa, Israel
   Agobard (779–840)
   Expulsions, High Middle Ages
   Middle Ages, Early (430–1096)
   Paul
   Visigothic Spain

Werner Suppanz
University of Graz
Graz, Austria
   Christian Social Party (Austria)
   Linz Program (1882)
   Pan-Germans (Austria)
   Schönerer, Georg von (1842–1921)

Adam Sutcliffe
University of Illinois
Urbana, Illinois
   Barruel, Augustin (1741–1820)
   Diderot, Denis (1713–1784)
   Memoirs Illustrating the History of Jacobinism
      (1797–1803)
   Philosemitism

Mark Swartzburg
University of North Carolina
Chapel Hill, North Carolina
   Aryan Paragraph
   Germanic Order
   Rathenau, Walther (1867–1922)

Reventlow, Ernst zu (1869–1943)
"Three Hundred," The
Thule Society

John F. Sweets
University of Kansas
Lawrence, Kansas
   Vichy

Marcia G. Synnott
University of South Carolina
Columbia, South Carolina
   Numerus Clausus (United States)

Guillaume de Syon
Albright College
Reading, Pennsylvania
   J Stamp
   Restitution (Switzerland)
   Switzerland

Bożena Szaynok
Wroclaw University
Wroclaw, Poland
   Kielce Pogrom (1946)
   Stalinization of Eastern Europe
   Slánský Trial

Melissa Jane Taylor
University of South Carolina
Columbia, South Carolina
   Evian Conference
   Long, Breckinridge (1881–1958)
   Oswego Camp

Susanne Terwey
Humboldt University
Berlin, Germany
   Britain (1870–1939)
   Maxse, James Leopold (1864–1932)

Tatjana Tönsmeyer
Humboldt University
Berlin, Germany
   Hlinka Guard
   Slovakia, Holocaust in
   Sudeten Germans
   Tiso, Jozef (1887–1947)

Leif P. Torjesen
California State University, Dominguez Hills
Carson, California
    Heidegger, Martin (1889–1976)

William Totok
*Study Group for the History and Culture of East
    Central and Southeast Europe*
Berlin, Germany
    Romania (1878–1920)
    Romania, Post-Soviet

Aryeh Tuchman
Anti-Defamation League
New York, New York
    Circumcision
    Dietary Laws
    Duke, David (1950–)
    Internet
    Talmud

Tzvetan Tzvetanov
Free University of Berlin
Berlin, Germany
    Bulgaria, Holocaust in
    Dahn, Felix (1834–1912)

Istvan Varkonyi
Temple University
Philadelphia, Pennsylvania
    Freud, Sigmund (1856–1939)
    Kraus, Karl (1874–1936)
    Schnitzler, Arthur (1862–1931)

George Vascik
Miami University
Hamilton, Ohio
    German Peasant League
    German Students, Association of
    Hahn, Diederich (1859–1918)
    Tivoli Program (1892)
    Sombart, Werner (1863–1941)
    Wagener, Hermann (1815–1889)

Nadia Valman
*Parkes Centre for the Study of Jewish/Non-Jewish
    Relations, University of Southampton*
Southampton, United Kingdom
    Coningsby (1844)
    Dickens, Charles (1812–1870)
    Dracula

English Literature from Chaucer to Wells
Svengali
Trollope, Anthony (1815–1882)

Petr Vašíček
Independent Scholar
Berlin, Germany
    Polná Ritual Murder (1899)

Jeffrey Veidlinger
Indiana University
Bloomington, Indiana
    Stalin, Joseph (1879–1953)
    USSR

Brian E. Vick
University of Sheffield
Sheffield, United Kingdom
    Christian State
    Dining Society, Christian-German
    Grimm, Brothers
    Verjudung

Clemens Vollnhals
*Hannah Arendt Institute for the Study of
    Totalitarianism, Technical University Dresden*
Dresden, Germany
    Gemlich Letter
    Hitler's Speeches (Early)
    Hitler's *Table Talk*

Dirk Walter
Münchner Merkur
Munich, Germany
    Culture-Antisemitism or Pogrom-Anti-
        semitism? (1919)
    Desecration of Cemeteries and Synagogues
        in Germany since 1919
    German Racial League for Defense and De-
        fiance
    Pudor, Heinrich (1865–1943)
    Scheunenviertel Pogrom (1923)

Henry Wassermann
Open University of Israel
Tel Aviv, Israel
    Caricature, Anti-Jewish (Modern)
    Fliegende Blätter
    Gartenlaube, Die
    Kladderadatsch
    Simplicissimus

Horst Weigelt
University of Bamberg
Bamberg, Germany
    Lavater, Johann Kaspar (1741–1801)

Richard Weikart
California State University, Stanislaus
Turlock, California
    Eugenics
    Racism, Scientific
    Social Darwinism

Gerhard L. Weinberg
University of North Carolina
Chapell Hill, North Carolina
    Hitler, Adolf (1889–1945)
    Hitler's "Prophecy" (January 30, 1939)
    Mein Kampf

Wolfgang Weiss
University of Munich
Munich, Germany
    Jew of Malta, The
    Shakespeare, William (1564–1616)

Edith Wenzel
*Institute for Germanistics and General
    Literary Sciences, Technical University of
    Rhineland-Westphalia*
Aachen, Germany
    Passion Plays, Medieval

Edward B. Westermann
School of Advanced Air and Space Studies
Montgomery, Alabama
    Commissar Order
    Einsatzgruppen
    Order Police

Cornelia B. Wilhelm
University of Munich
Munich, Germany
    German-American Bund

Benn Williams
University of Illinois at Chicago
Chicago, Illinois
    Vallat, Xavier (1891–1972)

George S. Williamson
University of Alabama
Tuscaloosa, Alabama
    Fries, Jakob Friedrich (1773–1843)

Andreas Winnecken
Reha-Zentrum Soltau
Soltau, Germany
    Youth Movement (German)

Victoria Saker Woeste
American Bar Foundation
Chicago, Illinois
    American Jewish Committee and Anti-
        defamation Efforts in the United States
    Dearborn Independent and *The International
        Jew*
    Ford, Henry (1863–1947)

Ulrich Wyrwa
*Center for Research of Antisemitism, Technical
    University of Berlin*
Berlin, Germany
    1848
    Emancipation
    Burschenschaften

Krista Zach
*Institute for German Culture and History in
    Southeast Europe*
Munich, Germany
    Codreanu, Corneliu Zelea (1899–1938)
    Cuza, A. C. (1857–1946)
    Goga, Octavian (1881–1938)

Lizabeth Zack
University of South Carolina, Spartanburg
Spartanburg, South Carolina
    Algeria
    Régis, Max (1873–1950)

Karl Zieger
University of Valenciennes
Valenciennes, France
    Zola, Émile (1840–1902)

INTRODUCTION

This encyclopedia is the first of its kind. Its mission is straightforward: to present to the educated reader the most accurate, thorough, and up-to-date information on antisemitism in an unbiased manner. That mission, however, is complicated in unique ways by the subject of antisemitism Although decisions about focus, selection, and length of entries are common to all encyclopedias, few if any works of this type have dealt with a phenomenon so capable of arousing our passions. Indeed, even the very definition of antisemitism is earnestly disputed.

Problems of Definition
Both antisemitism and its target, the Jews, elude convenient definition. Furthermore, antisemites do not accord Jews the right to define themselves. Early in his career, Leon Trotsky, Lenin's lieutenant in the Russian Revolution of 1917, ceased describing himself as in any way Jewish. Even so, his character and his deeds were subjected to repeated antisemitic attacks. On the strength of his participation and that of several others who did not acknowledge themselves as Jews, the politics and ideology of the entire Communist movement came to be considered by many as a sinister Jewish invention. Benjamin Disraeli, born a Jew, converted to Christianity yet continued to see himself (and was seen by most of his contemporaries) as somehow Jewish. Another convert, Karl Marx, retained no such obvious attachment, although he, too, attracted antisemitic attention and still does. Several historical figures who were clearly *not* Jewish, including popes, the black boxer Jack Johnson, Theodore and Franklin D. Roosevelt, and many scions of ancient Prussian aristocratic families, were "Jews," at least according to some antisemitic writers and politicians. By contrast, nearly every prominent reviler of Jews, from Torquemada and Luther to Hitler and Stalin, has at one time or another been identified by friends or foes as being "of Jewish blood." As in the past, Jews—both real and imaginary—are too diverse. The variety of their identities invites confusion and presents antisemites with welcome opportunities to "prove" whatever it is they feel called upon to prove. Just who is a Jew is, therefore, a question that needs to be addressed in *Antisemitism: A Historical Encyclopedia of Prejudice and Persecution.*

This work, which strives for comprehensiveness, has "solved" the problem of definition arbitrarily. It must be left to antisemites—moved almost exclusively by their fantasies, fears, and hatreds—to decide who shall be included for discussion in this forum. No matter how the target of these animosities defines him or herself, if a person's Jewish identity—self-acknowledged, denied, ignored, or totally fabricated—is at issue, then it is appropriate to include that person in these volumes. "The Jew Mark Twain," as he was labeled by Viennese antisemites in the late 1890s, is a case in point. Twain was not Jewish, but his response to antisemitic slurs is necessarily a part of the history of antisemitism and of this encyclopedia. Antisemites customarily deal in great generalizations, blanket indictments, and all-encompassing theories without respect for the laws of evidence or rational analysis. Indeed, antisemitism cannot survive the making of fine distinctions concerning Jews or what constitutes Jewishness. An encyclopedia of antisemitism must recognize this flawed mentality and give it adequate representation.

The other problem of definition is not so simply resolved. An encyclopedia of antisemitism's scope in time and space will depend on the conception of the word's meaning. The term *antisemitism,* used to describe an ideology and a politics, is only a little more than a century old. The word *antisemite* and the abstraction *antisemitism* in this sense first appeared in print in Germany around 1879, a somewhat belated response to the granting of equal rights to Jews. Initially, the new terms coexisted comfortably with older expressions such as *Jew-hatred, Jew-baiting,* or *Judeophobia.* But soon, anti-Jewish activists, their opponents, and neutral commentators all began making frequent use of *antisemitism,* thereby gaining acceptance for the new word in most modern languages. Its extremely rapid adoption after 1879—the process of its absorption into all the major European languages was complete by 1894—reflected a wide recognition that traditional patterns and motives of persecution had so changed that a new word was now needed to describe a new sort of anti-Jewish activist and activity and the institutions they hastily created: political parties, journals, newspapers, and reform clubs at the grass roots.

This is not to suggest that there was a clean break with the past in 1879 or that the changes were precisely or universally understood. The relationship between traditional Jew-hatred and antisemitism was sensed at the time, and it still has relevance for an encyclopedia dedicated to this subject: antisemitism proceeds from preexisting, deeply rooted anti-Jewish sentiments and is difficult to conceive of without the motivating force of antagonism. This connection notwithstanding, there are many who think it anachronistic to apply the term to the anti-Jewish prejudice and persecution found in antiquity or the Middle Ages. Others argue for a strict delineation between cognition and action, that is, between the ways Jews are thought of and the ways Jews are acted upon.

Popular usage is not so fastidious, however. Use of the word *antisemitism* to describe thinking and behavior intended to do harm to the reputation, rights, and/or physical well-being of Jews for a wide variety of motives and throughout history may lack absolute precision as a definition, but it has the advantage of allowing this encyclopedia to treat the subject broadly and usefully. Even so, many problems remain.

Antisemitism, anti-Jewish stereotyping, and Jew-hatred in whatever degree are phenomena of the Diaspora. As long as Jews had a country, there was little to distinguish between the kind of hostility they met with and that experienced by any other people who constituted a recognizable group, community, or nation. It is not sensible to describe the Canaanites as antisemites. Only from the third century BCE and *outside* ancient Israel did anti-Jewish hostility take on distinctive features. Thus, there is no need in this encyclopedia for an entry on the Jewish Wars (66–73 and 132–135 CE) waged by the Romans in Palestine: they were no different from Rome's other brutal wars of repression against rebellious peoples. However, the status of Jews *within* the Roman Empire does require treatment because it displayed unique characteristics that applied to no other people the Romans held in their power.

Antisemitism, broadly conceived, has not only a lengthier history, lengthier than any other species of ethnic or cultural enmity, but is also the only prejudice that has scriptural sanction. The English and Irish may despise one another, but neither group can open the Bible and find there that it is right and even divinely ordained to do so. The Balkan peoples' outbursts of genocidal fury, which so stunned the world in the last decade of the twentieth century, apparently required only minimal ideological or cultural justification beyond orally transmitted "folk wisdom" and inflammatory newspaper stories. Hostility toward Jews, by contrast, has produced an enormous body of literature; permeated Christian and, now, Islamic culture; found expression in the arts, high and low; and informed both the theory and the practice of politics all over the globe. Other ethnic groups, religious organizations, and economic collectives have been objects of suspicion and wild accusation, but rarely are they described as being able to exercise satanic evil as omnipotently, ruthlessly, and universally as the Jews.

Given the immense reach of anti-Jewish antagonism across time and space, it seems obvious that no reference work can do the subject total justice. The goal ought to be the highest attainable degree of completeness, breadth, and depth of coverage. But there is a pitfall inherent in the pursuit of this aim. The encyclopedia could become a compendium of people past and present who actually harmed or thought about harming Jews or said harmful things about them—a who's who of Jew-hatred. Alas, a reference work based on this catchall principle would require many, many volumes. But there is no need for such a compilation because something very much like it has already been done, although with a thoroughly jaundiced set of motives and evaluations. German antisemites at the end of the nineteenth century gleefully produced such tomes, combing the classics of world literature, canvassing celebrities for their views, and mining popular culture for anything even slightly insulting to Jews. There is no need to replicate this intellectually barren endeavor in the twenty-first century. Even when not motivated by malice, a reference work that seeks merely to compile a list of antisemitic offenders would be of little value because it cannot help us understand the rationales, functions, attractions, or effects of this prejudice.

To prevent this encyclopedia from becoming a crude who is/who is not exercise, a criterion of significant antisemitic and anti-Jewish thought or action has to be adhered to, and that standard ought to be set rigorously high. Personal quirkiness or the unthinking resort to inherited prejudice, for example, should not, by itself, qualify one for inclusion. Nor should imagined characters and comments found in deliberated but fictional texts necessarily suffice. Ernest Hemingway produced a notable antisemitic character in *The Sun Also Rises,* and F. Scott Fitzgerald's portrait of Meyer Wolfsheim in *The Great Gatsby* pointedly connected Jewishness and crookedness. Yet neither author often revisited this theme in his body of work, let alone attempted to mobilize anti-Jewish feeling for any detectable personal or political purpose. No doubt, they were prejudiced and influential individuals whose attitudes toward Jews need to be registered in a reference book on antisemitism. But many others involved themselves much more enthusiastically and systematically—and with greater effect—in "combating Jewish evil" than these individuals. It would be uninstructive to lump the two authors together with those others and accord them identical treatment. In the present work, this problem is addressed by means of a general essay on the representation of Jews in twentieth-century English-language literature rather than by separate entries on Hemingway and Fitzgerald.

Of course, individual contributors to this encyclopedia work from differing ideas of what constitutes antisemitism. With few exceptions, however, the terms *antisemite* and *antisemitic*

have been used sparingly and conservatively. Several figures commonly labeled antisemites, among them "the Jew Mark Twain," have that identification challenged by essays in these volumes. On the subject of antisemitism, perhaps more than most, it is important to bear in mind that intelligent people can disagree profoundly on its general and specific meaning, as well as the highly vexed questions it engenders.

In preparing an encyclopedia on antisemitism, decisions also have to be made on which general subjects to include. Two topics are particularly problematic. The first—the Holocaust—must, of course, be accorded its due importance. However, there are already encyclopedic works devoted to this widely ramified subject; it would be futile to try to duplicate them yet difficult to avoid some overlap. As far as possible—and it is not always possible—coverage in the present work is limited to the relationship between antisemitic ideology and the genocide of the Jews. No attempt is made to discuss the mechanics of the Final Solution, its intricate politics, bureaucratic organization, or public policy character. But in accounting for the decision to destroy the Jews of Europe and the participation of non-Germans in carrying out the Holocaust, it was deemed necessary to include entries on preexisting antisemitism in many countries. For instance, the place of Croatia in the Final Solution is examined in two essays, one dealing with the history of antisemitism in that land and another detailing the motivations, politics, and individuals who committed mass murder there.

The second difficult topic has to do with the hostilities awakened by the existence and policies of the state of Israel, which, in some ways, return us to the pre-Diaspora situation. Much of the hatred aimed at Israel is the product of states and peoples who are moved by "normal" conflicts and long-standing grudges in no way unique among nations. The line between criticism of Israel and antisemitism is not always easy to establish, but clearly, the two should not be conflated. Yet criticism of Israel frequently spills over to include all Jews, not just Israelis, and makes use of the materials, histories, and arguments set forth in this encyclopedia. For the first time in its century-long career, the *Protocols of the Elders of Zion* is more likely to be printed, quoted, and deployed in the Middle East than in Europe or the United States. For these reasons, several articles deal with antisemitism in the Muslim world, including its origins and special attributes.

Contributors

More than 200 men and women, spanning three generations and representing twenty-one countries, have written essays for this collection. They include independent scholars, officials in Jewish and non-Jewish secular and religious organizations, and academics from a great many disciplines. A concerted effort has been made to reflect the widest possible variety of viewpoints. Chosen for their expertise, the contributors have been allowed to have their say rather than being limited to the presentation of an imaginary consensus view of the issues at hand. In the process of editing submissions, no attempt has been made to censor their findings or mold them into a uniform scheme of interpretation. All that has been asked of each is a deep knowledge of the sources and a willingness to engage them critically.

This remarkable body of scholars would have been difficult and perhaps even impossible to assemble much before the present day because the study of antisemitism as a distinct research field is a relatively recent phenomenon. Magisterial histories of the Jews, such as those by Heinrich Graetz, Simon Dubnow, and Salo Baron had to deal with the persecution that is so much a part of the Jewish past. But they also dealt with issues in Jewish history that had little to do with hatred and prejudice. When they did turn their attention to these topics, they tended to focus on their effects upon the victims rather than the motivations of the Jews' enemies or the historical contexts, intellectual traditions, or political-religious motivations that shaped their hostility.

Antisemitism as a subject of scholarship has gathered force over time, spurred on by the manifestations of anti-Jewish prejudice and occasionally anticipating them. Bernard Lazare's *L'Antisémitisme: Son histoire et ses causes* (Antisemitism: Its History and Causes, 1894), the first methodical attempt to deal with the subject, was composed just before the Dreyfus Affair broke in France, an episode that not only divided the country but also introduced antisemitism as a potent force in national politics. The gradual recognition of the importance of antisemitism as a

freestanding area of research can be charted in the treatment accorded it in successive encyclopedias and lexicons. In 1894, the *Meyers Konversations-Lexikon* had no special heading for antisemitism, but it did include a half page on the antisemites and their writings. *The Jewish Encyclopedia* (1901–1905), in twelve volumes, devoted 8 of its 8,600 double-columned pages to the topic. Lucien Wolf, historian and activist in Anglo-Jewish affairs, contributed a 12-page account to the eleventh edition of *Encyclopedia Britannica* (1910–1911). During the Weimar years, the *Jüdisches Lexikon* (1927–1930) found 20 double-columned pages sufficient to cover the topic (although the *Grosse Brockhaus* of the same era needed less than one page). Many who participated in the *Jüdisches Lexikon,* having fled the Nazis, were part of the team reassembled in New York in 1939 to produce the most ambitious and elaborate essay on antisemitism to that point. The 68-page article in the *Universal Jewish Encyclopedia* sought to define the term, explain its origins, and consider its effects in the past, present, and future. A second section of the essay treated the history of antisemitism in the ancient and medieval worlds; the discussion of the modern period was divided by hemisphere, with the Eastern getting the greatest share of attention.

The attempted destruction of European Jewry during World War II rendered obvious the terrible potential of antisemitism and subsequently provided the most sustained stimulus for its separate study. Before the Holocaust, that study was confined almost exclusively to Jews. Now, it is a field of vital interest to scholars and nonscholars, Jews and non-Jews alike, in many countries and cultures, as the contributors to this encyclopedia amply show. The field commands the best efforts of many thoughtful people; for some, the study of antisemitism has become a lifelong commitment. This strong and growing interest is readily seen in an *antisemitism* keyword search of the World Catalogue database, which yields 7,000 book titles published since 1945 and 150 documentary collections. University institutes and independent research organizations conduct historical studies and track current outbreaks of antisemitism all over the world. They host conferences and publish scholarly journals, periodical reports, and bulletins; they provide data for parliamentarians in many countries and attempt to educate the public about the dangers of this particular form of hatred.

How to Use This Book

The 612 articles in these two volumes are alphabetically arranged. Each comes with a short bibliography of titles recommended for further reading. In many instances, the cited works not only provide more detailed information about the topic at hand but also include classic interpretations and/or other writings that contest traditional views of matters. The most recent literature on a topic has received preference. In an effort to conserve space, only rarely are the original works of antisemites cited in the bibliographies. These sources are usually not difficult to find.

An extensive and detailed general index will aid the user in finding information about individuals, events, and issues that have not been given their own entry. Thus, a reader seeking data on Generalissimo Francisco Franco's attitude toward the Nazi persecution of Jews will, upon consulting the index, discover that the subject is treated in the entry titled "Spain under Franco." To keep the main text uncluttered, the general index lists the birth and death dates, where ascertainable, of all the individuals mentioned in the entries. Finally, all of the articles appear in the index, indicated in boldface type.

Approximately 120 of the articles are syntheses of 1,000 to 2,000 words. These extended essays treat epochs, national entities, ideological movements, prominent individuals, and institutions. They are intended to complement and contextualize the more focused treatment of subjects that fall within these general categories. For example, the long survey on the Zionist movement provides a frame of reference for the shorter treatments of Theodor Herzl, Max Nordau, the concept of anti-Zionism, and a number of other linked themes. The survey on Arabic antisemitic literature will help the reader make sense of entries on the Constantine pogrom of 1934, Hamas, and the Iranian Revolution. At the conclusion of each essay, long or short, the reader will find an alphabetical listing of the most relevant related articles in a "See also" section.

In addition to survey treatments of national literatures and literary figures, this encyclopedia provides detailed information on the contents, publishing history, and reception of seminal texts—independent of the biographies of their authors. The biographical entry on Adolf Hitler, for example, is supplemented by analyses of his *Mein Kampf,* his early speeches, and his *Table Talk.* Fifty-five political pamphlets, theoretical works, novels, plays, magazines, and newspapers receive this close attention because of their significant role in the dissemination of anti-Jewish ideas, imagery, stereotypes, and political ideology.

Finally, despite the highly charged nature of the subject of this work, *Antisemitism: A Historical Encyclopedia of Prejudice and Persecution* is not an exercise in apologetics or special pleading. Scholarly rigor and an emotional subject matter coexist here. Every effort has been made to keep the focus on the search for truth and to base this search on respect for evidence. This has not, of course, been an easy task. Antisemitism has wrought such pain and suffering in the world and its proponents have done so much damage to individuals, communities, and ways of life that it is difficult to control one's feelings about the phenomenon. Furthermore and especially for students of the subject, knowledge of antisemitism's capacity to do harm, in the past and the present, awakens deep misgivings about its potential for causing future evil and prompts many to want to do something to overcome what is often called "the longest hatred." But the scholars gathered here know that ill-intentioned people will not be converted by any sort of moralizing or preaching. Telling readers how to feel about what they are reading is condescending, counterproductive, and ultimately futile. By contrast, it is our belief that if people of reasonably good will are given accurate, thorough, and honestly presented facts about this prejudice, most will arrive at the truth concerning the destructive nature of antisemitism and the injury it can still do to the human community.

Acknowledgments

A project of this magnitude owes thanks to many individuals and institutions. I would like to express my gratitude to Sander Gilman, Director of the Humanities Laboratory of the University of Illinois at Chicago, for bringing me together with the ABC-CLIO Press and for the laboratory's liberal grant that allowed the encyclopedia's board of editorial advisors to meet at an early stage of planning and conception. My thanks to them, too. The editors went well beyond the passive lending of their prestige to the enterprise; each wrote several articles for the volume and helped identify suitable contributors within their areas of expertise. They were, in every sense, a working committee—cooperative, professional, and collegial.

Roni Stauber of the Stephen Roth Institute of Tel Aviv University, Uwe Puschner of the Friedrich-Meinecke-Institut/Free University Berlin, Tom Kramer of the University of Sydney, and Frank Felsenstein of Ball State University were rich sources of good advice and always ready to share their wide-ranging knowledge of the field. Along with several of her associates, Dr. Krista Zach, Director of the Institut für deutsche Kultur und Geschichte Südosteuropas in Munich, Germany, supplied several high-quality articles on the subject of Romania, rescuing the project from what would have otherwise been an embarrassing failure. For their accommodating help I am indeed thankful.

I would also like to take this opportunity to acknowledge those—family, friends, and colleagues—who have given unstintingly of their counsel, help, and, especially, their patience. To my wife Linnea, thank you for putting up with a sometimes frazzled and abstracted mate. To David Jordan and Jonathan Marwil, loyal friends of forty years and my inspirations as scholars and writers, I once again owe much. For the past ten years, my colleagues on the electronic discussion list, H-Antisemitism, have helped me to think creatively about the problems and meaning of our common subject; they provided a sense of community in what sometimes seems a hostile world. Thanks also to Kimberly Tomlinson of the University of Illinois at Chicago for whom no computer problem, even those of my own making, proved insoluble.

Many people of ABC-CLIO have earned my appreciation and respect over the past three years. Simon Mason, Carol Smith, Joan Sherman, Sharon Daugherty, Rebecca Johnson, Terry Buss, and Elaine Vanater, committed professionals who care about what they are doing and do it extremely well, were a pleasure to collaborate with.

Finally, two individuals I could not have done without and whom I cannot thank enough. Matthias Brosch brought to the undertaking his boundless energy and tenacity, when I was about to run out of both. His crucial help at a crucial time, given unconditionally and certainly without sufficient reward, made it possible to find competent authors for the most rarefied topics. His knowledgeable suggestions changed my mind about the encyclopedia's content and method on several occasions; he is responsible for many of its improvements. Suzanna Hicks, a dear friend, read every word of every article. She provided that "extra set of eyes" absolutely necessary to an enterprise of this complexity and functioned as a most disciplined proofreader and vigilant gate-keeper, one who let pass neither murky prose nor sloppy logic. She is also that legendary "educated layperson" for whom one writes encyclopedias. I came to rely on her unfailing good judgment and intelligence.

What merit this encyclopedia has owes much to all those I have thanked here. For its defects, errors, and omissions I must take responsibility.

—*Richard S. Levy, Editor*

A

Action Française (1899–1945)

The Action Française was the most important organization of the extreme Right in France in the first half of the twentieth century. It brought together the anti-Dreyfusards defeated by the defenders of the French Republic at the beginning of the century, and by World War II, it had become the key ideological progenitor of the National Revolution launched by the Vichy government.

Action Française had its roots in a periodical launched on July 10, 1899, by Maurice Pujo, a young writer, and Henri Vaugeois, a professor of philosophy. Their goal was to research and debate the underlying social and political problems faced by France at the time. This publication evolved into the *Revue de l'Action Française,* a nationalist periodical that appeared every two weeks. Around the *Revue* the Ligue d'Action Française was founded in 1905, which was shortly followed by the cultivation of activist student groups and the creation in 1906 of L'Institut d'Action Française as an alternative establishment of higher learning. The daily newspaper *L'Action Française* was launched in 1908. The same year, the Camelots du Roi were created; they sold the paper and were the street soldiers of the movement. This organizational structure was able to integrate all nationalists and antisemites seeking an alternative to the republic, primarily attracting segments of the middle classes, the provincial nobility, the military, the magistracy, and the clergy. The newspaper appealed strongly to the cultivated classes by the quality of its writing and sold 100,000 copies in peak periods.

Although he was not originally a monarchist, Charles Maurras, a leading voice of the extreme Right, converted the organization to the theorems of his integral nationalism, which synthe-

sized populist xenophobia, exclusionary patriotism, and the reactionary elitism of royalism. Maurras provided a doctrinally coherent alternative to socialists, liberals, and conservatives. His assault on the revolutionary and democratic traditions, his view of nature as hierarchical and unequal, his anticosmopolitanism and cultural (as opposed to biological) racism, his adherence to monarchy as a principle of leadership and an institutional repository of order and authority, his bellicose nationalism, and his regionalism and corporatism made the tenets of the Action Française an amalgam of Joseph de Maistre's counterrevolution and Maurice Barrès's mystical nationalism. With this ideology, the organization united the revolutionaries of the Right opposed to the Third Republic.

Before 1914, the Action Française consolidated its monopoly on the royalist cause and was the best-structured, most vital nationalist movement in the country. However, it rallied to the *union sacrée* (sacred union) to defeat the Germans in World War I. By 1917, it had moved from cramped offices on the rue d'Athènes into spacious new accommodations on rue Caumartin, across from the train station at Gare St. Lazare, symbolic of its power but also indicative of the tempering of a movement that had become more integrated into mainstream conservatism, stressing patriotism and Catholicism as opposed to monarchism. Intransigent on the peace terms and resolutely anti-German, Action Française achieved the apogee of its power in the aftermath of the war. The group sent about thirty candidates to parliament, which indicated its influence but also its diminishing radicalism. In 1926, the Vatican condemned the movement's conflation of Catholicism and politics, initiating a major decline in the organization's popularity, which sank yet lower when younger adherents began to emulate Italian Fascism, with Georges Valois forming the Faisceau in 1925 and multiple other fascist parties arising in the 1930s. The period of the Vichy government, hailed as a "divine surprise," was an idyllic era for the Action Française, but Vichy's demise led to the end of the movement as a major force on the Right, even if its ideas have retained enduring influence.

—*Jonathan Judaken*

See also Barrès, Maurice; Camelots du Roi; Dreyfus Affair; France; Maurras, Charles; Vichy
References
Mazgaj, Paul. *The Action Française and Revolutionary Syndicalism* (Chapel Hill: University of North Carolina Press, 1979).
Weber, Eugen. *The Action Française: Royalism and Reaction in Twentieth-Century France* (Stanford, CA: Stanford University Press, 1962).

Adams, Henry Brooks (1838–1918)

Descended from a patrician Boston family, the grandson and great-grandson of presidents, Henry Adams was a historian and a capacious intellectual. His manifestations of antisemitism were a part of his complicated and intriguing thought, his animus arising from a convergence of social, intellectual, and psychological factors. As J. C. Levenson (1957, 225) noted, Adams's intelligence "was as cosmopolitan in its vices as in its virtues."

Antisemitism began to pervade Adams's personal (and, subtly, his public) writings in the early 1890s. He had grown increasingly pessimistic about the future of government and society in the United States in the face of the upheaval produced by industrial technology and emergent corporate capitalism. The depression of 1893 seemed to confirm his worries. Railing against the organized financial interests that he thought were responsible for this upheaval, Adams deployed the medieval stereotype of the Jew to reference these villains. National banking policy was "the Jew question"; the "commercial insanity" of contemporary America resulted from its "Hebraisation."

Adams's contempt for Jews as symbolic of capitalism and the evils of modernity meshed with the social contempt for them that was rampant in his Boston Brahmin circle, where nativist antisemitism arose from great discomfort with social and cultural changes accompanying the concentration of financial and industrial power. "The Jew [was] a howling horror and inevitable end of civilization" as Adams knew it (quoted in Chalfant 2001, 116). The diverse immigrants crowding U.S. cities represented the multiplicity of the modern world, which threatened to devolve into chaos. Likewise, fears for social stability—avoiding a "Jew War"—led Adams to support the French army against Alfred Dreyfus (guilt or innocence aside).

Adams's antisemitism was also of a piece with his philosophy of history, which was essentially a lament for the lost unity of the society that he imagined to have existed in the European Middle Ages. In the static, unified medieval world of his Eurocentric fantasy *Mont-St.-Michel and Chartres* (1904), Jews seemed out of place. Adams even attributed Judeophobia to his idealized Virgin Mary—"in spite of her own origin."

What pulled these strands together was Adams's acute self-consciousness about his own origins and his sense of failure and alienation. In the opening of his autobiographical masterpiece, *The Education of Henry Adams* (1907), he compared himself to the scion of a priestly family, born and raised by the Temple in Jerusalem, as "distinctly branded" by the past and equally "handicapped in the races of the coming [twentieth] century." On one level, Adams appeared to identify with the historical burden of Jewishness. Of a 1901 visit to Poland, he wrote, "The Jews and I are the only curious antiquities in it. . . . He ["the Jew"] makes me creep" (quoted in Chalfant 2001, 214). But "the Jew" was more than a symbol of Adams's own sense of cultural obsolescence. A residual Puritan identification with Jewish chosenness and mission helped spawn his resentment of inherited expectations he felt unable to meet. No doubt, that resentment was increased by the evident ability of many contemporary Jews to adapt to a world that, Adams believed, had left the Puritans' descendants behind.

—*Amy Hill Shevitz*

See also Capital: Useful versus Harmful; Dreyfus Affair; Poland; Twain, Mark; United States

References

Chalfant, Edward. *Improvement of the World: A Biography of Henry Adams, His Last Life, 1891–1918* (North Haven, CT: Archon Books, 2001).

Levenson, J. C. *The Mind and Art of Henry Adams* (Boston: Houghton Mifflin, 1957).

Solomon, Barbara Miller. *Ancestors and Immigrants: A Changing New England Tradition* (Cambridge, MA: Harvard University Press, 1956).

Young, James P. *Henry Adams: The Historian as Political Theorist* (Lawrence: University Press of Kansas, 2001).

Adversus Iudaeos

The eight sermons of Greek Orthodox preacher John Chrysostom (pictured here) have been handed down under the title *Against the Jews (Adversus Iudaeos)*. (Archivo Iconografico, S.A./Corbis)

The eight sermons of John Chrysostom, one of the most important preachers of the Greek Orthodox Church, have been handed down under the title *Against the Jews (Adversus Iudaeos)*. However, Jews represent only one of the polemical subjects of the work. His major target was "Judaizers," that is, Christians who, despite belonging to the church, participated in the life of the Jewish community. To separate them from the synagogue and the Jews, Chrysostom fiercely slandered the Jews themselves. The sermons must be understood as the product of their fourth-century context in the cosmopolitan city of Antioch, where a variety of peoples commingled on the social, cultural, and religious planes. Judaizers not only called into question the church's theological negation of Judaism, they also freely incorporated Judaic elements into their Christianity.

Conclusive theological grounds for sealing off the religions from one another were not immediately obvious—this much is clear from the polemics. The long existence of Judaism was especially problematic in antiquity because the age of an institution could give it great weight. Chrysostom and others therefore insisted that Judaism ought not to be venerated because of its age, but that it had instead become antiquated. Another feature of the sermons against Judaizing was their admonitions against participation in Jewish festivals. Notwithstanding the claims of the church authorities, a sizable number of Christians found it acceptable to take part in Jewish religious life, especially in the eastern parts of the Roman Empire, where the Jewish presence was significant. These superficial matters hid a more menacing problem for the church. If Christians consciously found themselves able to participate in Jewish sacred ceremonies and simultaneously take part in church life, then there was an obvious conclusion to be drawn: they simply did not see the differences between Jews and Christians that church preachers insisted were real.

In Antioch, the Jewish community was long established, comprising approximately 15 percent of the population and able to support many synagogues. Chrysostom's sermons bear witness to the attractiveness of Judaism. He apparently regarded Christianity and Judaism in a competitive situation, both intent on winning over the pagan part of the population. It should be remembered that the Christian churches were split into several groupings, whereas the Jews were unified. Even though the law promulgated by the Emperor Theodosius I in 380 had raised Christianity to a state religion, the religious constellation remained ambiguous. In retrospect, the fourth century can be seen as the beginning of the Christian era, but that fact was by no means obvious to contemporaries.

The eight sermons of *Adversus Iudaeos* belong to a cycle of addresses delivered between late 386 and late 387. Shortly thereafter, they appeared in book form. The sermons admonished Christians to shun Jews and Judaism. Chrysostom added nothing new to the stock arguments of Christian anti-Judaism, harking back instead to the familiar motifs. What was new about the work was the polemical intensity of the confrontation. Biblical imprecations abounded. The author applied the rebukes of the prophets to the Jews of his own times, ignoring their original historical context. He introduced pronouncements from the New Testament into the assault, adapting them with bold analogies to the present. He taxed Jews with their denial of the divinity of Jesus. From that, it followed that the blasphemers had killed God. The destruction of Jerusalem and the Diaspora were just punishments for the Crucifixion. Because it was his firm belief that there could be no knowledge of God without Christian faith, he disputed that Jews could know or worship God. Thus, the synagogue could not be a real house of prayer but only a dwelling place of the devil. He who went there put himself into the devil's hands.

Chrysostom sounded another traditional argument, stating that after the destruction of the Temple, it was no longer possible for Jews to fulfill the commandments of the law. Consequently, any attempt by Jews to lead a divinely ordained life went contrary to the law. In this tactic, he demonstrated how the Torah could be instrumentalized in the service of Christian anti-Judaism. But the attack went beyond the merely religious to castigate the social and ethical behavior of Jews. They were depicted as sexually dissolute, uneducated, and mad; they were enslaved to the tawdry pleasures, such as the theater and horse racing (an accusation Chrysostom also leveled at Christians in another sermon). The synagogue was a dwelling for demons, a bordello, a den of iniquity. He demonized the Jews and likened them to a disease that could infect Christians. Undoubtedly, his tirades were built on traditional theological arguments, but they also possessed an unmistakable manic, hate-filled character all their own.

An important subtext ran through the sermons. Their author did not represent himself or his cause as triumphant. Instead, he revealed a nagging sense of inferiority in relation to the historical claims and current attractiveness of Judaism, dread feelings he compensated for with a violent and extravagant rhetoric. It is not known whether Chrysostom succeeded in insulating Christians from Jews by means of his sermons; very probably, he did not. Perhaps a kind of peace through exhaustion settled on him later in life. Subsequent sermons contained the same total disapproval of Judaizing, but they lacked the impassioned tone. Over the centuries, *Adversus Iudaeos* exerted widespread influence in the Eastern Orthodox Church. The book was "rediscovered" by Christian antisemites of the nineteenth and twentieth centuries, who were happy to have the authority of a church father to legitimize their hatreds.

—Rainer Kampling
Richard S. Levy, translation

See also Deicide; Roman Empire; Supersessionism
References
Meeks, Wayne A., and Robert L. Wilken. *Jews and Christians in Antioch in the First Four Centuries of the Common Era* (Missoula, MT: Scholars Press, 1978).
Wilken, Robert L. *John Chrysostom and the Jews: Rhetoric and Reality in the Late 4th Century* (Berkeley: University of California Press, 1983).

African American–Jewish Relations

Even as African Americans and Jews enjoyed periods of impressive political and cultural cooperation, black antisemitism as well as Jewish racism emerged throughout the last three centuries to forge a complex black-Jewish relationship.

Soon after their arrival on American shores, Africans in slavery converted to Christianity and embraced many of the white South's antisemitic assumptions. Africans, and especially their African American children, and grandchildren heard sermons that blamed Jews for the death of Jesus. As Leonard Dinnerstein has reported, one African American writer noted that "all of us black people who lived in the neighborhood hated Jews, not because they exploited us but because we had been taught at home and in Sunday school that Jews were 'Christ killers'"(in Dinnerstein 1994, 198).

Antisemitic assumptions continued after African American emancipation. At the turn of the twentieth century, black-owned newspapers featured stories that identified Jews as unscrupulous businesspeople, a charge that stemmed from centuries-old European stereotypes about Jews as exploitative moneylenders. Even as African American leader and Tuskegee Institute founder Booker T. Washington adopted a strong assimilationist stance toward white America, he still confided antisemitic thoughts to his private circle of friends and associates. W. E. B. DuBois, who would join two leading Jewish philanthropists to form the National Association for the Advancement of Colored People in 1909, espoused antisemitic beliefs before distancing himself from them later in his life.

The popularization of scientific racism in the United States in the first thirty years of the twentieth century evoked a mixed reaction among African American leaders. Some joined white Christian leaders to argue that Jews possessed inferior genetic stock and should therefore be denied entry to the United States. Others saw in the antisemitic persecution of Jews a threat to their own African American community, rejecting both the xenophobic sentiments of many popular writers as well as the ideas espoused by Adolf Hitler.

Positive relations between Jews and African Americans peaked during the post–World War II era when the communal leaderships of each group joined in an unprecedented movement for racial equality in the United States. Abraham Joshua Heschel joined Martin Luther King Jr. in the famed Selma march to dramatize the common bonds between blacks and Jews. Jews funded and led many national civil rights organizations and could be counted as the majority of white volunteers during the most intense years of the civil rights struggle.

In the years after President Lyndon B. Johnson signed the landmark Civil Rights Act of 1964 and Voting Rights Act of 1965, relations between African Americans and Jews soured under the weight of competing charges of black antisemitism and Jewish racism. A growing number of African American civil rights activists resented what they considered the paternalistic approach of Jewish leaders, and northern Jews resisted residential and education integration in their own communities.

In 1966, the Student Nonviolent Coordinating Committee (SNCC) decided in a very tight election to purge whites and therefore Jews from leadership positions in the organization. Other civil rights groups followed suit, with some black leaders accusing Jews of complicity with Western imperialism and the evils of the capitalist system of the United States. After Israel's victory in the 1967 Six Days' War, Black Power advocates expressed public support for Palestinian leader Yasir Arafat and called for the destruction of the Jewish state.

King's accommodationist approach to interracial politics gave way to the flagrant antisemitism of Black Nationalists, the Nation of Islam leaders (especially Malcolm X), and even some black intellectuals. A series of high-profile confrontations between African Americans and Jews ensued.

Conflicts over the nature and limits of affirmative action programs, as well as widely publicized comments made by the then-presidential candidate Jesse Jackson and former United Nations ambassador Andrew Young, extended the era of African American–Jewish distrust into the 1980s. Attempts at interracial dialogue faltered in the last third of the twentieth century as more African Americans identified Jews with the attitudes and political views of the white majority. American Jews, who remained white America's largest liberal ethnic group, took particular offense at the vitriolic antisemitism of Nation of Islam leader Louis Farrakhan and Afrocentrist academics such as Leonard Jeffries.

In the early years of the twenty-first century, African Americans and Jews maintain a large measure of social isolation and only limited political cooperation. Expressions of black antisemitism remain rather limited in an era defined more by ethnic separation than by the accommodationist coalition building of an earlier time.

—*Marc Dollinger*

See also Black Nationalism; Farrakhan, Louis; Nation of Islam; Racism, Scientific; Student Nonviolent Coordinating Committee; United States

References

Dinnerstein, Leonard. *Anti-Semitism in America* (New York: Oxford University Press, 1994).

Forman, Seth. *Blacks in the Jewish Mind: A Crisis of Liberalism* (New York: New York University Press, 1998).

Friedman, Murray. *What Went Wrong? The Creation and Collapse of the Black-Jewish Alliance* (New York: Free Press, 1995).

Phillips, William M., Jr. *An Unillustrious Alliance: The African American and Jewish American Communities* (New York: Greenwood Press, 1991).

Agobard (779–840)

St. Agobard, the early ninth-century bishop of Lyons in south-central France, confronted Jews with anxiety. He feared their effects on Christians serving as domestics in their households and possibly advocated the quasi-forcible conversion of Jewish children. His main preoccupation was purity, which he believed was endangered by contact with Jews. In letters written between about 826 and 828—most of them to clergy and one to Emperor Louis the Pious—Agobard railed about Jewish abuse, especially about Jews dining with Christians. There were also intimations of sexual improprieties, Jewish proselytizing, and blasphemy in Jewish writings.

Agobard quite probably derived his ideas from the early third-century Cyprian, who feared that priests who had served at pagan altars during the Diocletian persecution of Christianity in the early third century had become impure (and therefore unfit to offer the Eucharist), and had also passed on this impurity to others. Agobard applied these ideas to contact with Jews, fearing that those who fraternized with Jews might later break bread with a priest who might then offer the sacrament in impurity. Extending this logic, he spoke against accepting gifts from Jews at holiday time, especially the Passover matzah—that surrogate for Christ's sacrifice, the true matzah, as Paul said in I Corinthians 5. Agobard saw virtually all social intercourse with Jews as *idolatriae autem iugo libertatem animi inclinarent* (leading to the yoking of the free to the harness of idolatry). He warned Christians to beware lest Jews seduce them "into their errors." In support of his contentions, he cited edicts of councils held at Agde, Clermont, and Laodicea in the fifth century, edicts reiterated at the 845–846 council at Meaux.

It is important to note that Agobard believed Jewish impurity threatened his ideal Christian *societas fidei* (society of the faithful), a society with no differences between peoples—by which he meant a wholly Christian society under church dominion. The Carolingian emperor, who, according to Agobard, should have set ecclesiastical policy seconded by important priests, disregarded him on the subject of the Jews. Incensed, Agobard openly rebelled.

Some Christians took his teachings to mean that Jews should be repressed at all costs and by any means. But Agobard himself did not preach violence. He sought to place limits on Jews through canon law, and for this reason, it appears he instructed his deacon Florus (a judicial official at that time) to gather the canons and texts he cited into a collection of restrictive laws. This collection has survived. Its contents reinforce our knowledge that nearly all the canons restricting Jews were on the books by about the year 900 or 1000; with but one or two exceptions, later councils did not innovate.

—*Kenneth Stow*

See also Church Councils (Early); Lateran Council, Fourth; Middle Ages, Early

Reference

Stow, Kenneth. *Alienated Minority* (Cambridge, MA: Harvard University Press, 1994).

Agrarian League

Imperial Germany's most powerful interest group was a bundle of contradictions. Launched in 1893 mainly by large estate owners of the Prussian east, the Agrarian League (Bund der Landwirte) cultivated its largest constituencies among smaller-scale farmers in Germany's central and western regions. In founding the league, Conservatives were, in part, responding to the challenge posed by Germany's antisemitic parties, whose recent electoral gains in rural areas threatened traditional strongholds. Yet the league's remarkable success was not a straightforward Conservative triumph, as the new venture, advancing an intransigently agrarian program of protective tariffs, bimetallism, and other palliatives, soon outstripped its Conservative Party sponsors in popular support and political resources. As the league grew into a genuinely mass organization, with its membership numbering over 200,000 by 1900, it generated its own nucleus of leaders—men such as Diederich Hahn and Gustav Roesicke, beholden largely to their own rising ambitions. With its burgeoning agitational apparatus, including several mass-circulation newspapers, more than 100 traveling agitators, and an annual budget of more than 1 million marks, the league came to dominate rural politics in many German regions. By 1907, its electoral clout was such that more than one-third of all Reichstag deputies had publicly signed on to its agrarian program. Yet this very success, which helped resuscitate Conservative Party fortunes in the short run, also pushed that party's appeal onto increasingly narrow agrarian tracks, as the league's stridency drove many middle-class and urban constituencies toward other parties instead.

In convening its first general assembly, the league pointedly declared its membership was open only to Christians, and over the organization's life span, antisemitism played an increasingly important role in its agitation. Yet many "true" antisemites, such as Hermann Ahlwardt and Otto Böckel, viewed the league with distrust, disparaging its anti-Jewish demagoguery as fundamentally insincere. The league, they argued, was using antisemitism chiefly as a rhetoric of convenience, not as an urgent priority unto itself. They condemned the league as a stalking horse for the landed elites, in a bid to undermine the authentic rebellion of the peasantry through spurious appeals to an imaginary community of agrarian interest. In this, they were largely correct; the Conservative notables who had long dominated Germany's rural politics made little effort to disguise the revulsion they felt for rabble-rousers such as Böckel and Ahlwardt, whose slogans had targeted "Junkers" as well as Jews. Antisemitism, Conservative agrarians argued, needed to be placed back inside "legitimate bounds," with its more radical exponents brought to heel.

And in this aim, the league was largely successful, though the disintegration and decline of Germany's antisemitic parties rested on other factors as well. Yet if the Agrarian League contributed to the gradual marginalization of the antisemitic parties, it simultaneously absorbed and preserved much of their venomous rhetoric and beliefs. Whatever their degree of "sincerity," league leaders and their press promoted an increasingly violent imagery of Jews, while gravitating toward a *völkisch* (racially grounded) nationalism. This ideological trend only hardened after the elections of 1912, when the league suffered sharp reversals in its political fortunes, losing fully 60 of the 138 mandates its electoral machinery had helped secure in 1907. As league agitation continued to absolve German agrarians of any responsibility for their problems, anti-Jewish scapegoating filled an inevitable and necessary role; this flight from reality continued through World War I, as the league press blamed "world Jewry" for everything from food shortages to the war itself. In January 1920, the league was reorganized into the Reichslandbund, which carried forth the former group's program and anti-semitism into Germany's Weimar years. Sections of the Reichslandbund went over to the Nazi Party in the early 1930s.

—*John Abbott*

See also Ahlwardt, Hermann; Antisemitic Political Parties; Böckel, Otto; Christian Social Party (Germany); German Peasant League; Hahn, Diederich; Liebermann von Sonnenberg, Max; Memminger, Anton; Ratzinger, Georg; Tivoli Program

References

Levy, Richard S. *The Downfall of the Anti-Semitic Political Parties in Imperial Germany* (New Haven, CT: Yale University Press, 1975).
Puhle, Hans-Jürgen. *Agrarische Interessenpolitik und preussischer Konservatismus im Wilhelminischen Reich, 1893–1914* (Hannover, Germany: Verlag für Literatur u. Zeitgeschehen, 1967).
Retallack, James. *Notables of the Right: The Conservative Party and Political Mobilization in Germany, 1876–1918* (Boston: Unwin Hyman, 1988).

Ahlwardt, Hermann (1846–1914)

Easily dismissed as a rowdy and a buffoon and often disavowed by mainline antisemites in the German Empire, Hermann Ahlwardt proved adept at holding the limelight in antisemitic politics, filling meeting halls, and scandalizing the respectable press with his flamboyant demagoguery. His early life gave no indication of such a career. Born in rural Pomerania, he received an excellent education, became a teacher in 1866, and was a school principal in Berlin by 1881. He was on friendly terms with Court Chaplain Adolf Stoecker, who confirmed one of his daughters, and with several Jewish and liberal notables. But then he fell into debt, resorted to short-term loans at high interest rates—he later admitted that the usurers were not Jews—and began embezzling school funds. Dismissed from his post and obviously foundering, he seized on antisemitic agitation as a way of saving himself.

Ahlwardt began leveling sensational and libelous charges against prominent public figures, including Chancellor Leo von Caprivi and Otto von Bismarck's personal banker, Gerson von Bleichröder, who was Jewish. Even as he sat in jail, having been convicted for slander, Ahlwardt prepared his next sensation. He claimed that the Jewish-owned Löwe munitions firm, in collusion with highly placed government officials, had knowingly supplied defective weapons to the German army. He laid out these charges in a pamphlet, *Neue Enthüllungen: Judenflinten* (New Revelations: Jew Rifles [1892]), which went through twenty editions and engendered a huge public outcry before being confiscated by the government. Ahlwardt was arrested, tried, and convicted, but before he could be imprisoned, he won, without organization or funding, a seat in the Reichstag; his parliamentary immunity allowed him to escape serving his sentence.

From 1892 to 1903, Ahlwardt represented a backwater Prussian district, rarely attending sessions of the parliament and making no significant contribution to the well-being of his constituents. Nonetheless, he remained unceasingly popular with his voters because he was able to understand and exploit their long list of grievances against a government they were certain favored Jews, city dwellers, and industry over hardworking small farmers. Ahlwardt also recognized their resentment toward the traditional leaders in the countryside; the Junker noblemen of Prussia with their large landholdings. His campaign slogan, adopted

by the antisemites in rural election districts elsewhere, effectively combined these two targets: "*Gegen Junker und Juden!*" (Against Junkers and Jews!) Ahlwardt's successes in populist politics greatly alarmed liberals and conservatives alike. Liberal doubts about the wisdom of letting simple folk vote were confirmed. His election victory was decried as a crime against reason and all upstanding German values of law, order, and honesty. When other antisemitic candidates also began to threaten their traditionally safe Reichstag seats, the Conservative Party leadership found it expedient to incorporate antisemitism into its own program in late 1892. More conventional antisemites also felt threatened by Ahlwardt's style and flaunting of the law. They pushed him to the fringes of the movement but never managed to undermine his popularity with the rank and file. Hailed as the "second Luther," he apparently was able to finance himself by charging admission to his meetings during never-ending national speaking tours.

Fortunately for all his enemies, Ahlwardt obliged them by self-destructing. Solving the Jewish Question never appeared to be his first priority. When his sensational antisemitic disclosures began to pall, he turned his attention to the Jesuits and Freemasons. In the late 1890s, while still technically a member of the Reichstag, he traveled to the United States, campaigned on behalf of William Jennings Bryan, and tried to establish an American antisemitic association based in Brooklyn, then a borough with a large German population. He returned to Germany to open a chain of *Judenflinten* cigar stores, which swiftly failed. In 1903, he successfully bequeathed his election district to Wilhelm Bruhn, another disreputable antisemite, and busied himself with the selling of fraudulent mining shares. In 1914, no longer of interest to German antisemites or interested in them, he was run over and killed by one of the first motorized meat trucks in Leipzig.

—*Richard S. Levy*

See also Antisemitic Political Parties; Freemasonry; Jesuit Order; Pückler, Count Walter von; Stoecker, Adolf; Tivoli Program

Reference

Jahr, Christoph. "Ahlwardt on Trial: Reactions to the Antisemitic Agitation of the 1890s in Germany," *Leo Baeck Institute Year Book* 48 (2003): 67–85.

Alexandrian Pogrom

By Alexandrian "pogrom," modern scholars refer to the persecution that Jews suffered in 38 CE in Alexandria, Egypt. The sole source of information for this episode is Philo of Alexandria, himself a Jew, who witnessed the riots and who afterward led the Jewish delegation to the Emperor Gaius Iulius Caesar Germanicus (Caligula) that requested the reestablishment of legal Jewish residence in Alexandria.

At the beginning of August 38 CE, King Agrippa I, whom Gaius had recently appointed king of a good part of Palestine, gave the Alexandrian citizens gathered in the gymnasium the occasion for mocking him qua Jewish king. Immediately thereafter, the same people went into a theater and called for the installing of images of Gaius in the synagogues. The Jews strongly and actively opposed this attempt. A few days later, the Roman prefect of Egypt, Flaccus, issued an edict declaring the Jews foreigners and immigrants, abolishing their rights to live in Alexandria. The Alexandrian population then pushed the Jews into a small district of the city, torturing and killing whoever attempted to leave it and destroying Jewish property anywhere else. Flaccus also arrested and punished some members of the Jewish council of elders.

The Jews had enjoyed legal residence in Alexandria since the city had, according to tradition, been founded in 331 BCE by Alexander the Great. Alexandria was later developed by Ptolemy I and his successors, who had allowed Jews to live according to their traditions and laws, or *politèia,* in a semi-independent enclave, or *polìteuma.* The Jews had their own civic institutions, which included magistrates and a court for the administration of justice. The Roman emperors later recognized and confirmed the legality of the Jewish presence in the city. Thus, the edict of Flaccus in 38 CE represented a breach in Roman policy.

Scholarly interpretation, with few exceptions, follows Philo's account. Flaccus, entangled in political troubles with the Roman court after the recent accession of Gaius, sought to enhance his position in Alexandria by making an alliance with the anti-Jewish factions and endorsing their persecution. Scholars who doubt that the Alexandrian citizens had enough weight to be a factor in the imperial policy of Rome have challenged this position. Until recently, there was also a general consensus on the Greek identity of the opponents of the Jews. However, a more careful reading of Philo's account has led some scholars to point instead to the Egyptians as the major perpetrators. The notion that Jews had a part in provoking the riots by demanding full Alexandrian rights is no longer widely believed.

In the winter of 38 or 39 CE, the Jews sent an embassy to Gaius to plead for the reestablishment of their rights; it is not clear what the emperor's response was, but it seems that nothing changed until Claudius's accession to the throne at the beginning of 41 CE.

—*Sandra Gambetti*

See also Claudius; Roman Empire; Roman Literature

References

Gruen, E. S. *Diaspora: Jews amidst Greeks and Romans* (Cambridge, MA: Harvard University Press, 2002).

Schäfer, Peter. *Judeophobia* (Cambridge, MA: Harvard University Press, 1997).

Algeria

Jews first arrived in North Africa 2,000 years ago after migrating west from Palestine. Later waves came from Spain during the Reconquista between the thirteenth and fifteenth centuries. For many centuries, Jews lived in relative harmony with Muslims and Christians in North Africa. They worked primarily as merchants and craftsmen; most resided in the larger coastal cities, such as Fez, Tunis, and Cairo. In terms of dress, language, and lifestyle, Jews in North Africa, unlike the Jews of Europe, often resembled their neighbors.

Beginning in the tenth century, however, Jews became a more distinctive community in North Africa. Islamic leaders formally separated the Jews (and Christians) as "protected persons" (*dhimmis*) and instituted special taxes and restrictions on them. During periods of hardship and war, urban masses sometimes directed their hostilities against the Jews because of their visible role in the economy. In response, Jews bonded together more tightly, withdrawing into their religious communities. Under Ottoman rule, between the sixteenth and eighteenth centuries, some Jews gained more economic power by extending their commercial networks into Europe and across the Ottoman Empire and by financing the privateering trade of Ottoman rulers. As the Ottoman government weakened in the late eighteenth and early nineteenth centuries, Jews became the target of attacks by local residents and military forces. Thus, Jews welcomed the French occupation of Algeria in 1830, and they became interpreters, suppliers, and conscripts. In 1870, the French government naturalized the Jews in Algeria through the Crémieux Decree. As a result, the Jewish minority, though small in relation to other European settlers and the Muslim majority, became a political factor in Algerian and French politics.

Although it was informed by European cultural prejudices and intellectual theories, antisemitism in French Algeria is best described as a popular political tradition. Supporters of *antijudaisme*—a special term used in Algeria to distinguish between Jews and Semitic Arabs—were drawn primarily from the European settler population in and around the large towns and cities in the north, such as Oran, Algiers, and Constantine. After 1870, anti-Jewish organizations, newspapers, and agitators appeared during election campaigns, in part the product of competition among settler political parties for Jewish votes (more than 10 percent of the total vote in some cities and towns). Anti-Jewish violence broke out in Algeria between 1881 and 1884 and again in 1889. After the Dreyfus Affair started in 1894, anti-Jewish political mobilization increased in Algeria. Led by the young and charismatic Max Régis, the Anti-Jewish League of Algiers sponsored petitions, boycotts, street demonstrations, and attacks on Jewish shops and neighborhoods; in 1898, it elected four anti-Jewish deputies, including Édouard Drumont, to the French National Assembly and swept the Algiers city council and mayoral elections. Moderate *antijuifs* (anti-Jews) hoped to limit Jewish influence, whereas the radicals demanded the abolition of Jews' citizenship rights or their expulsion from Algeria. Mixed in with these demands were calls for greater autonomy from France and regular verbal assaults on Parisian government officials. The end of the Dreyfus Affair, along with local scandals in Algeria in the early 1900s, brought an end to this phase of antijudaisme in Algeria.

Publicly disavowed by the Center and the Left in France, antisemitism in the twentieth century shifted squarely to the domain of the political Right in both France and Algeria. In Algeria, however, it retained its popular appeal. In the 1920s and 1930s, local politicians in Oran, Algiers, and Constantine branded the Jews as Bolsheviks and internationalists; electoral platforms called for the exclusion of Jews from public service, regulation of Jewish property, and abrogation of the Crémieux Decree. Spurred on by this atmosphere and by acute economic crisis, Muslim rioters killed several Jews in Constantine in 1934. Two years later, settler campaigns against the French Popular Front were marked by anti-Jewish violence and protests. The endorsement of Algerian antijuifs by right-wing organizations in metropolitan France culminated in the Vichy government's abrogation of the Crémieux Decree in 1940 (it was reinstated in 1943). Many Jews and Muslims in Algeria condemned these displays of prejudice and discrimination. In fact, ill treatment by Europeans fostered a solidarity between the Jews and Muslims that extended into the years of the Algerian War (1954–1962).

After independence in 1962, the majority of Jews in Algeria left for France, Israel, and North America. Today, with few Jews left in a Muslim-dominated country, the most common expressions of antisemitism appear in conjunction with condemnations of Israel's policies in the Middle East.

—*Lizabeth Zack*

See also Constantine Pogrom; Dreyfus Affair; Drumont, Édouard; France; Islam and the Jews; Régis, Max; Vichy

References

Ayoun, Richard, and Bernard Cohen. *Les Juifs d'Algérie: 2000 ans d'histoire* (Paris: Jean Claude Lattès, 1982).
Laskier, Michael. *North African Jewry in the Twentieth Century: The Jews of Morocco, Tunisia, and Algeria* (New York: New York University Press, 1994).

Alliance Israélite Universelle

In 1860, a group of acculturated French Jews established the Alliance Israélite Universelle as the first international organization dedicated to Jewish self-defense. The immediate impetus was the church's kidnapping of the six-year-old Jewish child Edgardo Mortara in Bologna and the inspiration was Adolphe Crémieux, the parliamentary deputy and minister of justice in the French governments of 1848 and 1870.

Intervention in the Damascus Affair of 1840 by Crémieux and Moses Montefiore, his English counterpart, had encouraged Jewish communities in the East to seek the continuing intercession of Western leaders. The French alliance with the Ottoman Empire in the Crimean War, along with an 1856 Turkish promise for Jewish emancipation, further stimulated interest among French Jews in the defense and modernization of their Eastern coreligionists and prepared the ground for the institutional innovation of the Alliance Israélite Universelle.

Alliance activities included diplomatic intervention, relief for the victims of pogroms and other disasters, aid to emigrants, and the establishment of an influential school system. Membership peaked at over 30,000 in 1885, and though 60 percent of the members were not French, authority always remained in Paris. Diplomatic influence was reduced by the defeat in the Franco-Prussian War of 1870, and in the following year, British Jews broke away to form their own Anglo-Jewish Association. The Alliance Israélite Universelle was sometimes an uneasy ally among the Jewish self-defense organizations that ultimately appeared in Berlin, Vienna, and New York as well.

From its inception, the new organization attempted to enlist the prominent Italian statesman Count Camillo Cavour to protect the young Mortara, and it protested the massacre of 11,000 Maronite Christians in Syria. Later attempts to intervene with the Turkish authorities over the proliferation of ritual murder allegations by Christians in the Ottoman Empire were partially successful, as were efforts undertaken with the Moroccan sultan in regard to the brutalities and depredations of his local officials.

The Alliance Israélite Universelle naturally became an advocate for the Jews of the Christian states that emerged from the disintegration of the Ottoman Empire. From 1861, the Serbian government dealt with the group as the virtual representative for its unemancipated Jewish community. Crémieux began his efforts for Romania's persecuted Jews in 1867 by obtaining the support of Napoleon III of France and Otto von Bismarck of Prussia. Alliance efforts contributed to the agreement reached by Bulgaria, Serbia, and Romania at the 1878 Congress of Berlin to extend equal rights to the Jews, an undertaking that Romania notoriously repudiated. The antisemitic movement of the 1870s and 1880s rendered this sort of high diplomacy even less effective.

By 1914, the educational system established by the alliance extended to 183 primary schools in fifteen countries, along with vocational, agricultural, nursing, and rabbinical schools and a Parisian teacher-training college. Controversy arose over the use of French as the language of instruction, the reduced role of religious studies, and the poor teaching of Hebrew by local rabbis. Yet by 1982, with a few of the schools still surviving in some Arab countries, approximately 650,000 students had been educated under the system. The effort enhanced social mobility for Ottoman, North African, and Middle Eastern Jews, enlarged the Jewish middle class, and emancipated young women.

The Alliance Israélite Universelle had its critics among both antisemites and Jews. Antisemites sometimes connected Crémieux to the *Protocols of the Elders of Zion*. During the Dreyfus Affair, the organization found it advisable to keep a low profile. Theodor Herzl, leader of the Zionist movement, feared that the existence of this far-flung (anti-Zionist) organization, with access to people in high places, nourished the myth that Jews maintained a secret organization plotting world domination. In all likelihood, however, the Alliance Israélite Universelle's anti-Zionist stance—ironically—nourished the Zionist movement by encouraging eastern European Jews to anticipate help in this enterprise from their brethren in the West.

—*Edward Bristow*

See also Damascus Blood Libel; Dreyfus Affair; Emancipation; Herzl, Theodor; Mortara Affair; *Protocols of the Elders of Zion;* Ritual Murder (Modern); Romania; Zionism

References
Laskier, Michael. *The* Alliance Israélite Universelle *and the Jewish Communities of Morocco, 1862–1962* (Albany: State University of New York Press, 1983).
Rodrigue, Aron. *French Jews, Turkish Jews: The* Alliance Israélite Universelle *and the Politics of Jewish Schooling in Turkey, 1860–1925* (Bloomington: Indiana University Press, 1990).
Weil, Georges. "The *Alliance Israélite Universelle* and the Emancipation of Jewish Communities in the Mediterranean," *Jewish Journal of Sociology* 24 (1982): 117–134.

Almohad Persecution

The Berber movement of the Almohads was founded by Ibn Tumart (d. 1130) in the High Atlas Mountains of North Africa. Claiming to be the *Mahdi* (divinely guided one), he followed a puritanical Islam insisting on the absolute unity of God, hence the name of the movement: *al-muwahhidun* (the Unitarians). Because he feared for the moral and religious decline of Islam and sought the foundations of Muslim law in the Koran and Hadith alone, Ibn Tumart can be considered one of the first fundamentalists in Islamic history. Under the leadership of his successor, 'Abd al-Mu'min (d. 1163), the Almohads conquered the whole Maghrib from Morocco to Tunisia and al-Andalus (Muslim Spain). In many ways, the rule of the intolerant and fanatical Almohads (just like that of their predecessors, the Almoravids, in the first half of the twelfth century) put an end to the more or less peaceful *convivencia* (living together) of Muslims, Christians, and Jews in Spain.

Non-Muslims were subject to persecution and inquisition, but Muslims were also targets of Almohad intolerance. Christians and Jews were given the choice of conversion, exile, or death. This situation led to the disappearance of the few Christian communities in North Africa and of the last Mozarabs (Spanish Christians living under the rule of Muslims) of al-Andalus who fled to the Christian north. As far as the persecution of the numerous indigenous Jewish populations of North Africa and al-Andalus is concerned, two periods can be distinguished. The first extended from the time of the conquest up to 1184, during which massacres of Jews took place at Marrakesh and Fez, forcing a large number of Jews to leave their country for Christian Spain, southern France, Sicily, Italy, Egypt, and Palestine. Among those fleeing to the Middle East was the future philosopher and physician Maimonides (Moshe ben Maymun), who left Fez in 1165 with his family. This flight of the educated at the end of the twelfth century initiated the intellectual decline of the indigenous Jewish population, by then already converted to Islam. It also deprived Muslim Spain and North Africa of some of its major intellectual and cultural resources.

The second period of persecutions began with the reign of Abu Jusuf Ya'kub al-Mansur (d. 1199). Under the influence of austere scholars, he suspected the Jews who had converted during the reign of his predecessor of only feigning belief in Islam. Therefore, he decreed that Jews could only marry among themselves and could not engage in large-scale business. In addition, "the Jews of the Maghrib had to wear clothing that would distinguish them from all others, that is dark blue garments with sleeves of an exaggerated length, reaching almost to their feet, and instead of turbans, caps of a very hideous appearance, [looking] like packsaddles, that fell below their ears" (Dozy 1881, 223; translated by the author). They also had to wear a distinguishing sign called the *shikla*. Al-Mansur's successor, Muhammad al-Nasir (d. 1214), allowed Jews to wear their normal style of clothes but only in yellow and once again permitted them to engage in trade. After suffering defeat at the Battle of Las Navas de Tolosa (1212), the Almohads lost their power in Spain, and the Jews were once more able to practice their religion openly. The situation in North Africa also improved. Under al-Ma'mun's reign (1228–1232), Jews started resettling in the cities.

—*Hans-Jörg Döhla*

See also Islam and the Jews; Islamic Fundamentalism; Yellow Badge
References
Corcos, D. "L'Attitude des Almohades envers les Juifs," *Zion* 32 (1967): 135–160 (Hebrew).
Dozy, Reinhart, ed. *The History of the Almohades* (Leyden, the Netherlands: E. J. Brill, 1881).
Kennedy, Hugh. *Muslim Spain and Portugal* (London: Longman, 1996), 196–266.

Tourneau, Roger L. *The Almohads Movement in North Africa in the Twelfth and Thirteenth Centuries* (Princeton, NJ: Princeton University Press, 1969).

Alsace

From the end of the eighteenth century until 1871, when most of the territory comprising the provinces of Alsace and Lorraine was annexed by Germany, debates over the Jewish Question in France, as well as physical violence against Jews, centered on the region of Alsace.

As part of the Holy Roman Empire, Alsace had remained open to Jewish settlement even after Jews had been expelled from medieval France. France acquired the region and its large Ashkenazi (Yiddish-speaking) population in the mid-seventeenth century. On the eve of the French Revolution of 1789, the Jewish population of Alsace numbered approximately 22,500, over half of the 40,000 Jews who lived in France at the time. Another 7,500 Jews lived in neighboring Lorraine, so together, these northeastern provinces constituted the heartland of French Jewry.

The distinctive cultural and economic profile of Jews in Alsace elicited debate even before the French Revolution. Although the Sephardi Jews, who had gone to southwestern France in the sixteenth and seventeenth centuries as New Christians, were highly acculturated and well integrated, the Jews of Alsace lived in a state of segregation, subject to a welter of medieval anti-Jewish regulations. Culturally, they retained distinctive customs and traditions within their own semiautonomous communities, which were governed by rabbis and Jewish lay leaders and adhered to Talmudic law. Barred from residing in major urban centers, Alsatian Jews lived scattered among hundreds of small rural hamlets and villages, where they sometimes constituted the majority of the population. Jews were banned from a wide range of occupations; they could not own land, join artisan guilds, or manage retail businesses. The vast majority of the Jewish population was therefore involved in petty trade, serving primarily as commercial intermediaries between the countryside and urban areas. Most significantly for the history of antisemitism, they functioned as the principal moneylenders in this region until the end of the nineteenth century. On the eve of the Revolution in 1789, Jews owned approximately one-third of all mortgages in Alsace, although they constituted only 3 to 4 percent of the region's total population. To the extent that they interacted with gentiles, it was to carry on business.

During the second half of the eighteenth century, several Enlightenment philosophes, most notably Denis Diderot and François-Marie Arouet de Voltaire, condemned Jews in general as misanthropic, rapacious, and culturally retrograde, thus raising the question of whether they could be integrated. It was, however, the Affair of False Receipts of 1777 that brought the question of Alsatian Jewry to the center stage of public attention. In that year, a local judge, François Joseph Antoine de Hell, orchestrated the forgery of hundreds of receipts, which were then distributed to the Alsatian peasantry to prove that they had repaid their debts to Jews. Two years later, Hell published a pamphlet justifying the forgery as a legitimate means of protecting the peasants against their Jewish oppressors, whom he excoriated as comprising an unassimilable "state within a state." In response to this campaign, which threatened Alsatian Jews with economic ruin, an appeal was made to Moses Mendelssohn to intervene on their behalf. Mendelssohn turned to his colleague Christian Wilhelm von Dohm, a Prussian civil servant and exponent of enlightened views. In this way, the Affair of False Receipts led to the publication of Dohm's *On the Civic Improvement of the Jews* (1781), an important milestone in the struggle for Jewish emancipation in both Germany and France.

In the 1780s, the administration of Louis XVI began to ease some anti-Jewish restrictions. In 1785, the royal society of Metz sponsored an essay contest on the question, "Are there means of making the Jews happier and more useful in France?" In 1787, three prizewinners, including Abbé Henri-Baptiste Grégoire, were announced. All three echoed Dohm in arguing that the Jews, despite their cultural and economic particularities, could be transformed into loyal citizens. In 1788, the king commissioned Chrétien Guillaume de Malesherbes, who had already prepared two memoranda on the status of Protestants, to compile a similar study of Jews. Malesherbes concluded that tensions between Jews and the Christian populace in Alsace would cease only when Jews no longer constituted a "nation within a nation." To achieve this end, he recommended that they be granted civil rights analogous to those being contemplated for Protestants.

Although Malesherbes's recommendations were never implemented, they set the stage for the debate over Jewish emancipation during the French Revolution. Jews, as well as other non-Catholic minorities, should have been granted citizenship automatically by the Declaration of the Rights of Man and Citizen of August 26, 1789. Nevertheless, full emancipation was delayed another two years: Protestants were granted citizenship in December 1789; the Sephardi Jews of southwestern France in June 1790; and the Ashkenazi Jews of Alsace and Lorraine only in September 1791. Although several prominent people, most notably Grégoire and Count Stanislas de Clermont-Tonnerre, ardently defended the right of Jews to become citizens, staunch opposition was voiced, especially in Alsace and Lorraine. The bulk of this opposition came from the conservative Right, represented by the clergy and aristocracy. But opponents could be found on the Left as well. The Jacobin deputy from Colmar, Jean-François Rewbell, emerged as the foremost exponent of antiemancipation views, warning his colleagues in the National Assembly that the Alsatian peasantry would turn against the Revolution if Jews were emancipated.

The debate over Jewish emancipation resurfaced under Napoleon Bonaparte. On his return from the Battle of Austerlitz in 1806, Napoleon passed through Strasbourg and was besieged with complaints about Jewish moneylending, which allegedly had worsened since Jews had purchased a portion of the *biens nationaux,* or nationalized properties, that had formerly belonged to the church and nobility. Although Jews had acquired no more than about 2 percent of all the biens nationaux in Alsace between 1789 and 1811 (10 percent if one counts land they acquired on behalf of Christians), the lament that Alsace had been delivered into Jewish hands found a sympathetic hearing among members of Napoleon's cabinet, as well as some prominent intellectuals,

such as Louis de Bonald, who argued that Alsace had fallen victim to a new form of feudalism—the "feudality" of Jewish money.

Although Napoleon's Council of State, as well as the Assembly of Jewish Notables convened in 1806, recommended against the imposition of specifically anti-Jewish measures, the emperor rejected this advice, continuing to regard the Jews of Alsace as having been degraded by their trade. In May 1806, he imposed a one-year moratorium on all debts owed to Jews in Alsace and Lorraine, and on March 17, 1808, he proclaimed what quickly became known as the Infamous Decree, which imposed stringent curbs on Jewish moneylending. This edict capped interest rates on loans made by Jews at 5 percent, barred Jewish immigration into Alsace and Lorraine, and stipulated that Jews from these provinces could move to the French interior only if they took up agriculture. Although the Infamous Decree initially applied to all Jews, the Sephardim in the south and the tiny Jewish community in Paris quickly won exemptions.

In 1818, after Napoleon's fall from power, the Infamous Decree was allowed to lapse. Nevertheless, debate over the role of Jewish moneylending continued to rage. In 1819, it appeared that the antisemitic Hep-Hep riots sweeping southwestern Germany might spill over into Alsace. In 1822, bands of men claiming to speak for the government and intent on undermining the "impious" Jewish community, encouraged the peasantry to renounce their debts to Jews, and the following year, both Alsatian departments considered whether to renew the Infamous Decree. In 1824, the Strasbourg Society of Sciences, Agriculture, and Arts sponsored another essay contest asking by what means the Jews of Alsace could be made to enjoy the benefits of civilization. Although the prizewinning essays did not demand the reinstatement of exceptional anti-Jewish legislation, they did advocate strict government control over usury in general, as well as state-sponsored measures to compel Jews to enter "productive" trades.

The periods of the July Monarchy (1830–1848), the Second Republic (1848–1851), and the Second Empire (1851–1870) were characterized by countervailing tendencies. On the one hand, urban middle-class Jews made enormous strides toward integration and acculturation, and state-sponsored antisemitism diminished significantly. In 1831, rabbis began to receive salaries from the state, which had been paying the salaries of Christian clergy since the first decade of the century, and in 1846, the *more judaico,* a special oath for Jews, was discontinued, greatly improving the legal status of Jews.

On the other hand, tensions continued to simmer in the countryside. As a result of the persistent problem of peasant indebtedness, compounded by the increasing number of small landholdings, every wave of revolutionary upheaval produced anti-Jewish uprisings. In 1832, in the midst of a severe food crisis following the Revolution of 1830, armed peasants, egged on by the local clergy, pillaged the Jewish communities of Bergheim, Itterswiller, and Ribeauvillé, forcing Jews to take flight. Even more widespread violence erupted during the Revolution of 1848, when at least 20 percent of all Jewish communities in Alsace experienced anti-Jewish violence. Troops ultimately were called in to restore order.

During the period when the territories of Alsace-Lorraine were incorporated into the German Empire (1871–1918), antisemitic violence abated. Popular antisemitism did not disappear, however. In the 1880s, the movement to create credit banks for small farmers, which had strong support from the Catholic clergy, invariably inspired antisemitic agitation, since one of its chief goals was to break the Jewish stranglehold over cattle dealing and moneylending. Catholic antisemitism was further stoked by the Dreyfus Affair (1894–1899), which had special resonance in this region because Dreyfus was an Alsatian Jew. Although Catholics and Jews had cooperated on behalf of the pro-French cause in Alsace-Lorraine since 1871, the Jewish population felt increasingly aggrieved by the fierce antisemitic and anti-Alsatian agitation that accompanied the affair in France. Many Alsatian Catholics insisted on Dreyfus's guilt, notwithstanding the evidence of a massive cover-up by the French army or the incessant anti-Alsatian agitation that French antisemites, such as Édouard Drumont, invoked to suggest that Alsatians, like Jews, were all Prussians at heart and could never be trusted.

Between the two world wars, when Alsace and Lorraine were returned to France, new political and economic tensions resulted in heightened antisemitism. The fact that some Jewish deputies supported extending the separation of church and state into the region revived blanket accusations from Catholics that Jews were enemies of the church. An even more contentious issue was the large-scale immigration of Jews into Alsace and Lorraine from eastern Europe and Nazi Germany. During the summer of 1933, local chambers of commerce and artisan associations in the major cities orchestrated street demonstrations calling on the central government to curb refugee settlement, since, they alleged, refugee-owned firms engaged in "dishonest" competition with local businesses. Sensitive to these middle-class protests, the central government closed Alsace and Lorraine to further refugee settlement by the end of 1933. The 1936 victory of the Popular Front government led by Léon Blum, who was a socialist and a Jew, as well as a new surge of Jewish refugees between 1938 and 1939 pushed tensions to dangerous levels. In 1939, the government even banned antisemitic propaganda on the grounds that it was abetting the Nazi propaganda machine and endangering national security.

After the fall of France in June 1940, Germany again took control of Alsace and Lorraine. Most of the 29,000 Jews who were living in these provinces in 1939 had already been evacuated to the interior when war broke out, but any remaining Jews were expelled. The displaced Jews found refuge throughout the unoccupied zone, and the majority survived the war. After the war, most of the survivors returned to the region and rebuilt their lives. Since then, relations with the non-Jewish population have generally been amicable, marred only by the xenophobia and antisemitism of Jean-Marie Le Pen's National Front Movement, which won nearly a quarter of the Alsatian vote in the 2002 presidential election and as much as 30 percent in some rural districts. Although Le Pen and his movement target primarily black and Arab immigrants rather than Jews, his talk of "France's Christian civilization" and his trivialization of the Holocaust continue to inspire unease among the region's Jewish population.

—*Vicki Caron*

See also Diderot, Denis; Dohm, Christian Wilhelm von; Dreyfus Affair; Drumont, Édouard; 1848; Emancipation; Expulsions, High Middle Ages; France; Grégoire, Henri-Baptiste; Hep-Hep Riots; Infamous Decree; Le Pen, Jean-Marie; State-within-a-State; Usury; Voltaire, François-Marie-Arouet de

References

Caron, Vicki. *Between France and Germany: The Jews of Alsace-Lorraine, 1871–1918* (Stanford, CA: Stanford University Press, 1988).

———. *Uneasy Asylum: France and the Jewish Refugee Crisis, 1933–1942* (Stanford, CA: Stanford University Press, 1999).

Hertzberg, Arthur. *The French Enlightenment and the Jews: The Origins of Modern Anti-Semitism* (New York: Columbia University Press, 1968).

Hyman, Paula E. *The Emancipation of the Jews of Alsace: Acculturation and Tradition in the Nineteenth Century* (New Haven, CT: Yale University Press, 1991).

Katz, Jacob. *From Prejudice to Destruction: Anti-Semitism, 1700–1933* (Cambridge, MA: Harvard University Press, 1980).

American Jewish Committee and Antidefamation Efforts in the United States

The American Jewish Committee (AJC) was organized in 1906 by a group of the most professionally successful and highly assimilated Jews in the United States. Its early mission was not concerned with the status of Jews in America, however, but rather with the fate of Jews in Europe and elsewhere, who were suffering persecution and dislocation. For decades, a persistent reluctance to play visible roles in fighting domestic antisemitism characterized AJC activism and, in the minds of its critics, meant that the fight to win full equality for Jewish Americans would be led by other organizations.

The AJC's longtime president, Louis Marshall (1916–1929), used his unassailable prestige to formulate the organization's cautious, nonconfrontational political style. Marshall believed in philanthropic and political activism on behalf of Jews abroad but in discreet, behind-the-scenes lobbying to redress antisemitic discrimination faced by Jews in the United States. His friends used the term *Marshall Law* in grudging tribute to his autonomy and his penchant for acting solely on his own judgment in representing the AJC.

When controversies arose in which Jews were publicly defamed or impugned, Marshall unhesitatingly fired off letters to public officials, demanding investigations and apologies. The "No Hebrews" advertisements of resort owners, the blood libel accusation against the Jews of Massena, New York, in 1927, the libelous antisemitism of Henry Ford during the 1920s—the AJC's response to all of these and other incidents put Marshall's personal influence and political judgment on display. He preferred leading through the example of his personal behavior, espousing the values of U.S. citizenship he wanted Jews to embrace. He was certain that if they demonstrated their fealty to constitutional ideals and legal traditions, pernicious antisemitism would eventually fade from the public sphere. Only when antisemitism threatened the fundamental civil rights of Jews did he advocate direct political and legal action.

Other religious and secular Jewish leaders, frustrated by what they saw as the AJC's passivity and elitism, organized the rival American Jewish Congress during World War I. The congress advocated the establishment of a Jewish state in Palestine, an issue on which the AJC's top officials exhibited nervousness. The AJC's reaction to another World War I–era Jewish cause, the sham trial and tainted conviction of Leo Frank on murder charges, remained consistent with Marshall's philosophy of indirect activism. He cautioned Jews against public protest and against sending money to Jewish organizations in the South, for fear of stirring up more anger. Marshall argued Frank's appeal before the Supreme Court, but that effort did not prevent Frank's lynching in August 1915. The Anti-Defamation League (ADL) of B'nai B'rith was formed in response to Frank's trial, and it took up the court challenges that the AJC declined to pursue in such cases.

After Marshall's death and under the rising threat of Nazism, the AJC redefined itself. The president now served as the public spokesperson for the organization, and actual policymaking was vested in an executive vice-president. Elected to that job in 1943, John Slawson was "determined to transform the AJC into a vibrant and socially relevant civil rights organization" (Ivers 1995, 43). Under his leadership, the AJC worked more directly through courts and legislatures to achieve equality for Jews, but it still stopped far short of the more activist programs of the American Jewish Congress and the ADL.

There was, however, still something of the old approach to be seen in one of the more successful episodes of Jewish antidefamation work. Together, the AJC and ADL confronted the antisemitism of Gerald L. K. Smith, a demagogue who was active during the 1930s and 1940s. Smith's inflammatory lectures attracted thousands and sparked widespread protests. Rabbi Solomon Fineberg of the AJC devised a strategy calling for "dynamic silence," arguing that if no one wrote about Smith or protested his lectures, his movement would die for want of publicity. Overcoming initial resistance, Fineberg finally persuaded other Jewish defense organizations to adopt the silent treatment. Smith's audiences declined drastically, and once the newspapers stopped covering the protests he engendered, his political career ended too.

The Holocaust and the more energetic enforcement of civil rights for African Americans after World War II continued to push the AJC toward a more public and proactive role. AJC lawyers became directly involved in the civil rights litigation undertaken by the National Association for the Advancement of Colored People. After 1945, the AJC signed amicus briefs in such cases as the challenge to the use of racially exclusive covenants in residential property sales. This practice broadened over the next sixty years to the point where the AJC now issues annual reports detailing the federal cases in which it has appeared.

In the latter years of the twentieth century, the AJC continued its legal work on civil rights even as the long-standing relationship between Jews and African Americans deteriorated. It continued to produce studies on the nature and scope of antisemitism in the United States, the status of Jews in higher education and the professions, and the perception of Jewish influence in the media and government. Widely regarded as one of the most influential Jewish organizations in the world, it

continues today to build its influence and authority as the premier U.S. Jewish activist organization.
—*Victoria Saker Woeste*

See also African American–Jewish Relations; American Nazi Party; *Dearborn Independent* and *The International Jew;* Ford, Henry; Frank, Leo; Restricted Public Accommodations, United States; Restrictive Covenants; Ritual Murder (Modern); Smith, Gerald L. K.; Zionism

References
Gerber, David A. *Anti-Semitism in American History* (Urbana: University of Illinois Press, 1986).
Ivers, Gregg. *To Build a Wall: American Jews and the Separation of Church and State* (Charlottesville: University Press of Virginia, 1995).

American Nazi Party

The American Nazi Party (ANP) was founded by George Lincoln Rockwell in 1959 and headquartered in Arlington, Virginia. The ANP was the first political organization in the postwar United States openly to use Nazi symbols, such as the swastika, and to defend the defeated regime of Adolf Hitler. Rockwell modeled his organization on Hitler's, with particular emphasis on the "leader principle." He, of course, was the undisputed "American Fuehrer."

The National Socialist White People's Party (NSWPP), as it was renamed shortly before Rockwell was murdered by his protégé John Patler in 1967, was poorly funded and never had more than a few hundred active members. Its attention-grabbing activities and Rockwell's flair for dramatic publicity stunts won greater national attention than its actual strength merited. The party's chief financial patron was Harold Noel Arrowsmith, an amateur anthropologist and obsessive antisemite. Arrowsmith, the son of a prominent Baltimore cleric, originally hired Rockwell to run his own creation, the National Committee to Free America from Jewish Domination, which had, as far as extant records can verify, precisely two members; Arrowsmith and Rockwell. The committee's chief function was to distribute flyers with caricatures of Jews (drawn by Rockwell, a gifted cartoonist) and to picket Dwight D. Eisenhower's White House. When enthusiasm for that activity waned, Rockwell proposed to Arrowsmith a party based on Hitler's

American Nazi Party Fuehrer George Lincoln Rockwell is shown here at his party's headquarters in Arlington, Virginia. Note the sign above the mailbox. (Bettmann/Corbis)

judged that the ANP could not long survive if it were denied publicity. He worked tirelessly, although not always with complete success, to convince Jewish community groups that the most effective way to neutralize the party was to ignore its provocations. Slowly, his message took hold, and by the mid-1960s, any threat the ANP might have posed seemed much diminished, a decline punctuated by Rockwell's death in 1967. The party struggled on under his successor but was unable to recapture public attention. From time to time, attempts are made by various antisemitic and neo-Nazi fringe groups to exploit the iconic value of the ANP. To this point, none have been successful.

—*Frederick J. Simonelli*

See also American Jewish Committee and Antidefamation Efforts in the United States; Christian Identity Movement; Militia Movement; Neo-Nazism, German; Rockwell, George Lincoln; Smith, Gerald L. K.; United States; White Power Movement

References
Higham, Charles. *American Swastika* (Garden City, NY: Doubleday, 1985).
Simonelli, Frederick J. *American Fuehrer: George Lincoln Rockwell and the American Nazi Party* (Champaign: University of Illinois Press, 1999).

own, with Storm troopers, swastika-emblazoned flags, and a plan to mobilize the white masses for a Nazi takeover of the United States by 1972.

The ANP's program was based on antisemitism, racism, and homophobia, and it seldom strayed from those themes. Its primary tactic was street theater, a calculated attempt to manipulate the media in order to grab the headlines. Outrageous provocations, brawls, planned confrontations with the authorities, and inflammatory rhetoric, Rockwell hoped, would result in wider membership and improved cash flow. For a while, the strategy worked. Every time ANP Storm troopers instigated a confrontation with police or with Jewish groups, the resulting publicity brought in what Rockwell called "Atta' Boy, George!" letters from sympathizers around the country. The letters often contained cash that was desperately needed to keep the fledgling ANP afloat.

Rockwell's primary target, American Jews, at first responded with outrage to every new provocation. Then, the American Jewish Committee, under the leadership of Rabbi Solomon Fineberg, devised a strategy of "dynamic silence," first used so effectively against Gerald L. K. Smith, one of the most vocal antisemites of the 1930s. Fineberg

Angriff, Der

Der Angriff (The Attack) was a savagely antisemitic newspaper founded by Joseph Goebbels in 1927. Under his direction, the paper rose from an obscure weekly to become the second-largest National Socialist newspaper in Germany.

In May 1927, the Nazi Party, because of its incessant rabble-rousing, was banned in Berlin. The party did not dissolve but rather went underground. As the city's *Gauleiter* (district leader), Joseph Goebbels was determined to maintain the party's visibility in the German capital. To this end, he established *Der Angriff*, which published its first issue on July 4, 1927. Goebbels hired Julius Lippert as editor to oversee the newspaper's day-to-day affairs and went about recruiting a highly educated staff, several of whom held doctorates. The most important *Angriff* employee was the talented political caricaturist Hans Schweitzer, who published his cartoons under the pseudonym Mjoelnir, the name of the pagan god Donner's hammer. Mjoelnir soon became famous for his remorselessly antisemitic cartoons, especially those lampooning the vice-president of the Berlin police force, Bernhard Weiss, whom the paper dubbed Isidor. Schweitzer later became one of the most important poster artists of the Third Reich.

Goebbels wrote much of the paper's antisemitic copy himself, although he usually left his articles unsigned in order to avoid libel suits. This strategy proved futile, however, and *Der Angriff* was sued numerous times, especially by Bernhard Weiss. At first, the paper languished, having a circulation of only 4,500, consisting mostly of Berlin's small number of Nazi loyalists. *Der Angriff* was always in dire financial straits, and its publisher repeatedly had to solicit loans and donations to keep it afloat. But Goebbels sank a great deal of the local party's resources into the project, with ultimately impressive results. The paper began to appear twice weekly starting in October 1929 and became a daily in November of the following year. Its fortunes rose along with those of the Nazi Party. *Der Angriff* circulation increased dramatically following the success of the party in the September 1930 elections, reaching its high-water mark of 110,600 in July 1932.

Recognizing that the majority of Berlin's citizens were from the working classes, Goebbels sought to target his newspaper's message at the proletariat, especially the unemployed. The appalling conditions in which the workers lived were the product, the paper insisted, of the Jewish-controlled "system" dominating the Weimar Republic. Following the Nazi seizure of power and his own elevation to the position of propaganda chief of the Third Reich, Goebbels lost interest in the paper. In 1934, he relinquished control. *Der Angriff* became the official organ of the German Labor Front and soon ceased playing a significant role.

—*Russel Lemmons*

See also Caricature, Anti-Jewish (Modern); Goebbels, Joseph; National Socialist German Workers' Party; *Stürmer, Der;* Weimar
References
Lemmons, Russel. *Goebbels and "Der Angriff"* (Lex-

ington: University Press of Kentucky, 1994).
———. "Hans Schweitzer's Anti-Semitic Caricatures: The Weimar Years, 1926–1933." In *Representations of Jews through the Ages.* Edited by Leonard Jay Greenspoon (Omaha, NE: Creighton University Press, 1996), 197–212.

Antichrist

Although references to Antichrist in the Christian Bible (1 John; 2 John) do not associate him solely with Jews—the term a*ntichrist* is defined as anyone who denies Christ (1 John 2:22)—early Christian exegetes did. Interpreting the symbolism of Revelation and other enigmatic New Testament passages, exegetes developed an apocalyptic scenario in which the human Antichrist, inspired by the devil, would appear in the last days shortly before the return of Christ to deceive and persecute the elect (Matt. 24; Mark 13; Luke 21). A vicious persecutor and persuasive false prophet claiming to be Christ (Matt. 24:5), Antichrist was first expected to convert Jews because, as Jerome argued, they still awaited the Messiah, having rejected Jesus for Barabbas (Mark 15:6–15). In medieval eschatology, Jews were to be Antichrist's most loyal disciples, preferring another who would come in his own name (John 5:43) to the true Messiah. Teaching a false doctrine and establishing a false church, called the "tabernacle of Antichrist" by Gregory the Great, Antichrist would reward his followers by rebuilding the Temple in Jerusalem (2 Thess. 2:4).

Exegetes wove together apocalyptic interpretations of numerous scriptural passages to create a prophetic biography of Antichrist, arguing, as one commentary on Revelation 11:7 stated, that he would come "from the bottomless impiety of the Jewish people" (from Pseudo-Alcuin's commentary, *In Apocalypsin,* edited in the *Patrologia Latina,* vol. 100, column 1148). Antichrist was expected to be a Jew from the tribe of Dan (Gen. 49:17; Jer. 8:16) who would be born either in Babylon or in Chorozaim, would be reared in Bethsaida, and would rule in Capernaum, an interpretation of Jesus' words in Luke 10:13, 15. Antichrist would be supported by the armies of Gog and Magog (Ezek. 38, 39; Rev. 20), which, identified as the lost tribes of Israel, were imprisoned by Alexander the Great behind the Caucasus. In the last days, they would break through the mountains to attack Christians, enlisting the Jews, who, according to Sir John Mandeville's *Travels,* would continue to speak Hebrew in order to communicate with Gog and Magog. Near the end of Antichrist's rule, Two Witnesses (Rev. 11:3)—identified as Enoch and Elijah, who had not died but awaited the last days in the earthly paradise—would come to preach against Antichrist, the beast from the abyss (Rev. 11:7). One version of the Antichrist legend expected Enoch and Elijah to convert the Jews to Christianity (Rom. 11:26).

In the mid-tenth century, Adso, abbot of Montier-en-Der, organized this disparate scriptural commentary, sibylline literature, and folklore into the *Little Book of Antichrist,* which served as a major source throughout the Middle Ages for inventive sermons, poems, plays, and theological compendiums as well as visual representations of the human Antichrist in sculpture, stained glass, wall paintings, and manuscript illustrations. The mid-fourteenth-century French play *Jour du jugement* (Day of Judgment) exemplified the widely popular understanding of Antichrist during the later Middle Ages. Beginning with a demonic parliament in hell, the play staged the conceiving of the Antichrist by a devil with a Jewish prostitute living in Babylon. Antichrist's followers included many Jews, and a usurer and his family were cursed in the play's concluding doomsday scenes. Medieval art similarly emphasized the close connection between Antichrist and Jews. Deluxe thirteenth-century moralized Bibles repeatedly portrayed Jews as accomplices of Antichrist, and fifteenth-century German block books pictured his circumcision by a Jewish priest and had him rebuilding the Temple in Jerusalem and being welcomed by Jewish disciples, who helped him burn books of Christian theology.

Later interpretations of Antichrist, such as the polemical apocalypticism of the Protestant Reformation—which identified Antichrist with the papacy and Catholicism—did not associate the apocalyptic deceiver specifically with Jews. Yet the medieval understanding of the single human Antichrist to come at the end of time and be supported by Jewish followers remained strong within Catholic tradition after the Reformation, as evident in *The Life of Antichrist* (1682) by Denis of Luxemburg. Since Antichrist was expected to dominate the world at the end of time, such notions also fed antisemitic tracts about Jewish world conspiracies, such as the *Protocols of the Elders of Zion.* Features of the traditional Antichrist also influenced twentieth-century evangelical millenarianism. Hal Lindsey's *The Late Great Planet Earth* (1970), for example, expected a Jewish false prophet to support an Antichrist-power, and Jerry Falwell, in a sermon delivered in January 1999, stated that Antichrist was a male Jew living in Israel, a sign suggesting the imminence of the end of the world.

—*Richard K. Emmerson*

See also Church Fathers; Gospels; Gregory the Great, Pope; Iconography, Christian; Nilus, Sergei; *Protocols of the Elders of Zion;* Reformation
References
Emmerson, Richard K. *Antichrist in the Middle Ages: A Study of Medieval Apocalypticism, Art, and Literature* (Seattle: University of Washington Press, 1981).
McGinn, Bernard. *Antichrist: Two Thousand Years of the Human Fascination with Evil* (New York: HarperCollins, 1994).

Antisemites' Petition (1880–1881)

During the summer and autumn of 1880, activists from the new antisemitic political parties and like-minded university students circulated separate petitions that were intended to serve as a plebiscite of the German people on the Jewish Question. The first and largest of these was the brainchild of Bernhard Förster (d. 1889), who claimed to have received his inspiration while attending Richard Wagner's Bayreuth Festival. The petition ultimately submitted to Prince Otto von Bismarck spoke in the urgent rhetorical voice of the day. An alien tribe was about to establish complete dominion over the Christian population; its exploitation of national labor had driven a wedge between classes of Germans; and revolution beckoned. The nation was in the process of being alienated from its true essence. The agitational literature that accompanied the document was equally shrill, stressing that mass violence against Jews was inevitable unless the government speedily took the four steps demanded in the petition: the prohibition, or at least the limitation, of Jewish immigration; the exclusion of Jews from positions of authority over Germans; an end to the employment of Jews as teachers in the national elementary schools; and a special census of Jews (later specified as "racially based"). Such a program meant the revocation of Jewish emancipation that had been granted in1869. Disenfranchisement along these lines became the basic agenda for all of the antisemitic political parties in Germany before 1914. The Nazis eventually achieved this goal with the promulgation of the Nuremberg Laws of 1935.

The petition's eager volunteers gathered the signatures of approximately 265,000 adult German males. Well over half came from the state of Prussia; Berlin/Brandenburg alone contributed 30,000; and Silesia, an eastern border province, provided nearly 50,000 signatures, perhaps because of a (statistically baseless) fear of being inundated by a flood of Jewish immigrants from the East. Beyond Prussia, Württemberg, a state noted for its liberal traditions, nonetheless supplied 7,000 signatures. The Antisemites' Petition was not a huge success in terms of the numbers of signatures—in fact, antisemitic leaders cautioned against trying this strategy again, lest it fall flat. But it was nevertheless an important moment in the history of political antisemitism.

The petition's appeal for the educated was dramatically demonstrated by the large number of university students who signed the document; half the student body of the University of Berlin supported the initiative, and the universities of Leipzig and Halle were also well represented. The enthusiasm for the petition in university circles provided the stimulus for the formation of an important carrier of antisemitism among the educated and future leaders of Germany; the Association of German Students (Verein Deutscher Studenten).

Between November 20 and 22, 1880—that is, well before it reached Bismarck (in April 1881)—the petition became the subject of a crucial debate in the Prussian parliament. When a Liberal deputy questioned the government about its intentions with regard to the inflammatory agitation, a minister in Bismarck's government responded with a lukewarm defense of the status quo. He assured the house that Jewish equality would be maintained but refrained from condemning the petition as an outrageous attack on human rights. This remote "neutrality" on the part of the government robbed those who fought against antisemitism of an important ally in their struggle.

—*Richard S. Levy*

See also Antisemitic Political Parties; Förster, Bernhard; German Students, Association of; Liebermann von Sonnenberg, Max; Nuremberg Laws; Stoecker, Adolf; Wagner, Richard

References

Jarausch, Konrad H. *Students, Society, and Politics in Imperial Germany: The Rise of Academic Illiberalism* (Princeton, NJ: Princeton University Press, 1982).

Levy, Richard S., ed. *Antisemitism in the Modern World: An Anthology of Texts* (Lexington, MA: D. C. Heath, 1991).

Antisemitic Correspondence

One of the great ironies of antisemitic politics in Germany and elsewhere was the inability of the antisemites to counter what they habitually described as Jewry's stranglehold on the press. Even Adolf Hitler's *Völkischer Beobachter* (Racial Observer) could not win a significant following outside Munich; its national circulation did not approach that of the great dailies, until the Nazi Party gained power over all publishing in 1933. From its appearance in the late 1870s, the antisemitic political movement never mastered the helter-skelter of its journalistic practices. Newspapers provided many antisemitic activists and Reichstag deputies with a (perilous) livelihood. Anyone with leadership pretensions had to have a newspaper at his disposal, and cutthroat competition prevailed against the obvious need to pool resources and centralize efforts against the "Jewish press hydra." Between 1890 and 1897, the period of political antisemitism's greatest strength, 36 new newspapers appeared; by 1898, only 7 were still in operation. The average life span of individual newspapers attached to the antisemitic political parties was two years. The enemies of the antisemites delighted in pointing out another irony: these publications sported exactly the characteristics attributed to the "Jew-press"—poor production values; excessive attention to automobile crashes and celebrity sex scandals; superficial, biased, inaccurate reporting; "coarseness of tone"; and an often fatal vulnerability to libel suits.

The *Antisemitic Correspondence* (*Antisemitische-Correspondenz*) could be called a success only in comparison to the jumble of short-lived, shabby newspapers produced by the antisemitic parties and associations of the German Empire. It was one of the few to appear throughout the period, surviving into the early years of the Weimar Republic. Even so, it changed ownership, location, frequency of publication, and name unusually often (*Deutschsoziale-Blätter* [1894–1914], *Deutschvölkische-Blätter* [1914–1924], *Reichs-Sturmfahne* [1924]). Founded in October 1885 by the era's most successful antisemitic publisher, Theodor Fritsch, the paper assumed an authoritative voice in the lull between the first and second waves of antisemitic grassroots organization. Fritsch opened the newspaper to a discussion of methods and goals, hoping to take over leadership of the movement as a whole. When his own antiparliamentary strategy lost out to those who wanted to prosecute the Jewish Question through conventional party politics, Fritsch sold the paper to Max Liebermann von Sonnenberg, a major figure in the antisemitic German Social Reform Party. Liebermann immediately began losing the 7,200 paid subscribers—and probably twice as many collateral readers—that he had inherited, thanks to his much more conservative approach to journalism. Gone were Fritsch's critical pieces on organized Christianity and his attacks on prominent people whose relations to Jews he found offensive.

A typical edition of the *Antisemitic Correspondence* bore on its masthead the epigram of Heinrich von Treitschke: "The Jews are our misfortune." The front page was given over to a feature article of topical interest, coverage of the doings of antisemitic deputies in the Reichstag and the state parliaments, organizational announcements, speaking tours, and other party matters. Regular columns dealt with "Israel in Conflict with the Law" and "Mosaic"—the exposure of Jewish misdeeds as yet unpunished. "The Conquest of Germany by the Jews" detailed the enemy's infiltration of medicine, law, and education. Book reviews, news from abroad, and letters to the editor were single-minded in their pursuit of a solution to the Jewish Question. Well before the war, only a few hundred subscribers could still be lured by these offerings.

—*Richard S. Levy*

See also Antisemitic Political Parties; Fritsch, Theodor; "Jewish" Press; Liebermann von Sonnenberg, Max; Treitschke, Heinrich von
Reference
Levy, Richard S. *The Downfall of the Anti-Semitic Political Parties in Imperial Germany* (New Haven, CT: Yale University Press, 1975).

Antisemitic Political Parties (Germany, 1879–1914)

One of imperial Germany's most important precedents in the organization of antisemitic sentiment came with the founding of political parties specifically dedicated to combating Jewish power. From the late 1870s, those whose first priority was solving the Jewish Question arranged themselves in small and fractious political parties appealing to Protestant peasants and small-town, lower-middle-class constituencies. Among the most durable was Court Chaplain Adolf Stoecker's Christian Social Party, founded in 1878, which took shape as an avowedly antisemitic party during the Berlin Movement. Stoecker, having squandered the tacit support of the Hohenzollern court, Otto von Bismarck, and the powerful Conservative Party by the mid-1880s, was forced to rely on supporters from rural Westphalia to hold his seat in the parliament. The populist Antisemitische Volkspartei (Antisemitic People's Party) established in Hessenland in 1889 by Otto Böckel; the Saxon-based Deutsche Reformpartei (German Reform Party [1880]) of Oswald Zimmermann; and the Deutschsoziale Partei (German Social Party [1889]) led by Max Liebermann von Sonnenberg united briefly as the Deutschsoziale Reformpartei (German Social Reform Party, 1894–1900). But personal rivalries, embarrassing scandals, and shifting fortunes at the polls led to frequent schisms, name changes, and a record of unrelieved failure in the Reichstag. Although the staunchly patriotic oratory of Stoecker and Liebermann could command the ear of parliament, the other antisemitic deputies, unable to meet the high standards of that body or contribute anything substantial to the legislative process, were frequently objects of ridicule.

Notwithstanding variations in rhetorical style and the personal respectability of their leaders, the antisemitic parties had much in common. For campaign personnel and as a source of always uncertain finances, they relied at the grassroots level on approximately 140 reform clubs. The German Conservative Party and the Agrarian League doled out support to chosen antisemitic candidates at election time but also kept their distance from rowdier and less politically reliable elements within the movement. Leaders earned their living by writing for or editing numerous, usually short-lived newspapers, twenty-five to forty of which were associated with one of the parties. The programs of the parties sought to solve the Jewish Question, while improving the lot of their constituents, through conventional legislative means. They all advocated the exclusion of Jews from governmental offices and employment in public schools, limitations on immigration, and the taking of a special, racially based census. None of these measures, which collectively would have amounted to a revocation of Jewish emancipation, came close to adoption in the national or state parliaments. Unable to penetrate the Catholic or working-class masses, the antisemites of the imperial era failed to build a strong mass movement. They achieved their high-water mark in the Reichstag elections of 1893 with sixteen deputies (eight from Hessenland and six from Saxony). Perhaps 350,000 votes (4.4 percent) were cast for identifiable antisemites from all parties. From that point, however, their percentage of the vote declined steadily. In the last Reichstag elections before World War I, they mustered only 131,000 votes, and during the course of the war, the six remaining antisemitic deputies disappeared into various right-wing formations, bringing an end to their autonomous existence.

This bankruptcy of conventional, parliamentary antisemitism led to a gradual radicalization of outlook. By the turn of the twentieth century, antisemitic politicians inside and outside the parliament began casting about for more effective methods in a struggle against the Jews that many of them thought they were losing. The institutions of the German Empire and the loyalty of non-Jewish government officials and public figures, as well as the legal, educational, and economic systems all came under attack. Continuing failure in the Reichstag and deaths among the older generation of leaders cleared the way for those who had never accepted the feasibility of solving the Jewish Question through party politics. For such deeply undemocratic men, parliaments and parties were symptoms of the Judaic disease afflicting Germany. According to them, all levels of German society would have to be infused with antisemitism before sweeping measures to cleanse German life of false values could be undertaken. Normal politics were useless in this struggle for survival.

—*Richard S. Levy*

See also Agrarian League; Antisemites' Petition; Berlin Movement; Böckel, Otto; Christian Social Party (Germany); Emancipation; Liebermann von Sonnenberg, Max; Stoecker, Adolf

References
Levy, Richard S. *The Downfall of the Anti-Semitic Political Parties in Imperial Germany* (New Haven, CT: Yale University Press, 1975).
Niewyk, Donald. "Solving the 'Jewish Problem': Continuity and Change in German Antisemitism, 1871–1945," *Leo Baeck Institute Year Book* 35 (1990): 335–370.
Rürup, Reinhard. "Emancipation and Crisis. The 'Jewish Question' in Germany, 1850–1890," *Leo Baeck Institute Year Book* 20 (1975): 13–25.

Antisemitism, Accusations of

Antisemitism remains a real and common problem in the world. Recognizing it, however, is not always easy. Is a film director who creates an obviously noxious Jewish character necessarily antisemitic? Do critics of the state of Israel, even harsh critics, warrant being suspected of antisemitism? Should someone who casually uses *Jew* as a verb be automatically labeled antisemitic? Answers to those questions will vary, and consequently, an unpleasant problem comes to the fore: in recent decades, the charges of being an "antisemite" or "antisemitic" have often been made too casually, if not irresponsibly.

The same has been true of "racist" and "racism" or "fascist" and "fascism." The problem with such mistaken charges is that they discredit the legitimacy of valid concepts. So, for example, the widespread employment of the term *fascist* by political groups since the 1960s to describe various governments and police agencies in Europe and the United States all but destroyed any meaning or relevance for the term. The great frequency with which the charge of racism is made has begun to raise concerns about the adequacy and even sometimes the fairness of the term itself. Similar concerns have been voiced about charges of antisemitism.

Complicating this problem has been Israel, a self-described "Jewish State" ardently supported by many Jews in the Diaspora, notably in the United States. As a consequence, criticisms of Israel (not to mention actual assaults on its citizens) have often been called "antisemitic," which has forestalled the willingness of many Israelis and many of Israel's supporters to examine the state's policies. Why, after all, should someone respond to those perceived as inherently hostile to one's existence?

The readiness of Jews today to label attitudes and behaviors as antisemitic arises from a long history of persecution, climaxing in the Holocaust. Now, with a fundamentally restructured sense of victimhood, it is not surprising that Jews have become keenly sensitive to how people and governments not only treat them but also speak of them. Nor is it surprising that Jewish communities and leaders today should be so outspoken in pointing out and combating what they see as antisemitism. Having the Holocaust in memory and possessing more prestige and political influence than ever before, Jews no longer choose to be silent.

On balance, that is a good thing, but there are dangers in this newfound willingness to know and name one's enemies. Mistakes can be made, mistakes that are not easily rectified because the accusation alone creates public shame. Beyond the possibility of unfairness lies perhaps a greater danger—a lack of understanding of and tolerance for the complexities of human actions and their motives. We may know antisemitism when we see it. Then again, what we see is itself often shaped by what we think we know.

—*Jonathan Marwil*

See also Antisemitism, Etymology of; Anti-Zionism
References
Arendt, Hannah. "Antisemitism." Pt. 1 of *The Origins of Totalitarianism* (New York: Harcourt, Brace and World, 1951).
Biale, David. *Power and Powerlessness in Jewish History* (New York: Schocken Books, 1987).

Antisemitism, Etymology of

The word *antisemitism* is not of ancient vintage. The earliest substantiated use of the term *antisemite* in a political sense came in late 1879. Wilhelm Marr, riding the popularity of his pamphlet *The Victory of Jewry over Germandom,* placed an advertisement on the last page of the twelfth edition to announce the first party dedicated exclusively to fighting Jewish power, the Antisemiten-Liga. Marr was not an original thinker, and the word may well have already been in circulation before he appropriated it for his party. There are at least two earlier documented uses of the term. In 1860, the Jewish scholar Moritz Steinschneider employed it in reference to Ernest Renan's views about Jews, accusing the French thinker of resorting to the euphemistic expression *Semitism* to mask his hostility. This essentially cultural usage can also be found in the influential *Staats-Lexikon* (Encyclopedia [1856–1866]), edited by Karl von Rotteck.

Semitism, attributed to the German Enlightenment figure A. L. Schlözer (1735–1809), had been in use since the end of the eighteenth century. Although there are those who claim that the term initially had a fairly neutral connotation, this was no longer the case by midcentury, when it had come to signify a body of uniformly negative traits supposedly clinging to Jews. The word may not have been value-free even at its inception, however. Schlözer clearly had more in mind than the objective linguistic differences between

Shem and Japheth, the sons of Noah. He presented the cultures of their progeny as polarities. A historian at the University of Göttingen, he also printed (but probably did not write) anti-Jewish articles in his influential journals. The transition from *Semitism* to *antisemitism* was effortless. Heinrich von Treitschke, one of the first among the intellectual elite to adopt the term *antisemitism,* had been using the word *Semitentum* pejoratively for at least ten years to contrast the "deeply creative German" with the "flighty and unfruitful" Jews (in Boehlich 1965, 244). If Marr cannot be shown to have minted the word *antisemite,* he can at least share credit for salvaging it as the essentially political concept we use today. Moshe Zimmermann (1986, 90–95) speculated that using the term *antisemite* as opposed to *anti-Jewish* served two purposes, both conditioned by immediate circumstances. First, it distinguished the Antisemiten-Liga from Court Chaplain Adolf Stoecker's organization. Second, Marr and his allies felt they needed to protect themselves from the dreaded wrath of the Jews. Despite the antisemites' demagoguery and cold calculation, they were convinced that the enemy possessed the strength of will and the iron discipline to retaliate against them. *Semite* was, like the term *Israelite* or *Hebrew,* a little more refined, a little less confrontational than *(anti-)Jew.* There was some hope that the litigious Jews might be better fended off with the more obscure and distancing *antisemite.*

Motives, appropriateness—many anti-Jewish activists then and later objected to the term as inaccurate and burdensome—and originality aside, the historical importance of *antisemitism* lies in its nearly universal and swift adoption. The term came into its own in the autumn of 1879 and not just among the followers of Marr or Stoecker. Treitschke, who scorned both of them, used the word in the first installment of his highly influential "A Word about Our Jews" in November 1879. *Antisemite* or *antisemitism* appeared in the prestigious *Neue Freie Presse* of Vienna in January 1880 and in the Catholic *Augsburger Postzeitung* and the Berlin-based *Germania* in November 1880. By 1883, the word had broken out of the German-speaking world, crossing the Rhine to grace the masthead of *L'Antisémitique,*

the first French weekly dedicated to antisemitism. During the next decade, it gained common currency in the titles of books and pamphlets in English (1882), French (1883), Italian (1883), Hungarian (1884), Dutch (1893), and Russian (1894). Eventually, variants of *antisemitism, antisemite,* and *antisemitic* made their way into nearly every European language.

A neologism is never an accident. This particular word represented a movement achieving consciousness of itself and convincing others that a new designation was needed to encompass it.

—*Richard S. Levy*

See also Antisemitic Political Parties; Marr, Wilhelm; Renan, Ernest; Stoecker, Adolf; Treitschke, Heinrich von; *Victory of Jewry over Germandom, The; Word about Our Jews, A*

References
Bein, Alex. *The Jewish Problem: Biography of a World Problem* (Rutherford, NJ: Fairleigh Dickinson University Press, 1990).
Boehlich, W., ed. *Der Berliner Antisemitismusstreit* (Frankfurt am Main, Germany: Insel Verlag, 1965).
Levy, Richard S., ed. *Antisemitism in the Modern World: An Anthology of Texts* (Lexington, MA: D. C. Heath, 1991), 2–11.
Zimmermann, Moshe. *Wilhelm Marr: The Patriarch of Anti-Semitism* (New York: Oxford University Press, 1986).

Anti-Zionism

Anti-Zionism is not necessarily antisemitic. In its early years, Zionism was opposed by many Orthodox Jews on theological grounds. They rejected the idea of human intervention in the restoration of Jewish sovereignty in the land of Israel. They also rejected the secular politics of Zionist activists in the early days of the movement. In the decades before the Holocaust, moreover, Jews in western Europe and the United States who identified strongly with their home countries were often ambivalent and sometimes hostile to the Zionist project. After World War II, however, and following the creation of the state of Israel, criticism of the Zionist idea by Jews faded.

A very different anti-Zionism began to replace it, shaped by a variety of events and agendas and involving many different peoples, most of them non-Jews. At first, this anti-Zionism was largely confined to the Arab world, which felt threatened by the creation of the new state. After the 1967 Six Days' War, which not only ensured the continued existence of Israel but extended its borders, new voices were heard. Left-wing political groups in Europe and the United States began siding with the Palestinians and charging that a nefarious "imperialist" partnership existed between Israel and the United States. Such views hardened after the 1973 war and gained international standing in 1975 with the passage of UN Resolution 3329, familiarly known as the "Zionism is racism" resolution. This resolution was supported by the Arab, Islamic, and Soviet blocs, with the tacit acquiescence of many Western countries.

By that point, anti-Zionism was suffused with the familiar arguments, symbols, historical stereotypes, and purposes of antisemitism. This new anti-Zionism rejected the very existence of the state of Israel and attributed its objectionable policies to Judaism, a supposed "Jewish essence," and/or a conspiracy conducted by "world Jewry." Despite the repeal in 1991 of the 1975 UN resolution and the efforts at Oslo and elsewhere to fashion a Middle East peace, such thinking gradually began to permeate all levels of Muslim society, finding expression in every form of media, from school textbooks to the Internet.

Since 2000, when a new intifada began after it was rumored that Israel was planning to destroy the Al-Aqsa Mosque on Jerusalem's Temple Mount, antisemitic anti-Zionism has been increasing—and not just in the Arab world. In 2001, a conference on racism and xenophobia sponsored by the United Nations and held in Durban, South Africa, served as a platform for a resolution labeling Zionism as racism. Two years later, the U.S. decision to invade Iraq was widely seen as further proof of "Zionist power." In a recent poll, Europeans ranked Israel as the country that posed the greatest threat to world peace; greater than Iran, Iraq, or North Korea.

It is not always easy to distinguish between antisemitism and anti-Zionism. For non-Jews, including Arabs, criticism of Israel—even harsh criticism—can seem less like an effort to demonize a people long persecuted and more like an attempt to restore political rights and economic opportunity to people who feel they have legitimate grievances. For Israel, however, which proudly describes itself as a Jewish state and sees itself forced by others into a struggle for its very existence, and for Jews elsewhere who strongly support its right to survive, the notion that anti-Zionism is a new form of antisemitism makes perfect sense.

—*Richard S. Levy*

See also Anti-Zionism in the USSR; Arab Antisemitic Literature; Arab Boycott; Arafat, Yasir; Hussaini, Mufti Hajj Amin al-; Islamic Diaspora; Islamic Fundamentalism; New Left; Zionism
References
Klug, Brian. "No, Anti-Zionism Is Not Anti-Semitism." *Manchester Guardian,* December 3, 2003.
Lewis, Bernard. *Semites and Antisemites* (New York: Norton, 1986).
Sharansky, Natan. "On Hating the Jews," *Commentary* vol. 116 (November 2003) 4:26–34.

Anti-Zionism in the USSR

The essentials of Soviet antisemitic anti-Zionism—distinctly different from other forms of anti-Zionism—emerged mainly in the years following World War II and was deeply rooted in Jew-hatred already long present in many Eastern European countries. Before antisemitic ideology could be deployed by the Soviet Union, however, it had to be integrated into the doctrines of Marxism-Leninism. It is this adaptation that accounts for the unique characteristics of Soviet antisemitism.

Anti-Zionist persecution, in the strict sense, was a post–World War II phenomenon. In the 1930s under Stalin, the USSR ceased the strenuous combating of antisemitism, and the anti-Zionism embedded in the ideology of Marxism-Leninism began to harden into specifically anti-Jewish policies. Perhaps the most dramatic harbinger of this transformation was the 1935–1938 Great Purge; a series of show trials meant to strengthen Stalin's rule. But lesser trends were also significant in this regard. The anti-Jewish measures of the era were still rationalized on a traditional basis, however, reflecting the residual effects of an inherited antisemitism. Controversies between communist and noncommunist Jewish organizations in the 1930s, which, issued in the persecution of the latter, played an important role. The Soviet Union's increasingly hostile stance toward all religious communities and cultural autonomy movements was particularly destructive to corporate Jewish life. Most synagogues were closed, along with Jewish cultural institutions, schools, and newspapers, and many rabbis were arrested and murdered. At the same time, however, many Jews qua individuals experienced a dramatic upward social mobility.

The high tide of anti-Zionist persecution came during the purges and trials staged in the USSR and all its satellite states between 1948 and 1953. Although not alone, Jews were proportionally overrepresented among the victims of these purges. In the trials, the accusation of Zionism gained increasing importance until, in the Slánský case in Czechoslovakia (1952), it became central. A further escalation was averted by the death of Stalin in 1953. The already planned show trial of Jewish doctors who supposedly plotted the murder of the Soviet leadership was aborted. Plans to deport Jews from major cities were also dropped. It remains unclear, even to the present day, just what further measures were being seriously considered or planned at the time.

The anti-Zionist campaigns presented a worldwide conspiracy theory in the tradition of the *Protocols of the Elders of Zion*, designed to strengthen the socialist and nationalist cohesion of the USSR and the satellite states. Foreign policy considerations also came into play. The Soviets supported the founding of the state of Israel both politically and militarily (through weapons deliveries via Czechoslovakia) in the hopes of damaging Great Britain and winning friendly support from Israel. The fronts during the Cold War formed differently, however. As it turned out, anti-Zionism was a commodity in great demand in the Arab states, and those states swiftly became the main importers of this propaganda product from the Soviet Union.

Certainly, later anti-Zionist campaigns never achieved the murderous dimensions seen in the years between 1948 and 1953, but the theme remained an essential element of Soviet ideology and practice. For Jews, it became virtually impossible to make careers in the party, military, or bureaucracy. The campaign against economic crimes (1961–1966) once again led to show tri-

als, accompanied by massive propaganda that highlighted the ethnicity of the preponderantly Jewish defendants, of whom perhaps 100 were executed. When Jews attempted to emigrate, many were treated as traitors or criminals and subjected to economic and other forms of ostracism. Anti-Zionism helped the USSR garner support in the Arab world after the Six Days' War and served to scapegoat Jews for the independence movements in Poland and Czechoslovakia (1968). These events, so menacing to the Soviet system, generated intense outbursts of anti-Zionist propaganda. In addition, there were a number of regional episodes and all the while a continuous outpouring of anti-Zionists newspaper articles and books.

Anti-Zionism as an ideology stemmed from the integration of antisemitism into Marxism-Leninism. This development occurred in the late 1920s and 1930s in conjunction with the Stalinization of the Soviet Union and many foreign communist parties. After Lenin and Trotsky's "world revolution" failed to materialize, Stalin developed the theory of "socialism in one country." Marxism-Leninism conferred legitimacy to the Soviet state (and later the satellite states) as the "socialist Fatherland." "People/Nation/State" became a concept with a positive valuation, and proletarian internationalism was accordingly redefined as the friendship between (working) people of various nations. Thus, after World War II, it was ideologically possible to legitimize both the socialist solidarity of newly arisen "people's democracies"—that is, the hegemony of the USSR—and the national autonomy of these states.

One example of the consequences of this ideological shift can be seen in the concept of cosmopolitanism. In the early years of the USSR, as well as in the thinking of Marx and Engels, the term had a positive connotation because it signified a universalist position untainted by bourgeois nationalism. After 1945, cosmopolitanism was rejected because it denied national sovereignty and patriotism. Responsibility for this imperialist cosmopolitanism was attributed especially to "the Zionists." Zionism was now understood to represent not a Jewish form of nationalism but rather a rootless, bourgeois cosmopolitanism closely allied to U.S. imperialism and bent on world domination. The true home-land of the Zionists was *not* Israel. It was Wall Street. Accordingly, Israel was not a true national state but an imperialist outpost.

Zionists appeared simultaneously as class and national enemies because they were identified with both capitalism and imperialism, as well as a de-nationalized universalism. In both aspects, there-fore, anti-Zionism could appropriate traditional antisemitic postulates. This fact was especially sig-nificant for the USSR, as well as for the satellites and Stalinist parties worldwide, because it vali-dated the Marxist-Leninist linkage of socialism and proletarian (inter)nationalism by establishing "the Enemy." Zionists were the enemies within, servants of foreign powers, and saboteurs of so-cialist progress. It was not the party or the state that was responsible for setbacks in the "building of socialism": that was the work of Zionist traitors.

Anti-Zionism indicted "the Zionists," not "the Jews." To be sure, the words *Jew* and *Zion-ist* were used almost interchangeably, but the fic-tion that Jews and Zionists were entirely different people was a necessity. Marxism-Leninism re-jected the notion that an entire people could be excluded on the basis of ethnic, racial, or cultural grounds. Officially, Jews were free and equal cit-izens of the USSR. Even Stalin found it repeatedly expedient to speak out against antisemitism. Thus, to mask the antisemitic character of anti-Zionism, the "Jew" was replaced by the "Zionist." Occasionally, it was even conceded that someone was a "good Jew," by which was meant that he or she was not a Zionist. Anti-Zionism's masking mechanism also facilitated the integration of the two most important elements in the figure of "the Enemy"—fascism and imperialism. Regularly, the claim was made that Zionists and Nazis had worked together. The Holocaust—the existence of which was never denied—was a plot by which the Zionists attempted to achieve a Jewish state in Palestine. Thus, Israel appears in anti-Zionist rhetoric as closely associated with National So-cialism or identical to it. Beyond this, the Zionists exploited the Holocaust to enrich themselves and also to deflect attention from their own conspir-ing. Properly viewed, "anti-fascist" anti-Zionism was really anti-antisemitism. Or so its creators and manipulators wanted the world to believe.

Such assertions appeared in hundreds of books and pamphlets, many with mass distribu-tions. Yet there was not a single serious, detailed Soviet portrayal of the Holocaust. Always ready to acknowledge the fact of the Holocaust, Soviet leaders at the same time prevented the general population from learning about or appropriately commemorating it. Although a small portion of the anti-Zionist literature was translated into Western European languages and had an impact on communist parties and leftist movements in the West, Soviet anti-Zionism as well as anti-Jewish persecution were strongly criticized time and again by Marxist and leftist intellectuals.

Relating anti-Zionism to the ideological needs of the USSR is an interpretation that not every-one accepts. An alternative explanation, based primarily on the work of Edmund Silberner, finds the origin of Soviet anti-Zionism in the pu-tative "antisemitic tradition of modern social-ism," beginning with its founder, Karl Marx. But this theory cannot, for example, explain why prior to the Dreyfus Affair, the French labor movement—so little influenced by Marx—was quite antisemitic, whereas the German Social Democratic Party—much under the influence of Marx—was relatively free of antisemitism and, in fact, consistently opposed it. Silberner's interpre-tation also cannot account for the USSR's pre-1930 combating of antisemitism. Seeking the genesis of Marxist-Leninist anti-Zionism in the writings of Karl Marx produces only the most nebulous results.

—*Klaus Holz*
Richard S. Levy, translation

See also Anti-Zionism; Doctors' Plot; Jewish Anti-Fascist Committee; Marx, Karl; *Protocols of the Elders of Zion;* Purges, Soviet; Slánský Trial; Social Democratic Party; Socialists on Antisemitism; Stalin, Joseph; Stalinization of Eastern Europe; USSR; Zionism

References
Holz, Klaus. *Nationaler Antisemitismus: Wissenssozi-ologie einer Weltanschauung* (Hamburg, Ger-many: Hamburger Edition, 2001).
Levin, Nora. *The Jews in the Soviet Union since 1917.* 2 vols. (New York: New York University Press, 1988).
Silberner, Edmund. *Sozialisten zur Judenfrage* (Berlin: Colloquium Verlag, 1962).

Antonescu, Ion (1882–1946)

Ion Antonescu was born in Romania in 1882, the son of an army captain. He attended the military school in Craiova in 1898 and became a lieutenant in the cavalry in 1904. He fought in the Balkan Wars of 1912 and 1913. During World War I, he was chief of operations with the northern army, taking charge of the attack on Transylvania, which ended in failure and retreat. He participated in the pacification of communist Hungary in 1919 and 1920. After serving in various posts during the 1920s, he achieved the rank of general in 1931.

At the end of December 1937, King Carol II commissioned Octavian Goga, leader of the Christian National Party, to form a government, in which Antonescu became minister of defense. The new government adopted a series of anti-Jewish laws. When Carol abdicated on September 6, 1940, the National Legionnaire State was proclaimed, and Antonescu declared himself leader; he formed a military government composed of loyal followers, generals, and members of the Iron Guard. From that point on, the state began the systematic persecution of the Jewish population. The "Romanianization" of the economy carried out the expropriation of Jewish businesspeople and manufacturers, and Jewish-owned agricultural and forestland was nationalized. Jewish assets were administered by a specially created office, the National Center for Romanianization.

In June 1941, Romania entered the war on the side of the Third Reich. Under Antonescu's command, Romanian and German units invaded Bessarabia and North Bukovina (which had been ceded in 1940). As a reward for its contribution to the attack on the Soviet Union, Romania received the occupation zone of Transnistria in the southern Ukraine. Between September 1941 and the end of 1942, approximately 150,000 Jews were deported from northern Romania (Bukovina, Bessarabia, and the Dorohoi region) into Transnistria, joining Jews already living there and those from the city of Odessa. Between 250,000 and 400,000 were murdered. Also in 1942, 25,000 Romanian Gypsies as well as 2,000 members of religious sects were deported to Transnistria.

Romanian army units suffered a devastating defeat at Stalingrad in late 1942. When the Red Army broke through the Romanian northern front in 1944, Antonescu was arrested by generals loyal to King Carol on August 23, 1944. He stood trial for war crimes in 1946, was condemned, and was executed in June 1946.

—*Brigitte Mihok*
Richard S. Levy, translation

See also Aryanization; Goga, Octavian; Iron Guard; Romania; Romania, Holocaust in; Versailles Treaty; White Terror

References
Hausleitner, Mariana. "War Antonescu ein Kriegsverbrecher? Zur aktuellen Diskussion über den Nationalismus in Rumänien," *Jahrbuch für Antisemitismusforschung* 8 (1999): 312–328.
Radu, Ioanid. *The Holocaust in Romania: The Destruction of Jews and Gypsies under the Antonescu Regime, 1940–1944* (Chicago: Ivan R. Dee, 2000).

Apion

A grammarian and scholar of Homer, Apion lived in Alexandria and taught in Greece and Rome in the first half of the first century BCE. He was Egyptian by origin but later took Alexandrian citizenship, and in this capacity in 38 or 39 CE, he led the embassy opposing the Jews before Caligula, who was to adjudicate the status of the Jews in the aftermath of the Alexandrian riots of the summer of 38. Apion wrote a *History of Egypt* and a treatise, *Against the Jews;* all of his works are lost and known only through excerpts in the writings of later authors. Most of the details of Apion's life and works come from the treatise *Against Apion,* which the Jewish historian Josephus wrote, in part, as a confutation of Apion's calumnious statements regarding the Jews. According to Josephus, Apion defamed the Jews by spreading false versions of the biblical Exodus story. He also wrote against the Jews of Alexandria, derisively questioning the origin of their community and arguing that they had no legal right to dwell in the city. Josephus countered that Apion was ignorant and that he had neglected to consult the documents by which Alexander the Great, the Ptolemies, and the Roman emperors had granted the Jews the right of habitation. Such a stark contrast in the positions of Josephus and Apion can, perhaps, be accounted for by reference to the legal situation that had developed earlier in the first century CE. Josephus reported in his *Antiquities of the Jews* that Jews were experiencing problems with regard to their status because the Persian and Ptolemaic grants—the legal basis for their claims recognized by the Roman authority—may have lacked official public registration.

—*Sandra Gambetti*

See also Alexandrian Pogrom; Manetho; Roman Empire; Roman Literature

Reference
Encyclopedia Judaica, 16 vols. 3: 178. Editor-in-chief, Cecil Roth (New York and Jerusalem: Macmillan, 1972).

Aquarius, Age of

Age of Aquarius is the astrological term for a coming era of spiritual enlightenment, also known as the New Age. According to this esoteric doctrine, human history has evolved through several epochs of roughly 2,000 years each, corresponding to succeeding astrological signs and dominated by a particular religious orientation. Many scholars credit occultist Alice Bailey with refining the concept. The term itself came into public awareness in 1969 through the hit song "Age of Aquarius," sung by the pop group Fifth Dimension (whose name refers to the dimension where the "Ascended Masters," the divine beings revered by Bailey, dwell).

The age now closing is the Age of Pisces, during which Christianity has been the dominant religion—the astrological sign of the fish connecting Pisces with a symbol of early Christianity. It is said that all those who hope to advance in their spiritual evolution must abandon Christian ideas as outdated spiritual hindrances that are destined to wither and die as the religion of the Aquarian Age takes hold. Those who fail to do so will wither and die along with the old age.

In this context, the Jewish religion is doubly outdated and a double hindrance. Judaism belonged to the cosmic age preceding Christianity, the Age of Aries. Here, the sign of the ram represents the pivotal experience of Abraham, father of the Jewish people, with the ram provided by

God at the Binding of Isaac, as well as the subsequent Jewish sacrificial system. Judaism was supposed to give way to the Christian age; failing that, it was supposed to die out from the force of spiritual evolution. That Judaism has done neither is attributed by Bailey to the strength of an evil cosmic energy called the "Jewish Force," which must be eliminated in order for the Age of Aquarius to arrive fully. To reinforce the negative destiny of Judaism, Bailey deliberately changed the astrological sign of the Jewish age from the ram to the scapegoat, which she thought colored all Jewish history.

—*Hannah Newman*

See also Bailey, Alice A.; Jewish Force; New Age

Arab Antisemitic Literature

Like nationalism, socialism, fascism, and other modern intellectual and political movements, antisemitism is a European import of fairly recent vintage into the Arab world. There was no lack of negative stereotypes of Jews in premodern Arabic literature, but these were of the traditional Islamic variety. Jews had "baseness and misery stamped upon them" (Sura 2:61). They had been the principal opponents of the Prophet, along with the idolaters, and were a treacherous lot. But they were people who had received a genuine divine revelation, like the Christians and Zoroastrians, and like the latter, they deserved tolerance, as long as they accepted the status of humble tributary *dhimmis* (protected persons). Though the image of Jews was, on the whole, even more negative and condescending than that of Christians, they shared the same legal status within the Islamic social system. Medieval Arab theologians devoted only a very small part of their polemics against other faiths to Judaism. There was nothing comparable in quantity and rarely in sheer vitriol to the *Adversus Iudaeos* literature of the church.

Modern antisemitic ideas made their first appearance in the Middle East among the Arabic-speaking Christians of Syria. Like other non-Muslims, they maintained close commercial and, to some extent, cultural relations with the European nations that made ever stronger inroads into the region. The Syrian Christians not only shared the Muslims' traditional contempt for Jews but also appropriated European antisemitic notions from French traders and missionaries. The European blood libel charge first appeared among Christians in Aleppo during the seventeenth century, but only gained widespread circulation after the notorious Damascus Affair of 1840 and with the active intervention of the French consul Benoit de Ratti-Menton, who brought in the Muslim authorities. However, neither medieval Christian European fantasies, such as ritual murder, nor the modern political and racial post-Enlightenment antisemitic ideas could make much headway among Muslims in the Arab world.

During the last three decades of the nineteenth century, antisemitic literature in the European mold but written in Arabic began to appear among the Syro-Lebanese Christians who were under strong French cultural influence. Most of these early antisemitic works were published in Beirut and were translations of European tracts—for example, Najib al-Hajj's *Fi al-zawaya khabaya, aw, Kashf asrar al-Yahud* (Clandestine Things in the Corners, or Secrets of the Jews' Unmasked [Beirut, 1893]), an adaptation of Georges Corneilhan's *Juifs et opportunistes: Le judaïsme en Egypte et Syrie* (1889). Antisemitic literature in Arabic developed slowly during this period and was still confined, for the most part, to Christian writers. Nevertheless, these early works laid the foundation for a much more extensive literature of this sort in the twentieth century, when a radical change took place in the general Arab perception of Jews. Its eventual impact owed much to Syrian Christians, who were the principal figures responsible for the renaissance of Arabic language, literature, and journalism known as the *Nahda* (Revival). They were active not only in Greater Syria but also in Egypt, which constituted the modernizing center of the Arab world at the time. It was in Egypt that one of the two most influential works of European antisemitic literature for Arab readers made its appearance in translation in 1899—August Rohling's *The Talmud Jew*. The Arabic translation, entitled *al-Kanz al-marsud fi-qawa'id al-Talmud* (The Guarded Treasure of the Principles of the Talmud), was made from the French edition, a translation from the German by the noted antisemite Édouard Drumont. The book became a classic and was reprinted several times throughout the twentieth century, as Arab authors increasingly made the connection between supposed Talmudic teachings and Zionism.

The other influential—indeed, the most important—European antisemitic work in translation was the infamous *Protocols of the Elders of Zion*. Arab nationalists in Palestine and Iraq were already citing the book in the early 1920s, and a complete Arabic translation, entitled *Mu'amarat al-Yahudiyya 'ala 'l-shu'ub* (The Jewish Conspiracy against the Nations), by the Lebanese Maronite priest Antun Yamin, was published in Cairo in 1925. This work was the first of a long line of Arabic editions and translations, and the book has been an enduring best-seller; praised and recommended by political leaders, it is widely available in bookstores from Casablanca to Baghdad.

Original works of Arab antisemitic literature did not appear in any substantial numbers until the second half of the twentieth century, after the establishment of the state of Israel and the defeat of Arab armies in 1948, 1956, and 1967. In addition to the hundreds of books on the conflict with Israel, many of which are replete with antisemitic imagery, dozens of books on Jews and Judaism are partially or thoroughly antisemitic. The authors are frequently rather eclectic, mingling traditional Christian and Islamic themes with those of post-Enlightenment antisemitism. Some works are completely imitative, such as S. Naji's *al-Mufsidun fi al-ard, aw jara'im al-Yahud al-siyasiyyah wa-al-ijtima'iyah 'abra al-ta'rikh* (Corrupters in the Earth, or the Political and Social Crimes of the Jews throughout History), published in Damascus in 1965. Much of the material in this book seems to have been lifted from German and French antisemitic writings of the 1930s and 1940s.

The most common charge leveled against Jews as a whole in this literature is that they are racists. Racism is depicted as one of the fundamental articles of their faith, based on both the Bible and the Talmud. The latter, following Rohling, is particularly singled out for attack. Muhammad Sabri's *al-Talmud: Shar'iat al-Yahud* (The Talmud: The Religious Law of the Jews), published in Cairo (n.d.), is typical of this genre. The Talmud is described as permitting Jews to lie to gentiles, to cheat them, and to steal from them; it considers non-Jews as animals who have human form only to serve Jews who may violate their women, and it makes the shedding of gentile blood licit.

Some works in this vein have a pseudoacademic flavor—for example, Sabri Jirjis's *al-Turath al-Yahudi al-Sahyuni wa-al-fikr al-Frawidi* (The Jewish Zionist Heritage and Freudian Thought), which purports to be a psychoanalytical study; or Hasan Zaza and Muhammad Ashur's *Al-Yahud laysu tujjaran bi-al-nash'ah* (The Jews Are Not Merchants by Origin), which was meant to be read as objective socioeconomic history. Both were published in Cairo in the 1970s.

One of the most noteworthy features of antisemitic literature in the contemporary Arab world is the ubiquity of the blood libel theme among both Muslim and Christian writers. Ostensibly scholarly treatments of Judaism present the myth matter-of-factly, such as Ali `Abd al-Wahid Wafi's *al-Yahudiyya wa 'l-Yahud* (Judaism and the Jews), in the section dealing with the Purim and Passover rituals. Jew-baiting tracts such as Iliya Abu 'l-Rus's *al-Yahudiyya al-`Alamiyya wa-Harbuha 'l-Mustamarra `ala 'l-Masihiyya* (World Jewry and Its Continuing War against Christianity), dwell on the blood libel at length and in morbid detail. Hasan Zaza, in his *al-Fikr al-dini al-Isra'ili: atwaruh wa-madhahibuh* (Israelite Religious Thought: Its Phases and Schools), devotes a learned discussion to the blood libel, observing that such a practice is forbidden by Jewish law, but then he notes that the accusation has followed the Jews throughout history and that people often act contrarily to their religious teachings; he finally cites the confessions of one of the accused murderers in the Damascus Affair as proof of the veracity of the charge. One of the most successful books touting the blood libel, *Fatir Sahyun* (The Matzah of Zion), by Syrian Defense Minister Mustafa Tlas, went into eight editions between 1983 and 2002. The last edition alone sold over 20,000 copies.

Antisemitism has become an integral part of Arab cultural discourse. Its imagery can be found not only in specialized tracts and monographs but also in school textbooks, articles in major newspapers and magazines, and television plays.

—*Norman A. Stillman*

See also Chrysostom, John; Damascus Blood Libel; Islam and the Jews; Islamic Diaspora; Islamic Fundamentalism; *Protocols of the Elders of Zion;* Ritual Murder (Medieval); Talmud; *Talmud Jew, The;* Zionism

References
Lewis, Bernard. *Semites and Anti-Semites: An Inquiry into Conflict and Prejudice* (New York and London: W. W. Norton, 1986).
Stillman, Norman A. "New Attitudes toward the Jew in the Arab World," *Jewish Social Studies* 37 (1975): 197–204.
———. "Antisemitism in the Contemporary Arab World." In *Antisemitism in the Contemporary World.* Edited by Michael Curtis (Boulder, CO, and London: Westview Press, 1986), 70–85.

Arab Boycott

The Arab boycott, which includes various measures of economic warfare taken by the Arab League against Israel, actually predates the creation of the Jewish state. On December 2, 1945, the Council of the League of Arab States called on all member nations and Arabs still under colonial rule to refrain from purchasing "products of Palestinian Jews" and thereby aid in thwarting "Zionist political aims." Like so many other anti-Zionist resolutions, the council's declaration employed the terms *Zionists* and *Jews* interchangeably. The Arab League boycott had its forerunners in resolutions calling for the boycott of Jewish businesses issued by the National Arab Congress held in Bludan, Syria, in 1937 and by the Fifth Palestine Arab Congress held in Nablus in 1922. Earlier still, the idea was proposed in 1908 in the Arabic newspaper *al-Asma`i,* published in Jaffa, and in 1911, the editor of the newspaper *al-Karmil* in Haifa attempted to organize a boycott in that city.

The scope and the mechanism of the Arab boycott developed substantially after Israeli independence. It was administered from the Central Boycott Office (CBO) established in Damascus in 1951, with regional committee offices under government auspices in each of the Arab states. The boycott came to be subdivided into primary, secondary, and tertiary actions. The primary boycott bars Arab states, corporations, or individuals from any commercial dealings with Israel. The secondary bans dealing with companies anywhere in the world that do business with Israel, and the tertiary blacklists individuals and organizations deemed sympathetic or supportive of Israel. Many individuals in the U.S. entertainment industry were blacklisted. In addition to Jewish actors and musical artists, the recordings and films of such famous personalities as Louis Armstrong, Eartha Kitt, and Marilyn Monroe were also banned. By 1976, 6,300 companies in ninety-six countries were on the CBO blacklist. However, observance of the boycott by firms worldwide and even the enforcement of the boycott within Arab states was always uneven. Some countries, such as Saudi Arabia, took the boycott to its most blatantly antisemitic lengths. In 1952, the Saudi government forbade business relations with any company that was owned or controlled by Jews or that even employed Jews. The following year, regulations were issued banning goods transported by Jewish-owned shipping companies. As Oil Minister Sheikh Ahmed Yamani explained, all Jews had to be considered Zionists unless proven otherwise. In the heyday of the Arab boycott during the 1950s and 1960s, many international corporations tacitly acquiesced to it, as did some non-Arab Muslim countries and countries with large Muslim populations, such as India.

By the 1980s, the effectiveness of the Arab boycott had been seriously compromised after corporations such as Coca-Cola, the Hilton hotel chain, and various airlines ceased to knuckle under. By the late 1970s, six Arab League members (Algeria, Morocco, Mauritania, Tunisia, Sudan, and Somalia) observed only the primary bans but not the secondary and tertiary ones. After signing a peace treaty with Israel, Egypt withdrew from the Arab boycott, as did Jordan in 1994. With the easing of tensions following the Madrid Conference and the Oslo Accords, a number of North African and Arabian Gulf states began to engage in tentative and discreet business relations with Israel, although most of these were frozen with the outbreak of the second intifada in 2001.

There are no precise figures as to the aggregate economic damage inflicted by the Arab boycott. In 1992, the Federation of Israeli Chambers of Commerce estimated the loss over the preceding forty years to be approximately $45 billion, whereas the CBO, wishing to show its own effectiveness, reckoned the figure at more than twice that amount.

—*Norman A. Stillman*

See also Anti-Zionism; Boycott of 1912; Boycott of Jewish Shops
References
Feiler, Gil. *From Boycott to Economic Cooperation: The Political Economy of the Arab Boycott of Israel* (London and Portland, OR: Frank Cass, 1998).
Prittie, Terrence, and Walter Henry Nelson. *The Economic War against the Jews* (London: Secker & Warburg, 1978).
Sarna, Aaron J. *Boycott and Blacklist: A History of Arab Economic Warfare against Israel* (Totowa, NJ: Rowman & Littlefield, 1986).

Arafat, Yasir (1929–2004)

Yasir Arafat, the founder and leader of Fatah, the Palestine Liberation Organization (PLO), was born in Cairo to Palestinian parents of the al-Hussaini clan; his original name was Abd al-Rahman Abd al-Ra'uf Arafat al-Qudwa al-Hussaini. His later nom de guerre, Abu Ammar, together with a nickname of his youth, Yasir, became his common appellation because of the association with a hero of early Islam. He is said to have run guns from Egypt to Palestine during his teens. In the early 1950s, he became active in Palestinian student activities at Fu'ad I University in Cairo and may have had some connection with the Muslim Brotherhood. During the late 1950s in Kuwait, Arafat, together with several close comrades, founded Fatah as a guerrilla organization, and after the Six Days' War, the group gained prominence from its center of operations in Jordan. In 1969, Arafat and his supporters took control of the Palestine National Council. His growing power and increasingly bold terrorist operations led to conflict with the Jordanian government, which drove him and the PLO from the country in 1970. Arafat took refuge in Beirut and reestablished PLO operations from southern Lebanon. After he was forced out by the Israeli army in 1982, Tunis became the new PLO headquarters. In 1988, the year following the first intifada, Arafat, seeing himself sidelined by the emergence of new, young, activist leadership in the West Bank and Gaza, agreed to recognize Israel's right to exist, to negotiation on the basis of territorial concessions, and to a renunciation of terrorism. Secret negotiations between the PLO and Israel led to the Oslo Accords in 1993, and Arafat became chairman of the interim autonomous entity, the Palestine Authority (PA).

Although Arafat frequently referred to Zionists and Jews interchangeably when speaking in Arabic, he usually made a careful distinction in English, and overall during the 1970s, 1980s, and 1990s, his public rhetoric was less given to the cruder antisemitic invective of many Arab nationalists and Islamic fundamentalists. Indeed, he often spoke in interviews for foreign consumption about Arabs and Jews as cousins who had lived in harmony prior to the advent of Zionism and who could someday live together in a democratic Palestine. But in PLO propaganda and in PA educational materials, radio and television broadcasts, and the print media, all of the stereotypes of essentialist antisemitism have been rife. A twelfth-grade teachers' guide published by the PA Ministry of Education lists as topics for in-depth study these themes: "The Jews' evil behavior causes antisemitic persecution," "Judaism is a racist religion," and "Jews welcome their own persecution because it is profitable." The Islamic education textbooks used in the PA schools dwell on the most negative depictions of Jews in the Koran, the Hadith, and other canonical literature. Given Arafat's penchant for micromanagement first of the PLO and later of the PA, it is unlikely that dissemination of these materials could have occurred without his approval. As with his covert support for terrorism after his public renunciation of it, Arafat's public restraint in employing antisemitic rhetoric was another example of his talent for having things both ways. Arafat died at age seventy-five of undisclosed causes in a Paris hospital on November 11, 2004.

—*Norman A. Stillman*

See also Arab Antisemitic Literature; Hamas; Islam and the Jews; Islamic Fundamentalism; Muslim Brotherhood; Zionism
References
Hart, Alan. *Arafat: Terrorist or Peacemaker?* (London: Sidgwick & Jackson, 1984).
Mishal, Shaul. *The PLO under Arafat: Between Gun and Olive Branch* (New Haven, CT: Yale University Press, 1986).
Rubinstein, Danny. *The Mystery of Arafat.* Translated by Dan Leon (South Royalton, VT: Steerforth Press, 1995).

Arch of Titus

The Arch of Titus, a monumental structure standing in the Roman Forum, was dedicated by Emperor Domitian (Titus Flavius Domitianus) sometime after 81 CE to commemorate his deceased brother, Emperor Titus Flavius Vespasianus. It was part of a major architectonic development undertaken by the Flavian emperors to establish public places in the space reserved by Nero for his private residence. Its relevance for the history of Judaism and antisemitism lies in the two large panels with reliefs representing the joint triumph the Senate granted in 70 CE to Titus and his father, the then emperor Vespasian, celebrating the recent defeat of the Jews in Palestine. The right-to-left panel portrays the Romans carrying off the spoils of the Temple in Jerusalem, which we know were later displayed in Vespasian's Roman Templum Pacis. The major recognizable feature of the booty is the seven-branched candelabra, or menorah, that once stood in the Temple. Together with an inscription unearthed in Jerusalem in the 1970s and carved with the same kind of candelabra, this is the earliest known representation of the menorah of the Temple. The right-to-left panel depicts Titus in a chariot proceeding through the triumphal procession. The ideological meaning of the triumph and of its representation on the arch is also stressed by the orientation of both panels toward the temple of Jupiter on the Capitol Hill, the final goal of the procession.

In 67 CE, Titus joined his father, who was the general in charge of the suppression of the Jewish revolt in Palestine. After his acclamation as emperor by the troops in Egypt and then in Palestine in 69, Vespasian left the Levant to return to

The Arch of Titus commemorates the military defeat of the Jews by the Roman Legions. The right-to-left panel portrays the carrying off of the spoils of the Temple in Jerusalem. (Werner Forman/Corbis)

Rome, delivering the command of the region into the hands of Titus. In 70, Titus successfully suppressed the revolt and took Jerusalem, destroying both the walls and the Temple. The following triumph in Rome served as the actual legitimization of the Flavian dynasty in the capital after some years of political incertitude.

—*Sandra Gambetti*

See also Roman Empire; Roman Literature
Reference
Kleiner, Diana E. E. *Roman Sculpture* (New Haven, CT: Yale University Press, 1994).

Argentina

Argentina has been characterized as a country where antisemitism has, at various times, permeated all social classes and political ideologies. Latent antisemitic sentiments have become activated through the teachings of the dominant Catholic Church, the diverse nationalist ideologies (from both the Right and the Left), and the policies of the ruling administrations. During times of crisis, antisemitism has become more visible and, especially under military regimes, more violent.

As early as 1881, when Jewish immigration was encouraged by Argentine political leaders, some groups denounced that immigration as pernicious and dangerous to the young nation. When the first contingents of Jewish colonists arrived in Argentina, a popular novel, *La Bolsa* (The Stock Market), depicted Jews as materialistic and held them responsible for the financial debacle of the times. Sentiments against Jewish immigration, fostered by important Argentinians, became entrenched in broad sectors of society.

At the outset of the twentieth century, the labor movement, under the influence of "foreign" left-wing ideologies, began to alter the traditional passivity of Argentine workers. Some Jewish socialists, syndicalists, and anarchists took an active part in the organizing of labor unions. As a result, Jews in their totality were branded as undesirables, particularly in the national capital of Buenos Aires. The fear of imported labor ideologies reached its climax at the end of World War I during the Semana Tragica (Week of Tragedy) of January 1919. The Jewish quarters of Buenos Aires were pillaged and largely destroyed. Several Jews died or were seriously wounded by mobs that had been incited to defend Argentina from an imminent Red takeover, supposedly led by Jewish Bolsheviks.

During the 1930s and through World War II, German propaganda and Nazi ideology (Argentina had a large German population), hand in hand with the growing local nationalism, created a suffocating atmosphere for Jews. Catholic education was made mandatory in the schools on December 31, 1943; government policies curtailed the admission of Jewish refugees from war-torn Europe; and public demonstrations against Jews continued. The popular novels of Gustavo Martinez Zuviria—*Oro* (Gold [1935]) and *Kahal* (from the Hebrew word for "Jewish Community" [1935])—played on the widespread suspicions of an international Jewish conspiracy; the novelist became secretary of education under the military government in 1943. By the 1940s, several factors were in place that continued to affect the Jews and, arguably, the country as a whole, negatively for the rest of the century: a military regime with strongly authoritarian, antidemocratic inclinations; a Catholic Church undaunted by the Holocaust and convinced that Jews posed a threat to Christian hierarchy, values, and traditions; and a deep-seated, broadly based xenophobia. Despite the obstacles posed by a hostile church and army, substantial numbers of Jews continued to enter Argentina during these years, hoping to find there the promising future that had traditionally characterized the country as a land of opportunity for immigrants.

During the late 1950s and early 1960s, Argentine nationalism fostered an even greater animus toward Jews, especially after Israeli agents captured Nazi war criminal Adolf Eichmann in Buenos Aires in 1961. His subsequent trial in Jerusalem and his execution led to renewed anti-Jewish demonstrations. The group Tacuara, which drew members from the upper classes of Argentinian society, became the pivotal neo-Nazi organization, taking inspiration from several European fascist movements. The antisemitism prompted by Tacuara and by the political group Union Civica Nacionalista (Nationalist Civic Union), as well as other smaller groups with similar outlooks, culminated in the kidnapping and swastika tattooing of a female Jewish student in 1962. This and other assaults prompted Jewish community representatives to call for a nationwide protest strike against Nazi-like terrorism. The success of this strike, with large-scale participation from the non-Jewish population, gave Jews a brief moment of dignity both as Argentines and as Jews.

But this show of solidarity did not last long. The military regime of Gen. Juan Carlos Ongania (1966–1970) was characterized by its repression of intellectual and artistic freedom. Following a well-established military tradition, antisemitism became an instrument of policy as well. The 1970s proved tumultuous, as the country threatened to split apart. Numerous revolutionary tendencies began to proliferate, especially among the urban, educated middle classes. A succession of authoritarian governments between 1974 and 1983 dealt savagely with the leftist guerrillas. During Isabel Perón's administration (1974–1976), the Triple A (Argentine Anti-Communist Alliance), a rightist terrorist group, waged a brutal campaign of suppression against the Left, focusing especially on Jews. In 1976, the military junta that deposed Perón dealt a death-blow to the Left in what became known as the Dirty War. More than 10,000 people were either killed or "disappeared," of which an estimated 10 percent were Jews, far exceeding the proportion of Jews in the population at large or even within the groups specifically targeted. Although the Dirty War was launched against subversives, it overflowed with antisemitic rhetoric that applied to the whole Jewish population. Jewish institutions were not attacked per se, but the impact on Jewish lives and on the Jewish community at large was much deeper than in previous episodes of overt antisemitism.

After the violence of the Dirty War, democracy returned to Argentina, and Jews became prominent in the political life of the country. However, two events during this democratic era adversely affected Jewish life there. In 1993, the Israeli embassy was bombed and destroyed, killing 29 people. In July 1994, another bomb demolished the building of the leading representative bodies of Argentine Jewry, claiming 100 lives, both Jewish and non-Jewish. Although there are strong suspicions regarding the identity of the perpetrators of these acts, some of whom are connected to the highest levels of government, the courts and the successive state prosecutors have yet (as of late 2004) to convict anyone of the crimes.

—*Victor A. Mirelman*

See also Buenos Aires Pogroms; Eichmann, Adolf; Judeo-Bolshevism; Tacuara

References

Avni, Haim. "Antisemitism in Argentina: The Dimensions of Danger." In *Approaches to Antisemitism: Context and Curriculum*. Edited by Michael Brown (New York: American Jewish Committee, 1994), 57–77.

Elkin, Judith Laikin. "Antisemitism in Argentina: The Jewish Response." In *Living with Antisemitism: Modern Jewish Responses*. Edited by Jehuda Reinharz (Hanover, NH, and London: University Press of New England, 1987), 333–348.

Mirelman, Victor A. "Attitudes toward Jews in Argentina," *Jewish Social Studies* 37 (1975): 205–220.

Armed Forces of the United States

Throughout the nation's history, the armed forces of the United States have usually reflected the traits, tone, and intensity of antisemitism prevalent in American society. Prejudice against Jews has ranged from the traditional negative religious, cultural, and political attitudes of the colonial era to an anti-Jewish engagement based on extremist racial theories in the early twentieth century. In the decades following World War II, such institutional antisemitism gradually devolved to the level of individual bias. The pace of change within the armed forces, however, has generally lagged behind the progressive transformations in attitudes toward Jews occurring within the broader society.

From the colonial era to the present, Jews have fought in all U.S. wars. They have served in numbers proportionate to their percentage of the general population, often distinguishing themselves with bravery on the battlefield. Despite such contributions, however, Jews have been suspected of disloyalty and cowardice. They have often been perceived and treated as permanent outsiders, as less than "true Americans" when measured against their Christian, predominately Anglo-Saxon compatriots. Uriah P. Levy, perhaps the first Jewish U.S. naval officer, found himself consistently isolated and ostracized by fellow officers, as well as institutionally sanctioned by the navy he served between 1812 and 1862. During the Civil War, when Jews served both the North and the South, antisemitism within the military rose, as it did in all sections of the country in times of fear and uncertainty. In December 1862, Gen. Ulysses S. Grant issued General Orders No. 11, expelling Jews from his military district and thereby making them scapegoats for procurement and other army scandals. Although President Lincoln rescinded the order, its very issuance reinforced images of Jews as traitors profiteering from the suffering of soldiers and impeding the war effort. Similar suspicions existed in the South, where some attributed defeats to the fact that Judah P. Benjamin, the Confederate secretary of war, was a Jew. Widespread sentiments that Jews had failed to bear their share on the battlefield lingered for decades thereafter.

By the late nineteenth and early twentieth centuries, Christian and social antisemitism was exacerbated and drastically transformed by the influx of millions of eastern European Jews and the embrace of racial theories by army officers. Applying Darwinian ideas to the new immigrants, army publications now depicted Jews generally as a biologically alien, inferior, and dangerous race. Jews had supposedly evolved into a race of parasites whose immutable inherited characteristics precluded their integration as either soldiers or citizens. Considered psychologically, morally, and physically deficient, weak and cowardly Jews could never become soldiers. Instances of Jewish military service and heroism were unknown, unrecognized, or dismissed as the exceptions. The few Jews who entered the military and naval academies in the early twentieth century confronted institutionalized antisemitism and harassment. In World War I, army advertisements, manuals, and military lore portrayed Jews as untrustworthy malingerers who evaded conscription and combat.

After World War I, army antisemitism underwent another significant change when the military began to identify Jews as threats to national security and geopolitical interests. Led by the Military Intelligence Division (MID), the army became actively engaged with the Jewish Question, especially regarding communism and immigration. Through systematic surveillance of Jews at home and abroad, military attachés, secret agents, and other officers concluded that communism was an "international conspiracy of Jews." Some officers accepted the *Protocols of the Elders of Zion* as evidence of a Jewish plan for world domination. Others held that in aiding Jews in eastern Europe, American Jews revealed their disloyalty by obstructing the U.S. struggle against communism. During the Red Scare of the 1920s, MID also prepared contingency plans for the suppression of an uprising of Jewish communists in New York City. Fears of Jewish subversion merged with racial antisemitism as the army entered the political contest over immigration. Invoking theories of Nordic supremacy, officers urged the passage of restrictive immigration legislation to halt the influx of the Jewish "scum of Europe," whose inferior racial traits and intrinsically dangerous behavior imperiled the genetic and political future of the United States. Into the 1930s, officers groomed for upper command at the Army War College received lectures and readings on racial theory and eugenics, which further legitimized and institutionalized racial and political antisemitism.

Army antisemitism had tragic consequences during the refugee crisis of the 1930s and the Holocaust. Some officers warned against allowing Nazi antisemitism to disrupt U.S.-German relations, possibly leading the country into a war that ran contrary to national interests. Invoking the subversive threat and "undesirable" characteristics of Jews, the army also effectively opposed admitting Jewish refugees into the United States. In World War II, the army used wartime security as a rationalization to hold up rescue of Jews from Nazism and keep Palestine closed to them. Long-standing antisemitism and indifference to the plight of Jews were factors in the army's refusal to bomb Auschwitz, and similar racial, geopolitical, and strategic considerations affected army policy toward displaced persons (DPs) after the war. Lack of sympathy, racism, and fear of subversion characterized the army's treatment of Holocaust survivors and resulted in the military's strong opposition to the admission of Jewish DPs into the United States. Predicting that Jewish immigration into Palestine would mean Soviet domination of the Middle East and the consequent loss of oil, the army likewise resisted the establishment of Israel.

Widespread antisemitism and the prejudiced treatment of Jews, especially among the top officers of the older generation, typified the army of the interwar years. World War II, however, witnessed momentous attitudinal changes in the greatly expanded and more ethnically diverse army that came into being during the 1940s. Abandoning officially condoned racial prejudice, War Department policies now began to promote toleration. Nazi racism and revelations of the Holocaust discredited antisemitism and racial thought in general. Moreover, the interaction of Christian and Jewish troops, especially during combat, created bonds of respect that eliminated or significantly reduced preexisting biases. This trend continued over the next several decades, as racial and institutionalized antisemitism gradually disappeared within the military. Although individual prejudice persisted and suspicions about Jewish loyalty and power occasionally surfaced thereafter, more Jews were able to make military careers, with some even rising to the highest rank. And the U.S. and Israeli armies became strategic allies.

—*Joseph W. Bendersky*

See also Eugenics; Evian Conference; General Orders No. 11; Immigration and Naturalization Laws; Jew Census; Jewish Question; Judeo-Bolshevism; Masculinity; Moseley, George Van Horn; Oswego Camp; *Passing of the Great Race;* Patton, Gen. George; *Protocols of the Elders of Zion;* Racism, Scientific; Social Darwinism; United States

References

Abzug, Robert H. *Inside the Vicious Heart: America and the Liberation of Nazi Concentration Camps* (New York: Oxford University Press, 1985).

Bendersky, Joseph W. *The "Jewish Threat": Anti-Semitic Politics of the U.S. Army* (New York: Basic Books, 2000).

———. "The Absent Presence: Enduring Images of Jews in United States Military History," *American Jewish History* 89, no. 4 (December 2001): 411–436.

Polmar, Norman, and Thomas B. Allen. *Rickover: Controversy and Genius* (New York: Simon & Schuster, 1982).

Arndt, Ernst Moritz (1769–1860)

E. M. Arndt's oeuvre devoted relatively little attention to the religion, history, or emancipation of the Jews, and the author did not make a career as a historian, writer, and politician out of his anti-Jewish views. Along with Johann Gottlieb Fichte and Friedrich Ludwig Jahn, Arndt was considered one of the German national movement's leading thinkers. It was his bristling hatred of the French, expressed in his propaganda writings during the Napoleonic occupation (1806–1814), that made him famous. Only with the emergence of political antisemitism in the German Empire after 1879 did Arndt become a well-known anti-Jewish ideologue.

Of his many works, two dealt specifically with the Jewish Question. In 1814, he published *Noch etwas über die Juden* (Something More Concerning the Jews). Thirty-three years later, he returned to the subject with *A Remark on the Jewish Question Being Discussed and Contested in the Prussian Parliament*. Both contributions addressed the debate about Jewish emancipation, which Arndt opposed with passionate eloquence. His animus was aimed first and foremost at Judaism, but he also regarded as inimical Jewish immigrants from eastern Europe. He conceived of the democratic movement during the Revolution of 1848 as the product of the Jews' cosmopolitanism and their deficient national feeling.

Arndt's writing on the Jewish Question was not altogether consistent. Deeply respectful of the Old Testament roots of Jewry, he found the Judaism of his own day to be an anachronism. Jews, he thought, were stiff-necked and rigid in their adherence to outmoded religious traditions. In contrast to the liberal-democratic champions of emancipation, Arndt maintained that citizenship in the German state could only be conferred on those of the Christian faith; he therefore expected Jews to convert.

His nationalist thinking, born in his opposition to the French occupation, developed into a culturally oriented racism that also influenced his anti-Jewish views. He was adamant that maintaining the purity of the German language and the vibrancy of the German nation required fending off all alien concepts and moral practices. The Germans, in his opinion, possessed the requisite purity. The Jews, however, were a bastardized people. Having lost their purity, they had also lost the capacity to develop into a virtuous, orderly nation.

Like many others, some of whom were more favorably inclined toward Jewish emancipation, Arndt attributed the supposed negative traits of the Jews to the long history of discrimination that had impeded their social and professional development. He also thought that the lack of their own territorial state had destroyed in them the ability to cherish a fatherland. Aside from these intellectual objections, Arndt voiced commonplace and popular prejudices: most Jews were prone to treachery; they were crooked; they were work-shy; they were interested only in quick profits. He likened them to flies, gnats, and other vermin. Such metaphors from the animal world, implying the biological inferiority of the Jews, became articles of faith for twentieth-century racists. Even though Arndt did not pursue this biological line of argument to its logical conclusion, his notion of bastardization bequeathed to the Nazis one of their most relied on "proofs" of Jewish degeneracy.

—*Jens Rybak*
Richard S. Levy, translation

See also Bauer, Bruno; Christian State; Dining Society, Christian-German; 1848; Emancipation; Fichte, J. G.; Jewish Question; *Ostjuden;* Supersessionism; Treitschke, Heinrich von; *Völkisch* Movement and Ideology; Young Hegelians

Reference
Rybak, Jens. "Ernst Moritz Arndts Judenbilder: Ein unbekanntes Kapitel," *Hefte der Ernst-Moritz-Arndt-Gesellschaft* 5 (1997): 102–142.

Aryan Paragraph

By the 1890s, the growth of racial antisemitism in German-speaking lands had led some middle-class organizations and parties to adopt a bylaw that excluded Jews on the basis of "race." The regulation required that members be of "Aryan" or Germanic racial descent and barred those of Jewish ancestry. This exclusion on racial rather than on religious or social grounds was new and controversial, and its acceptance was limited to organizations of the racist, or *völkisch*, Right.

The resurgence of antisemitism in Germany following World War I led to increased use of Aryan paragraphs in the bylaws of racist and nationalist organizations. Perhaps the most influential instance was the hotly disputed adoption of the paragraph by the nationalist student fraternities (Burschenschaften) in 1920. This paragraph required that prospective members prove Aryan descent back to the grandparents' generation and forbade marriage to Jewish or "colored" women. By the late 1920s, including an Aryan paragraph in bylaws was virtually automatic among German nationalist and rightist organizations.

After 1933, the Aryan paragraph was adopted by the Nazis as a matter of state policy, one of many tools used in the early years of the regime to exclude Jews from public life. The first official use appeared in paragraph 3 of the Civil Service Law of April 7, 1933, stipulating that only those of Aryan descent, without Jewish parents or grandparents, could be considered for civil service employment. This stipulation was quickly extended to education with the Law against Overcrowding in German Schools and Universities of April 25, 1933. Aryan paragraphs were included in the Hereditary Farm Law of September 25, 1933; in the Editor Law of October 4, 1933; and in all laws governing the professions, education, and health until, by the end of 1934, Jews had been driven out of mainstream German society. Nazi "synchronization" of German society extended the practice of including the Aryan paragraph to private organizations, which were forced to accept the paragraph or disband. There was little resistance to its introduction among private groups, a notable exception being the Pfarrernotbund (Pastor's Emergency League) of Martin Niemöller and Dietrich Bonhoeffer, whose main concern, however, was the fate of non-Aryan Christians.

The Aryan paragraph marked an important step in the disenfranchisement of German Jews, setting legal criteria for full citizenship based on race and thus anticipating the Nuremberg Laws of 1935.

—*Mark Swartzburg*

See also Austria; Nazi Legal Measures against Jews; Nuremberg Laws; Purge of the German Civil Service; *Völkisch* Movement and Ideology
References
Frei, Norbert. *National Socialist Rule in Germany: The Führer State 1933–1945.* Translated by Simon Steyne (Oxford: Blackwell, 1993).
Pauley, Bruce F. *From Prejudice to Persecution: A History of Austrian Anti-Semitism* (Chapel Hill: University of North Carolina Press, 1992).

Aryan Theater

From 1898 to 1903, Vienna's Christian Social municipal government, together with like-minded private individuals, sponsored an explicitly antisemitic theater called the Kaiserjubiläums Stadttheater (the Emperor's Jubilee Theater). Also known as the Aryan Theater of Vienna and sardonically as the Christian Social Asylum, this first antisemitic theater in history refused its resources to Jewish playwrights and actors—a rule that was occasionally broken—and produced a number of provocative antisemitic plays.

The Aryan Theater was controversial from the outset. Its history was characterized by fiascoes and blunders that demonstrated the cultural and artistic ineptitude of its sponsors and its director, Adam Müller-Guttenbrunn. A number of those who supported the theater were culturally illiterate. One Christian Social politician advertised his limitations in this regard by rejoicing that such "Jewish" authors as Alexandre Dumas, Émile Zola, and Henrik Ibsen could now be refused a stage in the new theater. On another occasion, in one of the party papers, a garbled version of Shakespeare's *Merchant of Venice* was hailed as the work of Austrian playwright Franz Grillparzer. When Müller-Guttenbrunn, sensing imminent financial ruin, attempted a conciliatory production of a legitimately philosemitic work, Karl Lueger, the antisemitic mayor of Vienna, intervened, forbidding its performance.

Party hacks bullied Müller-Guttenbrunn into

producing their lifeless dramas and became incensed when these failed to attract audiences. On one such occasion, only the playwright and his wife attended his production in a theater (today's Volksoper) that could seat 1,800. Though Lueger could boast that the Aryan stage was a welcome haven for Christian families seeking to escape implicitly Jewish-run theaters, Müller-Guttenbrunn was nonetheless called to task on a number of occasions for presenting unsavory or controversial dramatic fare.

The theater's greatest success was an adaptation of Henryk Sienkiewicz's *Sign of the Cross.* In an avowedly "Christian Theater," *Sign of the Cross* seemed a logical choice, but this production turned out to be an ideological defeat for the Christian Socials. An American, Wilson Barret, who was "culturally inferior" in the eyes of nationalistic theater sponsors, adapted the play. The staged persecutions, orgies, and flagellations permanently spoiled the taste of the audience, according to Müller-Guttenbrunn. The inherent antisemitism of *Sign of the Cross* and its ideological purpose were obvious. When "two [Jewish] sycophants whisper to each other that the Christians murder little children," one critic wrote, it was as if one "had been transported into the midst of a raucous Christian Social meeting resounding with anti-Jewish agitation" (Geehr 1973, 238).

The Aryan Theater failed for a number of reasons. Rivalries within the Christian Social Party continually underlined a serious confusion of purpose. Some of the project's supporters had invested in the undertaking only because Müller-Guttenbrunn had promised a relatively high rate of return, a promise he could not keep. Many backers were indifferent to the director's idealistic or ideological motives. Lueger himself seemed to be undecided about what the real purpose of the theater should be. Though he had supported an antisemitic theater project as early as 1890, he later seemed inclined to favor lighthearted, escapist fare that suited the tastes of the party rank and file. But the chief reason for the failure of the theater was very practical. Audiences of the era were uninterested in any sustained ideological effort on stage. The Aryan Theater did not meet their expectations either of entertainment or of edification. Successful antisemitic drama had to await the development of sound films and an audience brutalized by World War I and its aftermath.

—*Richard S. Geehr*

See also Austria; Christian Social Party (Austria); Kralik, Richard von; Lueger, Karl; Müller-Guttenbrunn, Adam; Ritual Murder (Modern)
Reference
Geehr, Richard S. *Adam Müller-Guttenbrunn and the Aryan Theater of Vienna: 1898–1903* (Göppingen, Germany: Göppinger Arbeiten zur Germanistik, 1973).

Aryanization (Germany)

Aryanization (*Arisierung*) was the euphemistic term used by the Nazi regime to describe its drive to strip Jews of their jobs and possessions, especially in Germany from 1933 to 1939. Originally presented as a self-defense measure against the supposedly destructive effects of Jewish "overrepresentation" in certain walks of German life, the program developed into a means of re-segregating Jews from the rest of the citizenry, then cashing in on their ultimate "removal" from German society. In the process, Aryanization benefited the Nazi state in two ways: it made numerous posts and goods available to covetous non-Jews, thus increasing popular support for Adolf Hitler's government, and it turned most Jewish-owned assets into money, which the regime confiscated via taxes, exit fees, and outright seizures, thus raising revenue for the Third Reich.

In the first years of Nazi rule, the party attacked the positions and property held by Jews intensely but in piecemeal fashion. Government edicts in the period between 1933 and 1935 excluded most Jews from posts in the civil service, state-controlled enterprises (including most of the country's largest banks), teaching, and the greater part of the nation's medical and judicial systems. Even more stringent laws barred all Jews from farming; public office; the military; and the national associations of journalists, musicians, and theater personnel that were prerequisites for employment in those fields. With regard to most of the private sector, however, the new regime generally preferred to proceed less overtly and precipitously, in part to avert damage to the German economy or the country's foreign relations. Only in a few dramatic instances, notably concerning prominent department store chains, publishing houses, and some armaments firms, did the government apply direct pressure at an early date to make corporations change hands at knockdown prices. Instead, intimidation at lower levels seemed adequate to the party's initial purpose, which was to persuade Jews to retire or sell out "voluntarily." Nazi decision makers, for example, routinely withheld contracts from firms owned or managed by Jews, and party activists among the enterprises' employees or stockholders loudly agitated for the dismissal of Jewish officers or directors. Fairly promptly, therefore, many of these individuals or their colleagues decided to acquiesce "for the good of the firm." Meanwhile, customers or clients were discouraged from patronizing Jewish-owned shops and professional practices, not only by the Storm troopers who stood ominously outside many stores during the infamous nationwide boycott of April 1, 1933, but also in the following period by local party organizations that publicly condemned anyone who did business with Jews. Behind all of this bullying stood the ever present menace of illicit violence, against which the courts provided no dependable protection. This mix of formal prohibitions and semiofficial harassment made deep inroads between 1933 and 1937 on the economic conditions of German Jews, although many still could obtain more or less standard severance and pension terms from former employers and something approaching legitimate prices for their companies. By the end of the period, perhaps one-quarter of the population remaining in Germany was dependent on Jewish welfare agencies for some form of sustenance; almost all the Jews still able to earn a living worked either for themselves or for each other. About 60 percent of the 100,000 Jewish-owned businesses in Germany as of 1933 (including about 30 percent of the major ones) had been sold or closed. The number of large German firms in which Jews held several leading positions had dropped by 83 percent, and the number in which they held any ranking post fell by over half; the total wealth of the Jewish populace,

estimated at 10 billion reichsmarks when Hitler achieved power, had fallen by 40 to 50 percent, whereas the Jewish population had declined by less than one-third. Moreover, the Nazi regime proved increasingly adept at skimming off the wealth of those who emigrated, primarily through the Reich Flight Tax that antedated Hitler's regime and consumed 25 percent of an emigrant's assets; discriminatory currency conversion rates for Jews that fell from 50 percent of the normal exchange rates in 1935 to 4 percent by 1939 aided the expropriation.

In early 1938, the Nazi regime began to close the gap between its overt and clandestine efforts to dispossess Jews and launched a full-fledged assault on their remaining livelihoods. No longer constrained by fear of unemployment but increasingly preoccupied with the likelihood of war, Hitler appears to have signaled Hermann Göring, the man principally responsible for the nation's economy, that the time had come to move forcefully against the Jews. By the spring, the Reich had defined what constituted a Jewish firm and threatened to cut off government contracts, raw materials, and foreign exchange from all enterprises that qualified, with the result that all remaining Jews in managerial positions and on corporate boards were forced out and most major Jewish stockholders had to begin divesting. Prohibitions on Jewish traveling salespeople, brokers, doctors, and lawyers followed, along with a requirement that sales of Jewish-owned companies had to be approved by the party's Regional Economic Advisors, who set narrow and larcenous parameters for the permissible prices.

In the aftermath of the so-called Night of Broken Glass pogrom of November 1938, the regime first imposed an "atonement levy" on the German Jewish population of 1 billion reichsmarks, most of it to be raised by a tax of 25 percent on all individuals' assets as of the preceding April; then, it began conducting forced sales or liquidations of the remaining Jewish-owned enterprises, requiring Jews to monetize virtually all their wealth. The proceeds of the forced sales, along with those from compulsory conversions of insurance policies, stockholdings, precious metals, and the like into cash, had to be deposited in blocked accounts under the control of Nazi trustees. As long as they remained in Germany, the owners could extract only minuscule monthly living allowances from these accounts. On a person's departure from the country, most of the balance went to the German state. By way of these procedures, at least half of the total wealth that remained to German Jews in April 1938 flowed into the Reich's coffers by September 1939 (a sum of nearly 3 billion reichsmarks). But the real total was probably even higher, and the proceeds may have come to as much as 5 percent of the Reich's expenditures in the year leading up to World War II. In the course of this ruthless plundering of the remnant of German Jewry, relatively modest portions of the loot were scattered among individual profiteers, including not only the recipients of the property taken, many of whom were prominent Nazis or well connected to the party, but also the numerous persons and firms that mediated the transfers, notably, real estate agencies, banks, pawnshops, and auction houses.

By mid-1939, about 200,000 Jews remained in Germany, out of a population of approximately 500,000 six years earlier. Only 16 percent were employed; the others who could work were increasingly dragooned into forced labor at low wages for municipalities or industries, and nearly all were being moved out of their homes and concentrated in "Jew houses" (*Judenhäuser*) in larger German cities. In the period prior to their virtually complete deportation by 1943, their property either was signed over to the National Representation of German Jews (Reichsvertretung der Deutschen Juden) and then collected by the Nazi regime or confiscated by the Reich outright under the terms of the 11th Citizenship Decree of November 1941. The latter fate also befell most remaining possessions in Germany of those who had succeeded in emigrating earlier.

—*Peter Hayes*

See also Boycott of Jewish Shops; German Big Business and Antisemitism; Göring, Hermann; National Socialist German Workers' Party; Nazi Cultural Antisemitism; Nazi Legal Measures against Jews; Night of Broken Glass; Purge of the German Civil Service; Restitution

References

Bajohr, Frank. *"Aryanisation" in Hamburg: The Economic Exclusion of Jews and the Confiscation of Their Property in Nazi Germany* (New York: Berghahn Books, 2002).

Barkai, Avraham. *From Boycott to Annihilation: The Economic Struggle of German Jews, 1933–1943* (Hanover, NH: University Press of New England, 1989).

Hayes, Peter. "State Policy and Corporate Involvement in the Holocaust." In *The Holocaust and History: The Known, the Unknown, the Disputed, and the Reexamined.* Edited by Michael Berenbaum and Abraham J. Peck (Bloomington: Indiana University Press, 1998), 197–218.

Hayes, Peter, and Irmtrud Wojak, eds. *"Arisierung" im Nationalsozialismus* (Frankfurt am Main, Germany: Campus Verlag, 2000).

Augustine of Hippo (354–430)

One of the four great "doctors" of the Latin church, Augustine is perhaps the most influential thinker in the history of Western Christianity. His influence on many aspects of Christian thought and practice, including Christian attitudes toward Jews and Judaism, has been immense. Indeed, his doctrine of "Jewish witness" might easily be regarded as the authoritative Western view from the time of his death in the fifth century until the Second Vatican Council in the twentieth.

Early in his writing career, Augustine, following a well-established Christian tradition, identified the biblical characters from the book of Genesis, Cain and Abel, as symbols of the Jews and Jesus Christ, respectively. For their guilt in the murder of Christ, the Jews (like Cain, who killed his brother Abel) were exiled from their land, and in exile, they would continue to live, in sorrow, anxiety, and servitude, until the end of time. Bearing "the mark of Cain," they were to be permitted to live (though, again, only in subjugation) by gentile emperors and kings in whose lands they were dispersed.

In Augustine's view, it was thus God's will that Judaism should endure and Jews not be slain. Biblically, the survival of the Jews and their dispersion were, Augustine argued, mandated by Psalms 59:12: "Slay them not, lest at any time they forget your law; scatter them in your might." The survival of the Jews and their continued practice of Judaism were intended, in several respects, to witness to the truth of Chris-

Augustine of Hippo was the most influential thinker in the history of Western Christianity on the subject of the Jews. In his view, it was God's will that Jews not be slain, so that they might bear witness to the triumph and truth of Christianity. (Library of Congress)

tianity. First of all, their condition of dispersion and subjugation served to authenticate the triumph and truth of Christianity and the displacement of the synagogue by the church. Second, by preserving their Scriptures, the Jews unintentionally would preserve the prophecies concerning Christ contained within them. In this way, they would prove to pagan critics of, or recent converts to, Christianity that the church had not forged those prophecies. Thus, Jews served unintentionally as custodians of the books that prove the messiahship of Christ and that contain prophecies of their own blindness and rejection. In short, if Jews had a continuing place in the drama of divine salvation, it was solely as

a witness people, to vindicate the truth of the new religion.

This "doctrine of Jewish witness" was charged with ambivalent meanings for Jews, especially since it helped to shape the ways that Jews were treated by Christian leaders and peoples for millennia. On the one hand, no potentate could coerce Jews into ceasing the practice of Judaism, although this proviso was not always observed, even by Christian clerics. (Comparatively, Augustine did not extend the same tolerance to nonorthodox Christians, such as the Donatists, against whom he condoned imperial punishment.) On the other hand, they were to be permitted to practice Judaism only as a service of witness to the church. According to historian Jeremy Cohen, the invocation of Psalm 59, with its mandate not to slay "them," served as a "prophetic policy-statement" that not only prevented their liquidation but also guaranteed them religious freedom (Cohen 1999, 36). Yet the second half of the Psalm—"scatter them in your might"—made their dispersion a matter of divine will and human obligation. Less ambiguously, it was simply assumed, according to the eschatological scenario laid out by Augustine, that the Jews would convert to Christianity at the end of time. Moreover, the doctrine underscored the sole responsibility of the Jews for the death of Christ, emphasized their supposed stubbornness and blindness in refusing to acknowledge Christ as Messiah, and viewed Jewish religion and the synagogue as essentially moribund.

The danger in this view of Jews and Judaism when put into practice, aside from the obvious psychological, social, political, and economic disabilities it could inflict, is that the religious and cultural presuppositions favoring and even demanding survival could change, wither away, or disappear altogether in different historical circumstances. A second, although less serious, danger (yet not unknown in the Middle Ages or in the modern period) is that the principle could be ignored even among those for whom it remained theoretically authoritative. Thus, the Augustinian doctrine was unable to prevent, in "Christian societies," instances of forced conversion, expulsion, and, in the Crusades and during the years of the Black Death, mass murder. Ultimately, in the Middle Ages, the tension between the two halves of Augustine's teaching proved difficult to maintain; in the modern period, that task proved tragically impossible.

—*Kevin Madigan*

See also Church Fathers; Deicide; Paul; Supersessionism; Vatican Council, Second
References
Cohen, Jeremy. *Living Letters of the Law: Ideas of the Jew in Medieval Christianity* (Berkeley and Los Angeles: University of California Press, 1999).
Fredriksen, Paula. "*Excaecati Occulta Justititia Dei:* Augustine on Jews and Judaism," *Journal of Early Christian Studies* 3, no. 3 (1995): 299–324.
Haynes, Stephen. *Reluctant Witnesses: Jews and the Christian Imagination* (Louisville, KY: Westminster John Knox Press, 1995).

Auschwitz Lie

The term *Auschwitz Lie* (*Auschwitz-Lüge*) was coined by the German Holocaust denier Thies Christophersen in the early 1970s. A former Waffen-SS man, Christophersen had been stationed in one of the Auschwitz subcamps in 1944. After the war, he became a leading neo-Nazi activist in Germany. By the end of the 1960s and in the early 1970s, he had founded the journals *Bauernschaft* (Peasantry) and *Kritik* (Critique), which became significant venues for Nazi apologists and Holocaust deniers. At the same time, he also established the neo-Nazi group Bauern- und Bürgerinitiative (freely translated as Town and Country Initiative).

The Auschwitz Lie was the title of his book, presented as an eyewitness report about Auschwitz. Christophersen claimed that he had neither seen nor heard of any gassing activity when he had served near Auschwitz and visited Birkenau. The book, published in Germany in 1973, was the first radical German Holocaust denial publication and had a powerful influence on extreme rightists in the country.

In the 1970s and 1980s, when Auschwitz came to be perceived worldwide as the embodiment of the unprecedented evils of Nazi Germany, it also became the main target for Holocaust deniers. As a result, the term *Auschwitz Lie*—the alleged Jewish fabrication that exterminations took place in Auschwitz—was embraced first by German deniers and neo-Nazis and later by their associates around the world. The claim that the facilities in Auschwitz and Birkenau were not capable of mass annihilation became obligatory in most of their publications. The "so-called gas chambers," they maintained, were used as delousing facilities and not for mass murder. The deniers' campaign to undermine the truth about Auschwitz culminated in 1988 during the trial of German Canadian Holocaust denier Ernst Zündel in Canada. Christophersen was one of the defense witnesses, and he repeated his Auschwitz Lie thesis. The main defense witness, however, was the American charlatan engineer Fred Leuchter, who claimed that the samples he had collected in Auschwitz and Birkenau demonstrated that people could not have been gassed there. Although his credentials as an expert witness were fraudulent and rejected by the court, the *Leuchter Report* had a huge impact on antisemites and Holocaust deniers. In early 1992, another Holocaust denier, the German chemist Germar Rudolf, claimed to have corroborated the Auschwitz Lie theory scientifically.

Christophersen was sentenced to prison in Germany in 1978 for disseminating Nazi propaganda. In 1986, he fled to Denmark in order to avoid further court proceedings. However, in 1995, he was forced to leave Denmark as a result of almost daily demonstrations against his presence, and two years later, he died in Belgium.

—*Roni Stauber*

See also Germany, Federal Republic of; Holocaust Denial, Negationism, and Revisionism; Leuchter Report; Neo-Nazism, German; Zündel, Ernst
References
Porat, Dina, and Roni Stauber, eds. *Anti-Semitism Worldwide, 1995/1996* (Tel Aviv: Project for the Study of Anti-Semitism, in Cooperation with the Anti-Defamation League, 1996).
Rembiszewski, Sarah. *The Final Lie: Holocaust Denial in Germany—A Second Generation Denier as a Test Case* (Tel Aviv: Tel Aviv University Press, 1995).

Australia

The Jewish community in Australia has unique historical legitimacy: Jewish convicts arrived on the first day of European settlement in 1788 and then as Free Settlers beginning in the 1830s. During this period, most of them came from Britain or other parts of the English-speaking world. Jews were elected to serve in the Australian parliaments two decades before they were permitted to contest seats in Britain. At least forty Jews served in Australian legislatures throughout the nineteenth century, a number of whom were vocal in support of Jewish rights and equal treatment for Judaism at the hands of Australian governments.

For much of the first century of the Jewish presence in Australia, there were indications of a low level of antisemitism, in the context of a more dominant philosemitism. Intermarriage rates were high, indicating a rare acceptance of Jewish people as members of society. In the late nineteenth and early twentieth centuries, Australians debated the suitability of east European Jewish immigrants—a debate generally framed in terms of the overall undesirability or desirability of non-English-speaking aliens, rather than specifically referring to Jews. In the 1920s, antisemitic ideas of European provenance gained some currency in Australia, centering on the identification of Jews as Bolsheviks and/or as archetypical capitalists. Between the world wars, during a period in which a number of Jews from central and eastern Europe began to arrive in Australia and many more sought sanctuary there, antisemitism reached the political mainstream: it was a product of the political tensions precipitated by the Great Depression and the emergence of Australian populism, which often adopted antisemitic rhetoric to bolster its arguments. Antisemitic propaganda came from a number of extreme right-wing political groups and from left-wing circles as well. However, there is little to indicate that antisemitism excited the Australian population or disturbed public life to the same degree that it did elsewhere in the world.

The outbreak of World War II effectively halted any prospect of an expanding antisemitic movement in Australia. With the country at war with Nazi Germany, extreme right-wing groups, those most likely to espouse Jew-hatred in politics, were clearly identified as enemies of Australia. But in the immediate postwar period, with many displaced persons, including many Jews, seeking refuge, antisemitism overtly and covertly entered once again into the discussion of immigration policy.

There was prominent opposition to the arrival in Australia of people who had been through the ravages of war, who did not speak English as their first language, and who were seen as likely to compete for Australian jobs. Jewish refugees who had just experienced the physical and emotional degradation of the war seemed to many to be less desirable than individuals who appeared fit, strong, and Christian. However, efforts by a number of active and prominent Jewish Australians made possible a limited Jewish immigration. Subsequently, antisemitism all but disappeared from the debate.

In the last half of the twentieth century, there were fundamental changes to Australian society, which had developed from a basically Christian, Anglo-Saxon community into a multicultural, ethnically and religiously pluralist society. Along with these changes came alterations in the nature of the antisemitism that arose from a variety of sources. Far-right-wing antisemitism operated on the political margins, advocated by racist groups that peddled views of Jews as un-British and un-Australian; neo-Nazi and like-minded groups, numerically weak, were nevertheless present in Australia, especially among segments of the immigrant communities of East and Central Europe. These groups rarely, if ever, worked in concert, but their propaganda, originating in a common fund of anti-Jewish stereotypes, was mutually complementary and reinforcing.

Growing antisemitism was also evident on the extreme Left, which included groups that saw the Jews as part of the capitalist establishment. Among these, a small but disproportionately significant element supported the Soviet Union and, in a number of cases, was supported by it. By this agency, Soviet antisemitic and "anti-Zionist" propaganda entered into the broader Australian political Left.

Since the 1970s, there have been a number of occasions when antisemitism, of a type otherwise unknown outside the political fringes in Australia, has impinged on Australian political life; its proponents are, by and large, Australians of

Arab and Islamic background. Arabic-language newspapers in the country have published Holocaust denial articles, repeated the blood libel, and excerpted the *Protocols of the Elders of Zion* for their readers, rarely making an effort to distinguish between Jews and Israelis.

The debate over whether individuals who committed crimes against humanity during the Nazi era should be prosecuted under Australian law also included a small but notable antisemitic element. Allegations raised by mainstream figures insinuated that those who sought to pursue justice in this matter were, in fact, motivated by "Jewish vengeance," which they contrasted with Christian compassion.

The Nazi war criminal issue reemerged somewhat later and in a different form. In 1995, Helen Darville, using the pseudonym Demidenko, published *The Hand That Signed the Paper,* a novel that she claimed drew on her own family's tragic history. In the book, brought out by the reputable publisher Allen & Unwin, a person charged with involvement in Nazi crimes against humanity was depicted as having done no more than what the Jews deserved because of their own behavior in the brutal Stalinist oppression of the Ukraine. Although praised by many at the time as "another voice" with ethnic authenticity, the novel was condemned by experts in the period of history it sought to evoke for its misrepresentation of that history and of Ukrainian society in general. Nevertheless, it gave a platform to Demidenko and enabled her to find some sympathetic audiences for her overtly antisemitic comments. When Darville was exposed as having no Ukrainian heritage whatsoever—she is the daughter of English immigrant parents—the ensuing debate raised disturbing questions. What, aside from its obvious antisemitism, could account for the literary fame of this invention? Why did it receive so much attention and praise from literary critics and other public figures, some of it continuing well after the fraud had been exposed?

One of the significant features in any study of Australian antisemitism is its minimal presence in the Australian church. There has been an active and strong engagement between Jews and Christians in Australia for decades, and problems that have arisen have generally been dealt with in a manner indicating a high degree of cooperation and mutual respect.

In the closing decade of the twentieth century, developing awareness of violence directed against all religious and racial minorities in Australia led to a reevaluation of the way the Jewish community's leading representative body, the Executive Council of Australian Jewry (ECAJ), analyzed and reported attacks on Jews. Since 1989, the ECAJ has maintained a comprehensive national database of antisemitic incidents directed at Jews and Jewish institutions: arson; vandalism; assaults on individuals; street harassment, particularly of Jews going to or from synagogues; threats and abuse through the mail and on the telephone; distribution of leaflets, posters, stickers, and electronic mail; and displays of insulting graffiti. The number of such attacks appears to be large, although none of them can be described as the product of any mainstream political, social, or cultural tendency. The physical manifestations of antisemitism have generally been condemned by the Australian public.

In both federal law and in the states of New South Wales and Victoria and the Australian Capital Territory, where laws have been put to the test, it has been determined that anti-Jewish propaganda is covered by measures drafted in terms of racism. In an important case that reached its final determination in the federal court of Australia in 2003, literature advocating Holocaust denial placed on the Internet was found to satisfy the illegality criteria for published material in a public space. The publisher of the material, who was living in Australia, was also found subject to Australian law. In an earlier decision, the federal court upheld a Human Rights and Equal Opportunity Commission finding that blaming Jews for bolshevism, as well as many other slurs, was also covered by federal antiracism legislation.

—*Jeremy Jones*

See also Anti-Zionism in the USSR; Britain; Crimes against Humanity, Trials; Holocaust Denial, Negationism, and Revisionism; Islamic Diaspora; Judeo-Bolshevism; *Ostjuden; Protocols of the Elders of Zion*
References
Jones, Jeremy S. *Antisemitism in Australia—Annual*

Reports 1993–2003 (Sidney: Executive Council of Australian Jewry, 2003).

Rubinstein, Hilary L. *The Jews in Australia: A Thematic History.* Vol. 1, *1788–1945* (Melbourne: William Heinemann Australia, 1991).

Rubinstein, William D., ed. *Jews in the Sixth Continent* (Melbourne: Allen & Unwin Australia, 1987).

Austria

As the legatee of the Holy Roman Empire, the "Austrian," or Cisleithanian, part of the Habsburg monarchy was also heir to the prejudices, acts of discrimination, and periodic violence directed against Jews that were characteristic of Christian Europe. During its final decades as part of the Habsburg monarchy and into the First Republic founded in 1918, Austria served as an incubator of various strains of antisemitic ideology and corresponding political movements, as well as a testing ground for antisemitic agitation. Although actual anti-Jewish laws were implemented in Austria only after the *Anschluss* (annexation) by Nazi Germany in 1938, the accumulated reservoir of traditional and modern anti-Jewish prejudice in the country made resistance to these measures unlikely. Indeed, any number of anti-Jewish motifs (religious, economic, cultural, and racial) offered sufficient grounds to justify the antisemitic political practice of the Nazis in terms consistent with the Austrian past.

Many "modern" antisemitic stereotypes in Austria can be traced to antiquity. Such beliefs inaugurated an exclusionary language that, once divorced from its ancient origins, became a set piece of anti-Jewish prejudice for centuries to come. In the Middle Ages, hostility toward Jews was expressed both in discriminatory acts and in physical attacks. Catholic Church councils discouraged or prevented contacts between Christians and Jews, required Jews to wear a distinguishing badge or mark, imposed restrictions on the exercise of occupations, and accepted protoracist notions such as the "purity of the blood." In the wake of the plague or in times of general dearth, accusations of well poisoning, host desecration, or ritual murder of Christian children were raised against Jews, sometimes leading to their massacre. Yet, as elsewhere in Europe, Jews lived peacefully enough with their neighbors for long stretches of time. A few, in position to offer their financial services to penurious secular princes, could purchase privileges and protection for themselves and others.

The word *antisemitism,* a neologism of the late nineteenth century, was introduced into political discourse in Austria in the late 1870s. Employed by movements and individuals that had adopted a new approach to the Jewish Question as it had been reframed following the legal emancipation of Jews (in 1867), the term also became a linguistic shorthand for the entire array of old and many new anti-Jewish prejudices.

The historical development of the German-speaking Habsburg lands gave antisemitism in Austria its distinctive character. The development of capitalism, the predominance of the Catholic Church, the short-lived ascendancy and disastrous fall of Austro-Liberalism, the specificities of the nationalities question in the empire, the migration of large numbers of Jews to Vienna, the growth of a powerful Social Democratic movement, and the emergence of mass political parties—all these elements determined the context and, to some extent, the nature of, antisemitism in Austria. Jews achieved leading and visible positions in the economy, especially in banking and on the stock exchange, in intellectual and cultural life (particularly the press), and in the legal and medical professions. They led the Social Democratic Party. Poor Jews were also seen as problematic; their marginal economic activities, it was said, undermined honest artisans and small shopkeepers. Some Jews wished to assimilate fully and, as bearers of German culture, came to believe that they had done so; others, the *Ostjuden* (eastern European Jews) from Galicia and elsewhere, stood out because they retained their traditional customs and dress. This spectrum of Jewish existence and identity, however, offered no antidote to the conventional wisdom about the uniform "essence" of the Jew; on the contrary, it formed the basis of the protean mixture of anti-Jewish religious, economic, cultural, and racial prejudice that ostensibly explained nearly every intractable social and cultural problem.

The three most significant political currents from the late Habsburg years up to the Anschluss of 1938 were embodied in the movements of the Christian Socials, the Pan-Germans, and the Social Democrats.

The Christian Social Movement was formed in 1887 as a coalition of constituent groups (artisans, lower clergy, and disaffected democrats, among others) and was molded into a potent electoral force principally by Karl Lueger, mayor of Vienna from 1897 to 1910. The program of Lueger's movement wove together several antiliberal elements, such as populism, social reform, antisemitism, and dynastic loyalty. Lueger's antisemitism was pragmatic rather than ideological, but its political legacy nevertheless legitimized antisemitic demagogy in Austrian public life.

Pan-Germanism in fin de siècle Austria came to be broadly identified with the politics of Georg von Schönerer. Schönerer was originally elected to the Reichsrat (parliament) as a progressive liberal, but he soon became a bitter critic of the liberal establishment. In 1882, along with Viktor Adler and Engelbert Pernerstorfer (both later leaders of the Social Democratic movement) and Heinrich Friedjung (a liberal historian), Schönerer drafted the Linz Program, which called for a closer union with Wilhelmine Germany. Schönerer became increasingly radical, both in his hostility to the multinational Austrian Empire and in his antisemitism: in 1885, he introduced a twelfth article into the Linz Program, excluding Jews. Although Schönerer himself never achieved any real political power, he shifted the focus of German nationalism in Austria away from mere cultural supremacy in the multinational state, linking its fortunes to those of the German Empire and pairing this integral nationalism with racial antisemitism.

Although Schönerer and his followers prided themselves on the "purism" of their antisemitism (much more so than did their competitors, in fact), the boundaries between the national racial form of antisemitism and the less systematic Christian Social variety remained fluid. Individuals who once were allied in the same groups fell out over a variety of political issues; they changed allegiances easily and often but rarely felt called on to jettison or even revise their antisemitism. Many Christian Socials who explicitly renounced racial antisemitism (in its Schönererian form) nonetheless expressed opinions with racist implications. One example was Karl von Vogelsang. From 1875, Vogelsang edited the conservative Catholic paper *Vaterland* (Fatherland), and he became a behind-the-scenes adviser for several Christian Social politicians and for some of the Catholic lower clergy. As a devout Catholic, he rejected racial antisemitism. Yet his writings contained recognizably racist elements. This "syncretic" antisemitism in nineteenth-century Austria also owed something to the efforts of priests such as Josef Deckert. In his later writings, Deckert argued that Christian teachings were compatible with racial antisemitism.

The shifting and overlapping boundaries between religious and racist currents within the antisemitic movement illustrated by Deckert's personal ideological migration continued into the Austrian First Republic, in which neither the (German) national camp nor the Christian Social camp strictly observed ideological differences over antisemitism. Christian Social politician Richard Schmitz, for example, fulminated against the "extraordinarily dangerous and spiritually unjustified phenomenon ... that the members of another people, even another race, appear as pseudo-Germans," whereas Leopold Kunschak of the Christian Social Laborers in Linz wanted to prohibit Jews from "denying their ethnic group membership merely by leaving their religious community" (quotations from Staudinger 1979, 29, 41). It is true that the sometimes extreme antisemitic propaganda of Christian Social politicians did not result in anti-Jewish legal measures. However, the ambiguous vocabulary of Christian Social antisemitism and its "language of hardness" offered arguments to justify the systematic exclusion of Jews from Austrian society.

Officially against all forms of discrimination, the Social Democratic Party in the Habsburg monarchy and the Austrian First Republic nevertheless exhibited an ambivalent attitude toward the antisemitic movement and sometimes had trouble distancing itself from antisemitic agitation. The Social Democrats' historical materialism convinced them that antisemitism was an ideological phenomenon corresponding to a particular stage of capitalist development. Instead of a struggle against Jewish capital, as the antisemites advocated, the Social Democrats proposed a proletarian fight against Jewish and non-Jewish capitalism. Tactically, however, they tried to exploit the confused anticapitalism of the antisemitic movement. This strategy, however, often minimized the significance of antisemitism, so that the party—many of whose leaders were Jewish—would not be seen to be defending specifically Jewish interests. At the same time, in their attempts to expose the Christian Socials' hypocrisy, the Social Democrats sometimes employed a language indistinguishable from that of their antisemitic opponents. As a consequence, they lent a new kind of respectability to the antisemitic stereotypes that equated "capitalist" and "Jew."

Writers and cultural critics were also part of the linguistic context of antisemitism in Austria, especially in Vienna, prior to 1938. The works of Otto Weininger, which contained passages contemptuous of Jews; the biting wit of Karl Kraus, who reserved his most derisory concinnity for Jews in leading positions in the Viennese press; and the curious writings of Arthur Trebitsch, who became a case study of "Jewish self-hatred," are merely the best-known examples of a much broader phenomenon. Whatever the origins or immediate causes of this type of writing, it also provided a kind of cover for the antisemitic prejudices of others.

These diffuse ideological currents helped create an everyday texture of antisemitic prejudice in Austria that ranged from generalizations about Jews in the professions to allegations of actual ritual murder to calls for the reimposition of legal disabilities against racially defined Jews. Moreover, antisemitism in Austria retained its syncretic character under the Nazi regime, even though racial elements—Hitler's "antisemitism of reason"—assumed a hitherto unheard-of prominence in official propaganda. In practice, however, the Nazis were not particularly doctrinaire in terms of their grounds for the intellectual and psychological stigmatization of the Jews that prepared the way for their political exclusion from the Third Reich and their physical elimination from Europe.

In Austria under the Nazis, the isolation and murder of the Jews entailed a series of steps in a process that met with little or no resistance. After the Anschluss, the zealousness of some Austrian antisemites surprised even the Germans when it came to the persecution of Jews. At no stage, however, would the concrete achievement of the Nazis' stated political objectives have required a purely racial justification or arguments that could not have been found among their Christian Social opponents. The Final Solution of the Jewish Question found a well-prepared soil in Austria.

—*Richard Mitten*

See also Antisemitism, Etymology of; Billroth, Theodor; Christian Social Party (Austria); Court Jews; Emancipation; Gemlich Letter; Host Desecration; Jewish Question; Kraus, Karl; Linz Program; Lueger, Karl; *Ostjuden;* Pan-Germans; Polná Ritual Murder; Ritual Murder (Medieval); Schönerer, Georg von; Self-Hatred, Jewish; Socialists on Antisemitism; Vogelsang, Karl von; Weininger, Otto; Well Poisoning; Yellow Badge

References

Arkel, Dirk van. "Antisemitism in Austria." Dissertation, University of Leyden, 1966.

Mitten, Richard. "'Synkretischer' Antisemitismus: Zur Kontinuität antisemitischer Vorurteile in Österreich." In *"Dreck am Stecken": Politik der Ausgrenzung.* Edited by Anton Pelinka and Ruth Wodak (Vienna: Czernin Verlag, 2002), 32–60.

Pauley, Bruce F. *From Prejudice to Persecution: A History of Austrian Anti-Semitism* (Chapel Hill: University of North Carolina Press, 1992).

Pulzer, Peter G. J. *The Rise of Political Antisemitism in Germany and Austria.* Rev. ed. (London: P. Halban, 1988).

Staudinger, Anton. "Christlich-soziale Judenpolitik in der Gründungsphase der österreichischen Republik." In *Jahrbücher für Zeitgeschichte (1978).* Edited by Karl Stuhlpfarrer (Vienna: Löcker Verlag, 1979), 11–48.

Wistrich, Robert S. *Socialism and the Jews: The Dilemmas of Assimilation in Germany and Austria-Hungary* (East Brunswick, NJ: Associated University Presses, 1982).

Auto-da-fé

The term *auto-da-fé* (in Spanish, *auto de fe*) signified the pronouncement of the sentence of the local Inquisition tribunal against a Christian suspected of heresy. The sentence could be pronounced in closed or public session. Until the mid-sixteenth century, there were no dispositions about the venue for the passing of the sentence. From that period on, it became common to choose the central place of a town—at least for death sentences—and to accompany the auto-da-fé with great pomp. All persons condemned had to wear a penitential robe (*sambenito*). The public reading and execution of the sentence was aimed at deterring potential heretics. Persons who refused to assist an auto-da-fé thereby opened themselves to suspicion of also adhering to heresy. Typical penalties included confiscation of property, public whippings, imprisonment, being sent to the galleys, or burning at the stake—the form of punishment that historical memory most closely associates with the Inquisition. The actual execution of death sentences was handed over to the secular authorities. Those who repented were strangled with the garrote; all others were burned alive. If the condemned was a fugitive at large, a puppet representing the individual was burned.

The procedures by which to prove innocence or guilt were strictly limited. Until the trial, defendants were held in secret jails. The witnesses remained anonymous, and sometimes even the content of the accusation was withheld. Rumors were acceptable as evidence, and confessions were extracted by torture. In the first decades of the Spanish Inquisition, acquittals were rare. Although severe by any standard, the proceedings of the Inquisition were not far different from those of ordinary secular tribunals of the period.

The most common accusation was not Judaizing—that is, practicing Jewish rituals—but blasphemy and the relapse of Moriscos to Islam. Following Lutheran ideas or superstitions, charges that occurred nearly as frequently as Judaizing (comprising 8 percent as opposed to 10 percent of the cases between 1540 and 1700), could also lead to punishment by the Inquisition. The numbers of those who fell victim to the auto-da-fé are difficult to determine. Most recent and reliable estimates say that 10,000 people were actually killed after the proclamation of the death sentence in an auto-da-fé. The vast majority of these deaths occurred in the first years of the Inquisition; thereafter, more indulgent sentences became the rule.

In the eighteenth century, the practice of the auto-da-fé declined, and only rarely did the process occur with great assistance from the public. The growing distance between the Spanish monarchy and the Inquisition was one of the factors that weakened the institution. Nevertheless, the last recorded instance occurred in 1826, and the auto-da-fé ceased formally only in 1834.

—*Bernd Rother*

See also Dominican Order; Inquisition; Torquemada, Tomás de
References
Abreu, Consuelo Maqueda. *El Auto de fe* (Madrid: Istmo, 1992).
Pérez, Joseph. *Crónica de la Inquisición en España* (Barcelona, Spain: Martínez Roca, 2002).

B

Bailey, Alice A. (1880–1949)

Alice A. Bailey, a British occultist and prolific writer, lived for decades in the United States. She is generally credited with building the framework for contemporary New Age philosophy. It was Bailey who popularized the term *New Age* and its globalist goals, now supported by many world-class institutions. Less publicized is the antisemitism that consistently ran through her vision for the new world. In her doctrine of "right human relations," she defined the Jews as one of "four world problems" to be resolved before the New Age could commence. In the political arena, she declared the United Nations a divinely appointed tool for uniting humanity, and she believed Zionism was a major obstacle to world peace.

A lapsed Christian, Bailey claimed a visitation from an "Ascended Master" at age fifteen (in 1895), the first of many psychic experiences that led her to embrace the occult divinity Maitreya as "the Christ." Sometime after discovering the Theosophical Society (in 1917), she experimented with channeling (taking dictation from spirit guides), resulting in her first book, *Initiation, Human and Solar* (1922). This debut was followed by no fewer than twenty-five other books, twenty of which she attributed to channeling (usually from "Djwahl Kuhl"). Her best-known work is "The Great Invocation" (1945), publicly presented as a universal prayer for peace but viewed by Bailey disciples as an occultic formula that empowers the "Masters" whenever recited. Bailey's more influential works, all attributed to divine dictation, include *A Treatise on White Magic* (1934), *Discipleship in the New Age* (1944, 1955), *The Problems of Humanity* (1947), *The Reappearance of the Christ* (1948), *Education in the New Age* (1954), *Externalisation of the Hierarchy* (1957), and *The Rays and the Initiations* (1960).

Although few have read these huge volumes in their entirety, they reveal unequivocal and pervasive antisemitism, as Bailey (in the name of the "Hierarchy") analyzed the destructive "Jewish Force," described the "Jewish Problem" and its solution, and presented the "Divine Plan" for human spirituality, which required the elimination of "separatist" Jewish identity. Like Helena Blavatsky before her, Bailey attributed Jewish suffering to racial karma, citing the Holocaust as proof and predicting future "purification" as well. Bailey, however, denied being antisemitic, claiming that her views were not born of hatred toward the Jews but of realism and a desire to free them of their spiritual handicaps.

Organizations and projects dedicated to carrying out Bailey's vision and directives are too many to list. The most prominent include Lucis Trust (originally Lucifer Trust, custodian of Bailey's writings and UN nongovernmental organization consultant), World Goodwill (distributor of "The Great Invocation"), Share International, New Group of World Servers, Arcane School, World Core Curriculum (UN-sponsored global education), and Robert Muller Schools. Alice's second husband, Foster Bailey, a Theosophist and published author in his own right, was an active partner in her work and continued to promote her teachings after her death.

—*Hannah Newman*

See also Blavatsky, Helena P.; Invocation, The Great; Jewish Force; New Age; The Plan of the Hierarchy

Reference

Washington, Peter. *Madame Blavatsky's Baboon: A History of the Mystics, Mediums, and Misfits Who Brought Spiritualism to America* (New York: Schocken Books, 1995).

Balzac, Honoré de (1799–1850)

One of the greatest of nineteenth-century French authors, Honoré de Balzac devoted his career to the completion of a vast literary project, including ninety-two novels designed to represent his society in its entirety and known since 1842 as *La comédie humaine* (The Human Comedy). In it, he aimed to observe every social actor or station, profession, institution, or condition of life and to analyze the forces underlying the enormous economic and social changes that he and his contemporaries experienced. Balzac's representation of French society covers the period from 1789 to 1848, when, despite retrenchments under Napoleon, Jews began to feel the beneficial effects of the proclamation of Jewish emancipation by the National Constituent Assembly in 1791. After 1830, all careers were open to Jews, and Jewish migration to Paris increased, with their numbers in the capital reaching 20,000 in 1853. Jews, therefore, had come to constitute an important new element in the society that Balzac set out to describe. About thirty Jewish characters make an appearance in *La comédie humaine,* with a few reappearing in several novels.

Although Balzac's fiction is less egregiously antisemitic than his personal writings, the novels reflect important negative preconceptions about Jews and Judaism. Despite the Jews' more active presence, especially in the Parisian society of his time, Balzac represents them as marginal to the French social body. They do not identify themselves as Jewish, but their origins are immediately apparent to non-Jews through physiognomy or accent or aura. Though they may attempt to become a part of French society, they inevitably retain their Jewishness despite conversion or assimilation; significantly, none of Balzac's Jewish characters has a French name. To be a Jew in Balzac's world, then, is a matter of foreign nationality or race rather than religion, an ineffaceable hereditary taint that marks one as an outsider. We therefore do not see Jews practicing their religion or interacting with their coreligionists, though they constitute a significant presence in the domains of the arts and sciences, the demimonde of the theater, and especially the world of finance.

Given these generalizations, however, it is important to differentiate between the representations of male and female Jews in *La comédie humaine.* In composing his work, Balzac set out to analyze an emerging industrial and capitalist society that he considered to be driven by money, at the expense of all traditions and values. In keeping with time-honored stereotypes that proved appropriate to his literary project, those Jewish men connected to the financial world and able to manipulate the markets to their own advantage—such as the Keller brothers, the moneylender Gobseck, and the financier Nucingen, who appears in more of the novels than any other character—epitomize the power of money and the social corruption attendant on the misuse of that power. Paradoxically, then, the male Jew is simultaneously placed both at the margins of French society and at the center of the negative forces generating social change. Moreover, these characters possess an energy and dynamism also evident in the Jewish men whose careers lead them to the arts and sciences. These traits are an obvious focus of Balzacian anxiety.

Balzac's Jewish women are the product of a different set of preconceptions that reflect an orientalist fantasy also characteristic of the romantic literature of the time. More marginalized than Jewish men, they are largely confined to the roles of actresses and prostitutes; they exude mystery, charm, and exoticism and possess a beauty beyond the conventional that evokes the biblical atmosphere of *The Song of Songs.* Unlike Jewish men, they are capable of great fidelity and generosity. At the same time, however, the power of their sexuality produces in their non-Jewish lovers a paralyzing fascination that constitutes an obvious analogue to the dominance enjoyed by Jewish men in the world of finance. Taken together, Balzac's male and female Jews embody a paradox that was central to nineteenth-century antisemitic attitudes.

—*Susan Rosa*

See also Belloc, Hilaire; Doré, Gustave; Drumont, Édouard; Fourier, Charles; France; Gougenot des Mousseaux, Henri; Proudhon, Pierre-Joseph; Renan, Ernest; Toussenel, Alphonse; Zola, Émile
Reference
Kupfer, Ketty. *Les Juifs de Balzac* (Paris: NM7 Éditions, 2001).

Banker, Jewish

Until the nineteenth century, many of the functions associated with modern banking were undertaken, inter alia, by merchants, money changers, moneylenders, pawnbrokers, stockjobbers, tax farmers, and minters. Historically, Jews were active in all of these areas.

In an agrarian culture rooted in classical and Christian values, basic mercantile functions such as currency exchange or long-distance trade created unease; this was even more true of moneylending. Although canon law sanctioned Jewish lending at interest to Christians, "usury" both aggravated existing religious tensions and implicated Jews in the host society's internal socioeconomic conflicts.

As a rule, Jewish moneylenders were perceived as functioning to extract revenue from peasants and artisans on behalf of the crown and nobility while engaging in unfair competition with burghers and guilds. In fifteenth-century Germany, Jews became pawns in the power struggles between emperors, the noble estates, and the urban communes—struggles frequently punctuated by blood libel accusations and expulsions. Similarly, in Renaissance Italy, Jewish pawnbrokers who supplied consumption loans to peasants and artisans (while powerful Christian banking houses concentrated on international mercantile loans and local manufacturing) provoked the ire of Franciscan preachers. Attacking Jews as "bloodsuckers" and "leeches," the friars instigated local expulsions and sought to replace the pawnbrokers with low-interest, consumer-loan banks (*monti de pieta*). Still, it should be noted that throughout the premodern era, the repeated public clamor to efface the scourge of Jewish moneylenders was countered by a fainter but equally persistent demand by segments of the European population to maintain or restore the Jews, whose financial services it deemed essential, or at least preferable, to those provided by their Christian counterparts.

Although Jewish involvement in protobanking activities such as pawnbroking, jobbing, and peddling persisted well into the twentieth century, modern Jewish high finance grew out of two distinct historical strands. The first was the tradition of Sephardic Jewish banker courtiers who, dispersed by the Iberian expulsions and the Inquisitions, pursued banking—as Jews or as nominal New Christians—in the Mediterranean basin and the Atlantic ports of Antwerp, Amsterdam, Hamburg, and London. Their efforts centered on currency and credit exchange, allied with long-distance trade and, later on, stock trading. The second was the small number of Ashkenazic Jews who provided banking services—state loans, minting, and military finance and supply—to the German absolutist states in the wake of the Thirty Years' War. These "court Jews" helped to revivify Jewish life in central and western Europe, though as agents of absolutist centralization, their actions intensified anti-Jewish hatred.

Nineteenth-century Jewish banking emerged from these "port Jew" and "court Jew" experiences. On the one hand, firms such as the Rothschilds helped to create a new type of international bond market that became a pillar of nineteenth-century European finance and politics. On the other, houses such as the Rothschilds, the Pereire brothers, and the Warburgs invested heavily in European railways and mines and played a significant role in industrialization—though how significant has been a matter of controversy. The extraordinary wealth and prominence of the Rothschilds contributed at least as much to antisemitic fantasies of a global Jewish conspiracy as to the evolution of modern capitalism. The Rothschilds were demonized by Alphonse Toussenel and Édouard Drumont as cosmopolitan "kings of the age" of money and mammon. Prominent bankers such as Gerson von Bleichröder in Otto von Bismarck's Germany or the houses of Goldman, Sachs & Company and J. W. Seligman in the postbellum United States became lightning rods for new antisemitic agitation in the late nineteenth century.

Despite local variations, what defined modern economic antisemitism was the scapegoating of Jews for capitalism's ills. In France, the predominance of nineteenth-century commercial development over industrial development inflated public perceptions of Jewish financial power, and in Germany and Austria, petit bourgeois class resentment targeted Jewish creditors and entrepreneurs as much or more than gentile industrialists. In the United States, Populists who bemoaned the disintegration of the self-sufficient farmer divined the cause in a bankers' plot to "crucify mankind upon a cross of gold." Yet as this last remark suggests, underlying many of the critiques of Jews and capitalism was a strong residue of traditional Christian animosity against the archetypal medieval Jewish banker—the usurious moneylender.

—*Jonathan Karp*

See also Caricature, Anti-Jewish (Modern); Court Jews; Drumont, Édouard; Expulsions, Late Middle Ages; Franciscan Order; Jud Süss; Populist Movement; Rothschilds; Seligman-Hilton Affair; Toussenel, Alphonse; Usury

References
Birnbaum, Pierre. "Anti-Semitism and Anti-Capitalism in Modern France." In *The Jews in Modern France.* Edited by Frances Molino and Bernard Wasserstein (Hanover, NH: University Press of New England, 1985).
Ferguson, Niall. *The House of Rothschild: Money's Prophets, 1798–1848* (New York: Viking, 1998).
Stern, Fritz. *Gold and Iron: Bismarck, Bleichröder, and the Building of the German Empire* (New York: Vintage, 1979).
Supple, Barry E. "A Business Elite: German-Jewish Financiers in Nineteenth-Century New York," *Business History Review* 31 no. 2 (1957): 143–178.

Escape tunnels used by Jewish rebels in the revolt of Bar Kochba in 132–135, Israel. (Richard T. Nowitz/Corbis)

Bar Kochba Revolt

Under the Principate of Emperor Hadrian (Publius Aelius Hadrianus), a Jewish revolt took place in Palestine led by Simon ben Kosiba, who is identified by the Christian tradition as Bar Kochba. Not much is known about him. On coins, he styled himself as *nasì* (prince), a title reserved at that time for the head of the Jewish community in Palestine—a fact that leads scholars to doubt Bar Kochba's claim.

The causes of the revolt are also obscure. Ancient sources mention Hadrian's prohibition of circumcision and his intention to build a Roman colony on the site of the destroyed Jerusalem. Some authorities hold these to be the consequences, rather than the causes, of the revolt; however, according to others, the presence of pro-Roman inhabitants in the area, supporting Hadrian's building plans, may have pushed the

tense relationship between the Roman power and the Jews to the breaking point. On the basis of other documentary evidence, another school of thought gives weight to the difficult economic situation for the Jews, who had to lease land from Roman landowners under onerous circumstances.

The chronology of events between the years 132 and 135 is confirmed both by written sources and by coins minted by Bar Kochba. The exact extent of the revolt, however, remains uncertain. It may not have occurred throughout all Palestine but only in Judea or, perhaps, just in Jerusalem and its environs. The revolt started with the occupation of numerous Roman fortresses but then seems to have been limited to guerrilla warfare tactics. Caves in the mountains near Jerusalem and in the area of the Dead Sea, where the rebels hid, have yielded valuable archaeological evidence that helps to reconstruct the revolt.

The final phase of the revolt concentrated around Eingedi on the Dead Sea and the fortress of Bethar, in the vicinity of Jerusalem. In these two places, the Roman army commanded by Iulius Severus crushed the rebels, having hunted down many of them or besieged their hiding places. Bar Kochba very likely died at Bethar. Resistance continued a little longer but was ultimately quelled by the Romans. Jews paid dearly for the revolt. Many were sold into slavery. They were forbidden entrance into Jerusalem, which was officially renamed the Roman city of Aelia Capitolina. Some ancient sources report that an altar of Jupiter was set up on the site of the former Temple, but modern scholars find this evidence rather dubious.

—*Sandra Gambetti*

See also Circumcision; Diaspora Revolt; Roman Empire; Roman Literature
Reference
Schäfer, Peter. *Der Bar Kokhba-Aufstand: Studien zum zweiten jüdischen Krieg gegen Rom* (Tübingen, Germany: Mohr, 1981).

Bardèche, Maurice (1909–1998)

Though less notorious than fellow authors Louis-Ferdinand Céline, Pierre Drieu La Rochelle, Robert Brasillach, and Lucien Rebatet, Maurice Bardèche was one of the few unrepentant French collaborators with the Nazis still publishing in the wake of his country's post-Occupation purge. Shielded partially by a cloak of respectability because of his widely read literary studies, he promoted neofascist ideology in a writing career that spanned seven decades.

Born to a family of modest means in Dun-sur-Auron (near Bourges), Bardèche was an excellent student who gained entry into France's most prestigious Latin Quarter schools (the Lycée Louis-le-Grand, the École Normale Supérieure, and the Sorbonne). His ties to the right wing surfaced early through high school friendships with his future brother-in-law Brasillach and Action Française stalwart Thierry Maulnier (1909–1988). Bardèche backed Francisco Franco during the Spanish civil war (1936–1939), and under Marshal Philippe Pétain's regime (1940–1944), he became a literature professor and contributed to the virulently antisemitic paper *Je suis partout* (I Am Everywhere). Imprisoned at the Liberation, he was eventually cleared of charges but stripped of his university post.

The next fifty years of his life were split between political and literary activities. On the ideological front, Brasillach's execution by the Liberation government hardened Bardèche's resentment toward the victors. He became the first Frenchman to adopt an openly negationist stance, with *Nuremberg ou la Terre Promise* (Nuremburg or the Promised Land [1948]). Seized and destroyed, the book asserted that the Final Solution sought solely to relocate Jews to ghettos in Eastern Europe and that the concentration camps were in most instances a *post facto* construction of Jewish technicians. He also published negationist pamphlets by Paul Rassinier, such as *Drame des juifs européens* (Tragedy of European Jewry [1964]), and Robert Faurisson's *The Problem of the "Gas Chambers"* (1978, translation in 1980). Bardèche helped form the neofascist European Social Movement in 1951, founded an extreme right-wing monthly, *Défense de l'Occident* (Defense of the West [1952–1982]), and wrote *Qu'est-ce que le fascisme?* (What Is Fascism? [1961]), which deemed racial commingling the century's true genocide. In spite of his ostracism from university ranks, he continued to produce works of valuable literary scholarship that are cited in bibliographies throughout France.

It would be misleading, however, to infer a divorce between Bardèche's right-wing propaganda and his literary criticism. His critical approach was arguably consistent with his ideological convictions. He favored a totalizing vision that organized the entirety of a writer's production into a sort of organic system working in the service of a specific overriding design. Critics have seen this aesthetic view of literary art as analogous to visions of a fascistic utopia, with the author posited as an absolute authority arranging elements hierarchically and moving toward complete unity at the expense of diversity and ambiguity.

—*Ralph W. Schoolcraft III*

See also Action Française; Brasillach, Robert; Céline, Louis-Ferdinand; Fascist Intellectuals; Faurisson, Robert; Holocaust Denial, Negationism, and Revisionism; Rebatet, Lucien; Vichy

References

Camus, Jean-Yves. "Nostalgia and Political Impotence: Neo-Nazi and Extreme Right Movements in France, 1944–1964." In *The Development of the Radical Right in France: From Boulanger to Le Pen*. Edited by Edward J. Arnold (New York: St. Martin's Press, 2000), 202–205.

Carroll, David. *French Literary Fascism: Nationalism, Anti-Semitism, and the Ideology of Culture* (Princeton, NJ: Princeton University Press, 1995).

Kaplan, Alice Yaeger. "Interview with Maurice Bardèche." In *Reproductions of Banality: Fascism, Literature, and French Intellectual Life* (Minneapolis: University of Minnesota Press, 1986), 161–192.

Barrès, Maurice (1862–1923)

Barrès was born in Charmes-sur-Moselle (Vosges) in the Lorraine region of France, soon thereafter to be annexed by Germany (1870). His native province became the model for the collective subject that is the foundation of much of Barrès's oeuvre: the Self occupied by foreigners must be born again through resistance and revenge. He attended the preparatory school in Nancy and completed his studies in Paris, where he went to pursue a career as a writer, launching his own journal *Les Taches d'encre* (Blots of Ink) in 1884, for which he wrote all the articles.

Barrès sought nothing less than to become the modern interpreter of the French spirit, revealing to the French people their indigenous genius. An iconoclast, he earned early fame with the publication of his *Culte du Moi* (Cult of Self) trilogy, in which his mouthpiece in the novel discovers the decadence of contemporary values, the vacuity of overcoming them through study, and the requirement of politics and action to energize the Self. This quest led him into involvement in the extremely diverse movement—with antisemitism sometimes serving as its only common bond—that united leftist and rightist antiparliamentarianism around the popular Gen. Georges Boulanger, who, it was hoped, would heroically save France from its perceived decline. Even after Boulanger fled France in 1889 and the threat of a coup d'état receded, the crusade continued, resulting in Barrès's election to the Chamber of Deputies from Nancy as a "revisionist socialist."

His failure in three successive campaigns led him gradually from socialism to nationalism, a development that crystallized during the Dreyfus Affair. Barrès emerged from the anti-Dreyfusard movement as a major theorist of exclusionary nationalism, weaving together the diagnosis of degeneration, the politics of revanche, a demand for a strong central authority, disdain for parliament, and the appeal of a populist socialism that he saw as a defense against the "Uprooted." These he defined as people who were individualistic, cosmopolitan, urbane, abstract, universalist—in a word, Judaicized. He infused nationalism with a mystical dimension incarnated in French traditions and *la terre et les morts* (the earth and the dead). The martyrs for France (the dead) served as progenitors for a resurrection promised when France returned to its roots (the earth). French culture thus served as a homologue for race in his integral nationalism. These themes were developed in essays and also fictionalized in his second trilogy, *Le Roman de l'énergie nationale* (The Romance of National Energy [1897–1902]). He advocated these themes in the League of Patriots, the League of the French Fatherland, and the League of the Action Française as well.

By the time of his parliamentary victory from the First Arrondissement in Paris in 1906, the same year he was elected to the Académie Française (he would occupy both seats for the remainder of his life), his stance had softened to a conservative nationalism. He spent his remaining days calling for the return of Alsace-Lorraine, supporting the church and Catholicism, propagandizing for the home front during the war, and shedding his antiparliamentarianism to embrace the Bloc National in its aftermath. Along with Charles Maurras and Édouard Drumont, Barrès is best remembered, however, as one of the fathers of extreme nationalism and a progenitor of French fascism.

—*Jonathan Judaken*

See also Action Française; Alsace; Dreyfus Affair; Drumont, Édouard; France; Maurras, Charles; *Verjudung*

References

Carroll, David. "The Use and Abuse of Culture: Maurice Barrès and the Ideology of the Collective Subject." In *French Literary Fascism: Nationalism, Anti-Semitism and the Ideology of Culture* (Princeton, NJ: Princeton University Press, 1995).

Doty, C. Stewart. *From Cultural Rebellion to Counterrevolution: The Politics of Maurice Barrès* (Athens: Ohio University Press, 1976).

Soucy, Robert. *Fascism in France: The Case of Maurice Barrès* (Berkeley and Los Angeles: University of California Press, 1972).

Barruel, Augustin (1741–1820)

Jesuit priest and anti-Enlightenment polemicist, Abbé Augustin Barruel was the first influential conspiracy theorist of the modern era. Born and raised in the small town of Villeneuve-de-Berg in southeastern France, where his father was a government official, he was educated at a Jesuit institution and committed himself to joining the order as a young man. When the Society of Jesus was expelled from France in 1764, Barruel went to Germany, where he pursued his Jesuit training and took holy orders. Following the general suppression of the Jesuit order in 1773, he returned to France, where he earned a living as a private tutor and established a reputation as a leading satirist and critic of the philosophes. Barruel's first major work, *Lettres provinciales philosophiques* (Provincial Philosophical Letters [1784]), attempted to turn the philosophes' rhetorical wit against them by exposing the supposed fallacies of Enlightenment rationalism in a piquant, ironic style. In 1788, he assumed the editorship of the *Journal ecclesiastique,* a widely circulated periodical, which, after 1789, polemicized vigorously against the antireligious oppression and violence of the revolutionary forces. In September 1792, having refused to take the secular oath of the clergy, Barruel fled to England, where he spent the next ten years.

During this period, Barruel wrote by far his most significant and successful work, *Mémoires pour servir à l'histoire du jacobinisme* (Memoirs Illustrating the History of Jacobinism [1797–1803]). This elaborate, five-volume opus purported to show that the French Revolution was the culmination of a long-standing secret conspiracy, spearheaded by an alliance between the philosophes, the Freemasons, and the Bavarian Illuminati. Although widely refuted, the text rapidly became an international best-seller, and it established the fame and also the prosperity of its author. Barruel's central concern, however, remained the state of the Catholic Church in his native France, to which, following the rise of Napoleon Bonaparte, he returned in 1802. His emphasis on obedience to the pope brought him enemies even within Catholic circles, and he was imprisoned for three weeks in 1810. In 1815, following the restoration of the monarchy and the reestablishment of the Jesuits in France, Barruel rejoined the order in Paris, where he died, disappointed by the moderation of the Restoration, in 1820.

—*Adam Sutcliffe*

See also *Biarritz;* Drumont, Édouard; Freemasonry; Gougenot des Mousseaux, Henri; Infamous Decree; Jesuit Order; *Memoirs Illustrating the History of Jacobinism; Protocols of the Elders of Zion;* Ultramontanism

Reference

Schaeper-Wimmer, Sylva. *Augustin Barruel, SJ (1741–1820): Studien zu Biographie und Werk* (Frankfurt am Main, Germany: Peter Lang, 1985).

Bartels, Adolf (1862–1945)

A prolific, ultraconservative writer and obsessive antisemite, Adolf Bartels became the main literary arbiter for the German-speaking radical Right between 1900 and 1933. In 1906, he led the successful campaign to prevent the public display of a monument to Heinrich Heine on the occasion of the fiftieth anniversary of the famous German Jewish poet's death. He actively supported the Nazis' rise to power and was rewarded with numerous honors in the Third Reich.

Bartels was a descendant of an ironworking artisan family in Dithmarschen, an isolated rural area of Schleswig-Holstein bordering on the North Sea. In 1882, his father lost his livelihood and had to sell the family home. This wrenching personal experience of industrialization and lost childhood was formative in Bartels's rejection of modernity and found later expression in the yearning quality of the *Heimatkunstbewegung* (rural art movement), which he helped found in 1899. The traditional way of life he remembered and idealized also served as the model for the *völkische Gemeinschaft* (national community) that he advocated throughout his life. In his historical novel *Die Dithmarscher* (The Dithmarschians [1898]), Bartels celebrated the patriotism, morality, and martial vigor of his rural ancestors, which he juxtaposed to the decadence, commercialism, and self-interest symbolized by the urban Jew.

Bartels failed, however, to achieve success as a creative writer and turned to literary criticism instead. Between 1895 and 1906, he published more than 300 articles and reviews in the respected conservative journal *Der Kunstwart* (The Guardian of Art) before his ever-increasing antisemitism and racism led to a parting of the ways with its publisher. By that time, Bartels had achieved financial independence from the sale of his popular books on the history of German literature, in which he championed nationalism, moral uplift, and *Heimatkunst*, defined broadly to include all literature that affirmed a powerful, ethnically homogeneous Germany, national pride, and love of the native soil. Firmly committed to racial doctrine, he excluded Jewish writers from his literary canon, even if their works endorsed conservative and nationalist values.

In 1910, Bartels founded his own monthly journal, *Deutsches Schrifttum* (German Literature), which survived, with interruptions, until 1933. His literary activities were always directed to the political goal of forging a unified *völkisch* (racist-nationalist) movement dedicated to the eradication of Jewish influence on German culture. He took a leading role in founding the Deutschvölkische Partei in March 1914, which called for putting all Jews under an aliens law. After the war, he was more active and popular than ever. His followers founded the Bartelsbund (Bartels Society) in 1920, which was later absorbed into Erich Ludendorff's Tannenbergbund (named after the victorious German battle against the Russians in September 1914). Hitler paid his respects to Bartels in Weimar in 1925.

Bartels's texts attained quasi-official status under the Nazis, but his fanatical antisemitism became something of an embarrassment when a number of writers complained that he had wrongly labeled them as Jews. He, of course, had come to believe that he could "instinctively" determine who was a Jew based on such evidence as physical appearance, an immoral lifestyle, or unwarranted literary success. The Reich Chamber of Literature ordered his publishers to make the necessary corrections and curtailed the distribution of the offending books. Nonetheless, Hitler personally conferred the highest civilian honor, the Adlerschild (Shield of the Eagle), on Bartels on his seventy-fifth birthday in 1937.

—*Roderick Stackelberg*

See also Antisemitic Political Parties; Class, Heinrich; Heine Monument Controversy; Ludendorff, Erich; Nazi Cultural Antisemitism; Pan-German League; *Völkisch* Movement and Ideology
Reference
Fuller, Steven Nyole. *The Nazis' Literary Grandfather: Adolf Bartels and Cultural Extremism, 1871–1945* (New York: Peter Lang, 1996).

Bauer, Bruno (1809–1882)

A prominent Hegelian philosopher and theologian in Prussia before the Revolution of 1848, Bruno Bauer became an advocate of political and racial antisemitism in the postrevolutionary period. His earlier work criticized Judaism for historical stagnation and national particularism, but it represented a theological approach more than a racialist doctrine. After 1848, Bauer asserted racial incompatibility between Europeans and Jews. Like G. W. F. Hegel, he stressed the derivation of Christianity from Hellenistic rather than Judaic sources, but unlike Hegel's *Philosophy of Right* (270), he did not condone the emancipation of Prussian Jews; that is, their admission to the civil service and universities.

In *Herr Dr. Hengstenberg* (1838), Bauer attacked conventional depictions of Christianity's indebtedness to Judaic sources. He distinguished the anxious, irrational prescriptions of the Mosaic law from the new, inclusive spirit of the Gospels and denied any historical continuity between Judaism and Christianity. In *Religion of the Old Testament* (1838), Bauer viewed religion as the unfolding of human self-consciousness, and he depicted Judaism as an arrested developmental stage, based on national egoism and, therefore, a dead end in historical evolution. Theologically, Judaism represented a lower level of consciousness, the external relation of humanity and God, mediated through law or arbitrary will; Bauer's model adapted Hegel's general view of Oriental society. The Jewish principle contained a limited inner mobility, shifting from legalistic to prophetic attitudes, but could not advance to higher forms of awareness. His three-volume *Critique of the Synoptic Gospels* (1841–1842) continued this line of inquiry and questioned the existence of messianic expectations among the Jews prior to the formation of the Christian community. Bauer's attitude toward Christianity became increasingly negative in these texts, as he identified it with the existing political order and saw in it a form of self-abasement and renunciation of freedom. In further studies published in the 1850s, he traced the evolution of Christian doctrine from Stoicism and late Hellenism. Insulating Christianity from non-Hellenized Jewish influences, he located the origin of the earliest Gospel under Hadrian (117–138 CE).

Two previous texts, *The Jewish Question* (first appearing as a journal article in November 1842 and then as a separate book in 1843), and "The Capacity of Present-Day Jews and Christians to Become Free" (in early 1843), expressed Bauer's critique of both religion and political reformism. The question was whether Prussia's explicitly Christian state could remove long-standing restrictions on Jewish participation in civil institutions. Conservative opponents contended that Jewish emancipation would entail the state's renouncing its confessional basis and becoming secular, thus undermining the hierarchical social order sanctioned by religion. Liberals and republicans almost unanimously advocated emancipation for the Prussian Jews. Bauer was an exception. As a result of his publications, which seemed to side with the conservatives, he forfeited his leading position in the reform movement. Criticizing all parties in the dispute, he insisted that his was the correct progressive stance. The state defended irrational privileges, using religion as a pretext for maintaining relations of subordination. Liberals viewed freedom as private interest, and they failed to grasp the danger of claiming rights on the basis of particular identities. Judaism was immutable, opposing historical progress; its practitioners' demand for emancipation was a claim to remain exempt from history and criticism. Bauer argued that genuine freedom required relinquishing all particularistic interests; thus, to win freedom, Jews and Christians both had to renounce their religious allegiances. Christians could do so more readily, however, because their religion represented a higher and more unendurable degree of alienation and so made a complete break with the past possible. Bauer's position has been described as republican rigorism (Moggach 2003), but his commitment to republicanism has also been challenged on this basis (Leopold 1999). Bauer's texts were attacked by Karl Marx in 1843.

After 1848, Bauer definitively abandoned republican politics as a failure. In his new reading, the political agenda changed as Christianity faded from doctrinal rigor to vapid moral consolation and as national interests were increasingly supplanted in power struggles among transnational elites. Europe would be unified in the wake of bloody wars, and national differences would be effaced. Race emerged as a defining element in a newly emergent era of political struggles. Bauer now reinterpreted religious and cultural differences between Europeans and Jews as an unbridgeable racial chasm. In an English-language publication, "The Present Position of the Jews" (*New York Daily Tribune*, June 7, 1852), he noted the prominence of Jews in both conservative and revolutionary camps, and he described their success in exploiting all political movements for their own careerist ends. He concluded that the ubiquity of the Jews in public positions would eventually incite Europeans to recognize the absolute incompatibility of the racial principles at stake.

In the 1860s, Bauer collaborated with Hermann Wagener on the conservative *Political and Social Lexicon,* extracts from which, elaborating the thesis of racial antagonism, were published as *Judaism as an Alien Phenomenon* (1863). Bauer's final editorial work was on a political-literary review, *Schmeitzner's International Monthly* (1882), which contained antisemitic articles by Eugen Dühring and possibly Bauer himself. These texts described Jews as idle usurers exploiting productive labor. The history of western Europe was characterized not as progress but as a tendential decline. Efforts to reverse this trend regularly failed, and the resulting dispiritedness and debility provided the atmosphere in which the Jews could flourish. These texts contributed markedly to antisemitic rhetoric in Germany, although Bauer's perspective was not that of German nationalism but of pan-European racial struggle.

—*Douglas Moggach*

See also Christian State; Dühring, Eugen; Emancipation; Feuerbach, Ludwig; Gospels; Hegel, G. W. F.; *Jewish Question, The* (1843); *Judaism as an Alien Phenomenon;* Marx, Karl; *Mirror to the Jews, A;* Wagener, Hermann; Young Hegelians

References
Leopold, David. "The Hegelian Antisemitism of Bruno Bauer," *History of European Ideas* 25 (1999): 179–206.
Moggach, Douglas. *The Philosophy and Politics of Bruno Bauer* (Cambridge: Cambridge University Press, 2003).
Peled, Yoav. "From Theology to Sociology: Bruno Bauer and Karl Marx on the Question of Jewish Emancipation," *History of Political Thought* 13, no. 3 (1992): 463–485.

Bayreuth Circle

The Bayreuth Circle coalesced in the mid-1870s around three key events that continued to shape its history and development. The first of these was the opening of the festival theater in Bayreuth and the premier performance of Richard Wagner's Ring cycle, which brought together a far-flung community of Wagner enthusiasts. Efforts that began on the plane of shared artistic values, however, then extended to much broader areas of concern.

The second foundational event, in the autumn of 1877, was the relocation to Bayreuth, at Wagner's behest, of Baron Hans Paul von Wolzogen, the figure who played the most influential role in the history of the circle and the development of its ideas. A dramatist and a music critic rather than a musician—he is said to have coined the term *leitmotif*—Wolzogen helped found and then edit the *Bayreuther Blätter* (Bayreuth Pages). For nearly sixty years, he functioned as the organizer, promoter, steward, and major interpreter of the cultural and intellectual body of thought

entrusted to him, preserving the master's legacy and pursuing its logic even further. He was, for example, one of the first to proclaim the "Aryan Jesus," even though Wagner had not dared to go that far when he questioned Jesus' Jewish descent in the *Bayreuther Blätter*. His antisemitism, too, went beyond what Wagner was willing to espouse publicly. He called for a ban on Jews in the professions and their compulsory emigration to the colonies; unlike Wagner, he signed the Antisemites' Petition (1880–1881). As early as 1924, he opened the *Bayreuther Blätter* to the Nazis.

After Wagner and his wife, Cosima, Wolzogen stood clearly at the top of the circle's hierarchy. Below him came many of the charismatic leader's "apostles of the Inner Circle," among them Houston Stewart Chamberlain, Ludwig Schemann, and Bernhard Förster, men whose antisemitism ranged from the radical to the paranoid. Wolzogen's eminence did not go unchallenged, however. There were enough controversies and crises, especially with Chamberlain, to keep the circle from developing into a disciplined league.

The third formative event in the history of the circle was the establishment of the *Bayreuther Blätter* in early 1878. Dedicated to the art and worldview of Richard Wagner, it was intended to serve as the literary vehicle for the cultural movement that would radiate out from Bayreuth into the world beyond, a mission the journal fulfilled until it ceased appearing at Wolzogen's death in 1938. Wagner's works established the themes and the tone, foregrounding the *völkisch* (racist-nationalist) and antisemitic nature of his views. Other "prophetic" Germans—Johann Wolfgang von Goethe, Friedrich von Schiller, Immanuel Kant, Johann Gottlieb Fichte, Ernst Moritz Arndt, and Paul de Lagarde—appeared frequently. Thanks to the efforts of Cosima Wagner, the race theories of Joseph Arthur de Gobineau were taken with utmost seriousness. It was Cosima who commissioned Wolzogen to give thorough exposure to Gobineau's *Essay on the Inequality of the Human Races*.

Antisemitism; racially defined nationalism; rejection of socialism and liberalism; and the reform of culture and "life," art, and religion were the constantly reiterated themes that produced a unique ideological amalgam in the *Bayreuther Blätter*. In its pages, Aryan Germandom was glorified and Jews denigrated, relegated to the role of the inimical counterrace. But it is, perhaps, inaccurate to speak of a single Bayreuth ideology, even in the matter of antisemitism; its proponents sometimes used racial arguments, sometimes religious, economic, or ethical ones. In their antisemitism, Wagner and his followers in the Bayreuth Circle doubtlessly belonged on the German Right, probably somewhere between the aesthetically inclined and those given over to Germanic religion.

After its first year, in which the *Bayreuther Blätter* was brought out by the antisemitic publisher and grassroots organizer Ernst Schmeitzner, the journal appeared from its own press until 1913, when it was farmed out to an external firm. It remained home to members of the circle but also opened its pages to many other prominent antisemites, such as Constantin Frantz, Ottomar Beta, Adolph Wahrmund, Friedrich Lienhard, Heinrich Pudor, and many others. These individuals can be considered extended members of the circle. Together, they stood for the segregation of Jews from the German national body politic. They normally kept their distance from "rowdy" antisemitism, but nonetheless, the ideological affinities to the antisemitic political parties of the German Empire and, later, to the Nazis were unmistakable. From the beginning, antisemitism was omnipresent in Bayreuth's milieu.

—*Matthias Brosch*
Richard S. Levy, translation

See also Antisemites' Petition; Antisemitic Political Parties; Chamberlain, Houston Stewart; Förster, Bernhard; Frantz, Constantin; Gobineau, Joseph Arthur de; Lienhard, Friedrich; Pudor, Heinrich; Schemann, Ludwig; *Völkisch* Movement and Ideology; Wagner, Cosima; Wagner, Richard

References

Large, David Clay. "Wagner's Bayreuth Disciples." In *Wagnerism in European Culture and Politics*. Edited by David C. Large and William Weber (Ithaca, NY: Cornell University Press, 1984).

Schüler, Winfried. *Der Bayreuther Kreis von seiner Entstehung bis zum Ausgang der wilhelminischen Ära: Wagnerkult und Kulturreform im Geiste völkischer Weltanschauung* (Münster, Germany: Aschendorff, 1971).

Beilis Case (1911–1913)

The blood libel trial in Kiev of Menachem Mendel Beilis (1874–1934) has widely been considered a Russian Dreyfus Affair. There were obvious similarities between the two cases, in that Beilis's arrest in July 1911 and his trial two years later on sensational charges gained the rapt attention of a large part of Russia's population and were front-page news in the press of Europe and the United States. His arrest and trial were widely seen, too, as an example of right-wing forces attempting to exploit antisemitism as a device to unite and mobilize diverse elements of the population against an emerging pro-Jewish Left.

By the late twentieth century, memory of the Beilis case came to be inextricably fused (and confused) with Bernard Malamud's celebrated 1966 novel *The Fixer* (made into a movie in 1969). In fact, however, Malamud's work had only a superficial resemblance to the Beilis case. The novel's main character, Jacob Bok, was an isolated drifter who stumbled into a frame-up, whereas Mendel Beilis was a more ordinary person with a large family, who was well liked and respected by Jews and non-Jews alike. The testimony of those who knew him was crucial to his eventual deliverance—not, however, before he spent an uncertain and often nightmarish two years in prison, awaiting trial and charged with the murder of twelve-year-old Andrei Yushchinsky.

Andrei's body, riddled with stab wounds and allegedly drained of blood, had been found on the outskirts of Kiev, not far from the brick factory where Beilis worked as manager. There was little credible material evidence to implicate Beilis, but in a sequence of complex and bizarre machinations by the authorities, lasting over four months, he was finally charged with the murder. In the Dreyfus Affair, the case for a widespread conspiracy to frame Dreyfus turned out to be weak, but Beilis was unquestionably the victim of appalling intrigues by certain tsarist officials, among them careerists who hoped somehow to win favor with the antisemitic tsar, Nicholas II, and others who were responding to pressure from antisemitic agitators and the right-wing press. Nonetheless, historians have found, even in this case, little evidence of a widespread or concerted conspiracy of tsarist officials; as in France, there was much blundering, with individuals and agencies often working at cross-purposes. The clearest culprit in high office was the reactionary minister of justice, I. G. Shcheglovitov. The chief minister at the time, Peter Stolypin, though no friend of the Jews, was almost certainly not involved, and others in the government actively opposed Beilis's arrest, helping to reveal how shoddy the evidence was.

Beilis's arrest and trial were met with immediate protests inside Russia and abroad. International agitation was sparked by Jewish activists in Germany and Austria, who, aside from their concern for the life of an innocent man, perceived a politically useful scandal; one that might serve further to discredit the tsarist government internationally and divide Russia from its French ally, thus alleviating the "encirclement" of Germany.

At the trial, from September 25 through October 28, 1913, the prosecution called an array of dubious witnesses, some obviously intimidated, others of unsound mind, and others transparently toadying. The defense had little difficulty in demonstrating Beilis's innocence, as well as making clear the guilt of a criminal band in Kiev. The evidence offered by the prosecution that Beilis had contacts with unidentified religious Jews who needed blood for Jewish rituals was particularly paltry and obviously less designed to convict Beilis than to attempt to disgrace Judaism and Russia's Jews before a credulous public.

As the trial progressed, the prosecution's case disintegrated, at times to the amusement of the large crowd in attendance. Indeed, even leading antisemites in Russia finally spoke up against the trial as a farce and a disgrace to Russia's good name. The jury found the ambiguously formulated charges against Beilis to be "not proven"—language peculiar to the Russian legal system that allowed the prosecution to claim a partial victory, in that it had supposedly demonstrated that some Jews, if not Beilis, did collect the blood of Christians for Jewish rituals. But at the time, many in Russia and abroad rejoiced in what they saw as another great victory against antisemitic libel and against the tsarist government in its efforts to exploit the hatred of Jews. Beilis, expressing amazement that so many non-Jews had finally come to his defense, nonetheless

concluded that he and his family were no longer safe in Russia. He soon emigrated to Palestine; unable to make a living there, he moved to the United States in 1920.

—*Albert S. Lindemann*

See also Dreyfus Affair; Pale of Settlement; Pranaitis, Justinas; Ritual Murder (Modern); Russia, Imperial; Russian Orthodox Church

References

Lindemann, Albert S. *The Jew Accused: Three Anti-Semitic Affairs (Dreyfus, Beilis, Frank), 1894–1915* (Cambridge: Cambridge University Press, 1991).

Rogger, Hans. "The Beilis Case: Anti-Semitism and Politics in the Reign of Nicholas II," *Slavic Review* 25 (December 1966): 615–629.

Belloc, Hilaire (1870–1953)

From 1906 to 1910, Hilaire Belloc, French-born British poet, journalist, political commentator, and prolific popular writer in many genres, served in the British Parliament as a Liberal, but he grew disillusioned with representation by political parties (as described in *The Party System* [1911], coauthored with Cecil Chesterton). In his 1912 book *The Servile State,* he proposed that society be reorganized into cooperatives as a means of equalizing the distribution of wealth. In 1912, the language of most British socialists derived either from Marx and the Fabians or from the Evangelical movement and the Christian Socialists, but Belloc's immediate inspiration was Pope Leo XIII's anticapitalist encyclical of 1891, *Rerum novarum.* Among all the Edwardian and early Georgian social reformers, Belloc was probably the only one who wrote from the point of view of a continental European—specifically, as a representative Frenchman of the late nineteenth century who was patriotic, authoritarian, deeply Catholic, and aggressively antisemitic. In the course of his long life, Belloc wrote approximately 150 books, and this was his persona in almost all of them.

His 1922 book *The Jews,* for example, argued that the existence of Jews represented a threat in itself to the people he sometimes called "the white race" and sometimes simply "us." He accordingly proposed that all Jews be regarded as members of an alien and permanently hostile polity. In his 1933 essay "Peace to Israel," he added:

I said [in *The Jews*] that sooner or later there was bound to be an explosion against the Jews in this or that white, western country yet to be decided. . . . The present trouble [in Germany] is an effect of the Dreyfus case at long range . . . . The new Prussian revolutionaries have access to all the archives; they know what a Jewish agitation may work against a nation and did work against France and the French army; they already ascribed to the Jews the evils Prussia had suffered through her own fault; they feared to suffer as France had suffered, and the result is before us. (155–156)

Unfettered by the facts, Belloc ignored the south German origins of Nazism and its many nominally Catholic adherents, preferring to define it as exclusively "Prussian" or "Protestant." That is, by 1933, Belloc's language was already as obsolete and provincial as his worldview. Today, his vast oeuvre survives only as a few fragments in Nazi websites, Tridentine Catholic nostalgia clubs, and anthologies of light verse. But his influence in his own time remains historically significant for three reasons.

First, Belloc helped to create a precondition for fascism by grafting French anti-Dreyfusard xenophobia onto a British reform tradition. Second, as a literary model whose books were taught in Catholic schools, he probably influenced the attitudes of educated Anglo-American Catholics toward Jews. And during the first half of the twentieth century, as Catholics were assimilated into the American middle class, Belloc's composite vocabulary of racist and theological Jew-hatred entered the language of secular antisemitism.

—*Jonathan Morse*

See also Dreyfus Affair; English Literature from Chaucer to Wells; Mosley, Oswald; Socialists on Antisemitism; Ultramontanism

References

Thal, Herbert van, ed. *Belloc: A Biographical Anthology* (London: George Allen & Unwin, 1970).

Wilson, A. N. *Hilaire Belloc* (London: Hamish Hamilton, 1984).

Benn, Gottfried (1886–1956)

Among other things, Gottfried Benn is an example of a formidable intellect—with close ties to antifascist thinkers—who embraced the Nazis' accession to power. In *Die Intellektuellen und der neue Staat* (The Intellectuals and the New State [1933]) and, to a lesser extent, in *Kunst und Macht* (Art and Power [1934]), Benn suggested that National Socialism would be an agent of great progress.

Benn was born into humble circumstances in 1886. His father, Gustav, supported eight children, of whom Gottfried was the second, on a pastor's salary in Sellin, a town of 700 inhabitants on the Oder River. Although Benn seems to have been fond of his siblings, the relationship with his father was characterized by mutual disdain. Benn pursued two careers: medicine and poetry. Success came early in both. His initial medical research earned him an award, and when his first book of poems, *Morgue und andere Gedichte* (Morgue and Other Poems), appeared in 1912, it elicited considerable critical attention. By the beginning of World War I, he had established himself as a leading Expressionist poet, publishing in highly regarded journals and invited to read his poetry in perhaps the most eminent Berlin salon, that of the prominent Jewish art dealer and publisher Paul Cassirer. He served as a military doctor in the war, while continuing to publish poems and essays, most frequently in the pacifist journal *Die weissen Blätter* (The White Pages).

In the Weimar Republic, he did more of the same from his home base in Berlin, where his social circle included antifascists such as George Grosz and Carl Einstein. Yet Benn displayed tendencies that distinguished him from such friends, and he revealed the intellectual basis for his brief enthusiasm for Nazism. Well before 1933, he began to meditate on the problem of nihilism in Western culture. This in itself was not a fascist activity, of course. Max Weber, Sigmund Freud, and many of the Frankfurt School theorists occupied themselves with the same question. But there is a mystical, eschatological tone in Benn's reflections and a fascination with a vague, yet still obviously illiberal ideal of "breeding," or *Züchtung*. Moreover, *Nach dem Nihilismus* (After Nihilism [1932]) seems to call for spiritual rather than material revolution. So when, in *The Intellectuals and the New State,* Benn contrasted what he perceived to be the regenerative spirit of the victorious Nazis with the misguidedness of Marxist intellectuals, it was not a matter of "spontaneous intoxication," as his later defenders claimed. Benn was elaborating on ideas he had articulated well before the Nazi triumph of January 30, 1933.

Benn's support for National Socialism was short lived. Some of what he wrote after 1934 can be read as an outright critique. He never actually joined the party. Nor did he attend political rallies or even read the Nazi Party program, as he often emphasized. He admitted being aware of the intensity of Nazi antisemitism, yet he did not exhibit any significant antisemitism in his own works. And unlike Martin Heidegger and Stefan George, Benn did not hold out any real attraction for the Nazis. Indeed, he fell into disfavor rather quickly. But he stayed in Germany during the Third Reich, eventually serving again as a military doctor in World War II.

After the war, he was briefly an object of suspicion. But he was soon rehabilitated—to such an extent, in fact, that he lectured widely, won the prestigious Georg-Büchner Prize for literature in 1950, and was short-listed for the Nobel Prize four years later.

—*Paul Reitter*

See also Fascist Intellectuals; George, Stefan; Nazi Cultural Antisemitism; Nazi Party Program; Weimar

References
Alter, Reinhard. *Gottfried Benn: The Artist and Politics, 1910–1934* (Bern, Switzerland: H. Lang, 1976).
Strauss, Walter A. "Gottfried Benn: A Double Life in Uninhabitable Regions." In *Fascism, Aesthetics, and Culture.* Edited by Richard Golsan (Hanover, NH: University of New England Press, 1992).

Berlin Movement

A loose alliance between various antisemitic and conservative parties and groups, the Berlin Movement started between 1878 and 1879 with Otto von Bismarck's antiliberal change of course. Formally established in 1881, its agenda included freeing the capital from the political domination of left-wing liberalism and laying Berlin "at the feet of the Hohenzollerns." With the populist Court Chaplain Adolf Stoecker as guiding spirit and covert government support, the movement won some initial successes during the early 1880s, but was never able to achieve its ambitious goals. It went into stagnation and decline as early as 1885 and ended in 1889 with Stoecker's forced, though temporary, withdrawal from party politics.

Despite its failure, the Berlin Movement was significant in the history of political antisemitism in Germany. It represented the first attempt to build a coalition between (moderate) conservative and (radical) right-wing parties based on the common political platform of antisemitism and antiliberalism. It also helped radically modernize the methods of conservative politics: from *Honoratiorenpolitik* (elitist politics) to populist mobilization of the masses.

With Stoecker and his Christian Social Party at the heart of the movement, other members included the German Conservatives, the radical antisemites led by Ernst Henrici and Max Liebermann von Sonnenberg, renegades of the Catholic Center Party such as the journalist Joseph Cremer, and middle-class organizations such as the reformed guild system for artisans. Representatives of these parties and groups came together in the Conservative Central Committee, established in April 1881. The committee nominated common candidates against left liberals and socialists in the national, state, and municipal elections. In the Reichstag elections of 1881, the committee candidates were able to triple their share of the poll (from 8.9 percent in 1878 to 27.1 percent), but they were still unable to win a single seat. In the two Berlin constituencies where a runoff ballot took place, the vast majority of socialist voters supported the liberal candidate rather than the movement's candidate. Stoecker's attempt to come to an agreement with the leaders of the socialists against the left-wing-liberal Progressive Party proved futile. The same constellation recurred in the following elections in Berlin, most visibly in the runoff between Stoecker and the prominent scientist and liberal luminary Rudolf Virchow in the national election of 1884. With support from socialist voters, Virchow won by a wide margin. Berlin remained a bastion of left-wing liberalism (and later Social Democracy).

Bismarck, who initially had misgivings about Stoecker's agitation because of its anticapitalist rhetoric, nonetheless used the court chaplain and his allies in the political fight against his political foes, supporting the movement with his secret slush fund (*Repitlienfond*). When the movement failed to live up to his expectations, however, Bismarck again began to distance himself from Stoecker and the antisemites. Other factors contributed to the movement's failure, most notably its ideological divisions and personal rivalries. In August 1881, after the riots in Pomerania, the Conservative Central Committee drew a line between itself and the militant, anticonservative Henrici. The differences between the various camps, especially between conservative reactionaries and Christian social reformists—only partially obscured by the common fight against Jews and liberals—reemerged once the movement lost steam in the mid-1880s, hastening its demise.

—*Christhard Hoffmann*

See also Antisemites' Petition; Center Party; Christian Social Party (Germany); Henrici, Ernst; Liebermann von Sonnenberg, Max; Neustettin Pogrom; Stoecker, Adolf

References
Levy, Richard S. *The Downfall of the Anti-Semitic Political Parties in Imperial Germany* (New Haven, CT: Yale University Press, 1975).

Massing, Paul W. *Rehearsal for Destruction. A Study of Political Anti-Semitism in Imperial Germany* (New York: Harper & Brothers, 1949).

Zumbini, Massimo Ferrari. *Die Wurzeln des Bösen: Gründerjahre des Antisemitismus—Von der Bismarckzeit zu Hitler* (Frankfurt am Main, Germany: Vittorio Klostermann, 2003).

Best, Werner (1903–1989)

Intellectually and administratively, Werner Best must be counted among the forerunners of the annihilation of the Jews. As early as 1931, he openly declared his belief that the Nazi Party's "struggle against Jewry" ought—as a matter of principle—to proceed "to the annihilation of the enemy." From 1935, working in a variety of military, police, and foreign office capacities, Best participated decisively in the preparations leading up to the deportation of the Jews. Nevertheless, immediately after the war, he successfully portrayed himself as having "opposed the evacuation of the Jews." In Denmark, where he served as the Third Reich's plenipotentiary from 1942 to 1945, he took credit for having sabotaged the planned deportation of Jews. Notwithstanding his claims, he was condemned to death in Denmark in 1948 because of his part in the persecution of Jews. A year later, however, he was acquitted of all charges. He died on June 23, 1989.

Best was born on July 10, 1903, in Darmstadt, the first of two sons of a senior postal official who died from wounds received on the Western Front soon after World War I began. The brothers grew up in a suburb of Mainz, where they finished prep school. Werner studied law between 1921 and 1925 at the universities of Frankfurt am Main, Freiburg, and Giessen. He received his doctorate from Heidelberg in 1927, became a district court judge, and married a dentist's daughter, who eventually bore him five children.

Politically, Best initially became active in the extreme nationalist and antisemitic German University Ring, an organization he maintained ties with long after his studies ended. From that point on, his political allegiance to the German Right never wavered. On November 1, 1930, he became member 341,338 of the National Socialist German Workers' Party. A year later, he joined the Schutzstaffel (SS) (member number 23,377). After Hitler assumed power in 1933, Best's rise in the ranks of the SS was meteoric. In the spring of 1933, as a police chief in Hesse, he established the first regular concentration camp at Osthofen. This success gained the attention of Heinrich Himmler, who took Best to Munich to work with Reinhard Heydrich in the construction of the Security Service (Sicherheitsdienst). Having performed his tasks in stellar fashion, Best continued his climb up the ranks of the SS within its various police agencies and in close association with Heydrich.

In August 1935, at a high-level meeting in the Economics Ministry called to discuss preparations for the Nuremberg Laws, Best presented his and Heydrich's ideas for solving the Jewish Question. Jews ought to be placed under an aliens law, they proposed, in order to hinder their ability to compete freely; their freedom of movement and domicile ought to be eliminated; and they should be separated from the German racial community (*Volksgemeinschaft*). At this time, Best instructed the police offices under his jurisdiction to construct registers of all the Jews in their zones.

In October 1938, acting as chief of police in charge of resident foreigners, he directed the (unsuccessful) attempt to expel 17,000 Polish Jews. Immediately following the Night of Broken Glass, which issued from this action, Best began planning the Reich Office for Jewish Emigration, which came into existence in January 1939.

From his position in the administration of the Military Command for Occupied France, he undertook measures that quickly developed into the first mass deportation of Jews. On March 24, 1942, the first train, carrying 1,112 Jews of various nationalities, left the internment camp at Compiègne for Auschwitz. The persecution of the Jews in France was supported by the Vichy government, but such was not the case in Denmark. Best went there in late 1942 as Reich plenipotentiary, with the rank of major general in the SS. He well knew that cooperation from the Copenhagen government in the matter of its Jews would not be forthcoming. Not until the German military commander declared a national state of emergency (on August 29, 1943) and removed the government from power could Best initiate his solution for the Jewish Question for Denmark. But because the preparations for the roundup of the Jews, scheduled for the night of October 2, could not be kept secret, over 7,000 were able to escape to Sweden. Only 481 Jews were deported from Denmark, primarily to Theresienstadt, and most of these survived. Best nonetheless claimed victory since Denmark was now "free of Jews." His superiors apparently shared this view. On April 20, 1944, he was promoted to lieutenant general of the SS.

—*Fritz Petrick*
Richard S. Levy, translation

See also Himmler, Heinrich; Holocaust; Nazi Legal Measures against Jews; Night of Broken Glass; Nuremberg Laws; *Ostjuden;* Vichy
References
Herbert, Ulrich. *Best: Biographische Studien über Radikalismus, Weltanschauung und Vernunft*

1903–1989 (Bonn, Germany: Verlag J. H. W. Dietz Nachf., 1996).
Rosengreen, Bjørn. *Dr. Werner Best og tysk besættelsespolitik i Danmark 1943–45* (Odense, Denmark: Odense University Press, 1982).

Bettauer, Hugo (1872–1925)

Hugo Bettauer wrote roughly two dozen novels, many of them set in post–World War I Vienna, fictionalizing contemporary social and political life. He was a newspaper journalist, magazine publisher, and editor in the early years of the First Austrian Republic. Born of Jewish parents in Baden, south of Vienna, he left the Jewish faith at the age of eighteen and converted to Protestantism. He was murdered in Vienna in 1925.

Although already successful as a novelist, Bettauer was motivated by the dire social and economic conditions of the early 1920s to found the first of two magazines in February 1924. *Er & Sie: Wochenschrift für Lebenskultur und Erotik* (He & She: Weekly for the Culture of Life and Eroticism) addressed contemporary issues such as unemployment, homelessness, alcoholism, abortion legislation reform, gender equality, sex education, and drug abuse. The weekly also included a "lonely hearts" feature, a column by a gynecologist, and an installment of the latest Bettauer novel. *Er & Sie* evoked a strong conservative and, in part, antisemitic backlash. The weekly was confiscated, and Bettauer was charged with spreading pornography and promoting prostitution, charges of which he was later acquitted. The often only thinly veiled antisemitic attacks on his publishing ventures became part of the "Bettauer scandal," which was accompanied by a political confrontation between the Christian Socials in the federal government under the chancellor, Prelate Ignaz Seipel, and the Social Democrats in the "red bastion" of Vienna. Following his acquittal in the fall of 1924, public threats were made against Bettauer's life. In March 1925, he was gunned down in his office by a twenty-one-year-old Nazi sympathizer named Otto Rothstock, who gave as his motive the wish to guard his generation from the likes of the "pornographer" Bettauer. The writer died ten days later.

The most noteworthy among Bettauer's novels is *Die Stadt ohne Juden* (*The City without*

Jews), a social and political satire that appeared in 1922. Intended as "an amusing little novel" with a "harmless plot," the book grasped the "topic of the day," as critics noted, satirizing rampant antisemitic sentiment. The story depicts the consequences of an "Anti-Jew Law" passed by the parliament. The economic situation deteriorates to such an extent that a popular movement soon arises, demanding the return of the Jews from "exile." With a jubilant crowd looking on, the Jews are welcomed back by the mayor, with the words: "My dear Jew, Vienna is once again Vienna" (Bettauer 1991, 189). A fanciful slap at antisemitism, the novel, it could be argued, inadvertently reinforced anti-Jewish stereotypes, seeming to confirm what antisemites had been saying for years—Jews with their power over money and control of culture had seen to it that Christians could no longer get along without them.

Bettauer is often regarded as a prophet of the Holocaust. After all, Vienna did become the "city without Jews" of his book title. Like eight of his other novels, *Stadt ohne Juden* was made into a movie. Panned by the critics, it nonetheless provoked demonstrations by Austrian Nazis. His ability to unleash antisemitic hatred, rather than predict the future, constitutes Bettauer's real historical importance. He should be seen as one of the first political victims of National Socialism in Austria. The scandal surrounding the writer and his works accentuated the charged antisemitic atmosphere in Vienna, one that had become so commonplace that it took a murder to illuminate it.

—*Murray G. Hall*

See also Austria; Christian Social Party (Austria); Freud, Sigmund; Pan-Germans

References
Bettauer, Hugo. *The City without Jews.* Translated by S. N. Brainin (New York: Bloch Publishing, 1991).
Hall, Murray G. *Der Fall Bettauer* (Vienna: Löcker, 1978).

Biarritz (1868)

In the third quarter of the nineteenth century, a Prussian postal official with connections to the Berlin court, Herrmann Goedsche (1815–1878), initiated under the pen name of Sir John Ret-

cliffe a successful new genre: the sensationalist novel of current events. He aspired to write fiction as exactly concurrent with events as possible, appealing to the readership with sex and violence. His resources included thugs, assassins, gangsters, atrocities in cloisters and catacombs, private detectives, hunts and chases, duels, sexual sadism and pornography disguised as folklore, varieties of torture, and the occult.

Few would remember him today if it were not for a scene of forty pages in the first volume of his cycle *Biarritz* (1868). In the Jewish Cemetery of Prague in 1860, as happened every 100 years, the representatives of the twelve tribes of Israel came together, joined by the Wandering Jew from New York, to plot the domination of the world by obtaining all the gold; drawing the aristocracy into debt; ruining the artisans by making them factory workers; transferring the people's savings to the capitalists via the stock exchange; arranging for easy bankruptcy and abolishing usury laws; taking religion out of the schools; destroying churches and armies; supporting revolutionary disaffection; dominating the arts, medicine, and philosophy; achieving influence through intermarriage; corrupting the virtue of gentile females; and controlling the press. All these purposes are achieved in the course of the novel cycle in alliance with English capitalists.

"Retcliffe's" fiction, devised in support of a policy of the Prussian monarchy to ally the guild artisans and craftspeople with the landed aristocracy against middle-class liberals and free labor, accounted for public affairs as the consequence of the machinations of secret societies and conspiracies in malignant alliances with one another. Jews were just one interest group, dispersed and deracinated and thus especially subversive and dangerous but not categorically different from the other competing nations and conspiratorial combinations, all dominated by the universal ambition for power and wealth. But the scene has had a long history as an allegedly genuine eyewitness report. Beginning with a Russian pamphlet in 1870, a series of publications in various languages conflated the points of Retcliffe's various speakers into a single discourse, commonly known as "the Rabbi's Speech" and offered as evidence of the international Jewish conspiracy. In this form, it became a base text of the *Protocols of the Elders of Zion,* as was promptly discovered in the 1920s and thus is significant proof of the origin of the *Protocols* in fiction.

—*Jeffrey L. Sammons*

See also *Protocols of the Elders of Zion; Rabbi's Speech, The;* Wandering Jew

References

Cohn, Norman. *Warrant for Genocide: The Myth of the Jewish World Conspiracy and the "Protocols of the Elders of Zion."* New ed. (London: Serif, 1996).

Neuhaus, Volker. *Der zeitgeschichtliche Sensationsroman in Deutschland 1855–1878: "Sir John Retcliffe" und seine Schule* (Berlin: Erich Schmidt, 1980).

Billroth, Theodor (1829–1894)

Theodor Billroth was born in Rügen, Germany, and became one of the most eminent professors of medicine in late nineteenth-century Vienna. He is credited with inventing an effective anesthesia consisting of ether and chloroform and also with bringing about advances in surgery, several medical procedures, and postoperative care. Billroth also helped found the Rudolfinerhaus, an interdenominational institute dedicated to modernizing the training of nurses. In the forefront of innovation, Billroth found certain changes in Viennese medicine unsettling. On hearing that the famous sexologist Richard Krafft-Ebing had performed hypnosis, Billroth denounced him as a swindler.

In 1876, with antisemitism on the rise in Austria, Billroth made a series of incendiary claims about the role of Jews in Austrian medicine. First published in that year, his book *On Teaching and Studying the Medical Sciences at German Universities* bemoaned the disproportionate percentage of Jewish students matriculating at the University of Vienna's medical school. He was especially concerned with the "problem" of eastern European Jews (*Ostjuden*), whose preparation he found inadequate and whose poverty and social aspirations he clearly despised. Beyond that, he argued that Jews were a separate ethnic entity and predicted that their efforts toward assimilation would be unsuccessful.

Billroth's status as a prominent scientist con-

Austrian surgeon Albrecht Christian Theodor Billroth (1829–1894). In 1876, Billroth made a series of incendiary claims about the role of Jews in Austrian medicine. (Getty Images)

ferred on such remarks a special credibility. And unsurprisingly, his book was widely cited and applauded in antisemitic circles, as, for example, in the nationalist German Students Reading Club. Yet Billroth's relation to antisemitism extended further and eventually took a sharp turn in a different direction. Not only did he later try to clarify his argument and sharpen it into a polemic aimed almost exclusively at Hungarian Jews, he also, in 1892, joined the Austrian League against Antisemitism (Abwehr-Verein). In all likelihood, the increase in Austrian antisemitism during the 1880s had alarmed him. Given that Billroth had Jewish friends and intimates, the move is understandable. But because he did not explain his new response to the Jewish Question, we can only speculate as to why he distanced himself from his earlier association with antisemitism.

—*Paul Reitter*

See also Aryan Paragraph; Austria; Freud, Sigmund; Hungary; *Ostjuden;* Pan-Germans
References
Johnston, William. *The Austrian Mind: An Intellectual and Social History, 1848–1938* (Berkeley and Los Angeles: University of California Press, 1972).
Pulzer, Peter. *The Rise of Political Anti-Semitism in Germany and Austria.* Rev. ed. (London: P. Halban, 1988).

Black Hundreds

The Black Hundreds, a generic name given to gangs that—under the slogan "Beat the Yids and save Russia!"—perpetrated violence against liberals, radicals, and Jews during and after the Russian Revolution of 1905. The movement was organized after October 1905, with the formation of loyalist right-wing groups; the most important of these was the Union of the Russian People (Soiuz Russkogo Naroda [SRN]), founded on November 8, 1905, and headed by Aleksandr Ivanovich Dubrovin. The SRN represented the first successful attempt to create a movement loyal to the idea of the autocratic state whose membership cut across the barriers of class and social estate. It successfully organized local branches throughout the empire and absorbed or cooperated with similar bodies in the provinces. The organizational activism of the SRN enabled it to elect a number of deputies to the State Duma (the Russian parliament) but it was plagued by infighting, and by 1910, it had split into three factions: the main SRN, headed by N. E. Markov; V. M. Purishkevich's Union of the Archangel Michael; and Dubrovin's splinter group, the True Union of the Russian People.

The SRN program was based on the demagogic appeals "For Tsar, Faith, and Fatherland" and "Russia for the Russians." It called for Tsar Nicholas II to reassert the autocratic powers that bound him in a patriarchal union with his people. The SRN opposed parliamentary democracy, and the actions of its Duma deputies, most notably Purishkevich, sought to discredit the system and make it unworkable. Hostile to "disloyal" nationalities such as the Poles, the SRN reserved special animus for the Jews. Drawing on existing currents of Russian antisemitism, it blamed the Jews for virtually all of Russia's social and political ills. It waged war against the Jews and their allies in the Duma who sought to enslave Russia by conspiring to create a democratic republic.

The Black Hundreds are often described as the organizers of the anti-Jewish and antirevolutionary pogroms that accompanied the Revolution of 1905 and its aftermath. The worst pogroms of 1905, however, predated the formal creation of the organization and appear to have been spontaneous clashes between loyalist "patriots" and demonstrators who hailed the October Manifesto of 1905 and called for the revolution to go further. After 1905 and often with the help of local officials, the SRN organized "fighting squads" (*druzhiny*), designed to intimidate enemies and battle against revolutionary activity. If these fighting squads did not actually organize pogroms on a wide scale, they did create an environment that encouraged their outbreak, and druzhiny members were frequent participants in such disorders. Most officials of the central government viewed the activities of the SRN with skepticism or distrust. The chief exception was the tsar himself: Nicholas II's willingness to accept an honorary membership in the organization and to maintain symbolic contacts with it helped to discredit him personally.

Members of the SRN, with the approval of Dubrovin, organized a small number of political assassinations, most notably of the Duma deputies M. Ia. Herzenstein and G. B. Iollos. Although both men were of Jewish origin, their political activities were apparently the main motive for their murders.

—*John D. Klier*

See also Krushevan, Pavolaki; Odessa Pogroms; *Protocols of the Elders of Zion;* Purishkevich, Vladimir Mitrofanovich; Russia, Imperial; Russia, Revolution of 1905
References
Klier, John D., and Shlomo Lambroza, eds. *Pogroms: Anti-Jewish Violence in Modern Russian History* (Cambridge: Cambridge University Press, 1992).
Rawson, Don C. *Russian Rightists and the Revolution of 1905* (Cambridge: Cambridge University Press, 1995).

Rogger, Hans. *Jewish Policies and Right-Wing Politics in Imperial Russia* (London: Macmillan, 1986).

Black Nationalism

The rise of Black Nationalism in the mid-1960s sparked a dramatic rise in African American antisemitic rhetoric. Frustrated by the reluctance of white liberals to press the movement for racial equality beyond the legal guarantees provided by the Civil Rights Act of 1964 and the Voting Rights Act of 1965, a small group of African American activists called for exclusively black civil rights leadership. In their speeches and publications, Black Nationalists invoked age-old antisemitic canards as they blamed Jews for the continued suffering of African Americans. Some black militants charged Jews with hypocrisy, arguing that they were the worst kind of white Americans because they boasted of their liberal activism even as they refused to acknowledge their complicity in the dominant power structure. In the June 1967 issue of the Black Panther Party's publication, *Black Power,* for example, editors warned: "We're gonna burn their towns and that ain't all, We're gonna piss upon the Wailing Wall. And then we'll get Kosygin and de Gaulle, That will be ecstasy, killing every Jew we see in Jewland."

Even as most national Jewish organizations condemned the antisemitic rhetoric of the Black Nationalist movements, many Jewish leaders advised against overreaction. Some empathized with African American frustration, and others believed it a temporary phase in the longer struggle for interracial cooperation. The American Jewish Committee went so far as to praise the new black movement for its commitment to ethnic identity as it paralleled developments in the African American community to Jewish historical experiences. "Black power," it held, "stresses black initiative, black self-worth, black identity, black pride" (in Dollinger 2000, 198). The Reform movement's Central Conference of American Rabbis proved especially understanding of the painful withdrawal into separatism and nationalism and the American Jewish Congress felt that black men had every right to seek to shape their own destiny. Representatives from other major national Jewish organizations echoed these sentiments.

The complex and seemingly contradictory relationship between Jews and the Black Nationalist movement was best described by Rabbi Arthur Hertzberg, who observed that "perhaps the saddest element in this whole frightening picture is in the fact that Jews are the people who are best able to understand the rhetoric of Black Power, even though they are most directly on the firing line of its attack" (Katz 1967, 72).

—*Marc Dollinger*

See also African American–Jewish Relations; American Jewish Committee and Antidefamation Efforts in the United States; Student Nonviolent Coordinating Committee

References
Carson, Clayborne. *In Struggle: SNCC and the Black Reawakening of the 1960s* (Cambridge, MA: Harvard University Press, 1995).
Dollinger, Marc. *Quest for Inclusion: Jews and Liberalism in Modern America* (Princeton, NJ: Princeton University Press, 2000).
Katz, Shlomo, ed. *Negro and Jew: An Encounter in America* (New York: Macmillan, 1967).
Van Deburg, William L., ed. *Modern Black Nationalism: From Marcus Garvey to Louis Farrakhan* (New York: New York University Press, 1997).

Blavatsky, Helena P. (1831–1891)

A Russian-born occultist, Helena P. Blavatsky is best known as a founder of the Theosophical Society in 1875, along with H. S. Olcott and William Q. Judge. After traveling through Tibet and other locales investigating esoteric lore, Blavatsky settled in the United States. She later moved to India with Olcott and established the world Theosophical Society headquarters at Adyar (in 1879) and the Theosophical Publishing House, allegedly under the direct inspiration of her spirit guides, the "Ascended Masters Morya and Koot Hoomi." The goal of the society, which eventually spread to fifty other countries, was to prepare human minds, organizations, and communication channels to receive a great religious world teacher, "the new torchbearer of Truth."

Blavatsky's first work was *Isis Unveiled* (1877), a promotion of "Ancient Wisdom" religion that reportedly sold all 1,000 first-edition copies

Helena Petrovna Blavatsky (1831–891), Russian traveler, mystic, and theosophist. (Bettmann/Corbis)

within two days. But Theosophists consider her greatest work to be *The Secret Doctrine* (1888), an occult treatise that glorifies Eastern and Luciferian religions as true enlightenment and denigrates the Jewish faith as harmful to human spirituality.

Much of Blavatsky's Theosophy ("god knowledge") is preserved in contemporary Theosophical literature and is borrowed from Hinduism, Tibetan Buddhism, Gnosticism, and Luciferian occultism. The first source contributed Theosophy's "racial cycle" theory, which calls for the periodic death and rebirth (*yugas*) of the human race, ridding humanity of weak and old "egos" and enabling spiritual advancement. At the top of humanity's current cycle are the Aryans; at the opposite end are the "Lemurians," an ancient race that embodies the "least evolved egos," which nevertheless defied the law of racial cycles by surviving several yugas up to modern times. In occultic tradition (as outlined, for example, by Blavatsky's spiritual successor Alice Bailey), the

Lemurians gave rise to the Jews. Each race carries its own peculiar karma as well, with the Jews' suffering presumed to be justly caused by their racial karma.

Blavatsky's influence ranged well beyond Theosophical circles and later contributed to Nazi ideology. One link was Baron Rudolf von Sebottendorf, a devoted Blavatsky fan and founder of the Thule Society (in 1918). The Munich-based organization borrowed heavily from *The Secret Doctrine* and counted several future Nazi leaders among its members or hangers-on. As early as 1920, Sebottendorf named the Jews as cosmic enemies to be "cleaned out" as a "final goal." Another link was Blavatsky disciple Karl Haushofer, whose "geopolitical" doctrines served the Nazis before and after 1933, and who some speculate may have introduced Hitler to *The Secret Doctrine* after their meeting in Landsberg Prison in 1924. However, yet another Blavatsky disciple, Dietrich Eckart, boasted that he had initiated Hitler into *The Secret Doctrine*. Hitler later dedicated *Mein Kampf* to Eckart.

—*Hannah Newman*

See also Bailey, Alice A.; Germanic Order; New Age; *Secret Doctrine, The;* Thule Society; *Völkisch* Movement and Ideology

Reference
Washington, Peter. *Madame Blavatsky's Baboon: A History of the Mystics, Mediums, and Misfits Who Brought Spiritualism to America* (New York: Schocken Books, 1995).

Bloch, Joseph Samuel (1850–1923)

Bloch was born in Dukla, in East Galicia. In 1883, he was an unknown Orthodox rabbi near Vienna when he publicly denounced August Rohling, an antisemitic professor of the Old and New Testament at Charles University in Prague. Rohling had testified at the recent Tiszaeszlar blood libel proceedings about supposed Talmudic passages that commanded Jews to commit ritual murder. Bloch labeled Rohling a fraud, declaring that he would pay him 3,000 florins if the professor could accurately translate a randomly chosen page of the Talmud. Rohling sued Bloch for libel, but then, two weeks before the scheduled trial date, he dropped the suit in disgrace, having never accepted Bloch's challenge.

The affair brought Bloch much praise as a fighter against antisemitism; the following year, he won a seat in the Austrian parliament from a Galician district that he represented for the next eleven years. Also in 1884, he began publishing the *Österreichische Wochenschrift* (Austrian Weekly), considered one of the most important Jewish periodicals in the country until it ceased appearing in 1920. In 1886, he cofounded the Österreichisch-Israelitische Union (Austrian-Israelite Union), an organization dedicated to combating antisemitism and defending Austrian Jews' legal rights. He authored a number of books, including *Der nationale Zwist und die Juden* (The Nationalities' Strife and the Jews [1886]). This collection of articles from his newspaper summarized Bloch's views on the Austrian political scene, his ideas about Jewish assimilation and ethnic identity, and his conception of a civic Austrian consciousness.

Prior to the mid-1880s, Austrian Jewish leaders had advocated a passive approach to antisemitic statements such as those of Rohling. Bloch demanded that Jews publicly refute antisemitic rhetoric, helping to usher in a new era of more assertive Jewish politics in central Europe. He also criticized Jewish assimilation, which entailed the denial of Jewish ethnicity. Bloch encouraged Jews to identify themselves not as Germans (or Czechs or Poles) of the Jewish faith but instead as members of the Jewish people, a separate nationality or ethnic group bound together by religious and historic traditions.

In addition, he urged his fellow Jews, as well as members of all the Habsburg nationalities, to see themselves as part of a multiethnic Austrian civic nation defined by citizenship and thus neutral regarding religion, language, or ethnicity. He sought to cultivate a civic Austrian identity that was fully inclusive. Building ties across ethnic lines and reducing tensions among all the peoples in Austria represented a key part of Bloch's strategy of fighting antisemitism and improving the lives of Austrian Jews.

—*Ian Reifowitz*

See also Austria; *Entdecktes Judenthum;* League against Antisemitism; Ritual Murder (Medieval); Ritual Murder (Modern); Talmud; *Talmud Jew, The;* Tiszaeszlar Ritual Murder; Zionism

References

Reifowitz, Ian. *Imagining an Austrian Nation: Joseph Samuel Bloch and the Search for a Supraethnic Austrian Identity, 1846–1918* (Boulder, CO: East European Monographs, distributed by Columbia University Press, 2003).

Wistrich, Robert. *The Jews of Vienna in the Age of Franz Joseph* (Oxford: Oxford University Press, 1989).

"Blood for Trucks" (Brand-Grosz Mission)

On April 25, 1944, Lt. Col. Adolf Eichmann, the Schutzstaffel (SS) officer responsible for deporting Hungarian Jews to Auschwitz, summoned a local Zionist leader, Joel Brand, to the first of several meetings in Budapest. According to Brand, Eichmann stated that Germany would release Hungary's Jews in exchange for a list of commodities; namely, 800 tons of coffee, 2 million bars of soap, unspecified minerals, and, in particular, 10,000 army trucks for exclusive use on the eastern front. Two days after the deportation of Hungarian Jews to Auschwitz began (on May 17, 1944), Brand, accompanied by a shadowy multiple intelligence agent, Andor "Bandi" Grosz, left Budapest under German auspices and arrived shortly thereafter in neutral Turkey.

After revealing Eichmann's "blood for trucks" offer to Zionist representatives in Istanbul, Brand left Turkey for Palestine in early June and—like Grosz shortly before—was arrested in Syria by the British and sent to Cairo for intensive interrogation. After several weeks of secret deliberations, during which both Britain and the United States exhibited confusion and uncertainty regarding an appropriate response, Joseph Stalin let it be known that he thought it was neither expedient nor permissible to negotiate with Germany.

Under British questioning, Grosz revealed that Brand's task of ransoming Hungary's Jews was a facade for Grosz's own, far more important mission, which was to arrange a meeting with representatives of the Allies in order to allow Heinrich Himmler to negotiate an anti-Soviet pact with the West. In mid-July, despite Winston Churchill's sympathy for European Jews and Franklin Roosevelt's concerns about the Jewish vote in the upcoming presidential election, the "blood for trucks" offer was rejected as a Machiavellian scheme to blackmail the Allies, disrupt the war effort in Europe, and smuggle spies and saboteurs into Allied territory.

A fervent antisemite, Himmler fully believed that an immensely powerful "international Jewry" controlled both Britain and the United States; that the West was fighting World War II on behalf of the Jews; and that, consequently, the Jews' plight was highly significant in all Allied considerations. From these absurd yet ingrained antisemitic articles of faith, Himmler concluded that negotiations with the West (the Grosz mission) depended on the release of Hungary's captive Jews, the only large, intact national Jewry still under German control. Himmler also knew that his proposed deal needed Adolf Hitler's approval and that, before letting Jews go, the Führer would require substantial deliveries of desperately needed war matériel—hence, his "blood for trucks" offer. For neither man did this signify a change of heart about the ultimate fate of Jews. Nazi "pragmatism" was to be only a temporary postponement of genocide.

Meaningful consideration of Himmler's overture was aborted by the West's unyielding focus on narrow self-interest, best summarized by Lord Moyne's questions to Brand: "What shall we do with a million [impoverished, alien] Jews? Where shall we put them?" (State of Israel Ministry of Justice 1993, 1067) However, some were saved through the offer. These included 1,700 Hungarian Jews who left Budapest by train, bound for neutral territory, on June 30, 1944 (the so-called Kasztner Transport), and 1,200 Jews from the Theresienstadt concentration camp who arrived in Switzerland in February 1945. Both groups were released by Himmler in a forlorn attempt to prove his sincerity and rehabilitate his reputation in the West.

The tragic paradox of this affair thus remains: for Britain and the United States, it was the prospect of a successful outcome of negotiations to save Jews that probably doomed the enterprise. Europe's Jewish remnant remained trapped between the relentless Germans and the impassive Allies.

—*Tom Kramer*

See also Eichmann, Adolf; Himmler, Heinrich; Hitler, Adolf; Holocaust; Hungary, Holocaust in; Stalin, Joseph; Zionism

References

Aronson, Shlomo. "The 'Quadruple Trap' and the Holocaust in Hungary." In *Genocide and Rescue.* Edited by David Cesarani (Oxford: Berg, 1997), 93–121.

Bauer, Yehuda. *Jews for Sale? Nazi-Jewish Negotiations, 1933–1945* (New Haven, CT: Yale University Press, 1994).

Kramer, T. D. *From Emancipation to Catastrophe: The Rise and Holocaust of Hungarian Jewry* (Lanham, MD: University Press of America, 2000), esp. chap. 6, "International Negotiations and the 'Rescue Matrix': Duplicity, Hidden Agendas, Calculated Tokenism, or Genuine Response?"

State of Israel Ministry of Justice. *The Trial of Adolf Eichmann: Record of Proceedings in the District Court of Jerusalem.* Vol. 3 (Jerusalem, 1993), 1067, col. 1.

Böckel, Otto (1859–1923)

After the waning of the Berlin Movement, Otto Böckel, the "peasant king" of Hessenland in west-central Germany, brought antisemitic electoral politics back to life, introducing a new style of populist agitation featuring torchlight parades, raucous open-air meetings, party badges, and incessant campaigning.

Born into a middle-class family in Frankfurt am Main, Böckel received his doctorate in modern languages from Marburg University (in 1882). While employed as a librarian there, the romantic nationalist wandered from village to village in the Hessian hinterland, collecting and preserving folklore. In pursuing his hobby, he got to know the troubles of a rural population in the throes of transformation from manorial to capitalistic agriculture. Like many of his contemporaries, Böckel blamed Jewish jobbers, moneylenders, and grain speculators for falling crop prices, peasant indebtedness, and the resulting foreclosures. But he went further than most when he claimed that Jews everywhere and throughout history were racially driven to exploit the honest labor of non-Jews. A spellbinding orator, he moved up within the organizational network of antisemitic clubs and newspapers that had sprung up in the early 1880s, and at the same time, he placed himself at the head of a peasant protest movement. In his own newspaper, the *Reichsherold* (1887–1894), he doled out homespun wisdom on the evil of Jewry, downplaying his own theoretical racism in favor of his constituency's more traditional, religiously based Jew-hatred. Supported by antisemitic reform clubs in Giessen, Kassel, and Marburg and by university student volunteers from the Verein Deutscher Studenten (Association of German Students), he ran for the Reichstag in 1887 on the slogan "Against Junkers and Jews" and won a stunning victory in the first balloting, displacing a Conservative Party notable and entering the parliament as the first avowed antisemite. When antisemitic competitors thwarted his ambition to form a unified national antisemitic party to solve the Jewish Question and rescue the peasantry, he settled instead for the Hessian-based Antisemitische Volkspartei (Antisemitic Peoples' Party, founded in 1889)—a power in regional politics, under a variety of names, until 1919. Böckel's agitation was at times boisterous, but his antisemitic ideology fell within the conventions of the period. His inflammatory pamphlet *Die Juden— die Könige unserer Zeit* (Jews—Kings of Our Times [1886]) promised the legal disenfranchisement of Germany's Jews. The Jewish Question would be solved when the German Constitution recognized that "two different Nations dwelt in Germany, Germans and Jews. The first [were] masters, the second guests, entitled to the rights of hospitality, but not to the rights of the masters" (in Levy 1975, 40–41). What made him an influential player in antisemitic politics was his creation of a fully developed agrarian movement. His Mitteldeutscher Bauernverein (Central German Peasant Association, with 15,000 members and 400 chapters in 1892) supported a youth group, consumer and producer cooperatives, "Jew-free" livestock markets, cheap insurance, and membership in savings and loan banks. None of these efforts was an unqualified success, and several involved questionable business practices, but they did achieve Böckel's main objective—the binding of the small farmer to his party.

Having alerted more powerful and betterfinanced political forces to antisemitic politics as a tool for mobilizing rural voters, Böckel was copied by Catholic grassroots organizations, especially in Bavaria. Given his limited resources and hounded by scandal, he proved unable to hold on to the leadership of his movement, watching helplessly as it was co-opted by the Junker-dominated Agrarian League. Poverty, poor health, and political obscurity marked the last twenty years of his life.

—*Richard S. Levy*

See also Agrarian League; Antisemitic Political Parties; Berlin Movement; German Peasant League; German Students, Association of; Riehl, Wilhelm Heinrich
References
Levy, Richard S. *The Downfall of the Anti-Semitic Political Parties in Imperial Germany* (New Haven, CT: Yale University Press, 1975).
Peal, David. "Anti-Semitism and Rural Transformation in Kurhessen: The Rise and Fall of the Böckel Movement." Dissertation, Columbia University, 1985.

Boer War (1899–1902)

The Boer War, also known as the South African War, lasted between 1899 and 1902 and involved Britain in its first major conflict since the Crimean hostilities of the 1850s. The British expected the South African fight to end quickly, but it dragged on. It required almost half a million British troops to secure victory.

The transformation of South Africa arose with the discovery of gold in the Transvaal, an area inhabited by the Boer descendants from earlier Dutch settlers and under the presidency of Paul Kruger. It has been claimed that the gold mine owners and managers, such as Cecil Rhodes, manipulated Britain into the war, fomenting a conflict to increase their power. However, no convincing evidence has been found to support the idea that the British government acted at the behest of the mine magnates or capitalists. Another claim, associated particularly with the radical journalist J. A. Hobson, is that the conflict amounted to a "Jews' war" fought at the behest of Jewish interests in the South African mining industry. During the war, that charge enjoyed strong support in socialist circles and appeared later in the poetry of Hilaire Belloc. However, this Jewish conspiratorial theory has been disputed by later scholarship.

Recent research suggests the war reflected the determination of the British government to assert its control over the Transvaal and its supremacy over South Africa in general. This emphasis switches the focus from South Africa to influences in London, although the British government received encouragement in its actions from the growing power of the *Uitlander* (non-Boer foreigners) in the Transvaal. The conflict can be viewed as part of the so-called scramble for Africa and a logical culmination of Britain's growing involvement in southern Africa, which, by 1902 and the Treaty of Vereeniging that ended the hostilities, had resulted in effective British control over the area.

The war gave rise to the first use of concentration camps, which Gen. Horatio H. Kitchener constructed for containing the Boers, a feature of the war that Nazi propaganda later exploited. The conflict also led to an orgy of jingoism, deplored at the time by Hobson. In addition, the war revealed the effectiveness of guerrilla tactics, at which the Boers proved adept, in the face of numerically superior armed forces. After the conflict, the British concentrated on reconstruction, and Lord Milner laid the groundwork for a political process that resulted in the Union of South Africa, effectively under Afrikaner control. Defeated militarily, the Afrikaners secured through this political settlement their language, culture, and own form of government, a development that carried enormous implications—particularly for black Africans, who would live until recently under Afrikaner rule.

—*Colin Holmes*

See also Banker, Jewish; Belloc, Hilaire; Britain; Hobson, J. A.; South Africa

References

Hobson, J. A. *The War in South Africa: Its Causes and Effects* (London: James Nisbet, 1900).

Judd, D., and K. Surridge. *The Boer War* (London: John Murray, 2002).

Smith, I. R. *The Origins of the South African War, 1899–1902* (London: Longman, 1986).

Boniface Society for Catholic Germany

The Bonifatiusverein für das katholische Deutschland (Society of St. Boniface for Catholic Germany), named for the apostle to the Germans (ca. 672–754), was founded on October 4, 1849, at the suggestion of Ignaz Döllinger, a Munich theologian, who had been a spokesman of the Catholic Right during the Revolution of 1848. The Boniface Society was organized by Count Joseph Stolberg-Stolberg, approved by Pope Pius IX in 1852, and repeatedly vested with privileges and indulgences by the Holy See. In 1918, the German Conference of Catholic Bishops resolved to establish the society in all parishes of the country; since 1967, it has been called the St. Boniface Mission of German Catholics.

During the nineteenth century, it was the declared aim of the society to help the "mission of the Church in Germany." Its main purpose was to support Catholics in the German diaspora by means of prayer and charity. The clerical and lay members of the association made it possible to build Catholic churches, chapels, schools, and presbyteries in foreign lands.

The Boniface Society was under the patronage of the bishop (or archbishop from 1930 forward) of Paderborn and managed by a general committee of this provincial diocesan town, one of the most important centers of Ultramontanism in Germany. As one of the church's most important institutional responses to the challenges of the modern era, the society helped mobilize Catholics against the new and threatening secular religions, such as liberalism, socialism, communism, and, later, even National Socialism. The association grew powerful as a medium of Catholic identity politics at all levels of society and as a tool for disciplining rank-and-file Catholics. Over the years, several subsidiary associations extended the organizational reach of the society to all segments of the Catholic milieu. Among these were the St. Boniface Academic Consensus (1867), an association for higher schools (1921), and the Guardian Angel's Association (1894) for children and elementary school students.

The Boniface Society made maximum use of an extensive and modern institutional network to pursue antimodern goals. Running its own bookstores, publishing houses, and magazines, such as the *Boniface Paper* (published since 1852, with a

The burning of "un-German" books on the Opera Square, Berlin, May 1933. (Bettmann/Corbis)

peak run of 640,000), the association defined and then confirmed "good" Catholics in their devotion to the church and pope. In the struggle against liberalism, socialism, and the Protestant domination of the German Empire, the society was able to make its voice heard. It was primarily in the antiliberal rhetoric of the organization that antisemitism came into play. The Boniface Publishing House issued several works that presented Jews as the purest example of the evils of liberalism. In 1876, it reprinted Konrad Martin's hostile critique of 1848, *A Look into Talmudic Judaism* (*Blicke ins Thalmud'sche Judenthum*). In the 1880s, it published no fewer than five editions and 20,000 copies of *Judenspiegel* (A Mirror to the Jews) by the Romanian Jewish apostate Ahron Briman (or Brimanus or Dr. Justus, as he was also known). Also part of the press's offerings were the widely distributed antisemitic works of Jakob Ecker and August Rohling.

Even though the Boniface Society refrained from and even condemned racist antisemitism, its dissemination of an essentially theologically based Jew-hatred in defense of Catholicism helped legitimize hostility toward living Jews.

—*Carsten Kretschmann*

See also Center Party; 1848; *Kulturkampf*; Pius IX, Pope; Rohling, August; Talmud; *Talmud Jew, The*; Ultramontanism; Vatican Council, First

References

Noack, Hannelore. *Unbelehrbar? Antijüdische Agitation mit entstellten Talmudzitaten: Antisemitische Aufwiegelung durch Verteufelung der Juden* (Paderborn, Germany: University Press, 2001), 163–173.

Smith, Helmut Walser. *German Nationalism and Religious Conflict: Culture, Ideology, Politics, 1870–1914* (Princeton, NJ: Princeton University Press, 1995).

Book Burning (May 10, 1933)

When Adolf Hitler "seized" power in Germany, the Nationalsozialistischer Deutscher Studentenbund (National Socialist German Students

Association), which had been in existence since the mid-1920s, almost immediately began to expand its organizational apparatus and to express its ideological commitments in bolder and more conspicuous ways. For example, just before the April 1, 1933, boycott of Jewish businesses, Oskar Stabel, the group's national leader, announced a boycott of lectures and seminars by Jewish instructors, apparently on the students' own initiative.

So, too, the infamous book burnings of May 10, 1933, grew out of student activism. In early April, the students association founded a press and propaganda section. Soon afterward, it settled on its first action. University students would publicly burn "destructive Jewish writings," thereby combating the Jews' "shameless" anti-German "incitement." A publicity drive was launched on April 12. On the next day, twelve "theses" spelled out the intended points of attack. The students mainly targeted books representing "the Jewish spirit." But they listed other subversive genres as well: Marxist books, pacifist books, and, somewhat cryptically, writings that "overemphasized instinctual life" (Friedländer 1997, 57). Members and collaborators posted the theses on university campuses throughout Germany.

On May 10, at 6 p.m., the burnings began, just as planned. In most German university towns and cities, bonfires were lit, and students cast large numbers of books into them. One historian of Nazism recently suggested that in most major cities, demonstrators burned between 2,000 and 3,000 books. The epicenter of the burnings was Berlin. In front of the Kroll Opera House, after a series of speakers—including Joseph Goebbels—inveighed against the pernicious influence of Jewish authors, a crowd of volunteers consigned to the flames over 20,000 volumes. Chanting antisemitic slogans, students and other participants threw into the fire works by Sigmund Freud, Maximilian Harden, Karl Marx, Kurt Tucholsky, and Heinrich Heine, who had said almost a century earlier, "Where books are burned, people will be burned too." In its coverage of the event, a prominent Jewish newspaper echoed that sentiment. Though noting that works by both Jews and non-Jews had been destroyed, it concluded emphatically, "The Jew will be burned!" (Friedländer 1997, 58)

—*Paul Reitter*

See also *Auto-da-fé*; Boycott of Jewish Shops; Goebbels, Joseph; Heine, Heinrich; Marx, Karl; National Socialist German Workers' Party; Nazi Cultural Antisemitism
References
Friedländer, Saul. *Nazi Germany and the Jews: The Years of Persecution, 1933–1939* (New York: HarperCollins, 1997).
Rose, Jonathan, ed. *The Holocaust and the Book: Destruction and Preservation* (Amherst: University of Massachusetts Press, 2001).

Boycott of 1912 (Poland)

The Russian Duma (parliament), created in response to the Revolution of 1905, was dissolved and reconstituted four times; each time, the electoral rules were changed to try to ensure a parliament that Tsar Nicholas II could work with. By the time of the fourth Duma elections in 1912, the rules were such as to limit severely the representation of national minorities and the urban working class, which tended to support radical parties. Elections were indirect: in each curia (electoral district), voters chose an electoral college, which in turn elected a single delegate to the Duma. The whole of Russian Poland was divided into only three curiae, one of which was Warsaw.

Because the franchise was subject to property qualifications, only a small proportion of citizens could vote; as a result, the Jews, with 39 percent of the city's population but a large middle class, controlled forty-six of the eighty-three electoral seats. The Jewish electors decided against choosing a Jew as the sole representative of the Polish capital, but they could not bring themselves to support the candidate agreed on by the Polish delegation—the antisemitic nationalist Roman Dmowski, who had represented Warsaw in the first three Dumas. Instead, they chose a hitherto unknown socialist named Eugeniusz Jagiełło. This action caused outrage among Poles, especially Dmowski's supporters, who retaliated by calling for a boycott of Jewish businesses. Dmowski had used the boycott weapon before, with limited success, but now, virtually the whole of the Polish press supported it, accompanied by intensely antisemitic rhetoric. Although the boycott did little economic damage, this sudden eruption of prejudice after a period of good relations shocked the Jewish community. Emigration to the United States and Palestine increased. The Warsaw Jews had been mainly divided between traditionalists (*Hassidim* and *Mitnagdim*) and the *Haskalah* assimilationists, but since the turn of the century, the socialist Jewish Workers' Bund and Zionist parties had made rapid gains. The boycott accelerated this trend, while assimilationism rapidly faded. As elsewhere in eastern Europe, a disillusioned Haskalah had become the mainspring of Jewish nationalism, which quickly attracted the support of the Jewish masses as well.

—*Steven Paulsson*

See also Dmowski, Roman; Poland; Russia, Imperial; Russia, Revolution of 1905; Zionism

References

Corrsin, Stephen D. *Warsaw before the First World War: Poles and Jews in the Third City of the Russian Empire, 1880–1914* (New York: Columbia University Press, 1989).

Levy, Richard S., ed. *Antisemitism in the Modern World: An Anthology of Texts* (Lexington, MA: D. C. Heath, 1991), 178–189.

Tomaszewski, Jerzy, ed. *Najnowsze dzieje Żydów w Polsce w zarysie, do 1950 roku* (Sketch of the Modern History of the Jews in Poland, to 1950) (Warsaw: Wydawnictwo Naukowe PWN, 1993).

Boycott of Jewish Shops (Germany, 1933)

On March 26, 1933, Adolf Hitler ordered a nationwide boycott of Jewish-owned shops and businesses, to begin the following Saturday, April 1, a major German shopping day. Hitler ostensibly called the boycott to counter what he decried as the "malicious hate propaganda" being directed against Germany from abroad. He was convinced that German Jews themselves were responsible for spreading lies about their supposed mistreatment at Nazi hands. His immediate focus was on New York, where a massive anti-German demonstration was scheduled for March 27.

Since Hitler's "seizure" of power on January 30, 1933, Nazi Storm troopers and undisciplined party thugs had been celebrating by terrorizing their supposed racial enemies. Their preferred targets were Jewish professionals and businesspeople. Foreign journalists brought reports of Nazi terrorist campaigns to the attention of the world abroad. The result was the prospect of a wave of protests stretching from New York to Warsaw.

Nazi leaders grew increasingly concerned about the specter of an international boycott of German goods. Efforts to call off the radicals perpetrating the anti-Jewish terror went largely unheeded. Calls for discipline were halfhearted; such spontaneous actions, moreover, were considered welcome evidence of healthy racial instincts. Nonetheless, the bad publicity needed to be countered. As a first step, Hermann Göring dispatched delegations of German Jewish leaders to London and Prague with instructions to deny reports of German mistreatment of Jews. He ordered others to call their counterparts abroad to refute rumors of Jews being brutalized.

The boycott of Germany's Jews, Hitler told his cabinet, was aimed at convincing them that the "atrocity propaganda" they were spreading abroad was about to backfire. It would also, he explained, steer the party radicals into a disciplined activity. For that reason, he appointed radicals to the boycott's steering committee. He named Julius Streicher, the publisher of a Jew-baiting scandal sheet, *Der Stürmer* (The Stormer), to be its chairman and an assortment of racist extremists to work with him.

On boycott Saturday, Storm troopers stood guard at Jewish-owned businesses to warn prospective customers they were about to enter a Jewish establishment. Jewish owners had been ordered to stay open so that the boycott's effect would not be avoided. In Berlin at least, the day went by quietly. Many shoppers refused to go along with the boycott. Reports from the provinces spoke of scattered violence, and in Kiel, there was at least one death.

Nazi leaders canceled the boycott before the day was out. The reason they gave was that its success obviated the need for its continuation. In reality, the boycott highlighted the recognition that prolonging it could only exacerbate Germany's

Nazi pickets outside a Jewish shop in Berlin during anti-Jewish campaign. (Hulton- Deutsch Collection/Corbis)

economic difficulties. Clearly, interference with business activity would add people, most of them Aryans, to the long lists of the unemployed. The boycott also demonstrated how difficult it was to define a "Jewish business." Did its owners have to be Jewish? What if some were Aryans? What if its employees were Aryans? These difficulties delayed for the time being the wholesale assault on the position of the Jews in the German economy.

—*Karl A. Schleunes*

See also Göring, Hermann; Streicher, Julius; *Stürmer, Der*
References
Barkai, Avraham. *From Boycott to Annihilation: The Economic Struggle of German Jews, 1933–1943* (Hanover, NH: University Press of New England, 1989).
Schleunes, Karl A. *The Twisted Road to Auschwitz: Nazi Policy toward German Jews, 1933–1939* (Urbana: University of Illinois Press, 1970).

Brasillach, Robert (1909–1945)

The most prominent French writer and critic to be executed by France's Liberation government, Robert Brasillach was an unabashed collaborator who used his position as editor in chief (1937–1943) of the fascist newspaper *Je suis partout* (I Am Everywhere) to revile democracy, communism, Jews, and the French Resistance. Seen as a martyred poet by the extreme Right and a failed writer seduced by the Nazi cult of virility by most others, Brasillach stands as a stark emblem of the significant role played by writers in the ideological divisions that nearly destroyed France in the 1930s and 1940s.

Brasillach was born in the south of France in Perpignan and lived briefly in Morocco, where his father, a lieutenant in the French army, was killed early in World War I. He began his journalistic career at the age of sixteen before graduating from the prestigious École Normale

Supérieure in Paris. He cast his allegiances with extreme elements from the very start, and his role as literary critic was soon overshadowed by his political diatribes. Inspired by Gen. Francisco Franco and Adolf Hitler, Brasillach called for a French brand of fascism to rid the nation of its "decadent" and "disloyal" elements. He attacked the Popular Front government (1936–1938) and its Jewish prime minister, Léon Blum, using racial antisemitism and "conspiracy theory" themes. Brasillach's gift for invective made him a name but also produced some of his most damning columns. When legislation prohibiting virulent racism in print was debated in the parliament, he wrote a piece on "the Monkey Question," recommending "antisimiatism" to the French people. Another article in 1941 urged that Jewish deportations should include small children. Although his writings were not as obsessively antisemitic as those of Lucien Rebatet and Louis-Ferdinand Céline, his approval of German and French efforts to expel Jews from western Europe was explicit. After the war, a jury found him guilty of collusion with the enemy, and he was sentenced to death. After French President Charles de Gaulle refused requests for a pardon, a firing squad executed Brasillach on February 6, 1945.

Attempts to rehabilitate Brasillach's reputation have followed a two-pronged approach. Since most of the evidence in his trial was culled from articles long out of circulation, his supporters have downplayed the contents of his polemical pieces. His brother-in-law, Maurice Bardèche, has been his principal champion, for his edition of Brasillach's "complete" works excises or distorts the most damaging texts. Thus, readers are left with the impression that he was a literary critic who dabbled in bad politics. The second approach has sought to characterize Brasillach as an ill-fated genius whose fiction nevertheless deserves admiration. His novels, for the most part hastily written, reveal occasional technical inspiration but overall have failed to establish his literary reputation. Given the public fascination with the history of the Vichy years in France and abroad, autobiographical fictions such as *Les sept couleurs* (The Seven Colors [1939]) and his memoirs, *Notre avant-guerre* (Our Prewar Years [1941]) are his best-known works.

—*Ralph W. Schoolcraft III*

See also Bardèche, Maurice; Céline, Louis-Ferdinand; Vichy

References

Carroll, David. *French Literary Fascism: Nationalism, Anti-Semitism, and the Ideology of Culture* (Princeton, NJ: Princeton University Press, 1995).

Kaplan, Alice Yaeger. *The Collaborator: The Trial and Execution of Robert Brasillach* (Chicago: University of Chicago Press, 2000).

Brazil

Antisemitism has never been a widely prevalent societal problem in independent (post-1822) Brazil. Indeed, most Brazilians historically have had little contact with "real" Jews or images of them. During the twentieth century, Jewish communal organizations were careful to keep internal Jewish issues (as opposed to ones related to Israel) out of the spotlight. Today, Brazil's strong rhetorical commitment to ethnic, cultural, and racial tolerance is backed up by law, making public antisemitism a potential crime. Furthermore, the active involvement of some Jewish community leaders in popular movements to combat hunger, poverty, and discrimination tends to present Brazil's Jews in a favorable, socially conscious light.

Understanding Brazilian antisemitism, which is most clearly found in the policy (rather than the popular) sphere, entails a realization that such attitudes tend to emerge from among Brazil's tiny elite and are then supported by a relatively small urban middle and upper class. While Brazil remained a colony of Portugal into the early nineteenth century, its anti-Jewish attitudes and actions were part of the Inquisition or the tradition it left behind. The history of modern antisemitism in Brazil, inspired more by central European rather than Iberian models, stems from 1930, when, during the Great Depression, a new nationalist regime led by President (and later the dictator) Getúlio Vargas rose to power. At that time, nativism, which included antisemitism as one of its components, became common among intellectuals and the elite press. A few organized groups that regularly attacked Jews and Jewish immigration also had access to the corridors of power.

From the mid-1930s, the government tolerated antisemitic acts and, during the early years of Vargas's rule, the Green Shirts of the Ação Integralista Brasileira (Integralist Party), which claimed 1 million members, began a virulently antisemitic campaign. When Vargas created the protofascist Estado Novo (New State) in late 1937, groups such as the Integralists were banned, but secret anti-Jewish immigration policies were regularized and formalized, a pattern that continued until Vargas was overthrown in 1945.

State-sponsored antisemitism in Brazil ended with the fall of the Vargas regime. As if to underline this change, when Vargas was elected president again in 1950, he chose an important member of the Jewish community, Horacio Lafer, as his finance minister. Since 1945, Jews have served in all areas of Brazilian political, economic, and military life.

In contemporary Brazil, much discussion has taken place over the publication of a series of books denying the Holocaust, written by Siegfried Ellwanger Castan, a wealthy industrialist living in the state of Rio Grande do Sul. Castan's publishing company, Editôra Revisão (Revision Publishing House), has distributed throughout the country books with titles such as *Holocaust: Jewish or German?* and *The Lie of the Century;* they are not available in any major bookstore chain. Editôra Revisão has also reprinted a number of antisemitic books from the 1920s, such as the *Protocols of the Elders of Zion* and Henry Ford's *The International Jew.* In spite of its restricted circulation, Castan's literature has been widely attacked and has consequently received disproportionate publicity.

Antisemitic publications would appear to be prohibited under Brazil's antiracism laws (Brazilian Constitution of 1988, article 5, paragraph 42). But attempts to enforce the laws have not been supported by politicians or judges. Indeed, when cases are prosecuted, the courts often find for the racists on the basis of Brazil's guarantees of freedom of speech and of the press. Thus, when Editôra Revisão was removed as a member of a publisher's consortium in Rio Grande do Sul, a local judge reinstated it. In April 2002, after a trial lasting several years, Castan received a two-year conditional sentence (carried out as community service) from a federal high court judge for "inciting racism." In December of that same year, however, the Supreme Court threw out the conviction, agreeing with a defense argument that since Jews were not a "race," there could be no racism against Jews in the juridical sense of the term as used in the constitution.

Flagrantly antisemitic movements in Brazil attract only a tiny number of participants. A formal neo-Nazi political party, the Brazilian National Revolutionary Party (PNRB), has about 200 sympathizers. A number of other groups are also popularly associated with neo-Nazism. Although their discourse is at times antisemitic, there is no evidence of violence specifically targeting Jews. Instead, their victims tend to be migrants from Brazil's impoverished northeastern states, those of African descent, and homosexuals.

—*Jeffrey Lesser*

See also *Dearborn Independent* and *The International Jew;* Holocaust Denial, Negationism, and Revisionism; Homophobia; Inquisition; *Protocols of the Elders of Zion*
References
Lesser, Jeffrey. *Welcoming the Undesirables: Brazil and the Jewish Question* (Berkeley: University of California Press, 1994).
Vieira, Nelson H. "Outsiders and Insiders: Brazilian Jews and the Discourse of Alterity." In *The Jewish Diaspora in Latin America: New Studies on History and Literature.* Edited by David Sheinin and Lois Baer Barr (New York: Garland Publishing, 1996), 101–116.

Britain (1870–1939)

Between 1870 and 1939, Jews in England did not suffer disabilities as members of the Jewish minority but as non-Anglicans, a status they shared with Nonconformists and Catholics. Jewish emancipation only became a separate issue after 1829, when Catholic emancipation was enacted, leaving Jews the only religious minority still subject to a handful of legal restrictions. The debate on Jewish political rights, specifically, admittance into both houses of Parliament, focused on the notion of "Christian England" and how far its very basis would be destroyed by allowing non-Christians to represent the nation. By 1871, however, Jewish emancipation was complete. It is crucial for the understanding of modern (racial) antisemitism in Britain that it did not come about in response to Jewish emancipation, as was the case, for example, in Germany.

Modern antisemitism circumscribes racial constructions of the "Jew" that subsume but go beyond Judaism. It also instrumentalizes these images and arguments, rendering them political. This variant of antisemitism surfaced in Britain during the Bulgarian crisis of the second half of the 1870s, voiced by the Liberal opponents of Prime Minister Benjamin Disraeli. London continued to support Turkey, even after massacres perpetrated by Turkish militias on Bulgarian Christians. Critics of Disraeli's policy seized on his Jewish background and the supposed Oriental blood ties between the Turk and the Jew to impugn his motives as anti-Christian and un-Christian. Antisemitic agitators claimed to speak for the (Christian) nation and for true patriotism. Disraeli's injection of the "Hebrew element," they said, threatened the English nation and English values.

Antisemitism reemerged in the course of the South African War (1899–1902). Once again, it became a tool of opposition to government policy from within the Liberal and Labour camps. The pro-Boers, as the antiwar party was derisively called, employed antisemitic imagery to buttress its opposition. Jewish financiers, crudely seeking capitalistic profit, were set against disinterested and true patriots, motivated by moral considerations and—pointedly—Christian values. English blood was spilled and English taxpayers' treasure was spent for a "Jew's war." In this political agenda, Jews served as the negative foil of the Boers, who were said to represent manliness, courage, honor, the simple life of the countryside, and love of homeland and nation. During the conflict over the war, another element entered into the rhetoric of the antisemites; an implicit and sometimes explicit questioning of current rules of citizenship, the *Jus Soli,* and naturalization. The Jewish financiers, attacked as greedy and treacherous, were also singled out as British subjects with a comparatively recent immigrant background. It became more common from that moment to subject English Jews to a

kind of denationalization, referring them back to their country of origin, no matter how distant in time. Jews whose families had once emigrated from Germany now became, in popular usage, "German Jews," with the distinct implication that they did not truly belong to the nation. The antisemitic interpretation of the driving forces behind the war was circulated in pamphlets, newspapers, and books. Member of Parliament John Burns carried it into the House of Commons, where his antisemitic utterances apparently moved none of his colleagues enough to contest him. Yet although voiced widely, antisemitism did not assume an organized form.

The Boer War controversy was part of a larger and intense public discussion of immigration and the need to control it, provoked by the arrival of approximately 140,000 Jews from eastern Europe starting in the 1880s. The "aliens debate" left its mark on antisemitic campaigns in the following years. Britons increasingly questioned the qualifications of citizenship in the face of immigration. Worry about the consequences for England and the nation's internal and external security assumed central importance for antisemitic discourse.

From the Boer War until the end of World War I, British antisemitism frequently combined with Germanophobia. The favored stereotypes included vague allegations of pro-German sympathies among Jews in England, the specific portrayal of "German Jews" as quintessentially "bad Jews," and the effortlessly arrived at equation of Jews with Germans. The embodiment of these sentiments in numerous images could be found in novels, newspapers, pamphlets, and treatises, reaching their peak after the outbreak of World War I. The journalist Leo Maxse and many less prolific and less well-known authors accused the Liberal government of subverting the nation to serve the schemes of "German" or, alternatively, "international" Jews. Antisemitic motifs went along with anxieties about degeneration, lack of patriotism, and youthful hedonism. Still, these expressions of antisemitism remained largely confined to national politics. Antisemites sought to criticize or influence government policy or the behavior of leading Jewish and non-Jewish politicians. Repeatedly, authors inquired via antisemitism into the nature of government decision making, insinuating or condemning what they took to be undue, unelected, outsider influence. It was the alleged power of the so-called Jewish element to manipulate government and thus endanger the country that bedeviled them.

This characteristic of British antisemitism continued on display after the Bolshevik Revolution of 1917. In the debate over the revolution, the terms *Jews* and *Bolsheviks* became synonymous to many. The evidence cited for the generalization was the presence of many Jews in the Bolshevik leadership. Again, however, what most preoccupied British antisemites was the potential influence this Jewish element might exercise over Russian government decisions and how these decisions might adversely impact England and its allies.

British antisemitism was a latecomer in the concert of organized antisemitisms and retained several peculiar characteristics. When it finally did become organized, it was relatively unsuccessful, never producing an antisemitic movement comparable to those on the Continent. Further, even though the vast majority of Jews in Britain had an east European background, the "aliens debate" never developed an exclusively or even a predominantly anti-Jewish emphasis, despite the best efforts of British antisemites. Antisemitism in Britain never fetishized the *Ostjuden* (eastern European Jews) to the same extent as that in France, Germany, and many other European countries. Perhaps most important, British antisemites never dared openly question the fact of Jewish emancipation.

During the interwar period, however, Britain saw the establishment of a handful of antisemitic organizations: the Britons, the Imperial Fascist League, and Oswald Mosley's British Union of Fascists (BUF). The Britons numbered 60 members in 1923; the Imperial Fascist League attracted some 140 in 1934. The Britons' prime importance lay in its circulation of the *Protocols of the Elders of Zion* immediately following World War I. But the *Protocols,* building on an atmosphere of conspiracy theory in vogue since the Boer War, enjoyed only a brief flurry of public attention before being so thoroughly discredited as to become useless for further antisemitic exploitation. Even the BUF found the forgery too compromised to employ for purposes of political mobilization. (This powerlessness of the *Protocols* highlights another profound difference between British antisemitism and that in the rest of the world, including the United States.) The failure of the BUF—the only overtly antisemitic political party—to garner many votes has been explained in various ways. One view suggests that it was the extremism of Mosley's group and its spurning of homegrown antisemitic themes in favor of the Nazi and Fascist models that severely limited its appeal to the British public.

Antisemitism's more general failure to achieve political strength in Britain may be a reflection of the well-established pluralist values and attitudes already in place in the Victorian era. Especially in the matter of religion, a reference point for many British antisemites, popular tolerance militated against antisemitic success. The organization of Jews into categories of "good"—national and English—and "bad"—international and German—was intended as a means of perpetuating antisemitic stereotypes. But the crucial point in the British discourse, as opposed to the German, was that the "good" Jew was identified as religiously observant, as well as patriotic and nationally minded. Since most east European Jews were also religiously observant, antisemites found it difficult to portray them to the public as completely inimical to Britain's well-being.

Finally, the reluctance of British antisemites to make an issue out of Jewish emancipation also needs to be explained. A close reading of antisemitic texts, from their appearance during Disraeli's premiership, reveals a racial conception of the "Jewish danger" that relegated the citizenship of Jews to a place of little importance. Antisemites feared the influence, mostly from behind the scenes, that Jews brought to bear on British political and governmental leaders and their policy decisions. Jews did not need the right to sit in Parliament or the cabinet in order to work their evil. Following this logic, revoking emancipation would not have rendered the Jews less effective in their efforts to conspire.

—*Susanne Terwey*

See also Boer War; British Union of Fascists; Disraeli, Benjamin; Emancipation; Gwynne, H. A.; Hobson, J. A.; Judeo-Bolshevism; Masculinity;

Maxse, James Leopold; Mosley, Oswald; *Protocols of the Elders of Zion*

References

Cheyette, Bryan. *Constructions of "The Jew" in English Literature and Society: Racial Representations, 1875–1945* (Cambridge: Cambridge University Press, 1993).

Endelman, Todd M. *The Jews of Britain, 1656 to 2000* (Berkeley: University of California Press, 2002).

Feldman, David. *Englishmen and Jews: Social Relations and Political Culture, 1840–1914* (New Haven, CT: Yale University Press, 1994), chap. 4.

Holmes, Colin. *Anti-Semitism in British Society, 1876–1939* (London: Edward Arnold, 1979).

Terwey, Susanne. "Stereotypical Bedfellows: The Combination of Anti-Semitism with Germanophobia in Great Britain, 1914–1918." In *Uncovered Fields: Perspectives in First World War Studies.* Edited by Jenny Macleod and Pierre Purseigle (Leiden, the Netherlands: Brill, 2004), 125–141.

British Brothers League

The history of the British Brothers League (BBL) and the immigration of Russian-Polish Jews into East London are inextricably entwined. The BBL's origins can be traced to February 25, 1901, although its official formation, together with a manifesto of its aims, came amid attendant publicity at Stepney Meeting House on May 9, 1901. Jewish immigration, increasing since the 1880s, had begun to have a discernible influence on parts of East London, especially in the housing market and among unskilled labor. The BBL emerged in response to these conditions.

In such circumstances, the organization attracted local support, but its membership did not consist of East Enders alone. According to one contemporary newspaper report, various Conservative members of Parliament (MPs), acutely aware of the possible dangers to their parliamentary majorities unless they adopted a firm stance on what was called alien immigration, took a leading role in the formation of the league. These members included Spencer Charington, Murray Guthrie, Thomas Dewar, and Maj. William Eden Evans-Gordon. The first president, drawn from outside these parliamentary ranks, was a city clerk, William Stanley Shaw, who had inspired the foundation of the league. In short, the BBL amounted to an alliance between East End workers and sections of the Tory Party, a union not without its tensions.

By June 1901, the league had established an administrative structure, and a revised statement of its aims had appeared. Moreover, underlining its links with Westminster, in its second full manifesto, issued in August 1901, the BBL declared its intention to work with the Parliamentary Alien Immigration Committee, formed in the same month and consisting of all the East End's MPs with the exception of Stuart M. Samuel, the Liberal MP for Whitechapel. This parliamentary pressure group urged immediate legislation to control immigration. Further evidence of the ties between East London and Westminster came when Sir Howard Vincent, the Tory MP for Sheffield Central and a leading campaigner against alien immigration, offered his support to the BBL.

By the autumn of 1901, the BBL's meetings became larger and more enthusiastic, all of which provided the background to the monster meeting on January 14, 1902, at the People's Palace in Stepney. A flavor of this occasion can be gleaned from the patriotic songs that opened the proceedings. Apart from East Enders, the meeting attracted not only the local Tory MPs who had earlier offered their support but also other well-known antialienists from among the Liberal camp.

Such bustle, however, proved short lived. Key activists died. Others lost interest or chose to concentrate on their own political advancement. And significantly, the Tory Party reined in its MPs who had earlier offered support. These politicians subsequently carried on with their campaign under the aegis of the more respectable Immigration Reform Association. Even so, representatives from the BBL gave evidence to the Royal Commission on Alien Immigration, which reported in 1903. However, the 1905 Aliens Act that followed this inquiry proved to be more muted than the complete cessation of alien immigration the league had sought. Overall, the BBL's brief history underlined and continued the tradition of nativism in East London, expressed in opposition to immigration and a willingness to employ antisemitism for this purpose.

—*Colin Holmes*

See also Britain; Maxse, James Leopold; *Ostjuden;* Webb, Beatrice
References
Fishman, W. J. *East End Jewish Radicals, 1875–1914* (London: Duckworth, 1975).
Holmes, C. *Anti-Semitism in British Society, 1876–1939* (London: Arnold, 1979).

British Union of Fascists

The British Union of Fascists (BUF) was founded in October 1932 by Sir Oswald Mosley after the failure of his New Party and was timed to accompany the publication of his fascist manifesto, *The Greater Britain* (1932). In the eight years of its existence, the BUF and the movement it engendered went through several phases, reflecting shifts in ideological emphasis and electoral strategy, decline of its public appeal, failures in organization, changes of personnel, legal censure under public order legislation, and opposition from a broad range of antifascist organizations and campaigns.

From its foundation to the violent Olympia Rally (on June 7, 1934), the BUF benefited from the publicity of Lord Rothermere's newspapers. It took its inspiration principally from Italian Fascism, establishing its national headquarters in the so-called Black House in Chelsea, London, as well as a women's section and regional headquarters and branches across England. Its membership stood between 40,000 and 50,000. British antifascists identified antisemitic themes in BUF propaganda from the start, and the movement alarmed British Jewry early on. But it was not until late 1934, with his speeches in Manchester on September 29 and at the Albert Hall in London on October 28, that Mosley openly embraced antisemitism. The conventional view is that he resorted to extreme antisemitism because the BUF was in need of an issue to revive its flagging fortunes and that this decision reflected opportunism as much as deep conviction. The Imperial Fascist League's Arnold Leese, for example, branded Mosley a "kosher fascist" because he did not share Leese's paranoid and genocidal vision of Nordic supremacy. But Mosley had never spurned the support of rabid antisemites such as William Joyce, founder of the National Socialist League (1937) and known later for his broadcasts from Nazi Germany as "Lord Haw Haw."

In 1936, the name of the movement was changed to the British Union of Fascists and National Socialists, abbreviated to the British Union (BU). The name change reflected a decided shift in influence and ideology from the Italian Fascist to the Nazi German model, underlined by the adoption of a new "Action Press" uniform modeled on that of the Schutzstaffel (SS). It was at this time, too, that the movement focused its efforts on London's East End—the locality with the highest concentration of Jews in Britain. The BU's canvassing, marches, and propaganda displays targeting the East End culminated in the battle of Cable Street (on October 4, 1936). The BU's planned march in commemoration of its founding four years earlier was met by a crowd of approximately 100,000 antifascist demonstrators and the construction of barricades. The "battle" turned out to be a struggle between the antifascists and the police. The BU's decline continued thereafter, especially following the promulgation of the 1936 Public Order Act that banned the wearing of political uniforms. Financial crises and a schism within the leadership over political strategy further hobbled the movement. However, the BU experienced a modest revival on the eve of World War II when it launched its peace campaign against the "Jews' War" and organized the large Earl's Court rally in July 1939. After the war began, the BU was officially outlawed, its publications were banned, and 747 of its members interned under Defence Regulation 18 B 1(a) in May 1940.

—*Julie V. Gottlieb*

See also Britain; Mosley, Oswald; Mussolini, Benito; National Socialist German Workers' Party
References
Linehan, T. *British Fascism, 1918–1939* (Manchester, UK: Manchester University Press, 2000).
Thurlow, R. *Fascism in Britain* (London: I. B. Tauris, 1998).

Bubis, Ignatz (1927–1999)

As the chairman of the Jewish community in postreunification Germany, Ignatz Bubis spearheaded ongoing efforts for German Jewish reconciliation and led the public campaign against antisemitism, real and perceived, in Germany in the 1990s. He also became embroiled in several public controversies.

Bubis, born in 1927 in the German city of Breslau (today's Wrocław, Poland), moved with his family to Dęblin, Poland, in 1935. There, he experienced the ghetto and labor camp before deportation to a labor camp in Czestochowa in 1944. After liberation, Bubis moved to Dresden and later to western Germany as the political situation in the East deteriorated. He established himself in the precious metal industry and in 1956 moved permanently to Frankfurt am Main, where he invested heavily in real estate. Bubis also became active in Jewish communal politics and helped with the establishment of communal schools and a nursing home. In 1965, he joined the executive board of the Frankfurt Jewish community, and he served as its chairman from 1978 to 1981 and again from 1983 to 1999. In the late 1970s, he joined the executive board of the national Central Council of Jews in Germany, becoming deputy chairman in 1989 and chairman in 1992, a position he held until his death.

As a real estate speculator in the late 1960s and 1970s, he drew the ire of many on the political Left, including those in the squatters' movement. In the play Der Müll, die Stadt und der Tod (The Garbage, the City and Death [1975]), German playwright and film director Rainer Werner Fassbinder satirized a "rich Jew" who took advantage of his Jewishness for business and political purposes. Many considered this characterization to be an oblique attack on Bubis, and he and other Frankfurt Jews staged a sit-in to prevent the play's Frankfurt debut in 1985.

As the outspoken leader of the Jewish community in Germany after 1992, Bubis gradually became a presence in German public life and discourse over the Nazi past. In 1993, some Center-Right politicians and journalists suggested that he run for German president on behalf of the classical liberal Free Democratic Party (FDP), which he had joined in 1969. Although he declined to do so, he remained politically active, serving on the board of the Hessian FDP and in the Frankfurt city council for the liberals after 1997.

Controversy marked the last year of Bubis's life. In February 1998, he demanded an end to the delay of the construction of the planned Holocaust memorial in Berlin, characterizing the issue as a matter of concern for all Germans, not just Jews. In October of that same year, German author Martin Walser, winner of the Peace Prize of the German Bookdealers' Association, criticized the instrumentalization of the Holocaust in German society. Enraged, Bubis accused Walser of *geistige Brandstiftung* (intellectual arson). After a series of well-publicized comments, Walser and Bubis met, and Bubis retracted most of his statements. A few weeks before his death, Bubis, who was then ill, proclaimed that he had failed as leader of the Central Council and that Jews and non-Jews in Germany had not overcome their differences. Fearing desecration of his grave if he was buried in Germany, Bubis requested burial in Israel.

—*Jay Howard Geller*

See also Desecration of Cemeteries and Synagogues in Germany since 1919; *Garbage, the City and Death, The;* Germany, Federal Republic of; Historians' Controversy

References

Bubis, Ignatz. *Damit bin ich noch längst nicht fertig: Die Autobiographie* (Frankfurt am Main, Germany: Campus, 1996).

Schirrmacher, Frank, ed. *Die Walser-Bubis-Debatte: Eine Dokumentation* (Frankfurt am Main, Germany: Suhrkamp, 1999).

Buenos Aires Pogroms (1910, 1919)

Among the great waves of immigrants that settled in Buenos Aires, Argentina, beginning in the latter decades of the nineteenth century were numerous socialist and anarchist sympathizers and ideologues, both Jewish and non-Jewish. The paternalistic aristocracy that ruled the country reacted with antiforeigner legislation in 1902 and in 1910. Workers' strikes, increasing in number, size, and forcefulness, were repeatedly dispersed by force. Violence peaked when a young Russian Jewish anarchist, Simon Radowitzky, assassinated Chief of Police Ramon L. Falcon on November 14, 1909, in revenge for the slaying of workers during the fierce repression of the strikes. On the eve of the centenary celebration of the May 10, 1810, revolution, which foreign dignitaries were invited to attend, heightened nationalist sentiment added to the menacing atmosphere in Buenos Aires. To forestall labor unrest, members of the upper classes assaulted key workers' institutions and, under the permissive eye of the police, attacked some Jewish quarters in the city. Many foreigners were deported at this juncture, among them several prominent Jewish labor leaders. These events proved to be a prelude to more serious anti-Jewish excesses.

A decade later, the fear of foreign leftists reached its climax during the Semana Tragica (Week of Tragedy) of January 1919. In response to a general strike that paralyzed the country's industries, commerce, and transportation system, the police and army were called on to restore order. President HipolitoYrigoyen, who had risen to power in 1916 as the candidate of the middle classes, was pressured by the traditional elite and the threatening circumstances to use extreme force to break the strike. Civilians belonging to the elite social classes, in organizations such as the Guardia Blanca (White Guard) and the Liga Patriotica Argentina (Argentine Patriotic League), launched additional attacks against radical workers, with particular vehemence against the Jews, most of whom were recent immigrants from Russia. The week of pogroms and plunder left the Jewish workers' neighborhoods with many dead and wounded. Union premises and workers' social halls and libraries were totally destroyed.

The upper classes remained convinced that the strikes had been planned abroad by Russian anarchists and "maximalists" (socialists and communists), and they accused some Jews of conspiring to introduce soviets in Argentina. Though there was no evidence of a Bolshevik plot and those arrested were finally liberated, this Red Scare was fueled by the events in Europe and by growing nationalism and xenophobia in Argentina. In addition, prominent Catholic clerics and representatives of lay organizations harangued the public on the Jewish danger, attacking Jews as traitors and importers of leftist ideologies that ran counter to the values of Argentine society and Christian belief. They branded socialism as a Jewish malady and demanded that Jews be expelled from the country.

In the absence of a communal structure, Argentine Jews offered no unified response to this attack on their existence. The more established Jewish institutions, representing middle-class businesspeople, denounced the strikers, justified the strikebreakers, and distanced themselves from the Jewish "hotheads," who did not typify the peace-loving Jewish community of Argentina. The local Zionist leadership was more resolute in organizing relief for the victims of the pogroms, defending their legal rights, aiding the imprisoned, and even framing a vision of Jewish unity for the future. However, even the Semana Tragica did not constitute a strong enough incentive for the centralization of Jewish institutional life in Argentina.

—*Victor A. Mirelman*

See also Argentina; Judeo-Bolshevism; *Protocols of the Elders of Zion*
References
Mirelman, Victor A. "The Semana Tragica of 1919 and the Jews of Argentina," *Jewish Social Studies* 37 (January 1975): 61–73.
———. *Jewish Buenos Aires, 1890–1930: In Search of an Identity* (Detroit, MI: Wayne State University Press, 1990).

Bulgaria, Holocaust in

Up to the 1930s, Bulgaria had been an inhospitable environment for antisemitic tendencies. *Bulgaria without Jews?* (1894) and other such journalistic forays into inflammatory politics remained fringe phenomena, unable to create a wider antisemitic climate of opinion.

Only after Bulgaria moved closer to the Third Reich in the late 1930s and began following its lead did nationalistic and ideologically based antisemitic organizations begin to appear, among them Defense of the Homeland, Union of the Bulgarian Legions, and Fighters for Progress and the Bulgarian Way. In imitation of Germany's major pogrom, the Night of Broken Glass, Sofia witnessed only minor and unpopular acts of vandalism against Jewish businesses in 1939. Historically, the coexistence of many national groups—Greeks, Armenians, Turks, Gypsies—militated toward ethnic toleration. Tolerance of Jews, the German ambassador reported in 1943, could be traced back to a modus vivendi a majority of them had reached with the broadest sectors of the Bulgarian working and artisan classes.

The Law for the Protection of the Nation, adopted on December 24, 1940, was based on racist principles that diminished the civil rights of Jews. Although several deputies argued against the necessity of such laws and warned against their unforeseen consequences, they were unable to prevent their promulgation. There followed a broad wave of protest in which many organizations took part, including the professional associations of merchant clerks, artists, war invalids, and lawyers. The Bulgarian Orthodox Church, twenty-one writers, and functionaries of the worker's party also joined the protest.

On March 1, 1941, Bulgaria joined with Germany, Italy, and Japan in the Three-Power Pact. In the following January, the Wannsee Conference determined that Bulgaria would surrender its 48,000 Jews to the Third Reich. German pressure led to the issuance of more anti-Jewish regulations and preparations for deportation. A Commissariat for the Jewish Question was established in August 1942; its task was to implement Berlin's decisions regarding the Final Solution, and its leader, Alexander Belev, underwent training in Germany before assuming his office.

On February 22, 1943, Belev signed an agreement with Adolf Eichmann's deputy, Theodor Dannecker, calling for the delivery of an initial 20,000 Jews, 12,000 from Thrace and Macedonia—the "new territories" given to Bulgaria to administer but controlled by the Nazis—and another 8,000 from "Old Bulgaria." The first 11,343 Jews, without Bulgarian citizenship and therefore regarded as under German territorial sovereignty, were deported to Treblinka and Auschwitz. Only 12 of them survived. A remarkable counterstroke was undertaken by the Bulgarian chief medical officer in Skopje, who managed to retrieve 57 Macedonian Jews from the transports, declaring them to be skilled medical workers.

On March 9 and 10, 1943, a total of 8,555 Jews living in several Old Bulgarian cities were arrested and put into improvised holding depots. But the trains to the death camps never departed. On the initiative of several influential Bulgarians—including the president of the parliament,

Dimităr Pešev, parliamentary deputies from many parties, and several church dignitaries, such as the Metropolitan Stefan of Sofia—and with the approval of the monarch, Boris III, the deportation order was rescinded. Remarkable in this context was the open letter of protest from Pešev to Prime Minister Bogdan Filov (on March 17, 1943), which was signed by forty-two deputies, primarily from the progovernment faction, and even by Alexandăr Zankov, the man who had championed the alliance with Nazi Germany.

On May 21, 1943, the government, once again being pressured by the Germans, decided to surrender the approximately 25,000 Jews of Sofia. When the plans to do so became public, another intensive protest was raised by prominent political, cultural, and clerical figures, including the Jewish religious leaders Daniel Zion and Ascher Hananel. On Education and Culture Day (May 24), Bulgaria's national holiday, a mass demonstration took place that even communist activists helped carry out. There followed a resettlement of Jews in the interior. Thus, the third attempted deportation had been foiled. This multifaceted mobilization of Bulgarian public opinion ought to be understood as an act of solidarity with fellow citizens under threat of death, men and women who over the centuries had shared equally in the unhappy fate of the Balkans. Until 1944, Jewish males capable of labor were held in preventive labor camps, where they were employed on public works. Arguing the pressing need for workers, Tsar Boris rejected Hitler's further efforts to deport these Jews.

Given the relentlessness of the Nazi persecution and then annihilation of the Jews of Europe, Bulgaria could not wholly escape a connection to the Holocaust. Yet it was not a willing participant in the Final Solution, and despite enormous pressure, it was largely successful in shielding its Jews from death. Even during the high tide of Bulgarian national feeling following World War II, antisemitism did not rise to the surface of public life. In the late 1940s, many Jews emigrated. Those who remained behind made their accommodation with the new leadership of the state and experienced no disadvantages because of their ethnicity.

—Tzvetan Tzvetanov
Richard S. Levy, translation

See also Croatia, Holocaust in; Eichmann, Adolf; Holocaust; Hungary, Holocaust in; Night of Broken Glass; Slovakia, Holocaust in; Vichy; Wannsee Conference

References

Bar-Zohar, Michael. *Beyond Hitler's Grasp: The Heroic Rescue of Bulgaria's Jews* (Holbrook, MA: Adams Media, 1998).

Cohen, David. *The Survival: A Compilation of Documents, 1940–1944* (Sofia: "Shalom" Publishing Centre, 1995).

Oliver, H. D. *Wir, die Geretteten oder wie wurden die Juden in Bulgarien den Todeslagern entrissen* (Sofia: Fremdsprachen Verlag, 1967).

Burschenschaften

Originally, Burschenschaften (fraternities) were organizations of university students in Germany that recruited volunteers to participate in the War of Liberation against Napoleon (1813–1815). This generation of students learned its politics on the battlefield, embracing the achievement of German nationhood as its special and heartfelt political mission. Following the foundation of the student association Teutonia in Halle in 1814, the first fraternity of the new sort, decidedly different from its traditional scholarly contemporaries, was formed in Jena in June 1815. Hostility toward France initially stood in the foreground, but another potential "enemy" soon became the center of controversy.

Under the influence of the romantic movement and its Christian German ethos, the question of Jewish membership was raised. Could Jews be accepted, or should they be excluded as foes of the Christian German fraternities? Those in favor of rejection drew considerable inspiration from the later icons of the *völkisch* (racist-nationalist) movement, Friedrich Ludwig Jahn and Ernst Moritz Arndt, as well as the philosopher Johann Gottlieb Fichte and the historian Friedrich Christian Rühs in Berlin. Within the German fraternities, it was paradoxically the democratic Giessen group under Karl Follen that fought the hardest against the acceptance of Jewish students. In contrast, at the University of Heidelberg, after a vigorous debate led by Friedrich Wilhelm Carové, a philosophy student and close associate of G. W. F. Hegel, the advocates of acceptance gained the upper hand. Jew-ish students also were granted admission to the fraternity at the newly founded University of Bonn, one of whose most active members was Heinrich Heine. However, the Wartburgfest, which the fraternities staged in October 1817 to celebrate the fourth anniversary of the Battle of Leipzig and the tercentenary of the Reformation, culminated in a dramatic anti-Jewish demonstration, during which cheering Christian German students burned the symbols of political repression and the book of a Jewish author (along with those of several non-Jews).

Disappointment with the lack of progress toward national unity drove segments of the fraternities into direct political action in order to gain public attention for their cause. When the theology student Karl Ludwig Sand murdered the allegedly "un-German" (non-Jewish) author and Russian spy August von Kotzebue, a political assassination celebrated by many fraternity members as a heroic act, the result was not the anticipated national uprising but rather the political isolation and prohibition of the fraternities in 1819. In the now officially illegal student groups, Jews were not only considered insufficiently German, they were also suspected of being spies for the forces of reaction. At the secret Fraternal Day (*Burschentag*) of 1820 in Dresden, Jews, it was argued, had no fatherland of their own and thus could not engage in the struggle for the German fatherland. But by the middle of the 1820s, the political persecution of the fraternities eased, and at the Fraternal Day of 1827 in Bamberg, those students who advocated the acceptance of Jewish students won increasing influence.

Students belonging to the fraternities participated in a revolutionary episode in Frankfurt in 1830, after which the organizations were again banned; they reemerged during the Revolution of 1848. When national unity was finally achieved through Prussian diplomacy and military action (between 1864–1871), the fraternities turned into enthusiastic supporters of the German Reich. Whatever liberal tendencies they might have exhibited previously now fell away. They revived their martial initiation rites as well as archaic battle and drinking rituals. Simultaneously, they also developed into strong and effective agitators on behalf of the new antisemitic political movement. They represented a potent force in the construction of the German völkisch mentality during the imperial era and in the Weimar Republic, rallying German students to the National Socialist movement.

—*Ulrich Wyrwa*
Matthew Lange, translation

See also Antisemites' Petition; Antisemitic Political Parties; Arndt, Ernst Mortiz; Christian State; Dining Society, Christian-German; 1848; Fichte, J. G.; Fries, Jakob friedrich; German Students, Association of; Grimm, Brothers; Hegel, G. W. F.; Heine, Heinrich; Hep-Hep Riots; *Völkisch* Movement and Ideology

References
Hardtwig, Wolfgang. "Studentische Mentalität—Politische Jugendbewegung—Nationalismus: Die Anfänge der deutschen Burschenschaften," *Historische Zeitschrift* 242 (1986): 581–628.
Wyrwa, Ulrich. *Juden in der Toskana und in Preußen im Vergleich: Aufklärung und Emanzipation in Florenz, Livorno, Berlin und Königsberg i. Pr.* (Tübingen, Germany: Mohr Siebeck, 2003).

C

Camelots du Roi (1908–1936)

Members of the paramilitary group known as the Camelots du Roi served as the street fighters for the royalist Ligue d'Action Française. The group's name literally means "street vendors of the king" and was sometimes spelled anachronistically as *Camelots du Roy,* indicating adherence to a mythic image of old France. The organization coalesced in November 1908, formed out of the student groups studying at the Institut d'Action Française, from workers with royalist sympathies and wealthy boys from the Seventeenth Arrondissement who sold royalist newspapers on Sundays. The titular president of the group was Maxime Réal del Sarte and later Marius Plateau, but the real chief was Maurice Pujo, who orchestrated the relations with the central organization and managed the corps.

The membership oath encapsulated the ideology of the Camelots:

French by birth, heart, reason and will, I shall fulfil the duties of a conscious patriot. I pledge myself to fight against every republican regime. The republican spirit disorganizes national defense and favors religious influences directly hostile to traditional Catholicism. A regime that is French must be restored to France. Our only future lies, therefore, in the Monarch, as it is personified in the heir of the forty kings who, for a thousand years, made France. Only the Monarchy ensures public safety and, in its responsibility for order, prevents the public evils that antisemitism and nationalism denounce. The necessary organ of all general interests, the Monarchy, revives authority, liberty, prosperity and honor. I associate myself with the work for the restoration of the Monarchy. I pledge myself to serve it by the means in my power. (Davies 2002, 83)

Within a year, there were sixty-five Camelot sections throughout France and about 600 members in Paris alone. In 1910, the Commissaires, an elite of the elite, was formed to keep order at meetings, march on either side of the Action Française at parades, guard the leaders and offices, and provide a task force for other activities.

The Camelots du Roi activists hawked the daily newspaper *L'Action Française,* guarded royalist meetings, and provided shock troops for conflicts with opponents. They armed themselves with canes, clubs, smoke and stink bombs and bolstered their courage with jeering songs. They attacked politicians, defaced icons, disrupted university lectures, rioted in national theaters against films and plays they considered unpatriotic, and demonstrated in the Latin Quarter against political enemies. They were dissolved by government order along with the Ligue d'Action Française after Léon Blum was attacked by the group's sympathizers in 1936. In its ideas and practices and certain of its personnel, the Camelots du Roi formed the bridge between the revolutionary royalism of the Action Française and the fascist groups of the 1930s.

—*Jonathan Judaken*

See also Action Française; Barrès, Maurice; France; Maurras, Charles

References

Davies, Peter. *The Extreme Right in France, 1789 to the Present* (London and New York: Routledge, 2002), 83.

Nolte, Ernst. *Three Faces of Fascism: Action Française, Italian Fascism, National Socialism* (New York: Holt, Rinehart and Winston, 1966).

Weber, Eugen. *Action Française: Royalism and Reaction in Twentieth-Century France* (Stanford, CA: Stanford University Press, 1962).

Canada

The history of antisemitism in Canada is characterized by a broad range of discriminatory acts, attitudes, and behaviors by individuals, businesses, and academic institutions, with a nearly total absence of civil disabilities. Restrictions imposed by the state on Jews, once they passed immigration authorities, largely disappeared in 1832 with the election of the first Jew to a legislative body. It was, however, a considerable time before another was elected to a Canadian legislature. There were no Jews in the federal cabinet and very few in provincial cabinets, and none was appointed to the high courts until after World War II.

Without discounting the hatreds and violence that run through its history, it can be said that Canada has distinguished itself from most countries where Jews live by an absence of pogroms or lynchings. Antisemitism was more pronounced in Quebec, where the Catholic Church associated Jews with modernism, liberalism, and a host of other "dangerous" doctrines. From 1880 through the 1940s, several Catholic journals denounced "the Jew." Abbé Lionel Groulx's condemnations of Jews influenced clerics, politicians, journalists, and teachers. The popular press fell into line with the Catholic press. The most notorious anti-Jewish violence occurred in Quebec City in 1910 when, following a particularly inflammatory address by a well-known antisemite, Joseph Plamondon, some of the audience attacked Jewish storekeepers and vandalized their businesses. The aggrieved Jews launched a civil action against Plamondon. Four years later, the courts awarded them minimal costs; but the disturbances continued. Jews who grew up in Toronto—one of the largest "Jewish cities" in the world (with a population of 179,000 Jews in 2001)—remember the Christie Pits riot of 1938 between Jewish and non-Jewish local baseball teams and the tardiness of the police in restoring order.

Antisemitism in Canadian history is found primarily in discriminatory attitudes that produce shunning (a lack of neighborly friendliness) and societally imposed exclusions initiated and cultivated by voluntary associations or religious bodies.

The Canadian Confederation as a compact between French Quebec and English (and Gaelic) Ontario and the Maritime Provinces was also a compact between Catholic and Protestant polities. Confederation was made possible by a series of constitutional protections for the French and Catholic minorities outside Quebec and the English and Protestant minorities inside Quebec. One major point of agreement between Catholic and Protestant clergy was the belief that Canada was a Christian society.

How did a confederation formed on this basis come to accommodate and accept a Jewish community? What was the real meaning of the antisemitism that did occur, and why did antisemitism not gain a greater foothold in Canada? Answering these questions requires a brief history of the Jews in Canada.

The earliest recorded evidence of Jewish settlement dates from 1759. Ezekiel Hart, son of a commissary officer in the British army during the Seven Years' War, was denied the right to take his seat in the legislature of Lower Canada after the elections of 1807 and 1808. In 1832, the United Canadas passed legislation giving almost full civil rights to Jews when Hart chose to take the oath of office on a Hebrew Scripture. Curiously, recognition of Jewish marriages did not occur until 1857.

From 1881 to 1914, the Jewish population of Canada rose from 2,393 to 6,414; most of the newcomers, refugees from eastern Europe, settled in Montreal, Toronto, and Winnipeg. Jewish merchants could also be found in almost every small town and in agricultural settlements on the prairies. The trend continued after the 1914–1918 war, especially after the United States restricted admission of immigrants in the 1920s. Canada also began to restrict immigration with the onset of the Great Depression. With the rise of Nazism, the Jewish Immigrant Aid Society and the Canadian Jewish Congress (CJC) pressed for greater numbers to be accepted. The government, however, maintained a policy that tied immigration to agriculture. From 1930 to 1940, Jewish immigration totaled 1,105, of which 900 were settled on farms.

Organized antisemitism emerged for the first time in both French and English Canada in the 1930s. The incipient fascist movement of Adrien Arcand in Quebec injected antisemitic overtones into its nationalist campaign. In western Canada, an antisemitic movement made major inroads into the Social Credit Party. The Ku Klux Klan offered Canadians a "galaxy of hatreds" in which Jews figured prominently but not exclusively. Prime Minister William Lyon Mackenzie King had primarily Jews in mind when he confided to his diary in 1938: "We must . . . seek . . . to keep this part of the Continent free from unrest and from too great an intermixture of foreign strains of blood" (in Abella and Troper 1982, 17).

The darkest hour in the history of antisemitism in Canada came with the onset of World War II. In 1940, Canada received and interned 2,000 individuals, mostly "enemy aliens," from Germany and Austria, who had previously been interned in Britain. In 1945, a senior Canadian official was asked, off the record, how many Jews would be allowed into Canada after the war. He replied, "None is too many" (in Abella and Troper 1982, v). Only when individuals or families found Canadian sponsors were they released from detention. Immigration continued to be restricted until the clothing industry and unions were allowed to recruit workers from the displaced persons camps. Of the 5,000 workers approved by the recruiting missions, 2,600 of them were admitted into Canada; of this number, 60 percent were Jews.

At the end of World War II, a variety of discriminatory practices persisted. Universities maintained admission restrictions that disadvantaged Jews. Property owners' associations engaged in restrictive covenants. Discrimination in rental housing and in employment remained commonplace until it was prohibited by law. Ontario, the most populous Canadian province, passed the Racial Discrimination Act in 1944, from which the comprehensive Human Rights Code developed during the 1950s. Other provinces and the federal government followed suit. From 1917 until the end of World War II, there were typically two or three Jews elected to the House of Commons, usually representing liberal or social democratic parties. By the late 1960s, when a Jew was elected from Newfound-land for the Conservative Party, Jewish identity had ceased to be a critical factor in electoral politics. Jews also began to attain important positions in both federal and provincial civil services in the late 1950s. The first Jewish member of the Supreme Court of Canada, Bora Laskin, became the chief justice in 1970.

In 1969, Canada adopted a criminal code amendment known as the Hate Propaganda Act. The bill sought a balance between free speech and the protection of vulnerable minorities by prohibiting speech acts likely to incite violence but requiring a high standard of proof for a conviction. The 1971 Royal Commission on Bilingualism and Biculturalism report devoted an entire volume to the "Cultural Contribution of the Other Ethnic Groups." The federal Multiculturalism Act resulting from this report gave nominal support for cultural programs but has been critically important for the recognition of minority cultural communities.

In 1982, a Charter of Rights and Freedoms was added to the Canadian Constitution, similar in principle to the U.S. Bill of Rights while maintaining the Canadian tradition of balancing individual rights with the recognition of community interests and the authority of government to maintain "peace, order and good government."

Without trivializing the violent incidents that have occurred, antisemitic attitudes have found no aid or comfort from any political leader or public office holder. When the leader of the Parti Québécois blamed the loss of a referendum on Quebec sovereignty on "the ethnic vote," his own party forced him to resign. A 1986 poll indicated that 6 percent of Canadians considered themselves antisemitic and 20 to 25 percent harbored some antisemitic feelings. Public expression of such sentiments remains typically unrewarding and is occasionally punished.

The "new antisemitism," confined largely to intemperate supporters of a Palestinian state, is no less troubling to Jews in Canada than to Jews elsewhere. At the same time, all the rational indicators suggest the balancing of individual and communal rights that has typified the Canadian outlook works against the capacity of antisemitism to disturb public life.

—*Michael Posluns*

See also Armed Forces of the United States; Immigration and Naturalization Laws; Ku Klux Klan; Multiculturalism; *Numerus Clausus* (United States); *Ostjuden;* Pogroms; Restricted Public Accommodations, United States; Restrictive Covenants; Ultramontanism; Zündel, Ernst

References

Abella, Irving, and Harold Troper. *None Is Too Many.* 3rd ed. (Toronto, Canada: Lester Publishers, 1997).

Betcherman, Lita-Rose. *The Swastika and the Maple Leaf: Fascist Movements in Canada in the Thirties* (Toronto, Canada: Fitzhenry & Whiteside, 1975).

Porter, John. *The Vertical Mosaic: An Analysis of Social Class and Power in Canada* (Toronto, Canada: University of Toronto Press, 1965).

Tulchinsky, Gerald. *Branching Out: The Transformation of the Canadian Jewish Community* (Toronto, Canada: Stoddart, 1998).

Capistrano, John of (1386–1456)

John of Capistrano studied jurisprudence and then entered the service of the king of Naples. After his political career foundered and his wife died, he entered the Franciscan order. In addition to handling important tasks undertaken for the order, he was active as an adviser, legate, and inquisitor for the papacy. He took an uncompromising position in all questions having to do with heretics and followers of contrary religions. On his numerous official visits of inspection, he always sought to safeguard the power of the church, applying the full force of his influence as a papal representative on the spiritual and secular authorities. He inspired the common people with his great oratorical talent and his supposed miracle-working powers. His diverse and large body of writings has not been edited, making it difficult to research his life and work.

For the Jews of Europe, he was the "scourge of the Hebrews," a title bestowed on him because of his preaching against them. His polemics elaborated on a stereotypical anti-Judaism that contested the right of the Jews to the Torah or to consider themselves still to be the chosen people. Apparently, he compelled Jews to attend sermons designed to effect their conversion. The baptism of a rabbi and fifty-two other non-Christians that is said to have resulted from John's ministrations in Rome (in 1450) remains unproven. He is thought to have exercised great influence on the papal bull of Nicholas V in 1447, which abolished all earlier privileges of the Jews and ordered the rigorous enforcement of canon law, specifying that they wear distinctive clothing and markings, restricting their social interactions with Christians, and defining their inferior legal status. Charged with the implementation of the bull, John began by challenging the rights of Jewish communities in Italy and Sicily.

After 1451, he extended his activities to Bohemia, Bavaria, and Silesia. While battling against the Hussites there, he attempted, with devastating effect, to undermine the rights of the Jewish population. The dukes of Bavaria expelled Jews in 1452. Bishop Gottfried IV of Würzburg soon joined in this action, even though just a few years before, he was still granting privileges to the Jewish community in his territory. Economic as well as purely religious motives may also have played a role in the expulsions. In Breslau, John intervened energetically against Jews accused of host desecration. Leading members of the community had their property confiscated and were tortured. In the summer of 1453, forty-one of them were burned at the stake. Others committed suicide. Survivors were driven from the city; their infant children were forcefully taken for baptism—a violation of existing canon law.

The anti-Jewish crusade continued in the Kingdom of Poland where Casimir IV had recently granted Jews special rights. In alliance with the Polish clergy, John demanded that the king revoke these measures, interpreting them as an assault on the church's own rights. After Casimir bowed to this interpretation in 1454, outbursts of violence against Jews took place throughout Poland.

John of Capistrano represented a traditional anti-Judaism based on theological grounds. But he was also a forerunner of modern antisemitism insofar as he sought the social isolation of Jews and held them up to popular contempt. His employment of economic accusations as a tool of mass mobilization, particularly his sermonizing against Jewish usury, also anticipated the techniques of modern antisemites. He was canonized in 1690 and is still venerated as a saint of the Roman Catholic Church.

—*Rainer Kampling*
Richard S. Levy, translation

See also Expulsions, Late Middle Ages; Franciscan Order; Host Desecration; Inquisition; Usury
References
Andreozzi, Gabriele. *San Giovanni da Capestrano e il terz'ordine di San Francesco* (Rome: Franciscanum, 1987).
Pasztor, Edith S., ed. "Giovanni da Capestrano: Un bilancio storiografico." *International Historical Conference held at L'Aquila, Italy.* (L'Aquila, Italy: Da Arti Grafiche Aquilane, 1999).

Capital: Useful versus Harmful

Some antisemites of the fin de siècle period devised a critique of laissez-faire capitalism that skirted the issue of class conflict by identifying Jews rather than the bourgeoisie as the principal exploitative element in contemporary society. In a speech before the German Reichstag in 1893, the antisemite and conservative Max Liebermann von Sonnenberg contrasted a useful capital, one that invigorated industry and agriculture and produced livelihoods for "millions of workers," with the harmful capital that was employed in speculative promotions (*Gründungen*) and sought merely profit instead of productivity. Although he denied that the terms *harmful* and *Jewish* were synonymous, he nevertheless insisted that, at that time, this latter form of capital was "mostly in Jewish hands" (Massing 1949, 277).

Such formulations resonated with peasants, artisans, and salaried commercial employees, as well as intellectuals who perceived their livelihoods and values threatened by a new economic order that, from both ideological and practical considerations, they were loath to identify with conservative landholders and industrialists. The sheer visibility of Jews in banking, stock brokerage, novel forms of commerce, and retail and the long-standing popular identification of Jews with usury made the dichotomy between destructive Jewish and productive Christian capital appear plausible. Moreover, the underlying duality of harmful and useful commerce or finance was reinforced by venerable traditions in Western economic mentalities. It recalled Aristotle's distinction between production for use (goods) and for profit and exchange (commodities), as well as the Scholastic differentiation between usurious and legitimate profit on monetary loans and the classical economic one between fixed and circulating capital. It similarly echoed Adam Smith's contrast of "productive" and "unproductive" labor and the anarchist Pierre-Joseph Proudhon's division of capital between its authentic fertile component, "attributable only to the creations of human industry," and its bogusly profitable one, which he identified with *tokos,* the Greek term for usury (Proudhon 1888, 306). Although these and similar oppositions emerged separately from the question of Jewish status, they nevertheless supplied a ready conceptual vocabulary for stigmatizing Jews as economic threats; one need only recall Shakespeare's juxtaposition of Shylock, the repellent Jewish usurer, with the "Merchant of Venice," Antonio, who epitomizes virtuous and honorable commerce.

The "socialism of fools," as Liebermann von Sonnenberg's brand of economic antisemitism was often labeled, had its more immediate roots in what Marx and Engels, in their *Communist Manifesto,* described derisively as the Christian, "aristocratic," and "utopian" socialism of the early nineteenth century. In contrast to Marx, who viewed capitalism through the lens of class conflict as a necessary prelude to the proletarian revolution that would bury it, these traditions sought to harness modern industrial productivity to the preservation of some precapitalist social institutions, such as guilds, that they wanted to shield from remorseless market forces. Adherents of these movements rejected Marxist "communism" along with capitalism, since Marx seemed to celebrate as inevitable and desirable what they most feared—the transformation of the peasantry and lower middle class into a propertyless proletariat. Moreover, because they often viewed Jews as emblematic of modern society's excessive embrace of commercial values, socialists of the most diverse outlooks at times manifested harshly antisemitic views.

Nevertheless, in no case was antisemitism the centerpiece of these socialist ideologies or movements. In contrast, the attenuated socialism of men such as Liebermann von Sonnenberg, Wilhelm Marr, and Adolf Stoecker—though often embracing progressive social welfare legislation—made restrictions on Jews the focal point of their reforms. Romanticizing and nationalizing the hierarchical but harmonious "estate" society of the Middle Ages as the counterweight to commercial capitalism, they wished to return Jews to the status of a tolerated but closely circumscribed alien minority. Along with the racialist economic critiques of the more radical antisemites who emerged in the 1890s, the older approach continued to exert significant influence. Indeed, just such an interpretation of the Janus-faced nature of capital was absorbed by Adolf Hitler from the lectures of his economics mentor Gottfried Feder to become, in his words, "one of the most essential premises for the foundation" of the National Socialist Party (Hitler, 1943, 210).

—*Jonathan Karp*

See also Banker, Jewish; Christian Social Party (Germany); Fichte, J. G.; Fourier, Charles; Liebermann von Sonnenberg, Max; Marr, Wilhelm; Marx, Karl; Proudhon, Pierre-Joseph; Rothschilds; Shylock; Socialists on Antisemitism; Stoecker, Adolf; Usury

References

Hitler, Adolf. *Mein Kampf.* Translated by Ralph Manheim (Boston: Houghton Mifflin, 1943).

Massing, Paul. *Rehearsal for Destruction: A Study of Political Anti-Semitism in Imperial Germany* (New York: Harper & Brothers, 1949).

Proudhon, Pierre-Joseph. *System of Economical Contradictions: or, The Philosophy of Misery.* Translated by Benjamin R. Tucker (Boston: Benjamin R. Tucker, 1888).

Wistrich, Robert. *Socialism and the Jews: The Dilemmas of Assimilation in Germany and Austria-Hungary* (Rutherford, NJ: Fairleigh Dickinson University Press, 1982).

Caricature, Anti-Jewish (Early)

As a graphic form of humor or wit, caricature depends on exaggeration for its effect. The origin of the word *caricature* stems from the Italian *caricare,* meaning "to accentuate or overcharge." "In the *Caricatura,*" wrote the English novelist Henry Fielding in 1742, "we allow all Licence. Its Aim is to exhibit Monsters, not Men; and All Distortions and Exaggerations are within its Province" (pref-

Figures of the statues of Ecclesia and Synagoga (Strasbourg Cathedral 1230). (Michael Freeman/Corbis)

ace to *Joseph Andrews*). Though the eighteenth and early nineteenth centuries are often viewed as the golden age of graphic satire (an art form that is particularly associated with Georgian England), it is possible to trace common motifs in the caricatural depiction of Jews to a much earlier era.

Allegorical representations of Jews occur quite widely on ecclesiastical carvings, stained glass, and friezes and in illuminated manuscripts from many parts of medieval Europe. The most familiar are the paired female statues of Ecclesia (church) and Synagoga (synagogue), in which the triumphant Ecclesia is often a crowned maiden holding a chalice or a cross, whereas the dejected figure of Synagoga appears blindfolded (perhaps as an incarnation of 2 Corinthians 3:13–16) and carrying the broken tablets of the Mosaic law. Good examples may be found on the exterior of the cathedrals at Strasbourg and Bamberg. In a wood carving on a choir bench at Erfurt Cathedral, Ecclesia is depicted riding a prancing horse and attacking Synagoga, shown astride a pig. A

Isaac of Norwich Drawing, 1233. The earliest known caricature of a Jew. Exchequer of Receipt, Jews' Roll, no. 87. (Courtesy of the Public Record Office, London)

more overtly caricatured representation of the putative conflict between Christianity and Judaism stems from the perverse association of Jews with swine, the flesh of which their religion strictly prohibits them from consuming. In medieval and later Christian depictions, Jews are often shown consorting or engaging in sodomitic practices with the pig. An infamous sixteenth-century German print of the so-called *Judensau* (Jew's pig; see *Judensau* entry for illustration) portrays a group of Jews sucking from the teats of a huge sow, while others are engaged in various acts of anal and labial intercourse.

Among the most widely studied delineations of medieval Jews is a thirteenth-century group caricature at the head of a vellum tallage roll in the Public Record Office, London. Here, a rich Jew, portrayed with three faces and identified as Isaac of Norwich, casts his eyes over a busy scene showing the interaction of Jews with devils. The horned demon at its center gestures with an index finger on the pronounced nose tips of both a male and a female Jewish figure. It is a signal both of their Jewishness and of their coalition with the devil, a kind of union sanctioned in hell. The drawing has elicited a variety of different interpretations yet with general consensus that it exemplifies the diabolization of the Jews in the late Middle Ages. Cecil Roth has identified and described several other caricatures of medieval English Jews.

In graphic caricature, an extraordinarily popular form from the eighteenth century, Jews are invariably distinguished by one or more of three main features; namely, their physiognomy, the clothes they wear, and the food they (should not) eat. In addition, they are often portrayed as sexually licentious, and when a caricature contains captions or a title, they are generally shown speaking a guttural lingo that—albeit appallingly—mimics Yiddish. During the same period, in English-speaking countries, the stage Jew also spoke with a similar dialect, which is sometimes referred to as *Jewish gibberish*. A common motif represents Jews as peddlers or street traders who are demonic in their zeal to sell their wares and ever unscrupulous and full of trickery in their dealings. Caricatures of this kind, which were often vended on the street and from the late eighteenth century in print shops, meld actual perceptions of contemporary Jews with traditional antisemitic slurs.

Among the earliest printed caricatures of a Jew, reference should be made to Elias Baeck's portrait of Nathan Hirschel (ca. 1620), president of the Jewish community of Prague (Rubens, no. 1564), one of a series of grotesque dwarflike figures done in the style of the French engraver Jacques Callot (ca. 1592–1635) and published in Augsburg in 1715 as *Il Callotto Resuscitato*. The figure of Hirschel was later copied by an unidentified London engraver to represent Crucible in

Engraving of "A Prospect of the New Jerusalem," 1753. (*Anti-Semitic Stereotypes: A Paradigm of Otherness in English Popular Culture, 1660–1830*, Felsenstein, Frank, Johns Hopkins University Press, p.195)

the alchemical print *Mercurius Sublimate a Chymist, and His Man Crucible*, one of nine engravings in the series *Lilliputian Humorists Drawn as Big as Life* (1730), a copy of which is in the New York Public Library. It is interesting that the London engraver merely borrowed Baeck's figure without any apparent significance given to the fact that the original on which it was based was a Jew. It is only from the middle years of the eighteenth century that the visual depiction of Jews in graphic caricature began to take on instantly recognizable features. What greatly enhanced this perception was the popularity of William Hogarth's prints, which provided important prototypes on which so many later representations of Jews were based, and also the string of caricatures of Jews that were spawned by the heated controversy occasioned by the Jew Bill of 1753. Hogarth abhorred caricature, claiming that his prints were manifestations of human

character, whereas he agreed with Fielding that caricature represented men as monsters. Nevertheless, later caricaturists both in Great Britain and across Western Europe, where his works were frequently reprinted, owe an immeasurable debt to Hogarth (see Hogarth, William for additional illustrations).

What is remarkable and frightening about the plethora of pamphlets, squibs, and prints in opposition to the Jew Bill was the facility with which they were able to reactivate stereotypes of the Jews that may be traced back to the medieval era. It is apparent that many such negative images had remained present in the popular consciousness and only needed a political flare-up to ignite them. A typical caricature in 1753 is *A Prospect of the New Jerusalem* (Rubens, no. 821), an anonymous print that shows a throng of Jews gazing with rapture at St. Paul's Cathedral, which it was imputed would become the chief synagogue once Judaism was established as the new official religion. "Christ save us," implores the caption, "from his Enemies the Jews!" who are depicted in league with the devil in employing their reputed massive wealth to secure political support and to buy up the nation. Another anonymous print, *The Jew Naturilized* (Rubens, no. 827), presents a latter-day version of the Judensau, with the caption "Buy Buy My Pork," mocking the street cries of Jewish peddlers.

After the repeal of the Jew Bill in 1754 and until the 1830 emergence of the protracted campaign to achieve Jewish emancipation, the majority of English caricatures of Jews were cultural and social and only rarely political. Increasingly, caricaturists showed an awareness of the social distinction between impoverished and moneyed Jews, even though both were ultimately perceived as cut from the same fabric. In general, this was also true of their representation in continental Europe. The most prevalent image was that of the heavily bearded and beaked or hook-nosed Jewish peddler, vending his wares from a sack or traveling box and more often than not linked to an underworld of petty larceny, low dealing, and trickery. Habitually, he was portrayed wearing a stack of hats on his head, simultaneously indicating his trade and also perhaps showing discernment of the need for a religious Jew to cover his skull. The wealthy Jew was often represented as an extravagant dandy, stylishly dressed but sometimes with more than a hint that his clothes are past the peak of fashion. In *Beau Mordecai Inspir'd* (Rubens, no. 842; B.M. Cat, no. 4525), a mezzotint published by Carrington Bowles in 1773, we see an excessively foppish Jew outside a fashionable brothel, a prostitute leaning on the windowsill and pointing with her index finger at her nose, the gesture both a sexual enticement and a reminder of his tribal Otherness. Sander Gilman's theories linking sexuality and the Jew's nose provide a useful reference here. The name Beau Mordecai was a common one for a stage Jew, employed among others by Charles Macklin in his farce *Love à la Mode* (1759), where he is derided as "a beau Jew, who, in spite of nature and education, sets up for a wit, a gentleman, and a man of taste." Other prints of the period, particularly works by Thomas Rowlandson, were very explicit in their equation of Jews with sexual depravity.

Of the approximately 20,000 separately published caricatures that appeared in England between 1730 and 1830, perhaps about 300 included depictions of Jews, who featured in the works of such artists as Hogarth, Rowlandson, James Gillray, Richard Newton, George Woodward, and Isaac and George Cruikshank. In the middle years of the nineteenth century, graphic illustration took on a new form with the advent of the satirical magazine *Punch* in 1841. In his later years, George Cruikshank switched from producing single-sheet caricatures and developed into a prolific book illustrator, counting among his commissions the illustrations for Charles Dickens's *Oliver Twist* (1837–1839). His engraving *The Jew & Morris Bolter Begin to Understand Each Other* (see Dickens, Charles for another Cruikshank depiction of Fagin), depicting Fagin striking his nose with his forefinger, reveals an easy familiarity with earlier caricatural portrayals of Jews. Similarly, many traditional antisemitic slurs found graphic reference in *Punch*—for instance, in *The House of Commons According to Mr. Disraeli's Views;* XII, 149, 1847), in which, reflecting the ancient prejudice that, given half an opportunity, the Jews would swamp the nation with their own, John Leech humorously portrayed sellers of old clothes turned Parliamentarians.

This ca. 1620 portrayal of Nathan Hirschel, president of the Jewish community of Prague, strongly influenced later demonizing caricatures of Jews. The emphasis on the figure's prominent beaked nose, shifty eyes, thick lips, and gesticulating hand became standard fare. (Courtesy of The Jewish Museum, London)

The most comprehensive collection of English caricatures is held by the Department of Prints and Drawings at the British Museum. This collection may be supplemented by George IV's collection, which was acquired by the Library of Congress in Washington, D.C., between 1920 and 1921. Two major collections devoted to the representation of the Jews in caricature are those of Alfred Rubens (1903–1998), which he presented shortly before his death to the Jewish Museum, London, and of Israel Solomons (1860–1923), a substantial part of which was acquired by the Library of the Jewish Theological Seminary of America in 1921.

—*Frank Felsenstein*

See also Caricature, Anti-Jewish (Modern); Dickens, Charles; Disraeli, Benjamin; Emancipation; English Literature from Chaucer to Wells; Hogarth, William; Iconography, Christian; Jew Bill; *Judensau;* Pork; *Punch;* Rowlandson, Thomas

References
Felsenstein, Frank. *Anti-Semitic Stereotypes: A Paradigm of Otherness in English Popular Culture, 1660–1830* (Baltimore, MD: Johns Hopkins University Press, 1995).
———. *The Jew as Other: A Century of English Caricature, 1730–1830* (exhibition catalog) (New York: Library of the Jewish Theological Seminary of America, 1995).
Fuchs, Eduard. *Die Juden in der Karikatur* (Munich, Germany: Albert Langen Verlag, 1921).
Gilman, Sander. *The Jew's Body* (New York and London: Routledge, 1991).
Mellinkoff, Ruth. *Outcasts: Signs of Otherness in Northern European Art of the Middle Ages,* 2 vols. (Berkeley and Los Angeles: University of California Press, 1993).
Roth, Cecil. "Portraits and Caricatures of Medieval English Jews." In *Essays and Portraits in Anglo-Jewish History* (Philadelphia: Jewish Publication Society of America, 1962), 22–25.
Rubens, Alfred. *A Jewish Iconography.* Rev. ed. (London: Nonpareil Publishing, 1981).
Stephens, F. G., and M. Dorothy George. *Catalogue of Political and Personal Satires Preserved in the Department of Prints and Drawings in the British Museum,* 11 vols. (in 12) (London: British Museum, 1870–1954).

Caricature, Anti-Jewish (Modern)

The early modern period in general and the Italian Renaissance in particular marked the threshold of the modern tradition of caricaturizing Jews, one branch of which eventually developed into what shall here be termed the *Stürmer* style of caricaturizing Jews and Judaism, after the abusive stereotypic graphic style that came to be identified with the Nazi newspaper *Der Stürmer* (The Stormer). This later, aggressively hostile, but short-lived tradition was an offshoot of an earlier, more general, and less offensive one, though it is not easy for the uninitiated to differentiate between them today.

Depictions of Jews and Judaism were uncommon phenomena in medieval Christian art, and the manner in which they were identified depended on the use of external signs, such as long beards, the Jewish badge, the Jewish hat, and other symbols. Jews could also be identified by negative roles, such as their participation in the flagellation of Jesus on his way to the Crucifixion. But when they fulfilled theologically positive roles, Jews were, as a rule, represented without external signs and with normal and even benevolent facial features. Thus, the depiction of Jews in medieval Christian art depended on their Christological function. This situational portrayal of Jews holds true for modern cartoons and caricatures as well. They are equally dependent on emotional, ideological, and political variables.

From its early modern and Renaissance beginnings, the art of caricature—in Italian, the word literally means "loaded picture"—had frequent recourse to personal parody and abuse. When coupled with social, regional, and ethnic criticism and satire, the art form lent itself easily to the creation and perpetuation of negative pictorial stereotypes, which became ever more well known thanks to the contemporaneous invention and spread of woodcutting, engraving, and printing. Thus, for instance, the European wars of religion beginning in the second half of the sixteenth century supplied both Catholic and Protestant graphic artists with manifold opportunities for creating easily recognizable depictions of the leading protagonists of the enemy camp in the company of the devil.

An early and well-known instance of such demonizing of a Jewish figure was *Nathan Hirschel, Primate of Prague Jewry,* often attributed to Jacques Callot (1592–1635), official court engraver of Louis XIII. The manner in which this prominent Jewish figure was depicted had an enormous impact on future artistic renderings of Jews, particularly the subject's protruding and beaked nose, shifty eyes, thick lips, and gesticulating hand. Callot's portrayal of Hirschel was part of a widely admired series of fifty grotesque figures from the lower depths of society—beggars, cripples, misfits of all types, court jesters, clowns, hawkers, and peddlers. The depicting of Jews grotesquely emerged as a characteristic of times that relished the grotesque. One memorable exception was the work of Rembrandt van Rijn, who frequently portrayed Amsterdam Jews

Je crois qu'ils devront, de gré ou de force, réintégrer leur pays d'origine...

Return of Jews to Palestine, an antisemitic caricature signed by "Bob," a pseudonym of right-wing novelist Gyp (Sybille de Riquetti de Mirabeaau, Comtesse Martel de Janville), 1849–1932. France, early twentieth century. (The Art Archive / Private Collection / Marc Charmet)

in their traditional garb and reveled in depicting both their exotic-Oriental and humane aspects, thereby establishing a minor, competing tradition in the representation of Jewry.

A number of scholars, influenced strongly by the great pioneer collector and publisher of caricatures Eduard Fuchs (1870–1940), have pointed out that the main modern tradition of stereotypic treatment of Jews in Western cartoons and caricatures emerged in German-speaking lands during the decade before and after the Congress of Vienna (1815), a period of upheaval in which both borders and political and social norms changed rapidly. One of these changes was the ease with which some wealthy Jews could now make their entry into the upper ranks of bourgeois and aristocratic society, a phenomenon that called forth immediate, invariably negative comment. One expression of the derision awakened by the social climbing of newly wealthy Jews was

Unser Verkehr (Our Crowd), by K. B. Sessa (1786–1813), a play that packed theaters in this period and presented delighted audiences with a full roster of nouveau riche Jewish figures.

The popularization of Jewish types at all levels of society gathered momentum beginning with the 1830s, thanks to the success of new mass-communication media, especially journals devoted to current affairs. The best known of these was *La Charivari* (Mock Serenade), in which the works of Honoré Daumier (1807–1879) and his competitors were published. These journals published relatively few caricatures of Jews, the exceptions being some of the Rothschilds, members of the richest family in Europe at the time.

But the French periodicals found avid imitators across the Rhine, the most important and influential of which were illustrated weeklies such as the nonpolitical Munich *Fliegende Blätter* (Flying Pages, 1844–1944), the highly politicized

Nazi racial stereotypes of the handsome, blond, healthy young Aryan German worker versus the fat, balding, greedy middle-aged Jewish profiteer. (Mary Evans Picture Library)

Berlin *Kladderadatsch* (loud noise, 1848–1944), and the Viennese *Kikeriki* (Cock-a-doodle-doo), to mention only those blessed by longevity, marked commercial success, and the ability to impress the public with a variety of graphic stereotypes, many of them unmistakably Jewish. These illustrated humor magazines reached audiences of hundreds of thousands and perhaps millions via reading clubs, coffeehouses, pubs, barbershops, and other social facilities. Practically no one could ignore the by now stock Jewish figures that they displayed: impecunious, shabbily dressed *Ostjuden* (eastern European Jews) displaying their own distinguishing signs and speaking a corrupt, Yiddishlike German; peddlers forever seeking to gull the customer; and rural cattle and horse dealers, equivalents of the modern used car salesmen. The most ubiquitous and popular of all was the *Protz,* a flashily dressed and prefer-

ably obese figure in a checkered suit, grotesquely self-satisfied and showing off his newly acquired wealth for all to see and envy; he visibly proclaimed, time and again and in innumerable variations, that money was the sole measure of all social, cultural, and moral values. Jews, given their historical association with money and their very prominent role in banking and finance, were deemed eminently, constantly, and ubiquitously suitable to convey this central message of laissez-faire capitalism.

The most prominent physiognomic aspect connected to this development was the invention of the "Jewish nose." A traditional attribute of otherness and ugliness in general and of disagreeability in particular was attributed to all illustrated Jews: "The idea that a Jew can be identified by means of his peculiarly ugly body structure is a modern and not a medieval one. It

Automobil, Patent Schmul.

Billigſter Betrieb!

Gänzlich gefahrlos¹

193. J. Bahr. **Der Scherer.** Innsbruck. 1900

An example of the Protz, lording it over honest gentile workers and farmers. The caption reads: "Automobile patent Schmul. Cheapest operation! Completely safe!" (Der Scherer [Innsbruck, 1900])

does not reach back longer than the seventeenth century. The development of a physiognomic stigmatization occurred, chronologically speaking, together with the gradual abolition of the Jewish Badge and of discriminatory restrictions concerning special Jewish clothing" (Erb 1985, 120, translated by the author).

The satirical representation of Jews in the modern era did not necessarily entail an ideological antagonism. Periodicals such as *Fliegende Blätter, Kladderadatsch,* and *Kikeriki* unequivocally supported political equality for Jews as well as their assimilation. This support did not, however, preclude the adoption of critical attitudes toward the ridiculous ways that the newly attained political, social, economic, and cultural equality sometimes manifested itself; no doubt, the increase in sales could also act as an inducement to pillory the social incongruities involved in the complicated processes of Jewish assimilation. But in order to evaluate these practices fairly, it is important to remember that Jews were

certainly not the only figures of fun. Others were absent-minded professors, students more inclined to drinking and fighting than to studying, servants who imitated their betters, and many others. The mid-nineteenth century also witnessed the emergence of caricatures and cartoons of national icons such as John Bull, the prototypic Englishman; the sleepy German Michel; and other "national" and "subnational" stereotypes, such as the Bavarians and Prussians. Few readers and commentators took much offense at the frequent use of such graphic stereotypes, presumably because they were an accepted part of a common subculture and considered devoid of malevolent and aggressive intent.

The appearance of antisemitic political parties in the 1880s and 1890s was accompanied by the dissemination of overtly antisemitic caricatures and malevolent representations of Jews that were the precursors of the *Stürmer* tradition. These graphic productions, produced in the short-lived and rather sleazy, antisemitic press, were more belligerent and abusive and—from a graphic point of view—much more primitive than the innocuous fare that had been purveyed for decades and with barely a ripple of protest from any quarter. During the decade or so before World War I, however, political antisemitism began to lose its popular appeal, as exemplified by the rehabilitation of Alfred Dreyfus in France, the acquittal of Mendel Beilis in Russia, and the disintegration of the ineffective antisemitic parties throughout Europe. The general decline of antisemitic politics threw into disrepute the gross graphic representations of Jews and Judaism that it had fostered. *Fliegende Blätter* distanced itself from its own tradition of purveying "Jewish" graphic humor and jokes and gradually decreased the quantity as well as the quality of this material. By contrast, however, *Kladderadatsch,* after shedding most of its original Jewish staff in the 1880s, drew ever closer to the nationalistic and antisemitic camp, and a similar development characterized the *Kikeriki.* The tasteful *Simplicissimus* gradually lost the little interest it had had in the Jewish Question altogether. It is often maintained that historian Heinrich von Treitschke's *A Word about Our Jews* (1880) succeeded in making antisemitism *salonfähig* (eligible for the drawing room) in Germany, but from the perspective of anti-Jewish caricature, his influence did not endure, at least not insofar as the graphic productions of the rabble-rousing antisemitic press were concerned.

Under the auspices of the Third Reich, the *Stürmer* style of antisemitic caricaturing and cartooning enjoyed a brief heyday, although the journal itself—a disreputable, low-circulation weekly throughout the Weimar era—never entirely shook off its reputation for crassness and bad taste. Nevertheless, the Nazi Party and regime simultaneously purveyed it as suitable for the masses. The caricaturing of Jews made its appearance in film as well, notable examples being Veit Harlan's *Jud Süss* and the pseudodocumentary *Der Ewige Jude.* The Nazis invested considerable resources in spreading antisemitic propaganda and stereotypical representations of Jews, including antisemitic comic books, within countries either under their control or under their influence. Two distinguishing features of the Nazified

Stürmer tradition were an emphasis on the threat that sexually predatory Jews posed to virginal Aryan maidens and the threat that "world Jewry" posed to international peace as the result of the Jews' machinations in Washington and Moscow.

The total defeat of Nazi Germany by the Allies, followed by the postwar trials of its criminal leaders, the wide support for the creation of the state of Israel, and, in particular, the growing interest in the Shoah (the Hebrew designation for the Holocaust) in the early 1960s, in effect militated against the use of caricatures identifiable as belonging to the *Stürmer* tradition. This embargo in the mass media of non-Communist Europe was the result of either direct legislation, as in the Federal Republic of (West) Germany, or the pressure of growing public opinion. Right-wing movements and periodicals, including neo-Nazi and neo-Fascist groups, which attempted to revive hypernationalist slogans and programs, refrained, with a few exceptions, from using these types of caricatures. Even Holocaust deniers felt it politic to keep their distance from the deeply discredited *Stürmer* tradition. Apparently, *Stürmer*-type caricatures could not survive in Europe without their Nazi cultural matrix.

The emergence of a viable Jewish state in 1948, its winning of the admiration and sympathy of the international community, and then its fall from grace in many parts of the world has encouraged the production of numerous but conflicting and fluctuating graphic images of the state of Israel, as well as Jews, in the press of Europe and the United States. Whether historical and current criticism of Israel constitutes a continuation of pre–World War II antisemitism is hotly debated today, although insofar as the use of graphic stereotypes is concerned, the absence of *Stürmer*-type cartoons and caricatures seems to indicate that a new phenomenon is at hand.

In the countries of the Soviet bloc and in Soviet Russia in particular, the anti-Zionist policies of the Communist governments after World War II and during the Cold War often employed graphic symbols and stereotypes that were similar to the ones once employed by the Nazis; this practice became more pronounced after the wars conducted by Israel in 1967, 1973, and 1982, and unequivocally supported by the United

States, the archenemy of the Communist bloc. Nevertheless, the similarities between these caricatures of Israel and Zionism and Nazi caricatures of world Jewry are superficial and should not be overemphasized; the discontinuities are as striking as the continuities. Thus, the sexual predator theme was totally absent, and the depiction of Zionism and Israel in the Communist media was wholly subordinated to political and ideological considerations; that is, the state of Israel as a vanguard of expansionist U.S. imperialism (a reversal of the Nazi formula). Analysis of this phenomenon should not be divorced from the context of the harsh propaganda confrontations of the Cold War, which vanished even before the collapse of the USSR.

The use of *Stürmer*-style caricatures and cartoons in the stereotypic depiction of Jews, Judaism, Zionism, and the state of Israel by the Arabic press—and specifically the Palestine press—was once common and endemic, and it was, in all probability, influenced initially by the strong impact that right-wing French and German nationalism, with its component antisemitism, had on the Arabic national movement in its initial stages. The *Protocols of the Elders of Zion* played a malicious role here, and the close connections that the early Zionist movement developed with Great Britain and that Israel subsequently developed with the United States did little to discourage conspiracy theories concerning hidden connections between Western and, in particular, U.S. imperialism, colonialism, and Zionism. Thus, for example, *Stürmer*-like figures have populated the nationalistic Arabic and Palestinian press, replete with sexual tropes; also sometimes present are insinuations that Zionist lobbies have "controlled" the United States by means of Jewish money doled out to U.S. legislators.

—*Henry Wassermann*

See also Antisemitic Political Parties; Anti-Zionism in the USSR; Arab Antisemitic Literature; Auschwitz Lie; Banker, Jewish; Beilis Case; Caricature, Anti-Jewish (Early); Dreyfus Affair; Emancipation; Film Propaganda, Nazi; *Fliegende Blätter;* Iconography, Christian; *Kladderadatsch; Protocols of the Elders of Zion; Punch;* Rothschilds; *Simplicissimus; Stürmer, Der; Word about Our Jews, A*

References

Dittmar, Peter. *Die Darstellung der Juden in der populären Kunst zur Zeit der Emanzipation* (Munich, Germany: K. G. Saur, 1992).

Erb, Rainer. "Die Wahrnehmung der Physiognomie der Juden: Die Nase." In *Das Bild der Juden in der Volks- und Jugendliteratur,* vol. 18, *Jahrhundert bis 1945.* Edited by Heinrich Pleticha (Würzburg, Germany: Königshausen & Neumann, 1985).

Fuchs, Eduard. *Die Juden in der Karikatur* (Munich, Germany: A. Langen, 1921).

Haibl, Michaela. *Zerrbild als Stereotyp: Visuelle Darstellungen von Juden zwischen 1850 und 1900* (Berlin: Metropol, 2000).

Klamper, Elisabeth, ed. *Die Macht der Bilder: Antisemitische Vorurteile und Mythen* (Vienna: Jüdisches Museum, 1995).

Nir, Y. *The Israeli-Arab Conflict in Soviet Caricature, 1967–1973* (Tel Aviv: 1973).

Rohrbacher, Stefan, and Michael Schmidt. *Judenbilder: Kulturgeschichte antijüdischer Mythen und antisemitische Vorurteile* (Reinbek bei Hamburg, Germany: Rowohlt, 1991).

Wassermann, Henry. "The Fliegende Blätter as a Source for the Social History of German Jewry," *Leo Baeck Institute Year Book* 28 (1983): 93–138.

Carto, Willis (1926–)

Willis Carto, a seminal figure in the postwar Holocaust denial movement in the United States, was born in Fort Wayne, Indiana, in 1926. He became involved in various right-wing groups and causes throughout the Midwest at an early age. In 1955, he founded *Right* magazine, followed two years later by the creation of the Liberty Lobby, an umbrella organization for his ultra-right-wing publishing and business interests.

During the 1950s, he closely associated with George Lincoln Rockwell, and although Carto never followed Rockwell into an overt embrace of Nazism, the two collaborated on the creation and dissemination of Holocaust denial material as a conscious strategy to discredit American Jews and the state of Israel. In 1964, Carto acrimoniously parted ways with Rockwell, establishing a pattern of behavior he repeated with many other collaborators.

In 1969, Carto's Noontide Press published *Myth of the Six Million* by David Hoggan, the first major book declaring that the Holocaust was a fabrication concocted by a Jewish-led conspiracy. The Noontide Press soon became the major publisher of antisemitic, revisionist, and racist texts in the United States.

Following Rockwell's murder in 1967, Carto took Rockwell's protégé, William Pierce, under his wing. The former college physics teacher and the American Nazi Party's house intellectual headed the National Youth Alliance (NYA), a Carto creation, and wrote and edited another Carto periodical, *Attack!* Pierce published his infamous apocalyptic novel, *The Turner Diaries,* in installments in *Attack!* In 1979, Carto created and funded the Institute for Historical Review (IHR) as a worldwide center for Holocaust "revisionism." He recruited antisemites with academic credentials in a failed attempt to give the IHR scholarly credibility. The IHR's slick pseudoacademic *Journal of Historical Review* became the clearinghouse for spurious rhetoric and suspicious research specifically designed to confuse the historical memory of the Holocaust. By the late 1980s, however, the board of directors of the IHR became uncomfortable with their benefactor and began to detach the organization from Carto. The ensuing breach turned public and nasty, resulting in an open repudiation of Carto by the organization, although its mission and motives remain indistinguishable from the founder's.

In 1988, Carto moved on to electoral politics. He funded the presidential campaign of former Nazi and Klansman David Duke, whose dismal showing prompted yet another public rupture of relations. Carto remains actively engaged in devising new tactics, schemes, and allies but always aiming at the same target: the Jews.

—*Frederick J. Simonelli*

See also American Nazi Party; Duke, David; Holocaust Denial, Negationism, and Revisionism; Liberty Lobby; Militia Movement; Rockwell, George Lincoln

References

George, John, and Laird Wilcox. *American Extremists, Supremacists, Klansmen, Communists and Others* (Buffalo, NY: Prometheus Books, 1996).

Simonelli, Frederick J. *American Fuehrer: George Lincoln Rockwell and the American Nazi Party* (Champaign: University of Illinois Press, 1999).

Cause of World Unrest, The

The Bolshevik Revolution of 1917 unleashed a multitude of fears in conservative circles in Europe. Such anxieties assumed especially acute proportions in countries such as Germany, which lay close to the new Communist state. The ripples created by the events in Russia also reached Britain, fed by the widespread belief that Bolshevism was Jewish-controlled. In such circumstances, it was no accident that an English-language edition of the *Protocols of the Elders of Zion,* a forgery manufactured in tsarist Russia detailing an alleged Jewish conspiracy to dominate the world, surfaced in Britain in 1920, when it appeared under the title *The Jewish Peril.*

H. A. Gwynne, then editor of the London-based *Morning Post,* took a keen interest in developments unfolding in Russia, and initially, the *Post* had welcomed the "thrilling events" that led to the overthrow of tsardom, believing "the freedom and orderly progress of a great nation" might result. However, as the Bolsheviks seized control, the mood of the paper's editors changed. Its Petrograd correspondent, V. E. Marsden, wrote about "Russian Jews of German extraction" allegedly controlling the country. In Marsden's view, Russia had gone over to "the Government of Tyranny" (in Holmes 1977, 13–21). *The Jewish Peril* appeared against this background in February 1920.

The *Post* treated it as "a very remarkable book" that could not be dismissed as "mere anti-Jewish propaganda" and spent time investigating its claims. That interest became more apparent in a series of articles published between July 12 and July 25, 1920. These essays, which were quickly published by the respectable house of Grant Richards, Ltd., as *The Cause of World Unrest,* were predicated on the belief that, for centuries, there had been "a hidden conspiracy, chiefly Jewish, whose defects had been and are to produce revolution, communism and anarchy, by means of which they hope to arrive at the hegemony of the world by establishing some sort of despotic rule" (*Cause,* VII). Yet the analysis drew back from a full acceptance of the *Protocols.* "It is necessary," Gwynne wrote, "to distinguish . . . between those Jews who have definitely adopted a single nationality and those to whom the Jewish nationality is the only one that counts" (*Cause,* preface).

The Cause of World Unrest gave no clue as to its contributors. But documentary evidence now available reveals that much of the work derived from Ian Colvin, a lead writer on the paper, although he refused to attach his name to it; other journalists on the *Post,* including Gwynne, also contributed, as did the well-known conspiracy theorist Nesta Webster.

On the surface, Gwynne's production suggested a more restrained approach to the existence of a Jewish conspiracy. However, in private, he continued to advance the claims of the *Protocols,* a new translation of which, produced by Marsden, now lay at hand. No matter the public nuances, all such publishing activity reflected the fears awakened by the Russian Revolution, a state of affairs that, in the autumn of 1920, led *The Spectator,* a venerable London periodical, to suggest the need for a royal commission to investigate whether a revolutionary conspiracy involving Jews could be traced.

—*Colin Holmes*

See also Britain; Gwynne, H. A.; Judeo-Bolshevism; *Protocols of the Elders of Zion;* Webster, Nesta
References
Cohn, Norman. *Warrant for Genocide: The Myth of the Jewish World Conspiracy and the "Protocols of the Elders."* New ed. (London: Serif, 1996).
Holmes, Colin. "New Light on the *Protocols of Zion,*" *Patterns of Prejudice* 11 (Nov./Dec. 1977): 13–21.
———. *Anti-Semitism in British Society, 1876–1939* (London: Arnold, 1979).

Céline, Louis-Ferdinand (1894–1961)

One of the twentieth century's most influential novelists, this "crippled giant" (to borrow Milton Hindus's phrase) compromised his renown with virulently antisemitic books in the late 1930s and early 1940s and compounded his disgrace after World War II with stubborn denials of any misconduct.

Born Louis-Ferdinand Destouches to lower-middle-class parents in a Parisian suburb, he was decorated for injuries sustained in World War I. After numerous travels and the completion of medical studies, he worked as a general practi-

tioner. In 1932, under the pen name Céline, he established himself as a major writer with the publication of *Voyage au bout de la nuit* (Journey to the End of the Night). His second novel, *Mort à crédit* (Death on the Installment Plan [1936]), can be seen as a moving but grim working-class companion to Marcel Proust's *Remembrance of Things Past* (1913–1927); like Proust's masterpiece, it chronicles the dying world of nineteenth-century France, revitalizes explorations of the world of the imagination, and revolutionizes novelistic techniques.

Championed *and* attacked across the political spectrum, Céline's critical look at French modernity was initially difficult to classify ideologically. However, in *Bagatelles pour un massacre* (Trifles for a Massacre [1937]), *L'École des cadavres* (The School for Cadavers [1938]), and *Les Beaux draps* (A Fine Mess [1941]), he gave vent to relentless racist tirades. Unavailable in English and long since banned in France (first by the occupying Germans, then by the French, and currently by the Céline estate), these political writings advocated sacrificing the Jews to maintain "peace" with Hitler's Germany. Fueled by exceptional paranoia and hatefulness, this degree of invective is unmatched in the works of any other French author of his stature. Near the end of World War II, Céline joined the Vichy government-in-exile in Sigmaringen, Germany, before fleeing to Copenhagen. In 1951, after protracted legal proceedings and eighteen months in a Danish prison, he returned to France, where he resumed publishing until his death. His postwar production, often loosely autobiographical, sold well but was not up to the standards of his early novels.

The question of how to assess Céline has become almost as controversial as his works. As George Steiner asked, can one be a great novelist while debasing the very values that, in large part, founded the tradition of the novel? No one disputes that the pamphlets are filled with violent, undisguised antisemitic propaganda written at a time when the fate of European Jews was worsening daily. But Céline's highly innovative style, characterized by its breathless slang delirium, ellipses, and misanthropic hyperbole, has muddied the issue. Moreover, attempts to maneuver around Céline's pamphlets have failed. For

Louis-Ferdinand Céline (1894–1961), avant-garde novelist, antisemitc propagandist, and Vichy collaborator. (Photographie Pierre Vals Photomania)

André Gide (writing, it should be noted, in 1938), Céline's ludicrous barrage of abuse was part of a pattern of provocation and was not to be taken seriously. Though an admirer of Céline before the war, Jean-Paul Sartre countered in 1945 that the form did not reduce the nefariousness of the content. Céline's apologists attempted to "sanitize" the author's first two novels by arguing that his rabid antisemitism developed only after his physical and mental health deteriorated in the mid-1930s. Philippe Alméras, however, has proved that Céline's antisemitism predated *Voyage*. The ideological debate about form and content has continued, even as Céline's entry into the hallowed Pléiade collection of great French works has been accomplished. With structuralism's valorization of transgressive discourses in the 1970s, the theorists Philippe Sollers and Julia Kristeva revived Céline's reputation by focusing on textual elements at the expense of sociohistorical context;

however, Philip Watts has undermined this approach by showing the form of Céline's discourse to be consonant with fascist ideology as well.

—*Ralph W. Schoolcraft III*

See also Bardèche, Maurice; Brasillach, Robert; Darquier de Pellepoix, Louis; Fascist Intellectuals; Sartre, Jean-Paul; Vichy

References

Hindus, Milton. *The Crippled Giant: A Literary Relationship with Louis-Ferdinand Céline* (Hanover, NH: University Press of New England, 1950, 1986).

Scullion, Rosemarie, ed. *Céline and the Politics of Difference* (Hanover, NH: University Press of New England, 1995).

Watts, Philip. *Allegories of the Purge* (Stanford, CA: Stanford University Press, 1998).

Center Party

The degree to which the Catholic Center Party of Germany (Zentrumspartei) espoused antisemitism has been a vexing question among historians. The tendency in the new research has been to emphasize the rootedness of antisemitism in Catholic political culture. Even if Catholic Center leaders such as Ludwig Windthorst, Ernst Lieber, and Matthias Erzberger defended the rights of Jews as a religious minority, it is nevertheless true that their electoral base expressed resentment against Jews. The second point of contention among historians is whether the antisemitism of the Catholic Center was religiously based and therefore more properly called anti-Judaism or whether it assumed a secular tint of racial exclusion, with antisemitism thus being its proper name. Here, too, the tendency of recent research has underscored how Catholic antipathy had, by the 1890s, become infused with racial images and arguments.

During the *Kulturkampf* (struggle for civilization) of the 1870s, important Center leaders, among them Franz von Ballestrem and Peter Reichensperger, publicly announced their party's opposition to "liberals, Freemasons, and Jews." This constellation of enemies suggests that during the Kulturkampf, Catholic antisemitism remained entangled in a defensive political stance. Yet the end of the Kulturkampf in 1878 did not end this defensive posture, nor did it still antisemitic sentiments. Instead, leading Catholic newspapers, such as *Germania,* continued to propagate prejudice. So, too, did the nascent Catholic peasant associations and the local branches of the largest organization of the Center Party, the Volksverein für das katholische Deutschland (People's Association for Catholic Germany), established in 1890. As the Center Party increasingly reached out to the working classes and competed with independent trade unions, it was also not above denouncing the competition as "Jewish."

World War I brought about a significant change in the politics of antisemitism. If at first Jewish sacrifice for the fatherland silenced antisemites, they once again became vocal as the war dragged on and casualties mounted. A new antisemitism—shrill, uncompromising, and vitriolic—emerged. The Center Party and its constituents did not participate in this new antisemitism as readily as conservatives and even liberals did. Under the leadership of Matthias Erzberger, the party came to stand for relative moderation and a negotiated peace. It also maintained distance from the antisemitic measures of the government and the rancorous demands of the Fatherland Party, newly constituted in 1917. Much the same may be said of the Center during the Weimar Republic. By the early 1930s, the constituency of the Catholic Center more readily resisted the incursions of the National Socialists than any other major group. Less clear and more doubtful is whether Nazi antisemitism played a role in bringing forth this resistance. When the Center dissolved itself in July 1933, it was in order to protect Catholic interests. Its opportunistic defense of religious minorities, including Jews, had not developed into an article of faith or of principle. That was the tragedy of the Center, a burden it did not carry alone.

—*Helmut Walser Smith*

See also Antisemitic Political Parties; Boniface Society for Catholic Germany; German Peasant League; *Kulturkampf;* Papacy, Modern; Ratzinger, Georg; *Talmud Jew, The;* Ultramontanism; Vatican Council, First; Weimar

References

Blaschke, Olaf. *Katholizismus und Antisemitismus im Deutschen Kaiserreich* (Göttingen, Germany: Vandenhoeck & Ruprecht, 1997).

Mazura, Uwe. *Zentrumspartei und Judenfrage 1870–1933: Verfassungsstaat und Minderheitenschutz* (Mainz, Germany: Matthias-Gruenewald, 1994).

Central Association of German Citizens of Jewish Faith

The founding of the Central Association of German Citizens of Jewish Faith (Centralverein deutscher Staatsbürger jüdischen Glaubens [CV]) on March 26, 1893, took place in response to a new wave of antisemitism in the early 1890s. The antisemitic political parties had launched an aggressive campaign aimed at overthrowing Jewish emancipation; the prestigious Conservative Party had adopted an antisemitic plank in its Tivoli Program in December 1892, and there had been disturbing instances of electoral alliances between fringe antisemites and mainstream National Liberals and German Conservatives, especially in Prussia. In the context of this renewed threat to Jewish civil equality, the journalist Raphael Löwenfeld published a pamphlet entitled *Protected Jews or Citizens?* (*Schutzjuden oder Staatsbürger?*) that admonished Jews not to go begging for protection from the state, as in the past, but to demand their constitutionally guaranteed rights. Löwenfeld's call for self-defense and the already existing League against Antisemitism (Abwehr-Verein), composed largely of liberal Christians, convinced German Jews to form their own organization.

The founding of the CV was not only an act of self-defense, however. It represented something of a public admission on the part of German Jews that neither social integration nor legal equality had been truly achieved. In spite of formal guarantees, Jewish emancipation was far from a practical reality. Positions in the administrations of the Reich, individual states, and municipalities, as well as in the army, judiciary, diplomatic corps, and universities, were routinely denied to Jews. These exclusionary practices were especially insulting given the contributions of highly acculturated Jewish intellectuals and politicians to the founding of the Reich.

From its beginnings, the CV sought effectively to represent the members of the Jewish religious communities of the German Empire. Its claim to do so, however, could never be fully realized. Lower-class Jews, many of them traditionally observant, were inadequately represented. The younger generation opted for Zionism or socialism. The great majority of CV members consisted of middle- and upper-middle-class, religiously liberal Jews, who identified themselves as unreservedly German. Even though the organization became the largest Jewish voluntary association in Germany, it included only a little more than 10 percent of all those who acknowledged Judaism as their religious denomination.

The CV conducted its activities on many fronts. It fought ideological and political antisemitism, educated the German public about Judaism and Jewish history, worked to strengthen the self-confidence of German Jews, and sought to enhance their German identity. One of its most important initiatives was to combat antisemitic candidates at election time, with campaign meetings and lectures and by throwing its weight behind countercandidates who would, it was hoped, defend Jewish rights in the Reichstag and state parliaments. The politics of the CV was essentially left-liberal, although from 1903, it also began, reluctantly, to consider Social Democratic candidates as worthy alternatives to antisemites. The CV also produced an impressive array of apologetic literature: a newspaper, large-circulation pamphlets, brochures, placards, and stickers. All these and the independent research financed by the organization were designed to counter the propaganda of the antisemites and committed to upholding the values of rational discourse in German political life.

The CV commitment to rational politics somewhat limited its understanding of antisemitism; official pronouncements continued to privilege socioeconomic analyses of the phenomenon while underestimating the strength of its irrational emotional and psychological appeal. Despite the abundant evidence that antisemites did not often respond to reasoned argument, the CV remained dedicated to the belief in a cure for antisemitism, one that could only be achieved through enlightenment and patient education. Another shortcoming of the organization was its insistence on demonstrating the exemplary patriotism of German Jews. Although the CV opposed German imperialist policies before World War I, it welcomed the chance to demonstrate its loyalties to the nation once the war began. The excesses of this stance, sincere though it was for most members, alienated some Jews of the younger generation who saw such "superpatriotism" as too craven and undignified. This generational and ideological conflict, one of many inner tensions in the Jewish community, resulted in a hostile relationship between German Zionists and the CV, preventing German Jewry from forming a united front against its enemies.

The democratic Weimar Republic that was born out of the upheavals of war and revolution brought de jure and de facto equality into line for Jews, but the rise of the National Socialist German Workers' Party (NSDAP) was met with much the same response from the CV as before the war. The dire threat posed by the Nazis, however, did, in 1929, produce a more concentrated response; a CV propaganda campaign of great scope that targeted the Hitler movement exclusively. This new departure necessitated a close alliance with the democratic representatives of German socialism. Only the dangers posed by Nazism could bring about such a reorientation of the CV, an organization that had remained essentially bourgeois in politics and outlook. Notwithstanding this opening to the Left, the CV remained largely isolated. Its partial legal successes in the prosecution of Nazi leaders and other antisemites and its continuing public enlightenment efforts did not significantly alter German politics in the desired direction.

After Hitler was named chancellor in January 1933, the organization adapted to the new regime as best it could, hoping, like many other Germans, that Nazi antisemitism would moderate now that the party had attained power. By September 1933, the situation of the Jews had deteriorated rapidly; the various Jewish organizations were forced to band together in the Reich Representation of German Jews (Reichsvertretung der deutschen Juden), under the leadership of Leo Baeck, and with the CV as its strongest constituent member. Even as it came under Gestapo surveillance, the CV continued to preach the virtues of assimilation and the need to maintain a Jewish presence in Germany. The leadership finally abandoned this position in November 1936 and began recommending emigration. In November 1938, the CV was dissolved.

—*Gregor Hufenreuter*
Richard S. Levy, translation

See also Alliance Israélite Universelle; American Jewish Committee and Antidefamation Efforts in the United States; Antisemitic Political Parties; Court Jews; Emancipation; League against Antisemitism; National Socialist German Workers' Party; Nazi Legal Measures against Jews; Tivoli Program; Zionism

References

Barkai, Avraham. *Wehr Dich! Der Centralverein deutscher Staatsbürger jüdischen Glaubens (C.V.) 1893–1938* (Munich, Germany: Beck, 2002).
Pätzold, Kurt. "Centralverein deutscher Staatsbürger jüdischen Glaubens e.V. (CV) 1893–1938." In *Lexikon zur Parteiengeschichte: Die bürgerlichen und kleinbürgerlichen Parteien und Verbände in Deutschland (1789–1945).* Edited by Dieter Fricke. 4 vols. (Cologne, Germany: Pahl-Rugenstein, 1983), 1: 418–426.

Chamberlain, Houston Stewart (1855–1927)

Houston Stewart Chamberlain, the son of a British admiral, became the most influential publicist of Germanic supremacy and racial antisemitism in Germany in the two decades preceding World War I. His major work, the two-volume *Die Grundlagen des neunzehnten Jahrhunderts* (1899–1900) (translated as *The Foundations of the Nineteenth Century* in 1912), sold 100,000 copies by 1914 and was reissued in twenty-eight editions by 1938. A confidant of Kaiser Wilhelm II, with whom he corresponded for over twenty years, and an early supporter of Hitler, Chamberlain personified the ideological link between the radical nationalism of the late Wilhelmian empire and the revolutionary extremism of the Nazis.

After the early death of his mother, Chamberlain was raised in France in the home of his aunt. A secure inheritance relieved him of the necessity of working for a living. His doctoral studies in botany at the University of Geneva ended abruptly, however, when he suffered a nervous breakdown in 1884. Enamored of Wagnerian music dramas and of German culture in general, he moved to Dresden in 1885, where he made the acquaintance of Richard Wagner's widow, Cosima. From 1889 to 1908, Chamberlain lived in Vienna, where he wrote the works that would make him famous: a Wagner biography published in 1896 and the 1,014-page *Foundations*. After divorcing his wife in 1906, Chamberlain married Wagner's daughter, Eva Bülow, and settled in Bayreuth in a home adjacent to Wagner's Villa Wahnfried. There, he completed his other major works, including a biography of Johann Wolfgang von Goethe in 1912. In 1916, at the height of the war, in which he supported the German cause in numerous militant pamphlets, he became a German citizen. Chamberlain lent his approval to the Hitler-Ludendorff putsch in 1923. After 1933, he was celebrated as the "seer of the Third Reich."

Chamberlain's extraordinarily successful *Foundations* appealed to German nationalist attitudes and prejudices that were already pervasive at the turn of the century. Written in a suave style that flattered an educated readership, the *Foundations* captured the buoyant, expansionist mood of Wilhelmian imperialism at the turn of the century. Not only did the book attribute all the great cultural achievements of the past 2,000 years to members of the Germanic race (broadly defined to include such non-Germans as Marco Polo, Shakespeare, Dante, Giotto, Leonardo da Vinci, and Lavoisier), it also exhorted Germans to pursue their divinely appointed mission of regenerating (and dominating) the world through their superior culture and spirituality.

Chamberlain interpreted all history since the death of Christ as a continuing conflict between the "Aryan-Christian worldview" and "Jewish materialism," to which he attributed the alleged degeneration of modern times. Like Richard Wagner and the French racial theorist Joseph Arthur de Gobineau, whose ideas on race he appropriated, Chamberlain viewed such aspects of modernization as industrialization, rationalization, secularization, and the growth of democracy and egalitarianism as symptoms of decline. His message, however, was optimistic. By adhering to laws of racial purity, avoiding western European influences, developing a specifically German national religion, and suppressing the subversive influence of Jews, Germans could reverse the supposedly regressive course of the nineteenth century and assume the role of leading world power in the twentieth. Despite its scholarly trappings and erudite references, the *Foundations* was intended not as a work of scholarship but as a call to action. Chamberlain claimed the artistic prerogative of shaping historical material to produce an inspirational work, thus disarming in advance those critics who insisted that his speculations on race failed to meet the rational standards of science.

In this version of history, the Germanic peoples and the Jews were the principal heirs of the brilliant civilizations of ancient Greece and Rome, whose decline resulted from racial mixing. Germans and Jews were locked in a struggle to determine the future course of the world. Typically exaggerating Jewish power and homogeneity, Chamberlain regarded Jews with a mixture of grudging admiration, anger, and fearful disdain.

The success of the Jews, despite their small numbers, lay in racial cohesion maintained through stringent marriage laws that Germans would have to emulate if they hoped to win the life-and-death struggle for global domination.

Chamberlain's description of Jews as mercenary, calculating, and self-seeking rehearsed familiar nineteenth-century stereotypes. In contrast to the Aryans' inward search for a meaning in life, Jews idolized the will that enabled them to seize external possessions and power. Jews supposedly pursued only material advantage—unlike Germans, who adhered to ideal goals at the cost of material comforts.

Chamberlain's celebrity status and consequent baleful influence can hardly be overstated. More than any other book, the *Foundations* helped to make antisemitism respectable among educated people. Nationalists esteemed its exaltation of Germanic superiority, conservatives appreciated its defense of tradition, and religious believers valued its affirmation of spiritual values. (Chamberlain helped to popularize the notion that Jesus had not been a Jew.) Among its most enthusiastic admirers was Wilhelm II, who distributed copies to members of his court and to officers in the army. Even critics who recognized the speciousness of his racial doctrine were captivated by the grand sweep of his historical imagination. The prominent American historian Carl Becker labeled it a book of great value. The Austrian writer Karl Kraus, who shared a hostility toward liberalism, invited Chamberlain to contribute to his iconoclastic journal *Die Fackel* (The Torch).

Aware of the lack of scientific evidence for his racial doctrine, Chamberlain denied that the concept of race required precise definition. He claimed race was an easily observable fact, like the colors blue or red, that could only be described but not explained. In the absence of objective criteria, he resorted to the subjective *consciousness* of race as the ultimate test of racial purity. For Chamberlain and his many followers and imitators, racialism served the ideological function of mobilizing Germans for the nationalist and imperialist cause. By insisting that right thinking was racially determined, Chamberlain could harness the prestige of Darwinian biology to conservative, monarchist goals. A generation later, one of his fervent admirers, the Nazi ideologue Alfred Rosenberg, attempted to develop a German religion of race in *The Myth of the Twentieth Century* (1929). Although it is hard to believe that Chamberlain would have approved of the Nazi genocide of the Jews, there is no denying that his works played a crucial role in creating the mental climate in which such barbarism could occur.

—*Roderick Stackelberg*

See also Bayreuth Circle; Gobineau, Joseph Arthur de; Kraus, Karl; Lagarde, Paul de; Lienhard, Friedrich; *Myth of the Twentieth Century, The;* Racism, Scientific; Rosenberg, Alfred; Wagner, Richard

References
Field, Geoffrey G. *Evangelist of Race: The Germanic Vision of Houston Stewart Chamberlain* (New York: Columbia University Press, 1981).
Lukács, Georg. *The Destruction of Reason.* Translated by Peter Palmer (Atlantic Highlands, NJ: Humanities Press, 1981).
Schüler, Winfred. *Der Bayreuther Kreis von seiner Entstehung bis zum Ausgang der wilhelminischen Ära: Wagnerkult und Kulturreform im Geiste völkischer Weltanschauung* (Münster, Germany: Aschendorff, 1971).
Stackelberg, Roderick. *Idealism Debased: From Völkisch Ideology to National Socialism* (Kent, OH: Kent State University Press, 1981).

Chesterton, G. K. (1874–1936)

A British man of letters and an anticapitalist conservative, the Anglican Chesterton converted to Catholicism in 1922, under the influence of his longtime collaborator Hilaire Belloc. As early as 1908, however, his book *Orthodoxy* had made the case for a fixed body of doctrine like that of the Roman Catholic Church. In the twentieth century, Ronald Knox, Dorothy Sayers, Graham Greene, Evelyn Waugh, C. S. Lewis, Hugh Kenner, and Marshall McLuhan were among many Christian writers and scholars influenced by Chesterton, and one contemporary Catholic intellectual who gratefully acknowledges a debt to Chesterton's theology is Garry Wills. In his own time, however, Chesterton was also known as a polemical journalist, and it was primarily in his journalism that he articulated his antisemitic ideas.

G. K. Chesterton never changed his mind about the Jews. Until the end of his career, he regarded them as a theological evil, endlessly reenacting their primal sin. (George Grantham Bain Collection, Library of Congress)

About the Jews, Chesterton's position was fixed from the beginning of his career to the end. He regarded them as a theological evil, endlessly reenacting their primal sin. So, for instance, he reacted to news of the suicide of one of the protagonists in the Dreyfus Affair with a poem, "To a Certain Nation," that interpreted the event as a second and worse coming of crime into the world.

> Though cowed by crashing thunders from
> all heaven,
> Cain never said, "My brother slew himself."

Likewise, some of Chesterton's articles about England's 1912–1913 Marconi scandal (in which four high-ranking government officials, two of them Jewish, were accused of using privileged information to make money in the stock market) amounted to religious pleas for Jewish blood. Out of any proportion to the gravity of the crime, the rhetoric of Chesterton's Jew phobia extended backward in history from the immediate situation to medieval denunciations of usury and from there backward to the prophetic cadences of the Bible itself. But it also partook of modern racist antisemitism. Addressing an open letter to one of the Jewish officials a full six years after the affair, Chesterton dropped dark hints about the workings of what he called the Jewish International and warned: "My fancy . . . is but one of many attempts I have made to imagine and allow for an alien psychology in this matter; and if you, and Jews far worthier than you, are wise they will not dismiss as Anti-Semitism what may well prove the last serious attempt to sympathise with Semitism" (Coren 1989, 198).

This passage was a representative item from the Chesterton bibliography. More important, however, it was a representative (if extreme) item from the bibliography of the Jew in English literature. As George Orwell observed in his 1945 essay "Anti-Semitism in Britain," literary Jew-hatred was simply the norm down the centuries from Chaucer to Hitler:

> And however little the average intellectual may have agreed with the opinions of Belloc and Chesterton, he did not acutely disapprove of them. Chesterton's endless tirades against Jews, which he thrust into stories and essays upon the flimsiest pretexts, never got him into trouble— indeed Chesterton was one of the most generally respected figures in English literary life. Anyone who wrote in that strain *now* would bring down a storm of abuse upon himself, or more probably would find it impossible to get his writings published. (*The Collected Essays, Journalism and Letters of George Orwell,* 1971, 3: 385)

Sixty years later, Orwell's argument still holds. In terms of the etiquette governing the word *Jew,* Chesterton was a man of his time, and it took the catastrophe of the Holocaust to make that etiquette change. In the aftermath of the change, Chesterton's continuing influence guarantees that his work will continue to be a primary resource for the history of antisemitism in Christian literature.

—*Jonathan Morse*

See also Belloc, Hilaire; Dreyfus Affair; English Literature from Chaucer to Wells; English Literature of the Twentieth Century; *Protocols of the Elders of Zion;* Usury

References
Coren, Michael. *Gilbert: The Man Who Was G. K. Chesterton* (London: Cape, 1989).
Sprug, Joseph W. *An Index to G. K. Chesterton* (Washington, DC: Catholic University of America Press, 1966).

Chmielnicki Massacres (1648–1649)

Bogdan Chmielnicki (or, as transliterated from the Cyrillic alphabet, Khmelnitsky [1595–1657] led the Cossack and Ukrainian peasant uprising between 1648 and 1649 against Polish rule in the Ukraine, wreaking havoc on hundreds of Jewish communities in the process. Traditional Jewish commentary placed "Chmiel the Wicked" in the ranks of Amalek and Haman— symbols of absolute evil and boundless, irrational hatred for Jews. Chmielnicki and his followers committed acts of appalling cruelty against Jews, although the Catholic Poles were the main enemy for him and his followers. Jews were attacked as allies of the Poles, since they often served as administrators of the estates of the Polish nobles.

To term these massacres antisemitic is problematic, not only in the obvious sense that Jews were not attacked because of their "Semitic race" (a concept that would have had no meaning at the time) but also even in the looser, more all-encompassing use of the term *antisemitic.* The hatred expressed by Cossacks and Ukrainian peasants seems to have emerged primarily from "real" or "normal" resentments over economic exploitation and from nationalistic fervor, as distinguished from a Christian hatred deriving from fantasies about Jews and an irrational demonization of them that had little relation to Jewish activity in the real world. That Jews were known to consider the Ukrainian peasants to be a lower form of humanity, little better than beasts of the field, no doubt stoked hatred for them, but such attitudes were hardly restricted to the Jews; they were the norm among the Polish, as well as the Russian, upper classes. Resentment found expression in religious terms, in that Jews were threatened with death if they would not convert to Christianity and synagogues were desecrated, but Christians acted with comparable cruelty and brutality to other Christians; Catholic priests were a special target of Chmielnicki and his Orthodox Christian followers. Still, the Jews, since they were the immediate agents of the Polish ruling classes in the exploitation of the Ukrainian peasants and were more numerous than either the nobility or the clergy, were often first in line, as it were, for violent retribution. It was a brutal age, one in which religious identities were closely linked to social and economic position, and in the end, it is impossible to untangle religion from other factors.

Contemporary Jewish accounts of the massacres placed the numbers of Jewish dead at around 100,000, a figure that mounted in subsequent accounts to hundreds of thousands. But most recent historians have scaled back considerably the probable number of deaths, in part simply because the population of Jews in the eighteenth century could not possibly have risen to the levels it did in Ukrainian and Polish lands if there had indeed been a mid-seventeenth-century massacre in which a major part of the Jewish population (which totaled approximately 350,000) was killed. Nonetheless, contemporary Jews considered the Chmielnicki massacres to be the third great destruction of the Jewish people, the greatest since ancient times, and a devastating blow to Jewish life in the area. Refugees clogged adjoining lands, and migration out of the Ukraine became more the norm than migration into it, as had been the case since the late Middle Ages (although, clearly, large numbers of refugees returned once the uprising had subsided). The messianic movement of Shabbetai Zevi that swept the area in the years after the massacres was no doubt influenced by them, although modern scholars differ in how powerful the impact was; some see the massacres as a gruesome but brief and not terribly significant interruption in the remarkably steady growth and expansion of Polish Jewry in the eighteenth, nineteenth, and early twentieth centuries.

It is revealing that Jewish deaths in the Chmielnicki massacres, whatever their actual numbers, were little noted in the histories subsequently written by Ukrainians, Poles, or Russians. For Ukrainians in the twentieth century, Chmielnicki became a national hero. He may, then, be counted as an example of how one people's villain is another's hero, one people's tragedy another's triumph.

—*Albert S. Lindemann*

See also Haman; Poland; Russian Orthodox Church; Shabbetai Zevi
References
Hanover, Nathan. *Abyss of Despair / Yeven Metzulah: The Famous 17th Century Chronicle Depicting Jewish Life in Russia and Poland during the Chmielnicki Massacres.* Translated by A. Mesch and edited by William B. Helmreich (New Brunswick, NJ: Transaction Books, 2002).
Israel, Jonathan I. *European Jewry in the Age of Mercantilism,* 2nd ed. (Oxford: Clarendon Press, 1989).

Christian Identity Movement

Christian Identity, a twentieth-century variation of British Israelism, was adapted to the antisemitic beliefs of those in the United States who sought a theological justification for their hatred of Jews.

Philosemitic and benign, British Israelism held that Anglo-Saxons were one of the ten lost tribes of Israel. The sect had a small following, some of whom migrated to Brooklyn, New York, in the late nineteenth century. In the 1920s, William Cameron, a protégé and employee of Henry Ford, seized on the core belief of British Israelism and from it reasoned that members of the Anglo-Saxon race were the true chosen people of God. Using that justification, he concluded that people who called themselves Jews and claimed to be God's chosen people were imposters and frauds. Another prominent American antisemite, Gerald B. Winrod, the "Jayhawk Nazi," followed suit. Christian Identity theology proved a potent recruitment tool for politically motivated antisemites, for antisemitism could now be theologically justified and clothed in religious values. (Christian Identity is not, however, recognized by any other denomination as a valid expression of Christianity.)

Wesley Swift, a former California Ku Klux Klan organizer and son of a Methodist minister, was the dominant figure in elaborating and organizing the Christian Identity movement in the United States in the 1940s. Swift integrated racial purity into Christian Identity doctrine. In the 1950s, he recruited Richard Girnt Butler, a former member of William Dudley Pelley's pro-Nazi Silver Shirt Legion, who quickly became his chief aide and most devoted adherent. As Swift aged, Butler took greater control of the Christian Identity movement, which, by the early 1960s, consisted of dozens of affiliated congregations across the country, with concentrations in the West and Southeast. Adding to Swift's introduction of racial purity to Christian Identity theology, Butler further refined the idea by designating Jews as the literal spawn of Satan.

In collaboration with George Lincoln Rockwell, Butler worked to merge neo-Nazi politics with Christian Identity religion, believing, as did Rockwell, that Americans' affinity for Christianity and Christian symbolism would be useful in the popularization of Nazi political beliefs and lay the groundwork for eventual electoral success.

—*Frederick J. Simonelli*

See also American Nazi Party; *Dearborn Independent* and *The International Jew*; Ku Klux Klan; Militia Movement; Pelley, William Dudley; Philosemitism; Rockwell, George Lincoln; Winrod, Gerald B.

References

Aho, James A. *The Politics of Righteousness: Idaho's Christian Patriotism* (Seattle: University of Washington Press, 1990).

Barkun, Michael. *Religion and the Racist Right: The Origins of the Christian Identity Movement* (Chapel Hill: University of North Carolina Press, 1994).

Christian Social Party (Austria)

The Christian Social Movement in Austria began organizing in the 1880s, mainly in reaction against the politically dominant liberals. Catholicism and loyalty to the Habsburg dynasty provided the basis for the movement; its general objective was to adapt modern economic and technological innovations to the premodern corporate society that most members believed to be the ideal. In 1891, the movement created the Christian Social Party to represent its values and pursue its goals on the political stage. In the urban sphere, it was predominantly the lower middle class that was attracted by the idea of a traditional corporate order, seeing in it a guarantee of protection from the market economy, industrialization, and the resultant influence of the proletariat. In the countryside, a majority of the peasantry came to regard the movement as a bulwark against secularization and the decline of agriculture. In both rural and urban areas, the lower clergy played the major leadership role. The party was less successful in attracting workers, the vast majority of whom supported the Social Democrats.

Antisemitism was central to the party's ideology. Jews were regarded as representatives of capitalism and cultural liberalism and, as such, antagonistic to Christianity. Christian Social rhetoric stigmatized liberal economics as the work of the "Jewish-liberal Manchester party." It portrayed the Liberal and Social Democratic Parties as the creatures of Jewish patronage and the "Jewish" press. The Hungarian elites, supposedly much too beholden to Jewish influence, provided another opportunity for the Christian Socials to vent their antisemitism. The so-called Judeo-Magyar clique was corrupt, disloyal (secessionist), and oppressive to the non-Magyar peoples in Hungary, according to the electoral manifesto of 1907.

The Christian Social Party rose to dominance in Vienna in the 1890s. Its charismatic leader, Karl Lueger, ruled the capital between 1897 and his death in 1910, borne aloft by his adoring Christian Social following. Mayor Lueger's masterful exploitation of antisemitic emotions later won him rare praise from Adolf Hitler, who witnessed his methods firsthand while living in the capital and later wrote about the "greatest German mayor" in *Mein Kampf*.

After 1918, in response to the influx of Jews from the former eastern territories of the defunct Habsburg Empire, the Christian Social Party strengthened its identity as a German Catholic party by opposing immigration and naturalization in order to preserve what it saw as the German character of Vienna. Jews, the Viennese Christian Social Party program of 1919 said, were a separate nationality. Jewish children

"German Christians, Vote Christian-Social, Save Austria!" says this election poster. The two-headed eagle symbolizing the Austro-Hungarian monarchy is here replaced by a serpent and a vulture with stereotypical Jewish features. (Courtesy of Richard S. Levy)

should be sent to separate schools or put in segregated classrooms, to guarantee German youth a proper Christian education. In Linz in 1923, the Christian Workers of Austria called on their compatriots to overcome the corrosive influence of Jewry in the intellectual and economic life of the German people. In 1926, the new party program declared: "The nationally minded Christian Socials demand the cultivation of the German way and fight the predominance of subversive Jewish influence in the fields of the intellect and the economy."

The focus of the Christian Socials' antisemitic discourse was not racist but rather economic and cultural, insinuating a distinct Jewish mind, values, and behavior, incompatible with Christianity or Germanness. In Austria's First Republic (1918–1938), the Christian Social Party was a major force, usually providing the country with

its federal chancellor. It is fair to say that the Christian Social Party was successful in establishing its brand of antisemitism as a central element of Austrian political culture both before and after World War I. The party continued until September 1934, when the launching of the "corporate state" led to its voluntary dissolution. However, its influence on Austrian antisemitism lived on.

—*Werner Suppanz*

See also Austria; Hitler, Adolf; "Jewish" Press; Lueger, Karl; *Mein Kampf;* *Ostjuden;* Vogelsang, Karl von

References

Boyer, John W. *Culture and Political Crisis in Vienna: Christian Socialism in Power, 1897–1918* (Chicago: University of Chicago Press, 1995).

Suppanz, Werner. *Österreichische Geschichtsbilder: historische Legitimationen in Ständestaat und zweiter Republik* (Cologne, Germany: Böhlau Verlag, 1998).

Christian Social Party (Germany)

In 1878, the Christian Social Worker's Party was founded by the court chaplain of the Hohenzollerns, Adolf Stoecker, in order to counteract the materialistic and "unpatriotic" socialist party and win workers back to conservative and Christian values. The Christian Social Party (CSP), as it was renamed in early 1881, only gained electoral support when it added antisemitism to its political platform. A core element of the Berlin Movement (1881–1886) and a political partner of the German Conservatives (1881–1896), the party played a crucial role in mobilizing mass support for antisemitism during the early 1880s. Its followers, however, were not the workers who solidly stood against Stoecker's socially conservative program but the *Mittelstand*—lower-middle-class shopkeepers, artisans, civil servants, traders—social strata that had suffered in the economic downswing of the mid-1870s and who were receptive to the antiliberal and anticapitalist message of the new antisemitic movement. After Stoecker addressed the Jewish Question for the first time in a public speech on September 19, 1879, he began to win a mass audience. Up to 3,000 men gathered to listen to the "tribune of the people." No other conservative politician could attract such crowds.

Antisemitism also paid off at the polls. It is true that the Berlin Movement never came close to unseating the solid majority of liberals and socialists in the German capital, but the numbers of conservative votes increased in Berlin, from 14,000 in 1878 to 46,000 in 1881 and 56,000 in 1884. It was Stoecker's appeal to the Mittelstand and his ability to obtain votes that convinced skeptics within the conservative camp that the CSP could be a useful ally, despite its "socialist" rhetoric. Influential figures, such as the later Kaiser Wilhelm II and the Prussian minister of the interior, Robert von Puttkamer, were among Stoecker's patrons. The position of the CSP as an independent political group within the German Conservative Party nevertheless caused friction, as its "democratic" and social orientation was met with suspicion by a party serving the interests of the big landowners. When Otto von Bismarck, between 1887 and 1890, based his domestic policies on an alliance between Conservatives and National Liberals, Stoecker's populist activities were curbed and the CSP lost political influence. After Stoecker's dismissal as court chaplain in 1890 and his exclusive focus on party activities thereafter, the CSP was able to shape the politics of the German Conservatives for a short time, most notably with the antisemitic Tivoli Program of 1892.

In the long run, however, the differences between the reactionary conservative establishment, on the one side, and the young and genuinely reformist (and not antisemitic) Christian Socialists, such as Helmuth von Gerlach and Friedrich Naumann, on the other, were irreconcilable. In the end, Stoecker lost the support of both elements: most young members left the CSP in favor of the newly founded Nationalsozialer Verein (National Social League), and the alliance with the German Conservatives broke off in 1896. The reorganized CSP never regained its former significance, although it was still represented in the Reichstag between 1898 and 1912 with one to three seats. In 1907, the party only had 9,000 members. After the Revolution of 1918, the CSP merged into the German National People's Party.

—*Christhard Hoffmann*

See also Berlin Movement; Christian Social Party (Austria); German National People's Party; Henrici, Ernst; *Our Demands on Modern Jewry;* Stoecker, Adolf; Tivoli Program
References
Fricke, Dieter, ed. "Christlich-soziale Partei." In *Lexikon zur Parteiengeschichte.* 4 vols. (Leipzig, Germany: VEB Bibliographisches Institut Leipzig, 1983-1986), 1: 440–454.
Massing, Paul W. *Rehearsal for Destruction: A Study of Political Antisemitism in Imperial Germany* (New York: Harper and Brothers, 1949).

Christian State

An important concept among German conservatives during the nineteenth century, the "Christian state" ideal was often deployed to justify the exclusion of German Jews from full civil and political rights, but it also carried broader implications. The idea was, in fact, a central pillar of the emerging conservative political ideology in this period, reflecting the revival of Christian religiosity among conservatives as well as their rejection of the secular liberal vision of politics associated with the Enlightenment and the French Revolution. As part of their defense of monarchical rule and traditional society, conservatives typically opposed any decoupling of church and state and insisted on the religious basis of political institutions. Conservatives also wanted to preclude the participation in politics and government of those deemed agents of secular liberalism, including deists, atheists, certain Protestant and Catholic sects, and—of most significance here—German Jews.

Conservatives' support for traditional religious values in political life thus also determined their stance on the so-called Jewish Question. Ideally, conservatives hoped to see Jews achieve emancipation by converting to Christianity, but many remained skeptical of this possibility and wanted Jews kept in their present civic status—tolerated but separate and subordinate. Some amelioration of Jewish civil rights might be allowed, but on political rights, the Christian state conservatives would not bend. A negative anti-Jewish stereotype was present among conservatives as in most other sectors of nineteenth-century German society and helped to motivate such anti-Jewish policies, but there were important differences from the liberal version. First, conservatives were more fearful of a *Verjudung*, (Judaization) of German society, which could only be combated by maintaining the Christian basis of politics. And second, they showed that they were more opposed to secular trends generally than to Jews in particular in that they often held a more favorable opinion of Orthodox Jews than of assimilated Reform Jews (just the opposite was true among liberals). A protected but separate status for Jewish communities thus seemed to conservatives to guarantee a more religious society for all parties.

The notion of the Christian state can be traced back to the early nineteenth century, but it was in the 1830s and 1840s that it became central to conservative ideology and Jewish policy. Historians have typically highlighted this trend among Prussian Protestant conservatives such as the Gerlach brothers or the converted Jew Friedrich Julius Stahl, but the same ideas were also found among Catholic conservatives, including Joseph Maria von Radowitz (adviser to Prussian King Friedrich Wilhelm IV) and the influential circle around Joseph von Görres in Bavaria. The Christian state concept attained its greatest practical significance for Jewish policy in Prussia during the 1840s, but it also influenced debates on Jewish emancipation in other German states, both in parliaments and in the pamphlet war going on in Germany at the same time. The concept continued to shape conservative opinion on the status of German Jewry during the second half of the nineteenth century, and some evidence suggests that it may have played a role during the Nazi period as well.

—*Brian Vick*

See also Bauer, Bruno; Churches under Nazism; Emancipation; Frantz, Constantin; *Jewish Question, The* (1843); Marx, Karl; Stahl, Friedrich Julius; State-within-a-State; Stoecker, Adolf; *Verjudung;* Vogelsang, Karl von; Wagener, Hermann

References

Katz, Jacob. *From Prejudice to Destruction: Anti-Semitism, 1700–1933* (Cambridge, MA: Harvard University Press, 1980).

Vick, Brian E. *Defining Germany: The 1848 Frankfurt Parliamentarians and National Identity* (Cambridge, MA: Harvard University Press, 2002), chap. 3.

Chrysostom, John (349–407)

John Chrysostom is counted among the greatest preachers of the Greek Orthodox Church. His epithet, Golden Mouth, bestowed on him posthumously, speaks to his significance not as an original theologian but rather as one of the most important Christian rhetoricians. He was born in Syrian Antioch in 349. Brought up by his mother, Anthusa, entirely in the Greek tradition, John never mastered a language other than Greek. He studied rhetoric with Libanius, an opponent of Christianity. On the completion of his studies in 367, he was taken into the circle around Bishop Meletius, who baptized him in 368. Thereafter, he continued to pursue theological studies.

From 372 to 378, he lived an ascetic hermit's life in the mountains near Antioch. He returned to the city as a reader of church lessons (lector), and in 382, he became a deacon. He entered the priesthood in 386 and became a preacher in the bishop's church. In this capacity, he earned the reputation of a brilliant rhetorician. His sermons, sometimes lasting two hours, were regarded as not only religious talks but also social events. Apparently, his oratorical gifts won him a huge following. Several of the surviving texts of his sermons come from copies made by his listeners—evidence of his popularity. His homilies treated whole books of the Old and New Testaments, individual biblical verses, and biblical figures. In 387, when the people of Antioch revolted against the Theodosian Code and the emperor's family because of a rise in taxation, John delivered twenty-two sermons from the church portal admonishing the citizenry to peace, obedience, and repentance.

In 386, he began a cycle of eight sermons entitled *Adversus Iudaeos*—meaning "against the Jews" or, more accurately, "against the Judaizers," those Christians who commingled with Jews and sometimes participated in Jewish ceremonies. His polemical ferocity was particularly on display in *Adversus Iudaeos,* which remained important in the Eastern Church and enjoyed a revival of popularity among nineteenth- and twentieth-century antisemites.

Named bishop of Constantinople in 397, an office he did not covet, John immediately showed himself too politically inept for survival in the imperial capital. His reform of the clergy, calling them to a simple lifestyle and the abandonment of luxury, created enemies. He alienated the wealthy and even the Empress Eudoxia when he called on them to live modestly and practice charity. He founded hospitals and hostels for foreigners, winning the support of the common people. But he remained remote from the court. The few times he attempted to exert political influence, he met with failure. He eventually fell victim to the intrigues of the imperial court and his many enemies inside the church. Deposed by a synod rigged by his opponents, John was banned, recalled, and then banned again for good in June 404. Exiled first to Cappadocia, he died on the way to Pityus on the Black Sea on September 14, 407.

—*Rainer Kampling*
Richard S. Levy, translation

See also *Adversus Iudaeos;* Roman Empire; Theodosian Code

References

Kelly, J. N. D. *Golden Mouth: The Story of John Chrysostom—Ascetic, Preacher, Bishop.* 2nd ed. (London: Duckworth, 1996).

Mayer, Wendy, and Pauline Allen. *John Chrysostom* (London: Routledge, 2000).

Church Councils (Early)

The church councils of Elvira, Nicaea, Antioch, and Laodicea were convened in a period during which Christianity was still undergoing a process of self-invention and definition. The kinds and number of decrees or canons issued by them are considerable. They treat all sorts of matters related to ritual, to discipline, and to dogma, as well as relations with non-Christians. None of these councils was convoked to deal specifically with the issue of relations with Jews. In fact, most dealt incidentally with that issue. Nonetheless, the canons issued on this matter were important and influential, sometimes being incorporated in later collections of canon law.

The Council of Elvira was almost certainly the first to occur on Spanish soil. Scholars dispute when exactly it was convoked, but the best guesses place it between the years 305 and 310. The council issued a large number of decrees,

eighty-one in all. Three of these treated the issue of Christian relations with Jews. The sixteenth banned intermarriage. The forty-ninth forbade Christians from having their produce blessed by Jews. The fiftieth prohibited clerics or any Christian from dining with Jews.

All three of these canons should be interpreted carefully. Read out of context, they seem to reflect an early form of Christian antisemitism. Actually, they may reflect something quite the opposite. Legislation such as this is almost always produced not prospectively but reactively. These laws were passed, in all likelihood, because Christians were, in fact, intermarrying and dining with Jews and having otherwise normal, even cordial, social relations with them. Thus, the production of these canons was motivated not so much by Jew-hatred as by the fear that Christians continued to find Judaism attractive and Jews amicable and hospitable. It is important to remember that this council occurred before the "triumph" of Christianity was assured and in an area where Judaism was vital and well represented. Its canons thus reflect fear that the church would lose some of its members to the synagogue. Indeed, evidence suggests that in the fourth century, a number of high-ranking Christians did convert to Judaism in Spain. In short, these canons, though hardly philosemitic, became antisemitic only when they were read out of context and then later incorporated into law books produced in entirely different conditions.

The Council of Nicaea was convoked in 325 by the Roman Emperor Constantine. Again, Christian dogma was still very much in flux in the early fourth century. The emperor called this council in order to encourage the assembled bishops to come to some agreement about the nature of the Deity, particularly on the issue of the ontological status of the Logos and its relation to God the Father. This was an issue that had been brought to the fore by the Alexandrian presbyter Arius and his followers, the Arians. The council was thus mainly concerned with the development of Trinitarian doctrine.

The council also tried to establish uniformity between East and West on the date of the observance of Easter, and it was in this regard that it tangentially touched on relations with Jews and

Judaism. Since the second century, some Eastern Christians (especially in Asia Minor) celebrated Easter on the fourteenth day of Nisan (the so-called Quartodecimans). In the West and in many Eastern provinces, it was generally observed on the following Sunday. Nicaea demanded that it be observed on Sunday. Part of the motivation for decreeing this was to differentiate Christian from Jewish observance. A letter from Constantine "preserved" by Eusebius makes this explicit. Again, we see Christianity in the process of religious self-definition. It is the desire for uniformity and the wish to distinguish Christianity from Judaism, rather than contempt, that motivated this decree.

The first canon of the Council of Antioch, which met in 341, proves that the Nicene decree regarding Easter was not being universally observed. For those observing Easter "with the Jews"—that is, when the Jews celebrated Passover—the council reserved harsh judgment. It excommunicated the laity. It also deposed any cleric from his ministry as a "cause of destruction and subversion to many." In addition, it excommunicated any person who associated with the deposed cleric. Again, this is the council's only mention of Jews. But by placing it in the first canon to be promulgated, the bishops indicated how urgent it was for them to distinguish Christian from Jewish religious practice.

The precise date of the Council of Laodicea is unknown. It occurred after the Council of Antioch and before the Council of Constantinople (in 381). Again, a large number of canons were issued—sixty in all. Only two treat relations with Jews. The thirty-seventh declared it unlawful to receive portions sent from Jewish feasts (or those of heretics) and forbade Christians to eat with Jews. The thirty-eighth forbade Christians to receive unleavened bread from the Jews, "nor to be partakers of their impiety."

Both canons are interesting because such legislation would not have been passed if the proscribed practices had not been occurring. Thus, it may be concluded that, in defiance (or ignorance) of earlier conciliar decrees, Christians were, in fact, still dining with Jews. Also, they seem to have participated in Jewish rituals, as the references to unleavened bread and "impiety"

suggest. The problem from the perspective of the bishops was that Christians continued to interact with Jews amicably and even to participate in their religious services. Other evidence from roughly the same time period, including the infamous sermons of John Chrysostom, supports this theory. Behind the surface of such legislation, which seems so antisemitic, lies a much happier picture of Jewish Christian relations in late antiquity. Indeed, it is a picture of cordial relations that the ecclesiastical laws, when decontextualized, serve only to obscure. However, such conciliar canons were often incorporated into later medieval law books. There, they took on an antisemitic meaning their original authors could not have foreseen or intended.

—*Kevin Madigan*

See also Chrysostom, John; Constantine, Emperor
References
Hefele, Karl. *A History of the Christian Councils from the Original Documents.* 5 vols. (Edinburgh: T & T Clark, 1871–1896).
Simon, Marcel. *Verus Israel: A Study of the Relations between Christians and Jews in the Roman Empire, AD 135–425* (London: Littman, 1996).

Church Fathers

Four ancient church fathers were recognized in the West as "doctors of the church": Ambrose, Jerome, Hilary of Poitiers, and Augustine. The essay that follows briefly explores the attitudes toward Jews and Judaism of the first three of these individuals (Augustine is discussed in a separate entry).

Ambrose (339–397) was made bishop of Milan in 374. At the time, Milan was one of the two most powerful episcopal sees in Europe. Much of Ambrose's episcopal and writing career was consumed by a confrontation with the Arians; nonorthodox Christians who did not believe in the divinity of Christ. He also had several clashes with the partisans of paganism. Finally, an incident that occurred far from his episcopal see involved him in a controversy surrounding Jews and Judaism. In 388, the bishop of Callinicum, a commercial town on the Euphrates River, was accused of having encouraged Christians of his diocese, supposedly in retaliation for an offense committed by certain Jews of the town against Christians, to burn the local synagogue. They did, and they looted the synagogue as well. An imperial official reported the incident to Emperor Theodosius, who commanded the bishop to rebuild the synagogue at his own expense. Those who started the fire were to be punished and stolen properties restored.

When Ambrose heard the emperor's decision, he wrote a long letter exhorting Theodosius to change his mind. If the bishop was forced to rebuild the synagogue for "God's enemies," Ambrose argued, he would be committing an act of apostasy. No synagogue, moreover, should be restored at the expense of the church: "Should a building be erected for perfidious Jews out of the spoils of the church?" he asked. How could the emperor give "the unbelievers" a triumph over the Christians? Theodosius backed down on his demand that the bishop rebuild the synagogue, decreeing instead that it be done at state expense. Still, he insisted that the criminals be prosecuted and all properties returned. Ambrose protested again. The deceitful Jews, he argued, had fabricated the robbery charges so that Christians would be condemned to the mines. The emperor would not relent. Further protests followed, and the emperor finally surrendered to the importunate and powerful archbishop of Milan. An ominous precedent had been set.

Jerome (ca. 340–420) was without doubt the greatest Christian scholar of the fourth century. His knowledge of the history, geography, and philology of Palestine was unrivaled. He wrote capaciously on the Bible; indeed, he was the most prolific commentator of his day. In 382, Pope Damasus commissioned him to translate the Bible into Latin. The result was the Vulgate, a Latin Bible translated from the original languages. To this day, it remains the edition of the Bible that has perhaps been most widely read in the West, where it exerted enormous influence on language, liturgy, art, architecture, literature, politics, and theology.

Jerome's attitudes toward Jews and Judaism were complex, and they raise scholarly questions even today. It is easy to find statements in Jerome that seem flagrantly antisemitic. He unequivocally blamed the death of Christ on the Jews. He admitted to loathing "men of the circumcision,"

calling their houses of worship "synagogues of Satan." He denounced Israel as a fornicatrix or adulteress and insisted, oddly, that Jews continued to persecute Christians even in his own day. Most strangely, he was convinced that Jews pronounced anathemas on Christians three times each day. By contrast, he sincerely respected Jewish scholarship, commented copiously on the Hebrew Scriptures, and took the time to learn Hebrew from a Jewish teacher in Bethlehem.

In an attempt to explain this contradiction, some scholars have argued that Jerome was defending himself against Christians who criticized him precisely for using Hebrew and for mastering Jewish traditions; they contend that the harshness of his anti-Jewish rhetoric was necessitated by self-defense. Another possible explanation is that Jerome's inconsistent remarks and attitudes reflected Christianity's own ambivalence toward a religious tradition that was, in fact, its progenitor yet remained a dangerous and attractive rival. When wrenched from its context, Jerome's antisemitic rhetoric was among the most vicious in Christian antiquity and was cited as authoritative against Jews in the very different conditions of the Middle Ages.

Hilary of Poitiers (d. 368) became bishop of his hometown in Gaul (France) around 350. Hilary's major episcopal and literary project throughout his life—for which he was exiled—was to oppose and eliminate the heterodox Arians. Jews and Judaism figured less prominently in his writings than those of Jerome, and he never faced a major controversy involving Jews as had Ambrose. His attitude toward Jews and Judaism was also much less complex and sympathetic than Jerome's. In his *Commentary on Matthew*, he wrote, "Before the Law was given, the Jews were possessed of an unclean devil, which the Law for a time drove out, but which returned immediately after their rejection of Christ." We are told by his biographer, Venantius Fortunatus, that Hilary would not dine with a Jew, nor even respond to a greeting on the street. This, however, was written of him more than two centuries after his death and may reflect realities of the sixth century rather than the fourth, when multiple councils decreed, unsuccessfully, that Jews and Christians should not eat together.

There is little that could be described as philosemitic in Hilary's writings on Jews and Judaism. Like Ambrose and Jerome and almost all ancient Christian writers, Hilary rarely referred to a *particular* Jew. Instead, the ancient church fathers referenced "the Jews" in the language of stereotype and generality. There was ample precedent in Greek and Roman ethnography for talking about "foreign" peoples this way. But the Christian fathers' ethnography of demonization was to have a duration and an impact of tragic dimensions that its classical predecessors never had.

—*Kevin Madigan*

See also Church Councils (Early); Roman Empire; Theodosian Code

References

Cohen, Jeremy. *Living Letters of the Law: Ideas of the Jew in Medieval Christianity* (Berkeley and Los Angeles: University of California Press, 1999).

Simon, Marcel. *Verus Israel: A Study of the Relations between Christians and Jews in the Roman Empire, AD 135–425* (London: Littman, 1996).

Churches under Nazism

In 1939, over 95 percent of Germans were baptized, tax-paying members of the two official churches—either the the *Evangelisch* (Protestant), in its Lutheran, Reformed, and united Lutheran-Reformed variations or the Roman Catholic. Protestants outnumbered Catholics by about three to two. Smaller Christian groups—Methodists, Baptists, Mennonites, Quakers, Seventh-Day Adventists, Jehovah's Witnesses, and others—accounted for fewer than 2 percent of the population. As institutions, the churches varied greatly in their responses to National Socialism, from the generally accommodating position of the Protestants and Catholics to the resolute opposition of the Jehovah's Witnesses. Individual church members differed even more widely, from eager perpetrators of Nazi crimes to victims of persecution and rescuers of those targeted for destruction. By 1945, the Christian churches could claim to be the only major institutions in Germany to have survived Nazi rule intact, but the price of survival was often high.

The German churches were implicated in Nazi crimes. Individual church members numbered among the perpetrators at every level. Hitler remained a nominal Catholic all his life. The Einsatzgruppen (mobile death squads) that murdered hundreds of thousands of Jews, Gypsies/Roma, and inmates of mental hospitals included in their ranks men with advanced degrees in Protestant theology. Indeed, one might argue that although not all Christians were perpetrators, the vast majority of perpetrators were Christians—in the sense that they were baptized and raised in homes and schools where the Christian Bible, the Lord's Prayer, and hymns were daily fare.

As institutions, the German churches were accomplices and enablers rather than hands-on perpetrators. By propagating notions of Jews as "Christ killers" and teaching contempt for Judaism, the churches helped build receptivity for Nazi antisemitism. Christian anti-Jewishness alone did not cause Nazi genocide, nor did it drive the top decision makers. But it helped justify the targeting of Jews for those who executed and tolerated antisemitic measures. Moreover, connections between Christian anti-Jewish tradition and secular antisemitism contributed to the metaphysical urgency and intensity of the Nazi assault on Jews.

Structural and historical differences shaped specific Protestant and Catholic responses, but the overall effect was similar: both major churches boosted the credibility of Hitler's regime at home and abroad. German Protestant leaders welcomed his accession to power in 1933. Mass spectacles in church buildings, such as the Day of Potsdam in March 1933 and the group weddings of uniformed Nazis with their brides, sent a message to lay Germans and foreign observers that the Protestant leadership blessed Hitler and his cause.

Some enthusiastic Protestants joined the so-called Deutsche Christen (German Christian movement) to seek an explicit synthesis of Christianity and Nazism. They attacked "non-Aryan" Christians and embarked on a campaign to purge all traces of Judaism from Christianity. In the spring of 1933, inspired by the ban on Jews in the civil service, Deutsche Christen tried to force non-Aryan clergy from Protestant pulpits. In protest, Martin Niemöller, a pastor from Berlin-

Countering a threat by Hitler to take action against the Catholic Party, 4,500 Catholics pledge allegiance to the church, the people, and the state at a ceremony in Grunwald, Germany, 1933. Here the priests have just blessed the crowd. (Bettmann/Corbis)

Jewish suffering as repayment for the "curse" of crucifying Jesus.

Germany's Roman Catholic leaders were initially less enthusiastic about National Socialism than their Protestant counterparts. Until 1933, the Catholic Center Party continued to contest the political arena, and some Catholic priests, worried that Nazi ideology elevated notions of race above loyalty to the universal church, refused to administer the sacraments to men in Storm trooper or SS uniforms. Although there were individual bishops who supported Hitler and endorsed the regime's measures against Communists and Jews, the euphoria typical of the Protestant hierarchy in early 1933 was not widespread in Catholic circles.

By mid-1933, the situation had changed. In July, Hitler's representatives signed a concordat with the Vatican. The papal nuncio in Berlin, Eugenio Pacelli (later Pope Pius XII), played a key role in the negotiations. This arrangement—Hitler's first major foreign policy success—served both to silence Catholic misgivings at home and to enhance the international prestige of National Socialism. The concordat effectively isolated those priests and bishops who had inveighed against Nazi racism and paganism from their parishioners, many of whom saw no contradiction between being good Catholics and good Nazis; it also isolated them from the Vatican, which embraced Nazi Germany as a bulwark against communism.

The Protestant and Catholic churches also helped isolate the Jewish targets of Nazi aggression. Although Nazi ideology claimed Jewishness was racial, the Nuremberg Laws of 1935 relied on the religion of one's grandparents to determine who counted as an "Aryan," who as a "Jew." It was the major churches that provided the papers, from baptismal and marriage records, that individuals needed to establish their "bloodlines."

A further example of the churches' complicity comes from the euthanasia program (involving the murder of people deemed handicapped), which began in 1939. Many of the estimated 70,000 Germans killed under this scheme lived in hospitals and homes run by the major churches, a great number of which complied with the authorities. There were administrators

Dahlem, organized the Pastors' Emergency League. Niemöller's organization grew into the Bekennende Kirche (Confessing Church), a movement within established Protestantism (not a separate church) that aimed to protect ecclesiastical integrity.

The contest between the Deutsche Christen and the Confessing Church for control of German Protestantism became known as the "church struggle." The bitterness of that dispute notwithstanding, members of both camps, as well as the numerous Protestant "neutrals," tended to accept old habits of anti-Jewishness. Even Niemöller, who spent years in Nazi prisons, characterized himself as an antisemite. He conceded that converts to Christianity had rights within the church but believed Germany suffered from a "Jewish problem" and described who refused to participate; individual doctors, nurses, and attendants who struggled with their consciences; and certain Protestant pastors, like some Catholic clergymen, who protested the killings from the pulpit. As an institution, however, the Protestant church provided neither encouragement nor protection for such resistance. In this regard, the record of the Catholic Church is somewhat stronger, though less than ideal.

Many scholarly and popular analyses depict the German churches as victims of Nazism. Indeed, although the Nazi leadership used Christian vocabulary and symbols for its own purposes, the regime demonstrated hostility toward institutionalized Christianity. Generally, Catholicism, with its international hierarchy, was perceived as more threatening than Protestantism. Nazi authorities harassed church organizations; imposed restrictions on activities such as youth work; and conducted negative propaganda accusing the churches and Christianity in general of being un-German, tainted by Jewishness, and enfeebling. Nevertheless, to use the label *victim* would be to exaggerate. Hitler's government continued to collect and distribute church taxes. Nazi authorities permitted the study of theology in public universities and left church property in ecclesiastical hands. As institutions, the German churches—with the exception of the Jehovah's Witnesses—cannot be numbered among the victims of Nazism.

Were the churches and church members rescuers of those targeted for destruction? The answer is mixed, but given the magnitude of destruction, the record appears dismal. Pastor Heinrich Grüber worked with elements of the Confessing Church in Berlin to help converts from Judaism and their families leave the country. He went to Dachau for his efforts. Even Grüber, however, considered the Holocaust to be God's punishment of the Jews. The Catholic priest Bernhard Lichtenberg prayed publicly for Jews being deported from Berlin to their deaths. He, too, was arrested, denounced to the Gestapo by members of his congregation. He died in 1943, in transport to Dachau. Bishop August Graf von Galen protested the murder of Germans deemed handicapped, and although the killings did not stop, the public attention he drew to the program forced its organizers to do more

to cover their tracks. Such examples are rare—and noticeably rarer within Germany than in the Netherlands, Belgium, France, Italy, and Poland. The German cases are typical, however, in their individual nature. There is little evidence that the churches as institutions supported rescue efforts.

Most discussions describe the German churches as bystanders to Nazi crimes. The usual charges against institutions and individuals cite their silence and failure to act. These criticisms assume that church leaders and members knew what was happening, from the escalating persecutions of the 1930s to the mass killings of the war years. Many sources confirm such knowledge, whether we consider the public nature of the Night of Broken Glass (November 1938 Pogrom) or the military chaplains who witnessed mass shootings of Jews in Ukraine in 1941.

A second assumption behind the "bystanders" label is that the churches could have done more. It is unlikely that the churches alone could have prevented or halted war and mass killing. But they might have made a difference. Hitler's sensitivity to public opinion, coupled with the prestige of the German churches at home and abroad, gave church authorities some power. Perhaps early, vigorous criticism of the Nazi regime could have weakened Hitler's hold on the population. Certainly, more widespread engagement on behalf of Jews and other victims would have communicated to those in need some assurance that the world had not abandoned them.

—Doris L. Bergen

See also Center Party; Deicide; *Deutsche Christen*; Einsatzgruppen; Holocaust; Jehovah's Witnesses; Night of Broken Glass; Nuremberg Laws; Pius XII, Pope

References

Conway, John S. *The Nazi Persecution of the Churches, 1933–45* (New York: Basic Books, 1968).

Ericksen, Robert P., and Susannah Heschel, eds. *Betrayal: German Churches and the Holocaust* (Minneapolis, MN: Fortress, 1999).

Gerlach, Wolfgang. *And the Witnesses Were Silent: The Confessing Church and the Persecution of the Jews.* Translated and edited by Victoria J. Barnett (Lincoln: University of Nebraska Press, 2000).

Phayer, Michael. *The Catholic Church and the Holocaust, 1930–1965* (Bloomington: Indiana University Press, 2000).

Circumcision

Throughout its long history, the Jewish practice of circumcision has been criticized—and sometimes suppressed—for a variety of reasons. Because circumcision is perhaps the oldest Jewish ritual, however, and is intrinsic to Jewish notions of self-identity, Jews have often interpreted opposition to circumcision as antisemitism. But motivations for the maligning or prohibition of circumcision are complex and may arise from antisemitism, general xenophobia, or the simple clash of cultural sensibilities, including changing attitudes toward the human body and sexuality.

Several pagan authors in the ancient world addressed Jewish circumcision with opinions ranging from the naked hostility of Tacitus—who described it, along with other Jewish customs, as a "base and abominable" practice that Jews had deliberately chosen to "distinguish themselves from other peoples" and express their "hate and enmity" toward them (*Histories* 5.5.2)—to Petronius—who poked fun at a practice that he compared with the outlandish customs of other peoples, such as ear piercing or face painting (*Satyricon* 102: 14). Literary, artistic, and legal evidence suggests that Greeks and Romans tended to view circumcision as a primitive act of mutilation unbefitting enlightened and civilized people. In certain periods, this view was shared by some Jews, who neglected to perform the ritual, and it was not unknown for circumcised Jewish men to voluntarily submit to a surgical procedure (epispasm) to eliminate this symbol of separateness.

Despite their general distaste for the ritual, Greek and Roman authorities prior to Emperor Hadrian did nothing to ban it—with the famous exception of Antiochus IV Epiphanes, who forbade circumcision, together with many other Jewish rituals, as part of his effort to Hellenize and politically stabilize the Judean region in 165 BCE. Although Antiochus's outlawing of circumcision was clearly aimed at Jews, Hadrian's later ban was bound up with legislation against castration, which suggests that he was motivated by moral, cultural, or economic concerns rather than anti-Jewish animus. This fact would have offered little comfort to Jews, however, and it is likely that the ban on circumcision played a role in fomenting the Bar Kochba Revolt in 132 CE. Hadrian's successor, Antoninus Pius, selectively repealed Hadrian's ban, so that Jews would be permitted to circumcise their children (though not their non-Jewish slaves), but for other peoples, it would still be a capital offense.

This arrangement held through the fourth-century rule of Constantine and Justinian's reign in the sixth century, and it was enshrined in canon law as well. Despite these legal protections, however, new attitudes toward circumcision had arisen in the Christian world by the Middle Ages. After some debate in the inchoate church, Christians rejected bodily circumcision, reinterpreting it as a spiritual doctrine symbolized by baptism; as Christian attitudes toward Jews hardened, the continued Jewish practice of the bloody ancient rite came to symbolize for Christians the backwardness and culpable blindness of "carnal Israel." Perhaps the nadir of the Christian perception of circumcision was reached by the fifteenth century, when it became linked with the blood libel and took on a demonic aspect; it was alleged that Jews coveted the blood of ritually murdered Christians for its salutary effect when applied to the wound of circumcision.

In modern times, with the relative decline in the importance of religion, opposition to circumcision was expressed from new and diverse perspectives. With the rise of nationalism and racialism, many non-Jews viewed the continued insistence on circumcision as exemplifying Jews' frustrating refusal to resolve the Jewish Question once and for all through assimilation. Criticism of circumcision also emanated from the newly developing field of psychology, because of the alleged ill effects that the practice inflicted on the psyche of the Jewish male. Many in the medical establishment condemned the ritual as unsanitary and promoting the transmission of syphilis and gonorrhea, which were widely believed to be "Jewish" diseases.

Circumcision has gone in and out of vogue in the general population and seems currently on the wane. Antisemites in the United States and elsewhere occasionally seize on the practice as a means of casting Judaism as an inhumane religion. This view is not widely shared.

—*Aryeh Tuchman*

See also Bar Kochba Revolt; Justinian Code; Masculinity; Misanthropy; Ritual Murder (Medieval); Roman Empire; Roman Literature

References

Gilman, Sander. *The Jew's Body* (New York: Routledge, 1991).

Hodges, Frederick M. "The Ideal Prepuce in Ancient Greece and Rome: Male Genital Aesthetics and Their Relation to Lipodermos, Circumcision, Foreskin Restoration, and the Kynodesme," *Bulletin of the History of Medicine* 75 (Fall 2001): 375–405.

Civiltà Cattolica

Founded in 1850 at Pope Pius IX's request as a means of spreading the pope's view of current events to the Catholic faithful, the biweekly journal *Civiltà Cattolica* has long been viewed as the unofficial organ of the papacy. It is run by Jesuits, who write all the articles and approve all drafts collectively. The drafts must then be approved by the Vatican itself prior to publication. The criteria for approval by the Vatican secretary of state's office include "conformity of the articles published in the journal with the official teaching of the Church" (Kertzer 2001, 135).

As modern antisemitism began to take shape in the 1880s, *Civiltà Cattolica* played an active role. From 1880 to 1883, the journal published thirty-six virulently antisemitic articles. A typical passage, from December 22, 1880, warned: "If this foreign Jewish race is left too free, it immediately becomes the persecutor, oppressor, tyrant, thief, and devastator of the countries where it lives." The journal urged that special laws be introduced to keep the Jews in their place. Jews were described as "eternal insolent children, obstinate, dirty, thieves, liars, ignoramuses, pests and the scourge of those near and far. . . . They managed to lay their hands on . . . all public wealth . . . and virtually alone they took control not only of all the money . . . but of the law itself in those countries where they have been allowed to hold public offices." Catholics were repeatedly warned that Jews were not simply members of a religion; they also constituted a hostile nation, dedicated to using every criminal means imaginable to rob and persecute them. An article in 1893 stated that the Jewish nation "does not work, but traffics in the property and the work of others; it does not produce, but lives and grows fat with the products of the arts and industry of the nations that give it refuge. It is the giant octopus that with its oversized tentacles envelops everything. . . . It represents the kingdom of capital . . . the aristocracy of gold. . . . It reigns unopposed."

Civiltà Cattolica was also active in promulgating the ritual murder charge, running many articles on the topic in the late nineteenth century and as late as 1914 (in connection with the Beilis case) charging that Jews were taught to regard the blood of Christian children as "a drink like milk."

A typical 1928 article continued to warn of the Jews' pernicious influence, lamenting that their emancipation had made them "emboldened and powerful, giving them, under the pretext of equality, a position that was increasingly predominant in prestige, especially in the economic sector, in modern society." To respond to this threat, *Civiltà Cattolica* championed racial laws introduced against Jews in the mid- and late 1930s across Europe. Following World War II, the journal's hostility toward the Jews remained, although in more muted form, until the Second Vatican Council.

In a June 2002 article, reflecting on its history, the journal rejected charges that it had ever been antisemitic, arguing that its former hostility toward the Jews was, rather, based on a combination of negative religious views of the Jews (as Christ killers, cursed by God) and a view of the Jews as responsible for the Russian Revolution. Ironically, in resuscitating the charge that the Jews had been behind the Bolshevik Revolution—a theme central to the Nazi campaign against the Jews—*Civiltà Cattolica*'s antisemitic legacy was once again revealed.

—*David I. Kertzer*

See also Beilis Case; Deicide; Emancipation; Jesuit Order; Judeo-Bolshevism; Pius IX, Pope; Ritual Murder (Medieval); Ritual Murder (Modern); Vatican Council, Second

References

Kertzer, David I. *The Popes against the Jews* (New York: Knopf /Vintage, 2001).

Rosa, Giuseppe De (S.I.). *La Civiltà Cattolica: 150 anni al servizio della Chiesa 1850–1999* (Rome: Civiltà Cattolica, 1999).

Taradel, Ruggero, and Barbara Raggi. *La seg-regazione amichevole: "La Civiltà Cattolica" e la questione ebraica 1850–1945* (Rome: Editori Ri-uniti, 2000).

Class, Heinrich (1868–1953)

The leader of the most radical of the many patriotic societies in imperial Germany, the Pan-German League, Heinrich Class radicalized the discourse concerning German nationalism and popularized theories of scientific racism and antisemitism.

Born in Mainz to a middle-class Hessian family, the son and grandson of senior judiciary officials, Class studied law in Berlin, where he absorbed the nationalist and antisemitic teachings of Heinrich von Treitschke, and at the University of Giessen, where he was introduced to the antisemitic teachings of Friedrich Lange and joined in the antisemitic campaigns of Otto Böckel. He returned to Mainz for his law practicum and, unable to find employment in the civil service, founded an independent law practice. Soon disillusioned with party politics, Class became active in the radical nationalist organizations that emerged in the mid-1890s. In 1894, he responded to Friedrich Lange's call for the formation of the antisemitic German Union (Deutschbund), helping to found a local "community" in Mainz, which he later converted into a local chapter of the Pan-German League (in 1897).

In just a few short years, Class became one of the leading figures in the league and was made its executive secretary in 1901. At the Pan-German national convention in 1903, he launched a vigorous attack on the government, which was later published as a pamphlet entitled *Die Bilanz des neuen Kurses* (The Balance of the New Course). He openly questioned the sole authority of the government to speak and act in the name of the nation and claimed for the league joint custodianship of national symbols. With the death of Ernst Hasse in January 1908, Class assumed the chairmanship and quickly moved to solidify the league's connections both to wealthy industrialists and agriculturalists and to sympathetic politicians in the right wing of the National Liberal Party and in the Free Conservative Party. The change in leadership also paved the way for the league to engage in more active political agitation in the sphere of domestic policy. As a self-appointed "national opposition," the Pan-Germans under Class's leadership openly criticized the government and, during the Daily Telegraph Crisis in 1908, even the emperor himself. Class also infused the league with the antisemitic ideas he himself had long promoted, most notably in his *If I Were the Kaiser* (1912), in which he called for stripping Jews of their civil rights.

Class remained active in nationalist politics during World War I and the Weimar era. He was a key player in the founding of the Fatherland Party in September 1917 and was later active in the German National People's Party in the Weimar Republic. Although Hitler and Class met on several occasions in the early 1920s and although the Nazis adopted much of the ideological program of the Pan-German League, Class viewed the Nazis with disdain. In his 1932 memoirs, *Wider den Strom* (Against the Current), he attempted to show that the Pan-German League was still relevant despite the rise of the Nazis, an untenable position after the Nazis attained power one year later.

—Elizabeth A. Drummond

See also Böckel, Otto; German National People's Party; *If I Were the Kaiser;* Lange, Friedrich; Pan-German League; Treitschke, Heinrich von; Weimar

References

Chickering, Roger. *We Men Who Feel Most German: A Cultural Study of the Pan-German League, 1886–1914* (Boston: Allen & Unwin, 1984).

Eley, Geoff. *Reshaping the German Right: Radical Nationalism and Political Change after Bismarck* (Ann Arbor: University of Michigan Press, 1990).

Claudius (10 BCE–54 CE)

At his enthronement as Roman emperor on January 25, 41 CE, one day after his predecessor Gaius Caligula's assassination, Tiberius Claudius Nero inherited a very tense situation in Alexandria, Egypt, where three years before, the Alexandrian Jews had lost their rights of residence. At the news of Gaius's assassination, the Jews of Alexandria took up arms to try to reverse their situation. It seems that the emperor intervened to restore order in the city, but riots probably broke out again later.

We know of Claudius's provisions from two pieces of evidence; both indicate that he eased the condition of the Jews. In his *Antiquities of the Jews,* the Jewish historian Josephus reported an edict carved on a stela exposed in Alexandria by which Claudius reestablished Jewish rights and customs in the city to what they had been at the time of Augustus (31 BCE–14 CE). Some scholars hold this decree to be authentic and to be Claudius's first intervention after the Jewish rebellion in the spring of 41. A factor arguing in favor of the authenticity of this edict is the decree the prefect Petronius issued in Dora, Phoenicia, when the Greeks there tried to erect statues of Claudius in the local synagogues. Petronius intervened in favor of the Jews recalling Claudius's Alexandrian edict, the principles of which he applied.

However, the unofficial language of the Alexandrian edict as reported by Josephus suggests to other scholars either that Josephus (or his source) embellished the original text in order to provide a more positive image of the relationship between the Jews and Roman power or that the edict never, in fact, existed and that Josephus was referring to a forgery. If so, the historicity of Petronius's actions in Dora also lose their credibility.

The *Letter of Claudius to the Alexandrians,* a most important papyrological document dated November 10, 41 CE (published in 1924), is certainly a historical document, a copy of the original deposited in the Alexandrian chancellery. It is the imperial response to the embassies that the Alexandrian citizens and the Jews sent to Claudius in order for him to adjudicate the unresolved conflicts in the city between the two parties. Some scholars deduce from the content of this letter that Claudius had taken measures earlier in the year—an argument for the authenticity of the edict mentioned earlier. The document's ambiguous language, however, leaves the discussion open as to the extent of the emperor's actual intervention. According to the text, Claudius decided to reestablish the Jewish customs in the city as they had been at the time of Augustus, but he also reminded Jews that they lived in a city that was not their own.

A comparative analysis of the vocabulary of the two pieces of evidence allows some observations. The edict called the Jews "Alexandrians," a descriptive Claudius carefully avoided in the *Letter;* the edict spoke of the reestablishment of Jewish customs *and* rights, whereas the *Letter* mentioned only of their customs—unless *customs* is semantically understood to include Jewish rights as well, as some think. Others hold these differences to be additional good reasons to doubt he authenticity of Josephus's edict.

Ancient historians also briefly reported two occasions on which Claudius is said to have expelled the Jews from Rome, in 41 and 49. But once again, the imprecise and sometimes controversial information contained in the sources make the truth difficult to establish. There is no unanimity among modern historians concerning these events; some scholars tend to minimize the involvement of the Jews.

—*Sandra Gambetti*

See also Alexandrian Pogrom; Roman Empire; Roman Literature
References
Pucci Ben Zeev, M. *Jewish Rights in the Roman World: Greek and Roman Documents Quoted by Josephus Flavius* (Tübingen, Germany: Mohr, 1998).
Schäfer, Peter. *Judeophobia* (Cambridge, MA: Harvard University Press, 1997).

Codreanu, Corneliu Zelea (1899–1938)

The Romanian nationalist politician Corneliu Codreanu was the oldest son of Ion Zelinski, who changed his Polish name to Zelea Codreanu and adopted the Orthodox faith. Zelea Codreanu provided his son with a pious and patriotic upbringing, sending him in 1910 to the military school Mănăstirea Dealului. The younger Codreanu went on to study law at Iassy, Jena, and Grenoble and took his doctorate under A. C. Cuza, the economist, writer, and right-wing politician. These formative influences in his life imbued him with a belief in elite leadership, work, discipline, and religiosity.

Codreanu was antisemitic. Like Cuza and many other intellectuals, he held "foreigners," that is, the Jews, responsible for the problems plaguing Romania after World War I. Even as a student, he had organized antisemitic actions. He also became an anticommunist during an episode of worker unrest in Iassy, and in 1919, he started his own short-lived anticommunist labor party, Bread and Honor, which championed national and Christian socialism. He was more successful organizing students than workers, however. The 1922 strike of his nationalist Association of Christian Students brought university instruction to a standstill. Peasants and students joined together in the LANC–National Christian Defense League, an organization that drew together all those opposed to granting Jews full rights of citizenship. Codreanu and his friends sought to mobilize opposition to the allegedly pro-Jewish policies of the liberals by attempting to assassinate six influential politicians and Jews. The attacks failed, but Codreanu then shot the Iassy chief of police. His subsequent trial and acquittal won him national notoriety for the first time. In 1926, he parted ways with Cuza and LANC and organized his own party.

He now rejected individual acts of terror as valid political means. He began to think beyond petty, everyday politics, proclaiming the need for a "national renewal" of the Romanian people and appointing himself as the instrument of Romania's salvation. In 1927, he and a few friends in Iassy created the Legion of the Archangel Michael to carry out this grandiose mission. To begin with, Codreanu was intent on saving Romanian youth from the deleterious influence of the ruling political parties, offering them an elaborately organized movement dedicated to hard work, friendship, mutual assistance, self-sacrifice, and discipline. The individual "nests," or cells, of the legion proved flexible and functional, equally adaptable to political campaigning and underground activities. Although Codreanu himself made an effort to keep the legion's activities within the bounds of the law, governmental authorities repeatedly banned or harassed the organization. From 1931, the league contested elections under a variety of names, including the Iron Guard. In 1937, it won sixty-six seats and nearly 16 percent of the vote.

After King Carol II imposed a royal dictatorship and because of the steady growth in the legion's membership, the government moved to put Codreanu on trial for high treason in May 1938 and to find him guilty, despite a lack of substantial evidence. He was sentenced to ten years of hard labor and shortly afterward, by order of the king, murdered. Codreanu's death launched the formation of his myth.

—Krista Zach
Richard S. Levy, translation

See also Cuza, A. C.; Iron Guard; LANC—National Christian Defense League; Romania; Romania, Post-Soviet

References

Heinen, Armin. Die Legion "Erzengel Michael" in Rumänien: Soziale Bewegung und politische Organisation—Ein Beitrag zum Problem des internationalen Faschismus (Munich, Germany: Oldenbourg, 1986).

Zach, Krista. "Rumänien." In Dimension des Völkermords: Die Zahl der jüdischen Opfer des Nationalsozialismus. Edited by Wolfgang Benz (Munich, Germany: Oldenbourg, 1991).

Coin Clipping

The most significant episode of Jewish coin clipping occurred between 1278 and 1279 under Edward I of England. By medieval standards, England policed and centralized the minting of its coinage to a remarkably effective degree. But in the 1270s, amid the fiscal pressures of Edward's Welsh war, concern mounted about recent deterioration of the currency. Edward was apparently convinced that royal judges, sheriffs, and mint masters were conniving with alien merchants, Jews, and goldsmiths to enrich themselves through clipping and counterfeiting. In 1278, he appointed special commissions "of oyer and terminer" (meaning, hearing and determination) to root out such practices as "shearing" (filing the edges of coins), "clipping" (cutting off entire slivers with forceps), and "forging" (melting the clippings into plate to overlay a base metal core with silver). That same year, he raised the maximum penalty for these offenses from banishment to execution.

On November 18, 1278, a mass arrest of Anglo-Jewry occurred, with over 600 imprisoned in the Tower of London and many more incarcerated throughout the country. After a special trial at the London Guildhall, some 269 Jews and 29 Christians (though historians disagree widely over the exact numbers) were hanged for offenses against "our Lord the King's coin." This numerical disparity probably resulted from the special status granted to the government's chief witness, Henry of Winchester, who, as part of the investigation, was engaged to pose as a customer of illegal coin and thereby gather evidence. As a Jewish convert to Christianity, Henry made use of his extensive contacts with Jewish merchants. This, combined with the fact that his testimony was granted the status of unimpeachable *recordum* (established matter of record) when directed against Jewish though not against Christian defendants, probably accounts for the far greater number of Jews who received the ultimate penalty.

It is estimated that the wealth confiscated from English Jews as a result of these arrests amounted to ā11,000, a financial blow from which, given the heavy exactions in taxes and fines of the preceding half century, medieval Anglo-Jewry never recovered. By so depleting their remaining assets—and thus rendering them fiscally useless—the coin-clipping prosecution helped pave the way for the Jews' general expulsion eleven years later. However, the expulsion from England did not solve the problem of coin clipping, which continued to plague the country for centuries.

The expulsion also failed to erase the memory of Jewish criminality in the nation's cultural consciousness, despite the lack of an overt Jewish presence. Amid renewed concerns about the abuse of the coinage in the 1500s, chronicles and pamphlets such as Raphael Holinshed's (a major historical source for Shakespeare) devoted significant attention to the monetary crimes of Edwardian Jewry. Seventeenth-century opponents of Jewish readmission, including the lawyer William Prynne, ransacked this literature to support their anti-Jewish claims. This antiquarian effort in turn provided historical source material for those who sought to overturn the 1753 Jew Bill, which would have allowed wealthy foreign-born Jewish merchants to become naturalized British subjects. One revealing bit of doggerel, for instance, likened Jewish coin clipping to the forced circumcision of Christians:

In brave Edward's days they were caught in
   a gin,
For clipping our coin, now to add sin to
   sin,
As they've got all our pelf, they'd be
   clipping our skin.
Those foes to the pork of Old England.
   (Shapiro 1996, 210–211)

Outside Britain, related charges of Jewish counterfeiting and the fencing of stolen goods were leveled frequently against pawnbrokers, whose occupation operated on the edge of the criminal underworld. Additionally, in the absolutist principalities of the seventeenth and eighteenth centuries, Jewish leasers of state mints (*Münzjuden*) sometimes debased the currency at the behest of their fiscally pressed rulers—a licit act but one that, like medieval coin clipping, fueled anti-Jewish denunciations.

—*Jonathan Karp*

See also Caricature, Anti-Jewish (Early); Court Jews; Expulsions, High Middle Ages; Jew Bill; Pork

References
Brand, Paul. "Jews and the Law in England, 1275–90," *English Historical Review* 115 (November 2000): 1–13.
Mundill, Robin R. *England's Jewish Solution: Experiment and Expulsion, 1262–1290* (Cambridge: Cambridge University Press, 1998).
Shapiro, James. *Shakespeare and the Jews* (New York: Columbia University Press, 1996): 210–211.
Spufford, Peter. *Money and Its Use in Medieval Europe* (Cambridge: Cambridge University Press, 1988).

Colonial America

During the fifteenth through the seventeenth centuries, antisemitism was on the rise in Europe, and Jews were forced to flee before the Inquisition. A group of Jews, finding sanctuary in Protestant Amsterdam, decided to try their luck in Brazil, but when the Portuguese took control there, they were forced to move on. Twenty-three of them wound up in the Dutch West India Company's colony of New Amsterdam (soon to be New York) in 1654, where they initially encountered resistance from Director General Petrus (Peter) Stuyvesant. The Puritans of New England refused to tolerate them, with the exception of those infamous for dissent themselves—the residents of Newport, Rhode Island. Despite the lukewarm welcome they received, Jews established a community in Philadelphia in the early 1700s and, by the middle of the eighteenth century, in the southern cities of Charleston, South Carolina, and Savannah, Georgia. In 1740, British officials decided that the empire would grow faster if Jews and other dissenters based in the provinces were allowed to become naturalized; their trade would then be easier to regulate, and a stronger front against French competition could be erected. Thus, a new law that applied only to the colonies allowed foreign Protestants and Jews (but not Catholics) to become subjects of the crown after they had lived in the colonies for seven years and provided they were not absent for longer than two months during that span. Still, there were fewer than 2,500 Jewish men, women, and children (perhaps 0.1 percent of the population) when Americans declared their independence from Great Britain. Most were members of the mercantile community.

Old World stereotypes also crossed the Atlantic Ocean. Many of their neighbors viewed Jews as dishonest, immoral money-grubbers who engaged in usurious business practices. But religion still generated most of the bigotry. Protestants discriminated against both Jews and Catholics; Puritans rebuked them from the pulpit. In 1669, Boston minister Increase Mather wrote that "the guilt of the bloud of the Lord of Heaven and Earth lyeth upon that nation," accusing Jews of "the most prodigious murther" of Jesus Christ (in Marcus 1970, 3:1119). William Shakespeare's play *The Merchant of Venice*, with its archetypal portrayal of Shylock, opened in Williamsburg, the capital of Virginia, in 1752 and in other cities thereafter. During the American Revolution, in 1778, a group of Jewish women and children fled from British soldiers in Georgia. When they arrived in South Carolina, "An American" wrote to the *Charleston Gazette* to warn the city's residents about "the *Tribe of Israel*" who had taken "every advantage in trade" before seeking "asylum with their ill-got wealth,

dastardly turning their backs upon the country, when in danger, which had given them bread and protection" (in Faber 1992, 96).

In the earliest years of colonization, Jews were occasionally and in some locales barred from owning land, required to live in their own small sections of town, and banned from retailing and practicing some crafts. There were instances of officials imposing heavy fines on Jews—and only Jews—who had committed minor infractions. At first, Jews were only allowed to worship in their own homes and had to petition the authorities before being allowed to have their own cemeteries, one of their first priorities.

Throughout the colonial period, Jews paid taxes to support the established churches in New England, New York, and the South, but they were barred in these places from both voting and holding office for failing to meet religious qualifications. The refusal of Jews to swear Christian oaths was also used against them. Despite such prohibitions, however, the most influential Jewish merchants probably did vote for local offices. By the eighteenth century, Jews could worship publicly, but they were still excluded from exercising political power. British policy forbade both Jews and Catholics from becoming members of the colonial assemblies. On a more personal level, Jews had to endure name-calling and public slander in newspapers, courts, and when business rivalries heated up. Enemies referred to them as "Jew merchants" or "devilish Jews," and a Christian who declared a Christian rival to be "rich as a Jew" was thought to have said something quite insulting. There were rare acts of violence, such as the beating of Naphtali Hart of Newport in the 1740s. On occasion, Jewish cemeteries were desecrated and vandalized.

Despite such examples of enmity, religious toleration was generally more widespread in North America than in Europe at that time. Jews and Christians engaged in business together and married each other. In terms of race, other colonists considered Jews fellow whites when it came to confronting Native Americans and those of African descent. By the late seventeenth century, Jews were allowed to trade freely, and their activities were recognized as economically beneficial. In the ethnically and religiously diverse colonies of Great Britain, for the most part, Jews functioned as one more group of Europeans engaged in the colonization of the Western Hemisphere. During the American Revolution, many Jews distinguished themselves as patriots, and they participated in the politics of revolution and constitution writing to claim political equality.

Following on the heels of such victories, however, Jews faced increased prejudice during the early American republic that paralleled the hardening of racial attitudes toward slaves and Indians in an era of growing nationalism. Still, the most virulent forms of antisemitism did not appear in the United States until the later nineteenth and twentieth centuries.

—*Kim M. Gruenwald*

See also Deicide; Emancipation; Shakespeare, William; Slave Trade and the Jews; Stuyvesant, Peter; United States; Usury

References
Faber, Eli. *A Time for Planting: The First Migration, 1654–1820* (Baltimore, MD: Johns Hopkins University Press, 1992).
Goodfriend, Joyce D. *Before the Melting Pot: Society and Culture in Colonial New York City, 1664–1730* (Princeton, NJ: Princeton University Press, 1992).
Marcus, Jacob R. *The Colonial American Jew, 1492–1776.* 3 vols. (Detroit, MI: Wayne State University Press, 1970).

Commissar Order

The Commissar Order (Kommissarbefehl) of June 6, 1941, was one of a series of orders given to the German Wehrmacht (armed forces), Schutzstaffel (SS), and police forces prior to the invasion of the Soviet Union on June 22, 1941, to prepare for the conduct of a racial war of annihilation in the East. The Commissar Order served as the charter for the notorious Einsatzgruppen (mobile death squads) as German forces prepared to enter Soviet territory on a mission of conquest, exploitation, and extermination. These units acted as the vanguard of Heinrich Himmler's SS forces, tasked with the elimination of the Third Reich's putative racial enemies in the pursuit of "living space."

To avoid conflicts between the SS and police forces and their Wehrmacht counterparts during the invasion of Poland, Adolf Hitler and the senior SS leadership drafted detailed military orders in the spring of 1941, outlining the duties and responsibilities of the various forces to be employed in racial war in the East. On March 3, 1941, Hitler clearly stated his intentions to the Wehrmacht leadership: "The impending campaign . . . entails a struggle between two ideologies. . . . The Jewish-Bolshevik intelligentsia, as the oppressor in the past, must be liquidated" (in Boog, Förster, and Hoffman 1998, 482). On March 13, at Hitler's direction, the chief of the German High Command, Field Marshal Wilhelm Keitel, issued Guidelines in Special Fields Concerning Directive Number 21 to the German armed forces concerning the forthcoming campaign, noting that "on behalf of the Führer, the Reich Leader of the SS (Heinrich Himmler) assumes special tasks in preparation for the political administration within the army's field of operations that arise from the final, decisive battle between two opposing political systems" (in Klein 1997, 365). In a meeting with his senior military commanders at the end of March 1941, Hitler provided explicit guidance on the nature of these "special tasks" assigned to the Wehrmacht and SS. The chief of the German general staff, Gen. Franz Halder, recorded in his war diary (on March 30, 1941), that Hitler repeated his earlier instructions by ordering the "extermination of the Bolshevist Commissars and of the Communist intelligentsia" (Halder 1988).

Hitler further ordered changes in the normal procedures of military jurisdiction, restricting the authority of military courts to examine Soviet citizens charged with criminal offenses. Consequently, such cases were placed in the hands of military and SS field units, eliminating any realistic hope of due process. On May 13, Keitel issued a decree that removed jurisdiction from the courts for criminal offenses committed by "enemy civilians." In essence, this decree created a situation in which Wehrmacht and SS forces literally became judge, jury, and executioner, thereby removing one further obstacle to the conduct of a racial war of extermination.

As Wehrmacht leaders finalized their marching orders, Himmler and the head of the Security Police and Security Service, Reinhard Heydrich, further developed the blueprint for the activities of SS and police forces. In a meeting with Reich Marshal Hermann Göring on March 26, Heydrich reported on SS plans for the "solution to the Jewish Question" in conjunction with the coming campaign. Göring expressed his concern that German forces be made aware of the danger posed by Soviet intelligence personnel (GPU—United State Political Administration), political commissars, and Jews so that they might know who was to be executed. In subsequent negotiations with the army leadership, Himmler and Heydrich finalized the role of SS and police personnel and their relationship to Wehrmacht forces. On May 21, Himmler issued a top-secret decree delineating the command relationship between SS forces and their army counterparts under the subject "Special Order from the Führer." These complex negotiations completed, the groundwork for the murderous activities of SS and police members in the following months was in place.

As German military, SS, and police personnel streamed across the Soviet border in the early hours of June 22, Hitler's vision of an apocalyptic clash between opposing ideologies removed the basic legal and moral limitations of warfare and created the conditions for mass murder. In the final analysis, the Commissar Order functioned as the keystone for a structure of measures that "legalized" the annihilation of the European Jews and the conduct of a racial war of extermination.

—*Edward B. Westermann*

See also Einsatzgruppen; Göring, Hermann; Himmler, Heinrich; Order Police

References

Boog, Horst, Jürgen Förster, and Joachim Hoffmann. *Germany and the Second World War.* Vol. 4, *The Attack on the Soviet Union.* Translated by Dean S. McMurry, Ewald Osers, and Louise Wilmot (Oxford: Clarendon Press, 1998).

Halder, Franz. *The Halder War Diary, 1939–1942.* Edited by Charles Burdick and Hans-Adolf Jacobsen (Novato, CA: Presidio Press, 1988).

Klein, Peter, ed. *Die Einsatzgruppen in der besetzten Sowjetunion, 1941/42* (Berlin: Druckhaus Hentrich, 1997).

Krausnick, Helmut, and Hans-Heinrich Wilhelm. *Die Truppen des Weltanschauungskrieges: Die Einsatzgruppen der Sicherheitspolizei und des SD, 1938–1942* (Stuttgart, Germany: Deutsche Verlags Anstalt, 1981).

Coningsby (1844)

Coningsby, or, The New Generation was the first of Benjamin Disraeli's political trilogy, a series of novels diagnosing the ills of 1840s England. The novels articulate a Conservative response to the new power of the manufacturing class, the grievances of the Chartists, who mounted an unsuccessful struggle for workers' rights, and the contemporary crisis of faith in the English national church. They formed a manifesto for the radical Young England faction of the Tory Party, asserting a renewed commitment to the ancient institutions of church and monarchy but also demanding that politicians engage directly with the modern problems of a nation irrevocably altered by constitutional change, industrialization, and capitalism.

The hero of the trilogy, Coningsby, is a young aristocrat alienated from a sense of national duty because of the decadence and corruption of his class. It is his good fortune, however, to meet Millbank, a manufacturer, and his daughter Edith, who exemplify the virtues of the middle class, which is misguidedly excluded from power and government. Coningsby visits Millbank's factory community, a model village that promotes the health and education of its workers and demonstrates a revival of the spirit of ancient feudalism. Millbank believes in a "natural aristocracy," one constituted by virtue, talents, and property rather than by the arbitrary power of the English ruling elite.

Coningsby is also elevated from his enervation by a chance meeting with the brilliant, cosmopolitan, and emotionally cold Jewish financier Sidonia, the figure in whom Disraeli invests his fantasies about Jewish racial superiority. Sidonia becomes Coningsby's other political mentor, offering him yet another model for reviving Conservative values. "The Jews," Sidonia informs him, "are essentially Tories"(*Coningsby,* chap. 10). In a chapter devoted to the genealogy and character of Sidonia, Disraeli expands the idea of a "natural aristocracy" and applies it to the Jews.

Sidonia is sprung from a Sephardic family of

international capitalists whose survival of the Spanish Inquisition through conversion gave them access to substantial political and economic power. Sidonia, who reverted to Judaism on migrating to tolerant England, holds an elaborate conspiracy theory of Jewish power and informs Coningsby that Jews occupy all the highest positions in European governments and universities as well as masterminding its revolutionary movements. The novel explains the survival of the Jews thus: "Sidonia and his brethren could claim a distinction which the Saxon and the Greek, and the rest of the Caucasian nations, have forfeited. The Hebrew is an unmixed race. . . . An unmixed race of a firstrate organisation are the aristocracy of Nature" (chap. 10).

In contrast to the liberal political strategy of contemporary Anglo-Jews, Disraeli echoed the racial thinking of the vehement antisemite Thomas Carlyle, who spoke of the "law of nature" that ordained a hierarchy of races. In his digression on the Jewish Question in *Lord George Bentinck: A Political Biography* (1852, 323), Disraeli reiterated this claim, arguing that the Jews "are a living and the most striking evidence of the falsity of that pernicious doctrine of modern times, the natural equality of man." By the same token, however, Disraeli assured the English of their ascendancy as an imperial nation, since "a Saxon race, protected by an insular position, has stamped its diligent and methodic character on the century. And when a superior race, with a superior idea to Work and Order, advances, its state will be progressive. . . . All is race; there is no other truth" (Disraeli, *Tancred* 1: 303).

—*Nadia Valman*

See also Disraeli, Benjamin; English Literature from Chaucer to Wells; Rothschilds; "Three Hundred," The

References

Bivona, Daniel. *Desire and Contradiction: Imperial Visions and Domestic Debates in Victorian Literature* (Manchester, UK: Manchester University Press, 1990).

Brantlinger, Patrick. "Nations and Novels: Disraeli, George Eliot, and Orientalism," *Victorian Studies* 35 (1991–1992): 255–273.

Endelman, Todd M., and Tony Kushner, eds. *Disraeli's Jewishness* (London: Vallentine Mitchell, 2002).

Constantine, Emperor (274–337 CE)

In 312, two claimants to the Roman imperial throne, Maxentius (d. 312) and Constantine, met in battle at the Milvian Bridge on the Tiber River in Rome. According to his apologist and biographer (and famous ecclesiastical historian), Eusebius of Caesarea, Constantine had a vision before the battle. In the vision, he supposedly saw a blazing cross and the words *In this sign you shall conquer*. The next day, his forces routed those of Maxentius. For reasons that were evidently tied up with politics and expediency, Constantine "converted" to Christianity, although, as was not unusual then, he deferred baptism until death. Among his first acts was to extend toleration to Christianity. After defeating the Eastern emperor Licinius in battle (in 324), Constantine became sole emperor, in which capacity he set out to strengthen Christianity materially and politically and even to unite it theologically; in the latter two enterprises, he achieved, at best, ambiguous success. Although his conversion was fateful for the future of Christianity and for the entirety of the empire, including the numerous Jewish communities spread out from Palestine to Spain, his attitude toward Jews and Judaism is easily misunderstood.

The central interpretive difficulty in describing Constantine's attitudes toward Jews and Judaism is that so much of what he is commonly believed to have thought and said was filtered through the writings of Eusebius. Like other church fathers, Eusebius wrote in a period when Christianity's "triumph" was far from secure. Just twenty years after his death, the crypto-pagan Emperor Julian (r. 361–363) moved vigorously against the newly tolerated religion. Judaism, moreover, was still cultically attractive to many Christians, and Eusebius and other intellectuals, responding to this competition, attempted to define Christianity, in part, by denouncing its parent religion. All of these factors have to be kept in mind when considering words and actions attributed to Constantine regarding Jews and Judaism.

This advice is especially relevant when considering Constantine's infamous letter concerning the correct day to commemorate the Resurrection of Jesus of Nazareth. Until the early fourth century, many Eastern churches, espe-

Constantine the Great at the Battle at Milvian Bridge (312). Legend states that a cross and the words "in this sign you shall conquer" appeared in the heavens and inspired Constantine to adopt Christianity. (Bettmann/Corbis)

cially in Asia Minor, celebrated it on Nisan 14—that is, on the day of the celebration of Passover; those Christians who so celebrated the feast were thus known as Quartodecimans. Most Western churches celebrated it annually on a Sunday, although others celebrated it on other days. (The whole problem was complicated by the Eastern and Western churches reckoning the vernal equinox differently.) In the letter, "preserved" by Eusebius, Constantine supposedly demanded that the Resurrection be celebrated on Sunday. Repeatedly, he warned his readers that they should "have nothing in common with the Jews"—in other words, they should not celebrate the Resurrection of Jesus on Passover. Indeed, they should "separate themselves from the detestable company of the Jews." After all, the Jews were guilty of the most fearful crimes, deicide. They

were irrational, delusional, blinded by error, and incorrigible. Therefore, Christian souls should not have been "tarnished with communication" with the Jews. Indeed, it was their duty to have nothing "in common with the murderers of the Lord" (Eusebius, *Life of Constantine* 3: 18–20).

Although this letter is often presented as proof of Constantine's hatred of the Jews and the social separation of Jews and Christians, it actually demonstrates nothing of the sort. We learn from this letter much more about Eusebius's attitude toward the Jews—and especially of those sympathetic to the authority of their ancient ritual practice—than we do of Constantine's. His rhetoric was, by any measure, antisemitic, but Eusebius's fury was likely motivated less by Jew-hatred than by fear of the continuing attraction of Judaism for many Christians, the lack of clear cultic and social distinctions between practitioners of the two rival religions, and the social relations that continued between them. Eusebius's anger, which he made Constantine express in this letter, was the result of frustration with "Judaizing" Christians, not with "the Jews" per se.

More clearly unfavorable to the Jews was Constantine's edict of October 315, in which he forbade Jews from attempting to proselytize Christians and at the same time forbade Christians from attending Jewish religious assemblies or converting to Judaism. An attempt to achieve religious and thus imperial unity, the edict was most certainly not an effort to eradicate Judaism or to discontinue Rome's traditional attitude of tolerance. However, Constantine clearly wanted Judaism to cease its missionizing. Eusebius also credited him with having forbidden Jews from owning Christian slaves, but again, whether this reflected Constantine's actual ambitions is ambiguous. Subsequent Roman legislation, not least of all Justinian's Code, would be considerably harsher toward Jewish "superstition" and Jewish economic and political interests.

—*Kevin Madigan*

See also Church Fathers; Deicide; Justinian Code; Roman Empire; Roman Literature; Theodosian Code

References

Barnes, Timothy D. *Constantine and Eusebius* (Cambridge, MA: Harvard University Press, 1981).

Eusebius. *Life of Constantine.* Translated by A. Cameron (Oxford: Oxford University Press, 1999).

Marcus, Jacob R. *The Jew in the Medieval World: A Sourcebook, 315–1791* (Cincinnati, OH: Hebrew Union College Press, 1999).

Constantine Pogrom (1934)

Between August 3 and 5, 1934, Muslim mobs went on a rampage in the Algerian city of Constantine, attacking Jews and Jewish property. In the attack, 25 Jewish men, women, and children were killed, most from having their throats cut or their skulls crushed, and 26 more were injured, according to official statistics. More than 200 Jewish-owned stores were ransacked. The total property damage to homes, businesses, and synagogues was estimated at over 150 million Poincaré francs. Some 3,000 people, one-quarter of Constantine's Jewish population, were in need of welfare assistance in the aftermath of the pogrom. During the rampage, anti-Jewish incidents were recorded in the countryside of the Department of Constantine, extending over a 100-kilometer radius. Jews were murdered in Hamma and Mila, and in Aïn Béïda, Jewish homes and businesses were looted. In all, 314 Jews left Aïn Béïda for good, seeking the relative security of larger communities. During much of the rioting, the French police and security forces stood by and did little or nothing to stop the rioters.

Differing analyses of the causes of the Constantine pogrom were offered by the French colonial administration, by Jews, by Algerian Muslims, and by later historians. All agree that the spark igniting the violence was an argument between a Jewish Zouave (infantryman), Eliahou Khalifa, and worshipers in a mosque adjacent to his home. Eyewitness accounts differed over the precise circumstances. The antisemitic French colonial authorities and press reported only the Muslim version that Khalifa was drunk, urinated on the Arabs, and insulted Islam. A report by the Jewish authorities claimed that he was not inebriated, that he had asked the Muslims to close some windows opening onto their ablution hall for the sake of modesty, and that in the ensuing argument, they had cursed him and his faith and that he in turn cursed them and their religion. ("God curse your religion" is a common imprecation in North Africa freely and frequently used by Muslims and Jews, even between members of the same faith.) Jewish public opinion at the time blamed the incident on a conspiracy between European antisemites in the Algerian colonial bureaucracy and on pan-Arab propaganda. In the official government account at the time, the rioting was described as a completely spontaneous event. The antisemitic *pieds noirs* (colonists) and some Muslims blamed the outbreak on the enmity of the native underclass caused by the arrogance of nouveau riche Jews, who supposedly flaunted their superiority as French citizens under the Crémieux Decree of 1870, and by the alleged exploitation of Jewish moneylenders.

French historian Charles-Robert Ageron has argued that though the violence was spontaneous, it resulted from the grave social and economic conditions at the time. André Chouraqui and Michel Ansky believed that the native mob, consisting mainly of poor, displaced migrants from the countryside, had been manipulated with the collusion of antisemitic colonists and self-serving Arab notables. However, in the most detailed and best-documented study of the pogrom, Israeli historian Robert Attal discounted the importance of the dire socioeconomic conditions and extreme antisemitic agitation. These factors may have provided the background to the event, but the scope and intensity of the violence, Attal suggested, may well have been the result of a cynical decision made in the highest ruling echelons of the country. There, it was decided to make the most of the fortuitous rioting (by doing almost nothing to restrain it) in order to discredit the increasingly vocal Muslim leadership and the continually truculent colonists who opposed any reform of the colonial administration. The Jews of Constantine and the surrounding area were the victims of this scheming.

—*Norman A. Stillman*

See also Algeria; Drumont, Édouard; Farhud; France; Pogroms; Régis, Max

References

Attal, Robert. *Les émeute de Constantine, 5 Août 1934* (Paris: Romillat, 2002).
Stillman, Norman A. *The Jews of Arab Lands in Modern Times* (Philadelphia: Jewish Publication Society, 1991).

Coughlin, Charles E. (1891–1979)

Born in Hamilton, Ontario, in 1891 and educated by the Basilian Fathers in Toronto, Charles E. Coughlin was ordained for the Roman Catholic priesthood in 1916 and then taught at Assumption College in Windsor, Ontario. In 1923, he was welcomed into the diocese of Detroit, where the young priest soon founded a parish in nearby Royal Oak, Michigan. Coughlin took up radio preaching in 1926 to raise money. His great popularity led the Columbia Broadcasting System (CBS) to offer him a contract in 1930. With the impact of the Great Depression spreading, Coughlin's radio sermons turned political. He denounced communism and delivered harsh criticisms of President Herbert Hoover. Although CBS and the National Broadcasting Company (NBC) refused to negotiate a contract with him in 1931, his fame and growing wealth facilitated the creation of his own network, the Radio League of the Little Flower.

Coughlin's calls for social justice in the early years of the Depression flowed naturally from the Catholic social doctrine's emphasis on the common good. He denounced the concentration of wealth and insensitivity to the plight of workers and farmers. At first an eager supporter of President Franklin D. Roosevelt and the early New Deal, he peppered his political sermons with slogans such as "The New Deal Is Christ's Deal!" His early economic prescriptions included cheaper and more abundant currency, abandonment of the gold standard, and the remonetization of silver. His proposals became more aggressive in 1934 when he published his *Sixteen Principles of Social Justice,* which urged the elimination of the Federal Reserve banking system dominated by private bankers and the creation of a bank of the United States that could expand the supply of currency. Coughlin lambasted the detrimental role of "international bankers," "financiers," and "plutocrats," who obstructed economic reform.

By 1934, he was receiving more than 10,000 letters a day, and his weekly broadcasts were reaching an estimated 10 million listeners. As his suggestions went unheeded in Washington, Coughlin began to voice ambivalence toward the New Deal. In November 1934, he launched his National Union for Social Justice to flex his political muscle. He urged its members to support only the candidates who backed his *Sixteen Principles.* In March 1936, he established his weekly, *Social Justice.* Uniting forces with followers of Francis E. Townsend and Gerald L. K. Smith, Coughlin backed Union Party candidate William Lemke in the presidential election of 1936. Staggered by Lemke's weak showing, Coughlin retired from the airwaves for six weeks but returned on New Year's Day in 1937 more embittered than before. His definitive break with Roosevelt significantly diminished his popularity, but the radio priest's core followers remained intensely loyal; they were, by and large, poor Catholics of Irish descent, and most lived in the cities of the East Coast and the Midwest.

Coughlin's violent denunciations of the New Deal for its "communistic" policies developed into an ugly and explicit antisemitism that pervaded *Social Justice* and his radio sermons in 1938. Although the archdiocese of Detroit had assigned Coughlin a censor in 1937, he appeared undeterred. He serialized the *Protocols of the Elders of Zion,* reprinted Nazi propaganda from Joseph Goebbels, and attacked bankers and New Dealers of Jewish descent—without ecclesiastical interference. Coughlin expressed his admiration for Benito Mussolini and Adolf Hitler, particularly their anticommunism. He held Jews responsible for Freemasonry, the French and Russian Revolutions, world communism, and attacks on Christian civilization. He nudged his followers to organize against the Red Menace, giving birth to the Christian Front that in eastern cities attacked Jewish stores and advocated violence. Meanwhile, his Christian Index worked to identify and boycott Jewish merchants. Notwithstanding this extremism, Coughlin collected $574,416 from his followers in 1938.

A strict isolationist, he railed against the "British-Jewish-Roosevelt conspiracy" when World War II broke out. By 1940, the National Association of Broadcasters enacted new codes that left him with no airtime. In the spring of 1942, following the Japanese attack on Pearl Harbor, the government banned *Social Justice* from the mails and warned his superior, Archbishop Edward Mooney of Detroit, that Coughlin faced sedition charges if his rancorous activities continued. Only then did the Catholic Church move to silence him, although he remained the pastor of his parish in Royal Oak until his retirement in 1966. He died in 1979.

—*Peter R. D'Agostino*

See also Goebbels, Joseph; Hitler, Adolf; Mussolini, Benito; Pelley, William Dudley; *Protocols of the Elders of Zion;* Smith, Gerald L. K.; United States
References
Bennett, David H. *Demagogues in the Depression: American Radicals and the Union Party,* *1932–1936* (New Brunswick, NJ: Rutgers University Press, 1969).
Brinkley, Alan. *Voices of Protest: Huey Long, Father Coughlin, and the Great Depression* (New York: Alfred A. Knopf, 1982).
Tentler, Leslie Woodcock. *Seasons of Grace: A History of the Catholic Archdiocese of Detroit* (Detroit, MI: Wayne State University Press, 1990).

Court Jews

At times during the Middle Ages, Jews had played prominent roles at princely, royal, and imperial courts under both Christians and Muslims—for example, during the golden age of Spanish Jewry. In the early modern era, more Jews performed these functions and faced many of the same challenges as their forerunners. They acted in important capacities for the numerous petty and grand ecclesiastical and secular courts of the German states, operating as agents of a growing absolutist and mercantilist economic system, supplying armies, minting coinage, and raising taxes; they served as diplomats; and they developed manufacturing, often in regions troubled by war and political intrigue, as during the Thirty Years' War, the struggle for the Polish Crown, or the defense against the resurgent Turks. In some cases, powerful Jews conducted operations simultaneously in several areas and under many rulers. According to some estimates, there may have been thousands of court Jews, at various levels.

Straddling a fine line between service to their overlords and commitment to their own Jewish communities, court Jews—their personalities, careers, and Jewish identities—have been the object of several scholarly investigations. They were generally shrewd businessmen but far from independent. They were subject to the whims of the ruler and often envied by others at court. Among the general population, they were hated because of their Jewishness and as the visible agents of often rapacious princes. Despite the extensive network of family and business contacts, leading occasionally to the establishment of influential dynasties and the accumulation of great wealth, court Jews often fell victim to one or another of the perils that surrounded them at all times. Although serviceable Jews were tolerated and even privileged, theories of toleration of Jews or Judaism played no role in the rulers' considerations. Jews were utilized primarily for practical and financial purposes. They could be readily sacrificed if expediency demanded.

Theirs was a dangerous business. The granting of monopolies produced resentment among non-Jewish merchants and craftspeople. Jews involved in provisioning armies could quickly become scapegoats for inferior equipment or poor food and pay. Coin clipping—a way of enhancing the prince's revenues—and devaluing of currency produced widespread popular anger that targeted Jewish mint masters. Acting as tax farmers put Jews in harm's way when the prince's subjects rebelled against his exploitation. Although court Jews enjoyed privileges related to residence, travel, and business prerogatives and benefited from protection that other Jews (and non-Jews) did not possess, they normally experienced great ups and downs in prosperity and sometimes in physical safety. Popular unrest that erupted in violence against powerless Jews did not always exempt powerful court Jews.

Some historians have portrayed the court Jews as secularists and precursors of Reform Judaism. Recent scholarship, however, has stressed the traditional and religiously observant life of most court Jews, as well as their strong ties with, work for, and devotion to the Jewish community.

—*Dean Phillip Bell*

See also Coin Clipping; Islam and the Jews; Jud Süss; Middle Ages, High
References
Israel, Jonathan. *European Jewry in the Age of Mercantilism, 1550–1750* (Oxford and London: Clarendon Press, 1998).
Mann, Vivian B., and Richard I. Cohen, eds. *From Court Jews to the Rothschilds: Art, Patronage and Power, 1600–1800* (Munich, Germany, and New York: Prestel, 1996).
Meyer, Michael A., Michael Brenner, Mordechai Breuer, and Michael Graetz, eds. *German-Jewish History in Modern Times.* 4 vols. (New York: Columbia University Press, 1996), especially vol. 1, *Tradition and Enlightenment: 1600–1780.*
Stern, Selma. *The Court Jew: A Contribution to the History of the Period of Absolutism in Central Europe.* Translated by Ralph Weiman (Philadelphia: Jewish Publication Society of America, 1950).

Crimes against Humanity (French Trials)

Crimes against humanity have had a complicated and controversial history in postwar France. In December 1964, the French parliament voted unanimously to suspend the statute of limitations on crimes against humanity as defined in article 6c of the charter of the International Criminal Tribunal at Nuremberg (ICT). With the statute of limitations running out on war crimes, the aim of the legislators was to bar Nazi war criminals permanently from French soil by holding the threat of prosecution over their heads. The law was not intended to be applied to French citizens and specifically those who had worked for the Vichy government. Therefore, when three Frenchmen—Paul Touvier, René Bousquet, and Maurice Papon—were later charged and in the cases of Touvier and Papon tried under the law, the accusations and trials created considerable controversy.

From the outset, the incorporation of crimes against humanity into French law raised a number of thorny legal and moral issues. First, the question as to which court would have jurisdiction in these matters was left unresolved, which would complicate and delay the prosecution of Paul Touvier for years after initial charges against him were filed in 1973. Second, the language of the ICT statute did not specify whether the law was intended to be applied to others besides citizens of the Reich, which complicated the legal and historical issues at stake when Touvier was finally tried in 1994. Third, the fact that the law could (and would) be applied retroactively and that it was imprescriptible seemed to many to run counter to the spirit of justice in which it was conceived. Finally, especially when Maurice Papon was tried in the 1997–1998 fall and winter in Bordeaux, many questioned the justice of putting a very old man in apparently fragile health on trial for crimes committed fifty years earlier.

The first individual tried for crimes against humanity in France was not, in fact, a Frenchman but the former Gestapo chief in Lyon, Klaus Barbie. Known as "the Butcher of Lyon" primarily for torturing and executing Resistance members—including France's greatest Resistance hero and martyr Jean Moulin in 1943—Barbie had fled France at the end of the war and worked for the Americans in Germany as an anti-Soviet agent. Eventually, along with his family, he escaped Europe with the help of elements in the Catholic Church and via the U.S. "rat line," a clandestine network for the "resettlement" of army counter-intelligence operatives. He turned up in South America in 1951, where, among other activities, he set up a successful export company and helped the right-wing government in Bolivia create a secret terrorist army, the Fiancés of Death, conceived along SS lines. Living under the name Klaus Altmann, Barbie led a very comfortable and secure life and remained completely loyal to Nazism and the memory of Hitler.

In the early 1970s, Barbie's identity was revealed primarily through the efforts of Nazi hunters Serge Klarsfeld and, especially, Beate Klarsfeld, but efforts to extradite him to Europe failed because he enjoyed the protection of the Bolivian president. In the early 1980s, a regime change in Bolivia resulted in a loss of Barbie's protection. Secret negotiations between the French and Bolivian governments made it possible to arrest Barbie and to secret him out of the country in February 1983. Once in France, he was imprisoned in Montluc Prison, where Resistance fighters had been jailed, tortured, and executed four decades earlier.

Barbie was immediately charged with crimes against humanity. Although this made it possible for him to be prosecuted for his role in the Final Solution—along these lines, Barbie was most infamous for ordering the arrest and deportation of Jewish children hidden by locals in the village of Izieu—his actions against the Resistance were not covered under the law. For many former Resistance fighters, to indict and try Barbie without reference to these crimes and especially the murder of Jean Moulin was not only ludicrous but a miscarriage of justice. But raising the issue of Barbie's crimes against the Resistance was a double-edged sword, which Barbie's lawyer deftly exploited. Moulin had, after all, been betrayed by members of the Resistance. To bring up the issue of Barbie's crimes against the Resistance and specifically the torture and murder of Moulin risked, therefore, not only exposing the Resis-

tance's "unheroic side" and tarnishing its memory but also stirring old animosities in the ranks of Resistance veterans.

Despite these difficulties, on December 20, 1985, the Criminal Chamber of the French Court of Appeals modified the definition of crimes against humanity to make it possible to include some crimes against the Resistance in the charges against Barbie. Henceforth, individuals acting on behalf of a "State practicing a policy of ideological hegemony" could be prosecuted under the law not only for persecuting individuals "because of their appurtenance to a racial or religious collectivity" but also for their actions against "adversaries" of this state, "regardless of the form of (the latter's) opposition." Although the prosecution's case now needed to be reconstructed, the trial could, in principle, at last move forward with the full range of Barbie's crimes taken into account.

The Barbie trial took place in Lyon from May 11 to July 4, 1987. The indictment included his role in the implementation of the Final Solution as well as his actions against the Resistance. No effort was made to distinguish between these two types of crimes, a factor that might have resulted in legal controversies except that the Resistance members mentioned in the indictment and victimized by Barbie were also Jewish. At the conclusion of the trial, he was found guilty and sentenced to life in prison. His conviction, moreover, accelerated the process of indicting and trying French citizens for crimes against humanity, because there was now a logical justification for using the same law against French defendants accused of similar crimes.

The next individual to be tried for crimes against humanity in France was Paul Touvier, an intelligence officer in Vichy's paramilitary and fascist militia, or *milice,* created in January 1943 to fight "France's enemies," especially Resistance fighters and Jews. Although Touvier was ultimately nothing more than a con man, thief, and murderer, his story is a fascinating one (fictionalized in Brian Moore's excellent 1995 novel, *The Statement*). Born into a fanatically reactionary, petit bourgeois Catholic family in the village of Chambéry, Touvier was one of eleven children. A ne'er-do-well before the war who worked primarily as a railway clerk, he joined Vichy's veteran's organization in 1940, quickly signed up with the milice, and began to climb the hierarchy. He attended the milice's leadership school at Uriage and assumed an important intelligence role in the Lyons, where in all likelihood he knew and perhaps worked with Klaus Barbie.

Although brutally efficient, Touvier was hardly a model policeman or soldier. He fleeced his victims, pimped for a mistress, and lived like a Mafia boss during the German Occupation. But he was also careful to preserve his close ties with the Catholic Church and especially its most reactionary elements. When the Germans fled Lyons, Touvier went underground but preferred "inner exile" to leaving the country. He robbed to survive in Paris, where he escaped once from the police, and when he needed help for himself, his wife, and his two children, he relied on the church, staying in convents throughout France.

From the beginning, Touvier was adept at convincing powerful figures in the church that he was an innocent victim and indeed a Christian martyr, and his tales of woe aroused the sympathy of other visible public figures, as well. In 1971, highly placed members of the clergy convinced President Georges Pompidou that Touvier had suffered enough for his activities during the war and that he should be pardoned. When news of the presidential pardon leaked out to the media, the public outrage was considerable. In September 1972, in an attempt to justify the pardon, Pompidou gave a press conference in which he asked if the time had not come "to draw a veil over the past, to forget a time when Frenchmen didn't like each other." As events would prove, that time had decidedly not come, and Touvier, now hounded by the public, was forced into hiding again. He was finally arrested for good in a monastery in Nice in 1989, where he was hiding under the name Paul Lacroix.

Touvier was not tried until spring 1994, and the numerous delays and legal controversies that took place before his trial confirm the extent to which many, including some in the judicial system itself, were reluctant to try the former milice member. In July 1991, public consternation greeted a decision by the Indictments Division of the Court of Appeals to release Touvier on his own recognizance because his imprisonment "was no longer necessary to the discovery of the truth." Given Touvier's long history of fleeing the law, speculation abounded that he would do so again.

A bigger bombshell fell in April 1992. The Paris Court of Appeals decided to acquit Touvier of all charges of crimes against humanity on the grounds that the Vichy regime that he served was not a regime that practiced a "politics of ideological hegemony." Under French law, as articulated in the 1985 definition cited earlier, only individuals acting on behalf of a regime that was "ideologically hegemonic" could commit crimes against humanity. In effect, the April 1992 decision not only allowed Touvier to walk, it also whitewashed the regime itself.

On November 27, 1992, the Criminal Chamber of the High Court of Appeals partially overturned the April acquittal of Touvier, retaining only one of several charges: that Touvier had ordered the execution of seven Jews at the cemetery of Rillieux-la-Pape in June 1944. The trial itself finally got under way on March 17, 1994, in Versailles, to intense press coverage. The prosecution successfully argued that Touvier had ordered the murder of the seven Jews and that he had chosen them *because* they were Jewish. (Touvier chose to spare one non-Jewish prisoner also slated for execution.) Moreover, the court rejected the defense's claim that Touvier had actually been ordered by his superiors to execute many more Jews and that, in supposedly sparing these lives, he could legitimately claim the title of the "French Schindler."

For the prosecution, the principal objective was to prove that Touvier had acted as a *German* agent, since the Vichy regime itself still remained out of bounds where crimes against humanity were concerned. Arno Klarsfeld (son of Beate and Serge), one of the lawyers for the civil parties, argued successfully that, since the head of the milice had sworn an oath of loyalty to Hitler, the milice—to which Touvier belonged and in whose name he had acted—could be considered an agency of Nazi Germany, a regime that unquestionably practiced a politics of ideological hegemony. If this was the case, then Touvier's crime could be considered a crime against humanity. As a result of Klarsfeld's successful argument, Touvier was convicted of crimes against humanity for the Rillieux murders and sentenced to life in prison.

To an important degree, the Touvier verdict underscored real difficulties in France's effort to come to terms with its Vichy past through trials for crimes against humanity. As noted, in order to convict Touvier, it was necessary to argue that he acted as a German agent. From a historical perspective, this was a highly dubious claim, as was the assertion made by the Paris Court of Appeals in its April 1992 acquittal of Touvier that Vichy was not a regime practicing a politics of ideological hegemony. Finally, questions remained as to whether the execution of the seven Jews at Rillieux was really a crime against humanity, in that they were murdered not in the context of a genocidal policy to exterminate Jews but as an act of reprisal for the Resistance's assassination the day before of Vichy's propaganda minister, Philippe Henriot. Although the conviction of Touvier was hailed as a victory for the memory of the victims and helped pave the way for the prosecution of "bigger fish" such as Maurice Papon, it left many historians, as well as legal experts, convinced that history and the law itself had suffered in the process. As one legal expert noted, crimes against humanity continued to be modified to suit the needs—and the accused—of the moment to the extent that they were rapidly losing legal specificity.

Unlike Paul Touvier, Maurice Papon had a distinguished postwar career as a Gaullist civil servant and government minister. Having served the Vichy regime in Bordeaux during the Occupation, where he had been responsible for rounding up and deporting Jews between 1942 and 1944, Papon stayed on briefly there in the post-Liberation government. He later served in the prefectural corps in Corsica and then in France's North African holdings, where he made a name for himself in putting down, often brutally, native unrest.

In March 1958, Papon became prefect of the Paris police, and he was asked to stay on when the Gaullists returned to power a few months later. His tenure was characterized by further brutalities, this time in the deadly suppression of pro-Algerian demonstrations (in October 1961). Papon retired to the private sector and then returned to political life as a Gaullist functionary and a representative of the Cher region. In 1978, he became minister of the budget under President Valéry Giscard-d'Estaing.

In May 1981, the satirical political newspaper *Le Canard enchaîné* published an article entitled "Papon, aide de camps" in which Papon's role in the deportation of Jews from the Bordeaux region during the Occupation was brought to public attention for the first time. In the months following, Papon lost the support of the Gaullists in his bid for reelection from the Cher, and relatives of the victims of the Bordeaux deportations accused him of crimes against humanity. An honor jury of former Resisters found him innocent of responsibility for the deportations from Bordeaux but acknowledged that he should have left his post rather than perform the heinous duties assigned to him.

For the next sixteen years, Papon's role in the deportations was the subject of media exposés, suits and countersuits, and charges and countercharges, as well as judicial wranglings. Following the convictions of Barbie and Touvier, as well as the indictment of René Bousquet on charges of crimes against humanity for his role in the deportations of the Jews to the death camps (see the later discussion), it became increasingly difficult for Papon to avoid prosecution. Finally, in December 1995, the prosecutor in Bordeaux, with prompting from the minister of justice, decided to try Papon in the city's Assizes Court, and in October 1997, the trial got under way, with worldwide media attention.

From a legal standpoint, the indictment of Papon avoided some of the obstacles of the earlier indictments of Barbie and Touvier. Papon was not charged with acts against the Resistance (in fact, former Resistance members testified on his behalf at the trial). Moreover, one could not argue, as had been the case with Touvier, that Papon's crime was a "French crime" and therefore not subject to prosecution as a crime against humanity. The deportations of the Jews from Bordeaux was clearly a German initiative. But unlike Touvier, Papon could not be characterized as a direct and willing accomplice, a requirement that was part of the November 1992 decision in the Touvier case. To circumvent this difficulty, the Court of Appeals ruled in January 1997 that it was no longer necessary for the accomplice of crimes against humanity to "adhere to the politics of ideological hegemony of the principal authors of the crime."

From the outset, the Papon trial generated fireworks. On October 8, 1997, the opening day of the trial, Papon's lawyer demanded his client's liberation from incarceration for the duration of the trial. If the request was denied, Papon would refuse to testify. The judge was thus forced to accede to the defense's request. Shortly thereafter, the trial was almost derailed by controversy surrounding Papon's role in the suppression of Algerian protestors in Paris in 1961. Some maintained that these actions should be considered crimes against humanity as well. Under any circumstances, the controversy regarding events in 1961 obscured, at least initially, the extent and nature of Papon's crimes during the Occupation.

The trial was also marred later on by the flawed memory of many witnesses, which tended, on occasion, to discredit their testimony and damage the prosecution. Similarly, misguided former Gaullist Resisters attacked the trial as a denigration of Gaullism and the memory of the Resistance, as well as an effort by the Germans to blame France for their crimes.

When the verdict was announced six months later, on April 2, 1997, Papon was found guilty of complicity in the "arrest" of thirty-seven individuals and the "arbitrary detention" of fifty-six more in relation to several convoys destined for the death camps between 1942 and 1944. To the consternation of many, he was found not guilty of complicity in the murders of these individuals. Papon was sentenced to ten years in prison for his crimes. In fall 1999, having failed in his appeal, he fled to Switzerland, where, living under an alias, he was quickly arrested and returned to France. In September 2002, a new French law requiring the liberation of infirmed prisoners was passed, and Papon was immediately released.

Although Papon's was almost certainly the last trial in France for crimes against humanity committed during the German Occupation, the irony is that the most important figure associated with Vichy's complicity in the Nazi Final Solution, René Bousquet, never went to trial. Bousquet, a successful young Radical Party politician and civil servant before the war who briefly served in Léon Blum's Popular Front government, was head of Vichy police between April 1942 and December 1943. In that capacity, he was responsible for the infamous roundup of Jews in July 1942 known as the Vel d'Hiv roundups. Some 4,500 French police rounded up nearly 13,000 Jews in Paris and held them in terrible conditions for several days at the Vel d'Hiv indoor bicycle-racing track before they were taken to Drancy, where most were deported to the death camps. Two weeks later, Bousquet negotiated far-reaching accords with Karl Oberg, SS leader in France, which created strong links between French and German police in the fight against the Resistance and the arrest and deportation of Jews in both the Occupied and Unoccupied Zones. Throughout the summer and fall, French police zealously arrested Jews in both zones, some as young as two years of age. Bousquet's direct orders enabled these actions.

In 1943, German authorities took increasing control of the deportations, and Bousquet's star began to wane, although his ties with influential Nazis remained strong. After the Liberation, Bousquet was imprisoned and was finally tried for treason in 1949. His role in the deportations was not a significant factor in the trial. He was sentenced to five years in prison, although the sentence was immediately commuted for acts of "important service" to the Resistance. Following his release, Bousquet became a wealthy and successful businessman and a personal friend of François Mitterrand, eventually the president of France.

In October 1978, Bousquet's role in the Vel d'Hiv roundups was revealed in a magazine interview with Louis Darquier de Pellepoix, a former Vichy minister of Jewish affairs. Thus exposed, Bousquet began to lose influential positions on corporate boards, but it took more than ten years, until September 1989, before a complaint alleging crimes against humanity was brought against him by Serge Klarsfeld. In 1990, the Indictments Division of the Paris Court of Appeals forwarded its findings to the prosecutor general, who, after initially ordering the Indictments Division to proceed with the case, reversed himself and stated that the Bousquet's case could only be handled by the High Court of the Liberation, which had tried Bousquet in 1949 and had long since ceased to exist. This was, of course, a subterfuge designed to bury the case. As it turned out, the prosecutor general was acting on indirect orders from President Mitterrand, who, it appeared, was seeking to protect his friend. Following public outcry, the Indictments Division ignored the prosecutor general's order and declared itself competent to proceed with the case.

By the end of 1992, Bousquet was formally charged with crimes against humanity, and his trial was scheduled for fall 1993. However, on June 8, 1993, a deranged publicity seeker, Christian Didier, entered Bousquet's apartment and shot him dead. Didier later told the press that he had the impression of "crushing a snake."

As the Barbie, Touvier, Papon, and Bousquet affairs reveal, crimes against humanity have a long and complicated history in postwar France. For some, the trials of Barbie, Touvier, and Papon fulfilled a sacred "duty to memory" and were entirely justified in that light. However, for many historians and legal experts, the historical distortions and repeated modifications of the law necessary to prosecute and convict these individuals cast a permanent shadow over France's otherwise laudable efforts to come to terms with its past and do justice to the victims of Vichy's complicity with Nazism.

—*Richard J. Golsan*

See also Darquier de Pellepoix, Louis; Holocaust; Vallat, Xavier; Vichy

References

Golsan, Richard J. *Memory, the Holocaust, and French Justice: The Bousquet and Touvier Affairs* (Hanover, NH: University Press of New England, 1996).

———. *Vichy's Afterlife: History and Counterhistory in Postwar France* (Lincoln: University of Nebraska Press, 2000).

Rousso, Henry. *The Vichy Syndrome: History and Memory in France since 1944* (Cambridge, MA: Harvard University Press, 1991).

Rousso, Henry, and Eric Conan. *Vichy: An Ever-Present Past* (Hanover, NH: University Press of New England, 1998).

Croatia

In medieval times, Jewish communities in Dubrovnik, Split, and Zagreb were small. The randomly recorded conflicts in these places reflected traditional animosity against Jews, rather than antisemitism of the modern variety. In 1502, Jews in Dubrovnik were accused of the ritual murder of an old woman. When some confessed under torture, seven were sentenced to death. Jews were probably expelled from Zagreb during the 1450s. The first expressions of more modern frictions occurred in Zagreb, where local Catholic merchants, in 1769 and 1780, protested against Jewish competitors, using traditional religious arguments but also claiming that their ancient rights had been infringed on.

When Jews began to move into northern Croatia at the end of the eighteenth century and the beginning of the nineteenth, antisemitism also appeared, nurtured by enmity between Christianity and Judaism, competition posed by Jewish merchants, and a general feeling of xenophobia against Jews as newcomers and aliens. In Croatia, an additional cause of mistrust had to do with language; Jewish immigrants at first usually spoke Hungarian and German. In the very complicated political and cultural circumstances of the late nineteenth century, this factor helped to alienate Croatian (and Serbian and Yugoslav) nationalists, who were sensitive to the claims of linguistic precedence.

The attitude toward the Jews of the great Croatian leader Bishop Josip Juraj Strossmayer (1815–1905) was ambivalent. Publicly, he expressed his admiration for Jewish ethics, culture, and other values. He had cordial relations with some rabbis. But in private letters, which were published long after he died, he called the Jews the "degenerates of mankind, enemies of Christianity, usurers, Hungary-lovers, national traitors, immoral and stinking individuals" (Vannutelli 1999, 311). Anti-Hungarian demonstrations in 1883 also targeted Jews, who were seen as foreigners and detested as merchants, especially by the peasant population.

The growth of antisemitic sentiment and its development into an ideology can be traced, in part, to Prague, where many Croatian students and intellectuals, who later adopted pronouncedly antisemitic stances, had gone to study at the turn of the twentieth century. During the Dreyfus Affair, some circles in Croatian political life called for the unmasking of Émile Zola "as a Jewish hireling." Others found the works of Houston Stewart Chamberlain worthy of praise. The most fervent antisemitic statements were made by the distinguished member of the Party of State Rights Grga Tuškan during the First Croatian Catholic Congress in Zagreb (1900). He cast all blame for the poverty of the people on the Jews. However, other members did not support his indictment. The case of Josip Frank, a Jewish convert to Christianity and a leader of the nationalistic, pro-Austrian Pure Party of State Rights, demonstrates the political uses to which antisemitism could be put in the country. Frank proclaimed himself the champion of a "firm" brand of Croatian consciousness. His opponents promptly attacked his Jewish roots, saying he worked on behalf of a modern Jewish liberalism, and they renamed his journal "*Kosher*" and labeled its reporters "kosher journalists."

Antisemitism was also strong in Serbian political circles of Croatia, especially in the Serbian Independent Party and its paper, *Srbobran*. The antisemitism of the Serbs stemmed largely from competition between Serbian and Jewish economic interests. In other Serbian-language newspapers of this period, the terms *kikes* and *Croats* were regularly paired, along with derisive descriptions of Croatia as the New Palestine.

At the end of World War I, the Habsburg monarchy disintegrated and the newly formed Kingdom of Serbs, Croats, and Slovenes (Yugoslavia after 1929) slowly came into being. During this period of uncertainty, the looting and vandalism of Jewish shops became common occurrences in northern Croatia. In some of the bigger towns, such as Bjelovar and Varaždin, Jewish communities were pressured into paying protection money in order to be allowed to stay and to avoid pillage. After 1919, Jews born outside the newly created kingdom, especially those from the former Austro-Hungarian Empire, found obstacles put in the way of achieving citizenship; the Yugoslav authorities wanted to banish them altogether. Only intercession by Jewish organizations within Yugoslavia stopped the expulsions. However, by this time, many Jews had already suffered irreparable economic harm.

Following this turbulent early period of statehood, antisemitic incidents were in abeyance. But the relative peace was shattered with new disturbances starting in the early 1930s, this time under the influence of the Nazis' propaganda and with their financial help. Nazi racist theory combined with traditional Croatian elements to constitute the basis of a new campaign of antisemitism, organized through marginal sensationalist newspapers, which were sometimes banned by the police. They fabricated a new vocabulary overrun with terms such as *Judeo-liberals, Judeo-usurers, Judeo-capitalists,* and *Judeo-Marxists*. But the campaign was far from universally welcomed in Croatia. In 1938, Vladko Maček, the leader of the powerful Croatian Peasant Party, condemned antisemitism as a "ridiculous phenomenon . . . there is no Jewish danger anywhere." He called it a hallucination to be found "in some circles" (in Goldstein 2003, 401).

Under Nazi pressure in September and October 1940, the Yugoslav government issued two decrees limiting the rights of Jews. The first was the Decree on Measures Concerning Jews and the Performance of Activities with Items of Human Nutrition, which, in fact, banned all wholesale enterprises dealing in foodstuffs whose owners or co-owners were Jews. The second was called the Decree on the Enrollment of Persons of Jewish Descent at University, Senior, Secondary, Teacher Training and Other Vocational Schools, which introduced the *numerus clausus* (fixed maximum number) for Jews. Although neither decree, particularly the second one, was rigorously enforced, members of the Jewish community could not escape the recognition that they were no longer equal citizens of the state.

When World War II began for Yugoslavia in April 1941, and the Independent State of Croatia was created, a fervent antisemitic campaign began immediately. Its accusations were either imitations of or direct transferences from Nazi propaganda. The scale of the effort was unprecedented. Hundreds of articles in the press and many booklets were published. The onslaught continued until the end of 1941, when the authorities declared that the Jewish Question had been solved, a euphemistic way to describe the mass murder of Croatia's Jews.

Antisemitism in post–World War II, Communist Yugoslavia differed markedly from that found in Eastern bloc countries. Having avoided Stalinization, the Yugoslavs also avoided many of the antisemitic consequences of that process, particularly the show trials and purges that targeted Jews. Anti-Zionism, for example, already rife in the USSR and elsewhere in the 1950s, did not affect Yugoslavia, where Jews could maintain contact with Jewish organizations in Israel and the United States. Only after the Six Days' War of 1967, when diplomatic relations with Israel were broken off and close relationships were formed with Arab countries, did a less intense form of anti-Zionism surface in Yugoslavia.

—*Ivo Goldstein*

See also Anti-Zionism in the USSR; Chamberlain, Houston Stewart; Croatia, Holocaust in; Dreyfus Affair; Expulsions, Late Middle Ages; Judeo-Bolshevism; *Numerus Clausus* (Hungary); *Numerus Clausus* (United States); Purges, Soviet; Ritual Murder (Medieval); Ustasha; Zola, Émile

References
Freidenreich, Harriet Pass. *The Jews of Yugoslavia: A Quest for Community* (Philadelphia: Jewish Publication Society of America, 1979).
Goldstein, Ivo. "Anti-Semitism in Croatia." In *Anti-Semitism, Holocaust, Antifascism.* Edited by Ivo Goldstein and Narcisa Lengel Krizman (Zagreb, Croatia: Zagreb Jewish Community 1997), 12–52.
———. *Židovi u Zagrebu 1918–1941* (Zagreb, Croatia: Novi liber, 2003).
Kerkkänen, Ari. *Yugoslav Jewry: Aspects of Post–World War II and Post-Yugoslav Developments.* Studia Orientalia 93 (Helsinki: Finnish Oriental Society, 2001).
Vannutelli, Serafin, ed. *Korespondencija Josip Juraj Strossmayer.* (Zagreb, Croatia: J. Balabanić–J. Kolanović.)

Croatia, Holocaust in

In the genocide perpetrated against the Jewish population of the Independent State of Croatia (ISC) from 1941 to 1945, somewhat more than 75 percent of the Jews in the territory of the present-day Croatia and Bosnia-Herzegovina were killed. Before the war, about 38,000 or 39,000 Jews lived on the territory of the ISC,

and only about 9,000 survived to the end of the war. The statistics according to region fall within the parameters of the national mortality rates: out of 14,000 Jews in Bosnia-Herzegovina, only 4,000 (or nearly 30 percent) survived, and out of 25,000 Jews in the northern parts of Croatia, only about 5,000 (or about 20 percent) were saved. The situation was a little better in Dalmatia, but there were only about 400 Jews living there before the war, out of whom about 250 survived.

Following the example of the Nazis, from whom they frequently received instructions, the Ustasha, the extremist nationalist movement that ruled the ISC during the war, added to their plans for killing Serbs even more severe measures against the Jews. Premeditation was apparent and again followed the German three-stage model: isolation, concentration, and extermination.

The ISC was established on April 10, 1941, following the German-Italian attack on Yugoslavia. Immediate and fervent antisemitic propaganda started to appear in newspapers. On April 30, the Legal Provision for the Protection of the Aryan Blood and Honor of the Croatian People was promulgated; it banned marriages between Jews and persons of "Aryan" origin. Jews could not get around this provision the way Serbs could, by converting to the Catholic faith, because the status of the Jews was clearly defined by the provision on "racial" grounds. All Jews over six years of age had to wear a yellow badge in public, and their movements were restricted.

In June, under the Legal Provision for the Protection of the National and Aryan Culture of the Croatian People, Jews were banned from "participating in the work, organizations and institutions of the social, youth, sports, and cultural life of the Croatian people in general, and especially in literature, journalism, the arts and music, town planning, the theater, and film."

Almost from the beginning of the Ustasha state, the authorities cast an eye on Jewish (and Serbian) property. Thus, special "legal provisions" were enacted according to which Jewish movables and real estate were declared to be "state-owned." In other words, looting became possible in the name of the state. However, in practice, even more open robbery was carried out by officials of the regime. A drastic example was the extortion of 1,004 kilograms of gold that the Jews of Zagreb had to turn over in May 1941 to save their lives. In some places, primarily in Slavonia and Bosnia-Herzegovina, members of the German minority (Volksdeutscher) took part in anti-Jewish activities.

Arrests of Jews began during the first days of Ustasha rule. At first, prominent and influential individuals of the Jewish community were taken away. In May, arrests were organized on a larger scale, and in June, there were still more. On June 21, for example, all the members of the Zagreb "Maccabi" sports club were arrested. The campaign was then intensified and channeled more purposefully toward the Final Solution. It was conducted under the slogan "In the ISC there is no room for Jews." In late June, Ante Pavelić stated in the Emergency Legal Provision and Order that "the Jews are spreading false information . . . and hindering the distribution of supplies to the population" and that they were "collectively considered responsible and therefore measures will be taken against them and they will be put away, because of their criminal responsibility, into prison camps under the open sky" *Narodne novine* (Zagreb), June 27, 1941; *Ustaša*, 3 (Zagreb), July 3, 1941). Throughout the ISC, this was the signal for large-scale arrests and deportations to camps on Croatian territory. Women and children were included. Varaždin, a town in northern Croatia, was declared to be the first town "cleansed" of Jews. The Ustasha regime made careful plans for this, the last stage of solving the Jewish Question. It established almost thirty assembly or transit camps, in which Jews who had been arrested were held until being deported to the death camps or concentration camps that were established at the same time. By the summer, a number of death camps were organized around Gospić in the southern province of Lika; in them, mass liquidations took place.

The location of these first camps was unfavorable, so in the autumn of 1941, a new complex of death camps was set up in the Jasenovac–Stara Gradiška area. The camps continued to function almost until the end of the war. Most of the approximately 18,000 Jews from northern Croatia and Bosnia were killed there. Many died of starvation. Taking and then shooting hostages also accounted for many Jewish deaths.

In early 1942, the Schutzstaffel (SS) in Croatia estimated that the Ustasha authorities, in spite of their cruelty, had not carried out the Final Solution thoroughly enough. Therefore, in August 1942 and again in May 1943, Germans took a direct and active part and together with Ustasha police captured between 5,000 and 6,000 Jews, most of whom were then transported to Auschwitz.

Only a few Jewish inmates of Jasenovac survived, and only rare individuals returned from Auschwitz. A small number of Jews survived on the territory directly ruled by the Ustasha, but this happened only by chance or because of the exceptional agility of the survivors or the people in their immediate environment. These included personal acquaintances and family connections, Catholic clergy who interceded on their behalf, and officials who could be corrupted.

In mid-1942, Ustasha ideologist Danijel Crljen proclaimed that the Jewish Question had been solved in Croatia, boasting of a thoroughness and persistence that ought to warn off all those who might contest the Ustasha movement.

Nevertheless, about 5,000 Jews saved their lives by fleeing to the Italian zone within the ISC and to the parts of Croatia occupied by Italy in 1941. After the capitulation of Italy in 1943, most of them joined Tito's Partisans or lived until the end of the war on territories controlled by the partisans.

—*Ivo Goldstein*

See also Aryanization; Croatia; Holocaust; Nuremberg Laws; Pavelić, Ante; Ustasha

References

Goldstein, Ivo. *Holokaust u Zagrebu* (Zagreb, Croatia: Novi liber—Židovska općina Zagreb, 2001).
Romano, Jaša. *Jevreji Jugoslavije, 1941–1945: Žrtve genocida i učesnici Narodnooslobodilačkog rata* (Jews of Yugoslavia, 1941–1945: Victims of Genocide and Participants in the National Liberation War) (Belgrade: Jevrejski Istorijski Muzej Saveza Jevrejskih Opština Jugoslavije, 1980).

Cross and the Flag, The

Gerald L. K. Smith founded *The Cross and the Flag* in 1942, claiming that an angel had whispered the title of the journal to him in a vision

Gerald L. K. Smith, editor and publisher of *The Cross and the Flag,* as he looks over the first copy of the publication with his associate editor, Bernard A. Doman (right). (Bettmann/Corbis)

after the U.S. government intervened to censure his inflammatory, isolationist radio talks during World War II. Whatever the inspiration, the title aptly summed up Smith's most important values. The monthly stood squarely "on the principle that Christian character is the basis of all real Americanism" (in Ribuffo 1983, 170). When Smith established the America First Party in Detroit on January 10, 1943, *The Cross and the Flag* became the party's official journal. The Canadian government, however, banned it from the mails, and the U.S. Department of Justice labeled it a source of subversion in the sedition indictment *United States v. Winrod* (1942, 1943).

Until the early 1950s, E. E. Manney of Fort Worth, Texas, served as Smith's printer, and Bernard Doman and his wife and Smith's wife and son were associate editors. By the late 1940s, Don Lohbeck, another Smith associate, served as editor, and after 1953, Charles F. Robertson took over the editorial position. Smith, however, wrote most of the copy for the magazine during its thirty-five-year run. As he once explained, "For ten years *The Cross and the Flag* has been my favorite ideological child. My soul gave birth to it, my conscience nursed it, and that first little handful of readers protected it from starvation, kidnapping and death" (in Roy 1953, 65).

For most of its life, the periodical spanned eight pages and sold for a quarter. Published on the fifteenth of every month and mailed to subscribers on the twentieth, it operated at a financial loss. Although Smith charged $2 for a yearly subscription ($3 after 1974), he refused paid advertisements. Still, *The Cross and the Flag* had the largest circulation of any periodical on the extreme Right and more subscribers than many mainstream liberal publications. It began with a circulation of 7,000; by 1951, it had 13,500. Soon after, the Antidefamation League estimated its circulation at 25,000.

Each copy included an editorial celebrating Smith's faith in Jesus Christ. Reflecting his political evolution after World War II, the monthly regularly attacked modernism, Jews, Zionists, Communists, the United Nations, and the civil rights movement. It folded in 1977, a year after its founder's death.

—*Peter R. D'Agostino*

See also American Jewish Committee and Antidefamation Efforts in the United States; Judeo-Bolshevism; Smith, Gerald L. K.; Winrod, Gerald B.; Zionism

References
Jeansonne, Glen. *Gerald L. K. Smith: Minister of Hate* (Baton Rouge: Louisiana State University Press, 1988).
Ribuffo, Leo P. *The Old Christian Right: The Protestant Far Right from the Great Depression to the Cold War* (Philadelphia: Temple University Press, 1983).
Roy, Ralph Lord. *Apostles of Discord: A Study of Organized Bigotry and Disruption on the Fringes of Protestantism* (Boston: Beacon Press, 1953).

Crusades

The year 1096 is notorious for pogroms of an unprecedentedly large scale in central Europe. They occurred during a time of widespread religious enthusiasm after the proclamation of the First Crusade by Pope Urban II at the reform Council of Clermont in November 1095. At its end, he suddenly propagated the idea of liberating the Oriental churches from Muslim rule or threatening to do so, a project that would—it was commonly understood—place the fate of the Holy Land at its center. Moved by the homilies of crusade preachers such as Peter the Hermit and the prospect of remission of their sins, masses of people were induced to risk the long and perilous journey to the Near East with the vision of reconquering Jerusalem and the Holy

Sepulcher before their eyes. Although the crusaders focused on the Church of the Sepulcher, they remembered the sufferings of Christ, for which Christians of the times held all Jews responsible. The violence against the Jews, however, was neither instigated nor sanctioned by Pope Urban II or by the competing "antipope," Clement III.

The first pogroms took place in France, but surviving detailed reports are all from Germany. At the end of the eleventh century, there were a few prosperous Jewish communities, boasting many famous sages, in the Rhineland, especially in the cathedral towns of Cologne, Speyer, Worms, and Mainz. Because Emperor Henry IV was staying in Italy at the time, responsibility for protecting the Jews fell to the local bishops. The power these prelates were able to exercise varied greatly from locale to locale. During spring 1096, crusaders arrived in Germany, intending ultimately to fight the Muslims, but they unhesitatingly integrated Jews into their conception of "the enemy." What followed is known from Latin and Jewish sources alike. Among historians, the exact dating and proper interpretation of the three extant Hebrew narratives about these events remain controversial, although they rely on the memories of eyewitnesses. Additional evidence in the form of Hebrew dirges lamenting Jewish martyrdom have also survived.

One of the first onslaughts against the Jews within the modern borders of France probably took place at Monieux in Provence. Later episodes occurred in the important cities of Rouen and Metz. But it is highly likely that there were many more places where blood was shed and baptisms forced. Aside from the Jewish centers of the Rhineland, Trier, Prague-Višehrad, and Regensburg were also affected. Although violence and repression were not unknown to German Jewry before this time, most Jews lived peacefully in the midst of a Christian environment—that is, until the situation was suddenly and completely reversed during the period from Holy Week until Pentecost and ending on the the week after St. John's Day (June 24) in 1096. Many of the traumatized Jews survived only because they accepted baptism. In their crusade narratives, they sought solace in their history of martyrdom, drew biblical parallels such as Abraham's sacrifice of Isaac, or used sacrificial metaphors from the Temple cult.

The high-ranking princes and noblemen took command of the main crusading armies after the pogroms had occurred and thus cannot be held responsible for them. Jews were attacked by the crowds that formed in the so-called precrusades under the command of lower nobles and clerics. In many places, townsfolk joined with them in their acts of plunder, desecration, homicide, and forced baptism. However, there are historical records of Christian burghers who tried to help their Jewish neighbors. All sources agree that the main argument of the crusaders against the Jews was that it made no sense to undertake a long and arduous pilgrimage to the Orient to fight one enemy of the Christian faith while leaving another equally inimical people at large in Europe. In cities such as Mainz and Worms, probably every sixth or seventh inhabitant was Jewish by the time of the First Crusade, prompting some Christians to worry that they themselves, instead of the Jews, might someday be in the minority.

Many crusaders who entered the German cathedral towns had never encountered major groups of Jews before. The majority of these Christians was poor and had suffered greatly during the periods of economic crisis in the late eleventh century. Now they were daringly on their way to begin a new life by becoming soldiers of the Lord. Their first experience of Jews, many of them grown rich through various sorts of business activities, struck them as contrary to God's will. Christian doctrine taught that the Jews ought to live in visible servitude among the Christians as a divine punishment for their alleged murder of God's son and as witnesses to the superiority of Christianity. The mentality of the crusaders was also influenced by the new piety movement of the later eleventh century, the dismaying investiture struggle between the papacy and the emperor, alarming natural catastrophes of the 1090s, and prospects of a sensational reconquest of the Holy Land with all its chiliastic implications. Ironically, many of these fears and hopes were shared by Jews, especially a conviction that the "final days" before the coming of the Messiah were at hand. Collective martyrdom

of their brethren only strengthened this expectation. In a French manuscript from the year 1100, Rabbi Schemaja calculated the year of the appearance of the Messiah to be 1102. Among his reasons were the crusade pogroms and the symbolic significance of the Christians' triumph in Palestine in 1099.

The known facts about the pogroms of 1096 can be summarized as follows. Peter the Hermit, having arrived with thousands of people in Trier on April 10 (Maundy Thursday), helped poison the relations of Christians and Jews, but no pogrom transpired at that time. On May 3, the Feast of the Finding of the Holy Cross, another band of crusaders, together with townspeople, assaulted the Jewish community of Speyer during the Sabbath. Eleven Jews were killed, but the great majority were effectively protected by the local bishop, who allowed Jews to take refuge in his palace. Afterward, Bishop John punished some of the perpetrators, living up to the great privilege he had granted the Jewish community in 1090. The less powerful bishop of Worms seemingly was not even present in the town and could not prevent the slaughter of up to 800 Jews as a result of two attacks on May 18 and May 25. After this massacre, Jews in Mainz feared the worst, along with many of the Christian inhabitants, when the local strongman, Count Emicho of Flonheim, appeared before the city gates at the head of an army of French and German crusaders. Finally entering the city, the crusaders annihilated a great part of the Jewish community. Archbishop Ruthard witnessed the death of hundreds of Jews and feared for his own life. He hoped in vain that the survivors would accept baptism to save themselves, but they are said to have instead chosen death by their own hands as an act of *kiddush ha-Shem* (sanctification of the name of God). More than a thousand died.

On June 1, 1096, many people went to Trier to celebrate Pentecost and to attend a special market. During these days, there was much agitation against the Jews, even after Archbishop Egilbert had courageously preached in their favor. He tried to protect them by offering asylum in his fortified palace. Jews in this case, acceding to his urgent requests, consented to baptism. There were random instances of bloodshed and of ritual suicide committed by Jewish women who jumped into the Mosel River. Similarly, the Jewish community of Regensburg survived the encounter with crusaders after being led to a nearby creek (or perhaps the Danube) and collectively baptized. It is also reported that Bohemian Jews, mainly those of Prague, were either killed or baptized by the crusaders and that some successfully defended themselves by force.

Another crusader army appeared in the Cologne region at the beginning of June. They destroyed the Cologne synagogue and plundered many Jewish homes. A number of Jews died in the violence. Archbishop Herman III evacuated the remaining Jews (several hundred persons) to villages in the neighborhood but in vain. Crusaders hunted them down some weeks later and confronted them with the alternative "Baptism or death!" Jews living in places such as Xanten or Eller near Düsseldorf are said to have preferred killing themselves or one another rather than enduring shameful apostasy or death at the hands of the gentiles.

Altogether, at least 2,500 Jewish men, women, and children died in the German lands in the wake of the First Crusade. Christian chroniclers almost unanimously refrained from condemning the fierce anti-Jewish violence or even sympathized with it. Albert of Aachen was an exception; he stressed that greed was one of the crusaders' major motivations. When the "official" crusading armies defeated the Muslims in Palestine in 1099, Jews were among the victims there also. However, it is hard to ascertain precisely how many of them actually died during the capture of Jerusalem and how many were taken prisoner, sold into slavery, or ransomed.

The Second Crusade (1147–1149) and its preparations established a clear pattern. Every new crusade would bring with it lethal dangers to the lives of Jews and the practice of their religion. Bernard of Clairvaux, the mighty abbot who made the Second Crusade possible, hoped for a worldwide resolution of the problem of the heathen. But when his fellow Cistercian Radulf went to the Rhineland and preached in an unrestrained manner against the Jews, Bernard hurried there himself to quash Radulf's outburst of vulgar theology, which had openly called for the killing of the Jews. Severe cases of violence against Jews during the years 1146 and 1147 are reported from Normandy, northern France, and Germany. One of them concerned Rabbi Simeon of Trier who, on returning home from England, became the victim of crusaders in Cologne who wanted to have him baptized. When he did not comply, he was decapitated. Among the fatalities in France was the great Rabbi Rabbenu Tam, on whose head the crusaders allegedly inflicted five wounds in remembrance of the five wounds of Christ.

Christian and Jewish sources concerning this crusade concentrate on a pogrom of 1147 that struck the Jews of Würzburg in Franconia. Crusaders generated an anti-Jewish climate by spreading rumors that the Jews had killed a Christian whose partial remains had been found in the Main River—the first ritual murder allegation on the Continent. Many Jews were robbed, tortured, killed, or baptized until the crusaders finally moved on at the beginning of Holy Week. The newly elected prince-bishop of Würzburg, Siegfried of Querfurt, in an act of sympathy, had the bodies of the slain Jews collected, washed, anointed, and buried in the grounds of his garden. During the crusades of the twelfth century many Jews found refuge with Christians, especially in fortified rural locations.

The fall of Jerusalem to Saladin in 1187 led to the Third Crusade. Although some isolated incidents of anti-Jewish violence occurred in Germany, Emperor Frederick Barbarossa and his son Henry took effective measures to protect their Jewish subjects. In this crusade, it was the turn of the Jews of England to be terrorized, once King Richard I had left the island for Palestine in December 1189. There had already been a pogrom in London at the time of his coronation on September 3 but with no discernible connection to the crusade. The London violence, however, proved to be only the overture to a whole series of attacks against the Jewries of Lynn, Norwich, Stamford, Lincoln, Bury St Edmunds, and other places during February and March 1190. The Jews of Dunstable underwent collective baptism. Rather than suffer this indignity, the majority of the Jews of York, assembled in Clifford's Tower, committed mass suicide before the mob could storm it on March 16, 1190. Evidence suggests that many of the crusaders who took part in the English pogroms were motivated by their indebtedness to Jews. As in the earlier crusades, some felt pity for the fate of the victims, but others relished it. Richard of Devizes, a Benedictine, used the word *holocaust* to describe the murder of the Jews.

The fall of Acre in 1291 signaled the end of the "numbered" crusades. But the crusade movement was multifaceted and endured until early modern times. A "crusade" could be directed against various politically and/or religiously defined enemy groups. The popular, unauthorized crusade of the so-called shepherds cost the lives of hundreds of Jews in 1251 and again in 1320 in France and northern Spain. Similar excesses are reported from the Netherlands in 1309. Crusaders on their way to fight the Hussites of Bohemia attacked Jews in the Rhineland in 1421. A much greater catastrophe, however, took place in the duchy of Brittany and the neighboring provinces of Anjou and Poitou in France in 1236 in conjunction with the preaching of a new crusade. More than 2,500 Jews were killed.

The history of the crusade pogroms shows certain patterns of behavior on both sides: Jews became an easy and early target of crusaders who wore the sign of the cross and perceived the Jews as the original and stubborn adversaries of everything the cross stood for. Because of the material well-being of many Jews, who increasingly became creditors of Christians during the High Middle Ages, envy could also easily be aroused and entangled with religious motives when Jewish quarters were attacked and plundered. The Jews stood in the greatest danger when Christian lords and authorities were temporarily unable to protect them. Normally, such forces for order would have attempted to do so, not only because it was their duty under law but also because it was in their own self-interest. During the reign of terror, Jews were often confronted with the alternative of death or baptism. Frequently, they chose death "to hasten the coming of the Messiah" and to avoid disloyalty to God.

—*Gerd Mentgen*

See also Augustine of Hippo; Deicide; Gregory the Great, Pope; Middle Ages, Early; Middle Ages, High; Paul; Ritual Murder (Medieval); Usury

References

Chazan, Robert. *God, Humanity, and History: The Hebrew First Crusade Narratives* (Berkeley: University of California Press, 2000).

Cohen, Jeremy. *Sanctifying the Name of God: Jewish Martyrs and Jewish Memories of the First Crusade* (Philadelphia: University of Pennsylvania Press, 2004).

Haverkamp, Alfred, ed. *Juden und Christen zur Zeit der Kreuzzüge* (Sigmaringen, Germany: Thorbecke, 1999).

Mentgen, Gerd. "Die Juden des Mittelrhein-Mosel-Gebietes im Hochmittelalter unter besonderer Berücksichtigung der Kreuzzugsverfolgungen," *Monatshefte für Evangelische Kirchengeschichte des Rheinlandes* 44 (1995): 37–75.

Riley-Smith, Jonathan. "Christian Violence and the Crusades." In *Religious Violence between Christians and Jews: Medieval Roots, Modern Perspectives.* Edited by Anna Sapir Abulafia (Basingstoke, UK: Palgrave, 2002), 3–20.

Cuba

The first Jews who went to Cuba were fleeing enforcement of the Spanish Inquisition (in 1492). Initially, the clandestine Jews who arrived were sailors; there are reports of Jewish merchants in Cuba from the mid-seventeenth century. The Inquisition was abolished in Cuba in 1834, yet there still was no true freedom of religion in the Spanish colony that tolerated only Roman Catholic worship. Although the defeat of Spain in the Spanish-American War of 1898 ushered in an era of official religious tolerance, the church monopoly continued concerning burial. Only after intervention by the U.S. government in 1912 was a Jewish cemetery opened in Guanabacoa, a Havana suburb.

Overt antisemitism first surfaced in postcolonial Cuba in the early 1930s. In the summer of 1932, the Centro Israelita (the main communal body of Jews established in Havana in 1925) tried to counter the antisemitism emanating from Europe by organizing the Comité de Intervención. In May 1935, this committee was superseded by the Jewish Community for Cuba, an umbrella organization encompassing several groups. After Adolf Hitler rose to power, the German embassy in Havana tailored its propaganda to appeal to and incite Spanish-born residents in Cuba who already supported Francisco Franco and his anti-Jewish pronouncements.

Several significant incidents in Havana in that period appeared to be antisemitically motivated. On October 5, 1933, for example, Havana's police chief, G. Granero, gave an interview to the newspaper *Mañana* in which he called Jews an immoral element. On December 17, 1933, a soldier accompanied by three men in civilian clothing killed two Jews and wounded another in a store on Calle Monte without any apparent provocation.

The most difficult period for the Jews of Cuba came a few years later, when Nazi supporters made continuous efforts to instill antisemitic feelings among Cubans. Particularly vicious was José Ignacio Rivero (1895–1944), who used his control of three newspapers to propagandize in favor of Spanish Falangism (fascism). His attempt to publish a local edition of the *Protocols of the Elders of Zion* was thwarted, thanks largely to the efforts of Adolph Kates, a prominent Jewish leader. A proposed ban on the ritual slaughtering of cattle, passed off as a measure to prevent cruelty to animals, was, in fact, antisemitically motivated. It, too, was defeated.

Antisemitism reached new levels of importance when the National Fascist Party of Cuba was legalized (on October 20, 1938) and received the blessing of a former president of Cuba, Grau San Martin. The party demonstrated its drawing power in May 1939 at a conference that an estimated 40,000 people attended. Its national radio hookup featured the well-known and inflammatory antisemite Primitivo Rodriguez, who implored his listeners to fight until the last Jew left Cuba.

International attention focused on Cuba when the government refused to allow Jews fleeing Nazi Germany to disembark from the SS *St. Louis*. The ship had sailed from Hamburg with 937 refugees, most of them Jewish, on May 13, 1939, arriving in Havana harbor on May 27. Political infighting and internal Cuban intrigue led the government of President Loredo Bru to void the visas of those on board the ship. Fewer than 30 travelers (including all of the non-Jews) were allowed to go ashore. The ship sailed past the lights of Florida and onward to Europe, where four countries eventually accepted the refugees so they would not be taken to virtually certain death in Germany. But Nazi propaganda had achieved something of a victory by being able to show that even countries such as Cuba and the United States did not want Jews.

The affair of the *St. Louis* jolted the Cuban conscience, however. Denial of entry to refugees was not repeated. Bru left office, and under the subsequent presidency of Fulgencio Batista, a thriving refugee community developed.

In the years after World War II, a few antisemitic tracts were printed in Cuba, but government policy clearly discouraged antisemitism in the public sphere. Still, antisemitism persisted on the social plane. According to one source, though it was possible for Jews to be guests at a prominent Havana country club, they were denied the right to be members. After Fidel Castro assumed power on January 1, 1959, the government ceased showing tolerance for antisemitic activities, public or private, and even the breaking off of diplomatic relations with the state of Israel in 1973 did not alter this policy. Since the legalization of religious practices in 1991, the situation of Cuban Jews has further improved.

—*Jay Levinson*

See also Inquisition; *Protocols of the Elders of Zion;* Spain under Franco
References
Bejarano, Margalit. "Anti-Semitism in Cuba under Democratic, Military, and Revolutionary Regimes, 1944–63," *Patterns of Prejudice* 24, no. 1 (Summer 1990): 32–46.
Levinson, Jay, and Dana E. Kaplan. *The Cuban Jewish Community: 1906–1958* (forthcoming).

Culture-Antisemitism or Pogrom-Antisemitism? (1919)

With the pamphlet entitled *Culture-Antisemitism or Pogrom-Antisemitism?* published on August 8, 1919, the Leipzig antisemite Heinrich Pudor wanted to accomplish three distinct goals. First, he intended a remorseless settling of accounts with the outmoded and, in his view, spineless "cultural" antisemitism of the prewar era. Second, he wanted to launch a new antisemitism whose keynote would be an explicitly condoned violence. Third, he sought to introduce the concept of the pogrom into antisemitic discourse. Viewed from a longer perspective, the pamphlet was an early example of the discussion among antisemites of the two major forms of Jew-hatred: one stressing worldview (*Weltanschauung*) and the other violence (*Gewalt*).

Pudor published the work at his own expense as part of a series between 1919 and 1920, most probably in a small edition of a few hundred copies. He sent the material to radical antisemites as well as to the more sedate conservative nationalist organizations, such as the successor to the Agrarian League (Reichslandbund). Pudor intended to answer the rejection of pogroms by Theodor Fritsch and the Berlin activist Richard Kunze. For this reason and despite its small print run, the pamphlet was vigorously and widely discussed, especially among the more radically inclined antisemites.

The antisemitism of prewar Germany, Pudor argued, was a total failure. No anti-Jewish laws had been passed. Under the new conditions of the Weimar Republic, it made no sense to stick to the old antisemitic party agenda. "Using legislative means against Jewry is no longer an option for us. Nowadays, the Jews make our laws" (all quotations are from *Kultur-Antisemitismus oder Pogrom-Antisemitismus?* [1920]). "Before we can pass antisemitic laws," he proclaimed, "Jewish hegemony [*Judenherrschaft*] must be broken." Challenging Fritsch directly, Pudor demanded that he demonstrate "a will to power over the Jews" and urged that "destruction be answered by destruction [*Vernichtung*]." What this meant in practice was that Jews had to be directly, violently attacked. "We openly and freely declare to one and all that every means is the right means if it frees us from the Jews and that we have nothing whatever against the pogrom if it serves this end."

Pudor's intervention did not go unnoticed. Adolf Hitler argued against the pogrom in his so-called Gemlich Letter (September 16, 1919). His newspaper, the *Völkischer Beobachter* (Racial Observer), entered into debate with Pudor, and throughout the 1920s and 1930s, *völkisch* (racist-nationalist) intellectuals continued to discuss the relative merits of "the antisemitism of reason" versus "rowdy antisemitism" (*Radauantisemitismus*).

Notwithstanding the debates, any attempt to make a sharp distinction between a violent and an allegedly nonviolent antisemitism—that based on duly passed legislation—remains artificial. The reality of the Third Reich demonstrates that both forms of antisemitism coexisted and reinforced each other. For example, the Night of Broken Glass of November 1938, supposedly an outbreak of pogrom violence "from below," was followed by a package of antisemitic ordinances "from above," including the incarceration of Jews in concentration camps.

—*Dirk Walter*
Richard S. Levy, translation

See also Agrarian League; Fritsch, Theodor; Hitler, Adolf; Night of Broken Glass (November 1938 Pogrom); Pudor, Heinrich; Weimar

References
Herbert, Ulrich. *Best: Biographische Studien über Radikalismus, Weltanschauung und Vernunft 1903–1989* (Bonn, Germany: J. H. W. Dietz Verlag, 1996).
Walter, Dirk. *Antisemitische Kriminalität und Gewalt: Judenfeindschaft in der Weimarer Republik* (Bonn, Germany: J. H. W. Dietz Verlag Nachf., 1999).

Cuza, A. C. (1857–1946)

A Romanian national economist, writer, and politician, Alexandru Constantin Cuza studied in Dresden and Brussels. Like many Romanian intellectuals, he at first inclined toward socialism but only until the Socialist Party merged with the liberals in 1899. Thereafter, he belonged to a series of conservative political groupings. Throughout his life, Cuza remained strongly engaged in Romanian public life, advocating extreme nationalist and antisemitic views in his lectures, speeches, and journalism.

Cuza published poetry, epigrams, and essays on cultural topics in a number of influential Romanian-language journals and literary periodicals. He was also an accomplished polemicist. Western European writers—for example, the French antisemite Édouard Drumont and the proponent of integral nationalism Charles Maurras—influenced his thinking. But Cuza also drew from a native school of ultraconservative political thinkers, among them the "national poet" Mihai Eminescu and the philologist Bogdan Petriceicu Hasdeu. Deeply mistrustful of democracy, they preferred an authoritarianism buttressed by strong nationalist and antisemitic sentiments.

As a professor of political economy at Iassy University from 1901 and as an authority on art, history, and politics, Cuza exercised immense influence over generations of Romanian students, especially in the 1920s and 1930s. He had no patience for social and economic problems, most of which he thought could be solved on the basis of an idealized nationalism and intolerant antisemitism. In numerous essays and his book *On the Populace* (1899), he sought to encourage the entrepreneurial spirit among Romanians and to exclude foreigners, first and foremost the Jews, who squeezed out the natives and denied them the fruits of their labor. He believed that the alcoholism afflicting the people could be cured through education and that the establishment of guilds would raise the level of craftsmanship. His *Nationality in Art* sought to demonstrate the existence of a natural law governing nationality, proving that it was an "expression of race and blood" as well as the creative life force of peoples. Every culture had its own homeland—with the sole exception of the uncultured and homeless Jews.

Cuza began his political career by founding, with Nicolae Iorga, the Nationalist-Democratic Party in 1909. In 1923, along with Corneliu Zelea Codreanu, he helped establish LANC–National Christian Defense League, but the group's popular appeal waned, and his relationship with Codreanu soured. In 1935, with pressure being applied by Alfred Rosenberg's office, Cuza's LANC and Octavian Goga's National Agrarian Party joined in the Christian National Party (or Bloc) and spoke out in favor of making common cause with Fascist Italy and Nazi Germany.

—*Krista Zach*
Richard S. Levy, translation

See also Codreanu, Corneliu Zelea; Drumont, Édouard; Goga, Octavian; Iron Guard; Maurras, Charles; Romania; Rosenberg, Alfred

References

Ornea, Zigu. *The Romanian Extreme Right: The Nineteen Thirties* (Boulder, CO: East European Monographs, 1999).
Weber, Eugen. *Varieties of Fascism: Doctrines of Revolution in the Twentieth Century* (Princeton, NJ: Van Nostrand, 1964).

D

Dahn, Felix (1834–1912)

Born February 9, 1834, in Hamburg, Felix Dahn spent an intellectually stimulating childhood in Munich in the company of his actor-father's cultured circle. He enjoyed reenacting knightly scenes from his historical reading and showed an early gift for lyric poetry. But this idyllic period ended with his parents' divorce in 1850.

At sixteen, he began the study of law and philosophy but also maintained his interest in literary pursuits. He drew inspiration from the German classics as well as Homer, Shakespeare, and Sir Walter Scott, whom he read in the original. An academic career in philosophy in Catholic Bavaria was rendered impossible for Dahn, a Protestant, because of his outspoken anticlericalism. He became a lawyer, a profession in which he succeeded brilliantly, earning his doctorate in 1855. In 1857, he finished a postdoctoral thesis on legal history that qualified him to lecture at the university level. The history and philosophy of law engaged his talents equally, and his interest in the earliest period of the Germanic migrations led him to become a pupil of Jacob Grimm. Years of struggle as an unpaid lecturer (*Privatdozent*) were rewarded finally with a professorship at the University of Würzburg.

Dahn volunteered as a nurse during the Franco-Prussian War (1870–1871). In the crucial Battle of Sedan, however, he picked up a rifle, was wounded, and was then decorated. His "collaboration" in the founding of the German Empire proved a life-changing experience, turning him into a devoted follower of Otto von Bismarck and affirming his national and liberal stance.

Following the war, he took a chair in Königsberg, married for a second time, and enjoyed the most fruitful period of his career, writing significant juridical and historical works. It was his literary production, however, that served to make him intellectually eminent. From 1888, he taught in Breslau at the Germanic-Slavic border, feeling himself to be at the forefront of the national struggle and lending his talents to the Association for Germandom in Foreign Lands (Verein für das Deutschtum im Ausland). He published novels and narrative tales, as well as his four-volume memoirs (1890–1895), a fifth anthology of poetry (1892), and his collected works "of a poetic nature" in twenty-one volumes (1899). Dahn died on January 3, 1912, having outlived the zenith of his popularity.

Although it is true that Dahn's scholarly work provided the raw material for his literary creations, it is also true that he injected his contemporary political concerns into his romanticized vision of the Germanic Middle Ages. A mythic reverence for Teutonic forebears coexisted with an obvious anti-Catholic and antisocialist patriotism. His fiction glorified the striving for a united national state and didactically portrayed the virtues of unquestioning, dutiful loyalty to it. His greatest publishing success was a ponderous novel in four volumes—*The Struggle for Rome,* which went through 110 editions before 1918. It describes the dramatic decline and fall of the Kingdom of the Ostrogoths in Italy, fully exploiting the tale's nationalistic lessons. The story sent a message to Dahn's contemporaries: the racial, blood-based singularity of virtuous Germans was constantly endangered. The survival of Germandom required warrior virtues and an unflinching willingness to take up arms in its defense.

The antisemitic undertones in Dahn's basic outlook ought not to be compared to the *völkisch* (racist-nationalist) antisemitism of his day. He pointed to his portrayal of "good Jews" alongside the obviously bad ones as evidence that he was not an antisemite. Further, he participated in various initiatives promoting tolerance. It should also be noted that though Dahn may appear to be an antisemite by the more exacting standards of the present day, he did not seem so to the radical antisemites of the interwar years. They condemned his view of Jews as "too full of compromises" and not sufficiently grounded in racial-biological principles.

—*Tzvetan Tzvetanov*
Richard S. Levy, translation

See also Bartels, Adolf; Fontane, Theodor; Freytag, Gustav; *Jews' Beech, The; Kulturkampf;* Lienhard, Friedrich; Riehl, Wilhelm Heinrich; Treitschke, Heinrich von; *Völkisch* Movement and Ideology

References

Mosse, George L. "The Image of the Jew in German Popular Culture: Felix Dahn and Gustav Freytag," *Leo Baeck Institute Year Book* 2 (1957): 218–227.

Tzvetanov, Tzvetan. "Felix Dahn: Das Mythologem des Nationalstaats im Deutschen Kaiserreich (1871–1914)." Dissertation, Free University of Berlin, under preparation.

Damascus Blood Libel (1840)

The blood libel trial in Damascus, Syria, may be seen as one of the first in a series of influential episodes in the nineteenth century involving attacks on Jews—in this instance, some forty years before the word *antisemitism* came into popular usage and before hostility to Jews in a racial sense was exploited as a modern political device. The Damascus trial developed into an "affair" in the sense that it engaged a large public, much beyond local or strictly legal issues. It is often considered a milestone in the prehistory of modern European antisemitism, primarily for the way that it brought up a range of issues having to do with Jewish power and powerlessness in Europe. It also marked a stage in the spread to the Islamic world of anti-Jewish themes that had originated in Christian Europe.

In early 1840, authorities in Damascus arrested eight Jews and charged them with ritually murdering a Capuchin monk, Father Tomaso, and his Muslim servant. Both had disappeared without a trace, and the Capuchins claimed that the two had been murdered by Jews to use their blood for Passover. Part of the reason that the case attracted such wide attention in Europe was that the initial newspaper accounts of it confidently reported that the Jews were, in fact, guilty. The first Jew arrested, a barber, had confessed and named seven others who then also confessed, providing elaborate, matching details in separate interrogations. Both the French and the English consuls in the area, representing modern, enlightened countries, similarly reported to their governments that the evidence for ritual murder was overwhelming. Only gradually did it emerge that the confessions were the result of torture and that the matching details of the confessions were the result of collaboration on the part of the interrogators.

The charges against the Jews quickly became entangled in great power rivalries in the Middle East. In 1840, Syria was ruled by Muhammad Ali of Egypt, who was in rebellion against the Ottoman Empire. By the late 1830s, he had expanded his rule over much of what was later known as the Sudan as well as Saudi Arabia and Syria. France was, at that point, a supporter of Muhammad Ali, whereas most other European powers, notably Britain, were trying to bolster the Turkish empire and undermine French influence in the region. The French had earlier acquired the right to protect Catholics in Syria, which meant that their consul, the Count de Ratti-Menton, participated in the investigation of the alleged murder, involving himself in the irregularities of the case. The premier of France in 1840, Adolphe Thiers, who was also foreign minister, was a moderate liberal and widely recognized by Jews as friendly. France had been the first country to offer Jews civil equality (in 1791) and was thereafter considered by Jews to be Europe's most progressive and tolerant nation in their regard. All the greater was their shock, then, at the French consul's report. In fact, Thiers initially viewed Ratti-Menton's account with suspicion, but before long, he concluded that the honor of the French nation was in question and therefore its national interests as well; he began to make known his own belief in the guilt of the Jews. In a private conversation with his Jewish friend James de Rothschild, who had approached him to help rescue the Jews of Damascus, Thiers described the Jews of the Middle East as fanatical and at a stage of development comparable to Europe's Jews in the Middle Ages—when, he added, they, too, had undoubtedly committed ritual murders.

It did not take long for the British foreign minister, Lord Palmerston, to perceive an opportunity to strike a high moral stance and to forward British national interests in the area by supporting the Jews and condemning the French. The British consul's report backing the ritual murder charges was an initial impediment to Palmerston's plans, especially since the consul also forwarded strongly worded testimony in support of the honesty and decency of the French consul and the local officials. The British consul also informed Palmerston of his conclusion that, in fact, passages of the Talmud justified ritual murder. Palmerston remained skeptical of the report but nonetheless hesitated to act.

That beliefs of this sort persisted even among the educated elites of Britain and France was one of the more remarkable revelations of these first months. Ironically, it was Prince Metternich of Austria and Tsar Nicholas I of Russia, leaders of Europe's two most reactionary major powers, who publicly expressed disbelief about the ritual murder charges, and both took measures to prevent the newspapers in their countries from spreading what they described as baseless and absurd charges. To be sure, Metternich and Nicholas shared with Palmerston the sense of an opportunity to discredit and weaken the French.

By 1840, many Jews, especially the upper classes in western and central Europe, had embraced values of the Enlightenment and European national identities, distancing themselves from Judaism's traditional emphasis on the Jews as a nation forever separate from the non-Jewish nations. That the charges in Damascus could be given credence seemed to them an almost unbelievable reversion to the climate of the detested Middle Ages. After various largely futile and disorganized efforts were made by Jewish leaders to discredit the charges and rescue the Damascus Jews, much hope was finally placed on a delegation that Muhammed Ali agreed to receive, including two of Europe's most illustrious Jewish leaders, Moses Montefiore from Britain and Adolphe Crémieux from France.

After complex negotiations, the surviving Jewish prisoners (two had died from the torture) were finally released. But they were not granted a retrial or declared innocent by the authorities. Both Montefiore and Crémieux returned with accounts claiming the importance of their individual efforts—while bitterly condemning each other as being completely ineffectual. But it is now clear that neither of their efforts were of decisive import, at least not in comparison to the pressure exerted by European powers at the time. War was imminent between Egypt and the Ottoman Empire, and Muhammad Ali decided that an act of goodwill toward the Jews would be seen as a sign of his willingness to distance himself from France and cultivate more friendly relations with the leaders of Austria and Britain, whose warships were cruising the eastern Mediterranean.

The outcome of the Damascus Affair enhanced the growing belief that the Jews, especially the fabulously wealthy leaders such as the Rothschilds, exercised decisive power behind the scenes in an emerging modern Europe where money ruled. But Jews themselves, to the contrary, saw the Damascus Affair as revealing their vulnerability and powerlessness—as well as the shocking persistence of ugly fantasies about their religion—in a Europe where rationality and toleration were supposedly emerging. Thus, Jewish leaders were ever more persuaded of the need for greater international cooperation and public activity on their part, both to protect Jews and to defend Judaism from ill-informed or malevolent charges.

—*Albert S. Lindemann*

See also Alliance Israélite Universelle; France; Islam and the Jews; Ritual Murder (Medieval); Ritual Murder (Modern); Rothschilds

References
Frankel, Jonathan. *The Damascus Affair: "Ritual Murder," Politics, and the Jews in 1840* (New York: Cambridge University Press, 1997).

Darquier de Pellepoix, Louis (1897–1980)

The story of Louis Darquier is a significant reminder that portions of the French population did not wait for the German Occupation during World War II to begin seeking state-sponsored persecution of Jews. Darquier's thuggish behavior, journalistic vitriol, zealous execution of Vichy's repressive policies, and negationist claims constituted a lifetime anchored in antisemitism.

Born in Cahors, he adopted the aristocratic name of Louis Darquier de Pellepoix and moved to Paris, where he joined the Catholic royalist group Action Française. In the antigovernment protest march of February 6, 1934, organized by the extreme Right, he was wounded by gunfire, along with fourteen others. Elected municipal councilor in 1935 for the Ternes district of Paris, he initiated an unsuccessful bill to annul all naturalizations granted since 1918, an effort obviously aimed at revoking the citizenship of Jewish immigrants. In 1938, he founded the Rassemblement Antijuif de France (French Anti-Jewish Assembly), which later received clandestine funding from Germany, and the Union Française pour la Défense de la Race (French Union for the Defense of the Race). His opinion paper, *L'Antijuif,* drew on the racist, inflammatory tradition of Édouard Drumont. Contemporary police reports recorded a number of his altercations with Jews in cafés and even at city council meetings; Darquier served a brief prison sentence in 1939 for "inciting racial hatred."

Under the Occupation, he entered the Vichy government to replace Xavier Vallat in 1942 as commissioner of the Commissariat Général des Questions Juives (General Commissariat for Jewish Affairs [CGQJ]). An important figure in Vichy's repressive measures, he directed economic Aryanization and the spoliation of Jewish property and in July 1942 helped organize the infamous Vel d'Hiv roundup of Jews to be deported.

In December 1947, the French purge courts, specially created to deal with collaborators, handed down a death sentence in absentia for Darquier, who had, in the meantime, fled to Spain, where Francisco Franco denied French requests for his extradition. In the 1950s and 1960s, when the Holocaust and Vichy's antisemitic policies were not significant concerns of French justice or the general public, Darquier was largely forgotten. In the 1970s, however, Holocaust historiography gained new prominence in the media. A journalist from the French weekly *L'Express* located the former collaborator and obtained an interview. Darquier's arrogant, unrepentant remarks provoked two important events. When asked about Vichy's persecution of Jews, he (correctly) identified Chief of Police René Bousquet as the principal architect, which led, a year later, to the indictment of Bousquet's liaison on Jewish affairs, Jean Leguay, for crimes against humanity. Had the accused's death in 1989 not cut short legal proceedings, this would have been the first trial of a French citizen under such statutes. The second matter was equally controversial. Darquier asserted in the interview that "only lice were gassed at Auschwitz." Seizing the opening, the leading French Holocaust denier, Robert Faurisson, followed with negationist claims of his own in a letter published by the French daily *Le Monde* (on December 29, 1978). This triggered a firestorm of debate in France that has yet to subside. After the interview, Darquier soon returned to obscurity, and news of his death on August 29, 1980, was not announced in the French press until 1983.

—*Ralph W. Schoolcraft III*

See also Action Française; Crimes against Humanity (French Trials); Drumont, Édouard; Faurisson, Robert; Holocaust Denial, Negationism, and Revisionism; Spain under Franco; Stavisky Affair; Vallat, Xavier; Vichy

References

Kingston, Paul J. *Anti-Semitism in France during the 1930s: Organisations, Personalities and Propaganda* (Hull, UK: University of Hull Press, 1983).

Paxton, Robert O. *Vichy France: Old Guard and New Order, 1940–1944* (New York: Columbia University Press, 1982).

Rousso, Henry. *The Vichy Syndrome: History and Memory in France since 1944.* Translated by Arthur Goldhammer (Cambridge, MA: Harvard University Press, 1991).

Dearborn Independent and *The International Jew*

The *Dearborn Independent,* a newspaper, and *The International Jew,* a set of pamphlets commonly published as a book, are forever linked in the history of American antisemitism. One gave birth to the other. Together, they constitute Henry Ford's contribution to the worldwide movement fomenting hatred toward Jews in the first half of the twentieth century.

In 1918, the *Dearborn Independent* was a small weekly in a sleepy town outside Detroit, Michigan. That year, Henry Ford, in search of a medium through which he could efficiently and directly reach thousands of ordinary Americans, purchased the newspaper and proceeded to convert it into his version of a mass-circulation periodical. The paper, accepting no advertisements, was sold by a few street vendors in major cities, but it was primarily distributed through Ford dealerships, which were required to sell subscriptions along with automobiles. Some dealers resented the imposition and groused that the money would be better spent on improving the Model T, whose sales dropped precipitously in the mid-1920s. By 1927, the *Independent* (like the car) was doing badly, losing more than $2 million. Ford did not care. He intended for the *Independent* to become the common folks' primer on American culture, literature, and political philosophy, all of which were first refracted through the prism of his small-minded dogmatism.

In reconfiguring the *Independent,* Ford created a media voice that he alone controlled, one that both spoke in the vernacular of Ford's limited ken and avoided the filtering effects of his increasingly unflattering national press coverage. The paper was physically retooled—Ford had new presses designed and made to order—and editorially redirected to reflect the America of the late nineteenth century in which he had come of age. Like many social conservatives, he idealized what he believed were the cultural and economic hallmarks of preindustrial society. The family farm, the one-room school, and racial and ethnic homogeneity all supported—and were, in turn, promoted by—a profoundly conservative and Christian fundamentalism. Articles extolled the virtues of Jefferson and Lincoln, superimposing anachronistic aspects of their political ideas onto the postwar culture of the United States in the 1920s. In short, the paper erected an intensely hostile critique of the modernist impulses of its own time, inveighing against new cultural trends that Ford personally abhorred: smoking, drink-

ing, newfangled dancing styles, and what he believed was the disproportionate influence of Jews on politics, culture, entertainment, diplomacy, industrial capitalism, and the state.

As it soon demonstrated, the paper's most important mission was to disseminate Ford's antisemitic beliefs. Beginning in 1920 and continuing for nearly two years, the *Independent* ran a series of ninety-one articles largely based on the *Protocols of the Elders of Zion,* an authorless document purporting to lay out the Jewish plan for world domination. Ernest G. Liebold, Ford's executive secretary, procured a copy of the *Protocols* and promptly handed it to the paper's editor, William J. Cameron. Several journalists, including Herman Bernstein, had attacked the authenticity of the *Protocols* before the *Independent* began its series. In 1921, the *Times* (London) hammered the nails in what should have been the literary coffin of the *Protocols* in an article that established the true sources of the literary forgery, as well as its reactionary and antisemitic political motivations. Liebold completely ignored all such evidence of the inauthenticity of the *Protocols.* So the *Independent* series continued, despite widespread public and media criticism, infuriated demands for retraction, and two libel lawsuits, one filed by Bernstein when the *Independent* asserted that he had supplied Ford with information about the nefarious activities of the "International Jew." Neither case ever went to trial.

The *Independent* broke off this initial antisemitic campaign abruptly in January 1922, apparently at the behest of President Warren G. Harding, who sent an emissary to Ford to prevail on the automaker to end the defamatory articles. The cessation proved brief, however. In November 1920, Dearborn Publishing, the paper's holding company, had already begun to issue the *Independent* articles in pamphlet form; after the series ended, the pamphlets were sold in sets of four volumes, affordably priced at 25 cents per set. This collection, titled *The International Jew: The World's Foremost Problem,* essentially put the Ford name— and the stamp of approval of the towering figure of American industrialism—on the *Protocols.*

The *International Jew* was an artless application of the arguments and claims of the *Protocols* to U.S. domestic politics, cultural issues, and social problems as identified by the Ford publishing machine. Each of the four volumes purported to take up a specific theme, so as to reinforce the perception that Jewish activities and influence were widespread, comprehensive, and sinister, but the volumes' titles pointed to their shared content and purpose: *The International Jew, Jewish Activities in the United States, Jewish Influences in American Life,* and *Aspects of Jewish Power in the United States.* War, peace, movies, sports, art, literature, music, money, bootlegging, farming, and even Columbus's voyage to America—few subjects escaped the book's single-minded accusation that the Jews were a nation unto themselves. The Jews controlled money, power, and influence in the United States. The Jews appropriated the business and labor of others. Supposedly ordinary Jews who claimed to have no knowledge of the intentions and movements of the "International Jew" nonetheless shared in the fruits of the Jewish conspiracy.

The International Jew was marketed with typical Ford ingenuity. It was published uncopyrighted, giving any other publisher license to reprint the book without paying royalties or becoming subject to any legal restraint. The work was translated and published in Germany by early 1923, and it appeared in at least a dozen other languages before 1930. During that time, the Dearborn Publishing Company sold out several domestic runs of 200,000 copies per printing.

The International Jew was poised to live on regardless of the future course of the *Dearborn Independent,* but subsequent antisemitic articles changed the book's fortunes as well as the newspaper's. Their attack on Jewish involvement in agriculture led to another libel lawsuit. This one, filed in federal court, actually went to trial; the case received nationwide press coverage and abundant editorial ridicule for Ford, who could muster in self-defense only the lame excuse that the paper's editor, Cameron, was solely responsible for all attacks on Jews. The litigation ended when Ford apologized to the Jews and agreed to cease all future published attacks. The attorney Louis Marshall, who negotiated the apology, included in the statement promises to withdraw *The International Jew* from circulation and to prevail on publishers everywhere to cease distributing the book.

Ford's apology and the *Independent's* retraction of its anti-Jewish articles had little impact on sales of *The International Jew.* Despite Ford's promise to do everything possible to restrain circulation of the book, it continued to be printed and sold all over the world. When Marshall complained, Ford Motor Company lawyers responded by writing letters of limp protest to antisemitic publishers, but otherwise, little was done to disassociate Ford's name from the book. Adolf Hitler's accession to power in 1933 renewed interest in *The International Jew,* as was pointedly acknowledged by publishers who began adding Ford's name to the frontispiece. The Ford staff denied that Henry Ford was the author of the work—a denial that actually represented the fact of the matter—but did nothing to discourage antisemites and Nazis from seeing Ford as fully sympathetic to their aims. The association between the book and the Ford name only strengthened over time. At the present moment, with the book universally available on numerous antisemitic Internet websites, there is little that the reinvented Ford Motor Company can do to rehabilitate its founder. It can only ignore the dark sides of his life and work.

It has been argued that the *Protocols* lacks a national context or identity, presenting a generic antisemitic theory that is marvelously adaptable to any specific national or political purpose or framework. If that claim holds merit, then it can also be said that Henry Ford's *The International Jew* gave the *Protocols* an American author, an American context, and an American identity. Wrapped in the Ford name, the *International Jew* has achieved an entirely undeserved literary permanence that yokes Ford and the *Protocols* together in infamy.

—*Victoria Saker Woeste*

See also Ford, Henry; Fritsch, Theodor; Internet; Judeo-Bolshevism; *Protocols of the Elders of Zion; Protocols of the Elders of Zion* on Trial; United States

References
Jardim, Anne. *The First Henry Ford: A Study in Personality and Business Leadership* (Boston: MIT Press, 1970).
Sward, Keith. *The Legend of Henry Ford* (New York: Atheneum Press, 1972).

Debit and Credit (1855)

Gustav Freytag's 1855 novel *Soll und Haben* (Debit and Credit) describes a world of commerce populated by German merchants adjusting to the new capitalist system. Half novel of business manners and half paean for the German bourgeoisie, *Debit and Credit* was an attempt to educate Germany in the view that the merchant, not the political radical of 1848, would be the creator of a modern, unified, progressive state. To Freytag, capitalism was both a threat to civility as well as a progressive force because the very capitalist system that held the potential to bring prosperity and unification could also reduce social relations to Thomas Carlyle's dreaded "cash nexus." Thus, capitalism had to be tamed by the retention of precapitalist virtues such as honor and character. *Debit and Credit* was therefore intended as a progressive political manifesto, but it is notable today primarily because Freytag portrayed Jewish greed as the essence of unrestrained capitalism. He created, in his memorable villain Veitel Itzig, perhaps the most poisonous stereotype of the greedy, utterly immoral Jewish businessman in nineteenth-century literature.

In *Debit and Credit*, the villain is the Jewish merchant who represents a threat to Germany in the sense that he simply amasses wealth while repudiating all civility and honor. For Freytag, there was something monstrous in Itzig's tireless pursuit of gain, something uncivilized in his joyless self-denial. Itzig embodied the greed and egoism traditionally ascribed to the Jewish merchant. When the novel's dark figures in caftans are not "gliding" through alleyways, they are "cringing" in the light of German bourgeois rectitude. At the other end of the economic scale, partially assimilated Jewish arrivistes ostentatiously display their wealth and lack of culture. The lesson of *Debit and Credit*, in the words of Jacob Katz, is that "Judaism alone is not capable of giving its adherents morality or culture" (Katz 1980, 205).

It is possible to argue that Freytag employed his stereotypes in the service of assimilation. As a noted liberal, he favored Jewish emancipation, criticized Richard Wagner for opposing it, and publicly denounced the antisemitic politics of the 1880s and 1890s as "that ancient evil, Jew-baiting." However, Freytag argued that civil emancipation could never bring about real assimilation; a deeper change in the nature of the individual Jew was required. Bernhard Ehrenthal, the one positive Jewish character in *Debit and Credit*, confesses, "It is only through contact with gentiles that a Jew can acquire an appreciation of any values beyond the coarsest material ones" (in Katz 1980, 205). In Veitel Itzig, Freytag created a more pernicious Jewish stereotype than Charles Dickens did with Fagin.

Debit and Credit enjoyed remarkable success and provided generations of German readers—Christian and Jewish alike—a powerful, if stereotyped, impression of Jewish life before assimilation and emancipation. But unlike Dickens, Freytag never expressed any regret for perpetuating Jewish stereotypes. He insisted that the Jewish characters he described in his novel were "realistic" portrayals of Jews he had known.

—Larry L. Ping

See also Dickens, Charles; Emancipation; Freytag, Gustav; Marx, Karl; Wagner, Richard

References

Katz, Jacob. *From Prejudice to Destruction: Anti-Semitism, 1700–1933* (Cambridge, MA: Harvard University Press, 1980).

Ping, Larry L. "Gustav Freytag and the Prussian Gospel: Novels, Liberalism, and History." Dissertation, University of Oregon, 1994.

Sammons, Jeffrey L. "The Evaluation of Freytag's *Soll und Haben*," *German Life and Letters* 22 (1969): 315–324.

Degenerate Art

The *Entartete Kunst* ("Degenerate Art") Exhibition, the most widely attended art exhibit of all time, focused on the supposedly Jewish, mentally corrupt, and communist inspiration of many of the most prominent examples of early twentieth-century German visual art. Opening in Munich in 1937 and closing in Halle in 1941, the show marked a crucial turning point in National Socialist antisemitic policy. Combined with other events of 1937, the Degenerate Art show signaled that Jews, already actively excluded from German social and political life, would be subjected to an assault on their essential humanity. The dehumanization of artists in

Hermann Göring and Adolf Hitler examine a painting at what is probably the exhibit "Entartete Kunst" (Degenerate Art) put together by the Nazi Party intending to illustrate that many artists were unworthy of the "higher race." (Corbis)

violent antisemitic and anti-Marxist propaganda ushered in Nazi policies that moved from textual and visual attacks on specific Jews to the systematic deprivation of European Jewry's right to exist during the years of genocide in World War II.

The Degenerate Art show followed on numerous regional art shows, beginning in Mannheim in April 1933, that attempted to exhibit the decadence of contemporary German cultural institutions. These exhibitions consistently noted the artist's identity when he or she was Jewish and indicated the dealer who sold the work, if Jewish. Most often, these regional exhibitions were meant to embarrass the previous cultural administrators of the democratic Weimar Republic and came in the wake of the general purge of the civil service. However, these localized initiatives did not necessarily represent policy at the national level, and many modernist artists who considered themselves apolitical or even staunchly pro–National Socialist still

thought there might be some place for them within the world of art.

The unresolved and inconsistent nature of art exhibition policy changed dramatically after 1936, when Germany entered a new and aggressive phase in cultural, domestic, and international politics. Although many artists (such as George Grosz) had already emigrated because of their politics, many others (including Max Beckmann and Otto Dix) remained in "inner exile" in Germany. The fate of their artistic careers was sealed, however, when, in June 1937, Joseph Goebbels (as head of the Propaganda Ministry and, by extension, the Reich Chamber of Culture, which controlled artistic production) gave the order to begin confiscating examples of "degenerate" art in state collections. Adolf Ziegler, chief of the painting division of the Reich Chamber of Culture, headed a committee of antimodernists who had been charged with putting together a show that would be used as a foil to highlight the first officially sanctioned Great

German Art Exhibition. Traveling around Germany for only ten days, the hodgepodge of modern art collected by the committee showed little consistency. The section devoted to nonrepresentative art included the work of the Surrealists and Berlin Dada and focused especially on the German Expressionists. The works themselves were hung in a random fashion with propaganda text along the walls, giving the viewer information about which artists were an insult to German womanhood, which bore the stigma of international Jewry, and so on.

The artwork shown included pieces by known Nazi Party members, such as the Expressionist Emil Nolde; by some with moderate politics, such as Dix; and by Jews, for example, Marc Chagall, although the majority of artists shown were not Jews. Notably, in spite of the propaganda about the Judeo-Bolshevik conspiracy, only one artist—Otto Freundlich—was both Jewish and a member of the German Communist Party. Hence, historical accuracy and consistency of message as related to individual biographies was clearly not the agenda for the Degenerate Art show. Rather, the grouping of these individuals, along with mentally handicapped artists, was part of a broader negative campaign to make clear what was culturally and socially objectionable to the German state. Although the destruction of the careers of specific modern artists was certainly a desired effect—Beckmann, for instance, left for Amsterdam when the exhibition opened—a much more significant goal of the exhibition was to use art as a means of convincing an outraged German public of the inherent inferiority of the social and political groups represented: Jews, communists, homosexuals, the deranged, and the morally unfit. The astounding popularity of the exhibition indicates a certain level of success for this mission. Jews and other victims were never killed simply because they were artists, but the denigration and racialization of artistic culture as Jewish and "degenerate" aided in the increasingly aggressive campaign to desensitize a German public that only a few years later became knowing perpetrators and bystanders in the genocide of the European Jews.

—*Paul B. Jaskot*

See also Goebbels, Joseph; Holocaust; Judeo-Bolshevism; Nazi Cultural Antisemitism; *Völkisch* Movement and Ideology
References
Barron, Stephanie, ed. *"Degenerate Art": The Fate of the Avant-Garde in Nazi Germany* (Los Angeles: Los Angeles County Museum of Art, 1991).
Steinweis, Alan E. *Art, Ideology, and Economics in Nazi Germany: The Reich Chambers of Music, Theater and the Visual Arts* (Chapel Hill: University of North Carolina Press, 1993).
Zuschlag, Christoph. *"Entartete Kunst": Ausstellungsstrategien im Nazi-Deutschland* (Worms, Germany: Wernersche Verlagsgesellschaft, 1995).

Degeneration

The concept of degeneration was developed in the mid-nineteenth century, most notably by the French psychiatrist Benedict Morel and the Italian (Jewish) criminologist Cesare Lombroso, in the wake of Darwinian evolutionary theory. The concept provided a positivist, medical-biological explanation for the persistence and even increase of retrogressive social elements, such as crime and mental disease, in an era of general progress. Degeneration remained a rather vague notion, and it was never standardized. It began to lose scientific credibility before 1900, and the mass experience of supposedly "degenerate" conditions such as shell shock in World War I made the concept politically and socially unacceptable in western Europe. However, it continued as an unspoken assumption in much social thought and enjoyed renewed prestige in interwar Germany. Ultimately, however, its use by the Nazi regime, especially with regard to anti-Jewish policies, fatally compromised degenerational theory, and since 1945, it has been utterly discredited.

Some adherents emphasized the role of heredity in allowing "primitive" and antisocial elements to survive in the populace, a line of thinking that led easily to eugenics and the "science" of racial hygiene. In the Nazi era, degeneration theory was used to justify euthanasia, sterilization, and the persecution and genocide of the Jews.

Other adherents, most famously Max Nordau in his 1892 *Entartung* (translated as *Degeneration* in 1895), though allowing a role for heredity, adopted a more Lamarckian approach, stressing the role of environmental deficiencies—poor nutrition and housing, alcohol and drug abuse, and the stress of modern urban living—in passing on so-called degenerate characteristics to the next generation. There was thus the potential for a negative synergy between heredity and environment that could be used to explain the social and moral problems of modern life, especially in the burgeoning cities. Most theorists of degeneration, however, including Nordau, thought that an improved environment would eventually, over the course of some generations, ameliorate the problem of degeneration for society as a whole.

Nordau's book has gained particular notoriety because he was among the first to indict "modernist" artists, composers, and writers as degenerate, a trend that led eventually to the Nazi concept of degenerate art and degenerate music. Nordau's role in fostering an idea so central to Nazi ideology is seen as deeply ironic because he was Jewish and was to become, a short time later, the deputy leader of Zionism. There is, though, a double irony, for in *Degeneration,* Nordau treated antisemitism itself as a hysterical symptom of degeneration, which he associated most closely with Germans and Richard Wagner. Jews are not treated as degenerate in Nordau's book, and in his later career as a Zionist, he attributed any physical degeneracy among Jews to poor living conditions and therefore saw it as corrigible. In contrast, for Nordau, it was those who would overturn rationalism and the concept of human solidarity, including notably the "ego-maniac" Friedrich Nietzsche, who were degenerate, hence reactionary and a danger to civilization.

Nordau was roundly condemned by contemporaries, including George Bernard Shaw, for trying to write off all the prominent artists of the age—among them Émile Zola, Leo Tolstoy, and Fyodor Dostoevsky—as insane, which was seen as a ludicrous undertaking. In retrospect and stripped of its pseudoscientific language, the book can be seen as a warning against the antiprogressive trends in modernism, which were indeed present in the work of writers such as Nietzsche and Dostoevsky. The final irony was that it was Nordau's prime target, Nietzsche—with his antirationalist, vitalist concept of degenera-tion, diametrically opposed to Nordau's concept—that was to be a much greater inspiration for the later Nazi approach to degeneration and the Jews.

—*Steven Beller*

See also Degenerate Art; Dostoevsky, Fyodor; Eugenics; Nietzsche, Friedrich; Nordau, Max; Social Darwinism; Wagner, Richard; Zola, Émile
References
Aschheim, Steven E. "Friedrich Nietzsche, Max Nordau and *Degeneration.*" In *In Times of Crisis: Essays on European Culture, Germans and Jews* (Madison: Wisconsin University Press, 2001).
Nordau, Max. *Degeneration* (New York: Appleton, 1905).
Pick, Daniel. *Faces of Degeneration: A European Disorder, c. 1848–c. 1918* (Cambridge: Cambridge University Press, 1989).

Deicide

Deicide interprets the death of Jesus, for which the Jews have been blamed, as the murder of God. The two presuppositions for this charge are the claims that Jesus was crucified by the Jews and that he was a divine being. Passages imputing Jewish responsibility for the death of Jesus are to be found throughout the books of the New Testament.

Given the political realities of the Roman Empire, it is clear that Jewish officials did not possess the power to condemn anyone to be crucified. Yet the literary accounts of the Crucifixion have presented Jewish officials in Jerusalem as the instigators. The book of Nehemiah (9:26), in the period of the Babylonian Exile, spoke of a prophet of God who would be rejected and even slain by his people. Rejection and death—attributes emphasized in the Passion (Luke 13:33)—were thus to be taken as signs of the true prophet. Because the first followers of Jesus interpreted his death as the murder of a prophet by his people, execution at the hands of the Romans presented significant difficulties, which were suppressed in various narrative accounts. Another historical-theological interpretation aided this endeavor. In harmony with the prevalent view in antiquity, divine retribution for the Crucifixion had been visited on the Jews in the destruction of the Temple and the city of Jerusalem. The very act of punishment was seen as having revealed the guilty.

This historical proof held sway in the theology of the antique period, gradually making it axiomatic for Christian anti-Judaism that the Jews had crucified Jesus Christ. Matthew 27:25 was crucial to this belief because it was understood as a juridical act of collective self-incrimination: "His blood be on us and our children." In medieval Christian iconography, this motif commonly appeared in depictions of the Crucifixion in which Jews, not Roman soldiers, crucified Jesus. Only with the Christological deification of Jesus could the conception of the Jews as murderers of Christ become equivalent to their being murderers of God. The charge was made explicitly for the first time by Melito of Sardis (ca. 180). Apparently, the motif became so widespread that it required its own word, the Greek *theoktoniā*. However, this term created theological problems that led to the coining of another word: *kyrioktonoi* (the murderers of the Lord). This term was used so frequently in polemical literature that it became synonymous with *Jews*. The Latin word *deicidae* was a translation from the Greek and first appeared in Augustine's commentary on Psalm 65:1. But Augustine rejected the notion because it would only have been valid if the Jews had known Jesus was the Son of God.

Even though lacking explicit theological grounding, the opinion was nevertheless constantly expressed in anti-Jewish polemics. Zeno of Verona made emphatic use of it to prove the moral depravity of Judaism. John Chrysostom warned Judaizing Christians to cease their consorting with the murderers of the Lord. Ambrose called on the temporal power to carry out God's judgment on the Jews. Especially consequential was the idea that Jewish guilt for the Crucifixion was heritable. All Jews who remained Jews thereby acknowledged their guilt in the murder of God, which was equal to that of their forebears. By this logic, every contemporary Jew could be accused and found guilty, according to Jerome.

The accusation continued to flourish in the altered situation of the Middle Ages. Deicide served as a legitimation for the crimes committed against Jews during the First Crusade as well as for localized pogroms. The debate over the real presence of Christ in the sacramental host fostered the legend of Jewish host desecration, which claimed that Jews, by torturing the wafer and causing it to bleed, were, in fact, reenacting the Crucifixion. Once again, Jews were negative witnesses proving a Christian truth, and a prejudice was enlisted to demonstrate a theological point: the Jews knew that Christ was present in the host. The medieval ritual murder legend also tied into the accusation of deicide. Building on the notion that Jews thirsted for blood, well established in late antiquity, the idea underwent further elaboration in the Middle Ages. As one variant had it, a punishment for the Crucifixion was that Jews suffered from anemia, which they needed to relieve by drinking Christian blood.

The consequences of deicide have been dire from the origin of the concept into the modern era. Those who murdered the Lord were incapable of morality. Any crime could be ascribed to them. One who laid hands on the Jew thereby made himself or herself an instrument of God's punishment. In Christian society, the inferior position of Jews had been justified since the fourth century by their guilt in the ultimate crime. Modern racism, without a religious foundation, was nonetheless influenced in its basic outlook by the religious motif of deicide. Secular racists did not charge Jews with the murder of the Son of God but were nonetheless certain that Jews wanted to kill "Aryan man." During the Third Reich, the so-called Deutsche Christen (German Christians), in the throes of racial delusion, conflated the myths, making Jesus into an Aryan.

—*Rainer Kampling*
Richard S. Levy, translation

See also Augustine of Hippo; Chrysostom, John; Church Fathers; Crusades; Deutsche Christen; Gospels; Host Desecration; Iconography, Christian; Ritual Murder (Medieval)

References

Davis, Frederick B. *The Jew and Deicide: The Origin of an Archetype* (Lanham, MD: University Press of America, 2003).

Kampling, Rainer. *Im Angesicht Israels: Studien zum historischen und theologischen Verhältnis von Kirche und Israel.* Edited by Matthias Blum (Stuttgart, Germany: Verlag Katholisches Bibelwerk, 2002).

Demonstratio Adversus Iudaeos

Demonstratio Adversus Iudaeos—or, by its Greek title, *Apodeiktiē pros Joudaious*—exists only in fragments (Patrologia Graeca 10, 787–794). The work is attributed to Hippolytus of Rome (ca. 170–235 CE). A presbyter of the church in Rome, he became involved in a long and drawn-out Christological controversy, which ended with his being exiled to Sardinia (in 235) by the Emperor Maximus Thrax.

Hippolytus wrote the *Demonstratio* in Greek, which drastically limited its reception in the western Empire. The short work took the form of a sermon. It explicated in historical-theological terms the situation of the Jews in the Roman Empire following the destruction of Jerusalem. A second purpose was to demonstrate from Scripture that Jesus was the Messiah. In this endeavor, Hippolytus aligned himself with the canon of the Septuagint, making use not only of the Prophets and the Psalms but also the Proverbs of Solomon. Reliance on the Septuagint makes clear the audience he was really addressing. Even though he spoke to a Jew at the beginning of the sermon, this was to be understood as a rhetorical device, not an attempt to reach actual Jews.

The argumentation of the sermon presupposed agreement with the Christian faith and addressed a Christian audience. Its scriptural evidence characteristically assumed what it claimed to be proving, that Jesus of Nazareth was the Christ. Compared to the other anti-Jewish sermons of Christian antiquity, Hippolytus indulged in relatively little verbal abuse of Jews. His main purpose was to present a Christological proof to his Christian readers. Resorting to a historical argument, he wanted to show that the disenfranchised situation of the Jews in the Roman Empire was divine punishment for the killing of Jesus. To make his point more emphatically, he exaggerated the deterioration of the Jews' status beyond what was really the case. The Diaspora was distinguished from earlier periods of exile because it was to be eternal—God would not grant forgiveness to the Jews. Killing the Son of God was so grievous a crime that there could be no salvation from its consequences (*Demonstratio*, 6–7). Thus, Hippolytus exploited the historical fact of the Diaspora to demonstrate a Christological dogma. The proof of the divinity of Jesus lay in the punishment meted out to those responsible for his death. This particular case carried no weight outside Christian circles, but within them, Hippolytus delivered what he considered an empirical "proof" that Jesus was the Son of God.

The *Demonstratio* was, in both argument and rhetorical style, thoroughly traditional. It is probable that Hippolytus was familiar with the work of Justin Martyr, *Dialogue with Trypho*. His sermon, though not widely read, is an important example of the "against the Jew" genre because it exemplifies the process by which theological argumentation developed into an anti-Jewish literary construct and iconographic symbol.

—*Rainer Kampling*
Richard S. Levy, translation

See also Deicide; *Dialogue with Trypho;* Roman Empire; Wandering Jew

References

Brent, Allen. *Hippolytus and the Roman Church in the Third Century: Communities in Tension before the Emergence of a Monarch Bishop* (Leiden, the Netherlands: Brill, 1995).

Cerrato, J. A. *Hippolytus between East and West: The Commentaries and the Provenance of the Corpus* (Oxford: Oxford University Press, 2002).

Desecration of Cemeteries and Synagogues in Germany since 1919

The normal pattern of cemetery desecration entails the overturning or breaking of grave markers; in the case of synagogues, the defilement includes the smearing of the building's exterior walls and, more rarely, the vandalizing of the interior. Because such deeds were regarded as heinous offenses, they drew special attention in the twentieth century.

In Germany, desecrations have a long tradition. As early as the fourteenth century, Jewish cemeteries were destroyed and their gravestones used for the building of churches and homes. However, the broad public, sensitized by the emergence of organized antisemitism, became conscious of these acts as something unusual only at the end of the nineteenth century. Since the foundation of Germany's first democratic republic in 1919, relatively exact statistics on these events have been kept; records of the vigorous public discussion engendered by these deeds are also available.

During the Weimar years (1919–1933), 200 cemeteries and synagogues were defiled, the high point of incidents being reached in the mid-1920s. In the Nazi period, acts of destruction escalated. Probably 80 to 90 percent of the approximately 1,700 Jewish cemeteries across Germany were totally or partially destroyed. The proportion of synagogues converted for use as garages and warehouses was also probably high, although no exact figures are available. On the night of November 9–10, 1938, the so-called Night of Broken Glass, more than 260 synagogues were set on fire. In the postwar Germanies, precise figures exist only for cemetery desecrations. From 1949 to the end of 1999, there were at least 1,000 such cases. Since the 1990s, annual occurrences have attained new levels, with a record 66 incidents in 1994. These high numbers are, to some degree, the reflection of greater public and official awareness. Alarmed by the growth of right-wing extremism, especially in the former German Democratic Republic, defilements that formerly would have gone unreported have instead been officially registered. In addition to the cemetery incidents, there are a few acts of vandalism targeting synagogues each year. Of late, the increasing militancy of the acts has become conspicuous. In 1998, the memorial tablet marking the burial place of Heinz Galinksi, former spokesman of the Jewish community in Germany, was blown up twice. In 2000, youths hurled Molotov cocktails at synagogues in Erfurt and Düsseldorf.

The offenders have often been underage youths. During the Weimar years, probably one-quarter of the crimes were committed by individuals under twenty-one. Their punishment, then and now, has posed problems for the police and the judicial system. Is the overturning of a grave marker a conscious political act or just a piece of stupidity? Not every case is difficult to assess, however. At least a portion of the youthful offenders belong to right-wing extremist groups, making it possible to establish decisively the presence of political—that is, antisemitic—motives. Among adult offenders, the connections to extremist groups are even more apparent. In the Weimar Republic, for example, perpetrators were frequently members of Hitler's paramilitary, the SA or SS.

The motivations for these deeds elude exact understanding. Expressing one's Jew-hatred by defiling a cemetery may testify to the antisemite's secret desire to kill. Most cemeteries lie on the outskirts of towns, making them relatively remote locations where violent fantasies can be acted out and still remain a secret. The remote cemetery has also served antisemites as a place of retreat, especially in periods when physically manifested antisemitism was strongly condemned, as was the case in the mid-1920s. But even the moral outrage over the defilements and the public discussion of such acts in the media can occasionally produce copycat occurrences by perpetrators in search of recognition.

Desecrations are crimes according to the German Penal Code—§168 (disturbing the peace of the dead) and §305 (misdemeanor damage to property)—punishable with sentences of up to three years in prison. When the crime concerns felony damage to property (such as the destruction of sacred objects), a weapons violation (as in a bombing), or the theft of a cemetery ornament, more severe penalties are possible. For youthful offenders, there can be additional school-related punishments, including expulsion. In historical and current practice, the penalties have been relatively severe. In the Weimar Republic, for example, sentences of up to six years of penal servitude were possible. In the Federal Republic of Germany, offenders as young as seventeen or eighteen faced several years in jail. The harsh sentences are consonant with the strong outrage produced in society at large by this sort of crime, reflected also in the morally charged adjectives commonly used to describe such acts: *brutish, vulgar,* or *cowardly.* But there is a paradox here as well. The socially and juridically sanctioned punishment for these crimes could often be more severe than that meted out for violence against living Jews.

—*Dirk Walter*
Richard S. Levy, translation

See also German Democratic Republic; Germany, Federal Republic of; National Socialist German Workers' Party; Neo-Nazism, German; Night of Broken Glass (November 1938 Pogrom); Weimar
References
Diamant, Adolf. *Geschändete jüdische Friedhöfe in Deutschland 1945 bis 1999* (Potsdam, Germany: Verlag für Berlin-Brandenburg, 2000).
Walter, Dirk. *Antisemitische Kriminalität und Gewalt: Judenfeindschaft in der Weimarer Republik* (Bonn, Germany: J. H. W. Dietz Verlag Nachf., 1999).

Deutsche Christen

The Deutsche Christen (German Christians) were a group of clergy and laypeople in Germany in the 1930s and 1940s who sought to synthesize National Socialism and Christianity. They aimed to purge Christianity of everything they deemed Jewish and to create a German church based on "blood." Most of the approximately 600,000 members were Protestant, although a few Catholics were involved. By mid-1933, Deutsche Christen had acquired key posts in the Protestant establishment—in national church governing bodies and university faculties of theology, as regional bishops, and on local church councils. Many kept those positions until 1945 and beyond.

Three impulses converged to form their movement. In 1932, a group of politicians and pastors met to discuss how to win the Protestant churches of Germany to the Nazi cause. They initially named themselves Protestant National Socialists but ultimately decided on Deutsche Christen instead. Meanwhile, in Thuringia, Siegfried Leffler and Julius Leutheuser, two young pastors and war veterans, had been preaching religious renewal along Nazi lines since the 1920s. They also called themselves Deutsche Christen. The two groups began to cooperate. A third initiative came from the Protestant, *völkisch* (racist-nationalist) associations that emerged after World War I. Dedicated to reviving church life through emphasizing German culture, antisemitism, and nationalism, some of those organizations merged with the Deutsche Christen.

Instead of breaking with the established Protestant churches, the Deutsche Christen tried to take over from within. Their main rival was the Confessing Church (*Bekennende Kirche*), another movement within official Protestantism. The Deutsche Christen also had opposition outside the church from neopagans who considered even Nazified Christianity "too Jewish." Although clergy normally spoke for the movement, the Deutsche Christen represented a cross section of German society.

They aimed to create a "people's church" that would provide a spiritual homeland for the "Aryans" of the Third Reich. Accordingly, they attacked every aspect of Christianity that was related to Judaism. They rejected the Old Testament, revised the New Testament, expunged words such as *Hallelujah* and *Hosanna* from hymns, and denied that Jesus was a Jew. Because they considered Jewishness racial, they refused to accept conversions from Judaism to Christianity as valid and insisted that only a hard, "manly" church devoid of qualities such as compassion could fight racial impurity.

Deutsche Christen ideas remained fairly constant, but the movement changed over time. From 1932 to late 1933, it enjoyed open Nazi support. It swept the Protestant church elections in 1933 and dominated the process that unified Germany's regional Protestant churches into one German Protestant church. One of their own, the naval chaplain Ludwig Müller, became the Protestant Reich bishop. But success was short-lived. Worried that the Deutsche Christen caused dissension, Nazi leaders withdrew their support. For 1934 and most of 1935, the movement was in shambles. But even though the national group splintered, the core ideas persisted. By late 1935, the movement began reorganizing, and by September 1939, almost all the factions had reestablished ties.

War fulfilled many of the aims of the Deutsche Christen. They wanted an aggressive Christianity; now they had the nation at arms. They demanded exclusion of "non-Aryans" and Jewish influences from German religious life; that goal was realized by default, through the isolation, expulsion, and murder of people defined as Jews. But the war also brought setbacks. Even Deutsche Christen experienced hostility from some Nazi authorities who resented Christianity in any form.

When Hitler's regime collapsed in 1945, the movement lost its credibility. To justify their involvement to Allied occupation authorities, de-Nazification boards, and even themselves, many former members claimed they had only wanted religious renewal. They rarely mentioned the antisemitism that had pervaded their program. Some pastors were ousted, but within a few years, almost all were back in the pulpit. Lay members easily reentered the Protestant mainstream.

Some scholars dismiss the Deutsche Christen because they constituted only about 1 percent of the population. In the Nazi context, however, their movement was significant. Through their quest for a "racially pure," anti-Jewish church, the Deutsche Christen echoed and endorsed the crimes of the Third Reich.

—*Doris L. Bergen*

See also Chamberlain, Houston Stewart; Churches under Nazism; Masculinity; Rosenberg, Alfred; *Völkisch* Movement and Ideology

References
Bergen, Doris L. *Twisted Cross: The German Christian Movement in the Third Reich* (Chapel Hill: University of North Carolina Press, 1996).
Conway, John S. *The Nazi Persecution of the Churches, 1933–45* (New York: Basic Books, 1968).

Devi, Savitri (1905–1982)

Savitri Devi was a French convert to Hinduism and a major proponent of occultic Nazi ideology. In the West, Devi is known for her identification of Adolf Hitler as an "avatar" (divine manifestation) who moved in harmony with Hindu tradition. In India, she is known as an early leader of the Hinduvta (Hindu Nationalist) movement.

Born Maximiani Portas, she was highly educated and particularly impressed by the antisemitic writings of the nineteenth-century French thinker Ernest Renan. She also followed the Nazi movement closely and was one of the few who actually read Alfred Rosenberg's ponderous *Myth of the Twentieth Century,* to which she gave high marks for its justification of antisemitism. At the same time, she immersed herself in study of the Hindu classics, the Vedas and the Upanishads, and eventually adopted the name of Savitri Devi,

an Aryan sun goddess. In 1940, she married Indian nationalist and esotericist A. K. Mukherjee, editor of the pro-Nazi publication *The New Mercury,* and settled in Calcutta, where she worked on her blueprint for a global Aryan religion combining Hinduism with Nazism. During a sojourn in Britain, she published several well-received works, including *The Impeachment of Man* (1946, reprinted in 1991), a manifesto for radical environmentalism and Aryan nature worship that is now regarded as a classic in neo-Nazi circles. Following World War II, while incarcerated in Germany for her Nazi activities, she wrote *Gold in the Furnace* (1949), an explicitly pro-Nazi autobiography, which she considered her greatest achievement.

In *The Lightning and the Sun* (1958), Devi declared Hitler a mystical embodiment of those two light sources, and she dedicated the work to him—"the god-like Individual of our times, the Man against Time." The latter tribute is explained within the book as the god-man who "lives in eternity while acting in time, according to the Aryan doctrine of detached violence." Devi believed that Hitler was the "one-before-the-last" such incarnation, a forerunner of "the one whom the faithful of all religions . . . await." This "last, great individual" would outdo Hitler by sparing none who "bear the stamp of the fallen ages." Devi claimed that Hitler knew both his own role and that of the "last Man against Time," for whom he would do "the preparatory work." With a peculiar twist of logic, she also described the forerunner role of Hitler in *Impeachment* as "messiah ben Joseph," a Jewish eschatological figure who presaged the final Messiah (ben David).

Devi's later years were dedicated to corresponding with admirers around the world, lecturing, and promoting Holocaust denial. She claimed an ally in Hindu leader Ramana Maharishi, who she said acknowledged Hitler as a *gnani* (sage). Devi died while on a lecture tour for the American Nazi Party, and her ashes were interred at the group's shrine in Arlington, Virginia. Her influence among neo-Nazis persists through her books and tapes, promoted by the American Nazi Party, British National Socialist leader Colin Jordan, Canadian Ernst Zündel, and New

Zealand's Renaissance Press, publisher of occultic-based fascist magazines and books.

—*Hannah Newman*

See also American Nazi Party; Aquarius, Age of; Hitler, Adolf; Holocaust Denial, Negationism, and Revisionism; *Myth of the Twentieth Century, The;* Renan, Ernest; Rosenberg, Alfred

Dewey, Melvil (1851–1931)

By 1905, when Melvil Dewey was involved in a sensational antisemitic incident, he was the most influential librarian in the United States and one of the best-known librarians in the world. He was born in Adams Center, New York. Both his mother, Eliza, and his storekeeper father, Joel, were devout Baptists, and their son began study at a seminary in Oneida, New York. Determined to enlist in the work of uplifting the masses, he entered Amherst College in 1870 and joined the movements to introduce the metric system and simplified spelling (changing his name from the too elaborate "Melville"). He took a job in Amherst's library and quickly decided that librarianship was the field in which he could best help to elevate humanity. In 1876, he published his famous "decimal system" for classifying and shelving library holdings. His ingenious method quickly displaced rival classification schemes and ensured him a lasting reputation among professional librarians.

Dewey was one of the founders of the American Library Association (in 1876), its secretary for fifteen years, and then its president and treasurer. In 1883, he became head librarian at Columbia University, and in 1887, he established there (without permission) the first library school in the world. Under fire at Columbia, he accepted an offer in 1889 to become the secretary to the regents of the University of the State of New York and, simultaneously, the state librarian.

In the mid-1890s, Dewey and his wife, Annie, built a recreational retreat at Lake Placid, in the Adirondack Mountains. In 1894, they started the Lake Placid Club and over the years transformed the place into a 10,000-acre complex with tennis courts, golf courses, concert halls, and 150 member families. Like other Adirondack resorts, Dewey's club excluded Jews: "No one shall be re-ceived as a member or guest, against whom there is physical, moral, social or race objection," announced one of its circulars. Rejecting "absolutely all consumptives, or other invalids," the club declared it "impracticable to make exceptions to Jews or others excluded, even when of unusual personal qualifications." When Henry Leipziger was barred from the meeting of the New York Library Association, held at the club in September 1903, he complained to Louis Marshall, who resolved to fight. Enlisting a group of prestigious and influential New York City Jews—men gathered around the American Jewish Committee and the *New York Times*—Marshall, in January 1905, petitioned the regents for Dewey's dismissal. No one denied the legal right of a private club to set its membership policies, but the petitioners contended that Dewey's open and arrogant prejudice rendered him unfit for the high positions he held in the state's educational system. The hearings before the regents were reported all over the country. In the end, the regents declined to fire Dewey but issued a strongly worded public rebuke of his conduct. A few months later, he was in trouble again over the issue, and in September, he resigned his positions, effective January 1, 1906. In 1927, he founded a second club in Florida, where he died two weeks after his eightieth birthday. His ashes were taken to Lake Placid.

—*David W. Levy*

See also American Jewish Committee and Antidefamation Efforts in the United States; Restricted Public Accommodations, United States; Seligman-Hilton Affair; United States

References

Wiegand, Wayne. "*Jew Attack:* The Story behind Melvil Dewey's Resignation as New York State Librarian in 1905," *American Jewish History* 83 (September 1995): 359–379.

———. *Irrepressible Reformer: A Biography of Melvil Dewey* (Chicago and London: American Library Association, 1996).

Dialogue with Trypho

Justin Martyr, author of the *Dialogue with Trypho,* was born of pagan parents around the year 100 CE in Nablus (Flavia Neapolis). He made a study of Middle Platonism, which he regarded as the logical precursor to the Christianity that he then accepted. Justin was martyred between 160 and 165 CE.

The *Dialogue with Trypho* appeared between 155 and 160 CE and took the form of a fictional dialogue, reminiscent of the Platonic school. The story that Justin met with a real Jew named Trypho in Ephesus shortly after the Bar Kochba Revolt (132–135 CE) is highly improbable. Fictional though the meeting likely was, Justin was familiar with at least some of the key Jewish arguments that he presented from his own perspective in the work: Christians interpreted the Bible arbitrarily (27,1; 79,1); Jesus was only a simple man whose Crucifixion demonstrated that he could not have been the messiah (32,1; 38,1; 68,1; 89,1); Christians did not obey the Torah, even though Jesus had lived according to its commandments (67,7). The reader's access to the Jewish perception of Christianity was, of course, mediated through Justin's own understanding of it.

Justin's apologetic thrust was to show that Christians, not Jews or pagans, were the one and true people of God. They were the true children of Abraham, the true Israel, in and for whom all God's promises would be fulfilled (82; 119; 123; 135; and elsewhere). The *Dialogue with Trypho* was an early expression of a fully developed Christian anti-Judaism. In the spirit of holy Scriptures, Jews were not really Jews. Rather, the real Jews were those who believed that Jesus was the Christ, no matter their ethnicity. Contemporary Jewry was thus deprived of its own tradition and religion. The church, as the true Israel, supplanted the Jews, contesting their claim even to call themselves Jews. This line of argument was presented to the readers of the Dialogue as a self-evident certainty.

But the work's initial purpose was to strengthen the identity of a still insecure church. The problem of Christian legitimacy led Justin to extreme claims—for example, that he understood the writings of the Jews better than they did themselves. That Jews should exist at all posed something of a cognitive dissonance for him, for their continued existence called the position of Christianity itself into question. Thus, Justin felt called on to pile on the textual examples in support of his case; whole stretches of the work read like a collection of testimonies in dialogue form. It is probable that Justin wanted to present arguments for inner-Christian discourse, but he seems to have overlooked that the "proofs" in his book only work if one already believed as a Christian. Another purpose was to proselytize among the pagans of the time, poised as they were between Judaism and Christianity. Justin hoped to persuade them to choose the latter as the "true Israel" (23).

After a highly stylized autobiographical prologue (1,1–8; 2), the dialogue unfolds over two days. Its major themes include the supersession of Jewish law by the law of Christ (10–47), Jesus as the true Messiah (48–108), and Christianity as the true Israel (109–141). Although elements of an irenic compromise are also present in the book—Jews are called brothers (96,2)—and although it ends on a note of reconciliation, the predominant tone is polemical and unyielding. Moral calumnies and the depiction of Jews as the deadly enemies of Christians, who curse them as a regular part of their synagogue services (16,4; 47,5; 95,4; 96,2), contribute to a sense of irreconcilable differences.

Giving voice to these claims, Justin supplied basic motifs for a pathological Christian anti-Judaism that would gain in strength and currency as Jews fell into a state of political powerlessness. His *Dialogue with Trypho* provided later theologians, including John Chrysostom, with a source of abundant arguments against the Jews.

—*Rainer Kampling*
Richard S. Levy, translation

See also Bar Kochba Revolt; Chrysostom, John; *Demonstratio Adversus Judaeos;* Roman Empire; Supersessionism

References

Allert, Craig D. *Revelation, Truth, Canon, and Interpretation: Studies in Justin Martyr's "Dialogue with Trypho"* (Leiden, the Netherlands: Brill, 2002).
Rokeah, David. *Justin Martyr and the Jews* (Leiden, the Netherlands: Brill, 2002).

Diaspora Revolt (115–117 CE)

In the last years of the principate of Trajan (Marcus Ulpius Traianus), the Roman Empire experienced Jewish revolts within the most important communities to which Jews had been dispersed following the fall of Jerusalem in 70 CE. Modern scholarship refers to these complex events as the Diaspora Revolt. The Jews of Mesopotamia, Cyprus, Cyrene, and Alexandria clashed with the local non-Jewish populations and the Roman authority. Ancient writers did not provide sufficient information to establish with certainty the causes of such widespread events, but there is scattered evidence from previous decades pointing to social tensions between resident Jews and non-Jews with the right of citizenship. This conflict, in all likelihood, spawned the explosive revolts. The better-known cases are those of Cyrene and Alexandria, where scholars think that the diffused messianism of the time may have generated expectations for a Jewish king who would lead the Jews out of the Diaspora.

In Cyrene, the Jews revolted in an apparently organized uprising and destroyed roads and public buildings, mainly pagan temples. Some of them then proceeded to Alexandria, led by a Jewish "king," Loukuas. Papyrological evidence shows that fights between citizens and Jews had already occurred there in 113. Other papyri, very likely extensively embellished by rhetoric, present a description of part of the events suspiciously reminiscent of those we know from the Alexandrian riots of 38 CE. Other sources report that this time the Jews attacked pagan monuments, destroying the temple of Serapis; their main synagogue was also destroyed, an action confirmed by a passage from the Talmud. Revolts also occurred in the Egyptian countryside, concerning which particularly gruesome details have been recorded.

The Jews were clearly well organized militarily and able to inflict defeats on their opponents, at least until a regular Roman army sent by Trajan arrived from Parthia. The Jewish revolt was then crushed, and the Jewish presence in Egypt, Alexandria, and Cyrene was drastically reduced.
—*Sandra Gambetti*

See also Alexandrian Pogrom; Roman Empire
References
Schürer, Emil. *The History of the Jewish People in the Age of Jesus Christ.* Vol. 3, pt. 1 (Edinburgh: Clark, 1986).

Dickens, Charles (1812–1870)

In the portrait of the Jewish fence Fagin in *Oliver Twist* (1838), Charles Dickens produced one of the most notorious anti-Jewish literary stereotypes of the nineteenth century. Already the most popular and best-paid novelist in England by that time, Dickens was also to become a champion of the causes of the oppressed. He abhorred slavery and was a supporter of the European liberal revolutions of the late 1840s, and in *Oliver Twist,* the story of an innocent workhouse orphan tempted into the world of crime, he attacked the New Poor Law of 1834. Reacting to the author's well-known liberal politics, a Jewish reader wrote to Dickens in 1863 and charged that he had "encouraged a vile prejudice against the despised Hebrew" and that the representation of Fagin was "a great wrong." Dickens, however, protested that "I have no feeling towards the Jewish people but a friendly one . . . always speak well of them, whether in public or in private, and bear my testimony (as I ought to do) to their perfect good faith in such transactions as I ever had with them" (Rosenberg 1960, 16). In the preface to the novel, Dickens wrote that he was aiming for a representation of criminals "as really did exist; to paint them in all their deformity, in all their wretchedness, in all the squalid misery of their lives." Such a sociological approach to crime, he considered, "would be a service to society."

Nonetheless, Dickens's representation of Fagin was drawn from both the idiom of stage melodrama and medieval images of the Jew as inherently evil. He is frequently referred to in the novel simply by the epithet "the Jew" and also as the "merry old gentleman," a euphemism for the devil. The reader first meets him in his dark, dirty, and vaporous den, hunched over a fire "with a toasting-fork in his hand"; he is described as "a very old shrivelled Jew, whose villainous-looking and repulsive face was obscured by a quantity of matted red hair." Fagin's red hair and toasting fork carry satanic associations, as does the apparent solicitude he uses to charm the naive Oliver into a life of pickpocketing and burglary. George Cruikshank's illustrations for the novel portray Fagin with a long, sharp nose, connoting shrewdness according to the physiognomic the-

Black-and-white engraving by George Cruikshank of the thief, Fagin, sitting in his jail cell, from an 1839 American publication of Dickens's novel, *Oliver Twist*. (Bettmann/Corbis)

ory of the day. The novel's figurative language links him with beasts: he is "lynx-eyed," a "wolf"; his hand is a "withered old claw"; he has "such fangs as should have been a dog's or rat's." He inhabits the night: "Creeping beneath the shelter of the walls and doorways, the hideous old man seemed like some loathsome reptile, engendered in the slime and darkness through which he moved: crawling forth, by night, in search of some rich offal for a meal." In Fagin's underworld, where "everything felt wild and clammy to the touch," the sliminess of the Jew is a sign not only of his physical repulsiveness and bestiality but also of his capacity to disorder representational boundaries.

—*Nadia Valman*

See also Caricature, Anti-Jewish (Early); English Literature from Chaucer to Wells; Iconography, Christian; *Jew of Malta, The;* Shylock
References
Rosenberg, Edgar. *From Shylock to Svengali: Jewish Stereotypes in English Fiction* (Stanford, CA: Stanford University Press, 1960).

Diderot, Denis (1713–1784)

A French philosophe and the leading editor of the landmark publication of the Enlightenment, the *Encyclopédie* (Encyclopedia[1751–1772]), Denis Diderot treated Jewish themes infrequently in his published works and even more rarely in his private correspondence: he showed none of the obsessive rhetorical venom toward Judaism exhibited by his contemporary Voltaire. However, his deprecatory attitudes toward ancient Jewish history and the Hebrew Bible reflected typical Enlightenment hostilities and have led some scholars to charge Diderot with antisemitism.

Many articles in the *Encyclopédie* sought to topple the biblical narrative of early Jewish history from its exceptional status. The authorial role of Diderot in various articles is not easy to ascertain, but as the key editor, he was to a large degree responsible for the overall tone of the work. The lengthy article entitled "Jewish Philosophy," signed by him, is most clearly illustrative of his stance toward Judaic themes. In it, he continually belittled the significance and creativity of Jewish thought, contrasting the sophistication of the Egyptians to the Jews' cultural inferiority. He was scornful of the supposedly arcane legalism of the Talmud, and he criticized the Jews for their "blind obedience" to this text. These attacks were stock themes in Enlightenment writings on Judaism and must be understood as part of a wider critique of revealed religion in general and of Christianity and its Jewish legitimating antecedent in particular. However, the especially persistent and sweeping dismissals of Judaism in the *Encyclopédie* reflected the unique intellectual difficulties posed by Judaism for Enlightenment thinkers such as Diderot. The mythic system of Judaism was impervious to Enlightenment critique, and this resilience readily provoked frustration. The repetition of familiar attacks on Jewish primitivism and legalism in several articles in this compilation revealed the inability of the philosophes to provide, within their rationalist schema, a conclusive alternative to the biblical account of Jewish history and survival.

In Diderot's philosophical fiction, there was one notable example of a negative Jewish stereotype: the lascivious Jew of Utrecht in *Rameau's*

Nephew (1761). In some of his critical writings, however, Diderot expressed a sustained admiration for the poetic power of the Jewish Bible. In the account of his travels in *Voyage to Holland* (1774), he also confronted with some sensitivity the reality of Jews as a contemporary social and political presence. He commented on the beauty of the Dutch Sephardic synagogues—though he was taken aback by the disordered noisiness of the services that occurred within them—and praised the toleration of religious diversity in the Dutch Republic.

In sum, Diderot's attitudes toward Jews and Judaism should be seen as eclectic and mobile, encompassing strains of idealism, denigration, and uncertainty. Although sharing the widespread Enlightenment tendency to posit a Jewish legalistic tribal atavism as the inverse of his own positive values of rational universalistic progress, he also, if only fleetingly, contemplated Jewish themes more positively in aesthetic and political contexts.

—*Adam Sutcliffe*

See also Bauer, Bruno; Dohm, Christian Wilhelm von; Emancipation; Fichte, J. G.; Hegel, G. W. F.; Herder, J. G.; Jewish Question; Kant, Immanuel; Michaelis, Johann David; Talmud; Voltaire, François-Marie-Arouet de.

References
Gendzier, Stephen J. "Diderot and the Jews," *Diderot Studies* 16 (1973): 35–54.
Schwartz, Leon. *Diderot and the Jews* (London and Toronto, Canada: Associated University Presses, 1981).
Sutcliffe, Adam. *Judaism and Enlightenment* (Cambridge: Cambridge University Press, 2003).

Dietary Laws

Judaism's dietary laws, which dictate every aspect of food preparation and consumption, have greatly interested non-Jewish observers throughout history. Although some anti-Jewish writers, such as Tacitus and Apion, referred to the laws with disdain, claiming that they set Jews apart and showed their hostility toward non-Jews, most others seemed to have viewed them as merely another ethnic peculiarity in a world teeming with these. The one known attempt in antiquity to outlaw some Jewish dietary practices was made by the Seleucid king Antiochus IV

Epiphanes, who forced the Temple priests to sacrifice and consume pigs; this decree was part of a larger failed effort to Hellenize and politically stabilize Judea. With the rise of Christianity and its notion that the old law had been superseded, Jews who continued to practice the kosher laws were derided, and church councils repeatedly prohibited Christians from partaking of food with Jews.

One aspect of the kosher laws that has proven particularly controversial since the Middle Ages is the Jewish method of slaughtering livestock. Although Jewish texts make clear that the prescribed kosher method—one quick cut to the neck with a very sharp blade—is designed to cause the animal to expire quickly, thereby sparing it unnecessary pain, the highly ritualistic manner of the slaughter and the copious amount of blood it produces may have contributed to several medieval anti-Jewish myths, including that of the blood libel. In modern times, kosher slaughter continues to be criticized as cruel, particularly because traditional Jewish law does not allow the animal to be stunned prior to its slaughter. In the nineteenth century, laws were passed in Germany and Switzerland (where they are still in place) prohibiting the slaughter of animals that had not been stunned; although antisemitic intentions should not automatically be attributed to the lawmakers, it is sometimes hard to tell where concern for animal suffering ends and antisemitism begins in the shrillest popular agitation for such laws.

In the twentieth century, a new libel regarding kosher laws evolved in some Western countries. To ensure the kashrut of industrial food establishments and prepackaged products, kosher certifying organizations have arisen. For businesses that request it—and are willing to pay a service fee—these organizations send trained rabbis to oversee their production processes. If a food product is properly supervised, the kosher certifying agency allows the business to incorporate a small trademarked symbol, at a nominal cost, on the packaging. Antisemites have decried this certification as a "kosher tax" that powerful Jews have enlisted the government to collect on their behalf; others have alleged that greedy rabbis threaten businesses with a Jewish boycott unless they accept their fee-based kosher certification. Some have gone so far as to post lists of kosher-certified products on the Internet, in an attempt to boycott businesses that have surrendered to the "kosher mafia."

—*Aryeh Tuchman*

See also Apion; Caricature, Anti-Jewish (Early); *Judensau;* Kosher Slaughtering; Pork; Ritual Murder (Medieval); Roman Literature
References
Brantz, Dorothee. "Stunning Bodies: Animal Slaughter, Judaism, and the Meaning of Humanity in Imperial Germany," *Central European History* 35 (2002): 167–195.
Schäfer, Peter. *Judeophobia: Attitudes toward the Jews in the Ancient World* (Cambridge, MA: Harvard University Press, 1997).

Dining Society, Christian-German

Established in Berlin in January 1811 and lasting until 1815, the Christian-German Dining Society (Christlich-Deutsche Tischgesellschaft) was a social club that drew together members from the Prussian intellectual and political elite, including the romantic writers Clemens Brentano and Heinrich von Kleist, the club founder Achim von Arnim, the philosopher Johann Gottlieb Fichte, the military theorist Carl von Clausewitz, and conservative political figures such as Leopold von Gerlach, Ludwig von der Marwitz, and cofounder Adam Müller. The organization was created in a spirit of xenophobic German nationalism and Prussian patriotism at the time of the Napoleonic occupation, but though anti-French sentiment was paramount, the group is most notable for its explicit exclusion of Jews—even baptized Jews—from membership.

The fact that even converted Jews were barred from joining has led some historians to cite the Christian-German Dining Society as an early instance of racist antisemitism in Germany; others have concluded that the opinions expressed in the club's statutes and discussions reflected more traditional forms of religiously motivated anti-Judaism. Arnim authored the club's bylaws and gave some particularly disturbing anti-Jewish lectures there, for which he has typically been seen as the prime instigator of the organization's anti-

semitism. More recent scholarship, however, suggests that even though Arnim did call for barring Jews from membership, he had proposed the admission of baptized Jews, only to be outvoted on that point by other founding members. The racial interpretation is still open to question, but it does seem clear from the club's transactions that the anti-Jewish sentiment shared by many of the members was at least ethnic rather than purely religious in nature.

When assessing the significance of the Christian-German Dining Society, it is also important to consider the larger historical context. The organization was, first and foremost, intended to provide an alternative venue for Prussian and German patriots during the French occupation. The membership was largely drawn from the patriotically inclined among Berlin's literary salons, and the exclusion of women (not just Jews) allowed the founders to form a more tightly knit all-male group, which marked an important shift in German political culture. Previous scholars also emphasized the society's role in facilitating cooperation between literary romantics and conservative opponents of the Prussian government's program of modernizing social, economic, and political reforms, which included a limited Jewish emancipation. This view, however, has recently been questioned, with two scholars pointing to the diversity of opinion among the club's members and seeing little evidence of organized opposition politics. The romantic writer Müller certainly worked with Marwitz and other Prussian nobles to oppose the reforms, and anti-Jewish rhetoric featured in their public arguments, but this need not indicate similar political ties and views for Arnim, much less Kleist or Fichte. In terms of the relationship with German Jews, although it is true that not all members of the Christian-German Dining Society supported its anti-Jewish stance, it is equally true that the club will remain of historical interest primarily because it highlights the presence of anti-Jewish xenophobia among German nationalists at a crucial juncture in German history.

—*Brian Vick*

See also Burschenschaften; Christian State; Dohm, Christian Wilhelm von; Emancipation; Fichte, J. G.; State-within-a-State

References

Härtl, Heinz. "Romantischer Antisemitismus: Arnim und die Tischgesellschaft," *Weimarer Beiträge* 33 (1987): 1159–1173.

Klessmann, Eckart. "Romantik und Antisemitismus," *Der Monat* 21, no. (1969): 65–71.

Kohn, Hans. *Prelude to Nation-States: The French and German Experience, 1789–1815* (Princeton, NJ: Van Nostrand, 1967).

Dinter, Artur (1876–1948)

The now nearly forgotten Artur Dinter was, on the strength of his novel trilogy *Sins of the Era,* one of the most widely read *völkisch* (racist-nationalist) authors of the 1920s and 1930s. A student of philosophy and the natural sciences, he earned a doctorate and went into teaching but then, in 1905, moved on to the theater world as an artistic manager and director. He helped found and lead the Association of German Stage Writers until the group expelled him in 1917 because of his strident racist preaching. Already a member of the Pan-German League, Dinter condemned the Writers' Association as an instrument of the Jewish "theater dictatorship" and proof of the "decadence" of the times. Meanwhile, the failure of his various theatrical projects inclined him more and more toward antisemitism. Eventually, he made antisemitic racism central to his understanding of the past, present, and future.

In 1917, he self-published 1,000 copies of the first volume of his trilogy. He described that volume, entitled *Sin against the Blood* (*Die Sünde wider das Blut*), as the "first race novel" and dedicated it to his mentor, the "German" Houston Stewart Chamberlain. Taken up by the youth movement publisher Erich Matthes, the book, full of sexually titillating moments and antisemitic clichés, became an immense success, reaching an estimated 1.5 million readers by the early 1930s. The novel luridly detailed the dire consequences of miscegenation for its readers, depicting Jews as the bearers of death and degeneracy.

Dinter participated in the founding of the German Racial League for Defense and Defiance. After it was banned, he joined the German Racial Freedom Party and then left it in April 1925 to join the Nazi Party, which, in recognition of his great services to the movement, gave him the extraordinary party membership number 5. But Dinter's goals were essentially religious rather than political, and he soon fell afoul of the Nazis. Dinter was a believer in the Aryan Christ, whom he regarded as the "greatest antisemite of all time." A prolific author, he wrote *179 Theses for the Completion of the Reformation: The Restoration of the Pure Doctrine of the Savior* (1926), an edition of the Gospels purged of "dogmatic falsifications" (1923), and several other books in this vein. He sought a religion cleansed of Jewishness and established the German People's Church to this end. This enterprise put him in direct conflict with Hitler, who, for the sake of political expediency, desired to steer clear of conflict with the established churches. Dinter was deposed from his position as *Gauleiter* (district leader) for Thuringia (in 1927), whereupon he conducted a running feud in print with Hitler. After the Nazis rose to power, he was briefly tolerated, but in 1937, Heinrich Himmler banned his church and his journal, *The Religious Revolution,* and prohibited him from further public speaking or writing. For the remainder of the Third Reich era, he was legally harassed and occasionally jailed. In 1945, as part of his de-Nazification proceedings, he was fined 1,000 reichsmarks, as one of the intellectual progenitors of the Nuremberg Laws.

—*Matthias Brosch*
Richard S. Levy, translation

See also Chamberlain, Houston Stewart; Deutsche Christen; German Racial Freedom Party; Himmler, Heinrich; *Myth of the Twentieth Century, The;* National Socialist German Workers' Party; *Sin against the Blood*

References

Kren, George M., and Rodler F. Morris. "Race and Spirituality: Artur Dinter's Theosophical Anti-Semitism," *Holocaust and Genocide Studies* 6 (1991): 233–252.

Disraeli, Benjamin (1804–1881)

Disraeli, the Earl of Beaconsfield (after 1876), was formally a Christian, but his parents were Jews, and his father, a freethinker in rebellion against Judaism and the Sephardic community in London, had his son baptized at age thirteen. Benjamin nonetheless remained fascinated by his Jewish descent and by the role of the Jews throughout history. His novels earned him recognition in the late 1820s and 1830s, but he gained much wider fame from his political career. He was first elected to Parliament in 1837, participated in various cabinets, and served as prime minister in 1868 and again from 1874 to1880. Fame meant that his pronouncements about Jews were widely noted—indeed, they were often cited by antisemitic authors. His reputation as a wily statesman and a conservative Jewish "wizard" who had somehow arrived at the helm of the British Empire added to a complex set of images about modern Jews—by no means only negative—that were becoming current by the middle years of the nineteenth century.

Disraeli's familiarity with things Jewish was, in many regards, superficial, but he spoke confidently about the decisive role that Jews had played in European civilization, and he proudly identified himself as a member of the pure Semitic race in spite of being a Christian. The Jewish characters in his novels were transparently designed to counter existing beliefs about Jews as cowardly or lacking a sense of honor. He asserted that Jews had survived over the centuries because they had maintained their purity of race and had collaborated across borders and empires. In his novel *Coningsby* (1844), modern Jews were portrayed as working steadily toward world power; the rich, wise, and generous Jewish banker Sidonia (generally considered a novelistic representation of Lionel Rothschild), declaimed that "all is race; there is no other truth." The racial genius and solidarity of the Jews was the secret of their success and the promise of their future.

Disraeli's belief in racial determinism was widely shared by his contemporaries in the second half of the nineteenth century, as was his belief in racial hierarchies; whether he influenced them in a racist direction or simply echoed and reinforced the growing fascination with the concept of race is a moot point. His political views emphasized hierarchies, too, with particular emphasis on the responsibilities of the privileged upper classes to aid and ally with the workers against the rapacious capitalistic class. In foreign policy, he opposed Russia and favored the Ottoman Empire, positions that his critics charged

Benjamin Disraeli's reputation as a wily statesman, a conservative Jewish "wizard" who had somehow arrived at the helm of the British Empire, added to a complex set of images about modern Jews—by no means only negative—that were becoming current by the mid-nineteenth century. (George Grantham Bain Collection, Library of Congress)

were motivated by the tsars' persecution of the Jews and the relative benevolence of the Ottomans in regard to their Jewish subjects.

In the course of his colorful and unorthodox career, Disraeli angered many of his compatriots across the political spectrum, but for the most part, he gained the support of the conservative classes, as well as the affection of Queen Victoria. The extent to which the hostility that he did encounter had to do with his Jewish origin, as distinguished from his politics, is not easy to determine, but that hostility obviously was not pervasive or strong enough to prevent him from having a brilliant career. The acme of that career, as Disraeli entered his seventies, came at the very point that modern racial-political antisemitism was making its appearance on the Continent. His death in 1881, a year after leaving office, came before political antisemitism gained momentum and broad attention. His racist ideas and conservative politics were atypical of Europe's Jews, and in subsequent years, they became an embarrassment to many of them.

—*Albert S. Lindemann*

See also Coningsby; Punch; Racism, Scientific; Rothschilds
References
Feuchtwanger, Edgar. *Disraeli* (London: Arnold Publishers, 2000).

Dmowski, Roman (1864–1939)

Born near Warsaw to a small-business family just after the failure of the January Uprising against tsarist Russia (1863–1864), Dmowski became active in the Polish independence movement at a time when it was growing increasingly narrow and inward-looking. He became the leader and chief theoretician of the right-wing National Democratic Party, founded in 1897. Because Germany was Protestant and relatively liberal, he advocated Polish reunification under tsarist Russian leadership as a step to full independence. Fluent in several languages, including English and French, he traveled to Paris in 1917 to press the Allies to support Polish independence. In 1919, he led the Polish delegation at the Paris Peace Conference. He served briefly as foreign minister in a Center-Right coalition government in 1923; after Marshal Józef Piłsudski's coup in 1926, he founded the fascist-style Great Poland Camp. Soon after, he withdrew from politics, and he died a few months before the outbreak of World War II.

Dmowski expounded his political ideology chiefly in his book *Thoughts of a Modern Pole* (1903). A typical Catholic conservative nationalist, he was mistrustful of democracy, left-wing ideas, and Jews. The core of his ideology was "national egoism," the belief that nations are entitled to act in their own self-interest without concern for others. He despised the Russian and especially the German occupying powers for their repressions against the Poles (he himself had been deported to Siberia), yet he felt that they were behaving according to the laws of nature and that Poles, once in power, should do the same to their national minorities. As a Pole, he claimed, he spoke as "a higher type of man." He advocated the assimilation of minority groups—other than the Jews, whom he considered "Asiatic" and therefore unassimilable. In general, Dmowski shared the antisemitic views of the Catholic Church at that time, seeing Jews as the linchpin of an anti-Catholic conspiracy involving communists, socialists, liberals, Freemasons, and Protestants.

Although his party never held sole power in Poland, Dmowski's views were very influential, and he continues to be admired by the political Right in Poland today. In theory, Dmowski opposed violence against the Jews, instead promoting economic boycotts, discriminatory legislation, and "voluntary" emigration, but antisemitic violence in interwar Poland was largely the work of his followers and was inspired by the kind of rhetoric in which he indulged.

—*Steven Paulsson*

See also Boycott of 1912; National Democrats; Poland; Ultramontanism; Versailles Treaty
References
Levy, Richard S., ed. *Antisemitism in the Modern World: An Anthology of Texts* (Lexington, MA: D. C. Heath, 1991), 178–189.
Polonsky, Antony. *Politics in Independent Poland, 1921–1939* (Oxford: Clarendon Press, 1972).

Doctors' Plot (1953)

A notorious provocation staged in the final years of Stalin's rule and fortuitously cut short by his death, the Doctors' Plot (*delo vrachei*, or "the case of the physicians") was publicly launched on January 13, 1953, with a report by the Soviet news agency TASS. Entitled "Arrest of a Group of Physician-Wreckers," the article announced the discovery and detention of a "terrorist group of physicians" who, by means of purposefully harmful diagnosis and treatment, "shortened the lives" of Soviet leaders A. Zhdanov (who died in August 1948) and A. Shcherbakov (who died in May 1945) and planned to do the same to other top-level Soviet civilian and military cadres. Several of the leading medical practitioners listed in the announcement were Jews (including the professors M. Vovsi, B. Kogan, A. Fel'dman, A. Grinshtein, and Ia. Etinger), and the antisemitic nature of the accusation was made clear by the added charge that the "physician-killers, outcasts of humanity," received their instructions, via the "bourgeois-nationalist" Jewish organization "Joint," from U.S. intelligence services. Both before and after the announcement, there were numerous arrests of physicians, Jews and non-Jews, in Moscow and elsewhere. Those imprisoned were ruthlessly interrogated and frequently subjected to physical and psychological torture. At the same time, Lydia Timashuk, a Kremlin Hospital physician and a state security informer who, in 1948, denounced alleged mistakes in the handling of Zhdanov's illness, was given an Order of Lenin award and elevated to the rank of a national heroine.

Jonathan Brent and Vladimir Naumov, who relied on previously unpublished archival documents, traced the origins of the case back to the death of Zhdanov and showed that it was part of a larger scheme by Stalin to subject the Communist Party, the government, and Soviet society as a whole to a new wave of legalized terror similar in scope to that of the 1930s. At the same time, the Doctors' Plot was rooted in Stalin's own antisemitism and was part of a broader pattern of postwar Soviet policy: dismissals of Jews from upper-level government and party posts; the campaign against "cosmopolitans" in education, science, and the arts (begun in 1947); the condemnation of Jewish nationalism and Zionism; the closing of Yiddish cultural institutions; the murder of Solomon Mikhoels (in February 1948); and the judicial murder of leaders of the Jewish Anti-Fascist Committee in August 1952.

In characteristic Stalinist fashion, the January announcement was followed by an orchestrated public campaign against the "murderers in white coats," involving the massive publication of the crudest type of antisemitic materials. This effort resulted in the spread of popular anger and hysteria in a population that still held, to a considerable degree, prescientific attitudes regarding illness and medicine. Throughout the Soviet Union, doctors—and Jewish doctors in particular—became feared, with patients frequently refusing treatment and accusing physicians of malpractice and outright criminality. Soviet Jews found themselves in an atmosphere of psycho-logical terror, with the threat of pogroms becoming tangible.

Although evidence regarding the full extent of Stalin's scenario for the Doctors' Plot is sparse, it is known that a major show trial was being planned. The physicians, inevitably condemned to death, were apparently to be executed by hanging in front of large crowds in Moscow and other major cities. According to Sergei Khrushchev and others who had knowledge of the affair, this would have been followed by the mass deportations of Jews—allegedly at their own request, to escape reprisals by the aroused Russian people—to camps in the Far East. Staged accidents and orchestrated attacks on the trains at various locations would have ensured that only some of them would reach their destinations. A new, Soviet-style holocaust was being planned. At the same time, given the broader ramifications of the Doctors' Plot, it is likely that the physicians would have been followed in the dock by many other government and party figures, including, as was the case during the Great Terror, some of Stalin's closest associates.

All these plans were abruptly terminated by Stalin's death on March 5, 1953; his successors, particularly Lavrenti Beria, quickly undid the Doctors' Plot. Within days, the interrogations ended. On March 17, M. D. Ryumin, a senior security official who had played a malevolent role in the entire affair, was arrested (and ultimately shot). On April 3, the accused doctors were released from prison. One day later, an official decree stating that the charges against the physicians had been false and that the doctors had been fully rehabilitated was read over the radio and printed in newspapers; it was also announced that Lydia Timashuk had been stripped of her award. On April 6, *Pravda* carried a lengthy editorial under the title "Soviet Socialist Law Is Inviolable," analyzing the role of the former Ministry of State Security in the frame-up.

For Soviet Jews, the Doctors' Plot was a traumatic experience. For Soviet society at large, it had lasting consequences. Notwithstanding the official refutation of the charges, it contributed to the demonization of Jews in the popular imagination; for many, the rehabilitation of the physicians was merely proof of the Jews' pernicious influence. Still, the turnaround by the government was a notable first in Soviet practice and may be regarded as the initial step toward the de-Stalinization of Soviet society.

—*Henryk Baran*

See also Anti-Zionism in the USSR; *Entdecktes Judenthum;* Jewish Anti-Fascist Committee; Purges, Soviet; Slánský Trial; Sorcery/Magic; Stalin, Joseph; USSR

References
Brent, Jonathan, and Vladimir Naumov. *Stalin's Last Crime: The Plot against the Jewish Doctors, 1948–1953* (New York: HarperCollins, 2003).
Rapoport, Yakov. *The Doctors' Plot of 1953.* Trans. by N. A. Perova and R. S. Bobrova (Cambridge, MA: Harvard University Press, 1991).
Ro'i, Yaacov. *Jews and Jewish Life in Russia and the Soviet Union* (Portland, OR: Frank Cass, 1995).

Dohm, Christian Wilhelm von (1751–1820)

A political writer and statesman, Dohm was the first major visionary of Jewish emancipation in Germany. In his treatise *Über die bürgerliche Verbesserung der Juden* (On the Civic Improvement of the Jews [1781]), he formulated a systematic plea for granting Jews equal rights and thoroughly integrating them into the political, cultural, and economic life of European states. His ideas unleashed heated debates in the German press from the 1780s and into the nineteenth century. Translated into French in 1782, Dohm's essay also played a role in shaping the French debates over Jewish emancipation before and during the Revolution.

The son of a Protestant pastor and from the northwest German town of Lemgo, Dohm studied at Leipzig and Göttingen Universities, where he began contributing reviews and articles for a variety of periodicals. In 1776, he and a Göttingen colleague launched the *Deutsches Museum* (German Museum), one of the most prominent political journals of the period. A great admirer of both British "public spirit" and the brand of enlightened absolutism cultivated in Prussia, Dohm was eager to play a more active role in the political world. In 1779, he secured a position working in the Prussian capital as an archivist in Frederick the Great's Ministry of War. After publishing his plea for Jewish emancipation and other notable works, he rose quickly in the Prussian civil service, was ennobled by Frederick William II in 1786, and spent twenty years in various diplomatic postings.

Dohm first became interested in the Jews' legal status as a result of his friendship with the Jewish philosopher Moses Mendelssohn, who felt that an argument for Jewish emancipation would be more effective if it came from the pen of a non-Jew. Dohm, like so many other Enlightenment intellectuals, saw contemporary Jews as morally and politically degenerate, but he rejected all theological explanations for their supposed corruption. Arguing from a secular and political perspective, he contended that the character of the Jews resulted solely from their treatment at the hands of Christians and could thus easily be reversed by a state-sponsored program of moral and political regeneration. Eager to make them "useful" citizens, he proposed a holistic program of "civic improvement" that included granting Jews immediate civil rights, requiring them to perform military service, and moving them away from trade and into the more "honorable" and "productive" fields of agriculture and the crafts. Although he anticipated that they would reform Judaism as a result of emancipation, he did not make rights contingent on religious reform, and he showed much more tolerance toward Judaism as a religion than many of his peers. For the most part, both intellectuals and state authorities in the German states adopted Dohm's project of regenerating the Jews yet rejected his recommendation that they be given rights unconditionally. German Jews did not gain complete political equality until 1871.

—*Jonathan M. Hess*

See also Alsace; Emancipation; Fichte, J. G.; Michaelis, Johann David; State-within-a-State
References
Hess, Jonathan M. *Germans, Jews and the Claims of Modernity* (New Haven, CT, and London: Yale University Press, 2002).
Vierhaus, Rudolph. "Christian Wilhelm Dohm: Ein politischer Schriftsteller der deutschen Aufklärung." In *Begegnung von Deutschen und Juden in der Geistesgeschichte des 18. Jahrhunderts.* Edited by Jacob Katz and K. H. Rengstorf (Tübingen, Germany: Niemeyer, 1994).

Dominican Order

A mendicant religious and preaching order of the Roman Catholic Church, the Dominican order was founded in the early thirteenth century by St. Dominic de Guzman (ca. 1170–1221) in response to the Cathar heresy in southern France. The traditional institutions of the church were proving inadequate to the needs of an increasingly urban and sophisticated Christian laity, and heresies were flourishing. The Dominicans, along with the Franciscans and other smaller mendicant orders, stepped into the breach, bringing the spiritual and intellectual rigor of monasticism into the streets of Europe.

Dominic and his followers sought to restore wholeness to the church and salvation to lost souls by preaching Orthodox Christian theology to heretics. Their original mission quickly expanded to include ongoing teaching of the Christian laity, correction of Christian error through preaching and inquisitorial process, and the conversion of Muslims and Jews. Believing that rational inquiry would lead inevitably to Christian truth, the order became renowned for its learning. Friars were trained in the scholastic theology of the universities and developed a highly systematized preaching style.

By the late thirteenth century, at the urging of Spanish friars, the order established language schools devoted to the needs of missionizing non-Christians. Recognizing that effective argument required the use of texts accepted as authoritative by their target audiences, friars studied Arabic, Hebrew, and Aramaic. Christian theology taught that the Hebrew Bible contained proof of Christian doctrine, but the friars also came to believe that portions of the Talmud, when properly read, confirmed that truth and that the rest of rabbinic tradition represented a deliberate obfuscation of it. In his massive *Daggers of Faith against Jews and Moors* Raymond Martini, the famed Dominican theologican and Orientalist, tried to distinguish "proofs" of Christianity from Jewish "absurdities."

Many Dominican-authored treatises against the Jews circulated during the Middle Ages. With names such as *Muzzle of the Jews, Quiver of Arrows against the Jews,* and *Errors of the Talmud,* these texts were meant as sourcebooks for preachers targeting Jews. Jewish converts to Christianity, among them Nicholas Donin, Pablo Christiani, and Bishop Paul of Burgos, actively participated in the onslaught, using their knowledge of Jewish tradition against their former coreligionists.

Although early Dominican optimism that preaching to the Jews would bring about large-scale conversion proved unfounded, Jews remained an important Dominican concern for centuries, with forced sermons and staged disputations as favored tactics to win Jewish converts. When the anticipated conversion did not result, some Dominicans became increasingly hostile toward Jews, whom they perceived as irrationally obstinate. A number of friars turned to virulently anti-Jewish preaching—in some cases, inciting Christian mobs to turn on their Jewish neighbors. St. Vincente Ferrer, passionate in his determination to convert the Jews, traveled to Spanish Jewish communities accompanied by hundreds of zealous Christian flagellants, causing many Jews to convert out of fear.

Dominicans continued to target Jews through the sixteenth century, engineering the Spanish Inquisition and expulsion, helping to censor Hebrew books, and combining efforts at persuasion with efforts to place additional restrictions on Jewish communities. Interest in converting the Jews began to fade in the eighteenth century. A progressive Dominican theologian, Yves Congar, was instrumental in the composition of the Vatican II document *Nostra Aetate* (1965), which began the Catholic Church's ongoing process of serious reflection on and dissociation from its historical intolerance toward Jews and Judaism.

—*Deeanna Klepper*

See also Ferrer, Vincente; Franciscan Order; Inquisition; Middle Ages, High; Spain, Riots of 1391; Talmud; Talmud Trials; Vatican Council, Second

References

Chazan, Robert. *Daggers of Faith: Christian Missionizing and Jewish Response* (Berkeley: University of California Press, 1989).

Cohen, Jeremy. *The Friars and The Jews: The Evolution of Mendicant Anti-Judaism* (Ithaca, NY: Cornell University Press, 1982).

Hinnebusch, William. *The History of the Dominican Order* (Staten Island, NY: Alba House, 1966).

Doré, Gustave (1832–1883)

One of the most famous and versatile French graphic artists and illustrators of the nineteenth century, Gustave Doré was self-taught and precocious. In 1847, at age fifteen, he was hired by the well-known publisher Charles Philipon to work on his satirical *Journal pour rire.* Working alongside the legendary Honoré Daumier, he regularly drew the title page of the journal and achieved great popularity in the process. One of these covers was the woodcut *Le Juif errant* (*The Wandering Jew*), which appeared in June 1852 accompanied by a satirical lament of the "eternal Jew." Artists throughout the nineteenth and twentieth centuries adapted Doré's exaggerated caricature of the Jew, sometimes further accentuating its antisemitic potential. The figure's angular facial profile, red hair, and slouching gait—all pictured in frantic forward movement—impressed the public, captured several elements of the anti-Jewish stereotype, and transposed them into a bold, negative visual image.

Doré dealt with the subject of the Wandering Jew several more times. He responded to anti-Jewish trends in French society and several popular works dealing with Jewish themes, such as Jacques Halévy's opera *La Juive* (The Jewess [1835]) and Eugéne Sue's novel *The Wandering Jew* (1845). In 1852, he presented a series of pictures entitled "The Wandering Jew, Lament in Eight Tableaux, with the Last Judgment, Raising of the Dead, Heaven, Hell, and All the Devils." Ten years later, on the basis of earlier compositions, he published another series of twelve, under the title "The Legend of the Wandering Jew." Here, he treated the theme in the manner of romantic nature paintings, while at the same time trying to render the tormented soul of the eternally recurring Wandering Jew. The Jew's proverbial loneliness and his isolation amid wild mountain landscapes made the series into a catchy example of "dark romanticism." The series preserved the set pieces of anti-Jewish prejudice and put them at the disposal of anti-Jewish representation in French, English, and German humor magazines.

In addition to his illustrations for periodicals and literary works—from Dante to Byron—Doré, who described himself as a "militant Chris-

Gustave Doré dealt with the subject of the "Wandering Jew" several times. Here he treats the theme in the manner of romantic nature paintings, while at the same time trying to render the tormented soul of the eternally recurring wandering Jew. (Dover Publications)

tian," created in the *Illustrated Bible* (*Bible illustré* [1866]) another influential series of images. He frequently clothed his Jewish figures in the tradition of Christian anti-Judaism. The rendering of Judas, for example, amounted to an antisemitic caricature and arguably introduced an embryonic racist visual vocabulary into late romantic European graphic art.

Doré was doubly effective in this respect. As the creator of woodcuts and lithographs published in large editions, he exerted significant influence in the world of high culture. As a caricaturist in popular journals, he reached a broad and appreciative bourgeois public that absorbed and then perpetuated his hostile distortions of Jewry. Doré's graphics combined formal motifs and modern techniques with an exaggerated visionary romanticism that only partially concealed its high measure of anti-Jewish imagery. His technical finesse helped mask the invidiousness of the representations of Jews. But, in fact, they disseminated and intensified the hostile stereotypes that remain usable and reusable in the antisemitic literature of the present day.

—*Michaela Haibl*
Richard S. Levy and Linnea H. Levy, translation

See also Caricature, Anti-Jewish (Early); Caricature, Anti-Jewish (Modern); *Fliegende Blätter;* France; *Kladderadatsch; Punch;* Wandering Jew
References
Doré, Gustave. *The Doré Bible Illustrations: 241 Illustrations by Gustave Doré* (New York: Dover, 1974).
Farner, Konrad. *Gustave Doré, der industrialisierte Romantiker* (Dresden, Germany: Verlag der Kunst, 1963).
Musée d'Art et d'Histoire du Judaïsme Paris, ed. *Le Juif Errant: Un Témoin du temps* (Paris: Société Nouvelle Adam Biro, 2001).
Renonciat, Annie. *La Vie et l'oeuvre de Gustave Doré* (Paris: ACR Edition, 1983).

Dostoevsky, Fyodor (1821–1881)

The problem of Fyodor Mikhailovich Dostoevsky's antisemitism has repeatedly vexed his admirers, especially in the West. Critics have taken turns in minimizing or excusing Dostoevsky's comments about the Jews and dismissing his works as irredeemably contaminated by it. They have also expressed wonder that an author who was so full of compassion toward all who suffered and so dedicated to Christian love and charity could forgot those sympathies and beliefs when writing about Jews.

Until the last five or six years of his life, Jews played only a small role in Dostoevsky's thinking. A comic but sympathetic portrait of a Jewish prisoner occurs in his semiautobiographical novel *Notes from the House of the Dead* (which fictionalizes Dostoevsky's experience in a Siberian prison camp). In *Crime and Punishment,* the villain Svidrigailov chooses to commit suicide in the presence of a (highly improbable) Jewish fireman, who tells him, with a thick Yiddish accent, "This is not the place!"—perhaps an allusion to the Jewish sense of eternal displacement. Dostoevsky's political novel *The Possessed* (more accurately, *The Demons*) includes among other radicals a Jewish figure. In short, in most of his fiction, Dostoevsky

Portrait of Russian novelist Fyodor Dostoevsky (1821–1881). (Bettmann/Corbis)

referred to Jews only in passing or as images to aid in making some other point.

Given the Russian context, his works through the 1860s do not justify the charge of antisemitism. Indeed, as an editor, he published criticisms of the antisemitism of another publication and called for Jewish rights. But his thinking took a decisive turn in the mid-1870s, and from that point until his death in 1881, he became an antisemitic propagandist whose writings have inspired numerous others. Even by the Russian standards of his day, Dostoevsky stood out as a particularly harsh critic of Jews.

What seemed to have changed in him was his attitude to history. Improbable as it seems, he became convinced that the world would literally come to an end in 1876 or 1877 (he made specific predictions) when the final battle between good and evil would take place, after which a reign of universal brotherhood would begin. In his odd, experimental collection of fiction, autobiography, and journalism, *A Writer's Diary*, written for monthly publication, Dostoevsky interpreted the prediction of Revelation—the last book of the New Testament plays a larger role in Russian Orthodoxy than in Roman Catholicism—almost novelistically, as a struggle among personalities incarnated as nations or peoples. He believed he could understand these nation-characters and anticipate the plot governing their actions.

He offered more than one version of the denouement of history. Catholicism (France), Protestantism (Germany), and Orthodoxy (Russia) would struggle until Russia's triumph; Christian Russia would battle the forces of Antichrist led by the pope; or the Christian principle of love would fight the Jewish principle of materialism, represented by Benjamin Disraeli, England, and the Russian financial community, as well as the Jews themselves. When this last fantasy gained ascendancy in his mind, Dostoevsky wrote that Jews would, if given the chance, exterminate Russians to the last person, as they did with Canaanite tribes in biblical times.

Dostoevsky may therefore stand as an apt illustration of Norman Cohn's celebrated thesis (in *The Pursuit of the Millennium*) that apocalypticism feeds antisemitism. In the final battle between good and evil, Jews are likely to be identified as the force of evil, as they are in that most famous of all Russian antisemitic documents, *The Protocols of the Elders of Zion*.

When the millennium failed to arrive on schedule, Dostoevsky ceased publishing *A Writer's Diary* and composed his greatest novel, *The Brothers Karamazov*. In it, the Apocalypse is interpreted not as imminent but as either metaphorical or impossible to predict. As in his earlier novels, Jews play essentially no role in the book, except for one passage in which the hero, Alyosha, says he does not know whether the charge of ritual murder is true. Actually, Dostoevsky entertained this charge as probable. In short, his antisemitism remained, but with its main source, belief in an imminent Apocalypse, gone, it seemed to be playing a smaller role. It is impossible to tell whether it would have receded to its earlier levels had Dostoevsky not died shortly after finishing *Karamazov*.

—*Gary Saul Morson*

See also Antichrist; Degeneration; *Protocols of the Elders of Zion;* Ritual Murder (Modern); Rozanov, Vasilii; Russia, Imperial; Russia, Post-Soviet; Russian Orthodox Church
References
Frank, Joseph. *Dostoevsky: The Mantle of the Prophet, 1871–1881* (Princeton, NJ: Princeton University Press, 2002).
Morson, Gary Saul. "Dostoevsky's Great Experiment," published as the introductory study to Fyodor Dostoevsky, *A Writer's Diary* (Evanston, IL: Northwestern University Press, 1993).

Dracula

Count Dracula, the east European villain of Bram Stoker's popular 1897 novel, is not explicitly identified as Jewish, although the novel's physiognomic language is suggestive of contemporary notions of the Jewish physique. Dracula is described by the novel's hero, Jonathan Harker, as having an aquiline nose, "peculiarly arched nostrils," "peculiarly sharp white teeth," and pointed ears; at other places in the novel, he is seen as tall and thin with a hooked nose and hard, cold eyes. Dracula can be read, however, as a monstrous composite of a number of fin-de-siècle discourses, including antisemitism.

The action of the novel shifts between Dracula's castle in Transylvania, where Harker, a young solicitor, is sent to assist with the count's house purchase in London, and England itself, where Harker and his allies attempt to defend the country and particularly its young women against invasion by the vampire. Dracula threatens to seduce and transform pure, virginal Englishwomen into voracious seductresses. At the same time as symbolizing a corrupt aristocracy, he also evokes, with his ease of mobility and lack of national allegiance, the rootless cosmopolitanism commonly ascribed to Jews.

Published during a period of increasing agitation against Jewish immigration to London, the novel presents the threat of the vampire as one of racial contamination and parasitism in terms that resonated with contemporary anti-Jewish hostility. In particular, the vampire is represented as degenerate. Stoker's intrepid vampire hunters explicitly discuss Dracula with reference to the theories of degeneration and criminality elaborated by Cesare Lombroso and Max Nordau. Like

gothic literature, Judith Halberstam has argued, late nineteenth-century racial antisemitism "unites and therefore produces the threat of capital and revolution, criminality and impotence, sexual power and gender ambiguity, money and mind, within an identifiable form, the body of the Jew" (in Ledger and McCracken 1995, 255).
—*Nadia Valman*

See also Britain; British Brothers League; Degeneration; English Literature from Chaucer to Wells; Maxse, James Leopold; *Ostjuden;* Svengali

References

Gilman, Sander L. *The Jew's Body* (New York and London: Routledge, 1991).

Ledger, Sally, and Scott McCracken, eds. *Cultural Politics at the Fin de Siècle* (Cambridge: Cambridge University Press, 1995).

Pick, Daniel. *Faces of Degeneration: A European Disorder, c. 1848–1918* (Cambridge: Cambridge University Press, 1989).

Dreyfus Affair

The arrest of Capt. Alfred Dreyfus (1859–1935) in Paris in the autumn of 1894 on charges of having passed military secrets to the Germans, led to one of the most famous and influential trials in modern history. His subsequent conviction was cheered by crowds shouting "Death to the Jews!" and it drew widespread commentary, overwhelmingly hostile to Dreyfus. But as evidence casting doubt on his guilt began to mount, "the Affair," as it came to be known, provoked passionate and revealing divisions in the French nation.

In some regards, France was a surprising place for an eruption of antisemitism. In the nineteenth century, French Jews were considered fortunate; they faced fewer obstacles to acceptance and ascent, especially in legal terms, than the Jews of any other nation. Granted civil equality in 1791, they had thereafter risen in remarkable numbers to prominent positions in state and society, especially after the establishment of the Third Republic in 1875. Even in the military, Jews were significantly overrepresented. By the 1890s, most of France's very small population of Jews (approximately 0.02 percent of the total population) had entered the ranks of the respectable bourgeoisie, and a number, including

On the front page of his inflammatory newspaper, the antisemite Édouard Drumont prepares to thrust Captain Alfred Dreyfus into the sewer. (Leonard de Selva/Corbis)

members of a branch of the Rothschild family, enjoyed fabulous wealth. Although anti-Jewish writers and theorists in France were numerous throughout the nineteenth century, efforts to launch antisemitic political parties during the 1880s were far less successful in France than in central Europe.

Those years did see, however, much negative publicity about Jews, often having to do with their being caught in financial scandals and in bribing parliamentary delegates. Édouard Drumont's book *La France juive* (Jewish France) became a runaway best-seller in 1886. Its main theme—that the devious "Semites" with their ill-gotten riches, working behind a shadowy "syndicate," were undermining the country and reducing its "Aryans" to servitude—was accompanied by a madcap compendium of rumors and anecdotes about the destructive role of Jews throughout history. Drumont's newspaper, *La Libre parole* (The Free Word), won admiration from both the Left and the Right for exposing political corruption, of which there was a great deal at the time. His paper was also well known for charges that the army was being fatally weakened by treasonous officers in its ranks, Jews prominent among them.

When Dreyfus was arrested, Drumont reported that the Jewish captain had initially "admitted everything" but would nonetheless be freed, as so many other Jewish culprits had been, through payoffs and behind-the-scenes manipulations. The key issue of motive—why would Dreyfus, who was from a very wealthy family, have sold military secrets to the Germans for paltry sums?—was dismissed by Dreyfus's accusers with the assertion that the "foreign" mind of a Jew was unknowable.

A crucial stage was reached in January 1898 with the appearance of the broadside *J'accuse!* (*I Accuse!*) by the famous novelist Émile Zola, charging French authorities, high and low, with malfeasance in the case. The defenders of Dreyfus, the "Dreyfusards," who stood largely on the republican Left, acclaimed Zola for taking up the cause of justice against a reactionary, antisemitic, antirepublican, and Catholic obscurantist Right. For these "anti-Dreyfusards," as they were called, Zola was a symbol of all that they hated, a typical element of the corrosive secular forces that were undermining social cohesion, religion, and patriotism. Some in the anti-Dreyfusard camp went so far as to assert that Dreyfus's actual guilt was of relatively little import compared to the catastrophe for France that would result from the victory of his corrupt and unprincipled supporters—an indication of how much the Affair had become a clash of blinding, deeply emotional symbols.

A number of historians have concluded that, contrary to widespread and persistent belief, Dreyfus's Jewish origin was not crucial to his arrest and conviction. No persuasive evidence of an initial conspiracy to arrest him has emerged. What appears to have happened is that his accusers in military intelligence, working under intense public pressure to uncover the officer who was passing secrets to the German military, jumped to conclusions on insufficient evidence. Once Dreyfus had been charged, the reputations of various officials became endangered, and in the effort to cover up initial incaution and incompetence, false testimony was given and material evidence forged, making his guilt seem clearer. Antisemitism emerged much more unequivocally once the campaign to free Dreyfus got under way—indeed, anti-Jewish passions erupted with shocking force. At the same time, the case was filled with ironies and contradictions. For example, it was conservative government officials, a few of them undoubtedly antisemitic, who discovered the forgeries and publicized the evidence of Dreyfus's innocence.

The colorful characters and dramatic twists and turns made the Affair irresistible: Dreyfus's harrowing years in solitary confinement on Devil's Island; the uncovering of the real spy (Ferdinand Walsin-Esterhazy); the confession and suicide of a military intelligence officer who had falsified evidence (Hubert Henry); a second trial in September 1899, at which, even after these revelations, Dreyfus was again found guilty; and his liberation and ultimate exoneration (with a pardon granted in 1899 and full rehabilitation in 1906), paralleled by the political victory of the Dreyfusards and the serious weakening of the Right.

The lessons of the Affair and its long-range meaning are still debated, and even some of the facts of the case remain uncertain; a number of key officials no doubt took secrets to their graves. At the broadest level, the question still remains whether the ugly emotions that came into play in the Affair were proof, as Zionists have claimed, that Jew-hatred lies everywhere beneath the surface, even in modern states and societies, producing violent explosions in times of crisis—an argument for a separate Jewish state. Later observers ask a disturbing question. Does Jew-hatred as manifested in the Affair possess some sort of mysterious power capable of uniting the previously hostile elements of a society, as Hitler's antisemitism did with such catastrophic results? What was the meaning, then, of the Dreyfusard victory? Can the Affair, in fact, be seen as a clash of Good and Evil, as distinguished from an avoidable conflict, based on blunders and misperceptions, involving fallible, emotional, and opportunistic people on both sides? These and many other lingering issues cast a long and ominous shadow over the following century, and they explain why the Dreyfus Affair retains the fascination of a mystery novel to this day.

—*Albert S. Lindemann*

See also Alsace; Drumont, Édouard; Emancipation; France; *France juive, La;* Gougenot des Mousseaux, Henri; Rothschilds; Vichy; Zionism; Zola, Émile
References
Bredin, Jean-Denis. *The Affair: The Case of Alfred Dreyfus* (New York: George Braziller, 1986).
Lindemann, Albert S. *The Jew Accused: Three Anti-Semitic Affairs (Dreyfus, Beilis, Frank), 1894–1915* (New York: Cambridge University Press, 1991).
Marrus, Michael. *The Politics of Assimilation: A Study of the French Jewish Community at the Time of the Dreyfus Affair* (Oxford: Clarendon Press, 1971).
Wilson, Stephen. *Ideology and Experience: Anti-Semitism in France at the Time of the Dreyfus Affair* (Rutherford, NJ: Fairleigh Dickinson University Press, 1982).

Drumont, Édouard (1844–1917)

Édouard-Adolphe Drumont was born in Paris into a lower-middle-class family. His father, Adolphe-Amand-Joseph, worked at the Hôtel de Ville (City Hall) as a copy clerk, and both parents were supporters of the Republicans (liberals) during the Second Empire of Napoleon III (1852–1870). Although Drumont never obtained university training, he received a good education at the Lycée Charlemagne preparatory school. He remained poverty-conscious his whole life and was a profoundly lonely man even after he had achieved the height of notoriety, perhaps because he had been orphaned at an early age, had no close relatives or friends, and had lost his wife soon after marrying and before having children of his own.

After writing for a smattering of modest newspapers, his breakthrough came in 1869 when he became a staff writer at *La Liberté,* a left-of-center newspaper of Saint-Simonian socialist predisposition owned by a Jewish banking family, the Pereires. His first book of note, *Mon vieux Paris* (My Old Paris [1878]), was a nostalgic lament for the lost charms of "old Paris," destroyed by railroad stations, department stores, and the

anonymous masses of modernity. Subsequent publications were in much the same vein.

Between 1879 and 1885, when the Opportunist Republicans (moderates) took control of the Third Republic, Drumont was rebaptized in his Catholic faith. He also became a convert to antisemitism. Spending these years doing research in the Bibliothèque Nationale, he amassed an impressive compendium of antisemitic charges and stereotypes about the Jews and Judaism. The following year, he published *La France juive* (Jewish France [1886]), which became the bible of the new antisemitism and the most widely disseminated book in France at the time.

Drumont fused three major strands of French antisemitism: (1) counterrevolutionary, Catholic anti-Judaism; (2) socialist anticapitalism; and (3) scientific racism. Drawing on the deicide myth, the anti-Jewish writings of the church fathers, and the medieval identification of Jews with Satan, he updated the theories of Abbé Augustin Barruel and, most important, Henri Gougenot des Mousseaux's *The Jew, Judaism, and the Judaization of Christian Peoples* (1869), which argued that Jews manipulated the ideas of the Enlightenment and exploited the secret society of Freemasons to advance the French Revolution, depose Christianity, and dominate the world. The identification of Jews with usury, the elevation of the Rothschilds as a symbol of Jewish wealth and power, and the economic antisemitism developed by French socialists Pierre-Joseph Proudhon, Charles Fourier, and Fourier's disciple Alphonse Toussenel were important strands in Drumont's narrative. Finally, he fashioned a new, specifically French brand of scientific racism, utilizing the modern disciplines of sociology, anthropology, criminology, physiology, and linguistics and drawing heavily on the theories of Gustave Le Bon, Gabriel Tarde, Jean-Martin Charcot, Cesare Lombroso, and Auguste Morel.

Having diagnosed the symptoms, Drumont prescribed his solution to the Jewish Question in a slew of publications, including *La Fin d'un monde* (The End of a World [1889]), *Le Testament d'un antisémite* (The Testament of an Antisemite [1889]), and *La Dernière bataille* (The Last Battle [1890]). He reached a mass audience in his newspaper, *La Libre parole* (The Free

Word), launched in 1892 with the masthead summarizing his doctrine, *La France aux francais* (France for the French).

On the basis of his notoriety as an antisemitic writer, Drumont moved into direct political agitation, founding the extraparliamentary Ligue Antisémitique de France in 1889, later led by his apostle, Jules Guérin, as the Ligue Antisémitique Française and then under yet another name, the Grand Occident de France. The Jeunesse Antisémite et Nationaliste (Antisemitic and Nationalist Youth) was formed under the double patronage of Drumont and the Marquis de Morès, a protofascist and violent activist and perhaps also the first national socialist. Associated with several other extraparliamentary groups, Drumont indirectly orchestrated a noisy assault on the republic and "Jewish France" from the Boulanger Affair (1886–1889) to the Dreyfus Affair (1894–1906). He ran unsuccessfully for parliament as a socialist in 1893 but then served as a deputy for Algiers on an antisemitic platform from 1898 until he was defeated in 1902. In the aftermath of the Dreyfus Affair, when the Radical Republicans (left-wing liberals) consolidated power in France, ending the civil war that Drumont did much to create, his fame began to ebb.
—*Jonathan Judaken*

See also Algeria; Barruel, Augustin; Church Fathers; Deicide; Dreyfus Affair; Fourier, Charles; France; *France juive, La;* Freemasonry; Gougenot des Mousseaux, Henri; Proudhon, Pierre-Joseph; Racism, Scientific; Rothschilds; Toussenel, Alphonse; Usury

References
Busi, Frederick. *The Pope of Antisemitism: The Career and Legacy of Edouard-Adolphe Drumont* (Lanham, MD: University Press of America, 1986).

Byrnes, Robert. *Antisemitism in Modern France.* Vol. 1, *The Prologue to the Dreyfus Affair* (New Brunswick, NJ: Rutgers University Press, 1950).

Dühring, Eugen (1833–1921)

In his autobiography, *Sache, Leben und Feinde* (Matters, Life and Enemies [1882]), Carl Eugen Dühring characterized himself as a "thinker, logician, mathematician, physicist, jurist, and political economist," as well as an objective historian and literary figure. He studied philosophy, law, and political economy in Berlin and took his doctorate in 1861; in 1863, he qualified as a university lecturer in philosophy and later in political economy. An unsalaried lecturer (*Privatdozent*), Dühring laid claim to competence in all "human interests."

His *Critical History of the Universal Principles of Mechanics* (1872, 3rd ed. 1970) was awarded a first prize by the Göttingen University Faculty of Philosophy. But in the second edition of this work, as was to be the case with all his publications after 1875, Dühring fulminated against universities and their professors. They were "decadent," "Chinese fossils," "used up and passé," "reptilian hangers-on," and given to "monkish sneakiness." In 1877, his license to teach was revoked.

When the Social Democrats wanted to establish a free university in Berlin, they offered Dühring a professorship. However, his social theories, which included a critique of Marxism, threatened to split the party and prompted Friedrich Engels to intervene: his essay "Herr Eugen Dühring's Overturning of Philosophy" appeared as the book *Anti-Dühring* in 1878. But it was Dühring himself who rendered further cooperation with the socialists impossible. His verbal abuse of the party led to a complete break.

Whatever professional or private setbacks befell him, he was quick to blame on professors, Social Democrats, and Jews. Later, he developed a four-part "enemies list": unscholarly professors; Hebrews; those infected by "Hebraism"; and so-called antisemites, that is, those who profited from his own "true and genuine anti-Hebraism." When the famed eye doctor Albrecht von Graefe could do nothing to cure his progressive blindness, Dühring assailed him (erroneously) as a "Jew half-breed" (*Judenmischling*) who owed his reputation to the Jewish journalistic rabble rather than any real merit of his own.

Dühring's tirades were more excessive than those of Heinrich von Treitschke and Court Chaplain Adolf Stoecker, although they partook of the same spirit and represented a significant penetration of antisemitism into the ranks of the cultural elite. But Dühring's proposed solutions to the Jewish Question were more radical than those of his antisemitic contemporaries. *The Jewish Question as a Racial, Moral, and Cultural Problem* (1881, 6th ed. 1930) and *The Replacement of Religion by Something More Perfect and the Elimination of Jewry by Means of the Modern Volk-Spirit* (1883, 4th ed. 1928) can be read as anticipating the Final Solution. Hitler, if he did not read Dühring directly, was likely familiar with his thought through the long excerpts in Theodor Fritsch's *Handbook of the Jewish Question.*

Friedrich Nietzsche, whom Dühring defamed in typically crass ways, answered in kind by referring to him as the "Berlin apostle of revenge," a man "who today makes the most indecent and offensive use of moralistic claptrap. He stands out, even among his own crew of antisemites, by the vehemence of his moralistic drivel" (*Genealogy of Morals,* third essay, chap. 14).

—*Birgitta Mogge-Stubbe*
Richard S. Levy, translation

See also *Handbook of the Jewish Question; Jewish Question as a Racial, Moral, and Cultural Problem, The;* Marr, Wilhelm; Nietzsche, Friedrich; Social Democratic Party; Stoecker, Adolf; Treitschke, Heinrich von

References

Mogge, Birgitta. *Rhetorik des Hasses: Eugen Dühring und die Genese seines antisemitischen Wortschatzes* (Neuss, Germany: Gesellschaft für Buchdruckerei, 1977).

Duke, David (1950–)

One of the best-known white supremacists in the United States, David Duke has, since the 1970s, promoted antisemitic ideologies as part of his efforts to "advance the white race." An activist and fund-raiser rather than an original thinker, Duke draws his antisemitic theories from a variety of sources: Holocaust denial from Mark Weber and the Institute for Historical Review, defamation of the Talmud and Judaism from Elizabeth Dilling and Israel Shahak, and allegations of Jewish control of the media from Edward Fields and William Pierce.

Duke began his career as a conventional neo-Nazi and Ku Klux Klansman but then worked hard to recast himself as the voice of conventional, if right-wing, mainstream America. Absent the swastika armbands and peaked hoods of his early

days and with his focus on hot-button political issues such as immigration and affirmative action and his appeals to race and class resentments, Duke won a seat in the Louisiana state legislature in 1989; he also obtained a majority of white votes in 1990 and 1991 bids for a seat in the U.S. Senate and the governorship of Louisiana. As he later admitted, however, his fundamental views—on the superiority of the white race, the degeneracy of "niggers," and attempts by the Jews to "destroy all other cultures"—never changed. Indeed, until the practice was publicly exposed, Duke sold extremist literature, including *Mein Kampf* and *The Turner Diaries,* from his legislative office in Louisiana in 1989.

As the skepticism of a public that repudiated his core beliefs increased, Duke's political machine broke down by the mid-1990s, and he turned his attention to his ideological base. In 1998, Duke self-published a 700-page autobiography entitled *My Awakening.* In it, he asserted the truth of social Darwinism and the existence of an inherent conflict between human races. It is this conflict, Duke believes, that has led to increasingly perfect forms of humanity, the apex of which has been reached in the white "Aryan" race. He views nonwhite races as substandard competitors to the white race but reserves special attention for the dangers presented by Jews. He elaborated on this view in *Jewish Supremacism,* claiming that Jews since ancient times have hated non-Jews and have sought to dominate them using whatever means possible. In turn, Duke claims that antisemitism is merely the natural and healthy response of non-Jews to the depredations of their Jewish oppressors. His second book's title suggests the motive for the predatory Jewish practices and attitudes: they result, Duke claims, from the Jews' belief that they are a superior race and therefore have a right to rule the world. He then reads this theme back into all of Jewish history. The Bolshevik Revolution, according to Duke, was not about economics or the pursuit of utopia; it was the Jewish attempt to triumph over the Russian people, whom they hated, and appropriate the resources and power of what would become the Soviet Union. The Holocaust was a hoax, a Jewish plot to extract sympathy and reparations from the rest of the world. Closer to home, American Jews so wholeheartedly endorse the separation of church and state, according to Duke, not because of Jewish historical memories of state-sponsored religious persecution but because they seek to diminish the religious and social cohesion of the Christian America, the better to exploit and control it. In an effort to shore up his allegations of Jewish perfidy, Duke reaches for the ultramodern theories of evolutionary psychology espoused by Kevin MacDonald, as well as to the medieval practice of defaming Jews by distorting passages from Jewish sacred texts, including the Talmud, and alleging that they express prescriptions that are accepted by large numbers of contemporary Jews.

In late 2000, Duke came under federal investigation for tax and mail fraud. Before he could be charged, he left the United States and lived for two years in Russia, which he called the "key to white survival," and then in the Ukraine, where he received an honorary doctorate. While there, he wrote and lectured to a variety of European extremist groups and some mainstream meetings as well.

With the September 11, 2001, terrorist attacks in New York and Washington, D.C., Duke discovered new material for his conspiratorial antisemitism. In a series of articles that appeared on his personal website and were promoted on the site of his "white civil rights organization," Duke alleged that the United States was targeted by Islamic extremists because it is dominated by "Jewish power," and he added that Israeli intelligence agencies purposely withheld foreknowledge of the attack from U.S. authorities. Duke's espousal of antisemitic 9/11 conspiracy theories gave him entrée to several Arab media outlets in the Middle East, and he even traveled to Bahrain and Qatar to lecture on the subject.

In December 2002, Duke returned to the United States and pleaded guilty in a New Orleans federal court to charges of mail and tax fraud. He began serving a fifteen-month prison sentence in April 2003.

—*Aryeh Tuchman*

See also Arabic Antisemitic Literature; Evolutionary Psychology; Holocaust Denial, Negationism, and Revisionism; Institute for Historical Review; Judeo-Bolshevism; *Mein Kampf;* Militia Movement; *Protocols of the Elders of Zion;* Russia, Post-Soviet; Social Darwinism; Talmud; White Power Movement

References
Anti-Defamation League. "David Duke." In *Extremism in America* (Anti-Defamation League, 2003). Available at http://www.adl.org/learn/ext_us/duke.asp?xpicked=2&item=4. (Accessed February 23, 2005).
McQuaid, John. "Duke's Decline." *Times-Picayune,* April 13, 2003. (New Orleans).

E

Eichmann, Adolf (1906–1962)

Adolf Eichmann, a lieutenant colonel in the SS, played a crucial role in the bureaucratic organization of the deportation of European Jews to their deaths. Born on March 19, 1906, in Solingen, Germany, he moved with his father to Linz, Austria, during World War I. From 1927 to 1933, he worked as a traveling salesman for the Vacuum Oil Company. He joined the Austrian Nazi Party in April 1932 and, in 1933, moved to Berlin and then Bavaria, where he worked in the Sicherheitsdienst (Security Service [SD]), the intelligence branch of the SS. After the annexation of Austria in March 1938, Eichmann was sent to Vienna, where he devised more efficient methods of coercing Jews to leave Austria. As leader of the Central Office for Jewish Emigration, he reduced the amount of time it took to arrange departures, refined the bureaucratic procedures of expropriation, and forced wealthier Jews to help pay the costs for those of lesser means. These techniques were extended to Germany after the pogrom of November 9, 1938, in order to accelerate efforts to rid the country of Jews. Eichmann implemented a similar program in Prague during the summer of 1939.

In the early months of World War II, Eichmann organized the first mass deportations, beginning with Moravia and Vienna. His achievements in this area met with the approval of his SS superiors and qualified him to take charge of evacuation affairs in the Referat IV D 4, in the newly founded SS Reichssicherheitshauptamt (Reich Security Main Office [RSHA]). Referat IV D 4 helped develop policies for dealing with Europe's Jews. As systematic plans for murdering them began to take shape in 1941, Referat IV D 4 became a strategic intermediary between officials in Berlin and regional administrators. At the Wannsee Conference of January 20, 1942, Eichmann participated in the broad bureaucratic coordination that was crucial for gathering millions of Jews and other victims and then transporting them to their deaths. By 1943, Eichmann's office had been involved in evacuation measures not only from Germany but also from central and Eastern Europe. In 1944, these were followed by actions against Jews in Greece, northern Italy, and Hungary.

Had this been the extent of Eichmann's criminal history, he might have been remembered as a significant but not overly distinctive perpetrator within the National Socialist state. However, after slipping out of Europe in 1946 on a Vatican passport, he was spectacularly tracked down in Argentina and kidnapped by Israeli agents in 1960. The 1961 Eichmann trial in Jerusalem attracted worldwide attention and highlighted the atrocities of the Nazi state through wrenching testimony by survivors. The banality of Eichmann's bureaucratic image combined with the shocking brutality of the evidence presented in court forced a general reassessment of the concept of criminal responsibility by scholars and the public alike.

—*Paul B. Jaskot*

See also Austria; Eichmann Trial; Holocaust; Hungary, Holocaust in; Nazi Legal Measures against Jews; Night of Broken Glass (November 1938 Pogrom); Wannsee Conference

References

Arendt, Hannah. *Eichmann in Jerusalem: A Report on the Banality of Evil* (New York: Viking Press, 1963).

Lang, Jochen von. *Eichmann Interrogated: Transcripts from the Archives of the Israeli Police* (New York: Da Capo Press, 1999).

Safrian, Hans. "Adolf Eichmann: Organisator der Judendeportation." In *Die SS. Elite unter dem*

Totenkopf. Edited by Ronald Smelser and Enrico Syring (Paderborn, Germany: Ferdinand Schöningh, 2000), 134–146.

Eichmann Trial

The year 1961 marked a significant turning point in postwar confrontations with the memory of the Holocaust in Israel. Adolf Eichmann (1906–1962) was put on trial in the District Court of Jerusalem from April 11 to August 15, 1961. Eichmann had been head of Department IV B 4 (formerly IV D 4) in the Reich Security Main Office in Berlin, whose role was to locate and deport Jews living in Germany, in Axis countries, and in Axis-occupied territories to concentration and extermination centers, as part of the Final Solution of the Jewish Question. Immediately after the war, Eichmann had eluded the fate of defendants who were considered high-level Nazi perpetrators at the Nuremberg trials in 1945 and 1946 by escaping to Argentina, where he had lived under a false identity in comfortable seclusion for almost fifteen years before Israeli agents captured and transported him to Jerusalem in 1960. In the Israeli court, presided over by Supreme Court Judge Moshe Landau, Attorney General Gideon Hausner presented an indictment of fifteen counts. It covered four categories of crimes as outlined in the Nazi and Nazi Collaborators (Punishment) Law of August 1950: crimes against the Jewish people; crimes against humanity; war crimes; and membership in a hostile or enemy organization, namely, the SS, which was defined as such at the Nuremberg trials.

How could one man be held responsible for the deaths of millions of Jewish men, women, and children? Eichmann's German defense attorney, Robert Servatius, submitted a long opening objection to the fundamental legal and philosophical bases of that question. He also challenged the illegal capture of Eichmann, the territorial jurisdiction of the court, and the alleged prejudices of the judges, all of which, he argued, severely compromised Eichmann's ability to receive a fair trial.

The trial proceedings produced sensational revelations. Unlike the perpetrator-dominated testimony of the Nuremberg trials, Eichmann's

Adolf Eichmann testifies in a specially bullet-proofed glass booth during his trial in Jerusalem in 1961. (Library of Congress)

trial focused on eyewitness testimony. The justices of the district court believed that by laying bare the effects of state-sponsored violence, persecution, and suffering, Eichmann's prosecution could have an educational effect and help shape Holocaust memory for decades to come. The prosecution utilized traumatic eyewitness testimony from dozens of survivors, whose narratives of separation from families, incarceration, and Nazi-inflicted torment reverberated far beyond the courtroom in Jerusalem. Images of the survivors' unresolved pain were televised in Israel, West Germany, and around the world, and they profoundly stirred public consciousness of the Holocaust as a victims' narrative for which justice was long overdue.

Eichmann was not a face-to-face executioner but rather a desk killer, or *Schreibtischtäter*, a role that complicated a hitherto dominant image of the Nazi perpetrator as a sadistic racist and ideologically committed fanatic. His crimes were classed as "administrative," and arguably, it was this "modern" type of crime that influenced Hannah Arendt's 1963 account of the proceedings, *Eichmann in Jerusalem*, in which she introduced into posttrial historiography and social discourse the phrase *the banality of evil*. The phrase proved controversial on a number of grounds but especially because it suggested that "ordinary" people, such as Eichmann, could commit mass murder while remaining ostensibly indifferent to the antisemitic ideology of the Nazis. Eichmann never admitted he was a racist, nor did he acknowledge that he performed his bureaucratic murders for any motive other than obedience to authority. He believed he was, as Servatius argued, a "cog in the machine"; his actions were justified according to the laws of the Nazi state, irrespective of their immorality and criminality or the resultant genocide.

Ultimately, Eichmann's cog-in-the-machine defense did not convince the judges, nor did the defense's allegation that the prosecution could not connect the harrowing eyewitness testimonies to Eichmann's specific administrative roles. After the announcement of the guilty verdict, Eichmann delivered a characteristic statement of moral ambiguity that nonetheless denied all responsibility: "The witnesses' statements here in the Court made my limbs go numb once again, just as they went numb when once, acting on orders, I had to look at the atrocities. It was my misfortune to become entangled in these atrocities. But these misdeeds did not happen according to my wishes. It was not my wish to slay people. The guilt for the mass murder is solely that of the political leaders" (*Trial of Adolf Eichmann*, vol. 5, sess. 120: 2216.)

Notwithstanding the protest of leading intellectuals, Eichmann was sentenced to death, and after a two-month appeal process, he was hanged on May 31, 1962. The debate about Eichmann's responsibility in perpetrating mass murder continues.

—*Simone Gigliotti*

See also Crimes against Humanity (French Trials); Eichmann, Adolf; Holocaust; Hungary, Holocaust in; National Socialist German Workers' Party; Wannsee Conference

References

Arendt, Hannah. *Eichmann in Jerusalem: A Report on the Banality of Evil* (New York: Viking Press, 1963).

Lang, Jochen von, and Claus Sibyll, eds. *Eichmann Interrogated: Transcripts from the Archives of the Israeli Police.* Translated by Ralph Manheim (New York: Farrar, Straus and Giroux, 1983).

The Trial of Adolf Eichmann: Record of Proceedings in the District Court of Jerusalem. 9 vols. (Jerusalem: Trust for the Publication of the Proceedings of the Eichmann Trial, in cooperation with the Israel State Archives and Yad Vashem, the Holocaust Martyrs' and Heroes' Remembrance Authority, 1992–1995).

1848

In the spring of 1848, a revolutionary movement originating in Paris swept through many parts of Europe, encompassing the territories of the Germanic Confederation, the Habsburg monarchy, Russian Poland, Scandinavia, and Italy. The upheavals did not have the same causes or follow the same patterns everywhere. Yet in all regions that were touched by revolution, activists sought the attainment of basic political liberties, the institution of parliaments elected by far-reaching suffrages, and the creation of constitutions in which the rights and duties of the citizens were defined.

The liberal and constitutional demands were especially attractive to the Jewish populations of these lands. In the general European struggle for emancipation, they hoped to eliminate ancient discriminatory regulations and to enjoy basic civil and human rights as well as equal protection under the law. Consequently, numerous Jews participated in the liberal revolutionary movement, became active in the new political organizations, fought in the streets and on the barricades, and utilized the unprecedented significance of newspapers and journals in the battle for public opinion.

In territories that had not yet established themselves as nation-states, the revolutions focused primarily on the question of national unity. In military conflicts such as the one between the Italian states and Austria or in the war of German volunteer units against Denmark, Jewish soldiers demonstrated their patriotism. In Hungary, too, Jews identified with the Hungarian national movement and enlisted in the Hungarian army.

The revolutionary movement was driven by the liberal bourgeoisie and democratically minded intellectuals. By contrast, revolutionary action in the streets was carried on by the lower classes in a sometimes violent expression of social protest.

The extent to which Jews were already integrated into society is evident by the fact that they represented all positions on the political spectrum as it took form during the course of 1848 and 1849. Indeed, one was as likely to find Jews in the camp of constitutional monarchists as among the democratic republicans or in the social revolutionary movements.

This unprecedented political activism in the Jewish population led to a fundamental change in the self-perception of European Jewry. Jews entered into politics, performed public functions, and were elected to parliaments. In the past, they had acted as representatives of corporate entities; now, they participated as independent individuals. Such was the case with Adolphe Crémieux and Michel Goudchaux in France, Isaac Pesaro Maurogonato and Leone Pincherle in Venice, and the tireless champion of Jewish emancipation in Germany, Gabriel Riesser. In Germany, Jews were elected to the Frankfurt National Assembly that deliberated on the fundamental legal precedent that civil rights could not be infringed upon on the basis of religious affiliation. The prominence of Jewish figures in the revolutionary arena and the promise of equal rights led numerous contemporary Jews to embrace the revolutions with near-messianic fervor. Even after many of its achievements and promises were overturned, 1848 remained enshrined in the memory of European Jews as a sublime moment.

Yet the development of the revolution was not free from contradictions and ambivalences for Jews. Even if the demand for their civil equality constituted a central issue in all European lands that were caught up in the revolutionary movement, the emancipation of the Jews was by no means guaranteed in the constitutions of the majority of states. The emancipation decree worked out by the Frankfurt National Assembly never went into effect. After suppression of the revolution, the king of Prussia and the emperor of Austria granted constitutions to their subjects in which some of the measures improving the status of Jews were retained. In the states of the German Confederation, Jewish rights were confirmed only in a few smaller principalities.

Beyond that, in the regions with competing minorities and diverse ethnic cultures, the Jews often fell between the lines of warring national movements. In Poznan (Posen), for example, they were wedged between German and Polish interests, and in Bohemia and Moravia, they were suspected of siding with the Germans.

Above all, what made the year 1848 something less than a "golden moment" for Jews were the widespread anti-Jewish excesses and violent attacks on Jewish residences. Initially, riots and assaults of lesser scope broke out in Alsace; spread to Baden, Württemberg, Hesse, Westphalia, Franconia, and Upper Silesia; and eventually extended into Bohemia, Hungary, and even into Italian lands. All of these protests expressed a deep-rooted hostility against the Jews and a refusal by ordinary people to acknowledge them as equal citizens. This dark side of the revolutionary period is seen by some historians as its most important aspect; others emphasize the era's more positive facets for the history of the Jews in Europe.

All the revolutionary movements of 1848 failed, and by the end of 1849, the Old Regime seemed to have regained full control. In fact, however, the political culture in all European lands had undergone fundamental change. This was especially true in regard to the Jews. Their demand for civil and legal equality had become a central issue, one that could no longer be avoided or ignored in any political conflict. Jews had also learned how to articulate their goals politically and to act in the public sphere.

—Ulrich Wyrwa
Matthew Lange, translation

See also Alsace; Drumont, Édouard; Emancipation; Jewish Question; *Judaism as an Alien Phenomenon;* Marr, Wilhelm; *Mirror to the Jews, A;* Riehl, Wilhelm Heinrich

References

Gailus, Manfred. "Anti-Jewish Emotion and Violence in the 1848 Crisis of German Society." In *Exclusionary Violence: Antisemitic Riots in Modern German History.* Edited by Christhard Hoffmann, Werner Bergmann, and Helmut Walser Smith (Ann Arbor: University of Michigan Press, 2002), 43–65.

Rürup, Reinhard. "Progress and Its Limits: The Revolution of 1848 and European Jewry." In

Europe in 1848: Revolution and Reform. Edited by Dieter Dowe, Heinz-Gerhard Haupt, Dieter Langewiesche, and Jonathan Sperber (New York and Oxford: Berghahn Books, 2001), 749–764.

Wyrwa, Ulrich. "Die Debatte über die Emanzipation der Juden und die jüdischen Erfahrungen 1848/49 in der Toskana," *Quellen und Forschungen aus italienischen Archiven und Bibliotheken* 81 (2001): 397–438.

Einsatzgruppen

The activities of the Einsatzgruppen (mobile death squads) during the German invasion of the Soviet Union have, in many respects, become emblematic of the National Socialist efforts to annihilate European Jewry. These units played a central role in Adolf Hitler's racial war in the East. The vanguard of Heinrich Himmler's SS forces, they were tasked with the elimination of the Third Reich's putative racial enemies to make way for the acquisition of *Lebensraum* (living space). Although best known for their activities in the campaign against the Soviet Union, Einsatzgruppen participated in the German occupation of Austria and the Sudetenland in 1938, as well as the occupation of Czechoslovakia and the invasion of Poland in 1939.

The Einsatzgruppen were composed primarily of members of the Sicherheitspolizei (Security Police), including personnel from the Gestapo and the criminal police, as well as members of the Sicherheitsdienst (Security Service [SD]) and the Ordnungspolizei (Order Police) and, later in the campaign in Russia, the Waffen-SS. In operations in Austria and Czechoslovakia, these combined police forces concentrated on confiscating important political materials and identifying, finding, and arresting political "enemies" of National Socialism, among them Jews, Freemasons, religious leaders, members of the Communist Party, and those who resisted the annexation of their countries. The invasion of Poland in September 1939 resulted in a profound shift in the scope and scale of the activities of the Einsatzgruppen. Under the code name Operation Tannenberg, these units received orders from Chief of the Security Police Reinhard Heydrich to combat "enemies of the German people and state in the rear areas behind the fighting troops"

(Krausnick 1981, 29). In real terms, these orders provided the Einsatzgruppen with the authority not only to identify and arrest but also to act as the instrument for the elimination of political and racial enemies of the Third Reich, including Jews, Polish nationalists, Catholic clergy, and members of the nobility and the intelligentsia.

The activities of the Einsatzgruppen in Poland provided a bloody precedent for the second act of the Nazi racial war in the East—the invasion of the Soviet Union on June 22, 1941. In contrast to the campaign in Poland, Hitler ordered the Einsatzgruppen entering the USSR removed from the control of the German army and placed under the authority of Reich Leader of the SS Heinrich Himmler for "special tasks." The Commissar Order (*Kommissarbefehl*) of June 6, 1941, outlined these special tasks by directing the execution of Communist functionaries, officials, and political commissars serving with the Red Army, while also targeting Jews in party and state positions. The Commissar Order served as the charter of the Einsatzkommandos (mission detachments) and Sonderkommandos (special detachments) within the Einsatzgruppen as German forces prepared to enter Soviet territory on a mission of conquest, exploitation, and extermination. After the initial invasion, the Einsatzgruppen rapidly expanded the definition of the term *political functionaries* to include Jewish men and, eventually, Jewish women and children, independent of any affiliation with the Communist Party; the Third Reich's propaganda campaign that inextricably linked Judaism with bolshevism made it only "logical" to broaden the categories of those Jews marked for death.

The Einsatzgruppen that entered the Soviet Union were divided into four groups, designated A, B, C, and D and assigned specific geographic areas of responsibility. Einsatzgruppe A operated in the Baltics and parts of White Russia (Belarus), Einsatzgruppe B in White Russia, Einsatzgruppe C in northern and central Ukraine, and Einsatzgruppe D in the southern Ukraine, Bessarabia, the Crimea, and the Caucasus. The units ranged in size from almost 1,000 personnel in Einsatzgruppe A to approximately 500 in Einsatzgruppe D. Operating primarily in detachments, the Einsatzkommandos and Sonderkommandos enthusiastically and methodically pursued their murderous mission and conducted actions ranging from individual executions to mass shootings, the most famous of which involved the murder of almost 34,000 Jews at a ravine in Babi Yar near the city of Kiev.

In a report detailing the activities of Einsatzgruppe A through October 15, 1941, an SS general, Walther Stahlecker, revealed the primary motive for his unit's mission in the East. He informed his superiors in Berlin that the "Security Police were determined by any means and with all decisiveness to solve the Jewish Question" (International Military Tribunal 1949, 672). In the prosecution of this goal, Stahlecker noted the cooperation of the Wehrmacht and highlighted the participation of local nationals in actions aimed at Jewish populations in the Baltics. By the end of 1942, the Einsatzgruppen had murdered approximately 750,000 Jews and increasingly cooperated with German army forces in antipartisan operations in the East—operations aimed not only at Jews but also at the entire spectrum of Nazi racial enemies. In the final analysis, the Einsatzgruppen played a key role in the Final Solution and left their mark as one of Himmler's most effective instruments in the annihilation of the European Jews and the conduct of a racial war of extermination.

—*Edward B. Westermann*

See also Commissar Order; Freemasonry; Himmler, Heinrich; Holocaust; Judeo-Bolshevism; Order Police

References

Headland, Ronald. *Messages of Murder: A Study of the Reports of the Einsatzgruppen of the Security Police and the Security Service, 1941–1943* (Rutherford, NJ: Fairleigh Dickinson University Press, 1992).

International Military Tribunal. *Trial of the Major War Criminals before the International Military Tribunal,* vol. 37 (Nuremberg: Secretariat of the Military Tribunal, 1949).

Krausnick, Helmut, and Hans-Heinrich Wilhelm. *Die Truppen des Weltanschauungskrieges: Die Einsatzgruppen der Sicherheitspolizei und des SD, 1938–1942* (Stuttgart, Germany: Deutsche Verlags Anstalt, 1981).

Rhodes, Richard. *Masters of Death: The Einsatzgruppen and the Invention of the Holocaust* (New York: Alfred A. Knopf, 2002).

Eliot, T. S. (1888–1965)

British poet, critic, and playwright T. S. Eliot, born and educated in the United States, moved to England in 1914. He established his reputation during the early 1920s with his long poem *The Waste Land* (1922), his editorship of the literary and political magazine *The Criterion* (1922–1939), and a handful of brilliant essays on criticism. In 1927, he was baptized into the Church of England, and his suite of religious poems, *Four Quartets* (1935–1942), established him as the most influential literary figure in the English-speaking world since Samuel Johnson. He was named Nobel laureate in literature in 1948. A strikingly original poet, he was also a deeply learned scholar, a political conservative, and a committed Christian. Some forty years after his death, his poetry and criticism remain central to the canon of modernist literature.

A very small proportion of this oeuvre appears to be antisemitic in tendency. Three poems published in 1920—"Gerontion," "Burbank with a Baedeker: Bleistein with a Cigar," and "Sweeney Among the Nightingales"—associate recognizably Jewish characters with images of vermin, disease, death, or decay. Anthony Julius has suggested that a fourth poem from the 1920 group, the obscure "A Cooking Egg," also contains antisemitic material. Bleistein the Jew reappears, dead, in the sadistic "Dirge," one of the fragments that Ezra Pound cut from the manuscript of *The Waste Land,* and antisemitic jeers fill Eliot's unpublished letters of the 1920s to Pound and the Jew-hating patron of the arts John Quinn. When Eliot praised the Jewish poet Isaac Rosenberg, his language was racist, and in a 1933 lecture at the University of Virginia, shortly after Hitler's seizure of power, he notoriously said: "The population [of a community] should be homogeneous. . . . Reasons of race and religion combine to make any large number of free-thinking Jews undesirable. . . . And a spirit of excessive tolerance is to be deprecated" (Eliot 1934, 20).

Eliot never repudiated or explained that opinion, even when offered the opportunity after the war. However, he soon withdrew the entire text of his Virginia lectures from publication, calling it "a sick book." Over time, the antisemitism disappeared from his letters to the pathologically antisemitic Ezra Pound, and in 1954, he put Pound on notice that an insult to the Jewish religion was also an insult to his own Christian religion. The preceding paragraph in this entry is a fairly complete summary of Eliot's antisemitic activities, and it is not long. As an antisemite, Eliot was minor. But historical circumstance made antisemitism an integral part of his life's work, even after he stopped writing about Jews.

The creative relationship between Eliot's language and his idea of the Jew ended with *The Waste Land*. After the early 1920s, only one more Jew was ever again to figure in Eliot's verse: the reverentially treated title character of "A Song for Simeon" (1928), an uninspired religious effort from the fallow period between *The Waste Land* and the *Quartets*. With the language problem of *The Waste Land* solved, Eliot the poet no longer needed his complex of metaphors for decay—which is to say, he no longer needed "Jews in his head."

He did not need them, either, when he wrote as a social critic. During the 1930s, his editorial comments in *The Criterion* sometimes expressed an irritable "anti-antifascism," but perhaps the most startling discovery to be made by reading through two or three bound volumes of the journal is its general quietism. In the age of Hitler and Mussolini, Eliot was a reactionary authoritarian who loathed democracy. But the central element of his eccentric politics was Christian theocracy, and he understood that Hitler and Mussolini were not Christian. Eliot published some antisemitic material in *The Criterion* and wrote sympathetically of the ideas of some Nazi sympathizers, but he was not a Nazi sympathizer. He seems to have regarded himself as a detached observer of the world, watching and waiting *sub specie æternitatis* (from eternity's point of view).

When the Christian poet Marianne Moore implored *The Criterion* in 1933 to raise its voice in support of what she called "that ancient and valuable race, the Jews" (*Selected Letters,* 305), the journal remained silent, just as it would later on. Antisemitism probably contributed to the silence. But the Eliot of the eve of the Holocaust was the poet of the *Quartets,* and his first allegiance was to their language. The *Quartets* did not require images of vermin or corruption, so

Eliot did not require Jews—and did not need to care whether they lived or died.

—*Jonathan Morse*

See also English Literature of the Twentieth Century; Pound, Ezra

References

Eliot, T. S. *After Strange Gods: A Primer of Modern Heresy—The Page-Barbour Lectures at the University of Virginia, 1933* (New York: Harcourt, 1934).

Gordon, Lyndall. *T. S. Eliot: An Imperfect Life* (New York: Norton, 1999).

Julius, Anthony. *T. S. Eliot, Anti-Semitism, and Literary Form* (Cambridge: Cambridge University Press, 1995).

Menand, Louis. "Eliot and the Jews." *New York Review of Books* 43, no. 10 (June 1996): 34–42.

Emancipation

The original Latin meaning of the concept of emancipation referred to the release of the son from paternal custody. In the Age of Enlightenment, the word *emancipation* underwent a semantic extension and indicated the self-liberation of the individual from intellectual tutelage and dependence. During the French Revolution, the meaning of the term was elaborated on yet again to include the collective processes of the liberation of social groups and their respective engagement for equal rights. At the beginning of the nineteenth century, the term became a central political slogan in the European public sphere, thanks to the highly visible battle of Irish Catholics for equal rights. From the second decade of the nineteenth century, the concept was also used to indicate the demand for equal rights for the Jewish population.

The emancipation of the Jews was not a one-time legal act but rather a continual process in all European lands with Jewish inhabitants. From a juridical perspective, emancipation marked the legal equality of Jews according to the principle that all citizens are equal before the law. From a social perspective, the concept also referred to the general advancement of the Jewish population, which moved collectively from the periphery into the mainstream of society and, in many individual cases, from marginality to great heights of wealth.

Even though the concept of emancipation surfaced in political discourse only at the beginning of the nineteenth century, its roots lay much deeper—first detectable in the protracted sociocultural evolution of earlier European polities. As the cultural, still religiously defined conventions that sustained the economic and social system of a preindustrial era dissolved, a civil society emerged to supplant the previous system of estates (*Ständestaat*). Because this new society was no longer based on religious practices, some thinkers began to urge that the relationship between the Jewish and Christian populations be redefined. In a secular society, no longer organized around religious-corporative institutions, it was not necessary or useful to segregate Jews on the basis of their religion. As part of this reorientation process, Jews themselves began to seek residential rights in places from which they had been previously expelled. In 1638, the Italian rabbi Simon Luzzatto pleaded for tolerance and the removal of limitations on Jews, arguing a mutually beneficial economic utility. From Amsterdam in 1655, Rabbi Manasseh ben Israel demanded the return of Jews to England, and in 1714, the English deist John Toland published his pamphlet, "Reasons for Naturalising the Jews in Great Britain and Ireland, on the Same Foot with All Other Nations." The most decisive programmatic essay that called for the integration of the Jews in civil society, which was read throughout Europe, came from the pen of the Prussian bureaucrat Christian Wilhelm von Dohm—*On the Civic Improvement of the Jews* (1781).

This document and the Edicts of Toleration in the Habsburg Empire, also in 1781, ushered in the Age of Emancipation, which gradually resulted in the constitutional acknowledgment of legal equality for Jews in Europe. The Age of Emancipation, from 1781 to 1878, can be divided into five phases. The first was characterized primarily by debates about the pros and cons of social integration and civic amelioration of the Jewish population. At the center of this exchange stood the Berlin triumvirate of Gotthold Ephraim Lessing, Moses Mendelssohn, and Friedrich Nicolai, whose emancipatory works were soon discussed in France and other European countries. The vigorous and at times acri-monious discourse focused on the possible consequences of liberation for both Jews and non-Jews. Even their friends, let alone their enemies, entertained doubts about whether Jews could be admitted into civil society, given what were generally perceived as their human deficiencies.

The second phase was marked by both progress toward and retreat from the achievement of Jewish equality. After the French National Assembly proclaimed the Declaration of the Rights of Man in 1789, it seemed only reasonable that Jews also be granted civil rights, a step that was finally taken in September 1791 and only after substantial opposition had been overcome. Shortly thereafter, however, the Jews fell victim to the general antireligious policies of the Jacobins. Although the reign of Napoleon brought the first emancipatory legislation beyond the French borders, in Venice and Rome as well as in the Kingdom of Westphalia and the Grand Duchy of Warsaw, the emperor also passed rigorous special regulations for Jews in France that diluted the principle of legal equality. During this era in Tuscany, political upheaval was accompanied by substantial anti-Jewish unrest. But even in territories outside Napoleon's direct control, the first stages of Jewish equality could be perceived. In Prussia, for example, the Edict of March 11, 1812, declared the Jews "Prussian Citizens."

The defeat of the French at Waterloo in June 1815 marked the transition to the third phase. This period was defined by the contest for political hegemony between the legitimist, Christian conservatives of the Old Regime, reinstated by the Congress of Vienna, and new political forces that emerged from civil society and whose champions declared them to be the true voice of progress. The old dynastic powers initially held the reins of power, and in numerous European lands, the first steps toward Jewish emancipation were quickly rescinded. Traditionally oriented populations maintained grave doubts about easing restrictions on Jews. They expressed their resistance to change and threatened change in a wave of violent pogroms, stretching from Alsace to Bohemia, from Copenhagen and Hamburg to Riga and Krakow—the so-called Hep-Hep riots of 1819. Meanwhile, the progressively inclined began to make headway against the repressive status quo. Although there were many local variations in this movement, in general it combined a desire to achieve national unity and self-determination by means of constitutional states in which liberal values would dominate. This agenda was especially appealing to Jews because nationhood on such a basis held out the surest promise of liberty and equality for them. With the July Revolution of 1830, the liberals took the offensive, and by the 1840s, the question of emancipation once again became a central topic in the European public sphere. A flurry of pamphlets and petitions favoring the emancipation of the Jews did not silence the opposition—there were some notable voices raised against the idea—but momentum toward Jewish equality seemed to be gaining the upper hand throughout most of Europe.

The revolution of 1848 and 1849 inaugurated the fourth phase of emancipation, in which the fundamental transformation in the self-perception of European Jews played a large role. Jews actively engaged in politics, assumed political offices, and were elected to parliaments. They found support primarily in the democratic and liberal parties and in all European countries that were seized by the revolutionary fervor. The emancipation of the people, which now was seen to include the emancipation of the Jews, became a central political demand. As in 1819, however, the movement toward equality provoked hundreds of cases of anti-Jewish violence over a very broad geographic expanse.

The suppression of the revolutions brought on the fifth and final phase. It began inauspiciously. In most places where revolution had achieved Jewish equality, it was promptly reversed. But it was no longer possible to ignore all that had just transpired. Liberals and democrats had learned from the revolutionary movement how to articulate their demands politically and influence public opinion. Although state institutions were dominated by conservative powers in many parts of Europe, the liberal movement exercised cultural hegemony in the political public sphere. Thus, after a decade of European reaction, a renewed liberal wave gathered strength. The political climate of the 1860s made it possible to es-

tablish Jewish emancipation throughout most of central and east-central Europe, this time much more solidly and with noticeably weaker resistance. At the Congress of Berlin (in 1878), an important milestone in the emancipation process was reached when the representatives of the Great Powers declared the legal equality of the Jewish population as a binding principle of international law. There were still places, particularly in eastern Europe, where Jewish emancipation had no reality, but its essential legitimacy had been forcefully pronounced.

The emancipation of the Jews in Europe resulted from the disintegration that overtook the corporative and caste order of the Old Regime. Within this general pattern of development, the various European state forms followed their own highly individualized paths to Jewish emancipation, essentially dependent on the ways in which they developed into secularized civil polities. Jews experienced these variations and many others, in relation to where they lived or emigrated. In places such as imperial Russia, where the secularization of society proceeded in fits and starts, they were unable to get out from under a host of onerous restrictions on their liberty. In North America, by contrast, Jewish immigrants effortlessly entered a pluralistic, mobile society without feudal or corporative traditions, one in which the equality of all citizens was firmly rooted. Further, inasmuch as the construction of a civil society was a European development, the Jewish experiences in Europe differed from those outside the European sphere. The Jews of the Ottoman Empire, Asia, and Africa were able to maintain their autonomy for a long period of time. In North Africa during the Age of Emancipation, Jews were economically privileged but not legally equal. Elsewhere, Jews remained virtually unaffected by the social and cultural upheavals of the nineteenth century; such was the case for the Jews of Yemen, whose situation under Muslim domination was precarious, and for the Falasha, the black Jews of Ethiopia. For the Jews of Persia, the issue of civil rights never became a question, even though they experienced religious intolerance and anti-Jewish persecution similar to that of European Jews. In India, as well, the issue of the political and civil rights of the Jews was irrelevant because the community lived in a segregated and isolated world within the Indian caste system. By contrast, the Jews of China had fully entered and all but disappeared into Chinese society in the first half of the nineteenth century.

The epoch of emancipation of the Jews of Europe was the product of liberal and democratic movements, secular values, and civil societies. It seemed a permanent, essentially unassailable achievement. But when these very same principles came under assault in the last decades of the nineteenth century, Jewish emancipation, too, was called into question, especially by the new antisemitic political movements dedicated to its overthrow. Following the collapse of European democracies and the rise of Nazism after World War I, one of the first casualties was Jewish equality.

—*Ulrich Wyrwa*
Matthew Lange, translation

See also Algeria; Alsace; Bauer, Bruno; Christian State; Dohm, Christian Wilhelm von; 1848; Fichte, J. G.; Grégoire, Henri-Baptiste; Hep-Hep Riots; Infamous Decree; Jew Bill; Jewish Question; *Jewish Question, The* (1843); Marx, Karl; May Laws; Michaelis, Johann David; Nuremberg Laws; Pale of Settlement; Philosemitism; Romania; Russia, Imperial; Stahl, Friedrich Julius; State-within-a-State; Toland, John; United States; Weimar

References

Brenner, Michael, Vicki Caron, and Uri R. Kaufmann, eds. *Jewish Emancipation Reconsidered: The French and German Models* (Tübingen, Germany: Mohr Siebeck, 2003).

Katz, Jacob. "The Term 'Jewish Emancipation': Its Origin and Historical Impact." In *Studies in Nineteenth-Century Jewish Intellectual History.* Edited by Alexander Altmann (Cambridge, MA: Harvard University Press, 1964), 1–25.

Rürup, Reinhard. *Emanzipation und Antisemitismus: Studien zur "Judenfrage" der bürgerlichen Gesellschaft* (Göttingen, Germany: Vandenhoeck & Ruprecht, 1975).

Wyrwa, Ulrich. *Juden in der Toskana und in Preußen im Vergleich: Aufklärung und Emanzipation in Florenz, Livorno, Berlin und Königsberg i. Pr.* (Tübingen, Germany: Mohr Siebeck, 2003).

English Literature from Chaucer to Wells

From the expulsion of the Jews in 1290 through their readmission in 1656 and into the modern era, the Jewish population of Great Britain remained tiny, only rising above 0.2 percent of the whole in the latter third of the nineteenth century. Yet throughout these centuries, Jews occupied a significant position in literary representation, and antisemitism was a productive resource for English writers.

The first historical accounts of Jewish figures in English literature, by Victorian critics, argued that there was a parallel between the rise and decline of Jewish persecution in England and the increasing realism of literary representations of Jews. Surveys written following World War II, in contrast, emphasized the continuity of stereotypes of the Jew across time, suggesting the persistence of cultural expressions of antisemitism. Most recent work, such as that of Bryan Cheyette, James Shapiro, and Michael Ragussis, analyzes the array of diverse and often contradictory depictions of Jews in given historical periods and argues that "the Jews" are repeatedly at the crux of wider questions of theological controversy, political inclusion, textual representation, and, above all, national identity. Rather than enduring, stereotypes are reinvented over and over again, and rather than being fixed and singular, the literary figure of "the Jew" is ambivalent and overdetermined.

The plot of "The Prioress's Tale" in Geoffrey Chaucer's *Canterbury Tales* focuses on the murder of a Christian boy in a Jewish ghetto. Despite his throat being cut, the child miraculously continues singing praises to the Virgin Mary, which leads to the discovery of his body and violent retribution on the Jews. The text draws on the anti-Judaism central to the medieval ritual murder libel and common to the genre exemplified by the tale "Miracle of the Virgin." In this genre, the pious reverence of the Virgin Mary is frequently conjoined with portraits of Jews as cruel, malicious enemies of Christianity. The Jews' refusal to accept Christ is set in opposition to the mystical body of the church, symbolized by the inviolable body of the Virgin. The tale, told by the sanctimonious Prioress Madame Eglantine, has been read in terms of the ironic narrative strategy of the *Canterbury Tales,* which characteristically questions the moral authority of the tales' narrators and frequently suggests a critique of the abuse of ecclesiastical office. Other readings see the Jews as figurative opponents of Christianity whose slaughter stands for the triumph of spirituality over literality; some view the murder charge as the projection onto Jews of intra-Christian violence.

Early modern representations of Jews allude to currents in both traditional theology and medieval popular culture. The characters of Shylock in William Shakespeare's *The Merchant of Venice* (1596) and Barabas in Christopher Marlowe's *The Jew of Malta* (1589) have their prototype in the medieval morality plays, where the Jew appeared in the allegorical roles of Avaritia and Usury. In Shylock, moreover, usury is conjoined with the threat of bodily mutilation, and Marlowe's Jew is even more conspiratorially murderous, his poisonous methods recalling the fourteenth-century charge that the Jews caused the Black Death by contaminating wells. The plays illustrate a struggle between medieval church teaching on moneylending, which ought, as Shakespeare's merchant Antonio believes, to be an act of Christian charity, and modern, usurious commerce. Moreover, *The Merchant* deploys the Pauline, anti-Judaic opposition between Shylock, who insists on the letter of the law in executing justice because of his hardened Jewish heart, and his self-sacrificing debtor Antonio. In Shylock's defeat, the play demonstrates the supersession of Christian grace over Jewish "law." Like Shylock, the merchants of Venice are motivated by the desire for gain; however, they are simultaneously dependent on the pursuit of commerce and threatened by its destabilizing effects. Such ambivalence is expressed in responses to Shylock and also to his daughter, Jessica. The incompatibility of Jessica's beauty with her Jewishness is a frequent source of humor in the play, but her uneasy conversion to Christianity suggests the uncertainties about identity provoked by the possibility of Jewish conversion.

In the eighteenth century, antisemitism was more present in popular culture than in literary publications, but the figure of the Jew was to present an important challenge to the Victorian realist novel. In *Oliver Twist* (1838), a novel indebted to stage melodrama, Charles Dickens revived the earlier Christian stereotype of the criminal Jew in Fagin, a lowlife receiver of stolen goods. Dickens's portrait of the dirty, red-haired Fagin, who lurks in an underground den, links the Jew iconographically to Satan and casts him as an outlaw. Luring the innocent young Oliver into a life of crime, Fagin recalls the Jew of the medieval blood libel, who similarly functioned as a foil to the inviolable innocence of the Christian child. Dickens's Jewish villain stands outside the sociological analysis of crime that the novel otherwise attempts.

As a symbol of an illegitimate and threatening economy, the fraudulent financier Augustus Melmotte in Anthony Trollope's *The Way We Live Now* (1875) similarly embodies Jewish criminality. "People said of him," Trollope wrote, "that he had framed and carried out long premeditated and deeply laid schemes for the ruin of those who had trusted him." Melmotte, a metaphor for the rapacious appetites of 1870s capitalism, has often been seen as a sign of that decade's prevalent Judeophobia. Yet in fact, it is the radical uncertainty surrounding Melmotte's identity, which is built entirely from what "People said of him," that makes him so sinister. In Trollope's England, increasingly subject to the power of the plutocracy, social order and identity were no longer guaranteed by the property of the landowning classes. Jews, therefore, symbolized not only the sinister force of capitalism but also the inevitability of social change. Trollope's other novels, such as *The Eustace Diamonds* (1873) and *Phineas Redux* (1874), seek to identify Jewish interlopers through their racial features, only to exclude them from English high society or have them acknowledge their inferior place within it.

Two of the most charismatic villains of the fin de siècle were gothic fantasies produced by the antisemitic imagination. In *Trilby* (1894), the biggest best-seller of the nineteenth century, the popular novelist George Du Maurier brought together fear and fascination in the predatory figure of Svengali, the Jewish mesmerist. The dirty, ill-mannered, but musically gifted Svengali turns the tone-deaf Irish artists' model Trilby O'Ferrall into a spectacular diva by hypnotizing her and making her dependent on him. The lure of foreign sexuality is also a key titillating feature of Bram Stoker's *Dracula* (1897). In the novel's monstrous east European vampire, who threatens to infect England with his bad blood, a number of late nineteenth-century fears concerning race, gender, and degeneration are condensed.

If Stoker's text articulates a typically fin-de-siècle fantasy of reverse colonization, such imperial anxieties preoccupied Edwardian writers even more obsessively. Liberal opposition to the Boer War at the turn of the twentieth century reinvigorated the image of the degenerate and unpatriotic Jewish financier, who was seen to be directing the war to further Jewish interests. In the fiction of John Buchan, who opposed the liberal pro-Boers, the Jews' racial instinct was what made them potentially ideal servants of the empire. At the same time, as in his story "The Grove of Ashtaroth" (1912), the Jew, like civilization itself, is perpetually in danger of reverting wholly to those more primitive instincts. The paranoiac Jewish conspiracy theory that opens *The Thirty-Nine Steps* (1915) is a warning of what might happen if Jews eschewed a noble colonial role (such as Zionism) and succumbed to their vengeful desire for domination of the world's economy.

Ambivalence similarly structured the work of socialist writers of the Edwardian period. Although resisting the 1890s' "socialism of fools" that identified Jews crudely with capitalism, George Bernard Shaw, in *Man and Superman* (1903) and *The Doctor's Dilemma* (1911), nonetheless deployed Jews as figures of philosophical and economic materialism, opposed to the "Superman" because they were incapable of a higher form of social evolution. H. G. Wells, by contrast, imagined a utopian future in which even Semitic particularities would be transcended by assimilation, and he dismissed the biological basis for racial categories. In his novel *Tono-Bungay* (1909), therefore, Wells lamented the ascendancy of the Jewish plutocracy as a sign of "the broad slow decay of the great social organism of England," but he regarded his scientific socialist hero as equally part of England's retrograde Judaization. In his nonfiction, however, Wells identified both an "exclusive" and an assimilatory tradition in Jewish history. In his futuristic fantasy *The Shape of Things to Come* (1933), he described the Jews' "traditional willful separation from the main body of mankind" as an initial obstacle to progress that was ultimately overcome in the rationalized universalist future state by the "success" of complete assimilation.

—*Nadia Valman*

See also Boer War; Capital: Useful versus Harmful; Caricature, Anti-Jewish (Early); Dickens, Charles; Dracula; Hobson, J. A.; *Jew of Malta, The;* New Age; Paul; Ritual Murder (Medieval); Shakespeare, William; Shylock; Supersessionism; Svengali; Trollope, Anthony; Usury; *Verjudung;* Well Poisoning; Wells, H. G.

References
Cheyette, Bryan. *Constructions of "the Jew" in English Literature and Society, 1875–1945* (Cambridge: Cambridge University Press, 1993).
Delany, Sheila. *Chaucer and the Jews* (New York: Routledge, 2002).
Freedman, Jonathan. *The Temple of Culture: Assimilation and Anti-Semitism in Literary Anglo-America* (Oxford: Oxford University Press, 2000).
Lampert, Lisa. *Gender and Jewish Difference from Paul to Shakespeare* (Philadelphia: University of Pennsylvania Press, 2004).
Ragussis, Michael. *Figures of Conversion: "The Jewish Question" and English National Identity* (Durham, NC: Duke University Press, 1995).
Shapiro, James. *Shakespeare and the Jews* (New York: Columbia University Press, 1996).

English Literature of the Twentieth Century

"The extremes lie close together," Blanchard Jerrold wrote of London in 1872.

How many minutes' walk have we between St. Swithin's Lane, and that low gateway of the world-famed millionaire; and this humble authority in Exchanges, in materials for shoddy, in left-off clothes cast aside by the well-to-do, to be passed with due consideration and profit to the backs of the poor? The old clothesman's children are rolling about upon his greasy treasure, while he, with his heavy silver spectacles poised upon his hooked nose, takes up each item, and estimates it to a farthing. (Doré and Jerrold 1993, 123)

When Gustave Doré engraved this scene, he illuminated the rag dealer's room from behind,

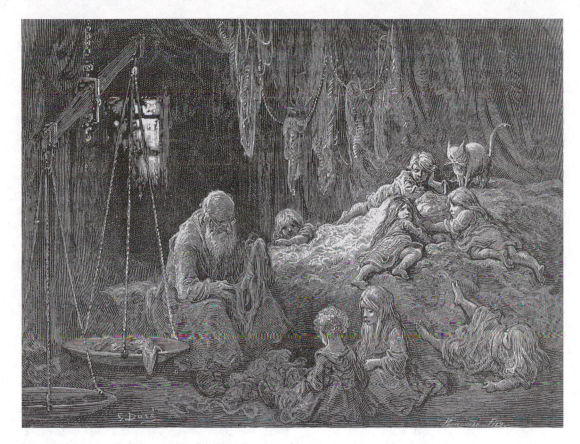

Gustav Doré's, *A Clothesman at Work* (1872). (Dover Publications)

with a single beam of daylight entering through a small window set high up and far back. Glinting on chains, the beam illuminates an enormous double-pan balance hanging from the ceiling: a tool of the rag dealer's trade. Behind the balance, hunched over the rag he is valuing, the dealer is as rapt as a priest contemplating the mystery of justice. He may be wearing a long apron or a Jewish caftan, but in the half-light of this scene, his garment has taken on the form of a robe—in fact, a robe out of one of Doré's illustrations to the Bible. Emerging from the blackness of the engraver's ground, Doré's Jew takes form at the meeting point of his two archetypal ways of being thought of: the allegorical and the stereotypical.

At the beginning of the twentieth century, these extremes lay close together through the whole range of literary representation. In British and American literature, the Jew was simultaneously rich and poor, a jeweled exotic and a denizen of Western civilization's underworlds.

The Jew is Dickens's Fagin and the auctioneer who disposes of other men's fortunes in William Makepeace Thackeray's *Vanity Fair,* but in the works of writers as different as Nathaniel Hawthorne, Benjamin Disraeli, and George Du Maurier, the Jew is also the possessor of an immemorial racial power over men and women. At either extreme, the Jew is something other than human. "I was a Jew once myself," remarks Trollope's silly character Bertie Stanhope to a bishop, and the bishop sensibly responds by pulling himself together and walking away (*Barchester Towers,* chap. 11).

Well into the twentieth century, some of these romantic and Victorian images retained their symbolic power, especially in popular culture. In *Goldfinger,* for example, Ian Fleming deployed all the technogadgetry available to him in 1959, but his Jewish villain was conceptually an antique, sired by William Jennings Bryan out of *The Merchant of Venice.* High literary culture, however, tended to modify the antisemitic archetypes that it had inherited. At the beginning of the twentieth century, for example, the expatriate American novelist Henry James returned to his country for the first time in thirty years and discovered that he and the changing language of his New York had entered into a distressing new relationship. Language always changes, of course, but James had not expected the new English to approach him from the direction of what he called "the terrible little Ellis Island."

"Truly the Yiddish world was a vast world," James mused in *The American Scene,* the record of his ten-month visit to the United States in 1904 and 1905. His vantage point at that moment was in New York, at one of "the half-dozen picked beer-houses and cafés in which our ingenuous *enquête,* that of my fellow-pilgrims and I, wound up."

> Truly the Yiddish world was a vast world, with its own deeps and complexities, and what struck one above all was that it sat there at its cups (and in no instance vulgarly the worse for them) with a sublimity of good conscience that took away the breath, a protrusion of elbow never aggressive, but absolutely proof against jostling. It was the incurable man of letters under the skin of one of the party who gasped, I confess; for it was in the light of letters, that is in the light of our language as literature has hitherto known it, that one stared at this all-unconscious impudence of the agency of future ravage. (chap. 3, sect. 3, "The Fate of the Language")

The key idea here is "impudence": the presumption of equality by an inferior. That the Jews around Henry James *were* inferior was simply a given. This unexamined assumption governed much of the representation of Jews in twentieth-century literature. In Edith Wharton's *The House of Mirth,* for example, the idea that a Christian woman could marry a Jewish man was treated as self-evidently absurd, and G. K. Chesterton saw no problem about writing a humorous poem that concluded, "We persecute these curly-headed men" (Wilson 1984). Occa-

sionally, in a book by a Christian such as Willa Cather's autobiographical novel *The Professor's House* or a book by a Jew such as Nathanael West's satire *The Day of the Locust,* an understated or unstated Jewish presence was essential to the design. Much more often, however, as in Ernest Hemingway's *The Sun Also Rises* or F. Scott Fitzgerald's *The Great Gatsby,* an author simply used a Jewish stereotype to keep his story moving along a clearly marked route. In fact, T. S. Eliot's antisemitism may remain controversial in the twenty-first century only because we still have not learned which way to read it: as a casual use of the idiom of the time like Hemingway's or Fitzgerald's or as a fundamental, constitutive part of a great poet's language.

But if antisemitism was a fundamental, constitutive part of Eliot's language, it functioned there in a way that must be almost unique. Jewishness was at the heart of two twentieth-century works that changed the technology of language forever: Ezra Pound's antisemitic *The Cantos* and James Joyce's philosemitic *Ulysses.* It functioned there only by reference to material outside the text: the author's personal pathology in the case of Pound, the author's national and religious culture in the case of Joyce. And such is the general case. With only a few exceptions (notably Henry Roth's novel *Call It Sleep* and some of the verse of Jerome Rothenberg), Jewishness remained peripheral to the *language* of twentieth-century literature in English. From one point of view, this means that Henry James's fears about "the agency of ravage" were not realized. From another point of view, it means that the large Jewish presence in modern literature has had little literary importance.

But it has had great importance as a sociological weather vane. In 1945, for example, Gwethalyn Graham's *Earth and High Heaven,* a trivial Canadian romance novel, became a best-seller in the United States because its didactic story—Christian girl falls in love with Jewish boy and discovers that antisemitism is a problem for Christians, too—suddenly became important to think about. With the revelation of the Holocaust, antisemitism was no longer in good taste. In 1951, the Jewish novelist Herman Wouk drove the point home by making the climax of his best-seller *The Caine Mutiny* a flag-waving speech about the Holocaust and the war, delivered by a Jewish character. For several years after that, best-sellers by Jewish authors such as Leon Uris and Harry Golden repeatedly explained to the public that Jews are sometimes square-jawed heroes (Uris) and sometimes wise and lovable ethnic clowns (Golden), but they are always and under every circumstance mankind's best friend. However, overt discrimination against Jews—in employment, in education, in housing—diminished almost to nothing during the 1950s, and that dramatic improvement in Jewish life brought with it a new self-confidence, which, in turn, called into question the need for any sort of literary public relations campaign.

In 1959, major publishers in Canada and the United States released two works of fiction that brought to a close an era of Jewish moral posturing. Mordecai Richler's *The Apprenticeship of Duddy Kravitz* and Philip Roth's *Goodbye, Columbus* were books by Jewish authors about Jewish characters—but these characters were throwbacks to pre-Holocaust, pre-Wouk/Uris/Golden stereotypes of the Jew. Vividly, shockingly, they were vulgar materialists, pushy climbers, scheming manipulators who provoked Christians' prejudices and then whined about them. The books' reviews communicated the North American Jewish community's dismay and fear. Yet Jewish assimilation into the social mainstream of the English-speaking world continued without a break to the end of the twentieth century, and literature continued to reflect the change.

Consider, for example, the protagonist of the 1971 British film *Sunday Bloody Sunday:* a man who was estranged from himself, unhappy, and Jewish. Twenty years earlier, the Jewishness would have been treated as a problem in itself. In *Sunday Bloody Sunday,* however, it functioned only metonymically, as a detail associated with the character's real problem. This, it turns out, was not that he was Jewish; it was that he was gay. In 1985, when the story was retold by another British film, *My Beautiful Laundrette,* its social setting was changed without any loss of authenticity from assimilated middle-class Jewish to immigrant Pakistani.

Another social signal was communicated in 1990 by Barry Levinson's *Avalon,* a story about an American family's life from the 1940s to the 1970s. With its wide emotional range, *Avalon* could have been about almost any middle-class American family, but the family in the film happened to be Jewish, and it had been touched by the Holocaust. For Jewish viewers, at any rate, there was no doubt about that. Yet the only holidays the family celebrated were Thanksgiving and the Fourth of July, festivals of the American cultural religion, and not one character uttered the word *Jew* even once. Toward the end of the screenplay (shot 241), a few lines alluded to the Jewish custom of naming a baby after a deceased relative, but these were not spoken in the final cut. Clearly, this deletion was not a case of censorship or squeamishness or fear of provoking hostility. No, the problem was simpler than that. Barry Levinson, author and director, wanted only to make a film that the general American public could understand, and to achieve that goal, he made a few cuts in his material. The material did not matter much anyway. By the end of the twentieth century, *Avalon* told us, the representative figure of the Jew had been assimilated for the first time into the language of high Western culture—and assimilated so completely that his Jewishness had lost its signifying force.

—*Jonathan Morse*

See also Chesterton, G. K.; Dickens, Charles; Disraeli, Benjamin; Doré, Gustave; Eliot, T. S.; English Literature from Chaucer to Wells; Hollywood, Treatment of Antisemitism in; Pound, Ezra; Svengali; Trollope, Anthony; Wharton, Edith

References

Doré, Gustave, and Blanchard Jerrold. *London: A Pilgrimage.* Facsimile reprint, 1872 (New York: Dover Publications, 1970).

Levinson, Barry. *"Avalon," "Tin Men," "Diner": Three Screenplays* (New York: Atlantic Monthly Press, 1990).

Wilson, A. N. "Hilaire Belloc," *Commentary* 78, no. 5 (November 1984).

Entdecktes Judenthum (1700, 1711)

Entdecktes Judenthum (Judaism Uncovered), the major work of Johann Andreas Eisenmenger (1654–1704), was the result of twenty years of labor. Jacob Katz characterized the book as the foundational text of scholarly antisemitism.

Although it purports to describe Jewish belief, the work is really a potpourri of accurate but literal translations of excerpts from over 200 Hebrew, Yiddish, Arabic, and Greek sources in their sixteenth- and seventeenth-century editions, embedded in tendentious, hostile interpretation. Eisenmenger insisted on the literal meaning of Jewish texts, refusing to read them according to midrashic or haggadic tradition or even in the metaphoric sense current in Christian theology. He charged that Jews believed God literally danced with Eve and braided her hair, wore phylacteries, and created humans' evil inclination (*yetzer hara*). He alleged, despite contrary evidence in prescriptive literature such as the Shulkhan Arukh, an early modern legal compendium, that Jews said Christians had no souls, called Christ "the uncircumcised God," and sought the ruin of non-Jews; further, Jews swore false oaths, killed children who converted, tested experimental remedies on Christians, and sold them spoiled meat. Despite his awareness of contrary Jewish readings of such texts and his acknowledgment that Jewish tradition emphasized that Christians, as followers of the Noahide commandments, were not subject to violence as idolaters, Eisenmenger charged that the presence of such prescriptions in Jewish texts was sufficient evidence that Jews followed them. Eisenmenger countered possible objections to his conclusions, frequently violating rhetorical conventions.

Eisenmenger's Jewish sources included the 1644 Amsterdam Babylonian Talmud; the 1603 Krakow Jerusalem Talmud; the 1684 Sulzbach Zohar; daily and holiday prayer books from Venice, Sulzbach, Frankfurt am Main, Prague, and Nuremberg, and the Tsena Urena (a seventeenth-century Yiddish compendium of prayers and Torah and Talmud texts); as well as works by Maimonides, Nachmanides, and several other Jewish luminaries. He named Rabbi Joseph Franco of Amsterdam as one of his teachers, explained the divergence between Sephardic and Ashkenazic Hebrew pronunciation, and was erudite enough to use arcane kabbalistic numerology in the service of his own arguments. His sources also included notorious books by converts such as Anton Margarita, reliable accounts such as those of Johannes Buxtorf, and classical anti-Jewish tales. Although his approach to Jewish literature was akin to later Enlightenment tracts critical of the Jews, he preserved remainders of medieval sentiment, recounting incidents of well poisoning and ritual murder.

Only four chapters of the book actually treated the beliefs of Jews, and these, too, were hostile. The work concluded with a reflection on why Jews persisted in unbelief and suggestions for accelerating conversions that included measures to increase the attractiveness of Christianity while restricting the freedom of Jewish religious practice.

On its publication in Heidelberg (in 1700), the work was immediately seized by the imperial government. Eisenmenger and his heirs agitated fruitlessly for its release; in 1711, Friedrich I of Prussia authorized a Königsberg edition, identical in content to the original but with orthographical changes, an index, and errata pages. An English translation was published between 1732 and 1734 and in 1748. The originally seized books were released in 1740.

—*Susan R. Boettcher*

See also Diderot, Denis; Liutostanskii, Ippolit; Pfefferkorn, Johannes; Pranaitis, Justinas; Ritual Murder (Medieval); Rohling, August; Talmud; *Talmud Jew, The;* Talmud Trials; Well Poisoning
References
Katz, Jacob. "The Sources of Modern Anti-Semitism: Eisenmenger's Method of Presenting Evidence from Talmudic Sources." In *Proceedings of the Fifth World Congress of Jewish Studies* (Jerusalem: World Union of Jewish Studies, 1972), 2: 210–211.
———. *From Prejudice to Destruction: Anti-Semitism, 1700–1933* (Cambridge, MA: Harvard University Press, 1980).
Levy, Richard S., ed. *Antisemitism in the Modern World: An Anthology of Texts* (Lexington, MA: D. C. Heath, 1991), 31–36.

Erasmus (1466–1536)

The leading humanist of his age north of the Alps, Desiderius Erasmus was born in Holland and educated under the auspices of the Brethren of the Common Life in the Devotio Moderna tradition. Inclined more toward a life of learning than one of priestly duties, Erasmus was a leading member of a far-flung circle of humanists devoted to improving piety and learning in their world. Prodigiously energetic, he oversaw multivolume, complete editions of the works of, among others, Cyprian, Ambrose, Augustine, and Jerome before embarking on the first critical edition, with a new Latin translation and commentary, of the Greek New Testament (1516).

In common with most Christian thinkers of the time, Erasmus held the Jews accountable for the Crucifixion, and he seems never to have deviated from this conviction. He considered Judaism at the time of Jesus' life a system of outward ceremonies and purity codes, valid as a provisional disposition before the Incarnation but empty after it. He condemned scrupulosity in ritual, without pious intention accompanying it, as Judaizing, whether by Jews or Christians. At points in his work, he echoed, with evident consent, the anti-Judaism of the late Middle Ages.

Such conventional commentary notwithstanding, Erasmus stands out among his contemporaries as an advocate of tolerance. Impatient with theological quarreling, he found the finer points of Scholastic disputations too elusive to support the strident contentiousness of rival theological factions. For Erasmus, the essence of Christianity, largely abandoned by his contemporaries, lay in a "philosophy of Christ," in contrast with the largely pagan philosophies undergirding the rational superstructure of Scholastic thought. The philosophy of Christ, for Erasmus, found its expression in an attitude of tolerance for differing religious viewpoints and even diffidence toward presumed certainties. Identifying Jesus as an example of charity toward outcasts, the Erasmian view articulated a solidarity with adherents of deviant beliefs that did not stop short at Judaism; as he stated in the catalog of his own works, his temperament was such that he "could love even a Jew."

Erasmian openness and contempt for rigid dogmatism may seem oddly discordant with his veneration of the church fathers, known for their attachment to the idea of orthodoxy and associated, much later, with an exclusive idea of patristic "consensus." Although it is possible to see Erasmus's simultaneous attachment to tolerance and to the formulators and anathematizers of the early church as another manifestation of his enigmatic personality, a more sympathetic reading of his work reveals a subtler but coherent thinker. Piety, for Erasmus, originated in the sprit and found its expression in outward devotion and ritual. Given the dominant contemporary impression of Judaism as uncritical and unfeeling adherence to "carnal law," Erasmus viewed that tradition as only another form of the "works-righteousness" that he and the Protestant Reformers who followed him found so objectionable in the Catholicism of their day.

—*Ralph Keen*

See also Augustine of Hippo; Church Fathers; Deicide; Philosemitism; Reformation; Supersessionism

References

Kisch, Guido. *Erasmus' Stellung zu Juden und Judentum* (Tübingen, Germany: Mohr, 1969).

Markish, Shimon. *Erasmus and the Jews.* Translated by A. Olcott (Chicago: University of Chicago Press, 1986).

Pabel, Hilmar M. "Erasmus of Rotterdam and Judaism: A Reexamination in the Light of New Evidence," *Archiv für Reformationsgeschichte* 87 (1996): 9–37.

Eugenics

Eugenics is an ideology dedicated to improving human heredity. Francis Galton, the founder of modern eugenics, promoted the idea in the 1860s after reading *The Origin of Species* by his cousin Charles Darwin. In addition to coining the term *eugenics*, Galton also was the first to use the phrase *nature versus nurture*. He and most eugenicists took the side of nature in this debate, insisting that most aspects of human character—including moral traits, such as diligence and thrift—are hereditary. They viewed many physical disabilities, psychiatric problems, and even criminal behaviors as hereditary conditions that could be eliminated by controlling reproduction. Eugenicists did not always agree on the best measures to improve human heredity, but they proposed various policies, such as incentives for the "fit" to have more children, marriage prohibitions or sterilization of the "unfit," and even infanticide for those born handicapped.

The eugenics movement reached its height in the first three decades of the twentieth century, when many eugenics journals and organizations were founded in Europe, the United States, and elsewhere. The first eugenics law was passed in the United States in 1907, when Indiana legislated compulsory sterilization for mentally disabled prison inmates. Many U.S. states passed compulsory sterilization laws targeting the mentally disabled, and other countries, such as Denmark and Sweden (both in 1934), followed suit. Germany passed its first compulsory sterilization law shortly after the Nazis came to power in 1933, and in 1939, Hitler expanded his eugenics program by authorizing the murder of the physically and mentally disabled.

Eugenics is not intrinsically racist or antisemitic, and quite a few Jewish physicians and scientists supported eugenics in the early twentieth century. The famous German Jewish geneticist Richard Goldschmidt promoted eugenics, as did Harold Laski, who formed the Galton Club at Oxford University to disseminate eugenics ideology.

Nonetheless, many leaders of the eugenics movement not only embraced antisemitism but also made antisemitic racism an integral part of their eugenics ideology. Galton claimed that Jews were "specialized for a *parasitical* existence," (in Pearson 1924, 2: 209) and his protégé, Karl Pearson, agreed. The geneticist Charles Davenport, the leading eugenics advocate in the United States, accused Jews of having criminal traits and suggested kicking them out of American society. The founding father of the German eugenics movement, Alfred Ploetz, toned down his prejudices in public but was intensely antisemitic in private, founding the secret Nordic Ring to promote racist and antisemitic eugenics. Fritz Lenz, appointed in 1923 to the first professorship in eugenics in Germany, also promoted antisemitic racism in his writings.

In the early twentieth century, U.S. eugenicists pressed for immigration restrictions against "inferior" races, including Jews. Many advocates for eugenics, including Madison Grant, supported the antisemitic Immigration Restriction League, and others testified before Congress in a successful bid to introduce immigration quotas in the 1920s. In 1939, the eugenicist Harry Laughlin warned in a report that the Jews were "human dross" that would corrupt the American racial stock; he recommended decreasing Jewish immigration quotas by 60 percent. During the 1930s, many American eugenicists praised the Nazi regime for introducing compulsory sterilization, though a good number distanced themselves from Nazi antisemitic measures.

The eugenics movement went into steep decline in the mid-twentieth century. By the late twentieth century, a new eugenics (often under a different label, such as genetic screening) reemerged, usually emphasizing individual choice rather than compulsory measures.

—*Richard Weikart*

See also Immigration and Naturalization Laws; Nazi Legal Measures against Jews; *Passing of the Great Race;* Racism, Scientific; Social Darwinism

References

Kühl, Stefan. *The Nazi Connection: Eugenics, American Racism, and German National Socialism* (Oxford: Oxford University Press, 1994).

Pearson, Karl. *The Life, Letters and Labours of Francis Galton.* 3 vols. (Cambridge: Cambridge University Press, 1924).

Proctor, Robert. *Racial Hygiene: Medicine under the Nazis* (Cambridge, MA: Harvard University Press, 1988).

Weikart, Richard. *From Darwin to Hitler: Evolutionary Ethics, Eugenics and Racism in Germany* (New York: Palgrave Macmillan, 2004).

Evian Conference

From July 6 to July 15, 1938, a conference convened in the French spa town of Evian to address the problem of Jewish refugees. President Franklin D. Roosevelt had called for the meeting shortly after Germany's annexation of Austria in March 1938.

Roosevelt initially invited twenty-nine countries to attend the conference, which was to promote the emigration of German and Austrian Jewish refugees. From the outset, he clearly stated that no country would be forced to change its immigration policies, although they would be asked to consider making such changes. Myron C. Taylor, a former president of United States Steel Corporation, served as the conference chairman, and James G. McDonald, former high commissioner of refugees from Germany, served as his deputy. Eventually, delegates from thirty-two countries attended, representing the United States, Great Britain, France, six smaller European democracies, Canada, the Latin American states, Australia, and New Zealand. In addition, forty private agencies, as well as twenty-one private Jewish groups, sent representatives. The expectation that the Jewish organizations would present a suitable immigration plan was unfulfilled when they proved unable to agree among themselves.

Not all of the invited countries were interested in attending the conference: Italy, for instance, refused Roosevelt's invitation. Romania requested that it, like Germany and Austria, be categorized as a producer of refugees. Along with Poland, it sent observers to Evian; both countries were particularly interested in the deliberations because they were eager to promote Jewish emigration.

The Evian Conference was marked by a lack of substantial progress toward the resettlement of refugees. During the first session, Taylor announced that the United States was working to consolidate the German and Austrian immigration quotas and would make every effort to fill them completely. Although this was a significant gesture for a limited number of Jews, the United States clearly was not altering its immigration quotas or creating a more liberal immigration policy. Having established no high standard for themselves, the U.S. representatives looked on as country after country offered excuses as to why they could not accept more refugees. Most representatives cited economic and unemployment crises or claimed that their countries were already saturated with refugees. Only the Dominican Republic took a meaningful step, agreeing to establish a large farming community to accommodate refugee resettlement.

The two primary problems faced at Evian were the funding of refugee relocation and the fear that countries in eastern Europe would imitate Germany's antisemitic policies in order to rid themselves of their Jewish populations. Organizers worried that successful resettlement options would simply encourage countries to drive out their unwanted populations, thus perpetuating and even intensifying the refugee problem.

One promising initiative of the Evian Conference was the establishment of the Intergovernmental Committee on Refugees (ICR), whose goals were to persuade Germany to allow for the orderly immigration of its Jewish refugees and to establish permanent settlements in countries that would provide a safe environment for them. Unfortunately, when it came time to implement the policy, the ICR lacked both the funding and the authority to have any sizable impact on the problem.

The Evian Conference marked the first time the Jewish refugee issue was seen to be an international concern. However, although the represented governments acknowledged the Jewish plight, it was clear that they were unwilling to offer substantial aid.

—*Melissa Jane Taylor*

See also Holocaust; Immigration and Naturalization Laws; Mussolini, Benito; Nazi Legal Measures against Jews; Poland; Romania; United States

References
Feingold, Henry L. *The Politics of Rescue: The Roosevelt Administration and the Holocaust, 1938–1945* (New York: Holocaust Library, 1970).
Marrus, Michael R. *The Unwanted* (New York: Oxford University Press, 1985).
Wyman, David. *Paper Walls* (Amherst: University of Massachusetts Press, 1968).

Evolutionary Psychology

A field of research and scholarship that views the human mind as the product of evolutionary processes, evolutionary psychology is the successor to mid-twentieth-century sociobiology. Evolutionary psychologists understand complex human learning structures and behavior patterns as having been conditioned by survival and reproduction pressures experienced by humans and their prehuman ancestors in prehistoric environments. The corollary field of behavioral genetics seeks to understand the relationship between specific patterns of behavior and inherited predispositions.

Some figures within the field, such as J. Philippe Rushton and Richard Lynn, have achieved notoriety by advancing arguments widely perceived as xenophobic, particularly with respect to Africans and people of African descent. The most extended attempt to apply the principles of evolutionary psychology specifically to Jews, however, was undertaken by Kevin MacDonald, a member of the Department of Psychology at California State University—Long Beach. MacDonald is also associated with the Charles Martel Society, an "intellectual arm" of the white supremacy/white separatism movement, and is a frequent contributor to its journal, *The Occidental Quarterly,* also serving (along with Lynn) on the journal's advisory board. He has published three books on Jews, Judaism, and antisemitism.

In *A People That Shall Dwell Alone* (1994), MacDonald argued that for roughly the last 2,000 years, Jews have engaged in strategic "cultural and eugenic practices" (1994, 19), in essence breeding for a population high in a set of genetically influenced psychological predispositions and other attributes, such as high "verbal intelligence," (19) that would enhance their ability to compete against non-Jews for resources and for reproductive success. These psychological predispositions allegedly include an array of traits that foster a strong sense of in-group commitment, including an attraction to authoritarian power structures and tendencies toward cultural separatism and ethnocentrism. MacDonald found that Jews are strongly marked by these traits, so much more strongly than other human groups that he consistently spoke of them as constituting the defining characteristics of what he called Jewish "hyper-collectivism," (299) the "intense commitment" to the group that is the "*sine qua non* of Judaism as a group evolutionary strategy" (1994, 257).

Separation and Its Discontents (1998b) offered MacDonald's theory of antisemitism, which he described as an essentially reactive phenomenon. Jews pursuing their group evolutionary strategy actively seek to prevent non-Jews from protecting and serving their own interests. Unless prevented by exceptionally severe restrictions on their activities, Jews engage in their group strategy by attempting to establish "economic, cultural and political domination" (MacDonald 1998b, 39) over other groups. In a pattern typical of his style, MacDonald framed his discussion of the perceptions of Jewish domination of non-Jews as "themes of anti-Semitism" (32) that need not be accurate in order to promote conflict, and he avoided explicitly stating whether such perceptions are indeed accurate. As his examination of each "theme" unfolded, however, he presented historical information in a way that implies that perceptions of Jewish economic and cultural domination of other groups are largely correct. Major manifestations of antisemitism in Western history, including "corporate Catholicism in the late Roman Empire" (91); "the Iberian Inquisitions" (121); and German National Socialism, "the anti-Jewish group evolutionary strategy" (133) all emerged in response to extended periods of Jewish exploitation of non-Jews. These movements typically take on the shape of "mirror images" (ix) of Judaism, as non-Jews adopt the group-serving behaviors and racialist assumptions Jews practice against them. The more these movements abandon the "universalistic, assimilatory tendencies" (163) of Western cultures in their natural state, the more closely they resemble Judaism.

Jewish attempts to avert the worst effects of the antisemitism generated by their own behavior include a variety of countermeasures: "crypsis" or "the pursuit of phenotypic similarity" (181), that is, the adoption of a deceptive non-Jewish identity to mask continuing identification with the Jewish group; manipulation of a culture's political and media apparatus in order "to make anti-Semitism a disreputable, unsavory enterprise" (190); and instilling in non-Jewish cultures "universalist ideologies" (193) while at the same time jealously defending Jewish particularity and exclusivity. They also attempt to circumscribe the activities of individual Jews likely to provoke hostility from non-Jews. These measures all share an agenda of deception, insofar as they are attempts to conceal from non-Jews behavior patterns that are, in fact, essential elements of the Jewish group evolutionary strategy. Moreover, as "hyper-collectivists," Jews are especially prone to engage in group-serving self-deceptions, typically by persuading themselves that Judaism is an ethical—indeed, an "ethically superior" (248)—religion, when in truth it is nothing more than a group strategy fitted with a religious veneer.

In *The Culture of Critique* (1998a), MacDonald applied his theory as an explanatory model, assessing a variety of historical movements as manifestations of the Jewish group evolutionary strategy. In all cases, he viewed these movements as efforts to facilitate or establish Jewish domination over non-Jewish populations. So the American school of anthropological thought founded by Franz Boas sought to delegitimize evolutionary explanations of human behavior, thus limiting the possibility that non-Jews would develop the perspective required to perceive and understand accurately the Jewish group evolutionary strategy (chapter 23). The Frankfurt School of sociocultural critique led by Theodor Adorno sought to stigmatize antisemitism as a pathological condition (169), and Freudian psychoanalysis declared "psychoanalytic intellectual war on gentile culture" itself (151). In the same vein, MacDonald discussed world communism as a protracted exercise in ethnic warfare perpetrated by Jews against the peoples of Eastern Europe. In the United States, Jews use their position of cultural dominance to prevent "gentile European Americans" (also variously referred to as "Western" or "Northwest Europeans") from recognizing their own ethnic group interests. By promoting both the ideology of "radical individualism" (101) and the ideology of multiculturalism (249–256), by manipulating immigration policy to create an ethnically heterogeneous U.S. population (243ff), and by exploiting the right to free expression to foster a debased, hypersexualized cultural climate (325), Jews force on "European-Americans" a debilitating environment designed to marginalize their attempts to cohere and develop an effective counterstrategy (chapter 7).

MacDonald explicitly asserted that "the continued existence of Judaism"(315) is detrimental to the long-term stability of Western society. If catastrophic social collapse is to be averted, policies entailing "intense social controls" (309) based on "ethnic group membership" will need to be implemented to achieve "parity between Jews and other ethnic groups" (307). These include "a high level of discrimination against Jews for admission to universities or access to employment opportunities and even entail a large taxation on Jews to counter the Jewish advantage in the possession of wealth" (307). Such measures would be consistent with a rising awareness of group identity among the "European peoples in the New World," who, in the best-case scenario, may be expected to become "more aware of themselves as a positively evaluated ingroup and more aware of other human groups as competing, negatively evaluated outgroups" (330).

There is no evidence that MacDonald conducted any original research on Jews for these works. Instead, they were entirely founded on citations of secondary sources, some of them of extremely dubious character. He grounded the critical distinction between Jews' supposed biological predispositions toward "hyper-collectivism" and Westerners' supposed biological predispositions toward assimilative individualism on arguments taken from the writings of the Nazi eugenicist Fritz Lenz. Elsewhere, he produced a profoundly distorted reading of David Irving's notoriously shoddy history of the anticommunist 1956 revolt in Hungary as evidence that under communism, Jews enjoyed "sexual and reproductive domination of gentiles" insofar as "Jewish males were able to have disproportionate access to gentile females" (99). When he did cite legitimate scholarship, it was often by way of a paraphrase that omitted and suppressed information contrary to the expectations raised by his theory.

There is every reason to conclude that MacDonald's project falls well short of the standards expected of scholarly inquiry and scientific research. He does not subject his hypotheses to rigorous scrutiny by evaluating them against contradictory data; he instead shields his theory from coming into contact with such data. The theory of Judaism as an evolutionary strategy is an exercise in propaganda masquerading as scholarship; its purpose is not to come to a clear understanding of the complicated and often fraught relationships between communities of Jews and non-Jews but instead to encourage "Europeans in the New World" to regard other human groups, particularly Jews, as "negatively evaluated outgroups." In short, it is an attempt to cultivate widespread hostility toward Jews predicated on distorted interpretations of historical events, an exercise that is, by definition, indistinguishable from any other form of antisemitism.

—*David Isadore Lieberman*

See also Irving, David; Racism, Scientific; White Power Movement

References

Gilman, Sander. *Smart Jews: The Construction of the Image of Jewish Superior Intelligence* (Lincoln: University of Nebraska Press, 1996).

Lieberman, David Isadore. "Scholarship as an Exercise in Rhetorical Strategies: A Case Study of Kevin MacDonald's Research Techniques," H-Antisemitism Occasional Papers. Available at http://www2.h-net.msu.edu/~antis/papers/dl/macdonald_schatz_01.html. Accessed on January 29, 2001.

MacDonald, Kevin. *A People That Shall Dwell Alone: Judaism as a Group* Evolutionary Strategy. (Westport, CT: Praeger, 1994).

———. *The Culture of Critique: An Evolutionary Analysis of Jewish Involvement in Twentieth-Century Intellectual and Political Movements.* (Westport, CT: Praeger, 1998a).

———. *Separation and Its Discontents: Toward an Evolutionary Theory of Anti-Semitism.* (Westport, CT: Praeger, 1998b).

Expulsions, High Middle Ages

In the later Middle Ages, Jews were expelled from all the major western European countries. And often, expulsions on a monarchy-wide scale were preceded by those from smaller regions. In 1289, Charles of Anjou, nephew of Louis IX and the protagonist of the forced conversion of southern Italian Jewry in the early 1290s, expelled Jews from the Duchies of Maine and Anjou. In his role as the Duke of Aquitaine, the English king Edward I expelled the Jews of Gascony, in France, a year prior to his expulsion of Jews from England, in 1290. Jews were expelled from France in 1306; in 1322, after a partial recall in 1315 (or so it seems); again in 1359; and finally in 1394. Each time, the pool of Jews to expel grew smaller. Expulsions in Germany were numerous, especially in the fifteenth and sixteenth centuries (Speyer in1435, Regensburg in 1519). German Jews were just as often massacred, a situation reflecting the lack of both centralized control and real authority in the Holy Roman Empire. The best-known expulsion is that from Spain in 1492, which was formally reversed only after the death of Francisco Franco in 1975.

Before Italian unification in the nineteenth century, expulsions were regional, notably from the Duchy of Lombardy in 1594, which was a possession of the Spanish Crown, and from small communities in Friuli-Giulia to the northeast of Venice toward the end of the sixteenth century. As put by the leaders of Udine, they had found an *occasione scacciare gli ebrei* (opportunity to be rid of the Jews). In the Papal State, which occupied about one-third of the peninsula, Jews were prohibited from all places save Rome and Ancona, first in 1569 and permanently in 1593. Jews were expelled from Sicily—under Aragonese rule—in 1492 and from the related Kingdom of Naples by 1510 and 1541. There was also the expulsion *into* the ghettos that began in Venice in 1516 and continued rapidly after the start of the Roman ghetto in 1555.

The Spanish expulsion drew great attention for two principal reasons: the size of the community and its great age, dating back to the Roman Empire. Myths grew up about the importance of the expulsion for the Spanish economy. Even today, historians debate whether the absence of Jews was economically determinant as Spain declined in the early modern period, but these debates often rest on mythical reasoning. Most agree the expulsion did not ruin the Spanish economy, if only because so many Jews—perhaps the majority (here again, there is great historiographical debate)—had converted, and so, de facto, many "Jews" and their alleged commercial acumen never left. Others, known as crypto-Jews, constantly moved in and out of Spain to carry on business. The "Jewish" role, whatever it was in Spain's economy, was largely uninterrupted.

Another issue was force. The Spanish Jews who fled to Portugal in 1492 were all forcibly converted five years later, opening a major ecclesiastical debate. Cardinal Pier Paolo Pariseo argued that even in the third generation, these conversions, the product of "absolute" force, remained illegal and hence invalid. Pariseo's opponents—who favored establishing the Portuguese Inquisition, which was notoriously violent—carried the day.

A common view is that Jews were expelled because of ecclesiastical pressure to rid Christendom of Jews, and rulers eventually bowed to ecclesiastical demands. This is not true. Jewish writers of the times said the opposite. Their real fear was the kings. The anonymous author of a fictional story about events in the year 1007 was specific. The Jews, he wrote with knowing exaggeration, fell under the jurisdiction of the popes. Kings, without papal authorization, tried to force Jews to convert, and by implication, they were the "evil kingdom" for whose destruction Jews prayed daily. The pope was legitimate authority; kings were capricious and untrustworthy. Another anonymous author, who penned letters ostensibly about the burning of thirty-one Jews in Blois in 1171 on a charge of ritual murder, had the king improbably telling his wife that her brother, the count who burned the Jews, had insulted the Crown. In fact, the letter was a satire. The king the author really intended, Philip Augustus, expressed his belief in libels of ritual murder and worse. The nobility, also satirized in this account, was not much different. The major dukes of thirteenth-century France protected only those Jews who might make a profit for them. In England, the king alone profited; the nobility believed that Jews posed a constant threat. Hence, the nobility pressed for expulsion, just as it sought to destroy the Jews of York in 1191, seeing in the Jews the king's hated financial agents.

There was ecclesiastical animus, but it must be contextualized. Legally, expulsion was a royal prerogative and it could be and was arbitrarily invoked, which explains any lack of either papal protest or expression of approval. By contrast, the formal church maintained a clear, ancient doctrine that made room for Jews, as long as they played a subservient role. Often, there was fear that Jews were doing otherwise or that their actions contaminated Christian ritual and threatened the *corpus mysticum* (Eucharist). But papal policy never abandoned fundamental principles of acceptance based on Pauline teaching. The church called for restriction, not expulsion.

It was in the kingdoms that fears about Jews were decisive. Philip Augustus is said to have heard, as a child, that Jews sacrificed Christian children and consumed their hearts—a full-blown blood libel. He expelled his Jews in 1182, only to call them back sixteen years later when it became clear to him that the exploitation of Jews by French barons was to his disadvantage. The desire to convert Jews, together with an inability to enforce restrictive legislation, eventually led to the more definitive expulsion of 1306. There was also royal piety. In 1179, Philip Augustus still questioned whether it was right to abandon the Jews' old privileges, allowing them to possess Christian servants or to build synagogues. In 1283, Philip III wrote the prohibition on synagogue building and on having Christian servants into a charter. In addition, from the mid-thirteenth century, the kings of France took the lead in such acts as burning the Talmud. The Jews, said Louis IX, were his to police. Meir ben Simeon insisted the king was harsher than the pope when it came to prohibiting lending at interest.

To all this was added the inability to insert Jews into the body politic, called in France the *corpus reipublicae mysticum*—the lay counterpart to the mystical body of the church, the *corpus ecclesiae mysticum*. Legally, Jews were *Judaei*, hence unique, and bound either to major barons or kings. Thought profitable in the short run, such a unique status could not endure in a society where participation in the civic body, viewed as the Corpus Christi, was vital. This was even truer in the *quasi res sacrae* (inalienable substance) of the English Crown, for in England, the Jews were the *quasi catallum* (veritable chattels) of the king alone. There could be no civil quiet or proper taxation as long as the barons feared that the king would exploit this special Jewish status to foreclose on their estates. Indeed, in gratitude, the act of expulsion led the barons to grant a tax worth ten to fifteen times the entire fortune of the Jews, a fiscal fact they probably did not know. What continually provoked the baronial fear of foreclosure was the English kings' early understanding that controlling the courts was the surest way to achieve stable power. To this end, the kings forced all disputes arising over loans made by their Jewish dependents, whose records the kings also held, to be aired in royal courts. However, by the late thirteenth century, the virtue of well-run courts was commonly appreciated, and nearly everybody turned to royal justice willingly. Even here, the Jews' special status became far more of a liability than a virtue. Getting rid of the Jews cost virtually nothing, provided for urgent royal financial need, and created a consensus the king desired in order to prosecute wars. Necessity seems to have overridden the fact that, theoretically, the "Jewish chattel" were a part of the putatively inalienable quasi res sacrae.

The Jews' civil dependency on rulers thus made their tenure in the medieval kingdom precarious. How this dependency arose is most visible in the case of Germany, where Jews once received individual charters of *tuitio* (special protection and privilege). These charters were granted only to permanent residents and members of a recognized *gens* (people). As feudal statuses developed, however, and there was no other way to accommodate Jews, the status of being "protected" became the Jews' only status and on a group, no longer on an individual, level. Yet by what right did they have this status? According to Emperor Friedrich I's statement in 1157, they had it because Jews pertained to the *camera* (the royal chamber), which symbolized royal continuity. However, such a status was demonstrably artificial—so artificial and weak, in fact, that Emperor Friedrich II in 1234 declared Jews to be *servi camerae nostrae* (the servants of this chamber; not real servitude or slavery). In reality, Friedrich had only given a name to what was otherwise ubiquitous. Jews were the *tanquam servi* (veritable servants) of the French kings, the *servi Regis* (royal servants) of Spanish monarchs, and, as said, the quasi catallum of the English. When pressure became too great, therefore, Jews could legally be expelled. This situation, not cynical and pragmatic explanations, explains the course of events; pragmatic cynicism, in fact, removes the expulsions from their proper medieval context.

—*Kenneth Stow*

See also Church Councils (Early); Expulsions, Late Middle Ages; Ghetto; Ritual Murder (Medieval); Spain under Franco; Talmud Trials

References

Jordan, William C. *The French Monarchy and the Jews: From Philip Augustus to the Last Capetians* (Philadelphia: University of Pennsylvania Press, 1989).

Langmuir, Gavin. "*Tanquam Servi*, the Change in Jewish Status in French Law about 1200." In *Les Juifs dans l'histoire de France.* Edited by Miriam Yardeni (Leiden, the Netherlands: Brill, 1980).

Stow, Kenneth. *Alienated Minority: The Jews of Medieval Latin Europe* (Cambridge, MA: Harvard University Press, 1994).

Expulsions, Late Middle Ages

Driving Jews out of their homes was not a phenomenon new to late medieval Europe, yet the many expulsions of the fifteenth century had a more profound effect on the subsequent development of both Jewish and non-Jewish societies. Beginning in the late thirteenth and early fourteenth centuries, Jews were driven out of England and France. During the fourteenth century, numerous expulsions and pogroms associated with accusations against Jews during the Black Plague, efforts to wrest money from them, and inflammatory anti-Jewish preaching also resulted in the significant demographic movement of Jewish individuals and communities.

But throughout the fifteenth century, Europe was disrupted by a wave of expulsions and attempted expulsions that changed the face of Jewry. In Germany, Jews were expelled from a variety of regions and cities under numerous pretexts and because of local conditions. Among the significant regional expulsions were those in the Palatinate (1390–1391), Thuringia (1401), Austria (1420–1421), Breisgau (1421), Bavaria-Munich (1442), Bavaria-Landshut (1450), Mecklenburg/Pomerania (1492), Carniola (1496), and Styria (1496). The phenomenon continued into the sixteenth century, with expulsions occurring in Brandenburg (1510), Alsace (ca. 1520), and Saxony (1540). The regional expulsions might include large archbishoprics, such as Cologne (1429), Mainz (1470), and Magdeburg (1493), or clusters of cities, as in the case of Bohemia in 1454. During the fifteenth century, Jews were expelled from the German cities of Vienna (1421), Cologne (1424), Augsburg (1438–1440), Mainz (1438 and 1470), Munich (1442), Würzburg (1450), Breslau (1453–1454), Erfurt (1453–1454), Hildesheim (1457), Bamberg (1478), Salzburg (1498), Nuremberg (1499), Ulm (1499),

Nördlingen (1504), Regensburg (1519), and Rothenburg ob der Tauber (1520). A mere list of place-names, however, does little service to an understanding of the dramatic social and communal effects of the expulsions. Jews were forced into new areas, many migrating eastward, and into new regional communal associations.

Various reasons might be given to justify the expulsions—from traditional anti-Jewish religious diatribes that accused Jews of blasphemy toward Christianity to more recent and sinister accusations of ritual murder or host desecration. In many cases, Jews were accused of subverting the common good with the practice of usury. In some cases, they were accused of treasonous behavior. In Augsburg, for example, Jews were labeled as evil, dangerous, and disobedient and were accused of conspiring against the city and being lazy and parasitical. In 1438, they were given two years to quit the city. In most cases, however, the underlying motivations for expulsion seem to have resulted from local political maneuvering and the acceding to popular pressure arising from virulent anti-Jewish preaching.

On the Iberian Peninsula, the terrible persecutions and pogroms of 1391 set the scene for complicated problems related to Jewish identity and the position of the Jews in Spanish society throughout the following century. Jews were segregated in Andalusia in 1480 and expelled in 1483. In 1483, the municipal council of Valmaseda in the Basque country banned marriages between resident and foreign Jews, and in 1486, following the Andalusian model, it expelled the Jews. With the expulsion of the Jews from Spain in 1492, the combined expulsions and forced conversions in Portugal in 1496 and 1497, and the expulsion from Navarre in 1498, Jews were essentially driven from the Iberian Peninsula. This created significant and dramatic changes for both Jewish and Christian societies. On one hand, some 200,000 Jewish exiles left Spain, attempting to integrate into a wide variety of far-flung communities where they were forced to learn new languages and occupations and adapt to diverse environments. The Spanish Crown as well as local and regional government, on the other hand, had to contend with a great number of economic and legal problems regarding the often complex property and business relationships left in the wake of the expulsions.

The Spanish expulsion edict issued by Ferdinand and Isabella focused on the alleged negative influence exercised by observant Jews on those who had converted to Christianity. The very extensive edict detailed the fundamental guilt of the Jews in a traditionally anti-Jewish religious context. According to the text:

"You know well, or ought to know, that because we were informed that in our realms there were some bad Christians who Judaized and apostatized from our holy Catholic faith, whereof the chief cause was the communication between the Christians and the Jews . . . we ordained that the said Jews should be set apart. . . . Thereby is established and made manifest the great damage to the Christians that has resulted and results from the participation, conversation, communication which they have held and do hold with the Jews, of whom it is proved that they always attempt by whatever ways and means they can to subvert and detract faithful Christians from our holy Catholic faith and separate them from it and attract and pervert them to their cursed belief and opinion." (translated in Beinart 2002, 49–50).

—*Dean Phillip Bell*

See also Dominican Order; Expulsions, High Middle Ages; Host Desecration; Middle Ages, Late; Ritual Murder (Medieval); Spain, Riots of 1391; Usury; Well Poisoning

References

Beinart, Haim. *The Expulsion of the Jews from Spain.* Translated by Jeffrey M. Green (Oxford: Littman Library of Jewish Civilization, 2002).

Bell, Dean Phillip. *Sacred Communities: Jewish and Christian Identities in Fifteenth-Century Germany* (Leiden, the Netherlands, and Boston: Brill, 2001).

Foa, Anna. *The Jews of Europe after the Black Death.* Translated by Andrea Grover (Berkeley: University of California Press, 2000).

Stow, Kenneth R. *Alienated Minority: The Jews of Medieval Latin Europe* (Cambridge, MA: Harvard University Press, 1992).

F

Farhud (1941)

A *farhud* in Iraqi Arabic designates a breakdown of law and order. The word became the name of the pogrom against the Jews of Baghdad that occurred on June 1 and 2, 1941.

As British troops approached Baghdad on May 29, the leaders of the pro-Nazi government of Rashid Ali al-Gaylani, including the Mufti Hajj Amin al-Hussaini, fled the country, leaving in charge the three-man Council for Internal Security. The Judeophobic minister of economics, Yunus al-Sab`awi, who headed paramilitary gangs, also remained behind and declared himself military governor of the capital. On May 30, al-Sab`awi summoned the president of the Jewish Community Council and ordered him to tell all Jews to remain at home and refrain from any communication with one another. Al-Sab`awi prepared an incendiary speech for broadcast by radio, calling for an uprising and a purge of the "enemy within," a clear reference to the Jews. However, before he could deliver the speech, he was arrested and expelled from the country. Convinced that the danger had passed, the Jews of Baghdad went out on June 1, the holiday of Shavuot, traditionally marked by pilgrimages to the tombs of holy men and visits to family and friends. Many also went out to welcome back the Hashemite regent, who had fled the pro-Nazi regime. Soldiers, soon joined by civilians, attacked this group of Jews, killing one and injuring others while the police looked on. Rioting spread throughout the city, and by nightfall, a major pogrom was under way. The rampage in the Jewish neighborhoods and business districts continued until the afternoon of the following day, when the regent finally gave orders for the police to fire on the rioters and Kurdish troops were brought in from the north. The British army encamped on the outskirts of the city did not intervene by order of the ambassador, Sir Kinahan Cornwallis, who did not wish to give the appearance of reinstating the pro-British regent by force of arms.

In the Farhud, 179 Jewish men, women, and children were killed; 242 children orphaned; 586 businesses looted; and 911 buildings housing more than 12,000 people pillaged. Total property losses were estimated by the Jewish community's investigating committee at $680,000 (some estimates were four times that amount). The Iraqi government commission of inquiry advanced considerably lower casualty statistics, although one of its members later acknowledged the government's desire to minimize the figures.

The Farhud dramatically undermined the confidence of all Iraqi Jewry and, like the massacres of the Assyrian Christians in 1933, had a highly unsettling effect on all the Iraqi minorities. The Farhud left an indelible mark on the Iraqi Jewish collective memory and is recounted in novels and memoirs by emigré writers in several languages.

—*Norman A. Stillman*

See also Constantine Pogrom; Hussaini, Mufti Hajj Amin al-
References
Stillman, Norman A. *The Jews of Arab Lands in Modern Times* (Philadelphia: Jewish Publication Society, 1991).

Farrakhan, Louis (1933–)

Louis Farrakhan has emerged as the most visible and vociferous African American antisemite on the contemporary scene. His charismatic style, ability to articulate the frustrations of the African American working class, and willingness to chal-

Minister Louis Farrakhan of the Nation of Islam addresses a crowd at Madison Square Garden while protected by his bodyguard. (Jacques M. Chenet/Corbis)

lenge the racial status quo have catapulted him into the public arena, despite the general unpopularity of his Nation of Islam movement within the larger African American community.

Farrakhan was born Louis Eugene Wolcott but changed his name to Louis X after he joined the Nation of Islam in 1955. A disciple of Malcolm X, he adopted the Muslim name Abdul Haleem Farrakhan. When Malcolm X and Nation of Islam leader Elijah Muhammed split in 1964, Farrakhan remained loyal to Muhammed and eventually came to head the religious organization.

Farrakhan connected the power of the ruling whites to age-old antisemitic canards. In several high-profile speeches, he claimed that Judaism was a "gutter religion," called Jewish landlords "bloodsuckers," and remarked that "Hitler was a very great man" (in Dinnerstein 1994, 220–225). National Jewish organizations such as the Anti-Defamation League pressed Farrakhan and the Nation of Islam to the top of their domestic political agendas, condemning his hate speech

and calling for unconditional public apologies for his conduct.

The Nation of Islam leader rose to prominence in an era when American Jews faced marginalization from their one-time allies in the African American community. Once considered white America's most committed social reformers, Jews endured charges of white racism and paternalism by a new generation of black leaders, most notably Farrakhan, who accused them of exploiting African Americans for their own communal gains. Critics of Farrakhan argue that the Nation of Islam has remained a tiny movement in the African American community and that Farrakhan's antisemitism has damaged his ability to attract wider support. They also agree that his ability to capture media attention, fueled in some measure by the organized Jewish community's public statements against him, keeps him and his message in the public eye.

In the 1990s, Farrakhan distanced himself from his antisemitic rhetoric and tried to forge alliances with local U.S. politicians, international leaders, and mainstream Muslim clerics. His successful effort to bring together 400,000 people at the Million Man March in Washington, D.C., offered him the opportunity to expand his message as well as his base of support.

—*Marc Dollinger*

See also African American–Jewish Relations; American Jewish Committee and Antidefamation Efforts in the United States; Nation of Islam; *Secret Relationship between Blacks and Jews, The*

References

Dinnerstein, Leonard. *Anti-Semitism in America* (New York: Oxford University Press, 1994).

Van Deburg, William L., ed. *Modern Black Nationalism: From Marcus Garvey to Louis Farrakhan* (New York: New York University Press, 1997).

Fascist Intellectuals (French)

Defining the phrase *French fascist intellectual* and cataloging the figures who meet the definition is problematic for several reasons. First, a lively debate among historians, including Zeev Sternhell and Robert Soucy, has focused on the question of whether an indigenous French fascism exists and, if it does, what its intellectual and cultural roots and identifying features are. Sternhell has argued that, historically, French fascism was essentially leftist in origin, growing out of the revolutionary syndicalism of Georges Sorel and the Sorelians. For Robert Soucy, French fascism was primarily a product of conservative and reactionary traditions exemplified in groups such as the Ligue des Patriotes and integral nationalists such as Maurice Barrès.

Another difficulty is that there is a tendency to confuse what Soucy has referred to as the "Second Wave" of French fascism with collaborationism with Nazism during the German Occupation of France from 1940 to 1944. For example, the modernist novelist Louis-Ferdinand Céline, author of classic works including *Journey to the End of the Night* and *Death on the Installment Plan*, was a rabid antisemite and admirer of Hitler. His antisemitic pamphlets published in the late 1930s and during the Occupation are still censured in France, and they were the primary reason Céline was forced to flee with the Germans at the Liberation and live in exile in Scandinavia for a number of years. But Céline

was not a fierce nationalist or a proponent of militarism, features commonly associated with the fascist mind-set. Finally, in speaking of fascist intellectuals, the common tendency is to assume that this category of intellectuals became extinct with the collapse of the Nazis and the demise of the Vichy regime at the end of World War II. In fact, in the immediate postwar years, a small but influential group of literary fascists achieved influence and prominence. Known as the *hussards,* the group was headed by the young novelist and literary critic Roger Nimier. Nimier successfully relaunched the careers of disgraced fascist and collaborationist writers after the Liberation and carried on a constant campaign against Jean-Paul Sartre and leftist "committed" literature. More recently, in the early 1980s, New Right intellectuals, including Alain de Benoist, were categorized as fascists. There have been other fascist or *fascisant* intellectuals before and since.

The most widely recognized group of fascist intellectuals is, of course, the generation of writers who played a dominant role in the interwar years and during the Occupation. This group included several figures clustered around the review *Je suis partout* (I Am Everywhere), such as Robert Brasillach, Lucien Rebatet, Alain Laubreaux, and Pierre-Antoine Cousteau, brother of the famous undersea explorer. Of this group, Robert Brasillach is the best known, and he was certainly the most influential in the interwar years and during the Occupation. Brasillach was a graduate of the prestigious École Normale Supérieure and was a successful journalist, novelist, and literary critic. His essays on classical writers such as Virgil and the French playwright Pierre Corneille are still considered astute in some quarters, and several of his novels are still praised by his admirers, although they are more widely viewed as dated and facile. Like many French fascists, Brasillach had early ties to Charles Maurras's royalist and Catholic organization Action Française.

In his role as journalist and fascist propagandist, Brasillach wrote of his journeys to Nazi Germany and sang the praises of the Nuremberg rallies in *Notre avant-guerre* (Our Prewar Years [1941]). He also visited Francoist Spain and wrote a hagiographic account of the defenders of the Toledo Alcazar, *Les Cadets de l'Alcazar* (The Cadets of the Alcazar [1936]). When World War II started, Brasillach was in uniform. He was captured by the Germans, briefly held as a prisoner of war, and then returned to Paris to edit *Je suis partout.* An archcollaborator throughout the Occupation, he was arrested and tried at the Liberation. His courage during his trial for treason earned him the respect even of those who despised his politics. He was executed on February 6, 1945, after an appeal for clemency signed by François Mauriac, Albert Camus, and others was rejected by Charles de Gaulle. Following his execution and largely as a result of the efforts of Maurice Bardèche (who himself became an apologist for fascism and a Holocaust denier after the war), Brasillach became a martyr for the extreme Right in France. His literary reputation was inflated, and his complete works were republished in expurgated form by Bardèche.

The other significant figure associated with *Je suis partout* was Lucien Rebatet, who served as music and cinema critic, writing under the pseudonym François Vinneuil, and authored a collaborationist, antisemitic best-selling essay, *Les Décombres* (The Rubble), in 1942. Rebatet's literary reputation rests on one massive novel, *Les Deux étendards* (Two Standards), published in 1952 and praised by the eminent critic George Steiner, who argued that it was a finer novel than any of the more recognized works of Céline. Admirers of Rebatet insist on the accuracy of Steiner's judgment, but this view is not widely held. Rebatet was imprisoned at the Liberation, but unlike Brasillach, he was granted clemency. He continued to write for right-wing publications after the war and became a fierce anti-Gaullist. He died in 1972, and his memoirs, *Mémoire d'un fasciste,* were published posthumously in 1976.

Of all the fascist intellectuals of his generation, certainly the most accomplished as a literary figure—and the one whose reputation in academic circles in France has improved considerably since the mid-1990s—is Pierre Drieu la Rochelle. Drieu's genealogy included the Surrealists and an early association with the Sorelians. A decorated veteran of trench warfare during World War I, he quickly made his literary reputation with novels celebrating the manly virtues of war and de-

nouncing the decadence of French culture and society in the interwar years. The best known of these works are *Le feu follet* (Will o' the Wisp [1931]), *La Comédie de Charleroi* (1934), (Comedy of Charleroi) *Rêveuse bourgeoisie* (Dreamy Bourgeoisie [1937]), and *Gilles* (1939). He also wrote a number of political essays and meditations on contemporary Europe. By the late 1930s, these tended to celebrate his commitment to fascism. The title of his book *Socialisme fasciste* speaks for itself, and Drieu's other profascist works include pamphlets and essays on Jacques Doriot, the former communist leader who switched sides and founded his own fascist party, the Parti Populaire Français. During the Occupation, Drieu edited a prestigious literary review, the *Nouvelle revue française,* and contributed pro-German pieces to the collaborationist press. The full extent of his virulent antisemitism only became apparent with the publication of his wartime journal in 1992. As the Liberation approached, Drieu took his own life rather than face trial.

The list of French fascist writers and intellectuals from the interwar years also includes a number of figures who did not necessarily trumpet their fascism or belong to fascist parties but were in sympathy with tendencies and attitudes commonly associated with fascism: the cult of war and virility, antisemitism, fierce nationalism, disdain for "decadence," and so on. Belonging to this group are novelist, essayist, and later playwright Henry de Montherlant and the novelist and short-story writer Paul Morand. Finally, a number of figures who claimed to be seeking a "third way" between fascism and democracy gathered around the 1930s review *Combat:* the left-wing novelist and essayist Maurice Blanchot, the Christian philosophers Emmanuel Mounier and Denis de Rougemont, and the critics Thierry Maulnier and Pierre-Henri Simon.

—*Richard J. Golsan*

See also Action Française; Bardèche, Maurice; Barrès, Maurice; Brasillach, Robert; Céline, Louis-Ferdinand; France; Maurras, Charles; Rebatet, Lucien; Sartre, Jean-Paul; Spain under Franco; Vichy

References

Carroll, David. *French Literary Fascism: Nationalism, Anti-Semitism, and the Ideology of Culture*

(Princeton, NJ: Princeton University Press, 1995).

Kaplan, Alice Yaeger. *Reproductions of Banality: Fascism, Literature, and French Intellectual Life* (Minneapolis: University of Minnesota Press, 1986).

———. *The Collaborator: The Trial and Execution of Robert Brasillach* (Chicago: University of Chicago Press, 2000).

Soucy, Robert. *French Fascism: The Second Wave, 1933–1939* (New Haven, CT: Yale University Press, 1995).

Faurisson, Robert (1929–)

A professor of French literature and a leading Holocaust denier for more than thirty years, Robert Faurisson was born in London in 1929, the son of a French father and a Scottish mother. Following his studies in the late 1960s and early 1970s, he was awarded his doctorate from the Sorbonne, and in 1978, he was appointed professor of French literature at the University of Lyon. He was highly influenced by the Holocaust denial theories of Paul Rassinier, with which he became familiar in the 1960s.

His emergence as a Holocaust denier occurred in 1974, when he published a provocative letter to the director of Yad Vashem (Israel's Holocaust Memorial Authority). The letter contained many of Faurisson's main arguments, which he later elaborated on in his articles and books. He claimed that extensive archival research had proved to him that the Nazis had never planned or implemented systematic genocide against the Jews. Testimonies of Nazi officials who were accused of being part of the extermination process such as Rudolf Höss, the commandant of Auschwitz, were full of contradictions, and details given on the extermination could easily be refuted. After the establishment of the international forum for Holocaust deniers, the Institute for Historical Review, at the end of the 1970s, Faurisson became very active at its conferences and in its publications. He traveled and lectured in various countries and tried to assist fellow deniers who were facing legal difficulties. Twice, in 1984 and in 1988, he testified at the trials of the Canadian-German Holocaust denier Ernst Zündel. It was Faurisson who, prior to the 1988 trial, proposed hiring an expert witness who could sci-

entifically undermine the alleged facts of the gas exterminations. The result was the publication of the *Leuchter Report,* one of the most influential works in the history of Holocaust denial.

Given his professorship at a prestigious university, Faurisson's denial of the Holocaust raised severe criticism among French intellectuals. Among those who spoke out against him was the eminent French historian Pierre Vidal-Naquet. However, Faurisson was also supported by French intellectuals from both the extreme Right and the extreme Left and even by prominent linguist Noam Chomsky, who defended his right to freedom of expression. However, Faurisson's ability to disseminate his ideas was restricted considerably when the French legislature passed the Gayssot Law against Holocaust denial in 1990. A year later, Faurisson was prosecuted, convicted, and fined, and in 1991, he was dismissed from his academic post. Undismayed by the decline of Holocaust denial in recent years and the devastating judgment against its fundamental allegations in the Irving trial (in 2000), Faurrison as recently as 2001 published an article combating "the creation of the Jewish genocide myth."

—*Roni Stauber*

See also Fascist Intellectuals; Holocaust Denial, Negationism, and Revisionism; Institute for Historical Review; Irving, David; *Leuchter Report;* Zündel, Ernst

References

Vidal-Naquet, Pierre. *Assassins of Memory: Essays on the Denial of the Holocaust* (New York: Columbia University Press, 1992).

Yagil, Limor. *Holocaust Denial in France* (Tel Aviv, Israel: Project for the Study of Anti-Semitism, 1995).

Ferrer, Vincente (1350–1419)

Vincente (Vicente in Spanish) Ferrer was born in Valencia in 1350. In 1368, he became a Dominican priest. In the 1370s, he published two treatises on logic and philosophy. After studies in Barcelona, he became father confessor to Queen Yolanda of Aragon. In 1399, following a short period of service to Pope Benedict XIII, Ferrer began to preach throughout Spain and other parts of Europe. He was said to have had a charismatic effect on his audience. Accompanied by priests and flagellants, he moved through numerous cities and preached the Gospels. Many miracles are ascribed to him, 873 of which are officially recognized by the Catholic Church. One of his main tasks was to missionize the Jews, with the aim of putting an end to the existence of Judaism by moral rather than physical force. Thus, he condemned the deadly anti-Jewish riots that swept through Spain in 1391. Ferrer reportedly succeeded in converting 25,000 Jews, as well as 8,000 Muslims, to Christianity.

Jews were subjected to the power of the state as well as Ferrer's powers of persuasion. Under his influence, several anti-Jewish rules were promulgated in 1412 in Castile (and in 1415 in Aragon): Jewish habitation was restricted to separate quarters, which Jews could leave only under guard; Jews had to wear distinguishing beards and were forbidden to appear in costly clothes; and they could not occupy public offices or work as physicians, pharmacists, tax collectors, carpenters, tailors, shoemakers, dealers, or in several other occupations. If these rules had been strictly enforced, Jewish life would not have been sustainable in the kingdoms. But even in their loose application, the regulations amounted to grave discrimination and sent a clear message that Jews who continued to practice Judaism would not be tolerated. Vincente Ferrer died in 1419 in Vannes, France, and was canonized in 1455.

—Bernd Rother

See also Dominican Order; Inquisition; Spain, Riots of 1391

References
Gheon, Henri. *Saint Vincent Ferrer* (New York: Sheed and Ward, 1954).
Mira, Joan F. *San Vicente Ferrer: Vida y leyenda de un predicador* (Alzira, Spain: Bromera Edicions, 2002).

Feuerbach, Ludwig (1804–1872)

Ludwig Feuerbach studied theology in Heidelberg and Berlin before transferring, under the direct influence of G. W. F. Hegel, to philosophy. He obtained his doctorate in Erlangen (in 1828), where he taught until he was sacked for his critical stance (in 1832). Associated with the Young Hegelians and writing for their periodicals, he reached the height of his fame with the publication of *The Essence of Christianity* in 1841. From the mid-1840s, he spent virtually the rest of his life as a recluse, living on a precarious income.

Feuerbach was not, strictly speaking, a systematic thinker, and his significance lies in the impulses he gave to others rather than in the substance of his thought. His ambiguity and conventional prejudices with regard to Jewry notwithstanding, the formulations on Judaism in his *Essence* (mainly in the eleventh and twelfth chapters) were, on the whole, rather more evenhanded and inoffensive than the few passages that are usually quoted would suggest. Having declared many of the characteristics previously identified primarily with Judaism to be typical of religion in general, he then considered the question of what remained to distinguish Judaism from Christianity. It was in this context that he portrayed Judaism as characterized by egoism and utilism. Where paganism took nature as given and sought to understand and interpret it, thereby ultimately submitting to it, Judaism, Feuerbach argued, posited that nature had been created expressly by a divine will. Israel, in turn, was the exclusive beneficiary of the divine purpose. Assuming, as Feuerbach did, that any deity was but a mirror image of the ideals aspired to by the human beings worshiping that deity, this, in fact, amounted to the assumption that nature existed solely to serve human aspirations (utilism) and, at that, exclusively those of Jewry (egoism).

Karl Marx readily adopted these two labels, and they reverberate in *Zur Judenfrage* (On the Jewish Question [1843]), his answer to Bruno Bauer. Feuerbach's genuinely formative influence on the young Marx was of a methodological nature and hinged on Feuerbach's "Provisional Theses for the Reformation of Philosophy" and his *Principles of the Philosophy of the Future* (both in 1843). Feuerbach's so-called transformative method, the notion that Hegel's thought could be turned on its feet if one exchanged the subject and the predicate of his contentions, had an inordinately more substantial influence on Marx's developing thought (including *Zur Judenfrage*) than his notion of Judaism's essential egoism and utilism. These two labels, however, took on a life of their own among thinkers and polemicists, who applied them to underscore their negative preconceptions with even less concern for the substance of Feuerbach's thought than Marx himself did in *Zur Judenfrage*.

—Lars Fischer

See also Bauer, Bruno; Hegel, G. W. F.; Jewish Question; *Jewish Question, The* (1843); Marx, Karl; Young Hegelians

References

Avineri, Shlomo. "The Hegelian Origins of Marx's Political Thought," *Review of Metaphysics* 21 (1967): 33–56.

Carlebach, Julius. *Karl Marx and the Radical Critique of Judaism* (London: Littman/Routledge & Kegan Paul, 1978).

Fichte, J. G. (1762–1814)

A major figure in the development of German philosophy from Immanuel Kant to G. W. F. Hegel, Fichte was also one of the great icons of German nationalism and the promoter, at one juncture in his career, of a distinctly philosophical brand of Jew-hatred.

Born to a family of weavers and peasants in a small village in Saxony, Fichte studied at Jena and Leipzig. After the publication of his *Versuch einer Kritik aller Offenbarung* (Attempt at a Critique of All Revelation [1792]), a work that extended Kant's philosophy into the realm of religion, he became an academic celebrity overnight and earned a professorship at the University of Jena. While at Jena, he published a controversial book defending the principles of the French Revolution in 1793 and the first of many versions of his seminal work, the *Wissenschaftslehre* (Doctrine of Knowledge [1794]). A popular lecturer, he wrote on issues of epistemology, law, ethics, and political economy. In 1798, an essay he published expressing radical views on religion resulted in a charge of promoting atheism. Under pressure, he resigned his post and relocated to Berlin, where he continued to write, lecture, and publish. In the years 1807 and 1808, during the Napoleonic occupation, he delivered his *Reden an die deutsche Nation* (Addresses to the German Nation), a call for German nationalism. Fichte was appointed head of the philosophical faculty at the newly created university in Berlin in 1810 and became its first rector in 1811.

In his defense of the ideals of the French Revolution in 1793, Fichte singled out Jews and Judaism as constituting a "state-within-a-state" that was "predicated on the hatred of the entire human race" and "spreading through almost all lands of Europe and terribly oppressing its citizens." In his critique of the ancien régime, he presented the alleged clannishness, misanthropy, and economic power of international Jewry as anathema to his ideals of human rights, legal equality, and human freedom. The only way to give Jews civil rights, he claimed in a moment of rhetorical excess, would be "to cut off their heads in one night and put others on them in which there would not be a single Jewish idea" (*Gesamtausgabe der Bayerischen Akademie der Wissenschaften*, 1964, 1: 292–293). Historians of philosophy have tended to ignore these comments. Fichte's contemporaries did not, however. In 1794, Saul Ascher, a Berlin writer and an early ideologue of Reform Judaism, charged Fichte with promoting a distinctly modern form of Jew-hatred that was secular, philosophical, and not without a basis in Kant's own philosophy. In the debates over Jewish emancipation in subsequent years, moreover, anti-Jewish writers frequently invoked Fichte's authority to deny Jews rights, casting him as a great philosopher of Jew-hatred.

Fichte's own relationship to Jews and Judaism over the course of his career was complex and ambivalent. There are few traces of such Jew-hatred in his *Addresses to the German Nation*, and Jew-hatred played a minimal role in his subsequent writings. While at the University of Berlin, he at one point prominently interceded on behalf of a Jewish student. If Fichte helped launch a novel form of Jew-hatred, it was because he denigrated Jews and Judaism as the antithesis of modern visions of political universalism, not because he cast Jews as the enemy of German nationalism.

—Jonathan M. Hess

See also Hegel, G. W. F.; Kant, Immanuel; Misanthropy; State-within-a-State

References

Hess, Jonathan M. *Germans, Jews and the Claims of Modernity* (New Haven, CT, and London: Yale University Press, 2002).

Sweet, Paul R. "Fichte and the Jews: A Case of Tension between Civil Rights and Human Rights," *German Studies Review* 16 (1993): 37–48.

Film Industry, Nazi Purge of Jewish Influence in

Once in power, the National Socialists immediately set about removing Jews from every level of the public sphere in Germany, including the entertainment industry. Already on March 29, 1933, the board of Germany's largest film studio, the Universum-Film A.G. (Ufa), fired all Jewish employees. Ufa's action preceded any formal order by the government and even the April 1 boycott of Jewish-owned businesses and professionals. On June 30 of that same year, the Aryan Paragraph codified the expulsion of Jews from the German film industry. This law was followed by the establishment of the Reichsfilmkammer (Imperial Film Chamber [RFK]) on July 14. The RFK functioned as a guild under the control of Joseph Goebbels's Ministry for Popular Enlightenment and Propaganda; membership was obligatory. No film could be publicly screened unless everyone who worked on it was a member of the RFK, and Jews and other "undesirable elements" were not eligible for membership. With the passage of the Nuremberg Laws of 1935, industry prohibitions on Jews were matched by a repeal of their rights as citizens.

There were occasional exceptions. The Propaganda Ministry could, at its discretion, issue *Sondergenehmigungen,* or special permission to allow film personnel with Jewish backgrounds or partially Jewish spouses to work in the film industry. An RFK document from 1936 even stated that some *Volljuden* (individuals of 100 percent Jewish origin) were members. The Nazis' racist antisemitism, based on genetic notions of Jewish or German "blood," rendered decisions about who would and would not be allowed to work in film a strange process of political alchemy. Director Fritz Lang, whose mother was born Jewish but later converted, was initially offered the post of head filmmaker for the Nazis by Goebbels himself. Lang declined. The popular comedic actor Heinz Rühmann was told he must divorce his Jewish wife before he would be accepted into the RFK. After years of exceptions, Rühmann relented in 1938; his wife survived the war in exile. Others were less fortunate. The actor Joachim Gottschalk, his Jewish wife, and his child committed suicide after he was unable to convince Goebbels to protect his family from deportation.

Those who were able to secure visas for the United States enriched Hollywood films with their diverse talents. A partial list of actors, directors, and film musicians who fled Europe, at least in part due to antisemitic persecution, includes Hanns Eisler, Erich Korngold, Fritz Kortner, Fritz Lang, Peter Lorre, Max Ophüls, Luise Rainer, and Billy Wilder. A young Werner Klemperer, son of the famous conductor Otto Klemperer, also escaped Nazi Germany. Ironically, he would go on to fame as Colonel Klink, the German commander of a prisoner-of-war camp in the television sitcom *Hogan's Heroes.*

—*Cary Nathenson*

See also Aryan Paragraph; Boycott of Jewish Shops; Emancipation; Goebbels, Joseph; Hollywood, Treatment of Antisemitism in; Nazi Cultural Antisemitism; Nuremberg Laws

References
Petley, Julian. *Capital and Culture: German Cinema, 1933–1945* (London: British Film Institute, 1979).
Rentschler, Eric. *The Ministry of Illusion: Nazi Cinema and Its Afterlife* (Cambridge, MA: Harvard University Press, 1996).
Wulf, Josef. *Theater und Film im Dritten Reich: eine Dokumentation* (Gütersloh, Germany: S. Mohn, 1964).

Film Propaganda, Nazi

Despite the prominence of antisemitism in National Socialist ideology and the dominance of film as the medium of propaganda and entertainment, the function of antisemitism in film in Nazi Germany was itself remarkably limited. Of the nearly 1,100 feature films produced under the Nazis, only a handful demonstrated explicit antisemitic content, and even there, the antisemitism was often secondary to the film's plot. Furthermore, the antisemitism portrayed in most of these features was often a more "traditional" anti-Jewish sentiment rather than the ideological racism specific to National Socialism. Typical films in this category were the comedy *Robert und Bertram* (1939), in which Jews are shown as bumbling and farcical, and the melodramas *Die Rothschilds* (1940) and *Wien 1910* (Vienna 1910 [1942]), in which they appear as greedy, coarse, and conspiratorial. Such films reproduced clichéd images of Jews familiar to German audiences from centuries of satirical theater and political caricature.

As repugnant an assault on Jews as these films provided, such anti-Jewishness predated fascism and was not particular to Germany. National Socialist antisemitism, by contrast, paired such ancient prejudices with a racist strain constructed out of crude biological theories of evolution and genetics. Thus, there was often a disconnect between the modern, racial antisemitism at the core of Nazi policy and the relatively harmless, traditional anti-Jewishness deployed in many of the films. Simply put, the bias was often structurally irrelevant to the film. The anti-Jewish potential of these films was diluted further by the failure to integrate it with filmic strategies that would have supported the message effectively. The hostility toward Jews in these films resided almost entirely in the language of their scripts. The figure of Mayor Karl Lueger in *Wien 1910,* for example, told the audience repeatedly that Jews were Vienna's misfortune, but the film neglected the opportunity to reinforce his statements through editing, shot composition, musical score, or lighting.

Two films, however, were designed to translate National Socialism's antisemitic ideology to a popular audience: *Der ewige Jude* (The Eternal Jew [1940]) and *Jud Süss* (Jew Süss [1940]). After the Night of Broken Glass (November 1938 pogrom) failed to trigger spontaneous acts of anti-Jewish fury, Joseph Goebbels was determined to initiate film projects that would raise the level of Jew-hatred in the populace. In *Der ewige Jude,* the director Fritz Hippler blended staged footage shot in the Lodz Ghetto after the German invasion of Poland with material from newsreels and feature films, creating a montage that "documented" Jews as a corrupt and parasitic "race." Bogus statistics and graphics lent the film an objective, scientific tone. Contemporary evidence of the film's reception suggests that audiences were more horrified and disgusted—particularly by the graphic scenes of the ritual slaughter of animals—than enlightened about the evils of Jewry. *Der ewige Jude* was quickly pulled from distribution and considered a flop.

Despite its failure at the box office, *Der ewige Jude* is significant for employing a variety of powerful images and techniques to represent Jews as outsiders culturally, socially, and, most important, biologically. In one sequence, the film exploits the technique of fading one image into another (dissolve) to argue that all Jews inherently shared several negative traits. Each shot begins by showing bearded Ashkenazi men in traditional, eastern European clothing and then fades into images of these same men clean-shaven and wearing Western suits. The narration explains that since Jews are easily recognizable in caftans and skullcaps, assimilation is an attempt to mask their Jewishness. The images reinforce this message and add an even more important one: a Jew remains a Jew (portrayed in *Der ewige Jude* as vermin), whether in the eastern shtetl or in Berlin's middle-class salons. Furthermore, the dissolve sequence acts as a kind of visual indoctrination: the sharp observer should be able to identify a Jew regardless of his attire, country of origin, or class. Thus, *Der ewige Jude* presents its viewers a filmic epistemology as well as a methodology of racial antisemitism.

Veit Harlan's *Jud Süss* repackaged the logic of antisemitism displayed in *Der ewige Jude* into a historical melodrama that audiences adored. Very loosely based on true events from the eighteenth century, the film portrays the infiltration of the court of Württemberg by the Jewish financier Joseph Süss Oppenheimer. Süss, played with smarmy charm by Ferdinand Marian, exploits the corrupt nobility in order to expropriate the state's coffers, institute a cruel and arbitrary tax policy, and lift restrictions on Jewish residency in Stuttgart. Eventually, Süss's protector dies, leaving the court Jew at the mercy of those he cheated. Süss is arrested and hung in the town square.

The film is effective for a number of reasons. It is an arguably entertaining story, cast with some of Germany's top stars of the day (Marian, Heinrich George, Kristina Söderbaum, Werner

Krauss). The antisemitic venom, though obvious, is integrated into the film's story and strategy, rather than overwhelming it (as in *Der ewige Jude*) or seeming to stand apart from the film (as in most other features with anti-Jewish motives). Marian, a dark-haired matinee idol, played Süss as an irresistible masher, and the figure's powerful erotic gaze captured women on and off the screen (fan letters to Marian/Süss would later be offered as evidence of the film's harmlessness and even its flattering portrayal of Jews!). Marian's sexualization of the Süss figure is powerful enough to lend to his rape of Dorothea (Söderbaum) at least a hint of seduction rather than brute coercion. Ultimately, Süss is executed not for his financial crimes but for sexual intercourse with a gentile, thus highlighting the Nazis' disproportionate anxiety about Jewish sexuality and Jewish-German miscegenation. This erotic ambivalence allows Süss's character to function as both evil and enticing—qualities that propelled the film's antisemitism while pulling in audiences.

The technique of the dissolve seen in *Der ewige Jude* is more subtly employed here. At the end of a speech vowing to open the gates of the city to all Jews, Süss is shown in dissolving shots transforming from beard and caftan to a finely dressed gentleman on his way to court. The message remains that Jews change their appearance at will yet remain ghetto Jews, here characterized as greedy, malicious, and licentious. The viewers of *Jud Süss* were likely to see Jews as devilishly amorphous and yet as real and compelling—and therefore, even more dangerous—figures.

Whereas *Der ewige Jude* rages ceaselessly against Jews, *Jud Süss* counters its negative portrayal with a positive "Aryan" hero for audiences to contemplate. Faber (Malte Jaeger) embodies National Socialist ideals of Germanness: he is youthful, strident, and incorruptible. He represents the rising power of the "productive classes," the guilds and estates (his name is from the Latin meaning "to make"), and therefore, he stands in clear opposition to the bloated and hedonistic nobility represented by Duke Karl Alexander (George). Significantly, Faber models the racist lesson learned from the dissolve technique: he alone is able to recognize Süss as a Jew, despite the latter's superficial conversion. Thus, Faber is cast as an identification figure for the audience—the only ones who share the knowledge of Süss's origins because they have witnessed his on-screen transformation. In this way, racist antisemitism was taught while the audience was invited to partake of the counterfantasy of German supremacy.

Jud Süss became one of the top-grossing films of the Nazi era, boasting 20.3 million viewers alone in its first year in theaters. The film was shown to German police forces and troops in occupied eastern Europe, with the intention of inciting and hardening them to violence against Jews. All the cast members would later claim to have been coerced into participating in the film. Director Harlan was twice put on trial for crimes against humanity (in 1949 and 1950). He was, however, acquitted, and he continued to work in the film industry, as did most Nazi-era actors and directors, after 1945.

—*Cary Nathenson*

See also Caricature, Anti-Jewish (Modern); *Fliegende Blätter; Gartenlaube, Die;* Goebbels, Joseph; Hollywood, Treatment of Antisemitism in; Jud Süss; *Kladderadatsch;* Kosher Slaughtering; Lueger, Karl; Nazi Cultural Antisemitism; Night of Broken Glass (November 1938 Pogrom); Nuremberg Laws; *Ostjuden;* Racism, Scientific

References
Albrecht, Gerd. *Der Film im Dritten Reich: eine Dokumentation* (Karlsruhe, Germany: Doku-Verlag, 1979).
Baird, Jay W. *To Die for Germany: Heroes in the Nazi Pantheon* (Bloomington: Indiana University Press, 1990).
Clinefelter, Joan. "A Cinematic Construction of Nazi Anti-Semitism: The Documentary *Der ewige Jude.*" In *Cultural History through a National Socialist Lens: Essays on the Cinema of the Third Reich*. Edited by Robert C. Reimer (Rochester, NY: Camden House, 2000), 133–154.
Welch, David. *Propaganda and the German Cinema, 1933–1945* (New York: Clarendon Press, 1983).

Fliegende Blätter

The illustrated humor weekly *Fliegende Blätter* (Flying Pages) was founded in Munich in 1844, and throughout the century of its existence, it remained true to its original policy of purveying material in full accord with the middle-brow tastes of the mainstream of the German *Bürgertum* (bourgeoisie). During most of its first two decades, sales remained stable at about 10,000; in the early 1870s, it reached 20,000 and then rose to 42,000 in 1882 and to 95,000 in 1895. After reaching this peak, it gradually declined despite a merger in 1928 with *Meggendorfer Blätter,* a once-popular competitor also published in south Germany and specializing in the same kind of rather innocuous illustrated humor.

The adjective *köstlich* (delicious) frequently came into play when describing the stereotypical stock-in-trade of the weekly: students dissipating their parents' money on wine, women, and song; absentminded professors; children imitating their parents and servants their social betters; vain aristocrats and haughty officers; foolish, fashion-mad females; cute, humanized animals of all types; Germans from different regions speaking their funny dialects; foreigners with their queer, characteristic habits; and, of course, Jews of many sorts. As was the case with the social types already mentioned, none of the Jewish exemplars were considered offensive by contemporaries. It was all just "good, clean fun," including the cartoons and caricatures of Jews.

Amid the many hundreds of caricatures and jokes published by the journal, most of the "Jewish" figures belonged to the commercial professions, generally either the upper or lower echelons thereof: beggars (*Schnorrer*), peddlers (*Hausierer*), and livestock traders on the low end and businessmen, bankers, and stockbrokers on the high. In this same general category, there was a strong admixture of caricatures of colorful eastern European Jews (*Ostjuden*), many of whom were depicted while engaged in commercial pursuits of various kinds. Judging from the frequency of his appearance, the favorite Jewish type of the *Fliegende Blätter* was the *Protz* (or, approximately in English, the Showoff)—the nouveau riche social climber who had made it economically. Often the Protz had acquired the much-coveted honorific title of *Kommerzienrat* (financial adviser), granted by the authorities to philanthropists and benefactors of society. He could usually be seen in the company of his wife and son, both of whom sported the same ridiculous characteristics.

During the first dozen years or so of the weekly's existence, "Jewish" items were a marginal feature, appearing less than half a dozen times per annum; during the late 1860s, the incidence increased to about ten per year. The number more than doubled during the so-called boom of the early 1870s (*Gründerjahre*) and the ensuing years of financial and economic recession; during the 1880s and up until the mid-1890s, between a dozen and fifteen Jewish subjects made their appearance annually. But thereafter, they gradually declined to barely perceptible levels of representation, indicating, perhaps, the editors' wish to distance themselves from the new and disreputable political and racist antisemitic movements. The antisemites had developed their own aggressive graphic stereotypes of Jews and were disseminating them for political purposes, a development frowned on by the *Fliegende Blätter.*

What do these many hundred "Jewish" depictions over the years signify? At least four interpretations are possible. Such representations: (1) constituted legitimate social commentary and satire on the growth of capitalism and on the admission of Jews into German society; (2) led to the creation, crystalization, and dissemination of stereotypes that were subsequently adopted by antisemitic movements and parties; (3) provide evidence of the deeply rooted animosity of German society toward Jews; and (4) demonstrate that increasing social contact produced friction between Germans and Jews. Other avenues of interpretation are also possible. The previously noted relationship of the rise and fall in the quantity of "Jewish" items in the *Fliegende Blätter*—the house journal, as it were, of the German Bürgertum—to the emergence of political antisemitism suggests that further research is required and may arrive at more tangible conclusions.

—*Henry Wassermann*

See also *Angriff, Der;* Caricature, Anti-Jewish (Modern); *Gartenlaube, Die; Kladderadatsch; Simplicissimus; Stürmer, Der*
References
Haibl, Michaela. *Zerrbild als Stereotyp: Visuelle Darstellungen von Juden zwischen 1850 und 1900* (Berlin: Metropol, 2000).

Wassermann, Henry. "The *Fliegende Blätter* as a Source for the Social History of German Jewry," *Leo Baeck Institute Year Book* 28 (1983): 93–138.

Fontane, Theodor (1819–1898)

Along with Johann Wolfgang von Goethe and Thomas Mann, Theodor Fontane ranks as one of the three most popular German novelists of all time. He was an early supporter of the 1848 rebels, and although he later softened this stance in deference to his largely bourgeois readership, he retained the reputation of a political progressive. Fontane continues to be viewed as an avatar of cosmopolitan urbanity and tolerance and as a social critic who never stooped to polemic.

In the West, Fontane was celebrated both for his aesthetic "finesse" and sophistication and for his critical stance toward the old Prussian aristocracy. Typically, he was much more candid about the passé nature of the nobility in his letters than in his generally more conciliatory novels. The distinction between the private and the public Fontane may help explain his enduring popularity.

Yet, as Gordon Craig obliquely put it, "Fontane always had a problem with the Jewish Question" (Craig 1999, 190). He was, at least in his correspondence, unambiguously and consistently antisemitic. Despite oft-quoted assurances about the importance of Jews to German culture and reminders of the friendly treatment he received at their hands, he considered them, in the end, capable only of material, as opposed to "spiritual," assimilation. He regarded baptism, generations of German civil service, and military decorations as mere veneer that could never successfully conceal the "core Jew" (*Stockjude*). Regarding the Dreyfus Affair, he insisted that he was initially entirely persuaded by Émile Zola, but he could not suppress his conviction that the scandal unmasked the European press as a total Jewish conspiracy. If scholars have generally treated Fontane's antisemitism rather gingerly—and here, Hans-Heinrich Reuter's frank designation of the author as "bigoted" (2: 754) contrasts refreshingly with Craig's all too encomiastic assessment—the Nazis were certainly not so coy. Fontane's derogatory views about Jews were approvingly quoted in the SS paper *Das Schwarze Korps* on September 19, 1935: "They are—despite all their talent—a horrible people; not the yeast enzymes that bring forth strength and life, but rather the ugly living organisms that promote fermentation."

As with his view on the obsolescence of the aristocracy, his antisemitism was given explicit articulation in the letters but more muted expression in the fiction. His antisemitic characterizations, such as that of Frau Salinger in *Irrungen Wirrungen* (Delusions, Confusions [1888]), are sometimes dismissed as Fontane's perhaps unfortunate but otherwise justified critique of the rising middle classes. As William Zwiebel argued regarding the opposition of the Poggenpuhl and Bartenstein families in *Die Poggenpuhls* (1896), "Scorn for the bourgeoisie and antisemitism were but two sides of the same skeptical attitude towards what he saw as the coarseness and materialism that had established themselves in the new Reich" (1992, 117). Fontane defended his use of "types" in order to characterize larger social groups. But even Craig admitted that this strategy descended into stereotypes in the case of the author's critique of the propertied middle class in *L'Adultera* (1882) and his decision to make both van der Straaten and Rubehn converted Jews (Craig 1999, 190).

In Fontane's masterpiece, *Effi Briest,* mild antisemitism presents itself just three times, and each of these instances could be read as the respective character's errant view being held up for criticism. For example, in the passage where Innstetten is described as a workaholic and neglectful husband, it is suggested that his preference for Richard Wagner is linked to the latter's stance on the Jewish Question (chap. 13). Then there is Güldenklee's toast at forester Ring's Christmas party, during which the character condemns G. E. Lessing's *Nathan the Wise* as a "Jew story" that, like so much other liberal rubbish, has caused social confusion and unrest (chap. 19). But Güldenklee is a minor and comical figure, and there is no hint in the novel that Fontane actually shared this view (which he did). Finally, when father Briest expatiates on his granddaughter's future marriage prospects, he expresses the hope that if Annie must one day marry a rich banker, she can still find at least one who is not a Jew (chap. 25). Though likable, Briest is himself a comical dimwit, so even this remark might be dismissed or qualified by the context. At any rate, the novel is too complex to reduce to any one character's utterance. One encounters a multilayered, ironic structure that is thankfully at odds with the author's unmistakable antisemitic prejudice.

—*William Collins Donahue*

See also Banker, Jewish; Dreyfus Affair; "Jewish" Press; *Schwarze Korps, Das;* Wagner, Richard; Zola, Émile

References

Craig, Gordon. *Theodor Fontane: Literature and History in the Bismarck Reich* (New York: Oxford University Press, 1999).

Reuter, Hans-Heinrich. *Fontane.* 2 vols. (Munich, Germany: Nymphenburger Verlagshandlung, 1968).

Zwiebel, William L. *Theodor Fontane* (New York: Twayne, 1992).

Ford, Henry (1863–1947)

Henry Ford ranks as the foremost purveyor of antisemitism in the United States. Biographers have spilled ink on hundreds of pages trying to understand the sources and meaning of Ford's hatred for Jews, but with few direct sources to reveal his thoughts and motives, they have had to rely largely on inductive speculation. What is known concretely is that Ford was first to circulate the *Protocols of the Elders of Zion* to a mass audience in the United States, a feat he accomplished through his newspaper, the *Dearborn Independent,* and by publishing articles based on the *Protocols* as a set of pamphlets entitled *The International Jew: The World's Foremost Problem.* By neglecting to copyright the pamphlets, he gave license to hatemongers all over the globe to disseminate the *Protocols* under his name, thereby significantly increasing its historical and philosophical credibility.

Most historians and biographers agree that World War I made overt what previously had been only latent for Ford—a tendency to blame Jews for things he found repugnant. Profiteering, media coverage of his pacifist crusade, and international diplomacy all seemed to him to be unduly influenced or conducted by Jews. During the war, the press criticized Ford harshly for the first time in his career for the failed "Peace Ship" voyage of 1915 and then for the mistaken report that the Ford Motor Company would not reemploy U.S. reservists deployed to Mexico. Public humiliation and his evident loss of popularity crystalized Ford's unsystematic prejudices into a sharp, focused conviction.

After the war, Ford used his manufacturing organization to finance and disseminate his antisemitic views. His enormous resources enabled him to carry out his public program of antisemitic attacks while keeping his own role sufficiently ambiguous to deflect attempts to hold him legally responsible.

The *Dearborn Independent's* content and management reflected Ford's increasingly narcissistic worldview. The *Independent* allowed him to communicate directly with the American public, free from what he complained was Jewish control of the mass media. Ford sought to staff the newspaper with men whose primary credentials were shared prejudices and absolute loyalty to their employer. When the *Independent's* first editor objected to the paper's increasingly antisemitic content, he was swiftly replaced by William J. Cameron, a former Detroit reporter and Ford Motor Company public relations official. It was under the compliant Cameron's watch that the paper became the platform for broadcasting Ford's antisemitic convictions by means of the *Protocols.*

During the 1920s, the *Independent* ran two series of articles that appropriated passages from the *Protocols* and interpreted them in light of recent world and national events. The first series (from May 1920 to January 1922) provoked harsh public criticism. Establishing a pattern of timely intervention to protect his boss, Ernest G. Liebold, Ford's secretary, turned away all critics with an ingenuous recommendation that they keep reading the paper because, he hinted, it would soon produce additional compelling evidence. The protests of the prominent attorney and president of the American Jewish Committee, Louis Marshall, drew only an unsigned letter on newspaper stationery calling him a Bolshevist and implying that he, too, was simply part of the

Photo shows Aaron Sapiro (left) and his attorney, William H. Gallagher, at the opening session of Sapiro's million-dollar libel suit against Henry Ford. This suit had its inception in a series of articles published in Ford's *Dearborn Independent.* (Bettmann/Corbis)

conspiracy. Ignoring public and media reaction, Ford continued his antisemitic campaign, with the Ford Motor Company entirely subsidizing the venture's considerable losses.

Marshall's exchange with Ford's newspaper touched off intense discussions among Jewish Americans all over the country. Though deeply troubled by the *Independent's* campaign, they expressed conflicting views about how (and whether) to respond. One approach, favored by Marshall, was to avoid direct and public confrontations with Ford personally, refrain from engaging the claims in the *Independent,* and instead focus the debate on the discredited *Protocols.* This view prevailed at a meeting of Jewish organizations in New York in October 1920, when leaders momentarily united against their common foe to endorse a statement written by Marshall that exposed the falsity of the *Protocols.*

Another less public approach, advocated by Ford's former neighbor Rabbi Leo M. Franklin, was to ask Jews whom Ford trusted to approach the automaker personally. Franklin and other Jewish leaders believed they had to strike a careful balance between a dignified defense and anything that might be taken as an implicit admission of guilt. As a result, they decided not to file suit or to support any independent investigation into Ford's allegations.

Yet others believed that forcing Ford to submit to the law was the only proper response to the personal damage caused by the *Independent's* libels. Many Jews, fearing a negative response from the public, opposed the use of lawsuits to fight discrimination generally, but in the case of Ford, this approach ultimately proved the most effective in eliciting a response from the man himself. Several Jews named in the paper filed lawsuits. One suit filed in New York by the author and diplomat Herman Bernstein produced an attachment against Ford that proved impossible to execute because the automaker stayed out of that state's jurisdiction. Another eventually led to a dramatic legal showdown.

The *Independent's* second antisemitic series attacked the work and legal conduct of Jewish lawyer Aaron Sapiro, who had gained fame through his work organizing farmers' marketing cooperatives with the economic powers of business corporations. In a twenty-article campaign, the *Independent* depicted this development as the implementation of plans to be found in the *Protocols.* "Jewish Exploitation of Farmers' Organizations," proclaimed one headline. Not only did the paper allege that Sapiro was part of a Jewish conspiracy to place U.S. agriculture under the control of Jewish speculators and financiers, it also claimed that he committed legal malpractice and defrauded his clients. Disregarding the counsel of Marshall and others, Sapiro decided to defend his professional reputation, his good name, and all Jews everywhere. He filed suit in federal district court in Detroit, where he could cross-examine Ford in person, a prospect he relished; he set his damages at $1 million, a sum that riveted the attention of the media. Unlike the other suits, Sapiro's grievance met the libel law requirement that false publications be accompanied by a show of malice, usually demonstrated by a refusal to consider evidence contrary to the published allegations.

Ford's lawyers sought to delay the case indefinitely, hoping Sapiro would lose heart, and then they attempted to drain his resources with expensive and prolonged pretrial discovery. Sapiro remained undeterred. The case finally proceeded to trial in March 1927, with one major source of drama: would Ford testify? During nearly four weeks of hostile cross-examination, Sapiro bested Ford's attorney, U.S. senator James A. Reed, in a performance that also won Sapiro a decided victory in the court of public opinion. Ordered by the judge to appear, Ford was promptly involved in a mysterious automobile accident and hospitalized. Sapiro then demanded that the judge appoint an independent official to determine Ford's condition and force him to appear if healthy. At

that point, the Ford forces moved quickly to bring about a mistrial. This they accomplished by planting an interview with a juror in the Detroit papers, after first charging that Sapiro had attempted to bribe her with a box of candy. The mistrial thus ended a bizarre series of events inside and outside the courtroom that point to at least one conclusion: Ford had no intention of ever taking the stand in the case.

Nor did he intend for the case to go back to court. Ford secretly dispatched intermediaries to Louis Marshall, requesting his services in settling the case. Marshall seized the opportunity and wrote a statement of apology, which Ford signed after it was read to him over the telephone. The apology incorporated Ford's claims that he was wholly unaware of the contents of the newspaper, that he had been betrayed by his employees, and that he was entirely repentant. The apology was greeted with such overwhelming expressions of acceptance and relief by Jewish spokespeople, organizations, and editorialists that both Sapiro and Herman Bernstein realized further litigation would be futile. Both settled their suits with Ford out of court in private agreements that provided each some compensation for legal expenses.

Marshall's goal in intervening in the case was not to serve the interests of any party to the litigation. He sought Ford's repudiation of *The International Jew.* This he got, together with Ford's promise to do all he could to revoke permission for antisemitic publishers to continue printing it. This promise proved empty. The Ford lawyers wrote desultory letters to South American and European publishers only as long as Marshall prodded them to do so. Marshall's death in 1929 ended serious efforts by the Ford Motor Company to make good on Ford's promise. *The International Jew* continued to circulate all over the world.

Ford proved ruthless in his efforts to mold the litigation to serve his interests. Interestingly, in order to end the case when and as he did, he willingly sacrificed what little public credibility he had left after a tumultuous decade of public missteps. The humiliation that Marshall hoped would serve as sufficient punishment in lieu of paying money damages appeared not to bother Ford. Indeed, on his seventy-fifth birthday in

1938, he accepted the Grand Service Cross of the Supreme Order of the German Eagle from Hitler's government, putatively in recognition of his achievements as a manufacturer and industrialist. Few contemporary observers missed the symbolism of the occasion. In his heart and mind, Ford remained obdurately unrepentant. As the Sapiro trial revealed, his strategy of evasion had proved effective. He hid behind subordinates who assumed responsibility for the injuries his newspaper inflicted, and during the endgame of the Sapiro case, he exploited the divisions among Jews to escape the authority of the legal process.

—*Victoria Saker Woeste*

See also American Jewish Committee and Antidefamation Efforts in the United States; *Dearborn Independent* and *The International Jew; Protocols of the Elders of Zion*

References

Lee, Albert. *Henry Ford and the Jews* (Briarcliff Manor, NY: Stein and Day, 1980).

Lewis, David L. *The Public Image of Henry Ford* (Detroit, MI: Wayne State University Press, 1976).

Wik, Reynold M. *Henry Ford and Grass-Roots America* (Ann Arbor: University of Michigan Press, 1972).

Förster, Bernhard (1843–1889)

An activist in the antisemitic movement in Berlin in the early 1880s, Bernhard Förster achieved considerable notoriety as the founder of Neu-Germania, a German colony in Paraguay from which Jews were to be excluded. The failure of his colonial project led to Förster's suicide in 1889.

As a young man, Förster fell under the spell of Richard Wagner, whose nationalistic and antisemitic zeal he shared. When Wilhelm Marr's Antisemiten-Liga (Antisemites' League) failed, Förster joined Max Liebermann von Sonnenberg in founding the antisemitic Deutscher Volksverein (German People's Association) in 1881, the proclaimed aim of which was to improve the lives of German artisans and peasant farmers. Förster took a leading role in preparing the Antisemites' Petition that would have essentially disenfranchised German Jews. One of the people he enlisted to collect signatures for his petition in the city of Naumburg was his future wife, Elisabeth Nietzsche, sister and later literary executor of the philosopher, whom he had first met at the premiere performance of Wagner's Ring cycle in Bayreuth in 1876. Although the petition gained more than a quarter million signatories, the Prussian government refused to act on its demands. In 1882, Förster lost his position as a teacher at a Berlin preparatory school after causing a public scandal by insulting Jewish passengers in a Berlin streetcar.

Frustrated by the failure of his antisemitic agitation in Berlin, Förster traveled to South America in 1883 to seek out land for a colony that would provide a refuge for true (read antisemitic) German patriots and the nucleus for a new, pure-blooded Germany. He was convinced that a regeneration of Germanic virtues was only possible on soil free of Jewish influence. Although he believed that the vast Russian Empire offered a more natural area for German colonization, the large Jewish presence there made such a project inadvisable. Förster hoped to divert German emigration from North to South America because he felt that Germans lost their national character too readily in the melting pot of the United States. Having identified an approximately 250-square-mile parcel of land in Paraguay as a suitable location for his colony, Förster returned to Germany in 1885 to marry Elisabeth, raise funds, and recruit followers for his new venture.

Before returning to Paraguay to launch the new colony in 1886, he published a pamphlet extolling the prospects of creating a new Germany in South America and denouncing his homeland as a "step-fatherland" that had succumbed to Jewish power. However, his colonial project failed to gain sufficient capital or attract enough settlers to become viable. Disgruntled colonists accused him of selling land he did not own, since under the terms of his contract with the government of Paraguay, he would gain title to the land only if he succeeded in settling 140 families within two years. Facing bankruptcy as the two-year deadline approached and unwilling to return to Germany as a failed man, Förster took a fatal dose of poison in June 1889.

Elisabeth Förster attempted to defend the integrity of her husband and carry on the enterprise for a few years. Despite her vigorous promotional efforts, however, control of Neu-Germania passed to a colonial company in Paraguay made up of members of various nationalities, and the colony lost its exclusively German character.

—*Roderick Stackelberg*

See also Antisemites' Petition; Förster-Nietzsche, Elisabeth; Liebermann von Sonnenberg, Max; Marr, Wilhelm; Nietzsche, Friedrich; Settlement *Heimland;* Wagner, Richard

References

Diethe, Carol. *Nietzsche's Sister and the Will to Power: A Biography of Elisabeth Förster-Nietzsche* (Urbana and Chicago: University of Illinois Press, 2003).

Macintyre, Ben. *Forgotten Fatherland: The Search for Elisabeth Nietzsche* (New York: Farrar, Straus and Giroux, 1992).

Förster-Nietzsche, Elisabeth (1846–1935)

Elisabeth Förster-Nietzsche's stance on antisemitism was largely opportunistic. She was probably telling the truth when she wrote, in 1913, that she never had negative feelings toward Jews during her childhood because "in Naumburg, there aren't any" (*Der einsame Nietzsche,* 259). However, she suppressed any misgivings she might have had about antisemitism when she married the openly antisemitic Bernhard Förster in 1885 and then backed the attempt to found a racially pure German colony in Paraguay. In defense of her late husband's colonial venture, Elisabeth railed against the "antisemites" for letting her husband down, but for her, the antisemites were simply a political faction in parliament who ought to have sent her husband financial help to save him from ruin.

Förster-Nietzsche subsequently confessed that she had simply mouthed obedience to her husband's views. "In this way, I developed into a warm defender of his colonial plans, finally even into a defender of antisemitism, which I actually found unpleasant and for which I never had the slightest cause," she wrote (*Der einsame Nietzsche,* 349). It must be noted, however, that when writing this, she was enjoying the financial backing of a Jewish banker, the Swede Ernst Thiel. She had also decided, soon after the death of her husband in 1889, that her life's task lay in acting as her brother's caregiver (until his death in 1900) and archivist, rather than as her late husband's apologist. In the financial crisis of 1922, Förster-Nietzsche lost most of her savings, as did Thiel. Within a few years, she once again switched her allegiance, this time to the National Socialist Party, correctly surmising that it would underwrite her operations at the Nietzsche-Archiv in Weimar.

Toward the end of her life, Elisabeth Förster-Nietzsche became friendly with Adolf Hitler, receiving money from his private purse. She was also an ardent admirer of Benito Mussolini. The attraction was not their politics but their power and social status. To demonstrate her support for her new paymasters, she even suggested, in her last book, *Friedrich Nietzsche und die Frauen seiner Zeit* (Friedrich Nietzsche and the Women of His Time [1935]), that Nietzsche himself would have approved of the National Socialist agenda had he lived to see it. Friedrich Nietzsche, of course, had been unremittingly hostile toward his brother-in-law's antisemitism and had virtually frozen contact with his sister after her marriage. A strong anti-antisemite, he was stung by her advice, in a letter dated September 6, 1888, not to become too friendly with the Jewish literary critic Georg Brandes because the latter had "looked into too many cooking-pots and eaten from too many plates."

Elisabeth Förster-Nietzsche did not go much beyond this pedestrian level in her antisemitism, perhaps because she never allowed herself to become fully cognizant of its destructive potential.

—*Carol Diethe*

See also Antisemites' Petition; Antisemitic Political Parties; Förster, Bernhard; Hitler, Adolf; Mussolini, Benito; Nietzsche, Friedrich; Wagner, Cosima

References

Diethe, Carol. *Nietzsche's Sister and the Will to Power: A Biography of Elisabeth Förster-Nietzsche* (Urbana and Chicago: University of Illinois Press, 2003).

Fourier, Charles (1772–1837)

François Marie Charles Fourier was a French social theorist and reformer who developed a system known as Fourierism, the goal of which was to rebuild society around small, cooperative agricultural associations called *phalanges* (phalansteries). Although he wrote no comprehensive treatise against the Jews, his socialist criticism of nineteenth-century economic and social evils included frequent attacks on Jews as economic parasites. This perspective was based on his belief that commerce, banking, and financial speculation were fundamentally immoral and the root of contemporary social ills. As such, Fourier's writings would later inspire late nineteenth-century antisemites in their economic arguments against the Jews.

Born in Besançon, France, to an affluent bourgeois family whose wealth derived ironically from commerce, speculation, and possibly fraudulent bankruptcies, Fourier eventually relocated to Paris and became an ardent critic of the mercantile life for which he was bred. He spent much of the revolutionary and Napoleonic periods in Lyon, where he witnessed firsthand the poverty of unemployed silk workers and became acquainted with many of the important social reform ideas of the day. Fourier's most important works include *The Social Destiny of Man, or, Theory of the Four Movements* (1808), *Treatise on Domestic Agricultural Association* (1822), and *The New Industrial World* (1829). In each of these works, he argued that the goal of human society should be to create a world consonant with human needs and human nature. His "System," as it was called, was meant to create a social order in better harmony with human nature, in which human desires and emotions would ultimately find fulfillment. This order organized people into agricultural phalansteries, small units in which all members would live and work together, share the benefits of their production equally, and take responsibility for the welfare of all. These phalansteries would remedy what Fourier perceived as the immorality, exploitation, boredom, and wastefulness of his world. In a way that somewhat foreshadowed Marx, Fourier criticized industrial society and the liberal economic and political theories that supported it as the source of contemporary poverty, vice, and emotional emptiness. In addition to his socialist critique of commercial capitalism, he inspired early feminists with his critique of bourgeois marriage and

family life. Fourierists attempted to put the master's theories into action by building cooperative agricultural settlements in France as well as abroad in the mid-nineteenth century.

Although Fourier himself never took direct action against Jews, his social critique was full of anti-Jewish rhetoric. He argued that the Jewish religion was responsible for all that he deplored in the Jews: their deceit, usury, concentration in professions he deemed "useless," and economic exploitation of non-Jews. He also advocated that Jews be stripped of their citizenship. In addition, one of his followers, Alphonse Toussenel, wrote a treatise inspired by Fourier called *The Jews, Kings of the Epoch* in 1845, which became a cornerstone for the arguments later developed by the influential antisemitic theorist Édouard Drumont.

—*Lisa Moses Leff*

See also Drumont, Édouard; France; Marx, Karl; Rothschilds; Socialists on Antisemitism; Toussenel, Alphonse

References

Beecher, Charles. *Charles Fourier: The Visionary and His World* (Berkeley: University of California Press, 1986).

Isser, Natalie. *Antisemitism during the French Second Empire* (New York: Peter Lang, 1991).

France (1789–1939)

The history of antisemitism in modern France is complex and ambivalent. France was the first European country to emancipate the Jews, not only in France itself but also in the vast territories conquered by Napoleon. At the end of the period considered here, the Vichy regime (1940–1944) enacted racial laws closer to the Nazi model than any European nation. After emancipation, the Jewish integration into every level of society in France was almost unparalleled elsewhere in Europe, as was most dramatically evident in France's two Jewish prime ministers, Léon Blum and Pierre Mendès France. Yet during the Dreyfus Affair (1894–1906), there were antisemitic riots in most major French cities.

The legislators of the French Revolution pushed the 40,000 Jews of France to the forefront of modern Jewish history as the first legally emancipated Jews in Europe, extending full citizenship to those who swore the civic oath and thereby renounced Jewish communal autonomy. Emancipation passed despite vehement opposition and in two stages, reflecting the ambivalence of revolutionary attitudes struggling between long-standing prejudices and Enlightenment principles. The acculturated Jews of southwestern and southeastern France were granted citizenship on January 28, 1790. The less acculturated Jews of Alsace-Lorraine and Paris had to wait until September 27, 1791.

The price of Jewish emancipation was cultural integration, with Judaism and Jewishness limited to the private sphere and individual rights deemed to conflict with Jewish communal identity. "One must refuse everything to the Jews as a nation, and give everything to the Jews as individuals," proclaimed Stanislas de Clermont-Tonnerre (in Katz 1980, 109). No subsequent regime until Vichy, whether republican, royalist, or Bonapartist, challenged the principle of Jewish citizenship, but the Jewish Question was raised anew in each succeeding period over the next 200 years.

As legally equal citizens, Jews were well positioned to ride the tide of modernization, spurred by industrialization and urbanization, which led to their integration into economic, political, and university institutions and to their progressive embourgeoisement. By the end of the nineteenth century, Jews were visible in every area of French life, especially after the advent of the Third Republic (1870–1940), to which they were zealously committed.

In response, two currents of anti-Jewish antipathy—right-wing and left-wing—emerged out of broader critiques of French modernization and the modern state. Each identified Jews as the symbols of what the critics opposed. First, a *counterrevolutionary*, conservative, Catholic tradition arose that named Jews and their purported republican, Masonic, and Protestant allies as the spirit and corrupting force of modernity and revolution. Catholic antisemites claimed Judaization advanced the destruction of the family and organic France, the true France of the peasant and the provinces. The proponents of this worldview pitted the counterrevolutionary vision of a traditional, aristocratic, hierarchical France ordered by the monarch against the France of the Revolution and its slogans of liberty, equality, fraternity,

and the universal rights of man. They sought to purge France of the corrupting influence of Judaized modernity that they identified with materialism, commerce, the stock market, industry, and the city—worst of all, Paris, where so many Jews were now centered; it was deemed a Babylon of vice and decadence, crime, unbelief, immigration, and cosmopolitanism.

The second trend of thought hinged on the socialist critique of industrialization and capitalism that created a new aristocracy of money. Its origins date from the July Monarchy (1830–1848), when Louis Philippe took the throne and the middle classes achieved new power; among them were a number of Jewish families, especially the Rothschilds, who became the new symbol of everything that a nascent socialism opposed. Although there was strong Jewish adherence to the Saint-Simonian strand of utopian socialism, the followers of Charles Fourier and Pierre-Joseph Proudhon began to identify the Jews with a new plutocracy of financial capitalism, likening them to the old aristocracy as parasites on the body of the people. The most influential socialist antisemite was Alphonse Toussenel, a disciple of Fourier and author of *The Jews, Kings of the Epoch* (1845), which argued that Jews dominated France through control over financial capitalism. His attacks on the Rothschilds resulted in a flood of pamphlets targeting the banking family as emblematic of what was wrong with capitalist modernity.

In the aftermath of the stunning defeat in the 1870–1871 Franco-Prussian War, with the amputated region of Alsace-Lorraine a perennial source of humiliation and with the firm establishment of the Third Republic on the principles of 1789, a politics characterized by *revanche* (revenge) arose on the Right that hinged on integral nationalism and antisemitism. This third variety of antisemitism fused elements of the other two strands to forge an indigenous French *racial* antisemitism. Although it incorporated elements of German racial biology, British eugenics, and social Darwinism, the French variant rested more heavily on culture and tradition than blood, more on sociological, medical, criminological, and psychiatric sciences than on "hard sciences."

The "pope" of this new antisemitism was the

muckraking journalist Édouard Drumont, who rose to prominence with what rapidly became the century's best-selling political work. *La France juive* (Jewish France [1886]) was a lengthy synthesis of socialist and counterrevolutionary Judeophobia, folk stereotypes, anecdotal evidence, and scientific theories of the day. Drumont's earnings from the book launched an antisemitic newspaper, *La Libre parole* (The Free Word [1892]), which served as the propaganda spearhead for several new antisemitic leagues that agitated for extraparliamentary solutions to France's decadence and degeneration. These leagues, their leaders, and the news organs that fostered their interpretation of French modernity formed the bridge between the Boulanger Affair (1886–1889) and the formation of the new revolutionary right-wing royalism of the Action Française.

The Action Française took form in 1899 during the ongoing Dreyfus Affair. The new mass political movements of the Right fused during these turbulent times, with antisemitism providing their most reliable bond. What started as a case about Capt. Alfred Dreyfus, a Jew on the army General Staff falsely accused and then convicted of selling military secrets to the Germans in 1894, had become, by 1898, a civil war. Long-simmering national, religious, political, and cultural conflicts broke into the open. Antisemitism now became a pivotal political weapon employed by the opponents of the Third Republic, a state the anti-Dreyfusards branded as *la France juive* and promised to supplant with a new national revolution.

The Dreyfus Affair also marked the abandonment of antisemitism on the Left and the transition of socialism into part of the democratic order. World War I saw a parallel decline of antisemitism on the Right, as all elements who opposed the Central Powers were accepted into the *union sacrée* (sacred union). In the aftermath of the French victory, there was a renaissance of Jewish culture in the 1920s. The influx of eastern European Jewish refugees before and during the war helped revitalize the Jewish community and allowed Zionism to exert a significant influence in Jewish affairs.

But these hopeful developments dissipated rapidly in the late 1920s. The Great Depression, political polarization, and xenophobia in a period of high Jewish immigration (from Hitler's Germany) fostered the fascist antisemitism of the 1930s. Fascists amalgamated the figure of the revolutionary and "the Jew," thus neatly epitomizing their dreaded enemy—"Judeo-Bolshevism." Building on the tradition of extraparliamentary agitation, a number of heterogeneous fascist groups arose in the 1920s and 1930s. All decried decadence, demographic decline, parliamentary disorder, the specter of communism, socialism, and the Jewish Syndicate. Their ultimate symbol was Léon Blum, the first Jewish and socialist prime minister, who rose to power as head of the Popular Front government in 1936. Although these diverse agitators never controlled the state, they eventually influenced the Vichy regime that installed itself after the defeat of France in June 1940. The end of the republic and the arrival of the Nazis inaugurated a sustained assault on the legacy of Jewish emancipation in France.

—*Jonathan Judaken*

See also Action Française; Algeria; Alsace; Dreyfus Affair; Drumont, Édouard; Emancipation; Eugenics; Fourier, Charles; *France juive, La;* Gobineau, Joseph Arthur de; Jewish Question; Judeo-Bolshevism; Proudhon, Pierre-Joseph; Racism, Scientific; Rothschilds; Social Darwinism; Toussenel, Alphonse; Vichy

References

Birnbaum, Pierre. *Jewish Destinies: Citizenship, State, and Community in Modern France* (New York: Hill and Wang, 2000).

Byrnes, Robert. *Antisemitism in Modern France.* Vol. 1, *The Prologue to the Dreyfus Affair* (New Brunswick, NJ: Rutgers University Press, 1950).

Hyman, Paula. *The Jews of Modern France* (Berkeley and Los Angeles: University of California Press, 1998).

Katz, Jacob. *From Prejudice to Destruction.* (Cambridge: Harvard University Press, 1980).

Winock, Michel. *Nationalism, Anti-Semitism, and Fascism in France.* Translated by Jane Marie Todd (Stanford, CA: Stanford University Press, 1998).

France juive, La (1886)

La France juive (Jewish France [1886]), a two-volume, 1,200-page synthesis of counterrevolutionary Judeophobia, socialist Jew-hatred, and scientific racism established the reputation of the journalist Édouard Drumont as the "pope" of French antisemitism. The book quickly became the best-selling political work of the century. It sold 100,000 copies in six months and went through more than 200 editions by 1900.

La France juive gathered together the themes of premodern and modern antisemitism, from Left and Right, Christian, secular, scientific, and folk sources. Littered with anecdotes, legends, rumors, and jokes, it was organized by a systematic interpretation of the history of old France in the process of degeneration as a result of the invasion and corruption wrought by the Jews, most emphatically since the beginning of the Third Republic in 1871. Advancing a conspiracy theory that also involved Protestants and Freemasons, Drumont seized on the scandals and hot-button issues that, he argued, were symptoms of French disease and decadence, the result of infection by an occult enemy—the Jewish Syndicate. He thus claimed to have unmasked the Jewish culprit in every sphere of public life: financial, political, and cultural.

The first 140 pages comprise a chapter aptly titled "*The Jew,*" which purports to "reveal the essential features distinguishing Jews from other men" by presenting "an ethnographical, physiological and psychological comparison of the Semite and the Aryan." This racial dichotomy then animates the long historical treatise on "The Jew in the History of France," which reinforces Drumont's basic thesis: "the Jew" has been the cause of every calamity the French have faced. Jews were responsible for medieval epidemics, the French Revolution, and all the destructive forces of modernity. With the rise of the Rothschilds and the reign of financial capitalism, Aryan opposition began to crumble before the Jewish assault, leading to the debacle of the Franco-Prussian War of 1870 and 1871. Defeat was contrived by German Jewish speculators, and it unleashed financial scandals such as the crash of the Catholic banking enterprise, the Union Générale (in 1882), which, in turn, sparked the economic depression of the late nineteenth century.

The final third of the first volume and much of the second is an invective against the anticler-icalism that had severed the French from their Catholic roots, thus sapping the sources of strength with which to resist the Jews and their allies. Half of the second volume is a diatribe against the decadence of the servile, immoral upper classes corrupted by *Paris juive* (Jewish Paris), the antithesis of the "old Paris" that Drumont idealized. The piece concludes with a chapter identifying the Promethean, villainous forms and deeds of "*Les Juifs*": deicide, blood sacrifice, the cult of Moloch, pornography, the iniquitous Talmud, and the spreading of Jewish disease and contagion. Without scrupling about the means, the mighty Jewish Syndicate sought to destroy "*la France aux français*" (France for the French) and to supplant it with "Jewish France."

—*Jonathan Judaken*

See also Drumont, Édouard; Freemasonry; Gobineau, Joseph Arthur de; Gougenot des Mousseaux, Henri; Racism, Scientific; Renan, Ernest; Rothschilds; Talmud

References

Byrnes, Robert. *Antisemitism in Modern France.* Vol. 1, *The Prologue to the Dreyfus Affair* (New Brunswick, NJ: Rutgers University Press, 1950).

Winock, Michel. *Nationalism, Anti-Semitism, and Fascism in France.* Translated by Jane Marie Todd (Stanford, CA: Stanford University Press, 1998).

Franciscan Order

The Friars Minor or Franciscan order, a mendicant religious order of the Roman Catholic Church, was founded when, after a sudden and dramatic conversion experience, Francis of Assisi (1182–1226) rejected his merchant family's position and wealth and embraced a life of radical poverty in imitation of Christ and the apostles. The charismatic St. Francis quickly attracted a small group of followers, who joined him in his mendicant life. They pursued poverty out of concern for their own salvation, but the apostolic model was an inherently conversionary one, and so they began working to bring other Christians to repentance and religious commitment. Recognizing Francis's potential to help address the changing needs of the Christian laity, Pope Innocent III supported him when his band of mendicants approached in 1209, presenting a primitive rule and asking for recognition and permission to preach the Gospel as they wandered. The rapid success of the new movement both reflected and further intensified the religious revival of twelfth- and thirteenth-century Europe.

Remaining firmly obedient to the church, the early Franciscans provided an orthodox antidote to similar heretical apostolic movements. Preaching to nonbelievers came to have a place in Franciscan mission as well; Francis himself tried to convert the Egyptian sultan, and second-generation Franciscan missionaries traveled as far away as India and China. For a variety of reasons, however, Franciscans did not pursue the mission to Jews that was so important to Dominican friars. Even when Franciscans became actively engaged in scholastic theology alongside Dominicans, the Franciscan concept of mission, based on the imitation of Christlike poverty and preaching of the Gospel message, was less suited to the endeavor than the Dominican style of direct confrontation and rational argumentation. An equally important factor was the strong apocalyptic element within Franciscan spirituality, particularly the influence of Joachim of Fiore's eschatology, which highlighted a critical role for Jews at the end of Christian salvation history. Traditional Augustinian toleration fit in well with Franciscan anticipation of a peaceful conversion of the Jews in God's time.

Though Franciscans remained aloof from the activities that led Dominican friars to missionary language study, an important group of loosely associated Franciscans did utilize Hebrew and Aramaic in their scholarship. Working to correct problems in the transmission of the Latin Old Testament or devising new literal-historical readings of Scripture, these scholars found the Hebrew Bible and Aramaic translations invaluable tools. The movement reached its height in the early fourteenth century with Nicholas of Lyra, whose Bible commentary made extensive use of the Hebrew Bible, Rashi's (Rabbi Shlomo Yitzchaki) commentaries, and other rabbinic texts to establish the literal meaning of Scripture. Though few in number, the Franciscan Hebraists of the thirteenth and fourteenth centuries were influential, and their work formed a bridge to the Hebraism of the fifteenth- and sixteenth-century humanists and reformers.

By the fifteenth century, anti-Jewish rhetoric made its way into the sermons of an increasing number of popular Franciscan preachers; in most cases, an imaginary, symbolic Jew stood as a rhetorical emblem of unbelief and rejection of Christ. The anti-Jewish sermons of Bernardino of Siena, for example, used the image of the Jew as usurer to prompt Christian audiences to repentance, to Christian charity, and to a return to a more rigorous Christian life.

—*Deeana Klepper*

See also Dominican Order; Innocent III; Middle Ages, High; Usury

References

Daniel, E. Randolph. *The Franciscan Concept of Mission* (Lexington: University of Kentucky Press, 1975).

Klepper, Deeana. "Franciscan Interest in Hebrew Scholarship." In *Nicholas of Lyra: The Senses of Scripture.* Edited by Philip D. W. Krey and Lesley Smith (Leiden, the Netherlands: Brill, 2000), 289–311.

Lerner, Robert E. *The Feast of Saint Abraham: Medieval Millenarians and the Jews* (Philadelphia: University of Pennsylvania Press, 2001).

Frank, Leo (1884–1915)

Leo Frank was the victim of the most notorious episode of antisemitic violence in the history of the United States. Born in Paris, Texas, Frank grew up in Brooklyn. He earned a degree in mechanical engineering from Cornell University before heading to Atlanta in 1908 to become superintendent of the National Pencil Company. Frank married Lucille Selig, the daughter of a well-to-do Atlanta family, and in 1912, he was elected president of the city's B'nai B'rith chapter.

On Confederate Memorial Day, April 26, 1913, the bloody body of thirteen-year-old Mary Phagan was discovered in Frank's factory. She had been raped. The day of her murder, Phagan had gone to receive her pay from Frank: this was the best honest evidence that the prosecution could muster. Yet through perjury and other prosecutorial malfeasance—combined with an inept defense and threats of violence against the jury—Frank was found guilty and sentenced to hang.

The main witness against Frank, National Pencil Factory janitor Jim Conley, was black (and according to the scholarly consensus, the likely murderer of Mary Phagan). One sign of the power of antisemitism in the case was the willingness of a white jury and the white public in the Jim Crow South to accept the testimony of a working-class African American male against the word of a wealthy white. Although the "racial" identity of early twentieth-century Jews in the United States was somewhat indeterminate, with Jews often seen as dark "Hebrews" and not authentically Caucasian, Frank was generally conceded to be white; indeed, his defense tried hard to play the race card, impugning Conley's integrity because he was supposedly an untrustworthy black man.

Soon, the trial's irregularities became the subject of intense public concern. Jews, northerners, and southern progressives presented a compelling argument that ultimately convinced Georgia governor John Slaton to commute Frank's sentence to life imprisonment. Thousands of white Georgians went on a rampage to protest this decision, eventually requiring the National Guard, operating under martial law, to restore order.

For many Georgians, Frank incarnated two odious and alien influences: the northern industrialist intent on exploiting child labor and "the Jew." In the words of Tom Watson, the populist demagogue who most effectively mobilized antisemitic fervor, Frank was "the typical libertine Jew who is dreaded and detested by the city authorities of the North for the very reason that Jews of this type have an utter contempt for law, and a ravenous appetite for the forbidden fruit— a lustful eagerness enhanced by the racial novelty of the girl of the uncircumcised" (Woodward 1938, 438).

The next step in the drama was perhaps inevitable. A mob stole Frank away from the prison farm where he was incarcerated, dragged him off to Marietta, Georgia (Phagan's hometown), and lynched him.

In the end, the Leo Frank case did not unleash a wave of antisemitism in the United States. The

The antisemitically motivated lynching of Leo Frank, who was convicted on flimsy evidence of raping and murdering Mary Phagan, an employee of his Georgia pencil factory. (Bettmann/Corbis)

lynching did, however, help lead to the creation of the second Ku Klux Klan, arguably the most powerful antisemitic organization in U.S. history; it also gave birth to an organization that showed Jews were ready to take up the challenge of self-defense, the Anti-Defamation League of the B'nai B'rith.

—*Robert D. Johnston*

See also American Jewish Committee and Antidefamation Efforts in the United States; Ku Klux Klan; United States; Watson, Tom

References

Dinnerstein, Leonard. *The Leo Frank Case* (New York: Columbia University Press, 1968).

MacLean, Nancy. "The Leo Frank Case Reconsidered: Gender and Sexual Politics in the Making of Reactionary Populism," *Journal of American History* 78 (December 1991): 917–948.

Woodward, C. Vann. *Tom Watson: Agrarian Rebel* (New York: Rinehart, 1938).

Frantz, Constantin (1817–1891)

Trained as a mathematician, Constantin Frantz became a philosopher, a political publicist, and a unique figure in the development of antisemitic theory. Frantz planned to unite the ideologies of conservatism, liberalism, and socialism, as well as the warring states of Europe. His federalism, based loosely on Friedrich von Schelling's philosophy, would bring together industry and agriculture and finally even Protestantism and Catholicism. For a time, Frantz was a publicist for the Prussian government, but after 1860, he vehemently disagreed with Otto von Bismarck's German and European policy and broke the connection.

Beneficiaries and instigators of this fatal political course were, he was certain, mainly the Jews. Frantz was a prolific writer, and he remained consistent in his views over the decades. His first publication on this topic, *Ahasverus or the Jewish Question* (1844), already contained many of the ideas that were developed at greater length in his *World Politics* (1883). In the years between these two works, he returned continually to the topic, most intensely in *National Liberalism and Jewish Dominance* (1874) and in *Federalism as the Governing Principle* (1879).

Frantz drew his ideas concerning the proper place of Jews from the sphere of religion; some of them seem to have come straight out his favorite time period, the Middle Ages. Although he explicitly rejected the fashionable racial antisemitism of the 1870s and even scoffed at the impreciseness of the term, Frantz thought conversion to Christianity would make no difference: "The Jews will always be Jews" (*Ahasverus,* 28). Thus, racial and religious elements were not distinctly differentiated in his theoretical universe.

In spite of his repudiation of organized antisemitism, Frantz shared many of the positions adopted by the antisemitic political parties of the 1880s. He believed that Jews should never be full citizens; that they could have no true allegiance to their countries of residence; and that they dominated the newspapers, international trade, and the stock exchange. Although he thought this to be the case all over Europe, it was most acutely so in Bismarck's Germany, which he was fond of calling a German Empire of Jewish Nationality.

For all his indulgence in anti-Jewish stereotypes, there are a few features in Frantz's system that are not typical of the antisemites in general: he was an ardent pacifist, and though he favored a European crusade to free Jerusalem from the Ottoman Empire, he abhorred the idea of a war within Europe because this would impede its "inevitable" uniting under the banner of federalism. And even though Jews would undoubtedly be second-class citizens in the Frantzian utopia—denied voting rights, intermarriage with Christians, military careers, or access to the civil service—he drew the line when he just as clearly stated that the basic human rights, including due process and the equal protection of the law in civil and criminal matters, must be guaranteed to all. In the last analysis, Frantz advocated a system of apartheid under the doctrine of separate but equal.

—*Michael Dreyer*

See also Antisemitic Political Parties; Center Party; Christian State; Dühring, Eugen; Glagau, Otto; "Jewish" Press; Jewish Question; Stoecker, Adolf; *Victory of Jewry over Germandom, The;* Wandering Jew

References

Dreyer, Michael. "Judenhass und Antisemitismus bei Constantin Frantz," *Historisches Jahrbuch* 111, no. 1 (1991): 155–172.

Freemasonry

"Freemasons control the world!" This assertion is to be found in numerous literary works that purport to reveal the powers that have ruled global events from behind the scenes ever since the French Revolution. In reality, Freemasonry is a widespread international humanitarian association that champions respect for human dignity and tolerance. It proceeds from the conviction that if trusting relationships between people of differing beliefs and cultures can be created, then human conflicts can be settled and their destructive consequences averted. In the past, Freemasonry worked for the improvement of society, and it has never directly or indirectly participated in conspiracies.

The starting point for conspiracy theories regarding Freemasons is the conviction that secret wire-pullers shape and determine political events and that the world is being directed by conspiratorial groups. The experience of military defeat, revolution, and civil conflict in the twentieth century engendered great feelings of anxiety and confusion and also produced the need to find scapegoats. These were swiftly found. Jews and Freemasons were well suited for this role because both were regarded as privileged minorities with suspicious international connections.

Also crucial to the emergence of the theory of a Jewish-Masonic world conspiracy was the position of the Jews in the medieval and early modern social order. Because Jews were held collectively responsible for the Crucifixion of Jesus in the eyes of Christians, they could not be fully integrated in a society defined by religious faith. Confined to ghettos, they pursued their livelihoods through petty trade or moneylending, occupations held in low esteem or condemned as un-Christian by the religiously delineated social doctrines of the era. These conditions favored the gradual rise of a socioeconomic antisemitism that complemented an existing Christian antisemitism.

Freemasonry's inclination toward the ideas of the Enlightenment and natural rights was seen by Christian conservatives after 1789 as preparing the way for the emancipation of Jewry. They tended to view Freemasons with distrust, as both beneficiaries and champions of Jewish emancipation. In a few portrayals of the time, it was claimed that the Jews were the "useful tools" of the Illuminati and the Jacobins who ruthlessly exploited the Jews' hatred of European governments. That such claims, when combined with traditional antisemitism, could be used effectively to provoke and channel aggression was demonstrated by the numerous documented anti-Jewish excesses.

The basic model for the theory of a Jewish-Masonic world conspiracy arose in the aftermath of the French Revolution. During the course of the nineteenth century, suspicions that the Jews were engaged in dark doings intensified to a point bordering on obsession. Social transformation and the continuing process of secularization strengthened the predisposition to see Freemasons and Jews at the root of menacing schemes.

Such beliefs became articles of faith for the elite of the Old Regime and for many clergy. Advancing industrialization, with its many casualties in the middle and lower classes, convinced the insecure and the anxiety-ridden that "jewification of the Christian State" was well under way.

Jews had come to represent many aspects of a deeply unsettling modernity. But equally important were the strong residual effects of the Christian medieval demonization of Jews that endowed them with uncanny, highly dubious characteristics. Together, these factors placed them at the focal point of conspiracy theories with antimodern and antiliberal agendas and in which they performed familiar scapegoat functions. The intimate association of Jews and Freemasons—they had become virtually synonymous—was axiomatic. Thus, Freemasons and Jews supposedly plotted the ruination of Germany by unleashing World War I and then administered the final blow with "Entente-Freemasonry," dictating the catastrophic Paris Peace Settlement. The compulsive need to expose the "inner connections" supposedly governing the actions of the Masonic lodges, capitalism, and bolshevism led to the construction of multiple conspiracy theories in the early decades of the twentieth century. The most successful of these was the *Protocols of the Elders of Zion*, which integrated a great variety of grotesque notions into a single, detailed global conspiracy scenario.

Scholars recognize in the *Protocols* the revival of a modernized version of demonological antisemitism. The "original" appeared in the book by the Russian pseudomystic Sergei Nilus, *The Great in the Small and the Antichrist as an Imminent Political Possibility*. No less a person than Alfred Rosenberg, Führer's Plenipotentiary for Supervision of the Total Intellectual and Ideological Schooling and Education of the National Socialist Party, based his anti-Freemason writings on the *Protocols*. As the manipulator of national politics and the real force stage-managing events, Rosenberg identified "all-Jewish high finance," hiding behind philanthropic and religious front organizations all over the world. To corroborate his diagnosis in all its details, he excerpted, commented on, and published his own version of the *Protocols* beginning in 1923.

In the 1920s, an ideologically tinged conspiracy theory appealed to certain sorts of people. Those who saw the traditional social order in terms of moral absolutes and whose basic outlook was deeply antiliberal viewed any challenge to their beliefs or interests as illegitimate, the work of evil minorities bent on destruction. Conspiracy theories serving this constituency cast the demonic powers as liberalism, democracy, socialism, and communism—all weapons ruthlessly wielded by Freemasons and Jews.

Historically, conspiracy theories have fed off social misery and political and economic uncertainties. Such theories serve a rationalizing function by providing a simple (and simplistic) explanation for all the existential anxieties of the moment. They reduce a complex reality to something more manageable. Obviously, they cannot function as objective tools of analysis, for their real purpose is to "unmask the enemy" and then to present themselves as political weapons in the battle against that enemy. Since conspiracies presuppose that a small minority can manipulate the great majority and decisively influence the course of events, it stands to reason that this minority possesses fearsome superhuman powers. This is why conspiratorial literature, especially that which portrayed Freemasonry as a satanic force, often bordered on the pathological. Filled with dread visions, it foretold the imminent destruction of everything sacred.

For those open to reason and research, it is obvious that Freemasonry never served as "the general staff of world revolution," nor was it ever guilty of the sins attributed to it by anti-Masonic propaganda.

—*Helmut Reinalter*
Richard S. Levy, translation

See also Ahlwardt, Hermann; Barruel, Augustin; Christian State; Coughlin, Charles E.; Deicide; Drumont, Édouard; Emancipation; *France juive, La;* Germanic Order; Hep-Hep Riots; Japan; Judeo-Bolshevism; Ludendorff, Erich; Maurras, Charles; Nilus, Sergei; Pius IX, Pope; Preziosi, Giovanni; *Protocols of the Elders of Zion;* Rosenberg, Alfred; Smith, Gerald L. K.; State-within-a-State; *Verjudung;* Versailles Treaty; Winrod, Gerald B

References

Pipes, Daniel. *Conspiracy: How the Paranoid Style Flourishes and Where It Comes From* (New York: Free Press, 1997).

Reinalter, Helmut. *Die Freimauer* (Munich, Germany: C. H. Beck, 2000).

———, ed. *Verschwörungstheorien* (Innsbruck, Austria: StudienVerlag, 2002).

Freud, Sigmund (1856–1939)

The Viennese sociocultural reality of Sigmund Freud's early youth was marked by the tension between maintaining a rigid loyalty toward the Habsburg dynasty and its strict clerical traditions and the ever-growing appeal of modern, secular, and bourgeois values that were sweeping through central Europe in the 1860s. When the Freud family moved from Freiberg (today Příbor), Moravia, to Vienna in the early 1860s, the metropolis was shedding its medieval appearance in both a literal and a figurative sense. The era was an age of wealth and grandeur in which Vienna, the imperial city of the Austro-Hungarian monarchy, and its newly rich bourgeoisie embraced a short-lived political liberalism that seemed destined to dominate Europe. The Ringstrasse era represented Vienna's rapid physical restructuring from what was once an ancient walled-city into a modern urban showpiece of neo-Baroque and neo-Gothic architecture. Along with its physical transformation, the city opened socially and politically, becoming, to all appearances, more tolerant of its Jewish population. By 1865, most, if not all, of the humiliating taxes and onerous controls placed on Jews had been lifted, and they were allowed to move freely. Great numbers of Jews, like the Freuds, moved from the hinterlands of the Dual Monarchy to opportunity-rich Vienna. Their children could now receive a secular education and gain admittance to the university.

The euphoria and rapid increase in personal wealth among Jews and gentiles alike, however, soon came to an abrupt halt with the devastating crash of the stock market on May 9, 1873. In the same year that Freud began his university studies, Vienna witnessed a frenzy of antisemitic scapegoating. In Vienna's press, Jewish bankers were vilified as culprits for the collapse. This scapegoating was Freud's first experience of a virulent public display of antisemitism, which continued to disrupt political life through the decade of the 1880s. Antisemitism reached its peak in the capital in the 1890s when Karl Lueger, the outspoken antisemite and demagogic Christian Social mayoral candidate, was finally seated by Emperor Franz Josef as lord mayor of Vienna (in 1897).

Freud's second experience of antisemitism came in this period as well and directly affected his professional life. A *Privatdozent* (unpaid lecturer) since 1885, he was nominated for a professorship by two influential colleagues, Hermann Nothnagel and Richard von Krafft-Ebing, in 1897. The medical committee unanimously endorsed Freud's candidacy, but the Ministry of Education flatly denied the promotion. Freud waited another five years before the emperor signed the promotion decree. Antisemitism also affected the new science of psychoanalysis for which he was largely responsible. So many of his early followers were Jews and so much of psychoanalytic theory dwelled on human sexuality that the movement as a whole presented an easy target for those who would disparage it as "typically Jewish."

Freud, however, faced his most menacing struggle with antisemitism as a frail, ill octogenarian. Even as the German Wehrmacht marched into the city on March 12, 1938, he was unwilling to leave the country for fear of the total collapse of his psychoanalytical organization. But just ten days later, his children Anna and Martin were arrested by the Gestapo, interrogated, and then, unexpectedly, released. More than anything else, this convinced Freud to leave behind the city and the work that he loved.

—*Istvan Varkonyi*

See also Austria; Billroth, Theodor; Emancipation; Jung, Carl Gustav; Lueger, Karl; Psychoanalysis
References
Diller, Jerry Victor. *Freud's Jewish Identity: A Case Study in the Impact of Ethnicity* (Rutherford, NJ: Associated University Presses, 1991).
Gay, Peter. *Freud: A Life for Our Time* (New York: W. W. Norton, 1988).
Grunfeld, Frederic V. *Prophets without Honour: Freud, Kafka, Einstein, and Their World.* Reprint ed. (New York: Kodansha International, 1996).

Freytag, Gustav (1816–1895)

Author of the popular novel of commerce *Soll und Haben* (Debit and Credit, [1855]), the Prussian historian Gustav Freytag represented the views of a generation of liberal nationalists in the debate over Jewish assimilation. Accused of prejudice by contemporary critics such as Theodor Fontane and charged with propagating literary antisemitism by modern academics, Freytag is a case study of the tensions within Prussian liberalism on the Jewish Question. Freytag's reputation as a liberal has been a casualty of his success as a novelist. There is no doubt that he created, in his memorable villain Veitel Itzig, one of the most poisonous stereotypes of the greedy, utterly immoral Jewish businessman in nineteenth-century literature.

Nevertheless, Freytag's real passion was history, and his cultural history of the German middle class, *Bilder aus der deutschen Vergangenheit* (Pictures out of the German Past [1857–1862]), and especially his biographical sketch of Martin Luther earned him a place in the Valhalla of Protestant historiography. *Pictures* provides the necessary context to bring his views on the Jewish Question into focus. If Freytag detected any conspiracies at work in German history, they were to be found in the machinations of the Jesuit order, the Catholic Church, and the Austrian Habsburgs. Like the Prussian middle class with which he identified, the Jews were also the historical victims of Catholic superstition, Habsburg power politics, and Jesuit resistance to progress.

To Freytag, Judaism was not so much evil as anachronistic. It was harmful only to the extent that it inhibited reason, progress, and the integration of Jews into German society. He encouraged Jewish assimilation, which he defined as largely a process of moral education into German bourgeois values. As one Jewish character in *Debit and Credit* puts it, "It is only through contact with gentiles that a Jew can acquire an appreciation of any values beyond the coarsest material ones." Freytag thus placed the burden of integration firmly on the Jewish community. Mere legal emancipation could never bring about real assimilation; a deeper change in the nature of the individual Jew was required. To be useful citizens of the new capitalist Germany, Jews did not have to become Christians, but in Freytag's view, they did need to exchange the caftan for the cravat, control their greed, and *behave* like Christian gentlemen.

Freytag did not ascribe Jewish greed to any racial characteristics or to any circumstances beyond mere historical backwardness. Far closer in spirit to Voltaire than to Hitler, Freytag was not an antisemite in the modern sense of the term. He married a Jewish woman, joined the League against Antisemitism (Abwehr-Verein), and publicly denounced antisemitism on a number of occasions. In a polemical exchange with Richard Wagner in 1869, he pronounced the process of Jewish assimilation "almost" complete. However, unlike Charles Dickens, who also created a famous Jewish villain, Freytag never expressed any regret for creating Jewish stereotypes. He insisted that Veitel Itzig and the other Jewish characters he described in *Debit and Credit* were realistic portrayals of Jews he had known. It is also true, however, that *Itzig* became a synonym for *Jew* in the Third Reich.

—*Larry L. Ping*

See also *Debit and Credit;* Emancipation; Fontane, Theodor; Jewish Question; League against Antisemitism; Philosemitism; Voltaire, François-Marie-Arouet de; Wagner, Richard

References

Carter, T. E. "Freytag's *Soll und Haben:* A Liberal-National Manifesto as a Best-Seller," *German Life and Letters* 21 (1967–1968): 320–329.

Mosse, George. "The Image of the Jew in German Popular Literature: Felix Dahn and Gustav Freytag." In *Germans and Jews: The Right, the Left, and the Search for a "Third Force" in Prenazi Germany* (New York: Howard Fertig, 1970).

Ping, Larry L. "Gustav Freytag and the Prussian Gospel: Novels, Liberalism, and History." Dissertation, University of Oregon, 1994.

Fries, Jakob Friedrich (1773–1843)

A philosopher at the universities of Heidelberg and Jena, Jakob Fries rose to prominence after the Napoleonic Wars and exerted a major influence on the newly formed nationalist fraternities, or Burschenschaften. His hostility toward Jews and Judaism was expressed most emphatically in the pamphlet *On the Endangerment of German Welfare and Character by the Jews* (*Über die Gefährdung des Wohlstandes und Charakters der Deutschen durch die Juden* [1816]), but it pervaded his writings on ethics, politics, and religion.

Born in 1773, Fries grew up and was educated among the Moravian Pietist Brethren in the Saxon town of Niesky. After declaring himself an advocate of enlightened "natural religion," he dropped plans for a theological career and dedicated himself to the study of philosophy. In 1805, he was appointed extraordinary professor at Heidelberg, where he taught for over a decade before being called to a professorship at Jena in 1816. Fries has usually been described as a neo-Kantian, although he abandoned the a priori universalist premises of Immanuel Kant's philosophy in favor of a system grounded in the certainties of human psychology. The consequences of this subjectivist approach were most evident in the realm of ethics, where Fries replaced the Kantian imperative to "act so that the maxims of your will could be the basis of a universal law" with the command to "act as you are convinced that you should act." This doctrine of "conviction" also informed Fries's conception of political life, which he believed should be based on the "republican" principles of honor, piety, equality, and public spirit. In his *Ethics* (1818), he favorably contrasted the "healthy" societies of the ancient Germans or North American Indians with what he saw as the degeneracy and corruption of the aristocracy, the Christian clergy, and the Jews.

Fries's foray into antisemitic polemics was occasioned by debates at the Congress of Vienna over granting civic rights to Jews in the German states. In 1816, the Berlin historian Friedrich Rühs published *On the Claims of the Jews to German Citizenship* (*Über die Ansprüche der Juden an das deutsche Bürgerrecht*), which declared Jews to be worthy of "human rights" but not "citizenship rights." Rejecting the logic of the gentile reformer Christian Wilhelm Dohm, Rühs argued that the supposed negative aspects of the Jews' character and livelihood were the result not of centuries-long oppression but of the Jewish faith itself, which constituted a "state-within-a-state." The only solution to this problem was for the Jews to convert to Christianity. Until that happened, they should be forced to remain separate from the Christian population, pay protection money to the state, and wear a special sign on their clothing.

Rühs's demands, harsh as they were, did not go far enough for Jakob Fries. In his review of Rühs, he insisted that no one who was unworthy of civil rights deserved state protection and that the Jews should either abandon their traditional practices or leave Germany. But for the philosopher Fries, religious conversion could only be a first step. In his eyes, Judaism was less a "faith" than a "commercial caste bound by theocratic despotism and sworn together through its own religion" (*Sämtliche Schriften,* 1996, 25: 162). Thus, he also demanded that the legal authority of the rabbis be destroyed and that Jews be forced out of occupations in areas such as finance and trade. Moreover, Jews could no longer be allowed to maintain their "physical separation" but would have to merge with the larger gentile population. Only in this way, Fries argued, would it be possible for Jews to "fuse with the Christians into a single civil union" (172). As Gerald Hubmann noted, this vision of Jewish assimilation (and self-annihilation) suggests that Fries did not see Jews as a biological race. Still, the language of his pamphlet was brutal and aggressive, with frequent references to Jews as "parasites" and "bloodsuckers" and a warning that if the German governments did not act quickly, the whole affair would end in "a terrible act of violence" (158).

Fries's fulminations sparked outrage among Jewish writers and among reform-minded officials in Germany. But they were well received by the more radical members of the Jena Burschenschaft, for whom Fries became both a mentor and a spiritual leader. The most notorious of his followers was the theology student Karl Sand, who absorbed his doctrine of ethical "conviction" and his hostility toward Catholics, Jews, and aristocrats. In 1819, Sand murdered the conservative playwright August von Kotzebue. That same year, the Hep-Hep riots broke out across Germany in an atmosphere galvanized by the tirades of Rühs and Fries. In response to these events, government authorities suspended Fries from his university position at Jena. He would not be fully rehabilitated until 1838, five years before his death.

—*George Williamson*

See also Burschenschaften; Dohm, Christian Wilhelm von; Emancipation; Hep-Hep Riots; Kant, Immanuel; State-within-a-State; Yellow Star
References
Hubmann, Gerald. *Ethische Überzeugung und politisches Handeln: Jakob Friedrich Fries und die deutsche Tradition der Gesinnungsethik* (Heidelberg, Germany: C. Winter, 1997).
Williamson, George S. "What Killed August von Kotzebue? The Temptations of Virtue and the Political Theology of German Nationalism, 1789–1819," *Journal of Modern History* 72 (2000): 890–943.

Fritsch, Theodor (1852–1933)

Eulogized by the Nazis as a pioneer of their movement and one of the few successful antisemitic publishers of the imperial and Weimar eras, Theodor Fritsch is best known as editor of the *Handbuch der Judenfrage* (Handbook of the Jewish Question [49th ed., Leipzig, 1944]) and the leading antisemitic journal, *Hammer: Blätter für deutschen Sinn* (Hammer: Journal of the German Way [Leipzig, 1902–1940]). Fritsch bridged two generations of antisemites, participating in the birth of the political movement during the German Empire and living just long enough to see Hitler take power.

Born to peasant parents in Prussian Saxony, Fritsch became a milling engineer, founded an organization for small-scale millers, and published its newspaper (in 1880); his earnings from these enterprises allowed him to finance his early antisemitic activities. He entered the antisemitic movement through lower-middle-class reform politics, helping to establish antisemitic clubs in Dresden and Leipzig in the early 1880s. In 1885, he started a newspaper, the *Antisemitic Correspondence* (Antisemtische-Correspondenz), which became one of the mainstays of parliamentary antisemitism. But Fritsch never favored parliamentarizing the movement. Earlier than most, he saw that conventional politics offered little prospect of solving the Jewish Question, a conclusion later shared and acted on by Hitler.

Viscerally antidemocratic and imperious, he had no faith in the judgment of the German masses and eventually advocated a "constitutional dictatorship" as the only suitable form for such poor material. Many of his most treasured projects were destined for the antisemitic elite and had an element of withdrawal or separatism attached to them. In 1894, he "retired" from party politics, unable to put up with the intellectual shallowness of the movement's popular leaders and their misguided emphasis on the spoken word—Fritsch himself could not deliver an effective speech. During the next thirty-five years, he devoted himself to the nonpartisan antisemitic indoctrination of all sectors of German society. Writing under his own name and the pseudonyms F. Roderich Stoltheim, Fritz Thor, and Thomas Frey, he published well over forty books and edited several more, including an early version of the *Protocols of the Elders of Zion* (1924) and a translation of Henry Ford's *The International Jew* (1922). These and his other publications were instrumental in establishing antisemitism as a legitimate part of German political culture.

In the 1880s, Fritsch developed an innovative way of financing his relentless publishing ventures, sending out half the edition of one of his works free of charge to youth groups, influential public figures, Sunday schools, and nationalist organizations; he capitalized on the interest thus engendered to sell the other half, using the proceeds to pay for a new edition. His deep hatred of Jews spilled over into denunciation of most aspects of modern culture. Contemptuous of the kaiser, the Reichstag, Christianity, education, and the press, he preached a "revolution of Germanic values" that would embrace tax reform, validation of the lower middle class as the "bedrock of the race," vegetarianism, temperance, and a return to the land. Only then could suitable legislation deny Jews the power to rule over Germans. After the 1912 Reichstag elections, which returned too many liberals and socialists, he began calling openly for "a holy Fehme of dedicated men" to kill off the leaders of a dreaded socialist revolution (in Levy 1991, 191).

Personally reinvigorated by the German collapse of 1918 and vindicated in all his direst prophecies of doom, Fritsch unleashed a new burst of activity. In the early years of the Weimar Republic, when he still hoped for its violent overthrow, he often crossed the boundaries of permissible behavior. He characterized and simultaneously justified the murder of Walther Rathenau in a 1922 article titled the "Desperate Act of a Desperate People" (in Levy 1991, 192–199). He brought libel suits against prominent men and was himself frequently sued, losing every time and then issuing long accounts of his trials that thundered against the "System" and the "Jew Republic." He overcame his detestation of parliamentary politics long enough to serve as a radical rightist member of the Reichstag (in 1924). But when the Weimar Republic seemed to stabilize in the mid-1920s, Fritsch fell back into his normal pose of despairing prophet. The rise of Hitler's movement did nothing to dispel his militant pessimism. To the resentful Fritsch, Hitler was the reincarnation of the mouthy leaders of prewar antisemitic politics, a man without political instincts who was able only to make fiery speeches to the feckless masses. After fifty years of indefatigable propagandizing against Jews, Fritsch thought his life had been wasted. He saw Germany as no closer to solving the Jewish Question than when he began. The masses, he grumbled, had learned nothing; they remained immune to serious antisemitism and incapable of the sustained effort required to overpower the Jewish enemy once and for all.

—*Richard S. Levy*

See also *Antisemitic Correspondence;* Antisemitic Political Parties; Ford, Henry; German Racial League for Defense and Defiance; Germanic Order; *Handbook of the Jewish Question;* Hitler, Adolf; Imperial Hammer League; *Protocols of the Elders of Zion;* Rathenau, Walther; Settlement *Heimland; Völkisch* Movement and Ideology; Weimar

References

Hartung, G. "Pre-Planners of the Holocaust: The Case of Theodor Fritsch." In *Why Germany? National Socialist Antisemitism and the European Context.* Edited by John Milfull (New York: Berg, 1992), 29–40.

Levy, Richard S., ed. *Antisemitism in the Modern World: An Anthology of Texts* (Lexington, MA: D. C. Heath, 1991).

Müller, Josef. *Die Entwicklung des Rassenantisemitismus in den letzten Jahrzehnten des 19. Jahrhunderts: Historische Studien.* Vol. 372 (Berlin: Ebering Verlag, 1940).

Fugu Plan

Fugu Plan is the name coined by Marvin Tokayer for schemes by Japanese military officers and diplomats to exploit Jews for the benefit of the Japanese Empire during the Asia-Pacific War. The term derives from Koreshige Inuzuka's comparison of Jews to puffer fish (*fugu*), which are considered a great delicacy in Japan but can be deadly if prepared incorrectly. In July 1939, Inuzuka, the navy captain responsible for the Jews of Shanghai from 1939 to 1942, joined army colonel Norihiro Yasue and Shanghai consul general Shirō Ishiguro to author the "Joint Report on the Jews of Shanghai." The report was developed in response to the influx of Jewish refugees into Japanese-occupied Manchuria and Shanghai. The number of Jews in Shanghai eventually exceeded 20,000.

The "Joint Report" was based on the exaggerated appraisal of Jewish power contained in the *Protocols of the Elders of Zion,* which Yasue had translated into Japanese in 1924, and it contained proposals to exploit "Jewish power" for the benefit of Japan. Jews were to be used to influence U.S. policy, to attract "Jewish capital" to the Japanese Empire, and to establish a Jewish settlement in Manchuria, where 30,000 Jews could exercise their talents to aid the Japanese war effort. Inuzuka had previously proposed that as many as 300,000 Jews be resettled. Although some desultory efforts were made by the authors to implement aspects of their scheme, including an abortive appeal to Rabbi Stephen Wise to intercede on Japan's behalf with the U.S. government, the "Joint Report" remained fantasy and never became Japanese government policy.

Japanese policy toward Jews was formulated on December 6, 1938, at a meeting of government ministers and had three basic principles: that no special effort be made to attract Jews, that Jews be expelled, and that Jews be dealt with on the basis of the same immigration policies as other nationalities. As an isolated island nation, Japan had little experience with immigration, however, and its policies were often formulated and implemented by local military and consular staff. The influx of masses of Jewish refugees to Shanghai was the result of ad hoc decisions made by officials such as Chiune Sugihara, who, on his own recognizance as Japanese consul in Kaunas, Lithuania, issued more than 2,100 transit visas to Jewish families fleeing the Nazis in 1940. Unwilling to liquidate the Jews as their Nazi allies urged, convinced despite all evidence to the contrary that Jews were powerful and well connected, and with little experience and few policies to govern their actions, the Japanese adopted a laissez-faire attitude toward the Shanghai Jewish community, which felt secure enough under their rule to develop a rich cultural life. Designer Peter Max, former U.S. Treasury secretary W. Michael Blumenthal, and former Israeli cabinet minister Zorach Warhaftig were members of the Shanghai Jewish community, which survived the war virtually intact.

—*David G. Goodman*

See also Japan; Lithuania, Holocaust in; *Protocols of the Elders of Zion*

References

Goodman, David G., and Masanori Miyazawa. *Jews in the Japanese Mind: The History and Uses of a Cultural Stereotype.* Expanded ed. (Lanham, MD: Lexington Books, 2000).

Sakamoto, Pamela Rotner. *Japanese Diplomats and Jewish Refugees* (Westport, CT: Praeger, 1998).

Tokayer, Marvin, and Mary Swartz. *The Fugu Plan: The Untold Story of the Japanese and the Jews during World War II* (New York: Paddington, 1979).

G

Garbage, the City and Death, The

Conservative historian Joachim Fest branded Rainer Werner Fassbinder's hastily written drama *The Garbage, the City and Death* (*Der Müll, die Stadt und der Tod*), a piece of left-wing antisemitism before it was even published in 1976. The charge stuck for several reasons, not the least of which was the presence of grotesque and undeniably antisemitic figures in the play. Two other factors included the general vulnerability of the Left in 1976 to charges of inappropriately confronting the Nazi past and the fact that numerous others, including prominent Holocaust survivor Jean Améry, joined in the chorus of condemnation. As a result of this outcry, the book was withdrawn, and Fassbinder was unable to raise the necessary funding to make a film out of the play. Furthermore, he refused to allow the play to be produced before his death in 1982. Ironically, then, the initial furor erupted over a play that few could have read and none had seen.

There can be no doubt—certainly, Fassbinder himself harbored none on this point—as to the play's forceful antisemitic content. The protagonist is "the Rich Jew," a rapacious, deceptive, and ultimately murderous Frankfurt real estate developer who has no other identity than this. He remains a nameless, Jewish "other" who fulfills the requirements of the antisemitic imagination. He avenges himself on Müller One, a transvestite, impenitent former Nazi who may have killed the Rich Jew's parents, by murdering Müller's daughter, the prostitute Lily/Roma B. He evades responsibility when the police arrest another likely suspect (the gentile Franz B.). Perhaps the most virulent antisemitic rhetoric is placed in the mouth of Hans von Glück, a competitor in the real estate business who expressly wishes that the

Rich Jew had been gassed during the Holocaust. Possibly more offensive still is the Rich Jew's bald assertion that in postwar Germany, he is "untouchable," a very cynical but perhaps insightful reading of some post-Holocaust sensitivities.

Antisemitism *in* the play is one thing; but is the play itself antisemitic? Fassbinder did not provide a ready-made realist perspective to "control" the play's reading, such as German viewers would get with the now famous 1979 broadcast of the television series *Holocaust*. Many critics were offended by the unsavory depiction of the Rich Jew and wished for more sympathetically drawn or more representative Jews. Fassbinder vowed never to present oppressed minorities (a category in which he included Jews) in a positive light, however, arguing that one must depict them precisely as a product of their social deformation. A plausible defense can be made by focusing on the play's formalist technique: the very artificiality of the generic "rich Jew" points to a social construct that has more to do with Germans' antisemitic imagination than the actual Jewish community of Frankfurt. Yet despite all elucidation regarding the author's experimental and nontraditional narrative technique, *The Garbage* remains, in part, clearly referential. This tension—modernist innovation versus realism—ran through Fassbinder's oeuvre and often proved very productive. In his greatest success, *The Marriage of Maria Braun* (1978), these two strands can be said to account for the film's broad appeal: the realist narrative served more traditional tastes (and depicted Germany as female victim), and the formal innovation (exaggerated use of melodrama and film noir citation, for example) could be recruited for more progressive readings.

The "realist" aspect of *The Garbage* was the

one that proved most objectionable, especially when, in 1985, director Günther Rühle chose to stage the play at last. Although several prominent German Jews supported the production, they did so with some ambivalence. The play's most eloquent proponent, Thomas Elsaesser, justified it, in the end, not as a work of art but as a "social text" capable of provoking a productive public debate. Many German Jews who had de facto assimilated to German society remained profoundly disturbed by the figure of a disreputable and nefarious Jew who was so fundamentally alien. In all of this, it is perhaps worthwhile to recall that Fassbinder never exempted himself from the phenomenon he referred to as "something like a second original sin," a relationship that bound Germans and Jews via the Holocaust and has continued to warp their relations down to the present.

—*William Collins Donahue*

See also Bubis, Ignatz; Germany, Federal Republic of; New Left

References

Elsaesser, Thomas. "Frankfurt, Germans and Jews: *The City, Garbage and Death.*" In *Fassbinder's Germany: History, Identity, Subject* (Amsterdam: Amsterdam University Press, 1996), 175–195.

Korn, Benjamin. "Shock and Aftershock." In *Jewish Voices, German Words: Growing Up Jewish in Postwar Germany and Austria*. Edited by Elena Lappin. Translated by Krishna Winston (New Haven, CT: Catbird Press, 1994), 19–37.

Gartenlaube, Die

During its heyday in the mid-1870s, the mass-circulation liberal weekly *Die Gartenlaube* (Garden Hut)—catering, as it never ceased proclaiming, to the interests of the whole family of the German *Bürgertum* (bourgeoisie)—was the most widely read periodical in Germany. In addition, it influenced the whole genre, promoting the appearance of half a dozen imitators and rivals and the introduction of family-interest supplements in many other periodicals. The *Gartenlaube* also exerted its influence on the German Jewish press.

The journal's long history falls into philosemitic and antisemitic phases. *Die Gartenlaube* was founded in 1853 by Ernst Keil (1816–1876).

He launched it as an ostensibly nonpolitical venture, soon had 100,000 readers (by 1860), and eventually reached a peak circulation of 210,000. During that period, Keil devoted much space to what Kirsten Belgum has defined as "Popularizing the Nation" (or *Volk*) to all segments of the Germany-to-be. This he did in accordance with the explicitly liberal worldview embodied in the Nationalverein (National Union), whose members championed the cause of German constitutionally based unity and whose liberal politics Keil found praiseworthy.

One not-too-subtle element of this national and social agenda of uniting the nation under the banner of the liberal bourgeoisie was popularizing Judaism in general and German Jews in particular. Judaism was praised for its family-oriented and picturesque religious practices. Works by the Jewish painter Moritz Oppenheim (1799–1882), much celebrated in Jewish circles for his kitschy depictions of Jewish family life, were featured. Articles on well-known Jewish figures emphasized their contributions to German letters, society, and state; even controversial figures, such as Ferdinand Lassalle and Heinrich Heine, also received their due. German Jews who had benefited the economic welfare of the nation came in for special attention. That he emphasized rather than obscured the Jewishness of these individuals suggests that Keil wanted to integrate Jews and Judaism—to be sure, in their explicitly liberal and bourgeois formats—into the German nation and state.

The second and longer phase of *Die Gartenlaube* followed the stock market crash of 1873. Keil allowed Otto Glagau, an antisemitic and scandal-mongering journalist who had hitherto published in rival journals, to write a series of sensationalist articles in which he insinuated that Jews had caused the crash and had benefited from it—almost exclusively—at the cost of ordinary Germans. Glagau subsequently published a best-selling brochure in which he denounced Keil for having toned down and even deleted some of his explicitly antisemitic declarations. Even with the editing of Glagau's articles, however, the antisemitism was unmistakable and, given the reach of *Die Gartenlaube*, damaging.

Glagau's sensation coincided with the cresting

of the journal's popularity. *Die Gartenlaube* published more and more articles with an expressly antisemitic coloration. But its turn to antisemitism coincided with a decline in readership. Attempts to stem the loss of circulation by fusing with other weeklies of a similar hue had little effect. A much-diminished *Die Gartenlaube* struggled on, finally folding during World War II.

—*Henry Wassermann*

See also Caricature, Anti-Jewish (Modern); *Fliegende Blätter;* Glagau, Otto; Heine, Heinrich; *Kladderadatsch; Simplicissimus*

References

Belgum, Kirsten. *Popularizing the Nation: Audience, Representation, and the Production of Identity in "Die Gartenlaube," 1853–1900* (Lincoln: University of Nebraska Press, 1998).

Wassermann, Henry. "Jews and Judaism in the Gartenlaube," *Leo Baeck Institute Year Book* 23 (1978): 47–60.

Gemlich Letter

The first preserved piece of political writing by Adolf Hitler and the first to mention the word *Jew* is the letter he wrote Adolf Gemlich on September 16, 1919, detailing his views on the Jewish Question. Hitler was then in the pay of the "News Bureau"—the cover name for a spy agency of the army in Munich—delivering civics lectures to soldiers and reporting on the German Workers' Party (later the National Socialist German Workers' Party), which he soon joined. The letter, a copy of which was placed in the army bureau's archive, most probably represents the answer to an inquiry from Gemlich that Hitler was called on to deal with as part of his duties. Doing so forced him to put his opinions in writing for the first time.

Political antisemitism, according to the letter, ought not be the product of "emotional impulse" but should instead be based on "knowledge of the facts." Like the *völkisch* (racist-nationalist) antisemites of the late imperial era, Hitler defined Jews in racial rather than religious terms. "The Mosaic faith, no matter how significant it may be for the survival of this race, cannot be the exclusive determinant of who is or is not a Jew" (all quotes from Jäckel and Kuhn 1980). Jews constituted a "non-German, alien race," unwilling or incapable of "giving up its racial peculiarities" or of adapting to the German nation. "Everything that prompted men to strive for higher goals, be it religion, socialism, or democracy, is for them only a means to an end, ways to satisfy their greed for money and mastery. As a consequence, they are the carriers of racial tuberculosis among the nations."

All these accusations, including the formulaic Jew as contagious bacillus threatening to suck the life out of the nations, were in keeping with the clichés of the *völkisch* antisemitism of Hitler's day. What is unusual in the letter is that Hitler still considered socialism and democracy to be "higher ideal values"; he would soon "discover" their connection to Judeo-Bolshevism, however.

From these general observations, it follows that "antisemitism based on purely emotional motives will find its logical expression in the pogrom. The antisemitism of reason, however, must lead to the systematic legal struggle for the abolition of the Jew's privileged status, that which distinguishes him from the other foreigners who live among us (Aliens Law). The ultimate goal, however, must be the absolutely final removal of the Jews altogether." Clearly, he was distinguishing between a short-term goal and a long-term goal. As a first step, the civil emancipation of the Jews should be rescinded. This demand made its way into points 4 and 5 of the Nazi Party program of February 24, 1920. Related measures were incorporated in points 6 and 8, denying Jews the right to hold public office and calling for the expulsion of all those who had arrived in Germany after the outbreak of World War I (primarily eastern European immigrants).

Exactly what Hitler meant by the "removal of the Jews altogether" (*Entfernung der Juden überhaupt*) is open to debate. In the context of his public oratory of the time, there is much to suggest that he meant expulsion, that is, emigration coerced by the state. Particularly persuasive in this regard is Hitler's "foundational" speech of August 13, 1920, "Why Are We Antisemites?" However, Hitler's seeming restraint may also have been the result of a prior cautioning from his army employers to proceed with utmost care when dealing with "certain matters." This, rather than innate moderation, may explain his distancing himself from pogrom antisemitism and his emphasis on legal measures to be taken against Jews.

—*Clemens Vollnhals*
Richard S. Levy, translation

See also Antisemitic Political Parties; *Culture-Antisemitism or Pogrom-Antisemitism?;* Hitler, Adolf; Hitler Speeches (Early); Judeo-Bolshevism; Nazi Party Program; *Ostjuden; Völkisch* Movement and Ideology

References

Deuerlein, Ernst. "Hitlers Eintritt in die Politik und die Reichswehr," *Vierteljahrshefte für Zeitgeschichte* 7 (1959): 177–227.

Jäckel, Eberhard, and Axel Kuhn, eds. *Hitler: Sämtliche Aufzeichnungen 1905–1924* (Stuttgart, Germany: Deutsche Verlagsanstalt, 1980), 88–90 (Letter to Gemlich).

Joachimsthaler, Anton. *Hitlers Weg begann in München 1913–1923* (Munich, Germany: Herbig, 2000), 231–235 (Facsimile of Gemlich's query, Hitler's answer, and related correspondence).

General Orders No. 11 (1862)

The Civil War was the context for the most egregious act of official antisemitism in U.S. history. On December 17, 1862, General Orders No. 11 was issued from Holly Springs, Mississippi, the headquarters of the Union army's Department of the Tennessee, under the command of Gen. Ulysses S. Grant. Signed by an adjutant "by order" from Grant, it decreed: "The Jews, as a class violating every regulation of trade . . . are hereby expelled from the department within twenty-four hours from the receipt of this order."

The incident developed from a larger issue in the war's western theater. To meet northern manufacturers' demands, the federal government authorized a limited cotton trade within those areas of the Confederacy under Union control, with the army responsible for enforcement of trade regulations. Speculation and corruption were soon rampant. As conflict increased, accusations against speculators crystalized into accusations against Jews. Recapitulating the long history of anticommercial Jewish stereotyping, *Jew* became synonymous with *speculator* in the language of both the military and civilians.

The Mississippi River, the main conduit of cotton shipment, was in Grant's command. Grant was neither more nor less prejudiced than the average American gentile of his time. But frustrated by widespread smuggling (and also, perhaps, embarrassed by his father's involvement in a legitimate cotton-trading partnership with some Cincinnati Jewish merchants), he singled out one group he could easily identify and thought he might be able to control.

In fact, the order was enforced only in Holly Springs and neighboring Oxford and in Paducah, Kentucky, where some thirty Jewish families were expelled. Paducah's Jewish leaders immediately sent telegrams of protest directly to President Lincoln and appealed to other Jewish communities and to the B'nai B'rith for help. In January 1863, Cesar Kaskel of Paducah met with Lincoln, who countermanded Grant's order.

Grant later admitted to having acted hastily. Contemporary evaluations of the incident and assessments of blame tended to reflect partisan politics, rather than attitudes toward Jews or civil rights; when Grant ran for president in 1868, Democrats publicized the order more to embarrass Grant than to defend principle.

The fate of General Orders No. 11 has registered in the annals of U.S. Jewish history as proof of the country's exceptionalism, compared to what would have been unexceptional antisemitism in Europe. Jews felt free to protest to their government, and they expected—indeed, demanded—that their grievances be remedied. The prominence of a Jewish issue in the 1868 campaign forced American Jews to begin reassessing their community's role in public life, furthering the emergence of a self-conscious American Jewish political voice.

—*Amy Hill Shevitz*

See also Armed Forces of the United States; United States

References

Ash, Stephen V. "Civil War Exodus: The Jews and Grant's General Orders No. 11," *Historian* 44 (1982): 505–523.

Isaacs, Joakim. "Candidate Grant and the Jews," *American Jewish Archives* 17 (1965): 3–16.

Korn, Bertram W. *American Jewry and the Civil War* (New York: Atheneum, 1970).

George, Stefan (1868–1933)

Stefan George was famous for the emotional intensity and formal rigor of his poetry, for his dreams of cultural purification and renewal, and, perhaps above all, for the abject loyalty he inspired in his accomplished, largely Jewish "circle" of disciples overawed by his shamanlike airs and stature. George was born into ordinary circumstances in Büdesheim, a village on the southwest bank of the Rhine. His father was a convivial, comfortably successful wine merchant, his mother a reclusive and devout Catholic. George seems to have gotten along with his parents reasonably well and then to have embraced his first opportunity to leave home in 1882 to attend the well-known Ludwig-Georg-Gymnasium (preparatory school) in Darmstadt.

The French symbolist poets exerted an early, decisive influence on George's writing. In the 1890s, he seriously considered living and working in France as an expatriate artist. But instead, he decided to commit himself to Germany and quickly developed into a cultural chauvinist. Indeed, by 1894, George's new attitude and his interest in avoiding foreign words and making the German language more Germanic had alienated some contributors to his *Blätter für die Kunst* (Art Pages), the journal that he founded in 1892 and that remained his artistic focus until 1919. Hugo von Hofmannsthal and Leopold von Andrian, two cosmopolitan-minded stars of Viennese letters, broke acrimoniously with George, for example. Von Andrian complained of George's antisemitism, although just what he was referring to remains unclear.

George had entered into a friendship with Ludwig Klages, who later became an important antisemitic thinker. But he also had begun to attract Jewish admirers. Karl Wolfkehl, Erich Kahler, Friedrich Gundolf, and Ernst Kantorowicz formed the nucleus of the vaunted "George circle." These German Jews were successful scholars and ardent enthusiasts of German culture. Yet neither George, who was one of the most widely acclaimed German poets during the Weimar Republic, nor his disciples were popularizers. Just the opposite was the case. They isolated themselves in an exclusive "secret society," energized by homoerotic attractions and a common desire to dwell in a rarefied artistic-intellectual-linguistic sanctuary.

Some critics see Stefan George as an antisemite. But on what basis do they make this assessment? There is no explicitly antisemitic content in George's poetry, and he had close Jewish connections. Nonetheless, he believed Jews to be culturally inferior to Germans. "They do not experience life as deeply as we do," he once remarked. Furthermore, he is said to have made flattering observations about Hitler and to have stated, just after the Nazis took power, "the Jews should not be surprised if I side more with the Nazis" (Norton 2002, 156).

More significant than these random comments and attributions, perhaps, is George's artistic vocabulary. His poetry celebrates autocratic "Führer" figures who would create a more Germanic "new Reich." George's enthusiasm for World War I, as well as his acidulous bitterness toward the French after it, are also sometimes adduced by those who see him as an antisemite. They argue that George conferred cultural legitimacy on themes, terms, and ideas that comprised core elements of Nazi political discourse. That is why some influential Nazis, for example, Ernst Bertram, publicly claimed George as their spiritual "prophet." In addition, Joseph Goebbels created the George Prize for literature in 1934. Yet unlike other highbrow seekers of Germanic renewal, such as Martin Heidegger, George never formally supported the Nazis, and he was clearly put off by the very prospect of having to join an organization that he had not designed and did not control. As Walter Benjamin put it just after George's death, "If ever God has punished a prophet by fulfilling his prophecy, then that is the case with George" (in Adorno 1994, 416).

—*Paul Reitter*

See also Austria; Benn, Gottfried; Goebbels, Joseph; Nazi Cultural Antisemitism; Weimar
References
Adorno, T., ed. "Lettter to Gershom Scholem, June 16, 1933" in *The Correspondence of Walter Benjamin.* (Chicago: University of Chicago Press, 1994.
Landmann, Edith. *Gespräche mit Stefan George* (Düsseldorf, Germany: Helmut Küpper, 1963).

Norton, Robert. *Secret Germany: Stefan George and His Circle* (Ithaca, NY: Cornell University Press, 2002).

German Big Business and Antisemitism (1910–1945)

By most indicators, Jews and Jewish-owned firms were well-represented in the upper ranks of German industry and finance prior to World War I, but this presence decreased during the Weimar Republic. Antisemitic attitudes surged in Germany in the 1920s, yet they appear to have played only an episodic part in the decline of the Jews' role. Rather, the downward trend resulted from (1) the falling birthrate of the German Jewish population, which led to a steady drop both in the percentage of Jews in the German citizenry after 1880 and in their absolute numbers after 1910 and to a rising average age level, and (2) economic developments that eroded the fortunes of family-owned or family-led firms and/or aborted the careers of veteran managers—notably, the hyperinflation of the early 1920s, the merger wave that followed, and the Great Depression. One consequence was that during Hitler's rise to power, most leading German entrepreneurs gave little credence to and saw little to gain from Nazism's charges that the nation's economy had become "Jewified" and could be improved by driving Jews from it. In fact, many Germans in big business had strong personal feelings to the contrary, having served with Jews in the war, rubbed elbows with them professionally, and found them loyal and cooperative in cartels and interest groups; many also had familial experience with intermarriage.

Nevertheless, certain strains of antisemitism persisted and even gained strength in German business circles as the Nazi Party ascended. The first among these was rooted in irritation at the prominence, both real and exaggerated, of Jews among the political opponents and intellectual critics of capitalism in the turbulent aftermath of World War I. The second fed on the discomfort caused by the arrival in Germany of some 100,000 largely traditionalist Jews from eastern Europe between 1917 and 1925. The result was a fateful ambivalence among corporate leaders in the face of Nazi racism. Opposed to infringements on the rights and livelihoods of people like themselves, German corporate executives were often receptive to restrictions on those Jews whose beliefs or customs challenged their own.

Once Hitler achieved power, even this selective form of solidarity collapsed. As the Nazis began pushing Jews from German economic life, the boards of most major banks, industries, and interest groups generally gave in, though sometimes haltingly, to demands to retire or dismiss most of their Jewish officers and employees. Such appeasement did not go unchallenged—among the famous magnates who opposed or tried to limit the persecution were Carl and Robert Bosch, Carl-Friedrich von Siemens, and, most eloquently, Georg von Müller-Oerlingshausen and Emil Kirdorf. But for the most part, corporate leaders concluded that discretion was the better part of valor. "The interests of the firm" usually argued for compliance, and abandoning one's Jewish colleagues seemed a small price to pay, however regretfully, in order to signal an enterprise's willingness to serve the New Germany and thus perhaps to deflect the Nazis from their more radical economic proposals.

In the years prior to World War II, as German firms adjusted to the state-directed economy of the Third Reich, they found increasing material reasons to cooperate in the persecution of the Jews. Antisemitism grew apace, even if distress over its application to old friends and colleagues remained. Participation in takeovers of Jewish-owned property at ever more advantageous prices brought rewards that otherwise might have fallen to competitors, demonstrated the ability of private enterprise to perform the nation's work, and enabled aggressive individuals to enrich themselves and build reputations.

After 1939, the abandonment of moral inhibitions toward Jews became virtually complete, and increasing cruelty directed at those caught in corporate sights in occupied Europe was only encouraged by their foreignness and the degradation to which the Third Reich reduced them, as well as by the effects of years of Nazi propaganda. Now, Jews' positions, assets, and even their persons devolved in the eyes of most German managers to mere factors of production, which could be used up like any other. Only a handful of business leaders showed any compunction about the use of Jewish slave laborers, when or wherever other workers were unavailable. Most German enterprises exhibited, moreover, a mounting readiness to extract every last portion of productivity from the laborers they had been allotted in order to offset the costs that using them entailed, such as payments per head to the SS and outlays for guards and barracks.

In the end, the historical record of the attitudes and behavior of the big business community toward Jews before and after 1933 suggests that antisemitic feeling may have been less a cause than an effect of the cruelty these executives meted out. Over time, they adopted the ideology that legitimated the conduct they thought their economic interests required. And for many years after 1945, the persistence of that ideology—along with considerable measures of amnesia, excuse making, and self-pity—contributed powerfully to the universal resistance of German business leaders to making restitution or paying compensation to those whose lives their actions had devastated.

—*Peter Hayes*

See also Aryanization; Judeo-Bolshevism; National Socialist German Workers' Party; Nazi Legal Measures against Jews; *Ostjuden;* Weimar

References

Fischer, Albert. *Hjalmar Schacht und Deutschlands "Judenfrage"* (Cologne, Germany: Böhlau, 1995).

Hayes, Peter. "State Policy and Corporate Involvement in the Holocaust." In *The Holocaust and History: The Known, the Unknown, the Disputed, and the Reexamined.* Edited by Michael Berenbaum and Abraham J. Peck (Bloomington: Indiana University Press, 1998), 197–218.

———. "Industry under the Swastika." In *Enterprise in the Period of Fascism in Europe.* Edited by Harold James and Jakob Tanner (Aldershot, UK: Ashgate, 2002).

Mosse, W. E. *The German-Jewish Economic Elite, 1820–1935* (Oxford: Clarendon Press, 1987).

———. *Jews in the German Economy* (Oxford: Clarendon Press, 1987).

Turner, Henry Ashby. *German Big Business and the Rise of Hitler* (New York: Oxford University Press, 1985).

German Democratic Republic (East Germany)

Founded in 1949 as the antifascist, socialist German state, the German Democratic Republic (GDR) was plagued by semiofficial antisemitism throughout its forty-year history. Despite the shared experience of persecution under the Nazis, many Communists in East Germany, governing through the Socialist Unity Party of Germany, or SED (Sozialistische Einheitspartei Deutschland), exhibited marked antisemitic and anti-Zionist tendencies.

Communists, predicating their hold on power on the claim to be the primary victims of Nazi persecution, felt threatened by the presence of the East German Jewish community, which vocally demanded support and reparations for the Holocaust. Moreover, the leader of the community from 1946 to 1953, Julius Meyer, was active in the SED and politicized the Jewish community. Support for Jewish demands, most notably reparations, became a point of contention in internal SED power struggles. Those Communists who had spent the war years with the Stalinist leadership in Moscow, including Walter Ulbricht, opposed reparations and used the issue to exclude their opponents from the ruling elite, including non-Jewish Politburo member Paul Merker, who had spent the war years in Mexico City (where he had ties to German Jewish refugees).

In December 1952, following a purge of Jews from the Czechoslovak Communist Party—most notably the party's first secretary, Rudolf Slánský—Ulbricht and his allies in the SED used supposed support for Israel and ties to the United States as a pretext to remove Merker and many Jewish Communists from public life. The high point of the purge coincided with the Doctors' Plots in the Soviet Union, and many leading Jews in the GDR fled to the West at the time. Although the worst persecution of the Jewish community ceased after Stalin's death in March 1953, the regime refused to offer reparations for Holocaust survivors or provide even minimal support to the Jewish community.

Following Soviet policy, many in the SED initially supported the establishment of a Jewish state in Palestine, but that support disappeared as the Soviet bloc came to support the Arab states in the Middle Eastern conflict. Official policy regarded (social democratic) Israel merely as a capitalist lackey of the United States. Espionage on behalf of the United States and Israel was one of the charges leveled at Slánský and other victims of Stalinist show trials in the early 1950s. Despite their experience under the Nazis, "antifascist" East German Communists made no effort to moderate the virulent antisemitism of their Soviet or Arab allies.

During the Six Days' War of 1967, East German officials compared Israel to Nazi Germany and regarded the Middle Eastern conflict as one against "Hebraic social-fascism" and the "spear point of US imperialism." Some historians, including Jeffrey Herf and Michael Wolffsohn, regard the GDR as essentially antisemitic. They claim that anticapitalism and anti-Zionism utilized anti-Jewish stereotypes and a preexisting basis of Marxist hostility toward religion as societal factors. Others, including Angelika Timm, differentiate between hostility toward Israel and domestic antisemitism. Unlike Poland, for example, East Germany did not overtly persecute its own Jewish citizens in 1967.

In 1973, the Palestine Liberation Organization (PLO) opened a bureau (later considered an embassy) in East Germany—the first in the Soviet bloc—and the GDR began to supply the PLO with arms and training. Two years later, the GDR voted for UN Resolution 3379, which equates Zionism with racism.

In 1987, seeking support for the weakening regime, SED leader Erich Honecker adopted a conciliatory tactic in dealing with foreign Jewish groups. In November 1989, after the fall of the Berlin Wall, the GDR began talks with the World Jewish Congress regarding reparations for the Holocaust. The East German government was not suddenly philosemitic; rather, it cynically hoped to shore up its international image and to gain the sympathy of the U.S. government by winning the favor of American Jews. The only democratically elected East German parliament, in office from March to October 1990, acknowledged both German responsibility for the Holocaust and the existence of antisemitism in the GDR.

Although the SED dominated the East German state, the GDR was officially a multiparty polity, and many former Nazis and Nazi sympathizers in East Germany found a political home in the Nationaldemokratische Partei Deutsch-

lands (National Democratic Party of Germany). Since German reunification, there has been a dramatic increase in extreme right-wing political activity in the eastern regions of Germany, although most of the physical violence has been directed against foreigners rather than German Jews. Nationalist, right-wing political parties have enjoyed success in local and state elections.

—*Jay Howard Geller*

See also Anti-Zionism in the USSR; Doctors' Plot; Germany, Federal Republic of; Slánský Trial; Socialists on Antisemitism; Stalin, Joseph

References

Fox, Thomas C. *Stated Memory: East Germany and the Holocaust* (Rochester, NY: Camden House, 1999).

Geller, Jay Howard. "Representing Jewry in East Germany, 1945–1953: The Jewish Community between Advocacy and Accommodation," *Leo Baeck Institute Year Book* 47 (2002), 195–214.

Herf, Jeffrey. *Divided Memory: The Nazi Past in the Two Germanys* (Cambridge, MA: Harvard University Press, 1997).

Wolffsohn, Michael. *Eternal Guilt? Forty Years of German-Jewish-Israeli Relations* (New York: Columbia University Press, 1993).

German Eastern Marches Society

One of many patriotic societies of imperial Germany, the German Eastern Marches Society (Deutscher Ostmarkenverein) focused its energies on the so-called Polish Question in the Prussian East. Although it advocated harsh anti-Polish measures, the society maintained a more ambivalent and flexible attitude toward Germany's Jews.

Ferdinand von Hansemann, Hermann Kennemann, and Maj. Heinrich von Tiedemann, prominent German nationalists from the eastern Prussian province of Poznania, founded the German Eastern Marches Society in November 1894; the organization was often referred to as the H-K-T Society and its members as *Hakatisten* because of the initials of its three primary backers. The goal of the society was to defend German interests wherever and whenever they were threatened by "the Pole" and to expand, strengthen, and solidify the German presence in the eastern provinces. The organization sought to mobilize the national loyalties of Germans in the region in support of harsher policies against

Prussian Poles—for example, the Germanization of schools and place names, economic aid for resident Germans, and the settlement of Germans in the provinces.

Although many nationalists, such as the members of the Pan-German League, viewed Jews as the cultural, religious, and national "Other," the statutes of the Eastern Marches Society did not exclude their membership. On the contrary, the society recognized the utility of Jews for the German cause in the Prussian East, reaffirming the Germanness of Jews, if only for pragmatic reasons. It was clear to the leaders of the society that a strong German presence in the eastern provinces required an alliance with the region's Jews, precisely because Jews represented a crucial—loyal, wealthy, and dynamic—part of the German population, particularly at election time. To ensure that the Jews maintained a German presence in the eastern provinces, the society admonished its members to reject antisemitism. Tiedemann repeatedly called for a fight against antisemitism whenever it surfaced, describing Jews as a pillar of Germandom. The Eastern Marches Society's condemnation of antisemitism was motivated primarily by politics and demography: with Jewish support at the polls, Germans would be able to stave off Polish advances. Jews would not support antisemitic candidates, however, and antisemitism might have forced them to leave the region, rendering German candidates vulnerable to defeat by a united Polish voting bloc.

Despite the Eastern Marches Society's professed nonconfessionalism and public condemnation of antisemitism, there were antisemites among its leaders and members. Yet antisemitism did not become a prominent feature of the society's ideology in the way that typified radical nationalist organizations elsewhere in the Reich. At least, this was the case until the loss of the eastern territories following World War I, when the society ceased practicing restraint on the Jewish Question and incorporated a discourse of scientific racism into its ideology.

—*Elizabeth A. Drummond*

See also Antisemitic Political Parties; Pan-German League; Poland; Racism, Scientific

References

Drummond, Elizabeth A. "On the Borders of the Nation: Jews and the German-Polish National Conflict in Poznania, 1886–1914," *Nationalities Papers* 29, no. 3 (2001): 459–475.

Grabowski, Sabine. *Deutscher und polnischer Nationalismus: Der deutsche Ostmarken-Verein und die polnische Straz, 1894–1914* (Marburg, Germany: Verlag Herder-Institut, 1998).

German National People's Party

The German National People's Party, or Deutschnationale Volkspartei (DNVP), was the most important conservative political organization of the Weimar Republic. Established in 1918, the DNVP traced its roots to the pre–World War I political Right. During the Weimar years, the party divided into two factions: a moderate wing that grudgingly accepted the republican constitution and was willing to cooperate with other parties in the German parliament and a reactionary wing that sought to replace democracy with an authoritarian form of government.

The DNVP, whose adherents were often referred to as the Nationalists, was one of numerous political parties organized in the months following the collapse of the German monarchy. Composed of industrialists, monarchists, members of the nobility, middle-class nationalist liberals, and lower-middle-class antisemites, the DNVP sought to widen its essentially elitist electoral base by appealing to the broadly defined middle class. In spite of its efforts, the party remained relatively small, although it did win 20.5 percent of the vote in the 1924 Reichstag elections. Thereafter, however, support eroded, and the party won only 8 percent of the vote in the Weimar Republic's last election. From 1918 to 1924, the Nationalists openly opposed Germany's democratic institutions, yearning for a Hohenzollern restoration. In the Reichstag, they aggressively opposed the Versailles Treaty and the obligations imposed by the victors. The Nationalists defiantly demanded that the government refuse to pay reparations and that Germany rearm as quickly as possible.

The party also perpetuated the antisemitic rhetoric typical of the imperial era. To the "real" antisemites further to the Right, this sort of antisemitism "in kid gloves" had become totally inadequate. Hitler, for instance, thought the Nationalists were demagogic rather than sincerely antisemitic and that they were only willing to fight for their own narrow economic interests. Their shopworn antisemitism was trotted out only at election time. Suspicions regarding their seriousness in the matter of the Jewish Question were confirmed when moderates gained control of the party, a process accelerated by the murder of Walther Rathenau (in 1922) and entailing the expulsion of several radical antisemites.

In the mid-1920s, the DNVP was an uneasy participant in a number of coalition governments. In October 1928, however, media mogul Alfred Hugenberg led a revolt of the party's right wing, and he became the new chairman. Under Hugenberg's leadership, the Nationalists moved swiftly rightward, openly denouncing the moderate policies of the previous four years and adopting a more radical brand of political antisemitism. In 1929, the DNVP was at the forefront of the opposition to the Young Plan, under which Germany agreed to a new schedule of reparations payments. Given its unimposing electoral base and its inability to reach the masses directly, the DNVP made room for the Nazis in the campaign against the Young Plan, hoping to exploit Hitler's popularity with certain elements of the middle class and, perhaps inadvertently, giving him more political legitimacy than he had been able to gain on his own. Although Hugenberg and the party leadership had misgivings about Hitler's economic and social radicalism, they found nothing to object to in his extremist antisemitism. In the end phase of the republic, it was often difficult to distinguish between Nazi and DNVP Jew-hatred.

The DNVP was at the center of the conservative movement throughout the Weimar years. Despite the moderate interlude, the party, representing the propertied and educated German elite, did nearly as much as the Nazis to destroy Weimar democracy.

—*Russel Lemmons*

See also Antisemitic Political Parties; German Racial Freedom Party; Hitler, Adolf; Hugenberg, Alfred; National Socialist German Workers' Party;

Pan-German League; Pudor, Heinrich; Rathenau, Walther; Weimar

References
Baranowski, Shelley. *The Sanctity of Rural Life: Nobility, Protestantism, and Nazism in Weimar Prussia* (New York: Oxford University Press, 1995).
Hertzman, Lewis. *DNVP: Right-Wing Opposition in the Weimar Republic* (Lincoln: University of Nebraska Press, 1963).

German National White Collar Employees Association (1893–1934)

Around the turn of the twentieth century, the number of commercial clerks in Germany increased dramatically: only 468,591 in 1895, the total number rose to 835,303 by 1907. The clerks' harsh working conditions led to the founding of numerous unions. Among them, the German White Collar Employees Association (Deutscher Handlungsgehülfen-Verband zu Hamburg), founded on September 2, 1893, was an exception because it combined sociopolitical demands with a strong antisemitic and anti–Social Democratic agenda. From its inception, it was closely allied to the antisemitic German Social Party (Deutschsoziale Partei). After a faltering start, the union intensified its propaganda effort and tellingly renamed itself the *German-National* White Collar Employees Association (Deutschnationaler Handlungsgehilfen-Verband [DHV]). Replacing the neutral *German* with *German-National* advertised the intensification of the group's antisemitic component and emphasized its separation from liberal and Social Democratic commercial associations.

On so-called White-Collar Days, combining lectures and sociable entertainment, the union promoted its economic demands and its "spiritual" goals, among them the educating of members to become "healthy national men." Jews were denied membership. The centrality of nationalism in the DHV outlook can be explained by the class-based thinking of the union's leaders, who saw proletarianization as the greatest danger facing the clerks. Although their actual working conditions and incomes hardly differed from those of the proletariat, they considered themselves "brain-workers" and identified themselves with the middle class. This status-consciousness reinforced the members' German nationalism and expressed itself politically in fighting against *international* socialism. But the clerks felt equally threatened by high finance, big business, and "unproductive capital"—all typified by the stereotypical "greedy Jewish capitalist."

Antisemitism was a distinguishing characteristic of the DHV and apparently helped recruit membership, strengthening the organization's political influence. In addition to its connection to the German Social Party, the DHV further embedded itself in the *völkisch* (racist-nationalist) movement through contacts with the German League (Deutschbund), the Pan-German League, and the Imperial Hammer League.

In 1911, the association entered a second phase, heralded by the resignation of its scandal-plagued chairman, Wilhelm Schack, and his replacement by Hans Bechly, who declared the union's political neutrality and withdrew it from völkisch politics and alliances. Bechly threw in with the Christian (nonsocialist) trade unions, which promoted the white-collar workers' economic and social interests without recourse to antisemitism or racist ideology.

But World War I led the DHV back to its original formula for success with a new wave of "*völkisch* educational work." Its Fichte Society of 1916, organized to promote racist and patriotic aims, gravitated toward Wilhelm Stapel, representative of a less extreme form of antisemitism that he, with the associations's help, popularized in conservative, nationalist, and Protestant circles. The DHV established its own Hanseatic Publishing Institute, an extraordinarily successful propaganda instrument that enhanced the impact of the union's already numerous professional publications. Following World War I, the DHV, in order to preserve its political influence in the democratic environment of the Weimar Republic, joined again with the Christian trade unions. The alliance precluded public espousals of a radical völkisch or antisemitic nature. But these sentiments were kept alive within the organization by means of elite groups, such as the Faithful Followers' Circle. The party leadership preferred to exercise its political options in the Protestant and nationalist milieu by means of the right-of-center and conservative parties. But in the later stages of the republic, DHV rank-and-file members clearly preferred the National Socialist German Workers' Party (NSDAP). In 1931 and 1932, the leadership made an abortive attempt to win Hitler over to the union's goals and to engineer a coalition of the Catholic Center Party (Zentrum) and the NSDAP.

Hitler's takeover in 1933 was, at first, effusively welcomed by the DHV, whose members felt certain that their own ideological and social demands would now be achieved. The white-collar workers, however, had not paid close enough attention to the socially retrograde and antiunion line of the NSDAP. The DHV was swiftly "coordinated," that is, forced into the German Labor Front. On February 20, 1934, a year after Hitler assumed power, the DHV was dissolved and its 400,000 members transferred into the Nazi unified trade union.

—*Alexandra Gerstner*

See also Antisemitic Political Parties; Capital: Useful versus Harmful; German National People's Party; Hugenberg, Alfred; Imperial Hammer League; Lange, Friedrich; National Socialist German Workers' Party; Pan-German League; *Völkisch* Movement and Ideology; Weimar

References
Edmonson, Nelson. "The Fichte Society: A Chapter in Germany's Conservative Revolution," *Journal of Modern History* 38 (1966): 161–180.
Hamel, Iris. *Völkischer Verband und nationale Gewerkschaft: Der Deutschnationale Handlungsgehilfen-Verband 1893–1933* (Frankfurt am Main, Germany: Europäische Verlagsanstalt, 1967).

German Peasant League

The first German Peasant League (Deutscher Bauernbund [DBB]), founded in 1885 by Ferdinand Knauer and Berthold von Ploetz, illustrated the potential and the pitfalls of German peasant politics—and its fluctuating relationship with regard to antisemitism—from the 1880s onward. The DBB's first leaders were "respectable" antisemites in the style of Adolf Stoecker, rather than that of Hermann Ahlwardt or Otto Böckel. The Prussian provinces provided the members, to whom the league lent material support by means of a network of buying cooperatives and whose votes were supposed to muster rural backing for Otto von Bismarck's government. However, the proindustrial policies of Bismarck's successor, Count Leo von Caprivi, threw the league into an existential crisis in 1890. Ploetz fled into the arms of the organizers of a broader, explicitly nongovernmental, and more radically antisemitic organization, the Agrarian League. The DBB was instrumental in the success of the Agrarians, contributing 40,000 of their original 162,000 members, the bulk of the treasury, and many of the original functionaries. Ploetz was elected president of the new association and also named leader of the antisemitic Economic Union (Wirtschaftliche Vereinigung), a caucus organized in the Reichstag after the elections of 1893.

The second incarnation of the German Peasant League (1909–1927) was engineered by liberal agrarian dissidents who had come under attack from the right-radical Agrarian League. Eastern peasant colonists, who also resented Junker domination of agrarian politics, allied with the dissidents. The leading personalities in the revived DBB were a Hanoverian estate owner, Friedrich Wachhorst de Wente, and a renegade Agrarian League functionary, Karl Böhme. The Bauernbund designation reflected the liberal belief that an exploitable gulf existed between the interests of peasants and aristocratic estate owners and that agrarianism did not have to translate automatically into right-wing politics or antisemitism. The organization never attained a large membership base or secure finances; it was underwritten by the industrial interest group the Hansa League (Hansabund), as a means of weakening the Agrarian League's hold on the countryside. In policy terms, the second league was most notable for its support of "moderate" tariffs, its willingness to work with the government, and its rejection of antisemitism. However, in 1911 and 1913, when the DBB incorporated several independent, largely antisemitic regional peasant groups, its opposition to antisemitism weakened.

During World War I, the DBB lobbied against government controls and supported the Reichstag's Easter Resolution in 1917 calling for peace without annexations. This opposition to the controlled economy and identification with the Left led to an alliance with the German De-mocratic Party (DDP) in December 1919. The DBB acted as the party's rural auxiliary, holding nearly one-fourth of its seats in the first postwar Reichstag. But the league split in 1924 over matters of tariff policy, and the issue of antisemitism once again contributed to the discord. Karl Böhme, supported perhaps by a majority of the DBB's members, moved to the Center-Right German People's Party (DVP). Wachhorst's supporters, who retained control of the league's treasury and newspaper, accused Böhme and his followers of covert antisemitism, a charge that Böhme vehemently denied and that remains unsubstantiated by the historical record. Acrimony reigned between the two factions until 1927, when the league dissolved.

—*George S. Vascik*

See also Agrarian League; Ahlwardt, Hermann; Böckel, Otto; Memminger, Anton; Ratzinger, Georg; Stoecker, Adolf; Weimar

References
Vascik, George S. "The German Peasant League and the Limits of Rural Liberalism in Wilhelmine Germany," *Central European History* 24 (1991): 147–175.

German Racial Freedom Party

During the course of the German Revolution of 1918, a number of rightist national groups and parties, finding themselves in somewhat desperate straits, came together in the German National People's Party (Deutschnationale Volkspartei [DNVP]). The DNVP embraced essential elements of the prewar antisemitic and *völkisch* (racist-nationalist) movements. Although the party must be considered fundamentally antisemitic, it was characterized from its inception by a great variety of often conflicting views on the Jewish Question. The leadership attempted to maintain good relations with Jewish members and contributors, and a few state branches of the party distanced themselves completely from open antisemitism. But many party members and the organizations that they were associated with engaged in radical antisemitic agitation. In time, the DNVP's internal divisions, especially concerning the Jewish Question, resulted in two factions. One hewed somewhat reluctantly to the line of legality. The other, including the völkisch antisemitic elements, chafed against the lack of radical action and publicly rejected the Weimar Republic as a creation of the Jews. It pushed relentlessly for radical solutions of the Jewish Question. The murder of Walther Rathenau in 1922 threw the party into crisis.

The moderate leadership moved to isolate and then expel the radicals led by the three Reichstag deputies Albrecht von Graefe, Reinhold Wulle, and Wilhelm Henning. First forming their own rebel faction in the Reichstag, the three joined with like-minded rightist radicals to form the German Racial Freedom Party (Deutschvölkische Freiheitspartei [DVFP]) in December 1922. The well-known radical antisemites Ernst zu Reventlow, Artur Dinter, and Theodor Fritsch soon joined the leadership of the new party, hoping to make it an umbrella organization for völkisch groupings and thereby fill the vacuum left by the recently banned German Racial League for Defense and Defiance.

The waxing and waning of the DVFP's fortunes had much to do with its relations to the rise of Hitler and his party. When the Nazi Party was banned in many parts of Germany in 1923, there was limited cooperation between it and the DVFP, and a number of individual Nazis gravitated to the party—especially in the north, where the DVFP was most active. But in March 1923, the DVFP was also banned by the government of Prussia, which declared it to be no more than a surrogate for already prohibited organizations under the Law for the Protection of the Republic. Several members participated in Hitler's attempted putsch of November 1923. The party's momentary importance in German political history came when Hitler was removed from the scene and imprisoned for his attempted overthrow of the republic.

The DVFP, again cooperating with the Nazis in several areas and with other rightist extremist groups, contested the Reichstag elections of 1924 and turned in an estimable success—winning 6.5 percent of the vote and thirty-two seats. In addition to the party's three original leaders, Fritsch, Reventlow, and Erich Ludendorff, also won mandates. But the promising coalition was riven by conflict, rivalry, and shifting political alliances, which compromised its political effec-

tiveness. Another election in December 1924 revealed the party's weakness. Now campaigning as the National Socialist Freedom Movement of Greater Germany, it managed to win only fourteen seats; the results of the Prussian state parliament elections that took place soon afterward were equally disappointing. After Hitler was released from prison and despite mediating efforts by Ludendorff, the party could no longer avoid schism. On February 2, 1925, Graefe, Wulle, Reventlow, and Fritsch announced the reestablishment of the German Racial People's Movement (Deuschvölkische Freiheitsbewegung [DVFB]). Ten days later, Hitler refounded the Nazi Party in Munich.

Hitler and his party were the clear winners in the struggle to monopolize völkisch antisemitic politics in the Weimar Republic, outmaneuvering the DVFB at every turn. While DVFB leaders argued and plotted, the rank and file began to drift away. By 1928, the party had lost nearly 45 percent of its membership, including some of its leaders, mostly to the Nazis. The Nazis had developed a new style of mass-party politics, while the DFVB remained mired in the old ways. Even though the two groups shared much the same outlook on the need to solve the Jewish Question and used antisemitism as a major tool of political mobilization, the DFVB failed to move with the times, and none of its old-fashioned leaders, schooled in the antisemitism of the prewar era, could match Hitler's popular appeal or political savvy. One by one, the prominent leaders left the party, were lured to the Nazis, or made their peace with them. Wulle, who remained with the DVFB, greeted Hitler's accession to power on January 30, 1933; nevertheless, his party was dissolved a few months later. He remained active as a writer until 1938 but kept his distance from the Nazis. He was then arrested and jailed, spending the years from 1940 to 1942 in the Sachsenhausen concentration camp. After the war, he attempted to use his imprisonment to stylize himself a resistance fighter.

—*Matthias Brosch*
Richard S. Levy, translation

See also *Culture-Antisemitism or Pogrom-Antisemitism?;* Dinter, Artur; Fritsch, Theodor; German National People's Party; National Socialist

German Workers' Party; Hitler, Adolf; Ludendorff, Erich; Reventlow, Ernst zu; Weimar

References

Striesow, Jan. *Die Deutschnationale Freiheitspartei und die Völkisch-Radikalen 1918–1922* (Frankfurt am Main, Germany: Haag & Herchen Verlag, 1981).

German Racial League for Defense and Defiance

In the early years of the Weimar Republic, no organization broadened the appeal of antisemitism more vigorously than the short-lived but tempestuous German Racial League for Defense and Defiance (Deutschvölkischer Schutz- und Trutz-Bund [DVSTB]). Founded on February 18, 1919, at a meeting of the Pan-German League, the DVSTB was no more than a catchall for various antisemitic splinter groups at first. Its further history developed in two stages. In the formative phase of its first year of existence, the organization actively fended off the leadership claims of all sorts of other antisemitic groups and personalities. Initially too weak to control the debate over antisemitism, the league was unable to prevent the maverick, right-wing extremist Heinrich Pudor, from taking the spotlight by openly advocating the pogrom as a legitimate solution to the Jewish Question. However, Alfred Roth, the active leader of the DVSTB, took steps to strengthen the organization, recruiting the Imperial Hammer League (Reichshammerbund) of his friend Theodor Fritsch, as well as another important antisemitic organization. By October 1919, the significantly bolstered DVSTB entered its second phase, operating for the next two years as the dominant force in the antisemitic camp.

Membership in the league reflected this dominance. Still only 30,000 strong at the end of 1919, it attracted 160,000 to 180,000 new members by 1922. Counting those who joined and then left the organization before its abolition following the murder of Foreign Minister Walther Rathenau (on June 24, 1922), at least 200,000 individuals participated in its activities. Close to 40 percent of them were university educated; that the ranks included many secondary school teachers, university professors, and even seminarians, such as the later resistance fighter Martin Niemöller, demonstrates the strong appeal the DVSTB had for the middle sectors of German society.

The political style of the organization harked back to the elitist politics of the Wilhelminian period. Several of the local branches resembled clubs, with regular lecture evenings and social gatherings; they did not, however, develop the all-important paramilitary or conspiratorial groups typical of other Weimar rightist movements, such as the Storm troopers attached to the Nazi Party. On the basis of its mass membership, the league was nevertheless able to set the parameters for antisemitic discourse in the early republic. Members excelled in the coarsest brand of antisemitism, maligning Germany's Jewish citizens and, at times, calling for their outright murder. If ever the league rose to power, Roth threatened, Jews would be "marched to the gallows." But the league reserved its major effort for the unremitting campaign against *Ostjuden* (eastern European Jews), demanding again and again the forcible expulsion of Jews who had immigrated to Germany from eastern Europe and the passage of an aliens law based on blatantly antisemitic principles.

Despite its crude fanaticism, the DVSTB ought to be considered the last gasp of a radicalized Wilhelminian antisemitism rather than the direct forerunner of the Nazis. Hitler always kept his distance from the organization, deeming the Munich branch of the DVSTB as little more than a "gentleman's club" or an outpost of the rival German National People's Party. The league was both too elitist and too timid for his tastes. In 1920, the Nazis challenged the more influential league in the matter of antisemitic radicalism, calling for the expulsion from Germany of *all* Jews, not just Ostjuden.

During its short existence, the league was weakened by constant internal conflicts and rivalries. As its public reputation dissolved, its rowdy tendencies gained the upper hand, until the assassination of Rathenau led to its official dissolution.

—*Dirk Walter*
Richard S. Levy, translation

See also Fritsch, Theodor; German National People's Party; Hitler, Adolf; Imperial Hammer League; National Socialist German Workers' Party;

Ostjuden; Pan-German League; Pudor, Heinrich; Rathenau, Walther; Roth, Alfred; Weimar

References

Lohalm, Uwe. *Völkischer Radikalismus: Die Geschichte des Deutschvölkischen Schutz- und Trutz-Bundes 1919–1923* (Hamburg, Germany: Leibniz Verlag, 1970).

Walter, Dirk. *Antisemitische Kriminalität und Gewalt: Judenfeindschaft in der Weimarer Republik* (Bonn, Germany: Dietz Verlag Nachf., 1999).

German Students, Association of

The Verein Deutscher Studenten (Association of German Students [VDSt]) was founded in the aftermath of Heinrich von Treitschke's infamous "the Jews are our misfortune" article, published in November 1879, and the antisemitic petition campaign of Berlin students in 1880. A Berlin chapter of the VDSt was formally established on January 18, 1881, the tenth anniversary of the founding of the German Empire, although the University of Berlin authorities refused to grant it recognition. The movement quickly spread to other universities. One of the largest and most dynamic chapters was in Leipzig, under the leadership of Friedrich Naumann and Diederich Hahn. On August 6, 1881, the Leipzig branch organized a huge national meeting on the Kyffhäuser, the mythic resting place of Friedrich Barbarossa. The VDSt branches joined together into a national organization, known as the Kyffhäuserverband. The association rejected the German party system of the day and characterized itself as "national, Christian and socially-aware." Its two major concerns were foreign influences and culture in the new Reich, most notably Jewish culture, and the social ills caused by Jewish industrialization. In this outlook, the founders of the association were closely allied with Adolf Stoecker and the "respectable" Christian conservative antisemites. The organization distinguished itself from the older style of student fraternity by not publicly "wearing colors" and not indulging in the cults of dueling or drinking. The local chapters conducted nationalist agitation and sponsored series of talks on ethical and social issues. More than anything else, the VDSt illustrated the pervasiveness of antisemitism as an explanatory model—not just on the Right—for many young Germans, who later carried this outlook into diverse agrarian, reactionary, pacifist, Christian Social, and Socialist politics.

Like the antisemitic political parties, the association was prone to intense and divisive ideological controversies. In 1891, the official motto, "With God for Emperor and Reich," was dropped in a pointed attempt to detach the VDSt from the Hohenzollern dynasty, while also making it possible for Austrian chapters to join. In 1896, the bylaws were revised to prohibit members whose parents were converts from Judaism, thus adding a distinctly racial strain to the group's largely cultural antisemitism. A further controversy erupted in 1906 when Naumann, after giving open support to a Social Democrat running for the Reichstag, felt it necessary to resign from the VDSt. The students reached a compromise in the following year, guaranteeing the members' freedom of political expression.

After World War I, the association made its antirepublican political orientation known by retaining the old black-white-red imperial colors. In keeping with such politics, the organization also began to focus more on the nation (*Volk*) than on the state, defining its new mission as the "defense of Germandom" in the areas recently lost to the Reich. Throughout the 1920s, antisemitic and reactionary tendencies became more pronounced, and well before its advent, the leader of the VDSt was calling for a "Third Reich."

Nonetheless, the independent existence of the organization ended in 1934, when it was subsumed into the National Socialist German Student League. Following World War II, it was banned in the U.S. zone until March 1947. The successor organization is today composed of forty-one chapters. Its antidemocratic past continues to haunt the revived VDSt, making it a controversial participant in university life for many German students.

—*George S. Vascik*

See also Antisemites' Petition; Antisemitic Political Parties; Aryan Paragraph; Germany, Federal Republic of; Hahn, Diederich; Stoecker, Adolf; Treitschke, Heinrich von; Weimar; *Word about our Jews, A*

References

Jarausch, Konrad H. *Students, Society, and Politics in Imperial Germany* (Princeton, NJ: Princeton University Press, 1982).

Kampe, Norbert. *Studenten und "Judenfrage" im Deutschen Kaiserreich* (Göttingen, Germany: Vandenhoeck & Ruprecht, 1997).

German-American Bund

In Buffalo, New York, at the end of March 1936, Fritz Kuhn, the newly elected "führer" of the German-American Bund (Amerikadeutscher Volksbund [GAB]), proclaimed the organization was the official successor to the Friends of the New Germany (FONG). The bund constituted the second phase (1936–1941) of Nazi Germany's attempt to utilize ethnic Germans in the United States for its own political purposes.

FONG was a merger of several pro-Nazi groups that had existed in the United States since 1923, composed mainly of recent German immigrants. Authorized by the Nazi Party's political organization, Heinz Spanknöbel, the leader of the Nazi locals in the United States, formed FONG in May 1933. The group took direction from the Nazi Party's Foreign Organization in Hamburg. By 1936, it had a maximum of 15,000 members, most of them German citizens. Notorious for its militaristic style, outspoken political propaganda, and antisemitism, the group sought to take over German ethnic organizations in the United States, utilizing a number of tactics.

By the end of 1935, however, Nazi Germany was forced to bow to U.S. diplomatic pressure to rein in FONG's propaganda. Another mode of political activism was clearly needed, one that would be less subject to official U.S. scrutiny. The founding of the bund in 1936 was the Nazis' solution to maintaining a presence in the United States. To escape surveillance, the coordination of German American groups was to be carried out by a *cultural,* rather than the former political, organization—namely, the German Foreign Institute (Deutsches-Ausland Institut) based in Stuttgart. The goal of tying German Americans to Nazism remained unchanged. Although the plan was to have the bund operate as a social-cultural body, coming out as a political force only at the opportune moment, it quickly turned into an even more aggressive political agent under the leadership of Fritz Kuhn and several other ambitious German American leaders. Even the Nazis found it difficult to control these self-appointed führers.

Almost immediately after its founding, the bund unleashed a vigorous antisemitic and anticommunist propaganda campaign. It found allies on the extreme Right in the United States, such as the Fichte-Bund, the German National Alliance, the Ku Klux Klan, William Dudley Pelley's Silver Shirts, Gerald L. K. Smith, George Van Horn Moseley, Father Coughlin, and many others. With an estimated 30,000 followers, the bund developed a network of organizations, owned training and recreational camps, and published a weekly newspaper, the *Deutscher Weckruf und Beobachter* (German Clarion and Observer) with a circulation of 10,000. It successfully coordinated several larger German American umbrella organizations, effectively damaging their reputations and ability to function as nonpolitical, cultural associations.

The bund's flagrant propagandizing on behalf of Nazism attracted congressional concern. In June 1938, the McCormack Act to register "agents of foreign principals" was passed to outlaw alien political activists in the United States. It was soon followed by several other laws, culminating in passage of the Alien Registration Act (on June 28, 1938), which reactivated the Alien and Sedition Laws of 1798. The First Amendment of the Constitution kept Fritz Kuhn from being tried for his political activities but not for his tax evasion and the misappropriation of bund funds. In December 1939, he was sentenced to two and a half to five years in prison, which seriously hurt the bund. Later, he was deprived of his citizenship and deported. It was left to his successor to preside over the bund's dissolution.

With Germany's declaration of war on the United States on December 8, 1941, all German nationals and those classified as being in the service of an enemy nation automatically fell under the special legislation of the Department of Justice. Organizationally, this constituted the end of the German-American Bund in the United States, although individual pockets of underground activity continued to exist. A few Ger-

A bumper sticker on a high school student's car stating he is a member of the German-American Bund, a Nazi movement in the United States during the 1930s that was especially popular in the Midwest. Omaha, Nebraska, November 1938. (Corbis)

man American Nazis became involved in German intelligence and sabotage activities in the country, of which Operation Pastorius in 1942, is best known.

—*Cornelia Wilhelm*

See also Coughlin, Charles E.; Judeo-Bolshevism; Ku Klux Klan; Moseley, George Van Horn; National Socialist German Workers' Party; Pelley, William Dudley; Smith, Gerald L. K.; United States
References
Diamond, Sander A. *The Nazi Movement in the United States, 1923–1938* (Ithaca, NY: Cornell University Press, 1974).
Wilhelm, Cornelia. *Bewegung oder Verein? Nationalsozialistische Volkstumspolitik in den USA* (Stuttgart, Germany: Steiner, 1998).

Germanic Order

The Germanic Order (Germanen-Orden) was an antisemitic and pan-German organization formed in 1912 by Theodor Fritsch as a "secret" sister organization of the Imperial Hammer League (Reichshammerbund). It was designed to attract well-connected individuals and provide an outlet for their activism, while keeping their identities secret. The branch organizations were given innocuous names, such as the Association for Northern Art or the Thule Society. They were structured on the model of the Masonic lodge because, it was thought, only a secret "Aryan" lodge could effectively combat the conspiracies of Jews and Freemasons. The leaders of the Germanic Order were heavily influenced by the occult Ariosophy of Guido von List. The order mixed Masonic rites and rituals from a variety of racist fringe groups and added a heavy dose of Wagnerian drama. Only those with ideal "Germanic" heredity and features were admitted. Its symbol was the swastika superimposed on a cross.

The Germanic Order's mission was to monitor the activities of Jews, combat Jewish influence, and provide a center for the distribution of antisemitic propaganda. Fritsch had hoped to make it the central command post for the entire antisemitic movement. Never very large before the war, its fewer than 1,000 members were found chiefly in northern and eastern Germany. World War I brought the organization to the brink of dissolution, as its members left to go to war and its finances dwindled. Squabbles between leaders led to fragmentation and schisms.

The postwar rise of the extreme Right revived the group's fortunes. A nationwide network was established, and close ties with other racist organizations were forged, particularly with the activist German Racial League for Defense and Defiance (Deutschvölkischer Schutz- und Trutz-Bund. In 1918, Rudolf von Sebottendorf formed the Thule Society as a branch organization of the Germanic Order in Bavaria that was involved in counterrevolutionary activities and the birth of the Nazi Party.

In 1921, members of the order, also associated with the shadowy Organization Consul, heeded Fritsch's call for a "Holy Fehme" (named after the secret medieval court) against the nation's enemies and assassinated Matthias Erzberger, a leading Catholic politician and signatory of the armistice ending World War I. Members of the order were involved with other radical nationalist organizations in the planning of further political assassinations, including that of the Jewish foreign minister of the Weimar Republic, Walther Rathenau, in 1922. The Law for the Protection of the Republic, together with the suspicion of other racist and nationalist organizations because of its Masonic structure and occultism, led to the Germanic Order's rapid decline. Notwithstanding Hitler's later disapproval of the order, the organization had helped establish the radical rightist and occasionally murderous atmosphere in which Nazism thrived.
—*Mark Swartzburg*

See also Freemasonry; Fritsch, Theodor; German Racial League for Defense and Defiance; Imperial Hammer League; List, Guido von; Pan-German League; Rathenau, Walther; Roth, Alfred; Stauff, Philipp

References

Goodrick-Clarke, Nicholas. *The Occult Roots of Nazism, Secret Aryan Cults and Their Influence on Nazi Ideology* (New York: New York University Press, 1992).

Lohalm, Uwe. *Völkischer Radikalismus: Die Geschichte des Deutschvölkischen Schutz- und Trutz-Bundes 1919–1923* (Hamburg, Germany: Leibniz Verlag, 1970).

Phelps, Reginald. "Before Hitler Came: Thule Society and Germanen Orden," *Journal of Modern History* 35 (1963): 245–261.

Germany, Federal Republic of (West Germany)

Since its foundation in 1949, the Federal Republic of Germany has struggled to allow freedom of expression while protecting both its citizens from abuse and the state from antidemocratic attack. Under the leadership of Konrad Adenauer from 1949 to 1963, the federal government attempted to reconcile with the Jewish community and to fight expressions of neo-Nazism. To this end, the West German parliament (Bundestag) enacted laws against antisemitic defamation. However, during the Adenauer era, the Center-Right elite, which included a number of former Nazi fellow travelers, wished to avoid a direct intellectual confrontation with the Nazi past. By the mid-1960s, as both the Social Democratic Party and the student movement grew in popularity, such a confrontation was irrepressible. Meanwhile, expressions of antisemitism, often couched in other terms, entered the general political discourse.

During the Federal Republic of Germany's first years, overt antisemitism manifested itself primarily through cemetery desecrations. However, more latent antisemitic attitudes persisted. In 1953, claiming fear of a backlash from the Arab states or West Germany's inability to pay, most of the country's parliamentarians refused to support Holocaust reparations to Israel or world Jewish organizations. Although the government slowly established a working relationship with Israel and Jewish groups abroad, the overall population was not enthusiastic about these ties, and by the late 1950s, some politically extreme, socially alienated elements reacted violently. In 1958, the synagogue in Düsseldorf was attacked, and on Christmas Eve 1959, extremists daubed antisemitic graffiti on the wall of the newly restored Cologne synagogue, unleashing a wave of similar acts, to the great embarrassment of Adenauer's government.

The years 1967 and 1968 signaled a turning point in West Germany's relationship to Israel, Jewry in general, and antisemitism. Prior to that time, the most vigorous German supporters of Israel had been on the political Left. Many on the political Right supported the oil-rich Arab states in the Middle Eastern conflict or had latent antisemitic tendencies. As a result of Israel's victory in the Six Days' War and the emergence of the student movement in Europe, these political positions largely reversed. Many on the Right admired Israel's military successes, and they valued its opposition to pro-Soviet Arab states. By contrast, many on the Left, embracing nascent Third World liberation movements and rejecting U.S. foreign policy, supported Palestinian groups against Israel, including the Palestinian Liberation Organization. They regarded Israel as an imperialist agent and an aggressor, not as the representative of historical victims. Their anti-Zionism often degenerated into overt antisemitism, and some politically leftist, German Jewish intellectuals left Germany for Israel at that time. In Frankfurt, student protestors and squatters targeted building developments owned by Jewish real estate speculator Ignatz Bubis, and their anticapitalist invective against Bubis occasionally drew on anti-Jewish stereotypes.

Widespread public debate over Germany's relationship to its past and to the Jews remained generally limited until the 1980s. During a visit to Israel in 1984, West German chancellor Helmut Kohl noted that he was the first chancellor to come of age after World War II and that, as a result of "the grace of late birth," he could not bear guilt for the Nazis' crimes. Kohl's comments, which he claimed were not intended to serve as an evasion of responsibility, ignited a controversy over complicity in the Holocaust and generational accountability. The following year, Kohl and U.S. president Ronald Reagan visited a German military cemetery at Bitburg, which contained the graves of Waffen-SS soldiers. The planned visit alienated Jewish groups worldwide,

and to mollify their critics, the two leaders first visited Bergen-Belsen concentration camp. Many Jewish leaders, including Nobel Prize winner Elie Wiesel and chairman of the Berlin Jewish community Heinz Galinksi, remained unconvinced by the gesture. Galinski regarded the insensitivity of the visit as emblematic of widespread latent antisemitism on the political Right.

In 1986, a fierce debate about the uniqueness of the Holocaust, known as the *Historikersteit* (historians' controversy), erupted among German intellectuals. During the debate, some mainstream scholars advanced positions that were insensitive and potentially antisemitic. Philosopher Jürgen Habermas attacked historian Ernst Nolte for his comparison of the Soviet gulags with Auschwitz and his assertion that the Holocaust was an explicable response to the Bolshevik threat in the 1930s. Many on the political Right decried any constant fixation on German guilt, and many on the Left accused conservative historians and politicians of being apologists for atrocities committed under Nazi German rule.

Ironically, the Historikersteit ignited a larger cultural war in which many on the extreme Left, in their critiques of U.S. and Israeli foreign policies, exhibited a far more pronounced antisemitism than those on the Right did in comparing the crimes of Hitler and Stalin. Charges of antisemitism have also plagued left-wing artists in Germany, including Rainer Werner Fassbinder. In 1985, Jewish groups, led by Ignatz Bubis, physically prevented a production of Fassbinder's play *Der Müll, die Stadt und der Tod* (*The Garbage, the City, and Death* [1975]), which drew on overtly antisemitic imagery and Nazi invective in its portrayal of an exploitative and murderous Jewish real estate developer.

Political parties exhibiting antisemitic tendencies have enjoyed success in local politics but done poorly on the national level since the early 1950s. During the 1960s, the right-wing National Democratic Party of Germany was the chief representative of most politically extreme voters and did particularly well in state elections in Bavaria and Hesse. Since German reunification, there has been a dramatic increase in the number of racially motivated crimes, including an arsonist attack in 1994 on the synagogue in

Lübeck. In the 1990s, some extreme right-wing electoral groups gained in popularity, including the Republikaner (Republicans) and the Deutsche Volksunion (German People's Union), which received enough support to seat deputies in several state parliaments. Article 9 of the German Constitution allows the state to ban organizations, including political parties that threaten the democratic order. Since 1952, numerous extraparliamentary groups and several political parties have been dissolved under this provision.

The Federal Office for the Protection of the Constitution, under the supervision of the Interior Ministry, has monitored radical political activity in Germany since 1950. Its officials document political extremism in Germany and provide public prosecutors with information needed to take legal action against antidemocratic organizations. Although the office initially concentrated on left-wing groups, it has focused more on radical right-wing groups in recent years.

—*Jay Howard Geller*

See also Bubis, Ignatz; Desecration of Cemeteries and Synagogues in Germany since 1919; *Garbage, the City and Death, The;* Historians' Controversy; Nazi Rock; Neo-Nazism, German

References
Herf, Jeffrey. *Divided Memory: The Nazi Past in the Two Germanys* (Cambridge, MA.: Harvard University Press, 1997).
Maier, Charles S. *The Unmasterable Past: History, Holocaust and German National Identity.* 2nd ed. (Cambridge, MA: Harvard University Press, 1997).
Office of Military Government of the United States (OMGUS). *Public Opinion in Occupied Germany: The OMGUS Surveys, 1945–1949.* Edited by Anna J. Merritt and Richard L. Merritt (Urbana: University of Illinois Press, 1970).
Wasserstein, Bernard. *Vanishing Diaspora: The Jews in Europe since 1945* (Cambridge, MA: Harvard University Press, 1996).

Ghetto

In medieval Christian Europe, Jews tended to reside in close proximity to each other in what was referred to as "the Jewish quarter." Various reasons have been given for the formation of such quarters. Most generally, Jewish residential patterns followed those of other foreign, minority, and occupational groups. Also, Jews wished to live close to relatives, friends, and coreligionists and near the synagogue and other institutions of the community. On occasion, authorities who wished to attract Jews for economic reasons granted them a specific location, and in some cases, that area was surrounded by a wall, with gates for their protection. However, for the most part, the Jewish quarters were neither segregated nor compulsory. The Frankfurt quarter, established in 1462, was one of the few exceptions. In late fifteenth-century Spain, Jewish quarters were increasingly made compulsory, segregated, and enclosed until finally, in 1480, all Jews and Muslims were required to live cordoned off from Christians. However, this policy was never successfully implemented. Thus, although a few compulsory, segregated, and enclosed Jewish quarters existed in medieval Europe, they did not represent the norm. And even these exceptions would never have been referred to by contemporaries as *ghettos,* for the term only became associated with Jews in early sixteenth-century Venice.

In the Middle Ages, the Venetian government permitted individual Jews to reside in the city but never authorized them to settle as a group, except for the brief period from 1382 to 1397. However, Jewish moneylenders lived on the adjacent mainland, and in 1509, when they fled into the city to escape the armies of the League of Cambrai, the government granted them refuge. Still, the Venetians were bothered that Jews now lived wherever they wished, all over the city. Consequently, in 1516, the Senate enacted a compromise between the new freedom of residence and the previous state of exclusion by requiring all Jews to dwell on the island known as the Ghetto Nuovo (the New Ghetto), so named because it was the dumping ground for the waste products from the adjacent Ghetto Vecchio (the Old Ghetto), the municipal copper foundry. (The noun *ghetto* derives from the verb *gettare,* meaning "to pour, or cast, metal.") This island was walled up and had a gate at each end that was locked from sunset to sunrise.

Because a few compulsory, segregated, and enclosed Jewish quarters had existed in Europe prior to 1516, the often heard statement that the first ghetto was established in Venice in 1516 is correct in a technical, linguistic sense but misleading in a wider context. A more accurate formulation would be that the compulsory, segregated, and enclosed Jewish quarter received the name *ghetto* as a result of developments in Venice in 1516.

In 1541, Ottoman Jewish merchants visiting Venice complained to the government that they did not have adequate room in the ghetto. After investigating, the government responded by ordering that twenty dwellings located in the Ghetto Vecchio on the other side of a small canal from the Ghetto Nuovo be walled up and joined by a footbridge to the Ghetto Nuovo. This development further strengthened the association between the Jews and the word *ghetto*.

The Counter-Reformation adopted a hostile attitude toward the Jews, and in 1555, Pope Paul IV issued a bull that sought stringent restrictions on them. Its first paragraph provided that henceforth throughout the Papal States, the Jews in a given area were to live together on a single street, separated from all Christians (or, should one street not suffice, then on as many adjacent streets as needed), with only one entrance and exit. Accordingly, that same year, the Jews of Rome were required to move into a new enclosed quarter, which was soon referred to as "the ghetto of Rome." During the following decades, almost all Italian authorities mandated special compulsory, segregated, and enclosed quarters for Jews, which, following the Venetian and, later, the Roman nomenclature, were given the name *ghetto*.

In 1630, the Jewish merchants of Venice requested that the ghetto be enlarged to house some additional wealthy Jewish merchant families who would come to the city if provided with adequate housing. The Senate decided that an area located across the canal from the Ghetto Nuovo would be enclosed and joined to it by a footbridge. Since Venice already had the Old Ghetto and the New Ghetto, this third ghetto became known as the Newest Ghetto (the Ghetto Nuovissimo). However, the Ghetto Nuovissimo differed from the Ghetto Vecchio and the Ghetto Nuovo in one important respect. Although the latter two designations had been in use prior to the residence of the Jews in those locations and owed their origin to the previous presence of a foundry in that area, the Ghetto Nuovissimo had never been associated with a foundry. Rather, it was called the *Ghetto Nuovissimo* because it was the site of the newest compulsory Jewish quarter. Thus, the word *ghetto* had taken on a generic life of its own, even in the city that gave birth to the term.

The word *ghetto* gradually came to be used in a more generalized secondary sense in reference to areas of dense Jewish residence, even if not compulsory, segregated, and enclosed with walls and gates. Then, in the nineteenth century, it assumed two different and indeed even opposing meanings. On the one hand, it was utilized positively in a romantic and nostalgic sense, stressing the richness of life in the preemancipation Jewish quarter with its warmth, close family ties, and communal solidarity, despite the frequently encountered material poverty and daily struggle for a livelihood. On the other hand, the term carried a negative connotation, especially among assimilated Jews and Zionists, for whom it represented the traditional pre-Enlightenment and preemancipation Jewish community that should have given way to more modern forms and values.

These varying usages of the word *ghetto* had the effect of blurring the important distinction between voluntary Jewish quarters and coercive ones. To distinguish between the two, at least in scholarly discourse, it became necessary to refer to different types of ghettos, as, for example, the "technical ghetto" or the "voluntary ghetto"—a distinction that certainly would have mystified inhabitants of the early modern Italian peninsula. These ambiguous uses of the word *ghetto* have rendered the understanding of Jewish historical reality more difficult, especially when the word is used loosely in phrases such as "the age of the ghetto," "out of the ghetto," "ghetto life," and "ghetto mentality," which are so often applied to the Jewish experience in the seventeenth, eighteenth, and even nineteenth centuries, especially in central and eastern Europe and almost always with negative valuation.

Actually, the word can be used in the original Counter-Reformation Italian sense of a compulsory and segregated Jewish quarter only in con-

Paper shop in a Jewish ghetto, Vilna, Russia, 1922.
(Library of Congress)

nection with the Jewish experience on the Italian peninsula and in a few places in the Germanic lands; it ought not be applied elsewhere. For example, up to the Revolution of 1917, many Jews in the Russian Empire lived in small towns and rural villages in the Pale of Settlement that were predominantly Jewish. Even though, with limited exceptions, no Jew was to live outside the restricted areas, the Pale never possessed the defining characteristic of the ghetto because Jews were not segregated in compulsory enclosed quarters from their Christian neighbors. Use of the term *ghetto* in this eastern European context, although common, is inaccurate.

On occasion, it has been claimed that the establishment of the ghetto was beneficial for the Jews, especially in fostering and facilitating Jewish cohesiveness, but very often, the Jewish residents had not wished to be compelled to live in a segregated area. Ghettoization was obviously not a necessary prerequisite for the functioning and survival of Jewish communities, for in innumerable locations during the Middle Ages and early modern times, Jews formed and maintained communities that endured creatively without forcible segregation.

The purposes of the ghetto seem not to have been realized. Thus, in Venice, for example, the establishment of a ghetto did not effectively seal Jews off from contacts with the outside world on any level, from the highest to the lowest—much to the consternation of church and state alike. The often alleged negative impact of the ghetto on the Jews also requires rethinking. To a considerable extent integrated into their environment despite its general anti-Jewish orientation, the Jews of Venice shared much of the general outlook and most of the interests of their Christian neighbors, although they retained their own religious identity, with all that it entailed. Actually, the decisive element determining the modes of Jewish self-expression was not so much the circumstance of whether Jews were required to live in a ghetto, but rather the attractiveness of the outside environment. In the case of cosmopolitan Venice, basking in the afterglow of the Renaissance, the stimulus to Jewish culture and intellectual activity was considerable. The negative impact of the ghetto on Jewish life has been, perhaps, too heavily emphasized.

In the twentieth century, the word and concept of *ghetto* received yet another meaning when employed by Nazi Germany during the Holocaust. These twentieth-century ghettos differed fundamentally in nature and function from those of Counter-Reformation Italy. The earlier ghettos were intended to provide the Jews with a clearly defined permanent space in Christian society in accordance with traditional Christian theology: Jewish existence in debased conditions testified to the validity and superiority of Christianity. Nazi ghettos constituted merely way stations on the planned road to the annihilation of Jews, in accordance with the doctrines of modern racial antisemitism. Christian anti-Judaism offered a way out of the ghetto through conversion. Nazi antisemitism provided no such escape.

—*Benjamin Ravid*

See also Augustine of Hippo; Emancipation; Expulsions, Late Middle Ages; Holocaust; Pale of Settlement
References
Bonfil, Robert. *Jewish Life in Renaissance Italy* (Berkeley: University of California Press, 1994), esp. 68–77.
Ravid, Benjamin. "From Geographical Realia to Historiographical Symbol: The Odyssey of the Word *Ghetto*." In *Essential Papers on Jewish Culture in Renaissance and Baroque Italy*. Edited by D. Ruderman (New York: New York University Press, 1992), 373–385.
———. "Curfew Time in the Ghetti of Venice." In *Medieval and Renaissance Venice*. Edited by E. Kittell and T. Madden (Urbana and Chicago: University of Illinois Press, 1999), 237–275.

Ghetto Benches

Polish universities in the interwar period were hotbeds of the National Democratic movement, particularly its radical wings. From the first years of independence, right-wing students agitated for restoration of the tsarist *numerus clausus,* the quota that restricted the admission of Jews to universities. Jan Kazimierz University in Lvov tried to introduce such quotas for the faculties of medicine and philosophy in 1922 and 1923, but this initiative was ruled unconstitutional by the Ministry of Religions and Education. Subsequently, the ministry canvassed forty-one university faculties; only twelve opposed the quotas. In the early 1930s, the radical rightist Great Poland Camp began to advocate the *numerus nullus* (complete exclusion of Jews from Polish universities), but as long as Józef Piłsudski remained alive, there was no chance that such extreme demands would be accepted, and members of the group lowered their sights. In 1931, their youth movement, the All-Polish Youth, demonstrated against allowing Jewish medical students to dissect Christian cadavers; the medicine faculty caved in and began supplying Jewish cadavers for Jewish students. Emboldened, the radicals began to demand the physical segregation of Jewish students in lecture halls. At first, they would ask the Jews to accept "voluntary" segregation; when the Jews refused, they would attack them and try to move them by force. Incidents of this sort led to violent clashes, which took place at nearly all Polish universities and even spread to the high schools. Violence also occurred in connection with local university elections and fee protests. The 1935–1936 school year began with demonstrations over the death of a Polish student in one of these clashes and led to more violence. Instead of disciplining the instigators, university administrators responded by suspending lectures, sometimes for weeks at a time, and by making other concessions. The Lvov Polytechnic introduced "ghetto benches," or segregated seating, in December 1935, but this measure was dropped after two months.

The 1936–1937 academic year was marked by the most serious disturbances to date, including a three-day "blockade" of the University of Warsaw by right-wing students. In January 1937, the minister of education spoke out in the parliament against separate seating and encouraged the universities to take steps to end the violence; a few months later, he dissolved the All-Polish Youth, the main instigator of the outbreaks. However, perpetrators were generally given only small fines or suspended sentences, even when the attacks led to serious injuries, as they frequently did. During the 1937–1938 academic year, most institutes of higher education introduced segregated seating for students. These included the Wawelberg and Rotwand school of engineering (Warsaw), founded by two prominent Jewish industrialists and donated to the state in 1919 with the explicit provision that it would not discriminate according to race, religion, or nationality.

About 100 Polish academics signed a protest against segregated seating, but most others took no position, and a few openly supported the radicals. By 1939, most institutions of higher education had adopted the *numerus clausus.*

—*Steven Paulsson*

See also German Students, Association of; National Democrats; *Numerus Clausus* (Hungary); *Numerus Clausus* (U.S.); Poland
References
Marcus, Joseph. *Social and Political History of the Jews in Poland, 1919–1939* (Berlin: Mouton, 1983).
Tomaszewski, Jerzy, ed. *Najnowsze dzieje Żydów w Polsce w zarysie, do 1950 roku* (Sketch of the

Modern History of the Jews in Poland, to 1950) (Warsaw: Wydawnictwo Naukowe PWN, 1993).

Żyndul, Jolanta. *Zajścia antyżydowskie w Polsce w latach 1935–1937* (Anti-Jewish Incidents in Poland 1935–1937) (Warsaw: Fundacja im. K. Kelles-Krauza, 1994).

Glagau, Otto (1834–1892)

Born in Königsberg, Otto Glagau studied philology and philosophy, worked as a private tutor for ten years, and in 1863 launched his career as a journalist covering the Danish War. A popular legend explained his "conversion" to antisemitism in the 1870s as the result of a personal financial disaster at the hands of a dishonestly run, Jewish-owned mining company. In fact, his Jew-hatred predated this event by many years. In a book recounting his travels in Lithuania in 1869, Glagau expressed many hostile opinions about *Ostjuden* (eastern European Jews) and also insisted that they be considered part of the same unwanted Jewish "race" that inhabited Germany. When the crash of 1873 struck, he managed to publish an exposé in Germany's largest-circulation magazine, *Die Gartenlaube*. The series of articles and a number of books on the same subject made wild claims regarding Jewish culpability for the crash and its human consequences. Fully 90 percent of the *Gründer* (fraudulent entrepreneurs), he said, were Jews. Glagau was widely believed, even though he offered only anecdotal evidence to back the charge.

From 1880 to 1888, he edited a journal entitled *Der Kulturkämpfer* (Battler for Civilization) and used it to help organize anti-Jewish feeling into a grassroots political movement. Like his colleagues Wilhelm Marr and Max Liebermann von Sonnenberg, Glagau had high hopes for antisemitism, seeing it as a means of integrating Germans of all political persuasions: the true "struggle for civilization" was to be waged by German Protestants and Catholics fighting together against "an alien tribe" and in defense of Germanic values. Proclaiming that "the social question is the Jewish Question," he hoped to lure working-class and lower-middle-class Germans into a great political party. "I don't want to destroy or slaughter the Jews, nor banish them from the land; I don't want to take away anything that once belonged to them, but I will check them, and that from the ground up" (in Niewyk 1990, 350).

Beneath Glagau's menacing rhetoric was an essentially conventional program. The antisemitic party he envisioned would win elections and gain enough seats in the Reichstag to undo emancipation and legislate Jews out of German national life. In 1883, at the Chemnitz Congress of antisemites he helped to organize, Glagau used his influence to defend this basically segregationist program against challenges mounted by the more radically inclined followers of Eugen Dühring, whose solution to the Jewish Question went beyond apartheid to embrace expulsion and, much later, physical elimination. Glagau thereby helped put political antisemitism in pre–World War I Germany on a hopeless path. The small and feckless antisemitic parties never came close to passing a single law. Glagau died a pauper in 1892.

—*Richard S. Levy*

See also Antisemitic Political Parties; Dühring, Eugen; *Gartenlaube, Die; Kulturkampf;* Liebermann von Sonnenberg, Max; Marr, Wilhelm; *Ostjuden*
References
Niewyk, Donald L. "Solving the 'Jewish Problem': Continuity and Change in German Antisemitism, 1871–1945," *Leo Baeck Institute Year Book* 35 (1990): 335–370.

Gobineau, Joseph Arthur de (1816–1882)

Marred by a troubled upbringing and hampered by his family's dedication to the Bourbon dynasty, Gobineau was reared in an aristocratic, Catholic atmosphere among people who despised the French Revolution and all it stood for. After serving in the postal administration, he turned to journalism in the 1840s, writing for a variety of Catholic and legitimist publications and upholding a profoundly pessimistic view of postrevolutionary France. He lauded the Germans for preserving their aristocratic traditions but feared that they would also soon succumb to bourgeois liberal tendencies and the mindless demands of the masses for greater democracy. Gobineau became the secretary to Alexis de Tocqueville in 1848 and followed him into the French Ministry of Foreign Affairs, where he remained until 1877, serving in its diplomatic corps.

The revolutions of 1848 sealed Gobineau's distrust and fear of the masses and their potential negative impact on state and society. A supporter of local politics and decentralization, he viewed Parisian society with extreme displeasure because of its deviation from familial ideals and traditional norms and its predilection for radical politics. The work he is best known for, *Essay on the Inequality of the Human Races* (1853–1855), expressed his disdain for the upheavals he had witnessed in French and European society.

Gobineau's *Essay* integrated anthropological, linguistic, and historical factors to support an all-embracing theory of race with which to explain civilizations' development and decline. His racial determinism limited the role of free will and human liberty. Moreover, he did not believe the races were equal. The white, yellow, and black races differed in value and in their respective contributions to civilization. Their characteristics were immutable unless they mixed with other races. Deriding theories based on class, religion, politics, or territory, he claimed that creative civilizations stemmed from the white race, specifically the Aryan branch of it, and "that a society is great and brilliant only so far as it preserves the blood of the noble group that created it" (in Biddiss 1970, 117). Because miscegenation was at the root of society's degeneration, the *Essay* repeatedly enjoined Aryans to guard the purity of the race and prevent the decline of civilization.

Miscegenation, the bane of societies and civilizations, provided the crucial link to Gobineau's critical stance toward contemporary French society. He depicted the masses as degenerates—the progeny of racial mixing—and believed their aristocratic superiors—those of true Aryan stock, who should have maintained rule over French society—were being thrust aside. In this gloomy view, Gobineau distinctly parted company with his mentor Tocqueville, who rejected racial determinism and continued to believe in humankind's ability to change the course of history.

Gobineau's *Essay* proved to be an important source for antisemitic writers and racial thinkers, although the work hardly concerned itself with the Jews and was not directed at them specifically. He regarded their steadfastness with respect, although he also saw them as agents of the miscegenation ("semitization") that he dreaded. Historians, in their quest to understand the intellectual evolution toward Nazism, have for good reason turned to Gobineau's thought, yet they are certainly at odds on the nature of his contribution to racial antisemitism.

—*Richard I. Cohen*

See also Bayreuth Circle; Chamberlain, Houston Stewart; 1848; Racism, Scientific; Schemann, Ludwig; *Verjudung; Völkisch* Movement and Ideology; Wagner, Richard

References
Barzun, Jacques. *Race: A Study in Modern Superstition* (New York: Harper Torchbook, 1965).
Biddiss, Michael D. *Father of Racialist Ideology: The Social and Political Thought of Count Gobineau* (New York: Weybright and Talley, 1970).
Mosse, George L. *Toward the Final Solution: A History of European Racism* (Madison: University of Wisconsin Press, 1985).

Goebbels, Joseph (1897–1945)

One of the most infamous leaders of the Third Reich, Joseph Paul Goebbels led National Socialist Germany's Ministry for Popular Enlightenment and Propaganda from 1933 to 1945. Controlling a vast media empire, he played a central role in efforts to drive Jews out of Germany's cultural life. A rabid antisemite, he incorporated anti-Jewish images into much of the Third Reich's propaganda, helping to prepare the German people for genocide.

Goebbels was born on October 29, 1897, in Rheydt, a small town in Germany's Rhineland. His parents were middle-class Roman Catholics who raised their son in a devout home and made certain he received an excellent education. A 1902 operation left him with a clubfoot, rendering him unfit for military service during World War I. As a consequence, the bright young man was able to pursue a doctorate from the University of Heidelberg in 1922, writing a dissertation on the romantic playwright Wilhelm Schütz. Unemployed and having little else to do, Goebbels wrote the autobiographical novel

Michael, eventually published in 1929. Joining the National Socialist German Workers' Party in 1924, Goebbels allied himself closely with Gregor and Otto Strasser, leaders of the party's left wing and critical of Adolf Hitler. The leader's charisma won him over, however, and Hitler appointed him *Gauleiter* (district leader) of Berlin in 1926. As leader of Berlin's Nazis, Goebbels sought to win over the city's proletarian population through a combination of ardent nationalism and crude antisemitism. In 1927, he established *Der Angriff* (*The Attack*), a newspaper in which many of his propaganda motifs made their initial appearance.

Goebbels, along with the paper's cartoonist Hans Schweitzer, launched a relentless antisemitic attack on the vice-president of Berlin's police force, Bernhard Weiss, climaxing in the publication of *Das Buch Isidor* (The Isidor Book) in 1928. The following year, Hitler appointed Goebbels to be the party's propaganda chief, and in that post, he proved instrumental in the rise of the Nazis during the end phase of the Weimar Republic. One of his most notable achievements was to fashion a secular hagiography around the Nazi thug Horst Wessel, who was murdered by Communists in 1930. Following Hitler's elevation to the chancellorship on January 30, 1933, Goebbels became the new government's propaganda minister. He used his office to promote antisemitism, employing all of the media under his control, including film. The venomous antisemitic films *Jud Süss* (Jew Süss) and *Der ewige Jude* (The Eternal Jew), which depicted Jews as parasites and vermin, were his personal projects. Goebbels also cultivated a myth of omniscience surrounding Adolf Hitler. Nevertheless, his influence on Hitler waxed and waned throughout the history of the Third Reich, although in the closing days of the war, Führer named him the plenipotentiary for total war. In this new position, Goebbels made every effort to convince the German people to fight the Allies to the bitter end. On May 1, 1945, after overseeing the poisoning of their six children, Goebbels and his wife, Magda, committed suicide.

As Nazi Germany's propaganda minister, Joseph Goebbels played an important role in justifying the regime's antisemitic policies, winning the overwhelming acquiescence of the German people for the Nazi persecution of Europe's Jews.

—*Russel Lemmons*

See also *Angriff, Der;* Caricature, Anti-Jewish (Modern); Film Propaganda, Nazi; Hitler, Adolf; National Socialist German Workers' Party; Nazi Cultural Antisemitism; Weimar
References
Bramsted, Ernest K. *Goebbels and National Socialist Propaganda, 1925–1945* (East Lansing: Michigan State University Press, 1965).
Reuth, Ralf Georg. *Goebbels.* Translated by Krishna Winston (New York: Harcourt and Brace, 1993).

Goga, Octavian (1881–1938)

Born into the family of a village schoolteacher and with relatives in the clergy, Octavian Goga grew up in Transylvania, attended both Romanian and Hungarian schools, and studied philology in Budapest. His ethnic heritage and longing for the national emancipation of Romanian Transylvania formed the inspirational basis for his early, highly successful volumes of poetry, *Poezii* (1905) and *Ne cheamă pământul* (The Earth Calls Us [1909]).

Before the war, he began to dedicate himself increasingly to politics and journalism, publishing most of his socially engaged nationalist and conservative essays in his own journal *Țara noastră* (Our Land [1908]). He became an unstinting admirer of Benito Mussolini, from whom he drew some of his ideas. Goga longed for the renewal of Romanian nationhood and saw it issuing from the peasantry. He compared Romania to a new wine, not yet fully fermented, and "the national idea" as the mystical means by which it would reach maturity.

Honored by the Romanian Academy (in 1923) as the poetic extoller of the nation, Goga simultaneously pursued a political career that was much more controversial among his contemporaries than his verse. He worked on behalf of the emancipation of Transylvania (from Hungarian rule); in 1912, he was jailed in Hungary, and in 1915, he sought exile in neighboring Romania, fighting on the Romanian side in the war. Afterward, he entered party politics, at first in a conservative government coalition. In the 1920s, he associated with a variety of groups on the Right, arriving in 1927 at uneasy membership in A. C. Cuza's LANC–National Christian Defense League. But Cuza's extreme antisemitism and Goga's Orthodox royalism were not suited for one another. Goga's personal slogan, "Christ, King, Fatherland!" became the basis for his own National Agrarian Party in 1932. Soon after Hitler gained power, Goga's party was persuaded by the Nazis to cooperate again with LANC. The electoral results were not impressive. Nevertheless—and in a surprise move—King Carol II named Goga prime minister (on December 28, 1937), even though his party won under 10 percent of the vote.

The new prime minister barely had time to inaugurate his government, with declarations of loyalty to Fascist Italy and Nazi Germany, before the king dismissed him after only five weeks in office. The naming of Goga in the first place may have been a ploy to demonstrate to the Romanian people the utter bankruptcy of parliamentary politics and to justify the king's assumption of dictatorial power as the "national savior."

—*Krista Zach*
Richard S. Levy, translation

See also Codreanu, Corneliu Zelea; Cuza, A. C.; Iron Guard; LANC–National Christian Defense League; Mussolini, Benito; Romania

References
Heinen, Armin. *Die Legion "Erzengel Michael" in Rumänien: Soziale Bewegung und politische Organisation—Ein Beitrag zum Problem des internationalen Faschismus* (Munich, Germany: Oldenbourg, 1986).
Livezeanu, Irina. *Cultural Politics in Greater Romania: Regionalism, Nation Building and Ethnic Struggle, 1918–1930* (Ithaca, NY: Cornell University Press, 1995).

Göring, Hermann (1893–1946)

Hermann Wilhelm Göring, son of an imperial era colonial official, was born on January 12, 1893, near Rosenheim, Bavaria, and baptized in the Lutheran Church. He attended several Prussian cadet schools and became a famous fighter pilot during World War I, winning the extraordinary Pour le Mérite medal.

This distinction and his popularity brought Göring to the attention of Adolf Hitler, who managed to recruit him for the Nazi Party. Like Hitler, he blamed "Jews and Communists" for the lost war. In May 1928, Göring won a seat in the Reichstag. On January 30, 1933, he entered Chancellor Hitler's government, filling the posts of Prussian minister-president and minister of the interior, both crucial for the success of the seizure of power. He used these positions ruthlessly to ensure the triumph of Nazism within Germany. One of his first acts in April 1933 was to help formulate measures for the purge of Jews from the German civil service, part of a broad occupational ban he had been demanding well before 1933.

In 1934, Hitler rewarded Göring for his accomplishments in the coordination of domestic politics by naming him his deputy and then his successor in the event of his death. He became the second most powerful man in the Third Reich. In the following years, he served as Hitler's special plenipotentiary on a number of important missions. At the end of 1934, he surrendered his police functions to Heinrich Himmler in order to devote himself to foreign affairs and the building up of the Luftwaffe, which he commanded from March 1935. His preoccupation with weaponry increasingly involved him in economic planning, especially the overseeing of the Four Year Plan for national rearmament.

As head of the Ministry of Economics, Göring issued a number of decrees concerning "Aryanization," providing the legal basis for forcefully ousting Jews from the national economy. Claiming that "the Jew" outside Germany was plotting to unleash war, Göring "was forced" to goad industry to greater rearmament efforts. Nonetheless and in spite of the propaganda slogans, he repeatedly exempted prominent Jews from the discriminatory effects of racial legislation. He reacted with annoyance to the Night of Broken Glass, the November 9–11, 1938, pogrom, because the party's unauthorized actions ran counter to his economic guidelines and damaged the rearmament program. He importuned Hitler to make him commissar in charge of the Jewish Question, in order to make sure that his economic directives were adhered to. His aim was not the destruction of Jewish assets, factories, and resources but their expropriation on behalf of the rearmament program. By the same logic, he opposed the imposition of cost-ineffective ghettos for Jews and instead strongly backed emigration as the solution to the Jewish Problem. Göring's antisemitism, which was basically nationalistic and economically rapacious, differed significantly from Hitler's Darwinist, racist, and ultimately genocidal Jew-hatred.

Göring's greater moderation in foreign and military policy matters began to alienate Hitler, and by 1939, he found himself excluded from a number of important decisions. To counteract his loss of power, he sought to demonstrate his unbreachable loyalty to Führer. Soon after the invasion of Poland, he cosigned Hitler's Germanization Decree of October 7, 1939, which Himmler used to legitimize his "special handling" of the occupied territories and which administratively enabled the territorial and racial reordering of Europe in the spirit of National Socialism. Göring also issued guidelines for the merciless exploitation of the East. In this connection, he composed his letter to Reinhard Heydrich of July 31, 1941, commissioning him to implement the Final Solution of the Jewish Question. Administratively, this letter marked the beginning of the Holocaust.

As the war dragged on and military deficiencies became increasingly obvious, Göring's loss of power accelerated. In the beginning of 1943, he had an open break with Hitler. Having lost faith in victory, Göring distracted himself with extended furloughs and travels, during which he became the greatest art collector in Europe—at the expense of Jews, foreign museums, and private galleries. In his *Political Testament,* written just before his suicide, Hitler expelled Göring from the Nazi Party and terminated all his official functions.

Captured by the Allies, Göring stood trial at Nuremberg. He denied that he had initiated the Holocaust or known anything about it. The tribunal nevertheless found him guilty on all charges and condemned him to death. On October 15, 1946, the night before his execution was to take place, he committed suicide by means of a cyanide capsule.

—*Alfred Kube*
Richard S. Levy, translation

See also Goebbels, Joseph; Himmler, Heinrich; Hitler, Adolf; Holocaust; National Socialist German Workers' Party; Nazi Legal Measures against Jews; Night of Broken Glass (November 1938 Pogrom); Nuremberg Laws; Purge of the German Civil Service

References

Kube, Alfred. *Pour le mérite und Hakenkreuz: Hermann Göring im Dritten Reich* (Munich, Germany: Oldenbourg, 1987).

———. "Hermann Goering." In *The Nazi Elite.* Edited by Ronald Smelser and Rainer Zitelmann (New York: New York University Press, 1993), 62–73.

Gospels

Answering the question of whether the four Gospels in the Christian New Testament could be considered antisemitic depends on how the term *antisemitism* is defined and on whether the question refers to the intentions of the authors and/or to the ways in which the New Testament has been used or abused over time.

All four Gospels were written near or after the Roman destruction of the Second Temple in 70 CE. They also were all written when the Jews who believed that the crucified Jesus had been raised to Lordship were still a subgroup within the diverse Jewish populations of the time. Some assemblies of such believers, or churches, had begun to admit gentiles into their fellowships (with varying membership requirements), and many were still predominantly Jewish in composition. In addition, to different degrees, most of the Gospel writers believed that God's kingdom was drawing near and that they were thus living at the end of human history.

The significance of this context is that some of the Gospel passages that were used to promote hostility toward Jews in later centuries actually originated in the midst of (1) debates within the churches about gentile admission requirements; (2) debates with Jewish contemporaries about the importance of Jesus, especially in a world suddenly devoid of the Temple; and (3) efforts to present the churches positively to Roman imperial eyes.

Gospel passages that were to prove particularly relevant to later relations between Jews and Christians include those that portray Jesus' interactions with his own Jewish contemporaries, especially in terms of debates over proper Torah observance, and those that tell of the circumstances of his execution (known as the passion narratives).

Widely considered to be the earliest of the Gospels (composed around the year 70), the Gospel of Mark presents a Jesus whose true identity as God's Son is not perceived by *any* human character—including his family, his disciples, his friends, and his foes—until his death on the cross. Most likely written in a church that had recently experienced persecution, perhaps under Emperor Nero between 64 and 66, the Gospel exhorts its readers to remain faithful to their beliefs even when threatened with death. Its attitude toward Judaism is distant, although the Pharisees seem especially hostile to Jesus. The author comments that Jesus has "declared all foods clean" (7:19), that is, eliminated kosher laws, but this probably reflects the practices in a largely gentile Marcan church, rather than the historical attitudes of Jesus himself. Later debates about Jesus' identity are reflected in such scenes as the high priest asking whether Jesus is "the Son of the Blessed One" (14:61). The chief priests and scribes demand Jesus' death in the passion narrative, but the Marcan motif that no human characters really understand Jesus diffuses the animosity of both the Pharisees and the Temple leadership.

Written perhaps a decade or two later, the Gospel of Matthew seems to come from a largely Jewish church. The Matthean Jesus does not abolish kosher laws but rather insists that anyone who teaches others to break the least of the commands of the Torah will be least in God's kingdom (5:17–19). For Matthew, Jesus is the one who definitively teaches the Torah. The author uses quotations and allusions to many personages from Israel's Scriptures, especially Moses, to make this clear. Matthew believes that God wants all Jews to live according to Jesus' teachings. He inveighs against competitors for influence in the post-Temple Jewish world, most notably the Pharisees who, in chapter 23, are called "blind guides," "hypocrites," and "white-washed tombs." Matthew argues that Jerusalem was destroyed by the Romans in 70 CE because its corrupt leaders, the Temple priests, had misled the people to demand Jesus' crucifixion. The so-called blood curse—"And all the people answered, 'His blood be on us and on our children!'" (27:25)—is Matthew's warning to his Jewish readers not to follow the blind Pharisaic guides of their generation but to follow Jesus' teachings instead. Many Jews blamed one another for the Temple's destruction in the last decades of the first century, and Matthew was among them. However, his words would acquire more destructive meanings in later centuries.

The Gospel of Luke and its companion volume, the Acts of the Apostles, evince a complex set of attitudes toward Judaism. On the one hand, the author stresses that Jesus, his family, and his followers are pious, Torah-observant Jews and that the church is the divinely willed outgrowth of Pharisaic Judaism. In the passion narrative, he usually distinguishes between Jewish leaders and the Jewish people, portraying the latter as sorrowful (23:48). On the other hand, in the Acts of the Apostles, he presents several speeches in which apostles prophetically confront Jewish contemporaries with such words as, "You killed the Author of Life" (Acts 3:15). As Acts goes on, the opposition of Jewish characters to the spread of the church intensifies. Again reflecting an intramural dynamic, Luke believes that Israel is being reconstituted into a community consisting of noble Jews who accept Jews and their gentile allies. Other Jews, he holds, "will be utterly rooted out of the people as the time of God's judgment nears" (Acts 3:21, 23).

The Gospel of John, written around the end of the first century, originated in a Jewish church that had been engaged in a painful break with a local Jewish community. The explicit claim of the Johannine church that Jesus was "equal to God" (5:18) was seen as a violation of monotheism and triggered some sort of expulsion from the Jewish community (9:22; 12:42; 16:2). The anger of the writer(s) over this conflict, combined with a delight in irony, results in the Gospel's frequent use of the collective phrase *hoi Ioudaioi*, usually translated as "the Jews." For this Gospel, "the Jews" are those in darkness who think they are doing God's will by opposing the truth of Jesus but who have shown themselves not to be authentic Jews at all. Jesus is portrayed as replacing such Jewish observances as the Sabbath (5:1–47), Passover (6:1–71), and Sukkot (7–9). Jesus denounces some Jews as having the devil as their father (8:44). Most ominously, it is "the Jews" who exclaim to the Roman governor, "We have a law, and according to that law he ought to die because he has claimed to be the Son of God" (19:7). Postresurrectional debates have undeniably shaped this scene. Of the four Gospels, John's is arguably the one that most expresses animosity toward Jews who do not believe in Jesus' Lordship.

Polemic found in the four Gospels is consistent with the rhetoric found in other Jewish literature of time, most notably at Qumran. Since this polemic occurs between Jews, the application of the later term *antisemitism* would be both out of place and anachronistic. However, there is no doubt that these aspects of the Gospels were put to antisemitic purposes in later centuries.

This potential was catalyzed in the patristic period (roughly the second through sixth centuries). Gentile Christianity extracted and collected various elements from among the Gospels in the service of an anti-Jewish theology called supersessionism. The church fathers combined the negative aspects of Jesus' debates with Jewish contemporaries together with Matthew's blood curse and with Luke's and John's collective use of "the Jews" to produce a portrait of Jews and Judaism as the degraded and even demonic enemies of Christianity. This religious picture of a delegitimated rabbinic Judaism would become imprinted on the imagination of Christian Europe and contribute to the marginalization of Jews in Christendom.

—*Philip A. Cunningham*

See also Church Fathers; Dietary Laws; Passion Plays, Medieval; Paul; Roman Empire; Supersessionism

References

Bieringer, R., Pollefeyt, Didier, Vandecasteele-Vanneuville, F., eds. *Anti-Judaism and the Fourth Gospel.* Papers of the Leuven Colloquium, 2000 (Assen, the Netherlands: Royal Van Gorcum, 2001).

Brown, Raymond E. *The Community of the Beloved Disciple: The Life, Loves, and Hates of an Individual Church in New Testament Times* (New York: Paulist Press, 1979).

Harrington, Daniel J. *The Gospel of Matthew.* Sacra Pagina Commentary Series (Collegeville, MN: Liturgical Press, 1991).

Johnson, Luke Timothy. *The Gospel of Luke.* Sacra Pagina Commentary Series (Collegeville, MN: Liturgical Press, 1991).

———. *The Acts of the Apostles.* Sacra Pagina Commentary Series (Collegeville, MN: Liturgical Press, 1992).

Gougenot des Mousseaux, Henri (1805–1876)

A devout Catholic and political legitimist associated with Ultramontanism, Henri Gougenot des Mousseaux was a noble who served in the court of Charles X of France in the 1820s. After the Revolution of 1830, he retreated to his chateau in Coulommiers and devoted his time to the study of what he considered the greatest dangers of the day: the Talmud, the occult, Freemasonry, and Satanism. Gougenot's most famous anti-Jewish tract was a book entitled *The Jew, Judaism and the Judaization of the Christian Peoples,* published in 1869. The book received only limited attention at the time of its publication and did not sell well, although it won the blessing of Pope Pius IX and appealed to French Ultramontanists. The book came into its own in the 1870s in Austria-Hungary and Romania, where political antisemitism was gaining a foothold at that time, and it became more important in France after 1886, when the leader of French political antisemitism, Édouard Drumont, helped bring out a new edition.

The Jew, Judaism and the Judaization of the Christian Peoples merged traditional Catholic myths about the Jews with anti-Jewish conspiracy theory. Regarding the latter, the book shows the influence of the writings of Alphonse Toussenel, despite the differences in their political sympathies (Toussenel was a left-wing Fourierist, Gougenot a right-wing legitimist). Gougenot argued that Jews were engaged in a secret plan to dominate and destroy the world through seemingly innocent modern institutions such as high finance, Freemasonry, the liberal press, and Jewish self-defense organizations, especially the Alliance Israélite Universelle. He criticized the French government for granting citizenship to the Jews during the Revolution (1791) and for agreeing in 1830 to support their religious expenses to the same extent as those of Christians.

Gougenot depicted Jews as "Satanic" practitioners of ritual murder, and he defamed the Talmud and the Kabbalah as weapons of black magic. Gougenot also developed new myths to buttress the old, arguing that the French revolutionary tradition, the republican movement, and especially the rise of secularism were part of the Jewish conspiracy against Christians—a claim that would later inspire the antirepublican, antisemitic movement of the late nineteenth century.

French Jewish leaders deplored Gougenot's book as an example of the worst kind of anti-Jewish prejudice. However, in marked contrast to their actions vis-à-vis Louis Veuillot in roughly the same period, members of the Central Consistory (the central administrative body of French Judaism) decided that the book would not significantly affect public attitudes. They therefore refrained from suing Gougenot for libel or even responding to his charges.

—*Lisa Moses Leff*

See also Alliance Israélite Universelle; Austria; Drumont, Édouard; France; Freemasonry; Hungary; Pius IX, Pope; Ritual Murder (Modern); Romania; Talmud; Toussenel, Alphonse; Ultramontanism; Veuillot, Louis

References

Isser, Natalie. *Antisemitism during the French Second Empire* (New York: Peter Lang, 1991).

Poliakov, Léon. *The History of Anti-Semitism.* 2 vols. Translated by Richard Howard (New York: Schocken Books, 1974).

Grégoire, Henri-Baptiste (1750–1831)

A native of eastern France, Abbé Henri-Baptiste Grégoire was a key figure in the granting of emancipation to Jews in France during the French Revolution. In 1788, while still a parish priest, he shared the prize in the Metz Academy's essay contest on whether Jews could be made "more useful and more happy." His entry, the *Essay on the Physical, Moral and Political Regeneration of the Jews,* brought him national attention and helped him win election to the Estates General in 1789.

During the Revolution, Grégoire became a key figure in the National Assembly. He wrote a motion in favor of the Jews in 1789 and helped introduce Jews desiring citizenship to his fellow

The abbé Henri-Baptiste Grégoire was a key figure in granting emancipation to Jews in France during the French Revolution. (Corbis)

deputies. The Jews were hardly his only interest during these years, though. He was also famous for his campaigns to obtain full citizenship for people of color and the poor, to wipe out non-French dialects, and to destroy the monarchy. Further, he was the leading proponent of a republican-Christian synthesis.

To his good fortune, Grégoire survived the fall of Maximilien Robespierre and the purge of other radical revolutionaries, and he remained an important figure in the postrevolutionary years. Though his major interests shifted away from the Jews, he continued to be interested in their fate. His more than 400 writings include pamphlets on the Jews of Germany and Amsterdam (1806 and 1807), and his multivolume *History of Religious Sects* (1814, 1828–1845) devoted several chapters to world Jewry.

Although Grégoire was long considered the father of Jewish emancipation and a hero to European Jews, he came under attack in the late twentieth century as post-Holocaust Jewish writers began to notice that his famous *Essay* contained antisemitic stereotypes. When Grégoire was honored by being placed in the Pantheon of Paris during the French Revolution's bicentennial (in 1989) as an exemplar of French ideals of tolerance and antiracism, Franco-Jewish writers pointed to passages in the *Essay* referring to the "spirit of greed which universally dominates [Jews]," their having "no idols other than money," and their "pallid faces" and "hooked noses." As a devout Catholic, Grégoire also ridiculed the Talmud and criticized Jews' "exclusive religion" and their "hatred for the nations." Indeed, as early as the 1930s, others had noted that Grégoire's efforts to help Jews rested on hopes that they would convert to Christianity.

At the same time, as some writers have pointed out, Grégoire was hardly the Jews' worst enemy at the time in which he lived, and in fact, he did much to help them. Although his idea of "regeneration" suggested that Jews were currently degenerate, it also placed much of the blame for this on Christian persecution and suggested that Jews were members of the same universal human family as Christians. Moreover, Grégoire insisted that Jews had the capacity to be like others if their circumstances were changed. Despite his critical view of Judaism and many Jews, he befriended a number of French Jews during his lifetime, and he disagreed sharply with other Christians who insisted that Jews were inherently inferior and devilish. Grégoire's denunciations of anti-Jewish violence were perversely acknowledged by the Nazis, who destroyed a statue of him when they occupied eastern France in 1942.

—*Alyssa Goldstein Sepinwall*

See also Dohm, Christian Wilhelm von; Emancipation; Jewish Question; Misanthropy; Talmud

References

Popkin, Jeremy D., and Richard H. Popkin, eds. *The Abbé Grégoire and His World* (Dordrecht, the Netherlands: Kluwer Academic Publishers, 2000).

Sepinwall, Alyssa Goldstein. *Regenerating the World: The Abbé Grégoire, the French Revolution, and the Making of Modern Universalism* (Berkeley: University of California Press, 2005).

Gregory the Great, Pope (590–604)

One of the traditional "doctors" of the Western church, Gregory I is one of two popes from antiquity to have had the honorific "the great" appended to his name. The scion of a patrician family, Gregory was born around 540 in Rome, where he became prefect in 570. Five years later, he converted his family's large Roman estates into a monastery, and he himself became a monk. In 579, Pope Pelagius II (r. 579–590) sent him as his emissary to Constantinople. Shortly after returning to Rome in 590, Gregory became an abbot and was then elected pope. As pope, he exercised strong political authority in the region of central Italy that eventually formed the Papal States, initiated the conversion of England, wrote an influential account of the life of St. Benedict (author of the Benedictine Rule), and made important innovations in liturgical chant. He is often regarded as the first medieval pope and a founder of the Christian Middle Ages. His influence on Christian attitudes toward Jews and Judaism was pivotally influential.

In his personal attitude toward Jews and Judaism, Gregory had absorbed the traditional antisemitism of the Western patristic theological tradition, to which he was quite capable of giving sharp and apparently heartfelt expression, especially in those of his writings (such as his biblical commentaries) that did not have the force of law or concrete empirical effect. Gregory could easily dismiss Judaism, as cultured Romans had early Christianity, as a ludicrous "superstition," and many of his attacks on Christian heretics began with the observation that they were blind or literal-minded like "the Jews." Beyond that, Gregory was also anxious to convert Jews to Christianity. On the one hand, he was emphatically opposed to the use of force and to any physical violence against Jews or the synagogue, even as coercion was being applied to Jews to convert in southern France at the very beginning of his pontificate. While demanding that bishops neither use nor condone violence, he urged them to preach to the Jews in the short interval that was left before the end-time, in order that they might convert to Christianity.

On the other hand, he pursued a practical policy that can otherwise be described, in context, as benign. He guaranteed religious toleration, both theoretically and practically, and did much to protect Jewish rights as enshrined in Roman law. His famously influential encyclical *Sicut Iudaeis* (598) is often seen (not entirely accurately) to have epitomized his policy: "Just as no freedom may be granted to the Jews in their communities to exceed the limits legally established for them, so too in no way should they suffer a violation of their rights." As has been observed by several scholars, if Gregory's personal attitude was informed by the traditional animus of patristic antisemitism, he was guided by the political and moral imperatives of Roman law in his actual dealings with Jews and Jewish communities. Even more significantly, it has been shown that he relied primarily on the older Theodosian Code rather than the more recently promulgated Justinian Code, which was notably less favorable to Jews. As one noted scholar has observed: "Thus, Gregory was not simply a legalist giving Jews their due, as might any unimaginative bureaucrat. Rather, he was an important political and ecclesiastical policy maker who chose a course of action that would seem to demonstrate a pro-Jewish stance regardless of the latest imperial legislation" (Bachrach 1977, 36).

In practice, this pro-Jewish stance led Gregory, on several occasions, to prevent the confiscation of synagogues and sacred vessels and books and to forestall interference in Jewish ritual practice. Although Jews were not permitted to hold Christian slaves by either the Justinian or Theodosian laws, Gregory usually allowed the practice when it occurred (as he mock innocently put it) "in ignorance" or "accidentally." This forbearance, however, may have been intended less to inconvenience Jewish merchants than to placate imperial officials, who certainly knew about the slave trade and were loathe to impede it. There are other instances in which Gregory acted on behalf of Jewish economic interests even when Roman law forbade him to do so.

Ironically, then, he, more than any other pope, happily violated his own injunction in *Sicut Iudaeis* not to go beyond legally established Jewish rights on behalf of the Jews. A pope who regarded Jews in his theological writings as "depraved" and "perfidious" and who attempted to convert them away from their "superstition," Gregory, in the end, demanded and achieved for individual Jews and Jewish communities—legally, economically, and politically—much more than either Roman law demanded or his pontifical successors would be willing to grant.

—*Kevin Madigan*

See also Captial: Useful versus Harmful; Church Fathers; Justinian Code; Middle Ages, Early; Roman Empire; Roman Literature; Slave Trade and the Jews; Theodosian Code

References

Bachrach, Bernard S. *Early Medieval Jewish Policy in Western Europe* (Minneapolis: University of Minnesota Press, 1977).

Cohen, Jeremy. *Living Letters of the Law: Ideas of the Jew in Medieval Christianity* (Berkeley: University of California Press, 1999).

Grimm, Brothers

Jacob (1785–1863) and Wilhelm (1786–1859) Grimm, usually referred to as "the Brothers Grimm," were among the most illustrious figures of German cultural and political life during the first half of the nineteenth century. They also often figure prominently in histories of German antisemitism, yet this view is problematic and needs to be set in its proper context. Moderate liberals, the Grimms did not differ from many other German liberals of the day in their ambivalence about German Jews. The brothers had imbibed many elements of the anti-Jewish stereotype so prevalent then in Germany, yet they did not support anti-Jewish measures in politics.

Examples of anti-Jewish stereotyping can be found in the Grimms' correspondence, but it is above all to that most enduringly famous of their works, the *German Fairy Tales,* that scholars have usually pointed when they identify the brothers as antisemitic. The brutal and degrading tale "The Jew in the Thorns" stands out in this regard, though it should be noted that similarly disturbing stories can also be found in the Grimms' collection of *German Legends,* including "The Jews' Stone" and "The Girl Who Was Killed by the Jews." Historians have debated whether these tales reflect the Grimms' own views or only those of the common people from whom the tales ostensibly came. In either event, it is important to recognize that such negative images of German Jewry were commonplace in German culture at that time and that they did not automatically entail political consequences, much less racial antisemitism. That the *Fairy Tales,* aimed at children as they increasingly were in later editions, may have played a role in the propagation of anti-Jewish prejudice into the later nineteenth century and fed the growth of actual antisemitism is another matter and one that deserves closer investigation.

For the Grimms, as with many other nineteenth-century German liberals, negative sentiments about Jewry could and did coexist with support for Jewish emancipation. Liberals sometimes supported emancipation as a means of "improving" the Jews and demanded reforms as its price; others did so without conditions and simply hoped for a certain degree of assimilation to occur afterward. The opinions of the Grimms on this question are hard to discover, but Jacob, at least, was among the delegates to the 1848 Frankfurt parliament who voted nearly unanimously for unconditional civic and political equality for German Jews.

The Grimms are also often noted in histories of antisemitism for their contributions in three other fields: the development of the ethnic *Volk* concept in German nationalism; the propagation of interest in a pure, mythic German prehistory; and the promotion of notions of a conquering diaspora of Aryan peoples defined by linguistic affinity. In none of these cases, however, did the Grimms actually apply these ideas to their thinking about Jews; rather, it was left to later interpreters of German nationalism to do so. Here, as with the *Fairy Tales,* the Grimms' legacy proved much more troubling than their original ideas.

—*Brian Vick*

See also Dohm, Christian Wilhelm von; 1848; Emancipation; Jewish Question; *Jews' Beech, The; Völkisch* Movement and Ideology

References

Snyder, Louis L. *Roots of German Nationalism* (Bloomington: Indiana University Press, 1978).

Vick, Brian E. *Defining Germany: The 1848 Frankfurt Parliamentarians and National Identity* (Cambridge, MA: Harvard University Press, 2002), chap. 3.

Gwynne, H. A. (1865–1950)

A number of early twentieth-century journalists assumed significance in the political narratives of their time. H. A. "Taffy" Gwynne was one such individual. Born in 1865 at Kilvey, near Swansea in Wales, the son of a schoolmaster, he received his education at the local grammar school and abroad. After a brief time as the Balkans correspondent for the *Times* (London), he became the Reuters news bureau representative in Romania. Special assignments kept him overseas for much of the 1890s, covering events such as the Boer War. In 1904, he became foreign director of Reuters. In that year, he left the agency and returned to Britain to assume the editorship of the *Standard.* He stayed with that paper until 1911, when a bigger prize loomed, and Gwynne was able to slide effortlessly into the editor's chair of the *Morning Post.*

From his new vantage point, he exerted more influence, becoming involved in much scene shifting behind the political stage. He helped to propel the career of H. H. Kitchener during World War I. He argued in favor of conscription (a novel departure in British military history), which was introduced in 1916. He also played a key role through his involvement in *The Cause of World Unrest* (1920), a collection of articles that had appeared in the *Post.* The book strongly suggested the existence of a menacing Jewish conspiracy, a claim that reflected, in part, Gwynne's lively fear of bolshevism. His support for the notions contained in the *Protocols of the Elders of Zion,* translated by his former Russian correspondent Victor Marsden, was instrumental in helping the forgery achieve some brief credibility among influential Britons. Despite his personal influence in national politics, however, his paper gradually lost ground with the public. After its merger with the *Daily Telegraph* in 1937, Gwynne left publishing. He died on June 26, 1950.

—*Colin Holmes*

See also Boer War; *Cause of World Unrest, The;* Judeo-Bolshevism; *Protocols of the Elders of Zion;* Romania

References

Koss, S. *The Rise and Fall of the Political Press in Britain.* Vol. 2, *The Twentieth Century* (London: Hamish Hamilton, 1984).

H

Hahn, Diederich (1859–1918)

Diederich Hahn was the most famous and controversial agrarian politician in Germany before World War I. He was born in 1859 into a bourgeois family of dike builders in the town of Oste, near the mouth of the Elbe River. He began his life steeped in the liberalism of his Friesian homeland and went off to university in Berlin with letters of support from prominent local liberal politicians. In Berlin, he fell under the spell of Court Chaplain Adolf Stoecker. He moved to Leipzig, where he was instrumental, along with Friedrich Naumann, in creating the antisemitic Association of German Students in 1881. After completing a doctorate in 1886 under the economist Adolph Wagner, he was helped by some of Berlin's leading liberals to acquire a position as an archivist for the Deutsche Bank. Hahn's ability to engage in highly visible antisemitic activities without sacrificing his connection to liberal sponsors in the early stage in his career underlines the equivocal relationship between liberalism and antisemitism in the Germany of the 1880s.

Ultimately, Hahn's ambition and his fealty to Otto von Bismarck led him to break with the liberal world. In 1891, the year after Bismarck's ouster as chancellor, Hahn managed his campaign in a Reichstag by-election. In 1893, at the age of thirty-four, he was himself elected to the Reichstag, joined the right-wing radical Agrarian League (Bund der Landwirte), and became one of the most vocal defenders of the economic interests of the landowning nobility of Prussia. He lent himself to a variety of extreme right-wing political causes, many of them antisemitic in nature. Hahn's maiden speech in the Reichstag was infamous for the phrase "Strike my lieutenant, I'll strike your Jew," uttered in a heated exchange over stock exchange reform.

From 1897 until his death in 1918, Hahn was the Agrarian League's national director in charge of its internal administration, press relations, and electoral agitation. A skillful and innovative organizer, he created the largest, best-financed, and most smoothly run political organization in the prewar period. Under his leadership, the Agrarian League grew to over 330,000 members, organized into a sophisticated network of provincial, regional, and local branches supported by an infrastructure of paid speakers and organizers, libraries, buying cooperatives, and insurance schemes. He imparted his own hyperbolic, emotionally charged speaking style to an entire cadre of rural activists and left a mark on rural political discourse that lasted far beyond his own lifetime, infecting it, in particular, with a harsh, aggressive, and antisemitic worldview.

It is difficult to arrive at a nuanced understanding of that worldview. With the exception of specific but rare outbursts, Hahn was careful to confine his public antisemitic utterances to general condemnations of the Jews. How personal this antisemitism was in his private life is also hard to ascertain because most of his papers have been destroyed. However, his remark to a newspaper editor is probably the best indication of his utter sincerity in the matter of antisemitism: "I hate the Jews and will strike them wherever I can" (Hahn 1908).

—*George S. Vascik*

See also Agrarian League; Antisemites' Petition; German Students, Association of; Stoecker, Adolf; Tivoli Program

References
Hahn, Diederich. *Papers,* no. 329, January 3, 1908. (Niedersachsische Staatsarchiv Stade).
Vascik, George. "Diederich Hahn and the Politics of Radical Agrarianism, 1859–1918." In *Be-*

tween *Reform, Reaction, and Resistance: Studies in the History of German Conservatism from 1789 to the Present.* Edited by Larry Eugene Jones and James Retallack (Providence, RI: Berg, 1993).

Haman

Identified as "the enemy of the Jews" almost as soon as he appears in the Bible (Esther 3:10), Haman reigned as the highest official in the Persian court of King Ahasuerus. According to the book of Esther, Haman grew enraged when the Jew Mordechai failed to follow local custom by paying him obeisance, and he sought revenge by plotting the first attempted genocide of the Jewish people. After persuading Ahasuerus not to oppose his plan, Haman was finally thwarted by an elaborate scheme in which Queen Esther—the king's wife as well as Mordechai's niece—revealed her previously concealed Jewishness and brought about Haman's downfall. Ahasuerus ordered Haman hanged on the gallows once intended for Mordechai, gifted Haman's estate to Mordechai and Esther, and granted the Jews of Persia the right to self-defense against their enemies.

Although scholars from ancient to modern times have attempted to identify Ahasuerus with the Persian kings Artaxerxes or Xerxes, there is virtually no evidence to support the existence of a historical Haman. Whether he actually lived or not, however, he has become an archetype of the antisemite, an outcome likely intended by the author of the book of Esther as well as its earliest rabbinic interpreters. The book of Esther gives prominent attention to Haman's lineage, referring pointedly to him as "son of Hammedatha the Agagite," an identification that inspired the sages of antiquity to construct a comprehensive genealogy for him that credibly linked him to Israel's most ancient enemies, Esau, Amalek, and Agag. Placing Haman in this context, the sages sought to elevate him from a wicked yet bumbling figure to a timeless representation of those enemies who for centuries had schemed to destroy the Jews and (symbolically) their God. One typical midrash, which begins "Accursed are the wicked, who all devise evil against Israel," compares Haman's failed plot to Cain, Esau, and Pharaoh's botched attempts to rid the world of the Jews; it concludes by linking Haman's defeat to God's triumph over Israel's enemies in messianic times (*Esther Rabbah* 7:23).

Such teachings account, in part, for the passion with which Haman is regarded even in modern times. However, the figure of Haman himself remains compelling in its own right. Here is a hateful man of virtually unlimited power, wishing to be worshiped as a god and consumed by ambition to destroy the people of God—arguably the ultimate example of the fearsome antisemite. Yet because Haman's defeat is known to us from the moment we meet him, because the book of Esther takes such delight in pointing out his blunders, and because he is a figure of history rather than a living, breathing enemy, Haman serves also as a catharsis; generations of Jews have projected onto him the names and qualities of their own more immediate foes, then symbolically conquered these foes by invoking Haman's downfall. For the sages of antiquity, Haman became identified with their despised Roman persecutors; for the Jews of Nazi Europe, Haman was said to be used as a code name for Hitler. Certainly, the roaring noise makers (groggers) and pounding feet that sound when Haman's name is heard during the Purim Megillah reading attest to the fascination Haman still holds for Jews today.

Although the biblical Haman is a single human being brought low simply by human ingenuity (indeed, God's name does not appear at all in the book of Esther), Jewish tradition has granted him an identity and a significance that span history, from the genealogies of Genesis to the time of the Messiah. According to one midrash, before being hanged on the gallows, Haman pleaded with Mordechai not to permit his name to be blotted out. Perhaps ironically, Haman's dying wish has been granted to this day.

—*Elaine Rose Glickman*

See also Hitler, Adolf; Roman Empire; Talmud
References
Glickman, Elaine Rose. *Haman and the Jews: A Portrait from Rabbinic Literature* (Northvale, NJ: Jason Aronson, 1999).
Grossfeld, Bernard, trans. *The Two Targums of Esther* (Collegeville, MI: Liturgical Press, 1987).

Hamas

The word *Hamas,* meaning "zeal" in Arabic, is the acronym for Harakat al-Muqawama al-Islamiyya (The Islamic Resistance Movement). The organization was founded in Gaza in December 1987, at the outbreak of the Palestinian uprising known as the first intifada, as the militant branch of local association of the Muslim Brotherhood. Under the leadership of Sheikh Ahmad Yasin, the brotherhood had previously focused its activities on spiritual and social revival among Palestinians, had refrained from anti-Israel resistance, and was hostile to the secular nationalist groups that comprised the Palestine Liberation Organization (PLO). The Israeli authorities had even given discreet financial support to the brotherhood's social welfare activities in the hope that it would provide a quietist alternative to the PLO. However, the groundswell of popular participation in the intifada convinced the brotherhood's leadership that the time had come for armed jihad. It refused to join the Unified National Command of the Uprising established by the PLO but did agree to operate with it as an independent organization. The Israeli authorities cracked down heavily on Hamas, imprisoning Sheikh Yasin and exiling other leaders.

Hamas opposed the Arab-Israeli peace talks that began at the end of 1991 and the 1993 Oslo Peace Accords, and it increased its terrorist activities against Israelis after the establishment of the Palestine Authority (PA). Its most dramatic weapon became the "martyr," or suicide bomber. This development had not been condoned by Sunni Islam and seems to have been inspired by Shi'ite groups such as the Lebanese Hizbollah and Amal. Hamas has continually posed the primary challenge to PLO rule in the PA.

From the beginning, Hamas espoused the antisemitism of the Muslim Brotherhood's leading thinkers, Hasan al-Banna and Sayyid Qutb. This fact is clear from its own ideological credo formulated as the Islamic covenant in 1988, which not only calls for Islam to eliminate Israel but also states "our struggle against the Jews is extremely wide-ranging and grave." It cites the Hadith (tradition attributed to the Prophet Mohammed) in noting that at the end of time, Muslims will fight the Jews and kill them. The covenant and other Hamas publications draw on the libels of the *Protocols of the Elders of Zion,* accusing Jews of a universal conspiracy for world domination. It also accuses them of instigating the French and communist revolutions and having their fingerprints on every war that has ever broken out anywhere. It claims that the Zionists control the imperial states and were behind the establishment of the United Nations and that the Freemasons, Rotary and Lions Clubs, and B'nai B'rith are all Zionist fronts. It brands Israel as "a vicious Nazi-like enemy" and opines that "the Nazism of the Jews does not skip women and children." Some of the antisemitic canards are backed in the covenant by koranic proof texts.

Hamas's anti-Jewish rhetoric has become increasingly violent since the second intifada. The art page of its website opens with a poster depicting an axe inscribed *al-Qassam* (for the organization's 'Izz al-Din al-Qassam commando squads) chopping in half the word *Jews,* scattered skulls, and the words "We shall knock on Paradise's Gates with the Jews' skulls."

—*Norman A. Stillman*

See also Anti-Zionism; Arab Antisemitic Literature; Arafat, Yasir; Freemasonry; Islam and the Jews; Islamic Fundamentalism; Muslim Brotherhood; *Protocols of the Elders of Zion*

References

Abu-Amr, Ziad. *Islamic Fundamentalism in the West Bank and Gaza: Muslim Brotherhood and Islamic Jihad* (Bloomington: Indiana University Press, 1994).

Alexander, Yonah. *Palestinian Religious Terrorism: Hamas and Islamic Jihad* (Ardsley, NY: Transnational Publishers, 2002).

Webman, Esther. *Antisemitic Motifs in the Ideology of Hizballah and Hamas* (Tel Aviv, Israel: Tel Aviv University Faculty of the Humanities, 1994).

Handbook of the Jewish Question (Antisemites' Catechism)

In November 1884, the Dresden antisemitic newspaper *Deutsche Reform* (German Reform) published a call for "a handy, pocket-sized guide with a wealth of information" on the Jewish Question. Theodor Fritsch, close to the Dresden antisemites, vowed to fill this suddenly discovered need in the near future. But it was only on May 31, 1887, that his publishing house issued the first 212-page edition of the *Antisemites' Catechism: A Compilation of the Most Important Material for the Comprehending of the Jewish Question.* Its author was Thomas Frey, one of Fritsch's many pseudonyms. The first edition nearly sold out within the week. There followed in rapid succession a second, improved edition and then two further printings in the same year.

Fritsch acknowledged his authorship in the tenth edition (in 1891). He steadily expanded his collection of material from edition to edition, so that by the time the twenty-fifth appeared in 1893 (in a run of 35,000 copies), the book had grown to 411 pages. Beyond its expansion, however, Fritsch made virtually no conceptual changes in his guide. Ever the systematic exploiter of his own works, he let excerpts appear as freestanding pamphlets, newspaper articles, or "little enlightenment writings."

The guide featured a catechism-like question-and-answer introduction to the Jewish Question "in everyday language." One of the book's essential features was devoted to the "sayings of famous men concerning the Jews." Fritsch included here anything negative about his subject that he could extract from scientists, artists, and writers, even if their alleged antisemitism consisted of no more than uttering the common prejudices of their day. Of course, authentic antisemites such as Richard Wagner, Arthur Schopenhauer, and Heinrich von Treitschke were also prominently represented. Fritsch included among the illustrious some far less well-known radical antisemites, such as Eugen Dühring and Adolf Wahrmund. His purpose was clear: to create the sense of continuity in antisemitism among the great from the days of Cicero to the present.

A complement to this feature was a section entitled "Jewish Self-Judgments and Sayings," in which Jews and Jewish character were allowed to convict themselves in their own words. In line with this aim was a series of Talmud extracts, taken from August Rohling's *The Talmud Jew.* (Fritsch knew no Hebrew and, like Rohling, was unable to read the original.) Here, readers could learn about the Jews' double morality and their

license to cheat gentiles, allegedly encouraged by the Talmud. "A History of the Jewish Race (*Volk*)" reinforced the idea of unchanging Jewish values and highlighted the Jews' stubborn unwillingness to accommodate themselves to the ways of others. "Jew-Statistics" supposedly proved the overrepresentation of Jews in key sectors of society, as well as their above-average participation in criminal acts. Taken together, these features of the *Antisemites' Catechism* served one basic purpose: to demonstrate the negative influence of Jewry on all aspects of German life.

Fritsch wanted his readers to draw the proper political conclusions from what they learned. He devoted a chapter to the history of the antisemitic movement. In the "Ten Commandments of Lawful Self-Help," he enjoined his audience to maintain the purity of Germanic blood and to isolate the Jews as a practical step toward this goal. Party politics, which Fritsch never really approved of, nevertheless received support from the *Catechism,* which reprinted the platform of the antisemitic German Social Party and provided a handy listing of antisemitic clubs and newspapers. After Fritsch had a run-in with authorities, the book was seized in 1888, and Fritsch was legally required to remove some passages that libeled the Jewish community. By 1889, a much-abbreviated version intended for mass distribution appeared as *Facts about the Jewish Question: An ABC for Antisemites—Taken from the "Antisemites' Catechism."*

In 1907, the twenty-sixth edition of the book assumed the title under which it is best known today: *Handbook of the Jewish Question: A Compilation of the Most Important Materials for Forming a Judgment on the Jewish Race.* By that time, Fritsch had sundered all connections to the party antisemites, announcing that the handbook stood above all political party strife and would henceforth devote itself to the purely objective and scientific study of society.

The *Handbook* adhered fairly faithfully to the structure of the l907 edition, but it also reflected certain trends of the day, such as the *Protocols of the Elders of Zion,* and occasionally gave more or less weight to traditional subjects. Beginning with the thirtieth edition of 1931 and the virtual retirement of Fritsch from an active role, individual features began to carry bylines. The *Handbook of the Jewish Question* survived until 1944, when it was in its forty-ninth edition and over 330,000 copies had been printed. During the Third Reich, it became a school textbook that Hitler himself fully endorsed. In a letter that appeared on the cover of the 34th edition of the *Handbook,* he wrote to Fritsch: "Even as a young man in Vienna, I studied the *Handbook of the Jewish Question.* I am convinced that this book, in very marked fashion, served to prepare the ground for the National Socialists Movement."

—*Matthias Brosch*
Richard S. Levy, translation

See also Antisemitic Political Parties; Bartels, Adolf; Dühring, Eugen; Fritsch, Theodor; Hitler, Adolf; Jewish Question; *Protocols of the Elders of Zion;* Rohling, August; Talmud; *Talmud Jew, The*

References

Fiebig, Paul. *Juden und Nichtjuden: Erläuterungen zu Th. Fritschs "Handbuch der Judenfrage" 28. Auflage* (Leipzig, Germany: Dörffling and Franke, 1921).

Hegel, G. W. F. (1770–1831)

Georg Wilhelm Friedrich Hegel began to develop his distinctive philosophy in Jena, where he had moved in 1801. As his funds dwindled, he left Jena in 1807 and became a secondary school principal in Franconia before securing a post at the University of Heidelberg in 1816. Two years later, he was appointed to J. G. Fichte's prestigious chair in Berlin, where he spent the rest of his life.

Hegel assumed that religion and philosophy were alternative modes of understanding and expressing truth. History consisted of a succession of religions and philosophies, each of which had been a more comprehensive and perfect representation of truth than the one before. Each new form of religion had not simply negated the one that went before. Rather, the valid elements of each obsolete religion were contained and developed further in the one that superseded it. Biblical Judaism had been one of these imperfect reflections of truth. It had been valid in its time, and Hegel, in fact, associated it with a particularly significant step in the development of human consciousness. Although Christianity had ultimately superseded all other religions, including Judaism, it did not directly supersede Judaism in his scheme of things. Provisos such as this one already indicated that the utility of his complex system for more common forms of political discourse was rather limited.

Hegel was by no means sparing in his characterization of what he held to be the deficiencies that had rendered Judaism obsolete, and he found postbiblical Judaism equally inexplicable and futile. He was more optimistic than most of his contemporaries, however, that Jews would assimilate if given a chance. Thus, he supported the granting of equal rights to Jews, even though he held to the common view that their current behavior did not as yet merit full emancipation. While Hegel was teaching in Heidelberg, the student fraternity there carried a remarkable motion permitting the admission of Jewish students. The initiator of that motion, F. W. Carové, was closely involved with Hegel. The transcript of Hegel's lectures on "The Philosophy of Right," delivered in Heidelberg in 1817 and 1818, shows that he already expressed his support for formal Jewish emancipation, thus boosting the case of those favoring the admission of Jewish students to the fraternity.

Probably the most influential aspect of Hegel's stance was the link it construed between the notion of Judaism's obsolescence (which tended to draw more attention than his assertion that Judaism had been valid in its time) and his concept of (irreversible) historical progress. Within the parameters of the Enlightenment discourse, the debate on Judaism's alleged inferiority could, at least in theory, be reopened if it could be proven that Judaism was not as immutably tied to its initial revelation as its critics claimed and was hence perfectible after all. But the Hegelian model rendered that option impossible, even in theory. His contention that Judaism was obsolete was not only meant as a qualitative judgment; it also supposedly represented a fact of history. Given that history obviously could not be turned back, this seemed to offer a watertight case.

—*Lars Fischer*

See also Bauer, Bruno; Burschenschaften; Emancipation; Feuerbach, Ludwig; Fichte, J. G.; Marx, Karl; Young Hegelians

References

Avineri, Shlomo. "A Note on Hegel's Views on Jewish Emancipation," *Jewish Social Studies* 25 (1963): 145–151.

Hodgson, Peter C. "The Metamorphosis of Judaism in Hegel's Philosophy of Religion," *Owl of Minerva* 19, no. 1 (1987): 41–52.

Smith, Steven B. "Hegel and the Jewish Question: In between Tradition and Modernity," *History of Political Thought* 12, no. 1 (1991): 87–106.

Heidegger, Martin (1889–1976)

Martin Heidegger was born in south Germany in the rural Catholic town of Meßkirch. In the course of a long life—and a world away from Meßkirch—he became the most famous philosopher of the twentieth century. Yet the remarkably complex issue of antisemitism in Heidegger's life and thought began in that small village.

The antisemitism Heidegger experienced as a youth in Meßkirch had its source in traditional Catholic views about Jews. But Heidegger's schoolteachers *rejected* the modern concept of antisemitism then making headway in German politics because it was contrary to Catholic doctrine. This new term *antisemitism* was purely secular and based on race. The church did not oppose Jews for racial reasons but because they had rejected Christ, which was a *religious* issue. However, this traditional Catholic hostility toward Jews was part of the landscape Heidegger grew up in and needs to be considered when explaining his choices later in life.

His family was part of the lower middle class. In Europe's rigid class structure, many in this economically and socially threatened grouping grew particularly vulnerable to extremist politics, including antisemitic politics. Heidegger, however, was not a victim of modernity. Even as a child, his genius was unmistakable. He was put under the care of local Catholic teachers, who saw to his schooling in a private elite academy and groomed him for the university, a trajectory totally at odds with that of most people of his social background.

Heidegger's university world was significantly Jewish. The adviser for his 1913 dissertation at Freiburg was the famous phenomenologist Edmund Husserl, who was a Protestant in religion but made no secret of his Jewish birth and his Jewish cultural heritage. Heidegger became known as a Husserl's brilliant assistant lecturer, and he soon developed a following among university students all over Germany, who read and passed on the notes from his lectures. Even more striking were the number of Heidegger's own students in the 1920s who were Jewish by birth. Many came from families with a markedly higher social status than Heidegger's own. Hannah Arendt came from such a background and became not only one of his best students but also Heidegger's secret lover for five intense years during the 1920s. Other of his Jewish students who went on to distinguished careers were Karl Löwith, Hans Jonas, and Herbert Marcuse.

In 1923, Heidegger received an appointment to teach at Marburg University. His lectures there eventually resulted in his most famous book, *Being and Time,* which was published in 1927 and led to his appointment as Husserl's successor at Freiburg in 1928. Three years later, Heidegger suddenly announced his interest in the Nazi movement and claimed to see parallels between its philosophy and his own.

In 1933, he joined the Nazi Party and was almost immediately elected rector of Freiburg University, an office that he conducted with considerable enthusiasm. As a Nazi, Heidegger imposed Nazi discipline on the university. Whatever the influence of antisemitism in his childhood milieu or that which he experienced in academic culture, the sort he now wholeheartedly practiced was of a different order. There is overwhelming evidence that, for a brief period, Heidegger zealously hounded Jewish professors and students in the university. Where and when possible, he saw that their careers were cut short or undermined in significant ways.

Within a year of his appointment as rector at Freiburg, for reasons still not entirely clear, Heidegger abruptly resigned and returned to teaching. Later in the 1930s, the Nazis became suspicious that he was not following the party line on important issues, and eventually, the Gestapo began monitoring his lectures. In 1944, he was forced into the *Volkssturm* (civilian militia) and had to fight against the invading U.S. and French armies.

German philosopher Martin Heidegger, one of the twentieth century's most influential thinkers, was a mentor to French existentialist Jean-Paul Sartre. Heidegger's central theme was man's inability to understand his own existence. His most famous work, translated as *Being and Time*, was published in 1927. (Bettmann/Corbis)

After the war, a German de-Nazification board declared him unfit to teach in a German university because of his membership in the Nazi Party and his activity as rector. He remained a private scholar until the early 1950s when he was granted formal retirement by the new West German government, which legally permitted him once again to give lectures at various German universities.

Heidegger's return to the academic scene coincided with his growing world fame. In the 1950s and 1960s, his admirers no longer came from the extreme Right but from the ranks of high-powered intellectuals on the Left, among them Jean-Paul Sartre. Later, his influence spread to U.S. universities, where his philosophy inspired many of the students who became involved in the civil rights movement and in protests against the Vietnam War. Heidegger's Nazi past was a matter of public record and the subject of occasional exposés published in obscure journals, but few of his new followers seemed much interested. He died in 1976, fully esteemed by the intellectual world.

Then, in 1987, the Chilean scholar Victor Farias published a book in French, *Heidegger et le Nazisme,* giving thorough exposure to Heidegger's involvement with the Nazi Party and his overtly antisemitic activities during the 1930s. Its publication stimulated an impassioned discussion and debate among thinkers of all schools. They asked the key question: who *was* the real Martin Heidegger? That debate continues to this day.

—*Leif Torjesen*

See also Nazi Cultural Antisemitism; Nazi Legal Measures against Jews; Nietzsche, Friedrich; Sartre, Jean-Paul

References

Farias, Victor. *Heidegger and Nazism.* Translated by Dominic di Bernardi (Philadelphia: Temple University Press, 1989).

Heine, Heinrich (1797–1856)

The first German Jewish creative writer of international reputation, whose poems went out into the world "on wings of song," in his own phrase, did not have intense experiences of antisemitism in his youth: there was no ghetto in his home city of Düsseldorf; his family was reasonably well integrated into the community; and from age eight to seventeen, he lived under Napoleonic occupation, which brought certain benefits to the Jews along with burdensome restrictions on commerce and military conscription. He did witness anti-Jewish disturbances in 1819, when the windows in the Hamburg townhouse of his millionaire uncle Salomon Heine were broken, and his private letters report recurrent anxiety from antisemitic insinuations, along with his own dismissive remarks about Jews that might sound antisemitic in another context. After Prussia restored legal restrictions on Jews in 1822, narrowing his career options, he had himself baptized shortly before completing his law degree at Göttingen in 1825—a step he came to regret as damaging to his dignity, al-

Drawing of German poet Heinrich Heine, (1797–1856). (Bettmann/Corbis)

though, when it suited him, he would project a persona as a Prussian Protestant. He came to fear being identified as Jewish in public. In 1829, the pathologically insecure poet Count August von Platen included some witless jibes about Heine's Jewishness in his comedy *Der romantische Ödipus* (The Romantic Oedipus), and Heine struck back within the year with a savage satire on Platen's homosexuality, *Die Bäder von Lucca* (The Baths of Lucca).

During much of his life, Heine, believing religious faith had been made obsolete by the Enlightenment, included Judaism with Christianity in a conspiracy to suppress sensual gratification and plentitude. In response to an accusation of Jewishness, he once wrote: "One does not turn to the excessively withered charms of the mother when the aging daughter no longer pleases" (Heine 1973–1997, 165). But an alteration was working within him under the surface; an early sign of it was a spirited defense of Shylock in his *Shakspeares Mädchen und Frauen* (Shakespeare's Maidens and Ladies, [1838]). A real shock came

with a ritual murder charge in Damascus in 1840, leading to a pogrom in the Middle East during which the government of France—for Heine, the guardian of the Enlightenment tradition—temporized opportunistically. He responded by publishing an extended yet incomplete version of a novel with a medieval Jewish setting that he had begun in his student days, *Der Rabbi von Bacherach* (The Rabbi of Bacherach).

His subsequent ventures into Jewish themes and his declaration of submission to a belief in God, though lively topics of inquiry to the present day, are not relevant here, and antisemitism played only a marginal role in his generally poor standing with the German public in the latter part of his life and for some years afterward. A collection of forty-two obituaries, some quite hostile, contains not a single overtly antisemitic note. He was regarded as frivolous, unpatriotic, and Frenchified—a view shared by many prominent Jews, who particularly resented his attack on his fellow dissident of Jewish descent, Ludwig Börne, widely regarded as Heine's moral superior. In the latter third of the nineteenth century, his reputation improved, both in general and among Jewish commentators. Simultaneously, with the rise of a more systematically articulated antisemitism, elaborate attacks were mounted against him. Notable among several zealots was Adolf Bartels, who strove in some two dozen publications to drive Heine out of German culture. Such agitators may seem more significant in historical retrospect than they appeared to be in their own time, when mainstream opinion regarded them as fringe crackpots. They would not have been so agitated if Heine's standing in German culture had not been substantial, as confirmed by nearly forty collected editions of his works published between the 1860s and the end of the Weimar Republic. The precipitous decline of his reputation among arbiters of taste around the turn of the century is owed not to antisemitism but to a modernist devaluation of his poetry, led not least by critics of Jewish origin such as Robert Neumann and Karl Kraus. The Nazis, of course, attempted to erase him altogether. (Although it has been reported that the "Lorelei" setting appeared in Nazi songbooks as "author unknown," in order to rescue the popular poem from its tainted Jewish authorship, no one has been able to find an example to support this claim.) In the vigorous revival of Heine studies in postwar German scholarship, antisemitism played no role except as a count of indictment against the bourgeoisie, although some uncompromising leftists continue to insist that he could not have had a Jewish identity or religious allegiance of any kind.

—*Jeffrey L. Sammons*

See also Bartels, Adolf; Damascus Blood Libel; English Literature from Chaucer to Wells; Heine Monument Controversy; Hep-Hep Riots; Kraus, Karl; Shylock

References

Heine, Heinrich. *Historisch-kritische Gesamtausgabe der Werke.* Edited by Manfred Windfuhr. (Hamburg: Hoffmann und Campe, 1973–1997).

Peters, George F. *The Poet as Provocateur: Heinrich Heine and His Critics* (Rochester, NY: Camden House, 2000).

Sammons, Jeffrey L. *Heinrich Heine: A Modern Biography* (Princeton, NJ: Princeton University Press, 1979).

Heine Monument Controversy

After the unification of Germany in 1871, monuments to inspirational figures of the past became important for defining national identity. Vigorous efforts beginning in the 1880s to erect a monument to Heinrich Heine (1797–1856) encountered moralistic, monarchist, and nationalistic opposition, to which accrued a rising tide of antisemitism. The issue generated recurrent scenes of political theater continuing into the late twentieth century. The most notorious of the endeavors, the Lorelei Fountain, intended for Heine's home city of Düsseldorf, was designed by a prominent monument specialist, Ernst Herter, whose fee was to have been paid by a fervent admirer of Heine, Empress Elisabeth of Austria. Although the project was supported by municipal government, the press, and majority public opinion in Düsseldorf, a minority of opponents forged an alliance with the Prussian government to thwart it; the empress, possibly as a result of pressure on Vienna from Berlin, withdrew her support. The project became a focus of antisemitic agitation, although an effort to move the fountain to Mainz was combated also by local Jews, including the chief rabbi. After epic adventures, a German American singing society eventually took the fountain to what is now Joyce Kilmer Park in the Bronx, where its restoration was celebrated in June 1999, exactly 100 years after the failed attempt in Düsseldorf.

Several other contentious episodes followed. In 1891, Empress Elisabeth had a statue of a seated, contemplative Heine, by the Danish sculptor Louis Hasselriis, erected at her estate on the island of Corfu; when Kaiser Wilhelm II acquired the property in 1908, he had it removed. An effort by the son of Heine's publisher to donate the sculpture to Hamburg failed; it is now in a park in Toulon. A tireless antisemitic campaign did not succeed in preventing a sculpture dedicated to Heine from being erected in Frankfurt in 1913, although it was moved to a Jewish neighborhood. The Nazis destroyed all the memorials that had not been hidden except, curiously, Hasselriis's bust on Heine's grave in Montmartre Cemetery in Paris, dedicated by a Viennese male chorus in 1901.

Quarrels reemerged after World War II. In 1953, Düsseldorf acquired by gift for the newly named Heinrich Heine Avenue one of the familiar nudes of the fascist sympathizer Aristide Maillol; titled *Harmonie,* this piece was scorned in some quarters for its incongruity. Düsseldorf seemed to have put the matter to rest in 1981 with what was regarded as a more adequate representation of Heine, a prostrate figure with broken body parts sculpted by Bert Gerresheim. But in 1983, a bitter dispute was ignited when a prewar work depicting Heine by a sculptor celebrated by the Nazi regime, Arno Breker, was erected on the island of Norderney. Another controversy arose over a life-size statue of Heine by the nationalist sculptor Hugo Lederer, originally erected in Hamburg in 1926 but destroyed by the Nazis; an abstracted version of this work was placed in front of the Heinrich-Heine-University of Düsseldorf, named for the poet in 1988 after a twenty-three-year conflict with the administration and faculty. Whether this dispute marks the end of monument controversies is difficult to predict.

—*Jeffrey L. Sammons*

See also Germany, Federal Republic of; Heine, Heinrich; Nazi Cultural Antisemitism
References
Reitter, Paul. "Heine in the Bronx," *Germanic Review* 74 (1999): 327–336.
Sammons, Jeffrey L. "The Restoration of the Heine Monument in the Bronx," *Germanic Review* 74 (1999): 337–339.

Henrici, Ernst (1854–1915)

Representing a radical racist, social reformist, and aggressively rowdy form of Jew-hatred (*Radauantisemitismus*), Ernst Henrici played only a short-lived role in the history of party-political antisemitism in the German Empire. He was born in Berlin, the seventh child of a retired soldier and fiscal official. With his special talent for languages and his extraordinary will and energy, he became a promising young scholar, writing a prize-winning essay at Berlin University in 1877 and earning his doctorate a year later with a thesis on medieval German literature. In July 1880, his study on Martin Luther's works took the even more prestigious prize of the Royal Prussian Academy, presented to him by the famous historian Theodor Mommsen. In the same year, dissatisfied with his life as a high school teacher and casual scholar, Henrici tried his luck in politics, first with the left-liberal Progressive Party and then, under the influence of his former teacher Bernhard Förster, within the new movement of antisemitism. In 1880, he founded a "liberal-minded antisemitic" association, which developed into the Soziale Reichspartei (Social Reich Party) in March 1881. Its program combined the demands of the Antisemites' Petition that Henrici had helped formulate, with social reformist planks such as the ten-hour working day and unemployment insurance, and chauvinist pleas for a more aggressive German colonial policy. The party failed by 1882.

Henrici was able to exert more influence, however, as a sensation-seeking antisemitic agitator in Berlin and the provinces. His inflammatory rhetoric and malicious ridicule of the supposed "racial traits" of Jews attracted mass audiences and provoked anti-Jewish disturbances on New Year's Eve in Berlin in 1880 and the burning of the synagogue and pogrom in Neustettin during the spring and summer of 1881. Henrici's antisemitic rowdyism soon cost him his job. Within the antisemitic movement, the violent excesses of 1881 led to a split between politically conservative antisemites, such as Court Chaplain Adolf Stoecker and Max Liebermann von Sonnenberg, and radicals such as Henrici, who were seen as threatening to the existing order. Henrici became increasingly isolated. At the First International Antisemitic Congress in Dresden (in 1882), he demanded that all Jews be expelled from Germany. Stoecker countered that a plebiscite on the question of whether Jews or antisemites should be expelled certainly would be decided in the Jews' favor.

In 1884, Henrici cooperated in founding the anticonservative and social reformist Deutscher Antisemitenbund (German Antisemites' League), another quick failure. Soon thereafter, he left the political stage for good, in his own mind both the hero and the martyr of the antisemitic movement. He spent much of the remainder of his unsettled life as a colonial adventurer, planter, and engineer in Africa, Latin America, and the United States. After his return to Germany in 1910, he held a succession of jobs, including the editorship of the inconsequential antisemitic newspaper *Frankfurter Warte* (Frankfurt Guardian).

—*Christhard Hoffmann*

See also Antisemites' Petition; Antisemitic Political Parties; Berlin Movement; Förster, Bernhard; Liebermann von Sonnenberg, Max; Neustettin Pogrom; Stoecker, Adolf
References
Hoffmann, Gerd. *Der Prozeß um den Brand der Synagoge in Neustettin* (Schifferstadt, Germany: Hoffmann, 1998), 247–281.

Hentschel, Willibald (1858–1947)

Willibald Hentschel was one of the most eccentric but influential propagators of racial hygiene and rural romanticism in the Wilhelmian and Weimar eras. Closely associated with Theodor Fritsch, with whom he founded the antisemitic periodical *Hammer* in 1903, Hentschel developed several utopian schemes for renewing the German race through selective breeding and polygamy in agricultural communities. His notions of "blood and soil" inspired the founding of the Artamanenbund after World War I, a rural work organization for young Germans that was absorbed into the Reichsnährstand (Reich Agriculture Corporation) under Hitler's minister of agriculture, Walter Darré, in 1933.

Hentschel studied biology under the Darwinian Ernst Haeckel at Jena and wrote a doctoral dissertation on the causes of hereditary variations. Having amassed sufficient wealth through a patent for the manufacture of indigo, he was able to devote most of his life to his publishing and political pursuits. In the 1890s, he served on the board of directors of Max Liebermann von Sonnenberg's antisemitic German Social Party. His two most influential books were *Varuna* (1901), a fanciful account of the origins of race from an "Aryan perspective," and *Mittgart* (1904), a proposal for breeding a new rural aristocracy on huge estates by settling 1,000 racially pure women and 100 men selected on the basis of athletic and military competition. The children resulting from these multiple temporary unions would leave the estates at the age of sixteen to replenish the declining racial stock in Germany's degenerate cities and provide superior soldiers for its armies. The scheme offended conventional religious sensibilities and also drew considerable criticism from other racial hygienists who deplored the dissolution of the family. The Artamanenbund, founded in 1923, was based on Hentschel's marginally more moderate postwar plan to re-Germanize the countryside and promote peasant-warrior values. Young volunteers were organized into rural work communities to displace migrant Polish workers on estates in the eastern part of the country and to open up new farmland for German colonization.

Hentschel collaborated with Fritsch in promoting political antisemitism. In 1904, the *Hammer* announced that *Varuna* contained the program of the journal and that acquaintance with this work would be required of all contributors. In *Varuna*, subtitled *On the Law of Ascending and Declining Life in the History of Peoples* in later editions, Hentschel warned that the Germanic race had become "Semitized" through racial mixing, contact with foreigners, industrialization, and the spread of alcohol and narcotics in the modern world. Commercialization, urbanization, and democracy were the deleterious consequences of this Semitism. Hentschel's immediate goal was to reverse the new Civil Code, adopted in 1900, which supposedly enshrined the "Roman-Jewish" institutions of real estate mortgage and mobile capital. He defined *Semitism* as everything that disjoined the heroic personality from its true nature. For him, Semitism stood not for a particular race (although Jews were its modern agents) but for an ethnic principle of moral and cultural degeneration that had corrupted the ancient Israelites and now threatened the Germanic race. According to Hentschel, ancient Greek and Roman civilizations had collapsed because they had been unable to mobilize effective antisemitic movements. Only a strong countermovement could prevent the triumph of Semitism all over the world. The urgent task for Germans was to overcome the Semitism within themselves, and racial hygiene was the means to this end.

—*Roderick Stackelberg*

See also Antisemitic Political Parties; Capital: Useful versus Harmful; Fritsch, Theodor; Imperial Hammer League; Liebermann von Sonnenberg, Max; Settlement *Heimland;* Social Darwinism

References

Löwenberg, Dieter. "Willibald Hentschel (1858–1947): Seine Pläne zur Menschenzüchtung, sein Biologismus und Antisemitismus." Dissertation, University of Mainz, 1978.

Mosse, George L. *The Crisis of German Ideology: Intellectual Origins of the Third Reich* (New York: Grosset and Dunlap, 1964).

Schmitz, Peter. *Die Artamanen: Landarbeit und Siedlung bündischer Jugend in Deutschland 1924–1935* (Bad Neustadt a. d. Saale, Germany: Verlag Dietrich Pfaehler, 1985).

Hep-Hep Riots (1819)

In August and September 1819, a series of anti-Jewish riots spread across Germany and beyond. For the first time since the Middle Ages, Jewish communities in Germany were exposed to the threat of large-scale violent persecution. The ominous and enigmatic slogan of the 1819 rioters—Hep-Hep—was to serve as a battle cry for Jew-baiters throughout the nineteenth century.

The riots started on August 2, 1819, in the Bavarian town of Würzburg. Large crowds systematically attacked Jewish-owned shops and private homes and abused and chased Jewish passersby. Even after the Jewish inhabitants had fled the town, the riots continued for several days before they were quelled by the police and military. There were no casualties among Würzburg's Jews, but a rioter and a policeman lost their lives.

The Würzburg riots triggered a wave of anti-Jewish unrest that, within a few weeks, spread across Bavaria, Württemberg, Baden, Hesse, and elsewhere in Germany. Severe riots occurred in a number of other major towns, including Frankfurt am Main, Heidelberg, Hamburg, and Danzig. In Heidelberg, the pillaging of the Jewish quarter went on for hours before it was finally stopped by a contingent of university students. In Danzig, a large crowd attacked two synagogues and several private homes on the Day of Atonement. In two Bavarian villages, the synagogues were demolished and the Torah scrolls destroyed. Elsewhere, Jewish villagers were threatened with arson attacks. In October 1819, a ritual murder allegation rekindled anti-Jewish disturbances in the Rhineland. Unrest spread beyond Germany to Alsace and to several Danish towns, most severely in Copenhagen and Odense.

The Hep-Hep riots occurred at a time of heightened political and social tension in Germany. On the eve of the repressive Carlsbad Decrees, the hunt for suspected demagogues was already under way, and rumors of revolutionary unrest were omnipresent. It was widely assumed by contemporaries that the anti-Jewish riots had been instigated by conspirators who hoped to use popular anti-Jewish bias to arouse general political unrest. Contributing to these suspicions were the swift and wide diffusion of the rioting, the uniformity of newspaper reports about incidents in places far apart, and the mysterious "Hep-Hep" slogan that rioters everywhere seemed to recognize as the starting signal. Much effort was devoted to deciphering this battle cry, which many believed contained a cryptic meaning whose decoding would reveal the identities of the instigators. The oft-repeated but erroneous assumption that the rioting in Würzburg had been initiated by university students is indicative of the conviction that the outbreaks were somehow related to political conspiracies and especially to revolutionary, nationalistic student activity.

The causes of the Hep-Hep riots are highly complex. The political frustrations of the years after the Congress of Vienna, the economic problems and social tensions that followed on the defeat of Napoleon, and the aftereffects of the famine of 1816 and 1817 may have facilitated the violent outbreaks against the Jews. However, more direct causes can be linked to the agitation for and against Jewish emancipation that peaked during these years. Liberals as well as Christian romantics participated in the acrimonious debates, together with journalists and playwrights. Anti-Jewish tracts written by university professors such as the historian Friedrich Rühs and the philosopher Jakob Fries were echoed by newspapers and even read out to people in taverns. For all their differences, most of the pamphlets, newspaper articles, and plays, as well as the public response they engendered, signified the emphatic rejection of Jewish emancipation.

The initial outbreaks of the Hep-Hep riots in Würzburg occurred just as the debate over Jewish emancipation in the Bavarian parliament had been concluded but before its outcome had been made public. At the same time, well-known Würzburg residents were conducting their own passionate arguments on the topic. Tellingly, the rioters in Würzburg chose targets primarily defined by these local debates over the legal status of the Jews in society and the civic community. Signs over Jewish-owned shops, first permitted in 1816, were systematically torn down by the rioters. Similarly, the riots in Frankfurt and in Hamburg began with Jewish pedestrians being chased away from public promenades and fashionable coffeehouses—places where Jews had been allowed only recently, occasioning much public rancor.

Despite some anti-Jewish restrictions temporarily imposed by authorities in Würzburg and elsewhere in response to the violent outbursts, the Hep-Hep riots did not have a lasting impact on the struggle for emancipation in Germany at large. Their long-term effects on the Jewish minority, however, are difficult to assess. Although the claim that the processes of acculturation among German Jews were manifestly accelerated by the riots may be overstated, they certainly strengthened the quest for reorientation among many Jewish intellectuals.

—*Stefan Rohrbacher*

See also Alsace; Arndt, Ernst Moritz; Burschenschaften; Emancipation; Fries, Jakob Friedrich; Heine, Heinrich; Jewish Question; Varnhagen von Ense, Rahel Levin

References
Katz, Jacob. "The Hep Hep Riots in Germany of 1819: The Historical Background," *Ziyyon* 38 (1973): 62–117 (Hebrew).
Rohrbacher, Stefan. *Gewalt im Biedermeier: Antijüdische Ausschreitungen in Vormärz und Revolution (1815–1848/49)* (Frankfurt am Main, Germany: Campus, 1993), 94–156.
————. "The Hep Hep Riots of 1819: Anti-Jewish Ideology, Agitation, and Violence." In *Exclusionary Violence: Antisemitic Riots in Modern German History*. Edited by Christhard Hoffmann, Werner Bergmann, and Helmut Walser Smith (Ann Arbor: University of Michigan Press, 2002), 23–42.
Sterling, Eleonore. "Anti-Jewish Riots in Germany in 1819: A Displacement of Social Protest," *Historia Judaica* 12 (1950): 105–142.

Herder, J. G. (1744–1803)

The German philosopher, theologian, and critic J. G. Herder had a particular interest in Jewish Scripture, which he read in Hebrew and passionately promoted in his own writings as the finest example of a national culture expressed through its poetry. Fullest understanding of Scripture, he argued, required that the reader have sympathetic awareness of the particular circumstances and experiences of its writers (*On the Spirit of Hebrew Poetry* 1782). The fundamental principle that each national culture develops organically as a distinctive entity and, as such, is intrinsically valuable underlies much of his thinking, including his condemnation of colonialist enterprises, his rejection of the notion that historical succession ought to be understood as a process of moral or cultural improvement, and his attack on state bureaucracies as artificial and inauthentic institutions that supplant the role properly belonging to organic national cultures. Taken in that context, Herder's expressions of sympathy for Jews and Judaism have traditionally been assessed as a significant departure from the thinking of his Enlightenment contemporaries, whose commitment to the ideals of liberty, equality, and fraternity was frequently tempered by ambivalence or open hostility toward Jews.

Recent scholarship, however, suggests that Herder's perspective on Jews was itself more ambivalent than has generally been acknowledged. His writings on contemporary Jews occasionally had recourse to the standard vocabulary of *Judenhass* (Jew-hatred). One particularly harsh passage appearing in the fourth volume of his masterwork, *Ideas for the Philosophy of the History of Humanity,* deploys the familiar imagery of Jews as parasites, sharp-practicing usurers who profited during the "barbaric centuries" of the Middle Ages by reinforcing Europeans' self-defeating pride in their ignorance of commerce; Herder describes this effect as "a more irritating leprosy" than the real thing, which the Jews are also (erroneously, according to Herder) thought to have introduced to Europe. Paul Lawrence Rose has argued that Herder's readiness to invoke such rhetoric, coupled with his view that Jewish populations ought to be restricted to such numbers as could be made useful to the "host" state, undermines his stature as a liberal humanitarian, putting him firmly in the camp of the statist conservatives.

Others have taken the position advanced by Bernhard Suphan, the nineteenth-century scholar who prepared the first and most comprehensive edition of Herder's works. Suphan claimed that the numerous passages in Herder's published works that were profoundly inconsistent with the rest of his thought reflected his need to mollify the authorities to whom he answered in his professional position as general superintendent and pastor of the court church for the Duchy of Saxony-Weimar. Indeed, Emil Adler found that comparison of the published version of *Ideas* with Herder's manuscript revealed a dramatic reversal; the manuscript version of the passage made no mention of parasites or usury, arguing that the Jews, dispersed throughout Europe in the centuries after the fall of Rome—through their wealth, intelligence, orderliness, and industry—played and continue to play an indispensable role in helping the European nations overcome the barbarism of the medieval era.

Even if Herder's manuscripts reveal a more consistently affirmative evaluation of Jews and Judaism than emerges from his published works, it must nevertheless be said that such suppressed sentiments are, by definition, irrelevant as a matter of historical reception. However, even at their most extreme, his passages of anti-Jewish rhetoric did not significantly expand on or deepen prejudices common at the time. Herder's most important contribution to the intellectual history of antisemitism was entirely unintended: his novel argument for the organic development of national cultures, which incorporated elements of geography, language, kinship, and historical continuity. Although Herder maintained (with occasional lapses) that no culture enjoyed a privileged position with respect to any other, his model of the organic national culture left Jews living in the Diaspora exposed, susceptible to charges that their culture was "inorganic" and therefore inauthentic. Herder's own attempts to overcome this difficulty and recover some claims for the legitimacy of Jewish culture were, in the end, not entirely convincing, which made them all the easier to reject when later generations of ardent German nationalists sought to apply his ideas to programs and policies he would certainly have abhorred.

—*David Isadore Lieberman*

See also Dohm, Christian Wilhelm von; Emancipation; Fichte, J. G.; Kant, Immanuel; Michaelis, Johann David; Usury

References
Adler, Emil. "Johann Gottfried Herder und das Judentum." In *Herder Today: Contributions from the International Herder Conference.* Edited by Kurt Mueller-Vollmer (Berlin: Walter de Gruyter, 1990).
Menze, Ernest A. "Herder's 'German Kind of "Humanity"' and the Jewish Question: Historical Context and Contemporary Criticism." In *Johann Gottfried Herder: Geschichte und Kultur.* Edited by Martin Bollacher (Würzburg, Germany: Königshausen & Neumann, 1994).

Herzl, Theodor (1860–1904)

A Viennese writer and journalist, Theodor Herzl is best known as the founder of political Zionism.

Antisemitism played a central role in Herzl's "conversion" to Zionism. However, the conventional view of him as an assimilationist shocked by the antisemitism of the Dreyfus Affair overestimates the role of antisemitism in this change of orientation and underestimates the extent to which Herzl's Zionism arose from his own negative assessment of modern European Jewry. This critique had a surprising degree of affinity with antisemitic accusations about Jews, but it arose from the quite different source of the emancipation ideology of central European Jewry.

Born into a prosperous "assimilated" Jewish family in Budapest in 1860, Herzl moved to Vienna in 1878, where he studied law. In 1883, he resigned from his dueling fraternity, Albia, over an antisemitic incident. After a brief stint as a lawyer, he eventually gained success as a journalist, being appointed Paris correspondent of the *Neue Freie Presse* in 1891. While in Paris, reporting on the Panama Scandal and other scandals with a Jewish connection, he became increasingly concerned about the Jewish Question and antisemitism—but as much, if not more, back in Austria than in France.

He became more and more critical of other Jews, from an emancipatory perspective: Jews still suffered from "inner insecurity" and the social flaws of a pariah parvenu class, including an obsession with money. He was deeply ambivalent about antisemitism, seeing it as useful as a way of making Jews behave more soberly but also as a dire threat to real Jewish emancipation and integration into modern, European society. He therefore advocated various ways to combat antisemitism, including duels, mass conversion, and the support of universal suffrage and socialism. Many of these themes are evident in his play *Das Ghetto* (The Ghetto), written in late 1894, but his conclusion by then was that Jewish self-emancipation could not succeed in the "new ghetto" caused by the antisemitism of the surrounding non-Jewish society, combined with the survival of many negative aspects of preemancipatory life among Jews themselves.

After the degradation of Dreyfus in January 1895 and, more significantly, the victory of the antisemitic Christian Socials in municipal elections in Vienna in April, Herzl concluded that if the

A painting of Theodor Herzl, the Austro-Hungarian Jewish writer and founder of political Zionism. (Bettmann/Corbis)

Jewish problem could not be solved in Europe, it could be solved by removing the Jews from the European context. If a state for the Jews could be created somewhere else, perhaps (but not necessarily only) in Palestine, then the emancipatory goal of Jewish self-betterment, materially and morally, could be realized without the encumbrances of the past. After Jews had been transformed into a modern people, with "inner freedom" and a sense of honor, they could then rejoin the rest of modern humanity, not as individuals but as members of their own state. Meanwhile, the emigration of Jews would relieve the antisemitic pressure in Europe and save the advanced societies there from its threat. As visitors, Jews would be greeted as friends in countries where they had been despised as pariahs. This is the argument of *Der Judenstaat* (The State for the Jews), which Herzl wrote in 1895 and published in 1896. This is also the rationale behind Herzl's subsequent campaign to form the Zionist movement.

After 1895, Herzl continued to press the argument that Zionism was the answer to antisemitism, both in saving Jews from persecution (in Russia and Romania, for instance) and in removing the problem that had caused antisemitism in the first place. That problem was that Jews *were,* for him, a separate people from their host societies and thus were understandably considered foreign, which was the basis of antisemitism. This pariah status had also created a deformed type of Jew, dubbed "Mauschel" in a Herzl essay. In their own homeland, by contrast, Jews would be on their own turf like everyone else and would form a normal society, indeed a model modern society, with cooperatives in agriculture and industry but without the former obsession with money. They would also, most probably, speak German and sing Wagner arias, as he prophesied in his utopian novel *Altneuland* (Old-Newland). Antisemitism would vanish because there would no longer be any Jews in Europe to cause it, and the Jews in Palestine would exemplify precisely the healthy, self-possessed, honorable people that antisemites and critical liberal emancipationists such as Herzl had claimed were not to be found in Europe. The Arabs in Palestine would welcome the Jews, because they would bring economic prosperity.

Thus, antisemitism played a central role in Herzl's thinking. But it did so in a far less straightforward way than is usually thought.

—*Steven Beller*

See also Austria; Christian Social Party (Austria); Dreyfus Affair; Emancipation; Hungary; Jewish Question; *Ostjuden;* Romania; Russia, Imperial; Zionism
References
Beller, Steven. *Herzl* (London: Halban, 1991).
Kornberg, Jacques. *Theodor Herzl: From Assimilation to Zionism* (Bloomington: Indiana University Press, 1993).
Pawel, Ernst. *The Labyrinth of Exile: A Life of Theodor Herzl* (New York: Farrar, Straus and Giroux, 1989).

Himmler, Heinrich (1900–1945)

As the leader of the SS, Heinrich Himmler wielded extraordinary power over the development, timing, and implementation of the Jewish genocide. Himmler was steeped in every aspect of the radicalization of antisemitic policy during the National Socialist era. His control over the policing functions of the Nazi Party and the state (including the concentration camp system) made him one of the key officials who both formulated and enforced policies of oppression.

Himmler was born on October 7, 1900, the second son of Professor Gebhard and Anna Maria Himmler. Gebhard was the tutor for Prince Heinrich of Bavaria, a member of the royal Wittelsbach family, for whom Gebhard's son was named. After failing to become a military officer, Himmler took up agricultural studies in 1919 at the Technical College in Munich. He also developed his anticommunist and antisemitic worldview in these early and turmoil-filled years of the Weimar Republic. Through his contact with Ernst Röhm, he joined the Nazi Party in August 1923, in time to participate in the Beer Hall Putsch in November of that year. Thanks to Himmler's administrative abilities and dogged personal allegiance, Hitler made him Reichsführer SS in 1929, a job that entailed turning the SS into a disciplined unit that could balance and control the unruly and much more haphazardly recruited SA under Röhm. Himmler's work was tested in the Blood Purge of June 1934, when SS men summarily murdered Röhm and other top Storm troopers.

Himmler's influence continued to grow. In June 1936, Hitler appointed him as head of the German police. As both Reichsführer SS and head of the police, Himmler exercised unprecedented power in the party and state, including oversight of the developing concentration camps. He reorganized the camp system, expanded its facilities, and combined the process of punishment with an increased emphasis on forced labor. Having acquired authority over the concentration camps meant that he also controlled the institutions that might be called on to implement specific policies designed to rid Germany of its Jews.

At the outbreak of war in September 1939, Himmler began to propose new ways (eventually including the use of gas) of eradicating not only German Jews but also other Jewish populations coming under German domination. In the early years of the war, the SS participated most actively in killing operations by the Einsatzgruppen (mobile death squads) in the East. These murders lacked a system, however, even if the numbers of victims reached extreme proportions. In 1941, after the stunning initial military victories, Himmler worked toward a more totalizing plan with his subordinate, Reinhard Heydrich, and in consultation with Hitler. Himmler was crucial at every stage of the decision-making process, instrumental to its brutally successful culmination in the death camps of occupied Poland and in the near destruction of European Jews.

Himmler committed suicide on May 23, 1945, his third day of custody in the hands of Allied forces.

—*Paul B. Jaskot*

See also Eichmann, Adolf; Einsatzgruppen; Hitler, Adolf; Holocaust; National Socialist German Workers' Party

References

Ackermann, Josef. *Heinrich Himmler als Ideologue* (Göttingen, Germany: Musterschmidt, 1970).

Breitman, Richard. *The Architect of Genocide: Himmler and the Final Solution* (New York: Alfred A. Knopf, 1991).

Tuchel, Johannes. "Heinrich Himmler: Der Reichsführer-SS." In *Die SS: Elite unter dem Totenkopf.* Edited by Ronald Smelser and Enrico Syring (Paderborn, Germany: Ferdinand Schöningh, 2000), 234–253.

Hirschfeld, Magnus (1868–1935)

Magnus Hirschfeld, one of the founders of the German homosexual rights movement, worked not only to overturn legal restrictions against male homosexuality but also to educate the German public on modern theories related to all areas of sexuality. Hirschfeld believed that the dissemination of scientific research on sex would overturn long-held prejudices and myths concerning sexuality and lead to changes in the German Penal Code regarding homosexuality, women's rights, abortion, birth control, adultery, and illegitimacy. His numerous books and pamphlets on these topics made him one of the world's leading sexologists of the early twentieth century.

A physician by profession, Hirschfeld espoused the theory that homosexuality was not an illness but an inborn, naturally occurring sexual variation, which he labeled the Third Sex. Though he later distanced himself from this notion, he continued in the firm belief that homosexuality was an innate predisposition and, as such, should not result in legal penalties. To this end, he founded Germany's first homosexual rights organization, the Scientific-Humanitarian Committee, in 1897, with the goal of repealing paragraph 175 of the Penal Code. That same year, Hirschfeld presented a petition to the Reichstag, signed by 6,000 prominent Germans, calling for the elimination of the law. His efforts led to the first Reichstag debate on homosexuality in 1905.

Despite his efforts, penalties for homosexual conduct were not eliminated in imperial Germany. In fact, Hirschfeld damaged both his and his movement's reputation before World War I by his participation in a well-publicized case, in which he claimed to know for certain that the defendant was homosexual without ever having met or spoken to him. The subsequent discrediting of his testimony made Hirschfeld a laughingstock to many. The fact that he was Jewish also linked the cause of gay rights with Judaism in the minds of many German conservatives of the time.

After the war, Hirschfeld continued his work with the committee, and in 1919, he founded the Institute for Sexual Science in Berlin to study all aspects of sexuality and to provide counseling on sexual matters. Though Hirschfeld continued to work for homosexual rights, much of his time was taken up with the work of the institute and with a busy speaking schedule that took him all over Europe. Catcalls, rude remarks, and stink bombs frequently greeted his lectures, and in 1920, members of an antisemitic group beat him into unconsciousness and left him for dead.

Hirschfeld was forced out of the leadership of the committee in 1929 for promoting useless medicines and birth control products in exchange for kickbacks from their manufacturers. Others in the homosexual rights movement who believed that the Jewish Hirschfeld was an unsuitable leader and a political liability greeted his departure with relief. Hirschfeld then left on a two-year international speaking tour. While he was out of Germany, the National Socialists came to power, making his return impossible.

One of the first targets of Nazi demonstrators was Hirschfeld's institute, which, on May 8, 1933, was sacked; its 12,000-volume library was destroyed. Hirschfeld died in exile in France on his sixty-eighth birthday.

—*James Kollenbroich*

See also Homophobia; Masculinity; Weimar
References
Steakley, James D. *The Writings of Dr. Magnus Hirschfeld: A Bibliography* (Toronto, Canada: Gay Archives, 1985).
Wolff, Charlotte. *Magnus Hirschfeld: A Portrait of a Pioneer of Sexology* (London: Quartet Books, 1986).

Historians' Controversy

From 1985 to 1987, a debate among historians (*Historikerstreit*) and other public intellectuals took place in the pages of German newspapers and magazines unaccustomed to airing protracted scholarly arguments. The controversy centered around three issues: (1) the origins of the Holocaust, (2) the comparability of the Holocaust to other genocides, and (3) the desire of many Germans to begin treating the Nazi era as a remote period of history like any other. Three works by distinguished German historians initiated discussions, which then erupted into a public and often acrimonious debate.

First, in 1985, Martin Broszat argued in "Plea for a Historicization of National Socialism" that the time had come to "historicize" the Nazi past and to cease treating it as a special case, exempt from the customary methods and demands of historical scholarship. He urged that the study of the Third Reich be normalized by placing it fully within the broadest historical context. Just as historians of phenomena much further in the past could treat their subjects with objective distance and employ approaches such as comparative history, scholars of the Nazi dictatorship ought now begin to normalize the period from 1933 to 1945.

Second, in *Two Kinds of Demise* (1986), Andreas Hillgruber evoked the suffering of Germans on the eastern front in the last year of World War II, a subject not much attended to in scholarly circles and never coupled with the book's other essay concerning the demise of Europe's Jews.

Both in the length of his discussion and in the degree of empathy he expressed, Hillgruber clearly accorded primacy to the agony of the German soldiers fighting the advancing Soviet armies.

Third, Ernst Nolte published a series of essays in 1986, including "The Past That Will Not Pass," and offered comparisons and outright linkages between the earlier mass murders perpetrated by Stalin and those of the Holocaust. In particular, Nolte partially explained the Holocaust as a defensive reaction by the Nazis to a perceived communist threat.

Social critic and philosopher Jürgen Habermas, joined, in turn, by several leading West German historians, responded to these and other works he believed trivialized the crimes of Nazi Germany. If the Holocaust's uniqueness was not recognized and if it had been a genocide like any other, then German history and identity would have been freed from any further need to reflect on the lingering traits in German culture and society that might have helped cause the Holocaust. Habermas challenged the motivations of Hillgruber, Nolte, and other historians and authors who had rallied to their side. Seeking to normalize German history in order to allow Germans to have national pride again seemed too great a price to pay for too slight a good.

Ultimately at stake in the controversy were the shared civic values of the Federal Republic of Germany. Germans' sense of their history was a key to these values. For Habermas and his allies in the Historikerstreit, the Nazi period could never be "normalized," for such a retreat from active confrontation with Germany's darkest chapter would likely mean a premature end to the country's still incomplete journey toward full and unquestioning acceptance of the liberal democratic values of the West. Only with a sense of history that continued to treat the Nazi period as unresolved and something that every German had the duty to face continually, Habermas believed, could German culture permanently internalize the values of peace and democracy. Some on the other side, such as historian Michael Stürmer, responded that a country without a settled past was also one without identity and hence infinitely malleable and capable of abandoning its Cold War allies for dangerous adventures.

Overt antisemitism was rarely in evidence in any of the debates. Instead, critics of the new historiographical tendencies worried that relativizing the Holocaust and normalizing the Nazi era would lay the groundwork for a new generation that would ignore the Holocaust and be more receptive to blatant expressions of antisemitism. The Historikerstreit demonstrated that German society had not yet matured to the point where people could discuss antisemitism and the Holocaust dispassionately, free of both excessive defensiveness on the Right or overzealousness on the Left. The mentality that had prefigured the Holocaust was thus still very much of concern among Germans of the day, and questions about the level of antisemitism among German elites would therefore remain unresolved.

—*Daniel Rogers*

See also Germany, Federal Republic of
References
Evans, Richard. *In Hitler's Shadow: West German Historians and the Attempt to Escape from the Nazi Past* (New York: Pantheon Books, 1989).
Maier, Charles S. *The Unmasterable Past: History, Holocaust, and German National Identity* (Cambridge, MA: Harvard University Press, 1988).

Hitler, Adolf (1889–1945)

Adolf Hitler was born into a family of a man who had worked his way up in the Austrian customs service. His years of indifferent performance in school were followed by half a decade in Vienna, where, after his application to the arts academy was rejected, Hitler bummed around until leaving for Munich in 1913, hoping to escape military service. In those years and possibly in school before that time, Hitler absorbed some of the antisemitic currents in the Vienna environment, although there is evidence that he had good personal and business relations with individual Jews.

At the beginning of World War I, he volunteered for the Bavarian army. He served on the Western Front and was decorated and wounded, but—unusual for a soldier who survived years of heavy casualties—he was promoted no further than private first class. He continued to paint and make architectural drawings as he had in Vienna and Munich. When the war ended, he was in a hospital, suffering from the effects of a poison gas attack. With his unit, like most of Germany's army, deep inside enemy territory, news of the military's acknowledgment of defeat came as a shattering blow to Hitler. This event would become a central element in his thinking. Germany, he believed, had not been defeated but had been stabbed in the back. Those who were trying to salvage what they could from defeat were, in fact, the authors of the collapse, and since the last legal restrictions on Jews in the German states were lifted, it was they who had brought on the defeat.

In the immediate postwar period, Hitler was first assigned to making indoctrination speeches and then to spying on local political movements. The first assignment gave him practice in public speaking; the second brought him to the political sect that eventually became the National Socialist Party. He used his oratorical talent to become the party's leader. By that time, Hitler's antisemitic views had become part of his core belief in the racial interpretation of history, and they were also a major theme of his oratory. Although he had attained a following, had received some financial support from the local military, and had sympathetic adherents in high social and government circles, a rash attempt to seize power in Munich failed ludicrously in November 1923.

While in jail for the coup, Hitler began to dictate the book *Mein Kampf.* In it, he outlined his view of history as a record of the struggle of races for living space (*Lebensraum*). In this struggle, the superior Germans would eventually dominate the globe, a point he made clear to his associates by 1927. The voters were not as enthusiastic as Hitler hoped when he resumed control of the party after his release from jail. The electoral defeat of May 1928 led him to dictate a second book, which he did not publish at the time for fear it would compete with *Mein Kampf;* nor did he publish it later because a year after writing it, he allied himself with the very people he had vehemently attacked in its pages. Hitler became part of their campaign against the Young Plan that was to settle Germany's reparations obligations and end military occupation of portions of the country five years early. The opponents of the Weimar Republic were terrified that the Young

Plan would be regarded as a great success and that it might help stabilize Germany; they saw in the Nazi Party a convenient ally. With new and powerful sponsors, Hitler was now able to appeal to ever more Germans; he drew increasing numbers of voters who liked his calls for a one-party state, wars to attain vast amounts of additional space for German settlement, and reversal of the emancipation of the Jews.

As leader of the party with the largest number of voters and masses of uniformed Storm troopers bullying opponents in the streets, Hitler was appointed chancellor by President Paul von Hindenburg on January 30, 1933. In the following months, he succeeded in persuading the president to suspend all constitutional liberties, in having parliament transfer legislative power to the cabinet, in abolishing all other political parties, and in establishing a terror apparatus that was publicized to overawe potential critics. Most important in view of his goals, a vast rearmament program was begun, and simultaneously, measures to discriminate against Jews and any individuals considered likely to have "racially deficient" children were put in place.

Because most of World War I had been fought outside Germany and investment had therefore gone into modernization rather than reconstruction and because all other combatants believed that one great war was more than enough for one century, Germany's rearmament provided the country with a head start over other countries. And since others had larger economies, Germany had an incentive to utilize its advantage while it lasted. Already in 1938, Hitler commented that he preferred war at age forty-nine than when he was older. In the same years that he pressed German armaments production, he pushed ever greater restrictions on Germany's Jews. His belief in the stab-in-the-back legend led him to favor expelling them before he began the first of his wars. They could always be killed later wherever they went, and a Germany without them and with only one party that he himself led was certain to win the wars he intended to fight.

In 1938, Hitler drew back from war at the last moment, an action he soon regretted and determined never to repeat. There would certainly be war in 1939. But as the annexation of Austria and the fringe areas of Czechoslovakia had already shown, German expansion was certain to add more Jews to the country. In this context, the pogrom of November 1938 was a means of expediting their departure while more drastic measures were under consideration. Having decided on war, he uttered his famous prophecy that war would bring about the extermination of the Jews.

The war Hitler initiated developed into one that Germany eventually lost. But during that conflict, the persecution of Jews was exported into whatever lands German forces reached. Before the attack on the Soviet Union in June 1941, orders were given that all Jews in the newly occupied lands were to be murdered. As Hitler believed victory in the East was in sight and as he saw the German military cooperating rather than complaining, the killing program was extended to all parts of Europe under German control or influence. Hitler hoped that it could be extended to the whole globe.

The war did not develop as he hoped, but he continued to push the killing of Jews into its last days. Before he committed suicide along with the mistress he had just married, he insisted in his will that the Germans continue to follow racial policies, and he designated as his successor Adm. Karl Dönitz, who shared his ideology.

—*Gerhard L. Weinberg*

See also Einsatzgruppen; Emancipation; Gemlich Letter; German National People's Party; Hitler's "Prophecy"; Hitler's Speeches (Early); Hitler's *Table Talk;* Holocaust; Ludendorff, Erich; *Mein Kampf;* National Socialist German Workers' Party; Nazi Legal Measures against Jews (1933–1939); Night of Broken Glass (November 1938 Pogrom); Versailles Treaty; Weimar

References
Kershaw, Ian. *Hitler: 1889–1936 Hubris* (New York: Norton, 1999).
———. *Hitler: 1936–1945 Nemesis* (New York: Norton, 2000).
Weinberg, Gerhard L. *Germany, Hitler, and World War II* (New York: Cambridge University Press, 1995).

Hitler's "Prophecy" (January 30, 1939)

In his speech to the German Reichstag on the sixth anniversary of being appointed chancellor, Adolf Hitler included in a lengthy speech the following: "Once again I will be a prophet: should the international Jewry of finance succeed, both within and beyond Europe, in plunging mankind into yet another world war, then the result will not be Bolshevization of the earth and the victory of Jewry, but the annihilation of the Jewish race in Europe."

Several aspects of this statement deserve attention. First, at the time Hitler made this speech, he had already decided that it had been a terrible mistake to draw back from war in 1938 and that he would most certainly go to war in 1939. No one would be allowed to cheat him of war, as Neville Chamberlain had done the preceding year. And the murder of Jews would be an integral part of the war on which he had already decided.

His thinking about the Jews fits in with a second aspect of the prophecy. When he referred back to it in speeches in subsequent years, for example on January 30, 1941, and January 30, 1942—at a time when the systematic killing of Jews was under way—he claimed to have made this prophecy on September 1, 1939, the day the war began. The war on which he had decided was always in his mind to effect a demographic revolution on the globe, a revolution in which the systematic killing of all Jews was a central part. In an analogous fashion, he backdated his October 1939 written authorization for the mass killing of the handicapped, the so-called euthanasia program, to the same date, September 1, 1939. A public speech and a secret document were both deliberately moved to the date that Hitler had picked for the initiation of World War II.

A third significant facet of this portion of Hitler's speech is his choice of terminology. The German word he used for "annihilation" was *Vernichtung*. Shortly before, on January 21, 1939, he had used a form of the same word in describing the future of Germany's Jews to the foreign minister of Czechoslovakia: *Die Juden wurden bei uns vernichtet* (the Jews living here would be annihilated). And Hitler used the terminology once more when promising the Grand Mufti of Jerusalem, in their lengthy meeting on November 28, 1941, that Germany's sole aim in the Middle East was the Vernichtung—the annihilation of all Jews living there; he made this pronouncement after he had explained to his guest the systematic removal of Jews from Europe and his hope of accomplishing the same objective with Jews living "among non-European peoples."

There are scholars who imagine that some event during the world conflict he unleashed led Hitler to implement a threat that was only theoretical when he first uttered it in public. Yet the contemporary evidence that his concept of eliminating the Jews was already worldwide in scope by November 1941 suggests otherwise. We do not know whether it had always been part of his view of global conquest. Implementation, of course, would depend on the course of the war.

—*Gerhard L. Weinberg*

See also Austria; Hitler, Adolf; Holocaust; Hussaini, Mufti Hajj Amin al-; Judeo-Bolshevism; *Mein Kampf;* National Socialist German Workers' Party

References
Weinberg, Gerhard L. *The Foreign Policy of Hitler's Germany: Starting World War II, 1937–1939* (Chicago: University of Chicago Press, 1980).
———. *A World at Arms: A Global History of World War II* (Cambridge: Cambridge University Press, 1994).

Hitler's Speeches (Early)

But the power which has always started the greatest religious and political avalanches in history rolling has from time immemorial been the magic power of the spoken word, and that alone. Particularly the broad masses of the people can be moved only by the power of speech. And all great movements are popular movements, volcanic eruptions of human passions and emotional sentiments, stirred either by the cruel Goddess of Distress or by the firebrand of the word hurled among the masses; they are not the lemonade-like outpourings of literary aesthetes and drawing room heroes. (Mein Kampf, translated by Ralph Manheim [Boston: Houghton Mifflin, 1943], 106–107.)

When Hitler wrote this passage, he already had gathered enough experience speaking before mass gatherings to believe in his own powers as an orator and in the history-making potency of demagogic speech. His oratorical gifts moved the "unknown corporal" of World War I, a man without formal education, money, or influential friends, into the spotlight of public life and then propelled him, in his own words, from "drummer" to "leader" of the fledgling National Socialist movement.

Beginning in September 1919, when he joined what was still the German Workers' Party, Hitler advanced swiftly to become its indispensable star speaker, the one who could fill the halls in the turbulent postwar years. By late 1920, he had already addressed thirty mass meetings with audiences ranging from 800 to 2,500 listeners. In addition, he spoke to numerous inner-party gatherings. On the basis of hastily composed notes, he typically spoke for two hours, sometimes even longer.

Hitler preached the Nazi movement "gospel," full of slogans that were vague on details but nonetheless clear on the basic message: all the misfortunes of the nation were the fault of Jews and Marxists! He played on the aggrieved sensibilities of the nation and promised national rebirth. Germany's resurrection, however, depended on setting aside the divisiveness that had been purposely injected into German life by Jewry, Marxism, democracy, and other alien forces. The party's melding of nationalism and socialism rejected the arrogance of class distinction that marred the Wilhelmine empire (whose downfall Hitler did not regret). National Socialism would, instead, take as its model the "community of the trenches" of World War I, a united "community of the race" (*Volksgemeinschaft*) embracing all social strata in a common struggle against the "yoke of Versailles."

Because all history consisted of race struggle for Hitler, the combating of the Jews occupied a pivotal place in his outlook. His manic obsession and undisguised Jew-hatred were the hallmarks of nearly all his early speeches: "The effects of Jewry will never disappear and its poisoning of the nations will never end as long as the instigator, the Jew, has not been removed [*entfernt*] from our midst" (in Jäckel 1981). In the early years, this was Hitler's basic credo; only after 1922 did anti-Marxism assume greater importance than naked Jew-hatred; the conquest of *Lebensraum* (living space) played scarcely any role in his speeches before 1927.

After the refounding of the party (on February 27, 1925), the Bavarian government banned Hitler from speaking before large audiences and for the next two years denied him his most effective weapon. The ban was adhered to by Prussia (until September 1928) and most of the other federal states, hampering Hitler politically and leaving him only the restricted venue of closed Nazi Party gatherings. But the "infamy" of the speaking ban also provided fertile propaganda opportunities for heroic self-stylization and the strengthening of Führer myth. The myth and its continuing elaboration functioned as the movement's integrating force, compensated for its programmatic vagueness, and covered over its organizational flaws.

The exclusive focus on Hitler's speech in a Nazi mass meeting was designed to proclaim a new political faith, one that aimed at conquering the audience through its emotions, rather than by appealing to its reason or engaging political opponents in rational debate. An important part of the experience was the cultic framework in which these events unfolded, the ever more refined and psychologically effective ritual of the "leader" bound to his "faithful band of followers." The Hitler salute, mandated inside the party in 1926, gave symbolic physical expression to the relationship.

The Hitler cult remained fundamental to the movement, but after the election breakthrough of September 1930, the emphases of the party's propaganda changed. Antisemitism, in Hitler's post-1930 speeches, lost its central significance, to be replaced by the crumbling Weimar Republic's economic and political-structural crisis. The transformation conformed to the Nazis' new electoral strategy, as it now assumed the profile of a people's protest party. However, this stratagem was sheer political opportunism. Hitler had not moderated his visionary goals. Neither was he prepared to abandon his commitments and grudges.

—*Clemens Vollnhals*
Richard S. Levy, translation

See also Hitler, Adolf; Judeo-Bolshevism; National Socialist German Workers' Party; Versailles Treaty; Weimar

References
Hitler: Reden, Schriften, Anordnungen: Februar 1925

bis Januar 1933. Edited by the Institut für Zeitgeschichte. 12 vols. (Munich, Germany: K. G. Saur Verlag, 1992–2003).

Jäckel, Eberhard. *Hitler's World View: A Blueprint for Power* (Cambridge, MA: Harvard University Press, 1981).

Jäckel, Eberhard, and Axel Kuhn, eds. *Hitler: Sämtliche Aufzeichnungen 1905–1924* (Stuttgart, Germany: Deutsche Verlagsanstalt, 1980). (See however "Neue Erkenntnisse zur Fälschung von Hitler-Dokumenten," *Vierteljahrshefte für Zeitgeschichte* 32 (1984): 163–169.)

Hitler's *Table Talk*

During lunch or dinner at Führer headquarters or at late-night tea parties, Hitler was in the habit of delivering monologues to his top-level military personnel or members of his most intimate circle. These free-wheeling commentaries were collected in the *Table Talk*. Presumably without Hitler's knowledge, one of Martin Bormann's adjutants recorded the contents of the talks, arranged them according to key terms, and afterwards compiled them into a longer memorandum. Most of these notes, which began on July 5, 1941, were written up by Heinrich Heim. Between March and July 1942, this task was taken over by Henry Picker. At the beginning of September 1942, a serious conflict between Hitler and his military leaders led to his growing withdrawal. The few entries from 1943 and 1944 were rendered by one of Bormann's men and by Bormann himself. (From a source-critical point of view, the most reliable version of the *Table Talk* remains Werner Jochmann's edition of 1980.)

Isolated from the German people in the closed and austere atmosphere of his headquarters, Hitler—physically in decline and frequently depressed as the war turned sour—used the round table as a forum in which he could lecture at length on his worldview, art, and politics. These occasions were also used to impart in a general way the "will of the Führer," which Bormann then fleshed out from notes. Hitler expatiated on the military situation and made known his desires on further actions to be taken. He pronounced on a wide range of subjects, including the position of the churches under National Socialism and policies for occupied eastern Europe.

He aired his criticism of the administration of justice, the bureaucracy, and the old elites.

In larger gatherings, Hitler, the autodidact, impressed his listeners with his immense knowledge of and memory for detail, especially in military matters. Even though surrounded by confidants in the seclusion of his headquarters, Hitler—always deeply mistrustful of his generals—frequently remained vague about what he was planning next. He left no doubt, however, about his intentions regarding the ruthless suppression and exploitation of the conquered East. "The struggle for hegemony in the world will be decided in Europe by the possession of Russian space. He will make Europe the most invulnerable place in the world" (September 17–18, 1941).The annihilation of bolshevism, the war for *Lebensraum* (living space), and the elimination (*Ausrottung*) of Jewry were interrelated aims. Thus, in the presence of Heinrich Himmler and Reinhard Heydrich, Hitler declared:

> In front of the Reichstag I prophesied to Jewry that, in the event of war's proving unavoidable, the Jew would disappear from Europe. This criminal race has on its conscience the two million dead of the World War, and [in this war] already hundreds of thousands more. Let nobody tell me that all the same we can't park them in the Russian wastes! Who's worrying about our troops? It's not a bad thing, by the way, that it is believed we are exterminating the Jews. Terror is a good thing. The attempt to create a Jewish State will be a failure. (October 25, 1941)

Hitler was more likely to unburden himself in the more relaxed nocturnal gatherings than in the lunch or dinner sessions. In neither context, however, did he admit to doubts about the increasingly dire military situation. In general, there was little discussion of current political problems. The repeated invocation of "unshakeable strength of will," historic mission, and National Socialism's heroic time of struggle was tantamount to self-hypnosis. The war, he reassured his intimates, would not be won by superior weaponry but by the most "unyielding resolve" and "fanatic will power." Should the German nation not be up to the challenge, however, then the consequences would be Darwinian: it would vanish.

Surveying the *Table Talk,* which must be seen as the distillation of hours of monologue, one conclusion is clear. During the war, Hitler made no substantial changes to the fundamental ideological positions he had held in earlier years. Yet, as Joachim Fest aptly observed in his great biography, a "tightening of the intellectual horizon" had taken place. The Hitler of the *Table Talk* "fell back on the vehement and vulgar phrases of the beer-hall demagogue" (Fest 1974, 696-697).

—*Clemens Vollnhals*
Richard S. Levy, translation

See also Churches under Nazism; Hitler, Adolf; Hitler's "Prophecy"; Hitler's Speeches(Early); Holocaust; *Mein Kampf;* Social Darwinism

References

Fest, Joachim C. *Hitler.* Translated by Richard and Clara Winston (New York: Harcourt Brace Jovanovich, 1974).

Jochmann, Werner, ed. *Adolf Hitler: Monologe im Führerhauptquartier 1941–1944—Die Aufzeichnungen Heinrich Heims* (Hamburg, Germany: Albrecht Knaus Verlag, 1980).

Picker, Henry. *Hitlers Tischgespräche im Führerhauptquartier 1941–1942* (Berlin: Ullstein Verlag, 1997).

Trevor-Roper, H. R., ed. *Hitler's Table Talk, 1941–44: His Private Conversations* (New York: Enigma Books, 2000).

Hlinka Guard

The Hlinka Guard (HG), a paramilitary unit of Andrej Hlinka's Slovak People's Party (HSPP), was formally established on October 8, 1938, although the first units were already functioning in the previous summer. Its roots can be traced back to the early 1920s and the so-called Rodobrana, the strong-arm squads established to defend the party's meetings.

The most important figure in the Rodobrana was Vojtech Tuka, a university law professor and editor of the party's organ, *Slovák.* The organization was outlawed in 1923 and again in 1927 but suffered the worst blow in 1929, when Tuka was charged with treason and taken into custody.

The first commander of the HG was Karol

Sidor; he was followed by Alexander Mach in March 1939, with Karol Murgaš as his chief of staff. Tuka remained a powerful force in the background. On the local level, HSPP officials and army officers were in charge. Although the ideology of the HG has yet to be studied in detail, two of its tenets are clear: the call for a social revolution and the solving of the Jewish Question.

Because the majority faction of the HSPP under the guidance of President Jozef Tiso had no enthusiasm for any kind of revolution, aside from anti-Jewish measures, an inner-Slovak struggle for power began. In the summer of 1940, Berlin intervened in this contest by forcing a cabinet reshuffling. Mach became minister of interior and Tuka became prime minister, as well as minister of foreign affairs. Berlin also sent the SS man Viktor Nageler as an adviser for the HG, along with others. Nageler became embroiled in the power struggle with those attempting a coup against Tiso, which prompted the pro-Tiso governmental majority to try to deprive the Hlinka Guard of its power. In May 1942, Tiso named one of his own followers, Karol Danihel, to lead the HG, and in August of 1943, the HG was completely subordinated to party jurisdiction. Its membership dropped from 100,000 in 1939 to 56,000 by 1943. Nageler's followers, who were fascinated by the idea of a "New Europe," wrote for a journal called *Náš boj* (Our Fight), but this ideological tendency probably had no more than 3,500 adherents.

The Rodobrana and later the HG are often said to have represented Slovak fascism, even though the ideological coloring of these formations is far from clear. Further, although violence as a means of achieving political ends was embraced in theory, the degree to which it was actually practiced still needs to be clarified. As far as is now known, the HG was less violent than the German SA or the Romanian Iron Guard. Another open question pertains to the social background of the HG members. These issues have not been addressed largely because of stereotyped thinking concerning Slovakia during World War II. The state has been written off as a "clerical-fascist" regime, with the HG representing its most radical elements. Such a formulation is too general, however, and does not leave

much room for a nuanced analysis of a troubled history. Of this much, however, there is no doubt: the Hlinka Guard participated in the looting of Jewish property, prepared the deportation transports, and ran the Slovak camps.

—*Tatjana Tönsmeyer*

See also Croatia; Croatia, Holocaust in; Hungary; Iron Guard; Ljotić, Dimitrije; Romania; Slovakia, Holocaust in; Szalasi, Ferenc; Tiso, Jozef

References

Jelinek, Yeshayahu. "Storm-Troopers in Slovakia: The Rodobrana and the Hlinka Guard," *Journal of Contemporary History* 6 (1971): 97–119.

Payne, Stanley. *A History of Fascism* (London: Taylor & Francis, 1995).

Tönsmeyer, Tatjana. *Das Dritte Reich und die Slowakei 1939–1945: Politischer Alltag zwischen Kooperation und Eigensinn* (Paderborn, Germany: Schöningh, 2003).

Hlond, August (1881–1948)

August Hlond was named archbishop of Gniezno and Poznan in 1926, became a cardinal in the following year, and was primate of Poland between 1936 and 1948. Hlond had a reputation for being relatively liberal but held views that were standard in the Catholic Church at the time. In the 1936 pastoral letter "On Catholic Moral Principles," he devoted a section to the threat posed by the Jews. Writing in the midst of a wave of anti-Jewish violence, he accused the Jews of promoting freethinking, godlessness, pornography, prostitution, fraud, and usury and then added, "But—let us be fair. Not all Jews are like that." He continued by listing the virtues of some Jews and warned against Nazi "unconditional" antisemitism, adding, "It is permitted to love one's own nation more, but it is not permitted to hate anyone. Including Jews." He praised the economic boycott but stressed that violence and "slander" were not permitted. He ended by warning against "those who incite anti-Jewish violence" because "a good cause gains nothing from these ill-considered deeds. And the blood that sometimes flows is Polish blood." Hlond's letter was strongly criticized by Jewish leaders as an endorsement and rationalization of antisemitism, but it was defended by nationalists as evenhanded.

Once war broke out, Hlond made his way to Rome, where the Vatican radio broadcast his descriptions of the persecutions of Jews and the Polish clergy. In 1940, he moved to southern France and was imprisoned there in 1944 by the Gestapo. On his return to Poland in 1945, he was named archbishop of Warsaw.

In July 1946, Hlond was asked to condemn the Kielce pogrom. In his official statement, however, he would say only that the church always condemned murder, "whether committed against Jews or against Poles, and whether in Kielce or in other parts of the republic" (Gutman and Krakowski 1986, 373–374). The local clergy had tried to stop the pogrom, he added, but had been blocked by the authorities. During the war, Poles had risked their lives to help Jews; the Jews were to blame for the deterioration of relations by playing leading roles in the communist government and trying to impose an alien system on Poles. In the resulting political struggle, "unfortunately some Jews die, but also a far greater number of Poles" (373–374). His personal posture toward Jews was known from his prewar statements, and while exiled in France, he had personally helped many Jews. He hoped that the Jewish Question would find its just solution in the postwar world.

Hlond has been proposed for beatification, the first step toward sainthood.

—*Steven Paulsson*

See also Jewish Question; Judeo-Bolshevism; Kielce Pogrom; Poland
References
Gutman, Israel, and Shmuel Krakowski. *Unequal Victims.* (New York: Holocaust Library, 1986).
Modras, Ronald. *The Catholic Church and Anti-Semitism: Poland 1933–1939* (Chur, Switzerland: Harwood Academic Publishers, 1994).

Hobson, J. A. (1858–1940)

John A. Hobson was born on July 6, 1858, in Derby, England, where his family founded and owned the *Derbyshire Advertiser,* a Liberal newspaper. Educated locally and at Oxford, he taught at schools in Faversham and Exeter between 1880 and 1887. Then, basing himself in London, he worked in the University Extension movement for the next ten years. This London period was crucial in his intellectual development and marked the beginning of his distinguished publishing career, with works such as *A Physiology of Industry* (1889, with A. F. Mummery), *Problems of Poverty* (1891), *The Evolution of Modern Capitalism* (1894), and *The Problem of the Unemployed* (1896).

These years also witnessed his first unfavorable observations on Jews. Jewish immigrants from Russian Poland, Hobson wrote in the *Derbyshire Advertiser* and especially in his *Problems of Poverty,* were "underselling the labor of the native poor." He portrayed them as admirable in their "domestic morality," but he believed their competition on the labor market seriously undermined the well-being of native workers. In view of these convictions, Hobson advocated the introduction of controls on immigration in the 1890s.

A decisive moment in his career came with the crisis in South Africa. The editor of the *Manchester Guardian* dispatched him there to report on the situation just prior to the outbreak of the Boer War. These experiences led to his *War in South Africa* (1900), *Psychology of Jingoism* (1901), and *Imperialism: A Study* (1902). Written in the heat of the controversy, Hobson's work gained the attention of his contemporaries and established him as one of the country's leading radical liberal intellectuals. His studies have continued to attract interest, and it is difficult even today to write on British imperialism without somewhere encountering Hobson's ghost.

In his reflections on imperialism, he returned to a discussion of Jews. He viewed the South African War as inextricably linked to "Jew power." He derided Johannesburg as the New Jerusalem and suggested Jewish financiers had unduly influenced the British government's policy for their own ends. Parasites that produced nothing, they had sunk their "economic fangs in the carcass" of South Africa, and British policy had danced to their "diabolical tune" (in Holmes 1979, 67–68). This emphasis, less evident in his major work, *Imperialism,* than elsewhere in his writings on South Africa, achieved a wide currency in Britain, particularly among socialist groups.

Overall, his work rejected individualist economics and also the proletarian attack on such doctrines. He devoted his activity to securing a

A Harlot's Progress, plate 2: "Quarrels with her Jew Protector" by William Hogarth. In the scene, Moll is shown deliberately upsetting the silver tea table in order to distract the Jew, while her secret lover creeps undetected from the room. (Burstein Collection/Corbis)

reformed capitalism, with some public ownership but allowing scope for private enterprise while recognizing the importance of social reform and social justice. Hobson died in London on April 1, 1940.

—*Colin Holmes*

See also Boer War; Britain; Maxse, James Leopold; *Ostjuden;* Socialists on Antisemitism; Wells, H. G.
References
Holmes, Colin. *Anti-Semitism in British Society, 1876–1939* (London: Edward Arnold, 1979).
Schneider, M. J. *A. Hobson* (London: Macmillan, 1996).

Hogarth, William (1697–1764)

William Hogarth was a painter and the most important English engraver of the eighteenth century. His xenophobia is well known and manifested itself most famously in his painting *O the Roast Beef of Old England* (1748; Tate Gallery, London), in which, following his arrest as a spy while sketching in Calais, he satirized what he perceived as the impoverishment of the French under the yoke of the Catholic Church. Hogarth's title for the work echoed Richard Leveridge's popular ballad (ca. 1730). The illustration was shortly after issued as an engraved print, sometimes with the alternative title *Calais Gate.*

Hogarth's best-known representations of Jews appeared in two series—*A Harlot's Progress* (1732) and *An Election* (1754) (engravings in 1755–1758)—both of which were issued as prints and enjoyed a wide circulation. In the six plates of *A Harlot's Progress,* Hogarth depicted the

Hogarth's antithesis to the rich Jew is the peddler in plate 2: "Canvassing for Votes" in the four-part sequence titled *An Election*. Here, Hogarth depicted the figure of a Jewish hawker as one of a crowd, peddling his wares from a traveling box. (The Art Archive / Harper Collins Publishers)

undoing of Moll Hackabout, a once innocent country girl who, when she arrives in London, rapidly descends into prostitution. In plate 2, she has become the paid mistress of a wealthy Jew. In the scene, Moll is shown deliberately upsetting the silver tea table in order to distract the Jew, while her secret lover creeps undetected from the room. The motifs of outtricking a Jew (which shows some indebtedness to *The Merchant of Venice*) and of Jews as notoriously lascivious in their desire for Christian girls are common in antisemitic discourse. Their combination in *A Harlot's Progress* prompted the late eighteenth-century German commentator Georg Christoph Lichtenberg to describe Hogarth's Jew as simultaneously "a deceived deceiver" and "a wealthy Old Testament sinner" (Lichtenberg 1966, 16–17). The print was the inspiration for a number of pantomimic and operatic entertainments,

in which the stage Jew sometimes appeared with the appellation Beau Mordecai. The outline of the story was also echoed in innumerable pamphlets, poems, and novels of the period.

Hogarth's antithesis to the rich Jew is the peddler in plate 2, "Canvassing for Votes," in the four-part sequence entitled *An Election,* which was prompted by the artist's observation of widespread bribery to secure votes in the election of 1754. Here, Hogarth depicted as one of a crowd the figure of a Jewish hawker, peddling his wares from a traveling box that he supports with straps over his shoulders. He stands next to a candidate who is buying from him amatory favors for two young women leaning from a balcony. Among the items in the Jew's box is a crucifix, alluding to the supposed willingness of the Jews to sell Christ. Hogarth also has in mind the infamous Jew Bill of 1753, at which time it was put out that the

"An Election," plate 1: "An Election Entertainment." Engraving by William Hogarth, published in 1755. In this plate, a mob can be seen through the window, carrying an effigy with a placard stating "NO JEWS." (Corbis)

Jews were preparing to take over the country. In plate 1 of *An Election,* "An Election Entertainment," a mob can be seen through the window, carrying an effigy with a placard stating "NO JEWS." At the time of the Jew Bill, a burlesque antisemitic ballad with the title "The Roast Pork of Old England" had been circulated, its name ironically echoing Hogarth's earlier satire of the French. Hogarth's peddler is among the earliest of at least 170 English prints depicting such figures, the most widely replicated of which is Francis Wheatley's mezzotint of the Orange Seller in his *Cries of London* (1794). Biblical figures of Jews were also represented in a number of Hogarth's works, including his only Old Testament painting, *Moses Brought to Pharaoh's Daughter* (1746; Thomas Coram Foundation, London; engraved 1752), and *Paul before Felix* (1748, Lincoln's Inn, London; engraved 1752).

—*Frank Felsenstein*

See also Caricature, Anti-Jewish (Early); Caricature, Anti-Jewish (Modern); Jew Bill

References

Felsenstein, Frank. *Anti-Semitic Stereotypes: A Paradigm of Otherness in English Popular Culture, 1660–1830* (Baltimore, MD: Johns Hopkins University Press, 1995).

Lichtenberg, Georg Christoph. *Lichtenberg's Commentaries on Hogarth's Engravings.* Translated and with an Introduction by Innes Herdan and Gustav Herdan. (London: The Cresset Press, 1966).

Paulson, Ronald. *Hogarth.* 3 vols. (New Brunswick, NJ, and London: Rutgers University Press, 1991).

———. "Some Thoughts on Hogarth's Jew: Issues in Current Hogarth Scholarship." In *Hogarth: Representing Nature's Machines.* Edited by David Bindman, Frédéric Ogée, and Peter Wagner (Manchester, UK, and New York: Manchester University Press, 2001), 236–263.

Rubens, Alfred. *A Jewish Iconography.* Rev. ed. (London: Nonpareil Publishing, 1981).

Solkin, David. "The Excessive Jew in *A Harlot's Progress*." In *Hogarth: Representing Nature's Machines*. Edited by David Bindman, Frédéric Ogée, and Peter Wagner (Manchester, UK, and New York: Manchester University Press, 2001), 219–235.

Hollywood, Treatment of Antisemitism in

Contrary to frequently heard antisemitic claims, the conspicuous economic and creative presence of Jews in the film industry has not translated into Hollywood foisting a specifically Jewish agenda on the movie-going public. Anticipating such criticism and seeking acceptance in American society, the first generation of American Jewish filmmakers used the new medium to reflect their faith in the civic equality promised by their adopted homeland.

Prior to the 1920s, these individuals strongly contrasted the oppression Jews were experiencing in tsarist Russia with the freedoms they enjoyed in the United States. A series of pictures contained plots revolving around anti-Jewish pogroms that had swept through the Pale of Settlement between 1903 and 1905. Usually, the surviving characters found refuge and prosperity in the United States. Their children often merged into American society through intermarriage. Other films treated the infamous ritual murder trial of Mendel Beilis in 1911, using it as a foil to highlight the fairness of the U.S. judicial system. These films faithfully reflected the American public's revulsion over patent injustice.

In the same period, however, gentile filmmakers implicitly warned of the negative impact of Jewish immigration on American society by reviving traditional negative stereotypes of Jews and Judaism. Thomas Edison's series about a Jewish character named Cohen depicted him as cowardly, dishonest, greedy, and vengeful. D. W. Griffith's epic *Intolerance* (1916) emphasized how the Pharisees opposed Jesus. Only pressure from the Anti-Defamation League persuaded Griffith to cut a scene showing Jews instead of Roman soldiers crucifying Christ. The Anti-Defamation League urged audiences to boycott Cecil B. De Mille's *The King of Kings* (1927) because it charged the Jews with deicide. Several scenes implicating Jews in the death of Jesus were deleted.

By the 1920s and 1930s, Jewish producers became reluctant to portray even foreign instances of antisemitism. The increase in anti-Jewish sentiment manifested itself in American isolationism, the Red Scare, the passage of restrictive immigration laws, and attempts to regulate the movie industry. Henry Ford popularized the canard of the international Jewish conspiracy seeking to destroy the American way of life by corrupting politicians, fomenting revolution, manipulating commerce, and undermining Christian morality through the libertinism glamorized by the mass media, particularly motion pictures.

Although Jewish producers owned four of the five major Hollywood studios, they tried to create films that appealed to mainstream audiences. When calls for film censorship accompanied a rise in popular antisemitism during the depression, the studios formed the Production Code Administration (PCA) in 1930, pledging "to maintain right moral standards," represent fairly "the history, institutions, prominent people, and citizenry of other nations," and not inflame "racial and religious prejudices." Producers were wary of funding movies that could be construed as defaming any minority group, religious denomination, or country. And films about antisemitism ran the risks of being charged with inciting it, jeopardizing relations with foreign countries that sanctioned it, or slandering groups that advocated it.

Consequently, movies from the 1930s minimized the role antisemitism played in depictions of anti-Jewish agitation. The script for *Black Legion* (1936) originally showed a group resembling the Ku Klux Klan recruiting a disgruntled factory worker who had lost a promotion to a Jewish coworker. Pressure from the PCA led to changing the Jewish character into a Pole and the antisemitic speeches of the group's leader into generic attacks on immigrants. *The Life of Émile Zola* (1937) chronicled the French novelist's crusade to free the unjustly convicted Jew Alfred Dreyfus, and the visual and verbal allusions in the film to Dreyfus's religious heritage were brief. PCA officials, however, expressed concern that the scene showing the burning of Zola's books to protest his defense of Dreyfus might evoke parallels with Nazi Germany's book-burning rallies (in May 1933) and could be interpreted as criticism of that country. Similarly, *They Won't Forget* (1937), a fictionalized account of the Leo Frank trial, contended that Frank was framed because he was a northerner who recently had moved to the South. The movie omitted any reference to antisemitism as a motive for his initial conviction and eventual lynching.

As late as 1940, Charlie Chaplin's caricature of Hitler in *The Great Dictator* sparked an official German protest and a Senate hearing into whether Hollywood was pushing the United States into a war with Germany. Things changed with the U.S. entry into the European conflict, enabling the major studios to make films such as *To Be or Not To Be* (1942), *Address Unknown* (1944), and *The Seventh Cross* (1944), which dramatized the plight of the Jews under Nazi rule. The corollary to condemning the Third Reich's racism was idealizing American pluralism. Jewish characters were cast as loyal soldiers in *The Purple Heart* (1944), *Pride of the Marines* (1945), and several others. The only wartime film that touched on American antisemitism was *Mr. Skeffington* (1944). In that film, the Jewish title character successfully pursues the heroine, Fanny, but his rivals for her heart suspect him of flaunting his wealth to win her love. When Fanny later divorces him, he moves to Germany to run a business. After being sent to a concentration camp, the saintly Skeffington returns and remarries Fanny, even though her beauty has faded.

The revelations of the Holocaust prompted a spate of films aimed at combating domestic antisemitism, among them *Crossfire* (1947), *Open Secret* (1948), and *Prejudice* (1948). The most successful of these films was *Gentleman's Agreement* (1947), in which a gentile investigative reporter is assigned to write an exposé on American antisemitism. Posing as a Jew, he discovers that otherwise decent people, even his fiancée, crack anti-Jewish jokes, refuse to hire Jews, or restrict where Jews can reside or vacation; when his son is beaten and taunted for ostensibly being Jewish, he realizes that antisemitic political movements are merely the tip of the iceberg. A survey of college students who saw the movie when it came out indicated that it left most of them with a more favorable impression of Jews.

Although films about antisemitism as a contemporary American social problem continued to be produced until the late 1950s, the systematic discrimination experienced by African Americans soon displaced antisemitism on the cinematic agenda. The casting of *Pressure Point* (1962) demonstrates the point. The prison psychiatrist treating a neo-Nazi sociopath was changed from a Jew to an African American. Although his patient despised Jews and blacks alike, his antiblack racism took precedence over his antisemitism. *The Pawnbroker* (1965) drew an analogy between the gang violence and poverty plaguing blacks in Harlem and the liquidation of European Jewry under Nazism. Recent Hollywood depictions locate antisemitism in the European or American past. *School Ties* (1992), *Quiz Show* (1994), *Liberty Heights* (1999), and *Focus* (2001) exemplify this new perspective. Typically in today's films, antisemitism comprises one component of the racist ideology of white supremacist groups depicted in films such as *Betrayed* (1988) and *American History X* (1998). With exceptions including *Boardwalk* (1979) and *Get on the Bus* (1996), the issue of black antisemitism seems to be too controversial to tackle in feature films today.

—*Lawrence Baron*

See also Beilis Case; Book Burning; *Dearborn Independent* and *The International Jew;* Deicide; Dreyfus Affair; Film Propaganda, Nazi; Ford, Henry; Frank, Leo; Immigration and Naturalization Laws; Ku Klux Klan; Pale of Settlement; Restricted Public Accommodations, United States; Restrictive Covenants; United States

References
Carr, Steven. *Hollywood and Anti-Semitism: A Cultural History up to World War II* (New York: Cambridge University Press, 2001).
Erens, Patricia. *The Jew in American Cinema* (Bloomington: Indiana University Press, 1984).
Friedman, Lester D. *The Jewish Image in American Film* (Secaucus, NJ: Citadel Press, 1987).
Gabler, Neil. *An Empire of Their Own: How the Jews Invented Hollywood* (New York: Doubleday, 1988).

Holocaust

The role of antisemitism in producing the Holocaust remains an ongoing source of debate among scholars. From 1933 to 1945, the Nazi regime persecuted, expelled, concentrated, and ultimately succeeded in physically eliminating most of Europe's Jewish population. There were also other victims of the Nazi regime—the physically and mentally disabled, homosexuals, asocials, Roma (Gypsies), Jehovah's Witnesses, and blacks—who were deemed enemies of the state and accused of embodying deviant biology, behaviors, and beliefs that were antithetical to the utopia of the promised Thousand-Year Reich. Jews were, however, the regime's primary victims, a stateless people targeted for their ethnicity, religion, and beliefs. The deliberately genocidal policy that destroyed almost 6 million Jews remains a devastating rupture in Jewish history and in the modern experience of crimes against humanity and mass atrocity.

The Nazi regime pursued the removal of Jews from European society with unmatched ideological fanaticism and bureaucratic meticulousness. Early explanations of the Nazi regime emphasized its racist ideology (see, for example, Leon Poliakov, *Harvest of Hate* [1954]), the role of Hitler as the principal architect of the regime of mass murder, and the supporting role of other high-level perpetrators. This approach was juxtaposed with heuristic studies. Hannah Arendt (*The Origins of Totalitarianism* [1958]) focused on European colonialism as the developing ground for twentieth-century regimes of state control and total domination of polity, society, economy, and culture. The denial of liberal principles and freedoms, submission of individuals to the state, elevated role of community, and charismatic leadership were all seen as central features of totalitarianism. Raul Hilberg (*The Destruction of the European Jews* [1961]) published an authoritative analysis of the bureaucratic foundations of the Nazi state. Inspired by Franz Neumann's *Behemoth* (1944), Hilberg used perpetrator documents to reconstruct a process of exclusion that was repeated in countries dominated or influenced by Nazi Germany: the identification, expropriation, concentration, and annihilation of Jews. This destruction process required individuals to implement and administer it, an involvement Hilberg labeled the "machinery of destruction." His suggestion that persecution could not be pursued without broad participation by the civil service, transport, and legal systems, among other departments, advanced a "normative" paradigm of the Holocaust's causality that distributed responsibility among elements of German society, beneath and beyond the high-level perpetrators prosecuted at the Nuremberg trials.

Hilberg thereby democratized explanations of the Holocaust. He removed the focus on individual agency and responsibility and gave the event's perpetrators anonymity and distance from the objects of their policy. Hilberg's paradigm exists alongside other explanations, such as totalitarianism and antisemitism, the latter of which has been radically challenged in Holocaust scholarship since the 1980s by the advent of the intentionalist/functionalist debate. This debate elucidates historiographical emphases between particularist and sociostructural explanations. Intentionalists, such as Lucy Dawidowicz (*The War against the Jews* [1975]) and Eberhard Jäckel (*Hitler in History* [1984]), insist that the destruction of the Jews was prophesied by Hitler long before his assumption of power in 1933 and that antisemitism, as explicated in his writings (*Mein Kampf* [1925]) and numerous speeches, was the primary sustaining agent of his ideology and *Weltanschauung* (worldview). Functionalists, by contrast, are less unanimous in their explanations of how the Holocaust originated or what Hitler's role in it was, although a telling point of agreement among them is the relegation of antisemitism as a significant motivating factor among perpetrators across occupations, ages, countries, and political orientations. Although functionalists acknowledge the role of the ideological elite around Hitler in authoring genocide, they emphasize that decision making did not follow a linear sequence or have central direction. Further, according to this view, the destruction of the Jews cannot be divorced from contingencies of war, general population resettlement policy, and territorial gains and losses.

Functionalists advance the metaphor of a twisted road to explain the protracted evolution of genocide. They refer to the inconsistencies of expropriations and expulsion policy in the prewar and early-war phases, the existence of Jews in ghettos for indefinite time periods (especially in the Lodz ghetto, which survived for four years from 1940 to 1944), the widely varying methods and sites of killings, and the emergence of a decision to seek a European-wide Final Solution between July and December 1941.

Functionalists also contest the antisemitism thesis as embodied by the singular identity of Hitler's victims. If Hitler zealously pursued an antisemitic agenda, how does one explain the murderous assault on Gypsies or the handicapped, the latter group in the so-called T-4 euthanasia program that provided the training ground for technicians and experience in chemical methods of killing that would be used in the industrial destruction of Jews? Functionalists contend that the multiple identities of Hitler's victims reflect a wider political assault against groups deemed inferior and unworthy of life. Their argument refers not only to the prewar targeting of homosexuals, blacks, the disabled, and Jehovah's Witnesses, but also to the evolution of the Final Solution in the policy of ethnic cleansing directed toward ethnic Germans, Poles, and Jews between 1939 and 1941. Götz Aly, Susanne Heim, and others have argued that the unmitigated physical destruction of the Jews emerged not so much from antisemitic ideology as from the ambitious plans of Nazi demographic experts who advanced a ruthlessly utilitarian population policy in the "undeveloped" territory of eastern Europe. Aly (Endlösung [1995]) later modified his model of the "economic Final Solution" to suggest that it was the failure of these population plans that led to genocide. Yet however compelling, this "modernization" theory is inadequate when stretched to fit, for example, the face-to-face killing methods of the Einsatzgruppen in the East, the targeting and deportation of the tiny island community of Rhodes, and the May to August 1944 deportations of 400,000 Hungarians to Auschwitz.

Updating Hilberg's paradigm, the sociostructural, or "universalist," interpretation was also evident in Modernity and the Holocaust (1989) by the Polish sociologist Zygmunt Bauman. He argued that the Nazis reinvented centuries-old Jew-hatred as a modern form of racial contamination and disease infecting the German body politic that needed urgent eradication. Bauman posited that "exterminatory antisemitism" emerged under the Nazis as a variant of traditional Christian anti-Judaism, and he hinged its legitimacy and practice on its modern birth and effective management: "Racism is a policy first, ideology second. Like all politics, it needs organization, managers and experts" (74). However, this argument fails to acknowledge that modernity had no monopoly on mass killing and that other comparatively modern European states did not produce genocides despite the existence of more virulent strains of antisemitism within them.

If Bauman premised the success of exterminatory antisemitism on bureaucratically managed racism, Daniel Jonah Goldhagen (Hitler's Willing Executioners [1996]) returned antisemitism to its "primitive" roots, alleging that a particular strain of it had been latent in German society since the nineteenth century but was finally unleashed under Hitler into a collective national project based on the elimination of Jews. Goldhagen's book was read by many as a reply to Christopher Browning's Ordinary Men (1992), a study based on postwar interrogations of Reserve Police Battalion 101 personnel and their killing activities in Josefow, Poland. Browning concluded that these men participated in mass murder not because of a preexisting ideological commitment to Nazism but rather because of their immersion in a social culture of conformism, careerism, and opportunism. Using the same documents but rejecting the Browning thesis, Goldhagen returned the Holocaust to the territory of comfortable monocausal explanations characteristic of early postwar histories. Scholars resoundingly criticized his book for its dogged insistence on antisemitism as a singular explanation and for confining its expression to "ordinary Germans," suggesting that Goldhagen denied that there were non-German perpetrators, that other segments of German society were also infected by years of ideological indoctrination, and that Germans targeted victims other than Jews. Saul Friedländer (Nazi Germany and the Jews [1997]) provided an additional interpretation of causality that he labeled "redemptive" antisemitism. Friedländer argued that Hitler was driven by "ideological obsessions that were anything but the calculated devices of a demagogue" (3). Although derived from preexisting elements of Christian anti-Judaism and racial antisemitism, redemptive antisemitism was different. Friedländer fused the religious ideal of redemption through destruction with the Nazi fear of racial degeneration from miscegenation, a fear related to the experience of European colonial racism.

A final point of contest between intentionalists and functionalists concerns the belief systems, morality, and values of individual participants in the Final Solution, who, whether by remotely bureaucratic or face-to-face killing, have been represented as ostensibly nonideological. To what extent can antisemitism be adduced from the bureaucratic management of killing and a range of inconsistent responses, embracing passive acquiescence, complicity, and conformity among segments of the German population? To what degree can such behaviors be declared "representative" of a normative attitude toward persecution and destruction?

As an ideology and explanatory model, antisemitism offers several interpretive dilemmas that become even more problematic when seeking links between its presence in Christian thought, its foundation in nineteenth-century anthropological and scientific discourse, its pre-1939 manifestations, and its viability as a causal paradigm of the Holocaust. There is no direct proof that one type or tradition of antisemitism conclusively produced the Nazi genocide of Jews. But the powerful influence of the many strains of antisemitism, it can be persuasively argued, helped produce the cultures and instances of routinized intolerance and persecution that the Nazi regime absolutely required in order to carry out the dehumanization and mass murder of Jews on such a comprehensive scale across Europe. How else can we explain the active and willing participation of countless individuals or the passivity of millions of bystanders?

Nevertheless, it must be conceded that the exact dynamic or relationship between antisemitism and the Holocaust, despite decades of earnest scholarly research and patient thought, continues to elude satisfactory or satisfying resolution.

—*Simone Gigliotti*

See also Commissar Order; Crimes against Humanity (French Trials); Degeneration; Einsatzgruppen; Himmler, Heinrich; Hitler, Adolf; Hitler's Speeches (Early); Hungary, Holocaust in; Jehovah's Witnesses; *Mein Kampf;* Nazi Legal Measures against Jews; Order Police; Poland; Wannsee Conference

References
Aly, Götz. *Final Solution: Nazi Population Policy and the Murder of the European Jews.* Translated by Alison Brown (London and New York: Arnold, 1999).
Bauman, Zygmunt. *Modernity and the Holocaust* (Ithaca, NY: Cornell University Press, 1989).
Dawidowicz, Lucy S. *The War against the Jews* (New York: Holt, Rinehart and Winston, 1975).
Hilberg, Raul. *The Destruction of the European Jews* (New York: Quadrangle Books, 1961).

Holocaust Denial, Negationism, and Revisionism

The attempt to obfuscate the reality of the Final Solution and the events surrounding it—the organized destruction of approximately 6 million Jews at the hands of the Germans and their collaborators during World War II—began shortly after the conclusion of the war, primarily in France and the United States. The deniers came from both the extreme Right and the radical Left. In the late 1940s, the French fascist Maurice Bardèche and the former socialist and inmate of the Buchenwald and Dora camps Paul Rassinier challenged the accepted belief that Jews had been systematically destroyed in the death camps. Historians David Hoggan and Harry Elmer Barnes were instrumental in boosting the development of denial literature in the United States in the 1950s and 1960s.

The allegations of the first deniers were gradually absorbed by the European and U.S. extreme Right as principal elements of their ideology and antisemitic propaganda. In 1974, a twenty-eight-page booklet entitled *Did Six Million Really Die? The Truth at Last* was published in the United Kingdom by Richard E. Harwood (also known as Richard Verrall), a leading activist of the racist National Front. It was sent to all members of Parliament and to many public figures, including the foremost members of the Jewish community. Another influential booklet denying the Holocaust, *Die Auschwitz-Lüge* (The Auschwitz Lie), was published in West Germany in 1973 by former SS man Thies Christophersen. Christophersen claimed that he had neither seen nor heard of any gassing activity when he had served near Auschwitz and visited Birkenau. Considered the first radical German Holocaust denial publication, his booklet had a powerful influence on extreme rightists in the country. It alleged that the claim of mass extermination was nothing more than a Jewish fabrication. The term *Auschwitz Lie* has become the shorthand designation for denial of the Holocaust in Germany and the rest of the world.

The full flowering of the phenomenon in West Germany occurred in the 1970s, with the broadcast of the television miniseries *Holocaust* (1978) providing unexpected additional stimulus to the movement. One prominent German denier was former judge Wilhelm Stäglich, who published *Der Auschwitz-Mythos* (The Auschwitz Myth) in 1979, which was disseminated together with Christophersen's booklet. Meanwhile, a milestone in U.S. Holocaust denial literature was reached with *The Hoax of the Twentieth Century* by Arthur R. Butz, a professor of electrical engineering at Northwestern University whose right to academic freedom was defended by members of his faculty.

Mutual support and links among those who claimed that the idea of the total destruction of European Jewry had been invented and cultivated only after the war began to consolidate in the 1960s and 1970s, strengthened at conferences held in the United States and Europe in the 1980s. In the United States, Willis Carto's well-funded antisemitic Liberty Lobby established the Institute for Historical Review in California (in 1979), which staged annual conferences of U.S. and European deniers and launched the *Journal of Historical Review,* a periodical that soon became the favored venue for World War II and Holocaust "revisionism."

Holocaust denial literature can be divided into two categories: (1) vulgar, blatantly antisemitic publications that often include caricatures and even pornographic materials, such as the leaflets of the Swede Dietlieb Feldere, and (2) pseudoa- cademic publications that display full scholarly apparatus in an attempt to prove the familiar thesis. Butz, French revisionist Robert Faurisson, British author David Irving, and others do not deny that Jews were persecuted, and they admit that a large number of them—tens or perhaps even hundreds of thousands or, according to Butz, probably even 1 million—were shot or died as a result of maltreatment, disease, air raids, and hunger. The deniers do, however, uniformly reject the historicity of systematic, industrialized extermination.

Holocaust denial evolved as part of a more general revisionist thesis that denied the distinct character of Nazi Germany, a complex of theories that appealed to a range of extremists, including American isolationists such as Barnes, French leftists such as Rassinier and his spiritual heirs in the radical left-wing publishing house *La Vieille taupe* (The Old Mole), and rightist authors such as Irving. Denial of the systematic machinery of destruction was intended to support another of their major projects, the relativizing of German wartime atrocities. By adopting the Holocaust denial theory, they could argue that German violence against civilian populations, including local massacres of Jews, was morally equivalent to the atrocities of the Allies. Neo-Nazis and their sympathizers on the extreme Right hoped that by denying the Final Solution, they could free the Nazi regime from its satanic stigma and obliterate any moral distinction between the Axis powers and the Allies. European authors associated with the extreme Left, however, sought to prove that when it came to war crimes, there was no difference between Nazi Germany—allegedly a product of the capitalist system—the liberal and democratic West, and the Soviet Union.

These assumptions were based on the following claims:

- The Jews had invented or used "wartime propaganda fantasies" about their systematic extermination to manipulate the world's guilt feelings in order to extort money and to further Zionist and Israeli goals.
- Both Britain and the United States had been pushed into the war by the Jews; the

"hoax" was inflated so that it might serve as a "moral alibi" for the disastrous decision to confront Germany to the bitter end.

- The Jews who allegedly perished during the war found refuge in the Soviet Union. Statistical projections from before and after the war prove that 6 million Jews could not possibly have died.
- The fact that no written order by Hitler to exterminate the Jews was ever found is a clear indication that no such operation was planned or carried out.
- The code words found in Nazi documents, such as the term *special treatment (Sonderbehandlung)*, have been misinterpreted to signify "extermination."
- Evidence from the Nuremberg tribunals and other postwar trials is unreliable. Some of the defenders were tortured, and others, subjected since the end of the war to "Holocaust propaganda," began to believe in the truth of the Final Solution.
- Survivors' recollections are unreliable. "Regular" historians, too, have confirmed that testimonies about gas chambers in camps such as Dachau and Buchenwald or about soap made from human fat are merely myths. Like Nazi criminals, survivors were also brainwashed by prolonged exposure to propaganda.
- The gas chambers in Auschwitz, Birkenau, and Majdanek were never used for mass exterminations but only as delousing facilities. (This claim was proven "scientifically" by the *Leuchter Report*, published in 1988 by Fred Leuchter, whose fraudulent credentials were exposed in a Canadian court and in the 1992 *Rudolf Gutachten* [Rudolf Report] by Germar Rudolf, a German chemist and an employee of the Max Planck Institute [who was dismissed for using its name to promote his theory]).

Holocaust denial reached a peak at the end of the 1980s and the early 1990s, attaining considerable notoriety when David Irving, the well-known World War II historian, joined the ranks of the deniers. Sowing doubt about the veracity of the Holocaust remained their goal, and they achieved a fair degree of success in disseminating their views, taking advantage of the gullible and the well-intentioned, who saw the issue as one of free speech rather than the willful distortion of history. In the United States, deniers became active on college campuses, advertising in student newspapers. In European countries such as Sweden and France, thousands of leaflets denying the Holocaust were distributed in high schools and universities, sometimes in joint ventures of the radical Right and Left. The movement was also able to reach beyond its normal European-U.S. orbit, establishing links to the Muslim world and Arab propagandists through the activities of the Sweden-based Radio Islam, headed by Moroccan-born Ahmed Rami. Following the collapse of the communist regimes in the early 1990s, Holocaust denial found new audiences among the nationalist parties and groups in these countries, mainly as a way to rehabilitate World War II leaders who had collaborated with Nazi Germany and implemented the Final Solution.

In the face of increased denial activities and the potential threat they posed as a neo-Nazi and antisemitic tool, Jewish organizations and communities as well as human rights groups launched an effective campaign against Holocaust denial. Several European countries, among them Belgium, Austria, Germany, France, and Spain, made denial of the Holocaust a punishable offense. In other countries, such as Canada, Australia, and South Africa, Jewish communities successfully opposed lecture tours by deniers. Internal dissension within the Institute for Historical Review, which had become the principal international forum for Holocaust denial in the 1980s and early 1990s, also contributed to the decline of denial activities and discussion. The antidenial campaign culminated in 2000 when a British court of law ruled against David Irving in the libel suit he had brought against historian Deborah Lipstadt, determining that he was a sham historian who misrepresented and manipulated historical evidence.

Nevertheless, as Holocaust denial waned, another no less disturbing aspect of Holocaust distortion gained prominence—the relativization of the Holocaust, meaning the rejection of its historical uniqueness. Espoused in the 1980s, mainly by conservative historians such as Ernst Nolte, who compared the Holocaust to Stalin's atrocities and mass killings, relativism became popular in the 1990s and at the beginning of the new century with many of the same people who had subscribed to the tenets of denial and for many of the same motives. It appeared as one weapon to be used in campaigns against Israel, and, perceived as a less radical form of denial, it occasionally penetrated the mainstream, particularly in Europe. The word *holocaust,* written with a lowercase *h,* emphasized that there was nothing unique about the genocide of the Jews; it was only one among many holocausts. Israel was described as a Nazi state that used Nazi methods against the Palestinians. Thus, relativization of the Holocaust led to its banalization and to the distortion of its true historical significance.

—*Roni Stauber*

See also Auschwitz Lie; Bardèche, Maurice; Carto, Willis; Crimes against Humanity (French Trials); Fascist Intellectuals; Faurisson, Robert; Germany, Federal Republic of; Historians' Controversy; Institute for Historical Review; Internet; Irving, David; *Leuchter Report;* Militia Movement; New Left; Sweden; Zündel, Ernst

References
Lipstadt, Deborah E. *Denying the Holocaust: The Growing Assault on Truth and Memory.* Repr. ed. (New York: Plume, 1994).
Rembiszewski, Sarah. *The Final Lie: Holocaust Denial in Germany—A Second Generation Denier as a Test Case* (Tel Aviv, Israel: Tel Aviv University Press, 1995).
Shafir, Michael. *Between Denial and "Comparative Trivialization": Holocaust Negationism in Post-Communist East Central Europe* (Jerusalem: Hebrew University of Jerusalem, Vidal Sassoon International Center for the Study of Antisemitism, 2002).
Stern, Kenneth S. *Holocaust Denial* (New York: American Jewish Committee, 1993).
Webman, Esther. "Rethinking the Holocaust: An Open Debate in the Arab World." In *Antisemitism Worldwide 1998/99* (Lincoln: University of Nebraska Press, 1999).

Homophobia

Until the last half of the nineteenth century, homosexuality was viewed solely as a moral failing on the part of an individual. With the scientific study of sexuality that began at that time, scientific and medical circles came to see homosexuality as a congenital degenerative condition. To many, this affliction posed a danger in that its spread could seriously damage "decent" society. In the minds of many antisemites at the turn of the twentieth century, the peril posed by homosexuals melded with that posed by Jews: both were seen as degenerate groups working toward the destruction of Christian society. More important, they believed that the cause of gay rights was one of the tools used by Jews to effect this downfall. Therefore, the fight against homosexuals was part of the fight against the Jews and vice versa.

Antisemites in the nineteenth and early twentieth centuries readily seized on what appeared to be incontrovertible proof of the connection between homosexuals and Jews. Most of the world's leading sexologists at the time, many of whom were Jewish—such as Marc Andre Raffalovich, who wrote the foremost attack on the French medical establishment's view of homosexuals as effeminate degenerates—advocated equal rights for homosexuals based on the inborn nature of their condition.

The connection between antisemitism and homophobia can be seen most clearly in Germany. Magnus Hirschfeld, the founder of that country's first homosexual rights group, the Scientific-Humanitarian Committee, was a Jewish doctor. His continuous and very public advocacy of equal rights for homosexual men at the beginning of the twentieth century united the concepts of Jew and homosexual rights in the minds of many Germans. Hirschfeld's lectures were disrupted by opponents, and he often faced physical attack. In 1920, he was beaten and left for dead by members of an antisemitic group. The National Socialists adamantly opposed gay rights, and their ire in this regard was mainly directed against the Jewish Hirschfeld rather than other equal rights advocates. Even within the German homosexual rights movement, Hirschfeld faced repeated antisemitic attacks from rival groups. When he stepped down as chairman of the committee in 1929, his departure was cheered because there was no longer a Jewish face on the movement.

The connection between Jews and homosexuals continues today among many antisemitic organizations. White nationalist groups in the United States believe that what they see as a proliferation of homosexual characters in television programs and movies is a direct attempt by Jews who use their stranglehold on the media to destroy white Christian society by making degenerate characters appear normal and acceptable. These groups advocate suppressing homosexuals as one of the best means of defeating the "Jewish threat."

—*James Kollenbroich*

See also Hirschfeld, Magnus; Masculinity; United States

References

Gilman, Sander. *Freud, Race, and Gender* (Princeton, NJ: Princeton University Press, 1993).

Kantor, Martin. *Homophobia: Description, Development, and Dynamics of Gay Bashing* (Westport, CT: Praeger, 1998).

Horthy, Miklós (1868–1957)

Adm. Miklós Horthy, son of a Calvinist Hungarian nobleman, entered the Habsburg naval academy in 1882, became aide-de-camp to Emperor Franz Joseph in 1909, and concluded his World War I service as commander in chief of the Austro-Hungarian navy. During Hungary's counterrevolution between 1919 and 1920, he commanded the White (anticommunist) militia and instituted a policy of "national purification," involving widespread atrocities and the murder of 5,000 to 6,000 perceived traitors, mainly Jews.

In March 1920, Horthy's reputation as a patriot, decisive military commander, and stalwart anticommunist led parliament to appoint him regent of Hungary, making him the head of state with powers similar to those of the recently deposed emperor. Under Horthy in September 1920, Hungary introduced the *numerus clausus,* limiting Jewish enrollments in institutions of higher education, the first major antisemitic legislation enacted in postwar Europe; the First and Second Jewish Laws (May 1938 and May 1939, respectively), statutes restricting Jews' civil, business, and professional rights; and the Third Jewish Law (August 1941), undisguised racialist legislation based on Germany's infamous Nuremberg Laws.

By late 1941, Admiral Horthy harbored doubts about an ultimate German victory. In March 1942, therefore, he dismissed his pro-German prime minister, replacing him with the anti-Nazi moderate Miklós Kallay. The Horthy-Kallay compact aimed to keep Hungary free of both German and Soviet domination. Hiding behind Kallay's initial pro-German public rhetoric but increasingly influenced by Germany's deteriorating military situation, Horthy approved a secret provisional armistice with Great Britain in September 1943.

Despite proclaiming himself a lifelong antisemite fighting tirelessly against Jewish power and influence, the patrician Horthy operated on the prejudices of his class rather than on an ideologically based antisemitism. He had contempt for the Nazi riffraff controlling Germany—proving his mettle in April 1943 in a bellicose confrontation with Hitler. Rejecting Hitler's furious onslaughts on Kallay's "defeatism," Horthy vigorously defended his prime minister and rebuffed Hitler's demands that the Jewish Question in Hungary be resolved by German methods. Summoned again by an enraged Hitler in mid-March 1944, Horthy capitulated to the German military occupation of Hungary.

In spite of his initial reservations, Horthy remained head of state, a decision that bestowed a facade of political legitimacy on the new pro-Nazi puppet regime. Moreover, his withdrawal from the executive aspects of public life removed a serious obstacle to the Germans' implementation of the Final Solution in Hungary. Beginning in mid-May 1944, under Adolf Eichmann's expert direction, 450,000 Hungarian provincial Jews—mainly the poor, unskilled, and Orthodox people that the callous Horthy considered parasitic—were deported to Auschwitz in the space of seven weeks. Responding to local and international pressure, however, Horthy courageously banned further deportations on July 7, 1944. His reemergence from political hibernation and his subsequent support for the Jewish community and its leaders helped ensure the survival of Budapest's acculturated and economically vital community. These were Jews he considered productive and essential for Hungary's future development. A German-led coup deposed Horthy on October 15, 1944, ironically on the same day this lifelong and militant anticommunist proclaimed an armistice with the USSR.

—*Tom Kramer*

See also Eichmann, Adolf; Hungary; Hungary, Holocaust in; Kallay, Miklós; *Numerus Clausus* (Hungary); Nuremberg Laws; Szalasi, Ferenc; White Terror

References

Braham, Randolph L. *The Politics of Genocide: The Holocaust in Hungary.* 2 vols. (New York: Columbia University Press, 1994).

Kramer, T. D. *From Emancipation to Catastrophe: The Rise and Holocaust of Hungarian Jewry* (Lanham, MD: University Press of America, 2000).

Sakmyster, Thomas. *Hungary's Admiral on Horseback: Miklós Horthy, 1918–44* (New York: Columbia University Press, 1994).

Höss, Rudolf (1901–1947)

Rudolf Höss was born into a merchant family in Baden-Baden on November 25, 1901. His father, described as "fanatically religious and militarily strict," made a solemn vow that his son would become a Catholic priest (in Deselaers 2001, 39–40). At age fifteen, Rudolf ran away from home so he could take part in World War I. At eighteen, he returned, a much decorated noncommissioned officer (NCO) but also an orphan. He cut the ties with his childhood milieu: "I found a home again and a sense of security in the comradeship of my fellows," he wrote in his autobiography (Höss 1959, 33). He fought with the Freikorps Rossbach on several fronts until this freebooter paramilitary group was disbanded. He left the church in 1922, met Hitler in 1923, and joined the Nazi Party.

The next year, he participated in a vigilante murder and was apprehended, tried, and sentenced to ten years in solitary confinement. After his release from prison in 1928, he joined the "blood and soil" Artamanen League, becoming one of its leaders. In this capacity, he got to know Heinrich Himmler, who after 1933 made Höss part of his plans to expand the power and influence of the SS. Höss began his SS apprenticeship in the Dachau concentration camp, then rose to vice-commandant of Sachsenhausen; following the attack on Poland in 1939, he received the commission to build a new concentration camp in Auschwitz.

The conversion of Auschwitz for the dual purposes of exploiting inmate labor and exterminating "enemies of the state" came to represent, according to Höss, his paramount mission in the war. In 1941, Himmler ordered him to step up preparations for the mass murder of Jews. "The problem itself, the extermination (*Ausrottung*) of Jewry, was nothing new," he confided to a psychologist who questioned him during the Nuremberg trials, "only that *I* should be the one to carry it out, gave me some initial concern" (Gilbert 1961, 247). Höss wrote in his autobiography that he carried out the will of Himmler by creating "the largest installation for the annihilation of human beings of all time" (Höss 1959, 135). From May through July 1944, he supervised Aktion Höss, the murder of approximately 400,000 Hungarian Jews. When asked at his trial in 1947 if he ever had qualms of conscience, he answered: "Later, yes, when the large transports arrived, when one, day in and day out, had to destroy the women . . ." (in Deselaers 2001, 184). However, he stifled his inner doubts.

After the downfall of the Third Reich, Höss went underground but was arrested in March 1946. He was one of the few SS men not to have denied his guilt. After testifying at the Nuremberg tribunal, he was delivered to Poland to stand trial himself. In prison, he wrote in his autobiography: "I remain now, as before, philosophically a National Socialist"(Höss 1959, 166). But later, in his last letter to his wife, he confided that the ideology and the deeds it resulted in were completely wrong. He reentered the Catholic Church and confessed his guilt. He was condemned to death in March 1947. The sentence was carried out on April 7, at the former Auschwitz death camp.

—*Manfred Deselaers*
Richard S. Levy, translation

See also Hentschel, Willibald; Himmler, Heinrich; Holocaust; Hungary, Holocaust in; National Socialist German Workers' Party; Weimar

References

Deselaers, Manfred. "*Und Sie hatten nie Gewissensbisse?" Die Biographie von Rudolf Höss, Komman-*

dant von Auschwitz, und die Frage nach seiner Verantwortung vor Gott und den Menschen (Leipzig, Germany: Benno-Verlag, 2001).

Gilbert, G. M. *Nuremberg Diary* (New York: Signet Books, 1961; orig. 1947).

Höss, Rudolf. *Commandant of Auschwitz: The Autobiography of Rudolf Hoess.* Translated by C. FitzGibbon. (New York: Popular Library, 1959).

Host Desecration

When the doctrine of transubstantiation was raised to a central sacrament of the medieval church at the Fourth Lateran Council in 1215, the stage was set for a harsh reaction to any objections to or alleged profanations of the host wafer. Heretics within the church had long been derided and attacked for their opposition to the belief that the Eucharist, after consecration, was the actual body of Jesus. But special animus was reserved for Jews, who were alleged to have stolen or purchased and then stabbed, "tortured," and burned the host. Jews were accused of attacking the very body of Jesus, reenacting the Crucifixion through the host. Guilty of violent acts against both Jesus and Christianity, Jews were also deemed duplicitous, for while they publicly denied the divinity of Jesus, they secretly believed in the power of Christ and central church doctrines. Why else would they defile the host?

Allegations of host desecration first occurred during the thirteenth century, with the earliest instance recorded in Belitz, near Berlin, in 1243. The charge was repeated across Europe well into the nineteenth century. Among the central episodes were those in Paris in 1290, in Deggendorf in Bavaria in 1337 and 1338, and at Knoblauch near Berlin in 1510. Host desecration accusations frequently resulted in literary narratives and artistic representations that demonized Jews. The tales and representations often stressed that the host possessed powerful and magical qualities and that it would defend itself against the attacks. As a matter of course, literary accounts noted the persecution, execution, or expulsion of the guilty Jews from the region of their crimes. Sites of pilgrimage for Christians were often established in these places.

According to a chronicle of the Bavarian dukes of 1338: "Jews cut up the Catholic host each in their synagogue and amongst other mockeries, pierced it with sharp thorns until it bled. Therefore, around the feast of St. Michael in all the towns of Bavaria and Austria except for Regensburg and Vienna they were miserably and cruelly killed by poor folk" (Rubin 1999, 36).

According to some scholars, allegations of host desecration represented one side of a two-pronged attack on medieval Jewry—the other being charges of ritual murder. Together, they marked a dramatic increase in popular anti-Jewish sentiment in the thirteenth century, stigmatizing Jews as the condign enemies of Christians and Christianity.

—*Dean Phillip Bell*

See also Deicide; Iconography, Christian; Innocent III, Pope; Lateran Council, Fourth; Middle Ages, High; Middle Ages, Late; Ritual Murder (Medieval)

References

Chazan, Robert. *Medieval Stereotypes and Modern Antisemitism* (Berkeley: University of California Press, 1997), esp. 71–72.

Rubin, Miri. *Gentile Tales: The Narrative Assault on Late Medieval Jews* (New Haven, CT: Yale University Press, 1999).

Trachtenberg, Joshua. *The Devil and the Jews: The Medieval Conception of the Jew and Its Relation to Modern Anti-Semitism* (Philadelphia: Jewish Publication Society, 2002; orig. 1943), 109–123.

Hugenberg, Alfred (1865–1951)

A leading nationalist politician, Alfred Hugenberg controlled a vast media empire in Germany. A tenacious opponent of the Weimar Republic and noted antisemite, he was a leading figure on the right wing of the German National People's Party, or Deutschnationale Volkspartei (DNVP). Hugenberg, his party, and his chain of newspapers were relentless in their attacks on the legitimacy of the republic and were instrumental in bringing Adolf Hitler to power.

Born in Hanover on June 19, 1865, Hugenberg was politically influential even before World War I. In 1890, he was among the founders of the Pan-German League, a powerful right-wing interest group that promoted German racism and extreme nationalism. From 1909 to 1918, he was chairman of the Krupp Corporation, one of Europe's largest arms manufacturers. In 1914, he founded the Scherl conglomerate, consisting of numerous newspapers and other media outlets, which he used as propaganda weapons in support of his country's war effort. A staunch supporter of a Hohenzollern restoration, he opposed the establishment of the Weimar Republic in 1918.

Hugenberg's concern flourished under the republic, and he became his country's leading media mogul, adding Ufa, Germany's largest film studio, to his string of newspapers in 1927. The following year, he led a revolt against the moderate wing of the DNVP, became the party chairman, and led the organization in an increasingly antisemitic and antidemocratic direction. Accumulating vast wealth, he used his resources in support of right-wing causes, most famously bankrolling the 1929 campaign against the Young Plan, under which Germany agreed to a revised schedule of reparations payments imposed after World War I. As a result of these actions, his party drew closer to the Nazis, although Hugenberg objected to what he saw as the socialist elements of Hitler's program. Ultimately, he found the prospect of a Hitler government preferable to what he considered the chaos engendered by the Weimar Republic and the greater threat from the Left. In January 1933, when Hitler became chancellor, Hugenberg agreed to serve as economics minister in his cabinet. He was among those on the German Right who believed that Hitler could be manipulated for the benefit of traditional German nationalism. His party allied itself with the National Socialists following the March 1933 elections, providing Hitler with the slim majority the Nazi leader needed to legitimize his new government. Hugenberg soon discovered, however, that efforts to cooperate with the Hitler regime were futile, and on June 26, 1933, he resigned from the finance ministry and then retired into political obscurity.

Following Germany's defeat in World War II, Hugenberg underwent de-Nazification proceedings. He was classified as a "fellow traveler" of the Nazis but received no punishment. Alfred Hugenberg died on March 12, 1951, at the age of eighty-five.

—*Russel Lemmons*

See also Film Industry, Nazi Purge of Jewish Influence in; German National People's Party; Hitler, Adolf; National Socialist German Workers' Party; Pan-German League; Weimar
References
Leopold, John A. *Alfred Hugenberg: The Radical Nationalist Campaign against the Weimar Republic* (New Haven, CT: Yale University Press, 1977).

Hugh of Lincoln

Little St. Hugh of Lincoln (d. 1255), along with St. Simon of Trent (d. 1475), is one of the most famous purported victims of ritual murder. Much of his renown stems from having been mentioned in Chaucer's *Canterbury Tales* and from the many surviving medieval ballads that tell versions of his story. (The boy martyr should not be confused with the more famous St. Hugh, Hugh of Avalon, who was bishop of Lincoln from 1181 to 1200.) The Prioress in the *Canterbury Tales* says that Hugh was killed "but a little while ago," although he died in 1255, more than a century before Chaucer wrote. According to the legend, he was lured by Jews of Lincoln while playing with a Jewish friend, then tortured and sacrificed. His body was tossed in a well or privy, where it was discovered a month later. The evidence came entirely from confessions produced under torture.

Jews had been gathering in Lincoln to celebrate the wedding of Belasset, daughter of one of the leading families of the area at a time of growing anti-Jewish hostility. In the previous decade, the Jews of England had been taxed so severely that by 1255 they made a formal request to leave the kingdom, but they were still too valuable an asset to be allowed to do so. The same year, Aaron of York, once the richest Jew in England, was declared bankrupt, prompting the king to mortgage the Jewish community to his brother, Richard of Cornwall. Twenty years later, the same Belasset was executed as part of an alleged Jewish conspiracy to clip coins.

King Henry III had written that he had no knowledge of the ritual murder accusation against the Jews (in 1235), but when he arrived in Lincoln in the summer of 1255 and heard from his official John of Lexington of rumors circulating in the city, he ordered one Jew tortured until he confessed and then had him executed; another eighteen were taken to London, where they were also executed. John of Lexington was trained as a churchman and had close family connections to the Lincoln minster. He helped spread the story of Hugh and confirmed that his body was buried in a place of honor in the south choir of the church.

Henry III's successor, King Edward I, eagerly supported the cult and ordered a shrine built to commemorate the boy, using the same royal masons who had constructed memorials for Queen Eleanor. Lincoln's memorial to Hugh was built just after the Jews were expelled from England in 1290 as part of the royal propaganda to emphasize Edward's Christian piety.

Hugh's story survives in annals, in the works of Matthew of Paris, and in the Anglo-Norman ballad of "Sir Hugh or the Jew's Daughter," which served to keep his name alive in the popular imagination. Little Hugh's story was widely known, but he was never canonized, and his feast day of August 27 was rarely observed. After the early fourteenth century, his cult faded, and the cathedral shrine was probably destroyed in the middle of the seventeenth century. Interest was revived in the early twentieth century, however, when a Lincoln homeowner created a fake well, printed advertising brochures, sold postcards, and charged an entrance fee to see the site where Little Hugh allegedly drowned. The hoax was exposed a couple of decades later.

—*Emily Rose*

See also Coin Clipping; English Literature from Chaucer to Wells; Expulsions, High Middle Ages; Middle Ages, High; Ritual Murder (Medieval); Simon of Trent; Sorcery/Magic; William of Norwich
References
Langmuir, Gavin. "The Knight's Tale of Young Hugh of Lincoln." In *Toward a Definition of Antisemitism* (Berkeley: University of California Press, 1990), 237–262.
Stacey, Robert C. "1240–60—A Watershed in Anglo-Jewish Relations?" *Historical Research* 61 (1988): 135–150.
Stocker, David. "The Shrine of Little Saint Hugh [of Lincoln]." In *Medieval Art and Architecture at Lincoln Cathedral*. Edited by T. A. Heslop and V. A. Sekules (Oxford: British Archeological Association, 1986), 109–117.

Hungary (1848–1944)

Prior to the failed revolution of 1848, widespread restrictions severely limited Hungarian Jews' social, professional, and business activities. The subsequent gradual elimination of discriminatory measures generated an extended mass movement into Hungary of mainly east European Orthodox Jews, attracted by superior socioeconomic opportunities and the absence of government persecution. Through this influx in the period between 1850 and 1869, Hungary's Jewish population soared from 350,000 to 542,000—an increase of over 50 percent in less than a generation.

The emancipation era between 1867 and 1918, often called the Golden Age of Hungarian Jewry, saw a massive expansion of Jewish involvement in the social, cultural, and economic affairs of the nation. Besides traditional commercial activities, such as wholesale and retail trade, Jews established banks, factories, and heavy industries; developed large rural estates; and became a force in the free professions.

Despite their semifeudal mentality, governments during the emancipation era adopted relatively progressive attitudes toward Jews largely to promote the growth of Hungary's economy. Jews comprised about 5 percent of the population (about 900,000 of the 18 million inhabitants in 1910); by classifying them "Magyars of the Israelite Faith," the percentage of Magyars (ethnic Hungarians) in the ethnically heterogeneous kingdom was boosted from a minority position (49 percent) to a slight majority status (54 percent). This statistical sleight of hand thus enabled ethnic Hungarians to retain their primacy in state and society, conferring a facade of political legitimacy on Hungary's notoriously chauvinistic, Magyar-dominated governments.

Jews thrived in this situation. By World War I, they comprised 60 percent of merchants, 50 percent of medical practitioners, 45 percent of lawyers, 40 percent of journalists, and 25 percent of those professionally engaged in the arts. In contrast, an unwritten agreement excluded most Jewish applicants from positions in the civil service, these being reserved largely for the sons of impoverished gentry.

In less than two generations, Hungarian Jews

had become distinctly middle class, particularly in the capital. By the twentieth century, because voting rights were dependent on educational and financial qualifications, Jews comprised nearly one-half of Budapest's electorate even though they constituted only one-quarter of its inhabitants. Although acceptable to Hungary's "progressive" nationalists, whose focus was on the Jews' critical contributions to Hungary's rapid development, the newly emerging ethnic, or "racial," nationalists considered that Jews fostered economic exploitation, urban decadence, and erosion of the country's Christian heritage. These new nationalists, in contrast to their "progressive" opponents, thought it illegitimate for the Jewish 5 percent of the population to own so large a portion of the country's banks, factories, and mines and to predominate in the free professions, commerce, and the press.

Notwithstanding such antagonism, it was the 1867–1918 emancipation era that generated and then consolidated the cultural, economic, and political symbiosis between Hungarian Jewry and their patrons, the country's "progressive" establishment. As a mark of government recognition, Jews received an estimated 20 percent of Hungarian ennoblements.

Despite several antisemitic episodes before World War I—the infamous 1882–1884 Tisza-eszlar blood libel resonated throughout the civilized world—Judaism was proclaimed an officially recognized religion, equal in rights to the Christian denominations, in October 1895. This legislation was enacted in the face of strong opposition from the Catholic Church, the déclassé gentry, and those whose position had declined through the growth of industrialization, capitalism, and liberalism. All of these modern developments were considered by Judeophobes to be elements of a Jewish conspiracy to undermine traditional Hungarian values. Until 1914, the foremost proponents of antisemitism were the Catholic Peoples' Party and certain minorities—particularly the Slovaks—who resented the Jews' alignment with the Magyar regime's repressive and hegemonic policies toward Hungary's numerous ethnic minorities.

Although Hungarian Jews, especially the Neolog (cautiously progressive in religious practice)

majority living in the large urban centers, were highly acculturated, many provincial Orthodox communities maintained their otherworldly lifestyle and attitudes. Yet the great majority of Hungary's Jews were firmly pro-Magyar and convinced Hungarian nationalists. Thus, even though Theodor Herzl, the founder of modern Zionism, was born in Budapest, his movement failed to achieve popularity in Hungary.

During World War I, Jews went to war, and 10,000 of them died in battle. Nevertheless, popular opinion increasingly viewed Jews in general as unpatriotic shirkers and profiteers. As the conflict raged, waves of ultra-Orthodox Jews fled to Hungary, trying to escape the fighting, as well as intensified tsarist oppression. The influx of these impoverished, distinctly alien refugees further inflamed the country's growing anti-Jewish sentiment.

With the end of the war, the victorious Allies subjected the defeated Central Powers to substantial geopolitical restructuring. As a defeated combatant, Hungary was forced to accept a punitive peace settlement, the Treaty of Trianon (June 1920), by which it lost two-thirds of its territory, 60 percent of the prewar population, one-third of its Magyar inhabitants, and enormous amounts of economic assets and infrastructure. Although the absolute number of Jews in Hungary declined by half to approximately 470,000, the relative number remained more or less constant at about 5 percent of the total population. The transfer of many provincial centers of Orthodoxy to newly created neighboring states increased the Neolog proportion to two-thirds of the community. As a result of Trianon, about half of Hungary's Jews lived in Budapest.

Trianon also transformed Hungary into an ethnically homogeneous nation, with Magyars now comprising some 90 percent of the postwar population. With the elimination of internal ethnic conflict, Jews ceased being a useful consolidating factor for the ruling Magyars and consequently became vulnerable to political exploitation, particularly scapegoating.

As with Germany, Hungary's military debacle of 1918 caused economic chaos, political turmoil, and a general revulsion against the Allies and their unilateral transformation of the nation into a mere "rump state." In March 1919, following a brief Center-Left coalition, Bela Kun, a Bolshevik of Jewish origin, formed a radical socialist regime, which, despite its initial popularity, quickly provoked a "White" counterreaction that advocated xenophobic policies of "national purification and regeneration." Even though Kun's Soviet regime collapsed within six months and even though the predominantly middle-class Jewish community suffered proportionately greater material losses than the population in general, the presence of thirty-two members of Jewish origin among Kun's forty-five commissars fed a virulent and effective antisemitic campaign by the White junta. Henceforth, popular opinion regarded Hungarian Jewry as synonymous with Kun's Soviet regime; Jews were reviled as the spiritual and financial advocates of Communist revolution.

Adm. Miklós Horthy, supremo of the 12,000-strong White militia, unleashed a reign of terror during which 5,000 to 6,000 Jews, left-wingers, and sundry other perceived traitors to "Christian" Hungary were murdered in cold blood. On March 1, 1920, an overwhelming majority of the Hungarian parliament appointed Horthy regent of the nation—in effect, the head of state. In September 1920, parliament passed the first major anti-Jewish statute in postwar Europe, the *Numerus Clausus* Law. Although its stipulations were somewhat ameliorated during the 1920s, the law limiting Jewish enrollments in institutions of higher education was not repealed.

The Great Depression and a growing, more active radical Right—both within and outside the parliament—increased pressure on the Jews. On June 17, 1933, Prime Minister Gyula Gombos, a veteran antisemite and prominent participant in the White Terror that suppressed the Kun regime, became the first foreign premier to visit Germany's new chancellor, Adolf Hitler. Subsequently, in both foreign and domestic policies and in economic relations, Hungary became progressively more enmeshed with Nazi Germany. This tilt to the Reich was based on both ideology and Hungary's fervent hope of regaining land lost by the Treaty of Trianon. Germany, expanding its power in the march toward hegemony, reinforced the new policies by ensuring

that Hungary regained some of the longed-for areas. Acquisition of these territories transferred to Hungary nearly 320,000 (mainly Orthodox) Jews: 146,000 from Slovakia, following the 1938 Munich Agreement; 164,000 from northern Transylvania (Romania), by means of the German-Italian arbitration of August 1940; and 14,000 from northwest Yugoslavia in April 1941. A subsequent national census indicated Hungary's Jewish population had increased from 470,000 in 1920 to 825,000 in 1941. The latter figure included 100,000 converts to Christianity, of whom about two-thirds resided in Budapest.

Encouraged by its German mentor and local ultrarightist agitation, Hungary progressively adopted aspects of the Reich's extreme anti-Jewish agenda. Thus, in May 1938, in an attempt to appease both Hitler and his followers in Hungary, the parliament overwhelmingly approved the First Jewish Law. Innocuously entitled "For a More Effective Safeguard of Equilibrium in Social and Economic Life," the statute limited Jewish involvement to 20 percent of the participants in each of a wide range of business and professional activities. The law expanded the definition of a Jew to include those who had converted to Christianity after the downfall of Kun's Soviet regime in August 1919.

A radical extension, the Second Jewish Law, was enacted in May 1939. More realistically entitled "The Law for Restricting the Place of the Jews in Public Life and in the Economy," it reduced Jewish business and professional involvement to 6 percent of all participants, potentially depriving as many as 200,000 people of their livelihoods. Shortly thereafter, Jews were banned from military service and conscripted into segregated Jewish Labor Service brigades, often commanded by sadistic, antisemitic army officers. To compensate those financially ravaged by institutional discrimination, Jewish leaders developed a comprehensive and widespread communal welfare system that later proved vital for Jews in their struggle to survive the German occupation. With poetic justice, the instigator of the Second Jewish Law, Prime Minister Bela Imredy, was forced to resign when he was unable to refute accusations regarding his distant Jewish ancestry.

Notwithstanding the restrictions placed on

Jewish business activities and civil liberties, the Second Jewish Law still permitted a Jewish presence—although substantially curtailed—within the Hungarian state. The government withstood radical Right demands for Jews to be expelled entirely from Hungary's socioeconomic structure. Facilitating this resistance was the relative parliamentary weakness of pro-Nazi groups, foremost of which was Ferenc Szalasi's Nyilas (Arrow Cross) Party, which secured just 49 of 260 seats in the openly corrupt, government-manipulated elections of 1939.

The government's escalating anti-Jewish policies failed to satisfy the ultra-Right's antisemitic fanaticism. Shortly after abandoning its noncombatant status by joining its German ally in attacking the USSR in June 1941, the regime sought to preempt further pro-Nazi agitation at home by introducing the Third Jewish Law. Officially termed the Race Protection Act of August 1941, the legislation, based on the Nuremberg Laws of 1935, segregated Jewry by designating the community as "racially subversive." To prove its antisemitic bona fides, the government arrested 30,000 "alien" Jews. (A Jew born in Hungary, it should be noted, was not automatically entitled to citizenship.) Some 20,000 of those arrested were swiftly deported to Kamenets-Podolsk in the German-occupied Ukraine. At the end of August 1941, the Germans and their collaborators murdered the large majority of deportees. This action constituted the first five-figure massacre of Jews in the Holocaust.

In March 1942, Horthy, already having begun to doubt an Axis victory, dismissed his pro-German prime minister, Laszlo Bardossy, and replaced him with his pragmatic ally Miklós Kallay. Apparently adhering to his predecessor's policies, Kallay authorized another major anti-Jewish statute in June 1942 when parliament, without debate and with support from the Christian churches, abolished the official status and constitutional equality of the Jewish religion, thus slashing the government's financial support for the community. With the tide of war turning against the Axis powers, Kallay, supported by Horthy, attempted a gradual withdrawal from the German alliance. Notwithstanding Hitler's personal hostility and intense domestic pressure,

Kallay rebuffed repeated German directions for Hungary to mark all Jews with a yellow star, confine them in ghettos, and deport them to the East. Tragically, Kallay's evident noncompliance reinforced Hungarian Jewry's collective perception of residing in an island sanctuary, insulated from the brutal treatment Jews received elsewhere in Nazi-dominated Europe.

In the period between 1918 and 1944, the overwhelming response of Hungarian Jewry to persecution could be described as one of passive legality. Considering antisemitic sentiment a transient phenomenon, the community's leadership rejected the formation of a specifically Jewish political party and remained steadfastly wedded to traditional measures, such as issuing increasingly emotional appeals for justice and fraternity. Similarly, ordinary Jews responded by reaffirming their traditional and heartfelt loyalty to Hungary, reminding their non-Jewish neighbors of the massive and diverse contributions made by "Magyars of the Israelite Faith" to their common homeland in both war and peace. To casual observers, the political consciousness of Hungarian Jews, developed and then fixated during the emancipation era that ended in 1918, appeared impervious to the menace of the Third Reich and its local allies. Hungarian Jews and their leaders seemed helpless to counter their ever more desperate circumstances.

On March 17, 1944, Horthy was summoned to Austria to consult with Hitler. Two days later, German forces occupied Hungary without resistance. On the brink of Germany's inevitable, catastrophic defeat by the Allies, Hitler was now in position to wage merciless war against the defenseless Jews of Hungary.

—*Tom Kramer*

See also Austria; Croatia; Emancipation; Herzl, Theodor; Horthy, Miklós; Hungary, Holocaust in; Judeo-Bolshevism; Kallay, Miklós; *Numerus Clausus* (Hungary); *Ostjuden;* Russia, Imperial; Slovakia, Holocaust in; Szalasi, Ferenc; Tiszaeszlar Ritual Murder; Versailles Treaty; White Terror; Yellow Star

References

Braham, Randolph L. *The Politics of Genocide: The Holocaust in Hungary.* 2 vols. (New York: Columbia University Press, 1994).

Kramer, T. D. *From Emancipation to Catastrophe: The Rise and Holocaust of Hungarian Jewry* (Lanham, MD: University Press of America, 2000).

Mendelsohn, Ezra. *The Jews of East Central Europe between the World Wars* (Bloomington: Indiana University Press, 1983).

Patai, Raphael. *The Jews of Hungary: History, Culture, Psychology* (Detroit, MI: Wayne State University Press, 1996).

Silber, Michael K., ed. *Jews in the Hungarian Economy, 1760–1945* (Jerusalem: Magnes Press, Hebrew University, 1992).

Hungary, Holocaust in

Motivated by political, economic, and military self-interest, Germany invaded its Hungarian ally on March 19, 1944, and was welcomed with considerable enthusiasm. Despite initial doubts, Hungary's powerful head of state, Adm. Miklós Horthy, decided to remain in office; his decision maintained the appearance of constitutional continuity and hence political legitimacy for the new German-imposed puppet government. In the period from March 19 to July 6, Hungary's freedom to maneuver, especially in foreign affairs and Jewish policy, was terminated; the anti-Nazi prime minister, Miklós Kallay, was replaced by a notorious pro-Nazi, Gen. Dome Sztojay, the former ambassador to Germany. Horthy withdrew almost entirely from public life. Sztojay's effusively collaborationist regime granted Germany carte blanche to "solve" the Jewish Question in Hungary. With few exceptions, the Hungarian bureaucracy implemented SS policy toward Jews with what the Germans themselves described as "Asiatic brutality."

In line with their Final Solution strategy, the occupiers immediately seized 3,000 Jewish hostages to ensure the compliant behavior of Jewish leaders and their community. Jews were banned from traveling without permission, and strict censorship allowed the SS to control the flow of information. The Germans established the Jewish Council (*Zsido Tanacs*) and made it responsible for conveying their orders to the Jewish community. The last measure was in accord with the Nazis' policy of forcing Jews, wherever possible, to participate in their own destruction.

On March 29, 1944, Jews were physically branded by being compelled to wear a 10-centimeter yellow star on their outer garment. Following their financial expropriation and loss of civil liberties, provincial Jews began to be herded into regional ghettos in mid-April; such establishments were often located near railway sidings at large factories, brickworks, distilleries, and other unhealthy sites. As a rule, these regional ghettos existed from three to seven weeks in near-total isolation and were therefore easily manipulated by the Germans, who were by then masters in the arts of manipulation, expropriation, disinformation, and crowd control. Typically, Jews were reassured that their "resettlement in the East" was for work purposes only, with women, children, and the elderly being transported so as to avoid the trauma of family separation.

Mass deportations to Auschwitz commenced on May 15, 1944, starting with Jews in northeastern Hungary and continuing with the sequential evacuation of individual provinces. Crucial in this process was the Interior Ministry and its much-feared *gendarmerie* (paramilitary police). Thoroughly brutalized, physically and psychologically, by these often sadistic collaborators, the ghetto inhabitants boarded the cattle cars without offering much resistance. On average, four trains per day carried between 10,000 and 12,000 Jews to Auschwitz, deporting 450,000 provincial Jews in the seven weeks from May 15 to July 6, 1944. In the whole history of the Final Solution, the Nazis had never approached this level of efficiency. Yet there were life-saving incongruities as well. Male Jews conscripted into the cruel Jewish Labor Service brigades by Hungary's pro-German military were spared Auschwitz.

Perhaps a great many more lives could have been saved. Even before the deportations began, Lt. Col. Adolf Eichmann, the SS officer in charge of the Final Solution in Hungary, revealed in the so-called Blood for Trucks proposal that Germany would release Hungary's Jews in exchange for badly needed commodities, including 10,000 army trucks for use on the eastern front. After desultory consideration until mid-July, by which time Hungary's provincial Jews had already been deported, the Allies—fully aware of the fate awaiting Jews trapped within Nazi territory—unanimously rejected the German overture. They proved equally impervious to heart-rending pleas from international Jewish leaders to save

Hungarian Jewry or at least to slow its destruction by either feigning to negotiate with the Germans over their extraordinary offer or bombing the Hungary-to-Auschwitz railway line and destroying the death camp's gas chambers and crematoria.

No longer able to wait on the Allies, local Zionist leaders managed to convince Eichmann's ultimate superior, Heinrich Himmler, that Western cooperation depended on proof of Germany's willingness to release Jews. Accordingly, a train known as the "Kasztner Transport" left Budapest on June 30, with 1,700 Hungarian Jews who, after several months in the "privileged" section of Bergen-Belsen concentration camp, eventually reached safety in neutral Switzerland.

On July 7, 1944, Admiral Horthy, subjected to growing international pressure and increasingly anxious at the prospect of an Axis defeat, emerged from fourteen weeks of political inactivity to challenge German hegemony in Hungary. Germany's continual military reverses presented Horthy with an opportunity to regain some degree of independence. Evidence of this came with his successful banning of further deportation of Jews to Auschwitz. Although this bold act occurred after the Germans had declared the provinces to be *judenrein* (totally "cleansed" of Jews), the measure saved Budapest's Jews from deportation. In August, Horthy dismissed the German-imposed puppet regime, appointed a trusted non-Nazi general as prime minister, and began secret negotiations with the Soviet Union, whose military forces were fast approaching.

The second phase of the occupation (July 7 to October 15) had begun, and conditions improved substantially for Hungary's surviving Jews, now overwhelmingly concentrated in Budapest. Jewish Council leaders regained access to Horthy and used their influence to strengthen his resolve that, despite Hitler's intense pressure, the ban on further deportations would be maintained. Moreover, significant support was provided by some neutral diplomats in Budapest, particularly the Swiss consul Carl Lutz and the Swedish consul Raoul Wallenberg, both of whom safeguarded Jews through the (necessarily limited) distribution of legally dubious "protective passports" (*Schutzpasse*).

Many have questioned whether Hungary's Jewish leaders did enough to defend their community once they realized that deportation meant extermination. Among civilized communities, the attempt to avoid catastrophe by capitulating to overwhelming force is hardly unknown in history, nor is it regarded as necessarily dishonorable or cowardly. As in every country crushed by Nazi Germany, Hungary's Jewish leaders surrendered to the initial realities confronting their community. Tragically, Hungary collaborated in full with the iron-fisted occupiers and their Final Solution; the Jews were already in a stage of impoverishment, thanks to previous Hungarian actions. Their social, political, and military isolation was nearly total; the churches were virtually silent, attentive only to the spiritual needs of Jewish converts. Finally, the core of any possible armed resistance—male Jews of military age—had already been forced into labor service brigades.

Nonetheless, during the occupation's second phase, Jewish physical resistance began in earnest, largely initiated and implemented by the underground Zionist youth movements, known collectively as *Halutzim* (pioneers). These groups, with a membership of only a few hundred fifteen- to eighteen-year-olds, established networks that eventually smuggled between 5,000 and 7,000 Jews across Hungary's borders, mainly to the relative safety of Romania. Furthermore, from June 1944 onward, the Halutzim printed and distributed gratis to tens of thousands of Jews all sorts of false identity papers. These documents enabled a wide cross section of the Jewish community to discard the compulsory yellow star and live under a relatively secure Christian Identity. In particular, during the brutal and chaotic third phase of occupation—the Szalasi era from October 16, 1944, to January 17, 1945—such false papers helped save thousands of Budapest Jews from Eichmann's winter death marches, the inhuman deportation of 80,000 Jews for forced labor on Vienna's fortifications. The Zionist youths' false document scheme was a mass rescue operation, a Jewish endeavor to evade the Final Solution unmatched anywhere within German-occupied territory.

Meanwhile, the Jewish Council, though officially rejecting "illegal" activities in an effort to preserve the 3,000 Jewish hostages imprisoned by the Germans, also engaged selectively in covert attempts to subvert the Final Solution. The council's paramount effort was a unique scheme, far greater in scale than anything undertaken by Jews elsewhere in Nazi Europe. Samuel Stern, head of the council, entered into a secret agreement with the noncommunist Hungarian Independence Front to help defend Horthy's proposed armistice by arming 25,000 Jewish Labor Service conscripts. The occupation's second phase ended, and the bold scheme came to nothing when Horthy himself was deposed by a German putsch on October 15, the day he announced on Radio Hungary his armistice with the USSR.

In the third phase of occupation, Horthy's replacement, Ferenc Szalasi, the brutal leader of the Hungarian pro-Nazi Nyilas (Arrow Cross) Party, ignored the Jewish Council's appeals for justice and humanity. The council did what it could under tremendous difficulties, managing to ameliorate the increasingly desperate circumstances of Budapest Jews by establishing public kitchens, collaborating with the few neutral diplomats remaining in Budapest, and utilizing false documents on behalf of its besieged constituency.

After a complete encirclement by Soviet forces, a destructive siege of Budapest began on December 24, 1944. The two recently established ghettos—the noncontiguous "International Ghetto" containing 30,000 recipients of (mainly false) documents and the walled "Common Ghetto" holding 70,000 Jews without foreign documents—were liberated by the Red Army on January 17, 1945. The same day, the U.S.-recruited Swedish consul Raoul Wallenberg disappeared forever into Soviet custody. On liberation, thanks to the efforts described here, over 120,000 Jews had survived in Budapest, more than in any other city occupied by the Germans. Yet this achievement cannot obscure the poignant counterreality: that Hungary's Jewish community, the last national Jewry to remain intact, had become the last to be destroyed by Nazi Germany and its Hungarian collaborators.

—*Tom Kramer*

See also "Blood for Trucks"; Eichmann, Adolf; Holocaust; Horthy, Miklós; Hungary; Kallay, Miklós; Szalasi, Ferenc; Yellow Star; Zionism

References

Anger, Per. *With Raoul Wallenberg in Budapest: Memories of the War Years in Hungary* (New York: Holocaust Library, 1981).

Braham, Randolph L. *The Politics of Genocide: The Holocaust in Hungary.* 2 vols. (New York: Columbia University Press, 1994).

Kramer, T. D. "*Arbeit Macht Frei?* The Hungarian Jewish Labour Brigades during World War II." In *Europe: Retrospects and Prospects.* Edited by John Perkins and Jürgen Tampke (Sydney, Australia: Southern Highlands Publishers, 1996), 41–47.

———. *From Emancipation to Catastrophe: The Rise and Holocaust of Hungarian Jewry* (Lanham, MD: University Press of America, 2000).

Hungary, Pogroms in (1946)

The Hungarian pogroms of 1946, unlike those that occurred in Poland at the same time, claimed only a handful of victims. The wave of violence was also short-lived, giving way to the return of political and economic stability. Yet the pogroms are significant for what they reveal about the society and politics of the time.

Although there were anti-Jewish demonstrations and attacks on individual Jews in at least a dozen places in 1946, the bloodiest and worst manifestation took place in Kunmadaras in May and in Miskolc in July. The Kunmadaras affair included the ancient anti-Jewish calumny of blood libel, which many, especially among the uneducated peasantry, still took on faith. The rumor spread in Kunmadaras that Jews made sausage out of Christian children and that several Christian children had mysteriously disappeared from the nearby town of Karcag. The pogrom against the town's seventy-three Jews, the remnant that had survived the Holocaust, began only when the police arrested a popular figure, who was also a former Nazi-collaborator, and attempted to transfer him to Karcag. The crowd attacked local Jews, killing two and wounding fifteen.

The situation was different in Miskolc, an industrial town, where the working class was in particularly dire straits. The ruling Communists crudely used local grievances for their own political purposes, sending prominent Communist leaders to harangue the workers on the evils of capitalism. The local Communist organization was aware of the antisemitic mood, but instead of attempting to combat that mood, it decided to remove party functionaries who came from the Jewish bourgeoisie. Violence broke out shortly afterward. News spread that three "speculators" had been arrested and that they were being moved to an internment camp outside the city. The crowds, probably tipped off in advance, intercepted the unfortunate men and killed one, wounded another, and let the third escape. He alone was not Jewish. After the tragic events were allowed to unfold, the police arrested some of the participants in the lynching. However, crowds again gathered, attacked the police station where the men were held, and lynched the Jewish Communist police lieutenant.

There are at least two explanations for this grassroots antisemitic violence. First, the power of Nazi propaganda obviously outlived Hitler, helping to convince many Hungarians who had collaborated with Nazism and many others who had passively witnessed the evil that Jews had deserved their fate: they were, in fact, an alien, subversive, and parasitical people. A second explanation for the wave of antisemitic outbursts had to do with the radically altered situation of Hungarian Jews as a result of Stalinization. In the minds of a great majority of Hungarians, Jews and Communists came to be identified as synonymous, undermining the credibility of both. The majority of Jews were not Communists, and the majority of Communists were not Jewish, but Jews, who welcomed the Red Army as liberators, were disproportionately represented in the party and also in the political police. The four most prominent and powerful leaders of the Hungarian Communist Party were Jewish.

The myth of Judeo-Bolshevism would predict that such a situation should have produced a "paradise for Jews." But on the contrary, postwar Hungary offers the clearest example of how Stalinists of Jewish descent employed antisemitism in an entirely self-serving fashion. The popular identification of Jews with Communists threatened to paralyze the party. Thus, leaders desperately sought allies with indisputably Hungarian credentials, even going so far as to recruit low-ranking members of the Hungarian Nazi Party (Nyilaskeresztes Part).

For the series of pogroms that took place in 1946, the Communist Party deserves considerable blame. Although they were not the creators of Hungarian antisemitism, the Communists nonetheless exploited and legitimized it. As a prelude to the violence, the party press attacked small traders as speculators, knowing that the common folk regarded them as Jews. It published posters in which the "enemy"—the capitalist, the speculator—sported recognizably Semitic features. The disturbances in Ozd, in February 1946, showed that the government's own antisemitism was not lost on ordinary people. Neither could it be contained to serve the Communists' limited purposes. What started as a protest at the murder of a Communist leader (a well-known antisemite) turned into something different. Workers and miners took the opportunity to demonstrate against Communists and Jews and looted Jewish-owned stores and apartments. When the police arrested some of the looters, the masses became increasingly incensed and maintained that there could be no solution to the social and political problems until Hungary got rid of the Jews.

—*Peter Kenez*

See also Hungary; Judeo-Bolshevism; Kielce Pogrom; Poland; Ritual Murder (Medieval); Ritual Murder (Modern); Stalinization of Eastern Europe
Reference
Hanak, Peter, ed. *One Thousand Years: A Concise History of Hungary* (Budapest: Corvina, 1988).

Hungary, Post-Soviet

Hungary today has approximately 80,000 Jews. However, for one reason or another, many choose not to reveal themselves as Jewish to the census takers. So, perhaps 80,000 understates the actual number. As time passes, the number will decrease because the Jewish birthrate is very low, far below what would be needed to replace losses from death or emigration.

Today in Hungary, Jews live almost exclusively in Budapest. The Nazis destroyed a far greater proportion of the provincial Jews, and those few who returned after the war to the small towns eventually left the countryside for the West, for Israel, or for the capital. Whatever their precise number, it is clear that outside the former Soviet Union, Hungary now has the largest population of Jews in Eastern and Central Europe. By any objective measure, Jews represent what might be viewed as a privileged minority: they are overrepresented in business, the professions, cultural life, and politics. Even the right-wing Small Holders' Party has some prominent Jewish politicians, and with one major exception, no political party is explicitly antisemitic. There are excellent Jewish periodicals, a Jewish publishing house, and Jewish schools supported by international funding. Unlike post-Soviet Russia, where pogroms are at least conceivable, such events seem remote possibilities in Hungary. It would be difficult to show that Jews face discrimination in any aspect of national life.

And yet, antisemitism is a significant force in contemporary Hungary. Although it is difficult to gauge the extent of popular antisemitism, it is fair to say that old stereotypes do not easily fade away. Now that the press is free, the ugly voices that had been repressed during the Communist era are again freely heard. As before, antisemites blame Jews both for playing dominant roles in the establishment of the Communist regime and also for unduly benefiting from the collapse of that regime by becoming the most successful members of the emerging capitalist class. Jewish graves have been desecrated repeatedly, even in the countryside, where there are no Jews still living.

The political home of antisemites is the ferociously antisemitic party, the extreme right-wing Magyar Igazság es Élet Pártja (Party of Hungarian Truth and Life [MIEP]). The very choice of name is revealing: the Party of Hungarian Life was a fascist, pro-Nazi party during World War II. MIEP can be classified as one of the many xenophobic, nationalist parties active presently in several European countries. The party got just over 5 percent of the vote in the national elections of 1998, which was enough to gain parliamentary representation. However, in the last elections, its vote total fell under 5 percent, disqualifying its candidates from taking their seats in the current parliament.

In one important way, however, MIEP is different from other right-wing extremist parties: it is pathologically preoccupied with Jews. In other European countries where the extreme Right is strong, the main attraction of these forces is anti-immigrant xenophobia. Jews are just one of the threats to their concept of nationhood and not even the most important one. The situation is different in Hungary. The problem of nonwhite immigration is relatively minor. Hungary is more or less ethnically homogeneous, if one discounts the significant social and ethnic problems posed by approximately 500,000 Gypsies. Hence, Jews get the lion's share of MIEP's attention. István Csurka, the charismatic founder and leader of the party, is a talented writer who even in the 1970s, when he was an artist in good standing with the relatively moderate Hungarian communist regime, did not hide his antisemitism. As is common with parties of this type, MIEP's antisemitic propaganda connects Jews with all sorts of trends that the extreme Right disapproves of. As nationalists, extreme rightists are foes of globalization, and in their view, Jews are behind this trend. MIEP politicians regularly talk about a New York–Tel Aviv axis. They attribute enormous power to the Mossad, the Israeli secret service, in influencing international events. In their conspiratorial view, it is the Jews who want to destroy national culture, undermine national traditions, and besmirch Hungary's good name. For example, when France gave asylum to some Hungarian Roma, implying that in the country of their birth they suffered discrimination, MIEP blamed the Jews for undermining the reputation of Hungary abroad. The party's periodical, *Forum,* is preoccupied with Israeli politics and habitually describes the Israeli government as fascist.

MIEP is a significant political force, and it cannot be dismissed as a movement of the old, the uneducated, or those who have been victimized by the postcommunist economic and political changes. Its major electoral support comes not from the politically less sophisticated countryside but from the most affluent districts of Budapest. In terms of antisemitism, MIEP has had an effect beyond what its vote would suggest. The leading party in the previous government, the Fidez (Fiatal Demokraták Szövetsége, or Alliance of Young Democrats), which in 2002 was engaged in a bitter and ultimately unsuccessful campaign, moved to the Right in order to attract MIEP voters. Mainstream politicians, such as Victor Orbán, the former premier, have regularly appeared on extreme rightist broadcasts, giving them respectability they are unable to get on their own. Lászlo Kövér, perhaps the second-most powerful Fidez politician, talks about a "Jewish problem" in Hungary, rather than an antisemitic problem. Maria Smidt, a historian and adviser to Orbán, trivializes the Holocaust, suggesting—remarkably for a historian—that the extermination of the Jews was not a German war aim.

Fidez, in attempting to use nationalism for its own electoral advantage by reconfiguring history, is rehabilitating the conservative, feudal, antisemitic interwar regime of Miklós Horthy. The nationalist Right is making heroes out of politicians of the World War II era who collaborated with the Nazis and were responsible for untold human suffering. For example, a plaque has been placed in the military history museum in memory of the Hungarian gendarmes, an organization whose record in the Holocaust, mutatis mutandis, can be compared to that of the SS. It is not surprising that the exclusivist nationalism that is popular in many circles makes Jews feel uncomfortable in contemporary Hungary.

—*Peter Kenez*

See also Horthy, Miklós; Hungary; Hungary, Holocaust in
Reference
Hoffman, Eva. *Exit into History: A Journey through the New Eastern Europe* (New York: Viking, 1993).

Hussaini, Mufti Hajj Amin al- (1895–1974)

The leading figure of Palestinian nationalism prior to the establishment of the state of Israel, Muhammad Amin al-Hussaini developed a virulent antisemitism as a corollary of his anti-Zionism. He took a leading role in the violent anti-Zionist riots in Jerusalem in 1920 and had to flee to Damascus. He was sentenced to prison in absentia but was pardoned the following year

on assuring British High Commissioner Herbert Samuel that he and his distinguished family would help keep the peace in the Arab sector. He was appointed mufti (chief Muslim legal authority) and thereafter president of the Supreme Muslim Council. The latter position gave him budgetary control over most Islamic public institutions. Already during the 1920s, the Mufti began casting Palestinian Arab opposition to Zionism in terms of a struggle between Islam and the Jews. He accused the Jews of attempting to usurp and dominate the Muslim sacred precincts in Jerusalem. It is open to debate whether he took part in planning the so-called Wailing Wall riots of August 1929, but at the very least, he helped incite them. The riots broke out in the wake of a perennial dispute over Jewish prayer at the Western (Wailing) Wall of the Temple Mount. The rioters massacred 129 Jews and injured over 300 more, most of them defenseless members of the old religious communities in Hebron and Safed.

Throughout the 1930s, the Mufti endeavored to foster anti-Zionist and anti-Jewish sentiments throughout the Arab and Islamic world by calling for solidarity in the defense of Arab Palestine and its Islamic holy places. In December 1931, he convened the World Islamic Conference in Jerusalem. Among the resolutions adopted were a number calling for the defense of the Holy Land against the *Jews* (not just Zionist Jews). After the conference, the Mufti actively disseminated anti-imperialist, anti-Zionist (frequently antisemitic) propaganda materials through organizations such as the Young Men's Muslim Associations, the Muslim Brotherhood, and nationalist groups all over the Muslim world.

Like other Arab nationalists, the Mufti viewed Hitler as an ally against both Anglo-French imperialism and Jewish Zionism. Shortly after Hitler's appointment as chancellor in 1933, the Mufti met with the German consul in Jerusalem. In 1937, he was dismissed from office by the mandatory authorities for his role as a leader in the Arab general strike, which broke out in 1936 and soon erupted into outright rebellion. He fled to Lebanon and thence to Iraq in 1940, where he became active in extremist Arab nationalist circles and in anti-Jewish agitation. He helped plan the coup that brought the pro-Axis government of Rashid Ali to power in 1941 and was in close contact with the German ambassador. He fled, once again, with the regime's leaders on May 29, 1941, as British troops closed in on Baghdad. The pogrom, known as the Farhud, that followed two days later had apparently already been planned. The Mufti eventually reached Berlin, meeting with Mussolini in Rome on the way. In Berlin, after conferring with Hitler, he stayed on to work for the German war effort. His radio broadcasts called on Arabs and Muslims to "Kill the Jews wherever you find them, for the love of God, history, and religion." He also helped to recruit Muslim volunteers from the Balkans and Soviet Muslim territories into special units in the German armed forces. One of these units of Bosnian Waffen-SS played a role in the destruction of Yugoslavian Jewry.

Captured by the French at the war's end, the Mufti again escaped and moved between Cairo, Beirut, and Damascus, where he helped direct Arab opposition to the partition of Palestine. After the Palestinian and Arab failure to destroy the nascent state of Israel and to establish a Palestinian state, the Mufti gradually lost all political influence and lived out his life as a religious scholar in Cairo and Beirut.

—*Norman A. Stillman*

See also Anti-Zionism; Arafat, Yasir; Farhud; Hamas; Islam and the Jews; Muslim Brotherhood; Zionism

References

Hirszowicz, Lukasz. *The Third Reich and the Arab East* (London: Routledge & Kegan Paul, 1966).
Schechtman, Joseph B. *The Mufti and the Fuehrer* (New York: Thomas Yoseloff, 1965).
Stillman, Norman A. *The Jews of Arab Lands in Modern Times* (Philadelphia: Jewish Publication Society, 1991).

I

Iconography, Christian

The graphic representation of Jews in Christian art has for centuries exercised a determining influence on the perception of Jews. ("Christian art" here refers to images with explicit Christian content employed in a religious context.) It has helped shape the way Judaism is imagined, giving graphic expression to the images of Jewry found in literary and polemical texts. This is most readily seen in the artistic renderings of biblical themes. The artist's attempt to illustrate a biblical story often went beyond the literal text and revealed instead a personal interpretation or that of the patron. Art, therefore, can tell us important things about the history of antisemitism. It can document the developments taking place in politics and society.

Tracing the popular Ecclesia et Synagoga (church and synagogue) motif over time reveals the increasingly pronounced negative valuation of Judaism. During the Carolingian era, two royal ladies placed in opposition recalled the common theological ground shared by Christianity and Judaism. But with the passage of time, the depiction of Synagoga became ever more unsympathetic, ever more disparaging. Thus, Benedetto Antelami's marble relief of the Deposition from the Cross illustrates an angel robbing Synagoga of all her dignity, an apt representation of the worsening situation of European Jewry in the twelfth century. A similar decline can be traced in artistic interpretations of the Passion narratives. From late antiquity through the Carolingian period, graphic illustrations of the Passion were without a Jewish presence. A mid-fourth-century sarcophagus from the catacomb of Domitilla shows the Passion as a Roman affair. Even Pilate's interrogation lacks

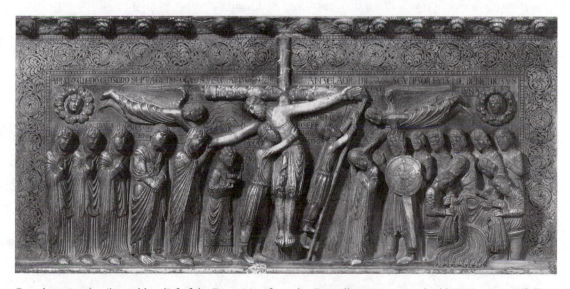

Benedetto Antelami's marble relief of the Deposition from the Cross illustrates an angel robbing Synagoga of all her dignity, an apt representation of the worsening situation of European Jewry in the twelfth century. (Scala /Art Resource, New York)

Following the anti-Jewish tendencies of literary texts, depictions of Jews, such as this scene from the Naumburg Cathedral, often made them recognizable by their "Jew hats" or other prescribed identifying markers. (Foto Marburg/Art Resource, NY)

the obligatory Jewish accusers. From the eleventh century, however, the image began to alter. Following the anti-Jewish tendencies of literary texts, the perpetrators were now Jews, often made recognizable by their "Jew hats" or other prescribed identifying markers.

Illustrations of the Crucifixion, in which Jews were seen as actors, were influenced by the reading of literary texts. However, a change in the relationship of text and image gradually became noticeable, with the image becoming the dominant element. The obscure comments in the New Testament, under the powerful influence of graphic representation, acquired a clarity not to be found in the text. Art supplanted text in the determining of reality. Moreover, because the images were of the moment and unambiguous, they impacted contemporary Jews negatively. The portrayal of Judas, the betrayer of Jesus, as a Jewish moneylender (from the Naumburg Cathedral), was one

such contemporary adaptation of the past. Representing Jews as cruel and brutal strengthened the impulse to treat them unjustly, inhumanely, and even criminally. It legitimated such misdeeds and paved the way for new ones.

Depictions of Jews underwent historical development. Absent from the literary sources of late antiquity and the early Middle Ages and also missing in the arts was a specific Jewish type. In neither literature nor art was it claimed that Jews had recognizable physical appearances, facial expressions, or gestures that distinguished them from others. Difference was solely related to religious and social practices. The so-called Jewish type came into existence as a construct of Jew-hatred, which maintained that Jews should first be isolated through physical markings and then forced into a special inferior status. The contention that Jews could be distinguished from others by their pale skin, hooked noses, and other features developed parallel to efforts to make them readily identifiable through physical symbols. As with other forms of prejudice, Christian anti-Judaism did not rest on empirical reality but rather constructed the reality of "the Jew" to fit its needs. Graphic representations accepted this construct and lent it its own reality. Thus, Christian iconography confirmed the prejudice out of which it grew. Illuminating in this respect were the depictions of the ritual murder legend in direct imitation of the Passion illustrations. The type already existed; it needed only to be adapted to a new context. The long tradition of iconographic representation made such connections credible, as in the combined rendering of a ritual murder with the *Judensau* (Jew's pig; see entry on *Judensau* for illustration).

Without oversimplifying the historical connection, it is nevertheless difficult to deny that Christian graphic materials readied many of the themes to be found in modern antisemitism and also palpably influenced their expression. Aside from the "Jew as murderer" motif, modern antisemites could draw on traditional iconographic associations of Jews with demons, Satan, and the Antichrist. A central reference point for this particular trope was the interpretation of the biblical story of the Adoration of the Golden Calf. Christian authors from late antiquity found in Exodus 32 indisputable proof of the enduring inclination of Jews to abandon their faith and to venerate demons. Such traditional modes of interpretation established the Jewish fascination with the demonic and later produced one of the vilest of antisemitic images, the Judensau, in which the pig served as a symbol of satanic evil.

Overtly anti-Jewish iconography is, however, only one side of an artistic tradition which contains many additional elements that produce and foster hatred of Jews. More subtle anti-Jewish messages can be conveyed, for example, by the portrayal of them in "Oriental" garb, the Turkish costumes featured in numerous medieval paintings. Even conceding that artists merely wanted to provide local color, the effect on viewers was to associate Jews with Turks. Jews dwelling in Christian lands were thus linked to a deadly enemy, and dread of "the terrible Turk" merged with dread of Jews. The Jews of Europe were made into strangers and enemies who might easily betray what, ironically, their Christian neighbors denied them, the homeland.

In the history of antisemitism, the calumny concerning the treachery of the alien Jews is a particularly stubborn theme and one that is constantly reanimated in the literature and in the arts. Christian iconography has been especially influential in portraying Jews as aliens, either by placing them outside society or by not representing them at all. Very few Western paintings make explicit the Jewishness of central figures. Perhaps eight medieval illustrations of the Supper at Emmaus portray Jesus wearing the Jew's hat. There are a few pictures of Saint Joseph wearing the hat, as well. Aside from Rembrandt's paintings of identifiable Jews, Raphael's *Betrothal of Mary* (1504) can also be mentioned. These few examples stand out by way of exception, however, and probably had little effect on the cultural perceptions of Europeans with regard to Jewish subjects. Much more common was the alienation of Jewish figures from their Jewish contexts, as was typical with Moses, the Prophets, Jesus, Mary, and the Apostles. However, the enemies of these figures—the Pharisees, priests, and torturers—were presented as Jews.

The art of the Renaissance left historical Jewry even further behind. Biblical genres were chosen in order to represent the perfection of the human form. Biblical events were "antiqued," as, for example, Michelangelo's sculpture *David,* which presents an uncircumcised king of Israel. The artistic tradition that interpreted biblical subjects was molded by a Christian iconography that either depicted Jewry in a negative light or ignored it altogether. The visual experience of these artistic formulations influenced viewers' judgments regarding Jews, at least latently and often overtly, in a negative way. Christian iconography obscured rather than highlighted the commonalities that existed among Christians and Jews. Western Christian art appropriated the portrayal of biblical subject matter and laid claim to sole possession of Holy Scripture. European Christian art helped estrange and alienate Jews and Judaism from the Western cultural tradition.

—*Rainer Kampling*
Richard S. Levy, translation

See also Antichrist; Caricature, Anti-Jewish (Early); Gospels; *Judensau;* Lateran Council, Fourth; Pork; Ritual Murder (Medieval); Yellow Badge; Yellow Star

References

Amishai-Maisels, Ziva. "The Jewish Jesus," *Journal of Jewish Art* 9 (1982): 84–104.

Claman, Henry N. *Jewish Images in the Christian Church: Art as the Mirror of the Jewish Christian Conflict, 200–1250 CE* (Macon, GA: Mercer University Press, 2000).

Frojmovic, Eva, ed. *Imagining the Self, Imagining the Other: Visual Representation and Jewish-Christian Dynamics in the Middle Ages and Early Modern Period* (Leiden, the Netherlands: Brill, 2002).

Kampling, Rainer. "Bilder des Mißverstehens: Dokumente der Judenfeindschaft in der europäischen Kunst." In *Christen und Juden gemeinsam ins dritte Jahrtausend: "Das Geheimnis der Erlösung heißt Erinnerung."* Edited by Hubert Frankemölle (Paderborn, Germany: Bonifatius, 2001), 99–129.

Lipton, Sara. *Images of Intolerance: The Representation of Jews and Judaism in the "Bible Moralisée"* (Berkeley: University of California Press, 1999).

Schreckenberg, Heinz. *The Jews in Christian Art: An Illustrated History* (New York: Continuum, 1996).

If I Were the Kaiser (1912)

Published under the pseudonym Daniel Frymann in 1912, Heinrich Class's *If I Were the Kaiser* (*Wenn ich der Kaiser wär*) was a systematic expression of the ideological program of the Pan-German League. It laid out a series of radical reforms, regarded as necessary by German extreme nationalists, to save the empire from catastrophe.

In what amounted to a manifesto, Class decried the socialist victory in the Reichstag elections of 1912 as evidence of a much more significant crisis in German society. Jews, he warned, had infiltrated German society and constructed a powerful alliance of enemies of the state, including socialists, national minorities, the Catholic Center Party, and the left-liberal Progressive Party, which was dedicated to subverting German society and the German national community from within. Although the charges presented in *If I Were the Kaiser* were familiar, Class's solutions were more startling and original. He called

for the constitutional reform of the political system, whereby universal and equal suffrage would be replaced by a class or plural voting franchise. The new system would ensure that representatives elected to parliament would have the appropriate—that is to say, upper-middle-class—education, wealth, and culture to speak and act in the name of the nation. From this elite, a select few would serve as advisers to the emperor and to the nation as a whole. *If I Were the Kaiser* also detailed a number of specific remedies to address the "threats" posed by social democracy, Jews, and the national minorities living in Germany. Class called for a new law outlawing socialist and anarchist assemblies, organizations, and publications; all socialist and anarchist activists were to be expelled from the country. National holidays and festivals were to fill the gap left by the suppression of social democracy in the lives of workers. Class also called for the censorship of all newspapers, except for the "national press," whose loyalty was assured.

Most significantly and most ominously, Class's book called for the eradication of "Jewish influence" in German society. Germany's borders were to be closed to Jewish immigration, and all foreign Jews were to be expelled, "to the last man." German Jews, moreover, were to be stripped of their civil rights and governed according to an "Aliens' Law." Jews would not be allowed to serve in public office, in the military, or in the professions and would be barred from owning rural property. They would also be required to pay double the taxes of Germans, "as compensation for the protection Jews enjoy as foreigners." Similar measures, including expropriation and draconian language laws, were proposed for the resident Polish, French, and Danish minorities. Foreshadowing the brutal population transfers later carried out by the Third Reich, Class wanted all non-German aliens to be expelled and to make up for these lost numbers by encouraging the return of ethnic Germans from abroad. Finally—and again prefiguring later events—he demanded forceful German expansion to the East.

The Pan-German League subsidized the publication of *If I Were the Kaiser,* and its local chapters distributed 20,000 to 25,000 copies before the outbreak of World War I. The Nazis later took up many of Class's recommendations in their own ideological program, although distancing themselves from his upper-middle-class milieu.

—*Elizabeth A. Drummond*

See also Antisemites' Petition; Antisemitic Political Parties; Class, Heinrich; Nazi Party Program; Pan-German League

References

Chickering, Roger. *We Men Who Feel Most German: A Cultural Study of the Pan-German League, 1886–1914* (Boston: Allen & Unwin, 1984).

Peters, Michael. *Der Alldeutsche Verband am Vorabend des Ersten Weltkrieges (1908–1914): ein Beitrag zur Geschichte des völkischen Nationalismus im spätwilhelminischen Deutschland* (Frankfurt am Main, Germany: Lang, 1996).

Immigration and Naturalization Laws (U.S.)

Although economic concerns most often dictated the direction of federal immigration and naturalization laws, Congress also used its legislative authority to control the racial, ethnic, and religious makeup of American society. For Jews, that meant the creation of a national origins quota system designed to limit the immigration of eastern Europeans and preserve what contemporaries termed a purer Anglo-Saxon genetic stock. In the late 1930s, these restrictive quotas prevented most European Jewish refugees from gaining admission to the United States. The government did not reassess the national origins system until Lyndon Johnson's Great Society in the mid-1960s.

Eighteenth- and nineteenth-century U.S. immigration and naturalization laws discouraged or even prevented a variety of American peoples, including American Indians, African Americans, Chinese Americans, and Japanese Americans, from achieving full civil equality. By the turn of the twentieth century, Congress began investigating ways to limit the immigration of peoples from southern and eastern Europe, which included most Jews. In 1907, the year that marked the greatest influx of Jews into the United States, Congress created the Dillingham Committee, charged with the responsibility of studying immigration patterns and recommending legislative changes. Rooted in the belief that immigrants from southern and eastern Europe possessed inferior genetic stock, the Dillingham Committee recommended that Congress institute a literacy test as a means to limit the number of "undesirable" arrivals. In 1911, 1913, 1915, and 1917, the literacy test passed Congress only to be vetoed by the chief executive. When xenophobic sentiment spiked after U.S. entry into World War I, Congress overturned President Woodrow Wilson's veto and instituted a literacy test for all European immigrants.

High literacy rates among the immigrants inspired Congress to reexamine the question in a December 1920 emergency session. The nativists' initial call for a one-year immigration moratorium ended in a compromise agreement, creating a national origins quota system that would limit the number of new arrivals to 3 percent of their group's representation in the 1910 census.

Three years later, the U.S. Congress reevaluated the 1921 law. Influenced by even greater xenophobic sentiment, Congress reduced the national origins quota from 3 percent to 2 percent and abandoned the 1910 census in favor of the 1890 count. By basing quota calculations on the earlier census, Congress sought to limit eastern European Jewish immigrants (as well as immigrants from other countries deemed unsuitable for Americanization). Because most Jews immigrated after 1890 and before 1910, the net effect of the 1924 Immigration Law was an almost total cessation of Jewish immigration to the United States.

The restrictive quotas established in 1921 and 1924 compounded the immigration challenges of Jews seeking asylum from the Nazis during the 1930s and 1940s. Even as the federal government expanded the number of available quota spots for Jewish refugees, it rarely issued visas for more than 10 percent of the allowable numbers. It was not until the postwar era, with the Displaced Persons Act of 1948, that restrictions on Jewish immigration eased. President Lyndon Johnson offered the first major overhaul of the structure of exclusion when he signed the Immigration Act of 1965, a Great Society program that reversed a century-old restriction against

Asian immigrants and eased the national origins-based discrimination of the earlier laws.

—Marc Dollinger

See also Eugenics; *Ostjuden; Passing of the Great Race;* Racism, Scientific; United States
References
Divine, Robert. *American Immigration Policy, 1924–1952* (New York: Da Capo Press, 1972).
Lissak, Rivka Shpak. *Liberal Progressives and Immigration Restriction, 1896–1917* (Jerusalem: American Jewish Archives, 1991).
Wyman, David. *The Abandonment of the Jews* (New York: New York University Press, 1997).

Imperial Hammer League

Beginning in 1905, the staff and readers of Theodor Fritsch's *Hammer: Journal of the German Way* banded together in local "Hammer communities" or "Hammer alliances." In December 1907, Fritsch declared to his readers that he intended to establish a strong, tightly knit organization. At about that time, he and Willibald Hentschel reactivated their German Renewal Community, the goal of which was the creation of racial, life-reforming settlements. Hammer communities of anywhere from ten to thirty members took root in Berlin, Bochum, Breslau, Charlottenburg, Chemnitz, Danzig, Dresden, Duisburg, Frankfurt am Main, Fürstenwalde, Grossröhrsdorf, Hamburg, Hanover, Leipzig, Lübeck, Magedeburg, Nuremberg, Stettin, Stuttgart, Weissenfels, Zeitz, and Vienna. They held regular public readings or lectures, recruited new members, and sold Fritsch's "Hammer-Pamphlets" and other publications. Typically, members belonged to one or more racist (*völkisch*), antisemitic organizations, such as the Pan-German League, the German National White Collar Employees Association, the German League, or the Young German League. The effectiveness of the local communities as conduits for antisemitic propaganda varied according to the personality of the individual head man (*Obmann*) and the dedication of the membership. Although the organization never had much direct effect on German politics, it contributed significantly to the diffusion of racist and antisemitic attitudes in the public sphere.

On May 24, 1912, in the wake of the Reichstag election and the antisemitic revival it engendered, the Imperial Hammer League (Reichshammerbund) was established in Leipzig to serve as the umbrella organization for the existing Hammer communities. The first *Bundeswart* (league overseer) was the former cavalry captain and lawyer Karl August Hellwig (1855–1914). Fritsch, the honorary overseer, authored the constitution of the organization, which he conceived of as a rallying point for the antisemitic movement. Although open to all parties and social strata, the league, in fact, spoke most effectively to the lower middle class. The bylaws of the organization called on members to "profess their German blood and German ethos," to shun contact with Jews and their businesses, and to promise the same for their dependents. Fritsch's *Hammer* served as the official organ and periodically sent out questionnaires to gather information. On the basis of one such polling at the end of 1919, the league claimed a membership of 5,000. But this number was almost certainly an exaggeration. More probably, the organization had no more than 3,000 members.

The ideological activists and leadership of the Imperial Hammer League reached out to other like-minded groups, striving to overcome the antisemitic movement's notorious tendency toward schism, personal rivalry, and political ineffectiveness. From the start, the league paid special attention to the German youth movement. Representatives attended the national congress of Free German Youth in October 1913, distributing antisemitic pamphlets. In the spring of 1914, free copies of the *Hammer* were sent to 700 leading figures in the youth movement.

After Hellwig's sudden death in June 1914, the businessman Alfred Roth took over as leader. At the end of the war, Roth used his position in the league to work for the creation of a powerful racist and antisemitic central body. With the blessing of Fritsch, who had called for such an "offensive and defensive alliance" as early as 1913 and whose *Hammer* now got a significant boost in subscribers, the German Racial League for Defense and Defiance (Deutschvölkischer Schutz-und Trutz-Bund) absorbed the Imperial Hammer League. On April 1, 1920, the league ceased to exist as an independent organization.

After the murder of the Jewish foreign minister Walther Rathenau in 1922 and the resulting dissolution of the League for Defense and Defiance, there were fitful attempts to revive the Imperial Hammer League, based on the continuing existence of local chapters and Hammer reading circles. Fritsch's interests lay elsewhere by that time, however, and an effective organization could not be refashioned. Many of the former members of the league eventually made their way into the Nazi Party.

—*Christoph Knüppel*
Richard S. Levy, translation

See also Fritsch, Theodor; German National White Collar Employees Association; German Racial League for Defense and Defiance; Germanic Order; Hentschel, Willibald; Lange, Friedrich; Pan-German League; Rathenau, Walther; Roth, Alfred; Settlement *Heimland;* Youth Movement

References
Lohalm, Uwe. *Völkischer Radikalismus, Die Geschichte des Deutschvölkischen Schutz- und Trutz-Bundes 1919–1923* (Hamburg, Germany: Leibniz-Verlag, 1970).
Weissbecker, Manfred. "Reichshammerbund (Rh) 1910/12–1920." In *Lexikon zur Parteiengeschichte: Die bürgerlichen und kleinbürgerlichen Parteien und Verbände in Deutschland, 1789–1945.* Edited by Dieter Fricke (Cologne, Germany: Pahl-Rugenstein, 1985), 3: 681–683.

Infamous Decree (1808)

One of three decrees pertaining to the Jews of the French Empire issued by Emperor Napoleon I on March 17, 1808, the so-called Infamous Decree forbade Jews to borrow or lend money for a period of ten years. The decree came as a response to the publication of a number of pamphlets in Alsace demanding that the Jews, described as antisocial usurers, be stripped of the citizenship they had won in 1791 and expelled from the realm. The decree was meant to end Jewish moneylending, long a source of prejudice, hatred, and violence against the Jews of the region, as part of Napoleon's program to reform the Jews "so that there will no longer be any difference between them and the other citizens of the Empire" (article 18). The decree explicitly exempted the Sephardic Jews of Bordeaux and the Landes region from its provisions because they, unlike the Jews of Alsace and Lorraine, had not "provoked any complaint, nor had they participated in any illicit trade" (article 19). Jews of Alsace and Lorraine, it should be noted, were heavily concentrated in commercial trades because until the Revolution, legal disabilities had prevented them from doing much else.

Other than lifting the 1806 temporary suspension on repayment of debts to Jewish creditors, the terms of the decree were unequivocally harsh. The edict annulled all debts to Jews that had been contracted by minors, married women, soldiers, and military officers without the consent of their legal trustees or superiors. It suspended payment on all debts to Jewish creditors unless they could prove that they had indeed lent the money to the debtor, a difficult task given the lending practices of the day and the high rate of illiteracy among French peasants. The decree fixed the legal rate of interest at 5 percent; debts previously contracted at a higher rate were annulled as "usurious." Further, it forbade Jews the right to borrow money, including mortgages, unless they had received special permission from the local prefecture, for which they would have to furnish proof that they had not "engaged in any illicit commerce."

The decree also strictly limited Jewish migration. Jews would not be allowed to immigrate to Alsace, nor could Jews not currently resident in the French Empire immigrate there unless they proved their intention to practice agriculture. Finally, the decree forbade Jews the right possessed by all other French citizens to send a paid replacement for military conscription, a measure that would create many problems for religiously observant Jews. The effect of this decree on the economic well-being of the Jews of Alsace and Lorraine was momentous, driving many who had previously depended on commerce and moneylending into dire poverty. Jewish leaders immediately condemned the decree and campaigned against it for the entire period of its application. With help from members of the emerging liberal camp in the Chamber of Deputies, the decree was not renewed when it expired in 1818.

—*Lisa Moses Leff*

See also Alsace; France; Grégoire, Henri-Baptiste; Usury

References

Hyman, Paula. *The Jews of Modern France* (Berkeley: University of California Press, 1998).

Schwartzfuchs, Simon. *Napoleon, the Jews and the Sanhedrin.* (New York: Routledge and Keegan Paul, 1979).

Innocent III (1160/61–1216)

Born Lotario dei Conti di Segni in 1160 or 1161, Innocent III became one of the most influential popes in the history of the Latin Christian Church. Following his early clerical training in Rome, Innocent was one of the first popes to study at the schools (soon to become the university) of Paris. He served as a member of the papal curia from 1187 and was elected pope in 1198 at the age of thirty-six or thirty-seven. He frequently stated that the two aims of his pontificate were the reform of Christian society and the recovery of the Holy Land, most of the latter lost to Latin Christians since the victory of Saladin at Hattin in 1187. Innocent launched two crusades, both failures, and was preparing yet another (which later became the Fifth Crusade) when he died in 1216. In terms of the reform of Christian society, he patronized a number of new religious pastoral movements, the early Franciscan order being the best known of them; he vigorously enforced criminal sanctions against clergy guilty of misdeeds, opposed secular rulers and heretics, and, most spectacularly, convened the Fourth Lateran Council in November 1215. Innocent's ideas about Jews and Judaism, themselves the subject of a large and contentious scholarly literature, must be understood in terms of both his pastoral concerns for the whole of contemporary Christian society and his concept of papal authority in the world.

At the outset of his pontificate, Innocent subscribed to—and reissued—the conventional papal statement concerning the rights of Jews, the *Constitutio pro Judeis;* this permitted Jews protection of their rights to security and their religious practices but prohibited them from enjoying any rights beyond these, particularly any activities that might appear to threaten the stability of Christian society, including, of course, actions considered insulting or injurious to Christianity, illegitimate exercise of power over Christians, and attempts to convert Christians. In this respect, however, Innocent's sharp perception of Jews as hostile and dangerous to Christian society dominated his reissuing of the papal privilege. His later correspondence also showed him far more hostile and less energetic in protecting Jews than many of his predecessors had been.

Twenty-nine of Innocent's letters, most of these directed to powerful spiritual and temporal rulers, deal with Jewish issues, and these, too, illustrate the extent to which he invoked traditional ecclesiastical positions while reacting forcefully and with considerable hostility toward contemporary perceptions of Judaism. Innocent's letters repeat—but with increased emphasis—the themes of Jewish guilt for the Crucifixion of Christ, the comparison of Jews to the murderer and condemned wanderer Cain, Jewish blasphemies against Christian truth, and the perceived dangers of Jewish moneylending in a new economy, which he perceived exclusively in moral terms.

Much of Innocent's attitude toward Jews reflected contemporary heightened fears of Jewish hostility toward Christians. These suspicions were summed up in the canons of the Fourth Lateran Council, which enacted into law the developments in theology and canon law that had been developed in the schools during the twelfth century and shaped the Latin Christian Church for the next three centuries. Canons 67–70 of IV Lateran sternly regulate Jewish moneylending (67), prescribe distinctive Jewish dress (68), forbid Jews to appear in public on certain Christian holy days (68), criminalize Jewish expressions deriding Jesus (68), prohibit Jews from holding public offices and therefore exercising power over Christians (69), and prohibit Jewish converts to Christianity from continuing to use Jewish rites (70). The inclusion of these canons, traditional as some of them were, in the influential pronouncements of IV Lateran marks, if it does not create, the decline of the European Jewish community in an increasingly articulated and legally defined Christian Europe.

—*Edward Peters*

See also Crusades; Deicide; Franciscan Order; Lateran Council, Fourth; Middle Ages, High; Usury; Yellow Badge

References

Chazan, Robert. "Pope Innocent III and the Jews." In *Pope Innocent III and His World*. Edited by John C. Moore (Aldershot, UK, and Brookfield, VT: Ashgate, 1999), 187–204.

Grayzel, Solomon. *The Church and the Jews in the XIIIth Century*. Vol. 2. Edited by Kenneth Stow (New York: Jewish Theological Seminary in America, 1966; Detroit, MI: Wayne State University Press, 1988).

Moore, John C. *Pope Innocent III (1160/61–1216): To Root Up and to Plant* (Leiden, the Netherlands: Brill, 2003), 140–145.

Synan, Edward A. *The Popes and the Jews in the Middle Ages* (New York: Macmillan, 1965), chap. 6.

Inquisition

The Latin term *inquisitio* had as one of its meanings a legal procedure in which a single magistrate supervised all stages of a case, from investigation to sentencing. When Roman law began to influence jurists and legislators in western Europe in the twelfth century, the inquisitio began to be used in many instances in place of the older procedure of private accusation. Pope Innocent III (1198–1216) introduced the procedure into courts of the Latin Christian Church, first in the cases of clerics who had committed grave offenses. Innocent and subsequent thirteenth-century popes also approved the use of the procedure in the investigation of heterodox beliefs and created the specific office of the *inquisitor hereticae pravitatis* (inquisitor of heretical depravity), a papal judge subdelegate specializing in the discovery and examination of heretics. The office was usually entrusted to members of the Dominican or Franciscan orders.

Until the mid-thirteenth century, there had been very little ecclesiastical jurisdiction over Jews and then usually in cases of relapse into Judaism after conversion to Christianity. Between 1239 and 1242, however, Pope Gregory IX (1227–1241) commanded an investigation and later a burning of the Talmud. He and his successors asserted ecclesiastical jurisdiction over what they considered Jewish heresies against the Christian understanding of Jewish Scripture and over cases of rabbinical failure to discipline moral offenses in the Jewish community. Canon lawyers gradually expanded claims of ecclesiastical authority over Jews—but not always or often by inquisitors of heretical depravity.

In 1267, Pope Clement IV (1265–1268) issued the bull *Turbato corde,* which dealt with both converts to Christianity from Judaism who had reverted to Judaism and hence apostatized and Jews who had urged or assisted in the reversion. Later versions added born Christians who converted to Judaism and Jews who retained unexpurgated copies of the Talmud. In 1391, a wave of riots in the Iberian Peninsula caused many Jews to convert to Christianity, and over the next several generations, these New Christians, or *conversos,* came to be perceived as a uniquely Iberian problem, one that centered on suspicions that the conversos had remained crypto-Jews and that unbaptized Jews both supported them and attempted to revert them to Judaism. In 1478, Pope Sixtus IV (1471–1484) permitted the rulers of Castile and Aragon to appoint two inquisitors to investigate the problem, and in 1482, seven more inquisitors were appointed, including the Dominican Tomás de Torquemada, who became inquisitor general in Castile and Aragon; he wrote the first handbook of Spanish inquisitorial regulations, the *Instrucciones,* which was later supplemented by his successors. In 1483, the new Spanish Inquisition was formally made a council of state, the Council of the Supreme and General Inquisition.

From 1478 to 1530, the Spanish Inquisition concentrated on various aspects of the problem of Judaizing, including blasphemy. The council (La Suprema) was the first institutionalized inquisition, issuing its own rules, assuming operational and jurisdictional control over all other inquisitorial tribunals, requiring reports from them, and supervising their activities. With the expulsion of all unbaptized Jews from Spain in 1492, the Spanish Inquisition could focus on conversos and converso families and other offenses that came within its purview. By the mid-sixteenth century, there were over twenty inquisitorial tribunals in Spain and the Spanish dependencies, including the Americas. Each tribunal included two in-

The expulsion of the Jews from Spain in 1492 by command of the Inquisition. Undated engraving. (Bettmann/Corbis)

quisitors, a legal official, a constable, a *fiscal* (prosecutor), and a network of familiars, especially privileged lay assistants. Particularly important are the archives meticulously kept by all tribunals, containing detailed accounts of the lives, possessions, relationships, investigations, trials, and sentences of thousands of individuals. Although investigations and trials were secret, sentences were read publicly in a ceremony called an *auto-da-fé* (act of faith).

Between 1534 and 1540, an inquisition was instituted in neighboring Portugal, which focused longer on Judaizing than did the Spanish Inquisition. In 1561, the Portuguese established an inquisition at Goa, in India. The two inquisitions survived into the nineteenth century, the Portuguese office being abolished in 1821 and the Spanish in 1834.

In 1542, Pope Paul III (1534–1549) estab-

lished an inquisition in Rome for the Papal States and nominally over Catholic Europe. In 1588, when the papal government was divided into fifteen congregations, the Inquisition became the Congregation of the Holy Roman and Universal Inquisition, or Holy Office. In 1908, Pius X (1903–1914) renamed it the Congregation of the Holy Office, merging it with the Congregation of the Index (established in 1571). In 1965, Paul VI (1963–1978) renamed it again as the Sacred Congregation for the Doctrine of the Faith, abolishing the Index in 1966. The Roman Inquisition, under its several names, dealt with Jews far less frequently than those of Spain and Portugal. Much more active in this regard was the Inquisition of Venice, established in 1571, which survived until 1797.

Following the reformations of the sixteenth century and the concerns of the post-Tridentine Catholic Church to discipline both clergy and laity, the concerns of inquisitorial tribunals with Jews and even conversos gradually declined during the seventeenth and eighteenth centuries.

—*Edward Peters*

See also *Auto-da-fé;* Dominican Order; Franciscan Order; Innocent III; Papacy, Modern; Raymund of Peñafort; Spain, Riots of 1391; Talmud Trials; Torquemada, Tomás de

References

Edwards, John. *The Spanish Inquisition* (Stroud, UK: Tempus, 2003).

Kamen, Henry. *The Spanish Inquisition: A Historical Revision* (New Haven, CT, and London: Yale University Press, 1998).

Kelly, Henry Ansgar. *Inquisitions and Other Trial Procedures in the Medieval West* (Aldershot, UK, and Burlington, VT: Ashgate/Variorum, 2001).

Peters, Edward. *Inquisition* (New York: Free Press, 1988).

Roth, Norman. *Conversos, Inquisition, and the Expulsion of the Jews from Spain* (Madison: University of Wisconsin Press, 1995).

Institute for Historical Review (IHR)

The principal international forum for Holocaust denial in the 1980s and early 1990s, the Institute for Historical Review (IHR) was founded in California in 1979 by Willis A. Carto, head of the extreme right-wing and antisemitic Liberty Lobby. During the 1980s and early 1990s, the

IHR sponsored annual conferences that became the main forum for Holocaust deniers worldwide. The lectures delivered at these conferences were published in the IHR's *Journal of Historical Review* (JHR). In addition, the IHR produced audio- and videotapes and distributed a variety of books and pamphlets. Underlining the academic tone of its publication and conferences, the IHR sought to present itself as a legitimate historical institute. It claimed to establish a new school in the historiography of World War II and the Holocaust—the "revisionist approach"—which, it alleged, had succeeded in undermining the accepted narrative about the extermination of European Jewry.

Deniers from numerous countries were drawn to the IHR, one of the few venues that could afford them a degree of public exposure. Regular lecturers included Robert Faurisson and Henri Roques from France; the German Canadian Ernst Zündel; the British author David Irving; Ditlieb Felderer and the Moroccan-born Ahmed Rami from Sweden; Carlo Mattogno from Italy; Fredrick Toben from Australia; Jürgen Graf from Switzerland; and the Americans Arthur Butz, Mark Weber, Greg Raven, and Bradley Smith. Among the participants were Nazi fugitives such as Otto Ernst Remer and leading white supremacists and neo-Nazi activists such as David Duke and Ewald Althans.

From the outset, the IHR was beset by internal dissension, mainly between Carto and senior IHR staffers. The latter described Carto as a dictator who censored articles according to whim. No less important for both sides was the controversy over a $10 million inheritance left to the IHR by Jean Farrell, the granddaughter of Thomas A. Edison. In September 1993, the IHR editorial staff and the board of directors voted to terminate the IHR's association with Carto. This decision led to a prolonged litigation process, during which Carto established a rival "revisionist" journal, the *Barnes Review*. In 1996, a California court ruled against him and awarded the IHR's parent corporation, the Legion for the Survival of Freedom, $6 million. The appeals process continued until mid-2001, when the Liberty Lobby was denied bankruptcy protection and forced to liquidate assets and pay damages to the IHR.

The IHR never fully recovered from its internal squabbling. In May 2000, it held its first conference since 1992, but a year later, it was involved in an unsuccessful attempt to organize a Holocaust denial gathering in Beirut, Lebanon. It continues to play a role in Holocaust denial, inter alia, by expanding its archive of articles from the JHR on its website; new issues of the journal, however, have grown increasingly sporadic, and no new IHR conferences had been held or announced as of early 2005. If in the 1980s and early 1990s the IHR acted as the nexus of most Holocaust denial activity worldwide, by 2000 it had become merely another component in a loose federation of independent deniers with their own websites and narrowing range of activities.

—*Roni Stauber*

See also Duke, David; Faurlsson, Robert; Holocaust; Holocaust Denial, Negationism, and Revisionism; Internet; Irving, David; Zündel, Ernst

References
Anti-Defamation League. *Embattled Bigots: A Split in the Ranks of the Holocaust Denial Movement* (New York: The League, 1994).
Porat, Dina, and Roni Stauber, eds. *Anti-Semitism Worldwide* (Tel Aviv, Israel: Project for the Study of Anti-Semitism, in cooperation with the Anti-Defamation League, 2001–2002).
Stern, Kenneth S. *Holocaust Denial* (New York: American Jewish Committee, 1993).

Institute for the Study and Eradication of Jewish Influence on German Church Life

The Institute for the Study and Eradication of Jewish Influence on German Church Life (Institut zur Erforschung und Beseitigung des jüdischen Einflusses im deutschen kirchlichen Leben) was a center of anti-Jewish, theological scholarship and activism in Nazi Germany from 1939 until the end of the war. Headquartered in Eisenach, the institute was under the academic leadership of Walter Grundmann, professor of New Testament and *völkisch* (racist-nationalist) theology at the University of Jena. Siegfried Leffler, a founder of the Deutsche Christen (German Christians) movement and subsequently head of its Thuringian wing, served as official director. A 1941 institute publication described the de-Judaization of the church as an "inescapable and decisive duty," central to the survival of Christianity.

In keeping with its "de-Judaizing" mandate, the institute produced and disseminated new versions of Scripture, revised hymnals, liturgical guides, collections of devotions, and other materials, all purged of evidence of Christianity's Jewish roots. For example, *Die Botschaft Gottes* (The Message of God), a compilation of the synoptic Gospels, appeared in December 1939. It avoided the word *Jew,* opting instead to present Jesus in a geographic and historical vacuum and to reduce Christianity to a collection of familiar sayings. Within six months, the institute sold 200,000 copies. A year later, the new hymnal, *Grosser Gott, wir loben Dich!* (Holy God, We Praise Thy Name!) was released after an institute committee reviewed over 2,000 songs for Jewish content, dogmatism, and "tastelessness." The result included new material and familiar hymns from which words such as *Hallelujah* and *Hosanna,* along with references to the Old Testament and Jesus' Jewish lineage, had been expunged. The institute also organized conferences and gatherings for pastors, academic theologians, and other church people in various parts of Germany and engaged in outreach abroad. Funding came from individuals and groups in the "circle of supporters," central organs of the Protestant church, and regional Protestant church governments. Moreover, the institute claimed the backing of important National Socialist Party offices, although Nazi authorities kept their distance.

The institute enjoyed broad support beyond Deutsche Christen circles. High-ranking church officials cooperated with its efforts; and many unaffiliated theologians, students, and laypeople participated in its activities. Even most members of the Confessing Church (Bekennende Kirche), who criticized the institute's rewriting of traditional Christian texts, accepted its underlying premise: that Christianity stood in sharp, "unbridgeable" opposition to Judaism. During the war years, the propaganda and practices of the Nazi regime provided another kind of credibility to the institute and its work. Persecution and, beginning in 1941, the expulsion of Jews and people defined as Jews from Germany gave new meaning to attempts to destroy so-called Jewish influence on the religious front. Interpretations of the war as a struggle against "international Jewry" lent urgency to the institute's claims to be part of a mortal combat against an ancient foe. Representatives of the institute played up their contribution to the anti-Jewish cause, although after the collapse of Nazi Germany, many claimed they had only sought to defend the church against anti-Christian hostilities. The myth that the institute was not a collaborator with Nazi antisemitism but an effort to protect the church from neopagan assault persists in some historical accounts. As Susannah Heschel in particular has shown, however, that notion cannot withstand scrutiny of the archival record.

—*Doris L. Bergen*

See also Churches under Nazism; *Deutsche Christen*; Gospels; *Völkisch* Movement and Ideology
References
Bergen, Doris L. *Twisted Cross: The German Christian Movement in the Third Reich* (Chapel Hill: University of North Carolina Press, 1996).
Heschel, Susannah. "Nazifying Christian Theology: Walter Grundmann and the Institute for the Study and Eradication of Jewish Influence on German Church Life," *Church History* 63 (1994): 587–605.
———. "When Jesus Was an Aryan: The Protestant Church and Antisemitic Propaganda." In *Betrayal: German Churches and the Holocaust.* Edited by Robert P. Ericksen and Susannah Heschel (Minneapolis, MN: Fortress, 1999), 68–89.

Internet

The Internet has been a boon for antisemites, who have used it since its inception to communicate with one another and disseminate their beliefs. They have embraced every aspect of Internet technology, from simple text-based websites to sophisticated Flash videos and streaming multimedia. Virtual bulletin boards allow antisemites to post their thoughts online, share their ideas, and set up meetings, private E-mail lists, and public listservs at minimal cost. Small groups or even individuals can now hide behind impressive websites and "compete" with more established groups. Conferences devoted to antisemitism, which in the past would not have had audiences beyond the basements in which they were held, are now being webcast around the globe, accessible to anyone with an Internet connection.

Although no reliable estimates of the number of websites containing antisemitic material exist, a Google keyword search for *Jews* or *Israel* immediately reveals the existence of an astonishing number of them. Virtually every major extremist and racist group based in the United States has some form of Internet presence, and many groups based overseas utilize servers located within the United States to circumvent local laws prohibiting racist, extremist, and antisemitic content. Antisemitic and anti-Western terrorist groups increasingly utilize the Internet to recruit new members, share technical expertise, and post videos of their successes. Although many terrorist groups have recently found Internet providers in the United States to be less willing to host their antisemitic and violence-promoting materials, they continue to find them in less regulated corners of the globe.

The use of the Internet by antisemites has affected the nature of antisemitism itself. The free exchange of ideas afforded by the Internet has promoted cross-fertilization of antisemitic ideologies. Holocaust denial, for example, has migrated from its traditional home among neo-Nazis and Hitler apologists to the websites of radical anti-Israel groups, White Power advocates, and left-wing organizations as well. By allowing instant communication of even the most bizarre theories, the Internet has also contributed to the rise of a conspiratorial mind-set that frequently sees the hidden hand of Jews, Zionists, or "Mossad agents" behind world events.

The commingling of anti-Israel/Zionist rhetoric with antisemitism has led to an increase in expressions of antisemitism in forums and events targeting Israeli political decisions. The co-opting of antisemitic images and ideas and the conflating of Jews with the state of Israel, so common in the virtual world of the Internet, is becoming more popular in the "real world," too.

The antisemitic materials that are shared online often spread to a variety of lists and sites—including those that are not antisemitic in nature. The pervasiveness and persistence of antisemitic materials on the Internet and the speed with which they can be posted online, downloaded, and reused by anyone anywhere pose daunting new tasks for those who would combat this old evil.

—*Aryeh Tuchman*

See also American Jewish Committee and Antidefamation Efforts in the United States; Anti-Zionism; Australia; Carto, Willis; Holocaust Denial, Negationism, and Revisionism; Irving, David; Militia Movement; Nazi Rock; Neo-Nazism, German; New Age; *Protocols of the Elders of Zion;* White Power Movement; Zündel, Ernst

References
Stern, Kenneth S. "Hate and the Internet." American Jewish Committee Publications. http://www.ajc.org/InTheMedia/PubAntisemi tism.asp?did=135. (Accessed February 25, 2005).

Invocation, The Great

"The Great Invocation," the poetic New Age prayer for world peace and oneness, was formulated by occultist Alice A. Bailey (in a final version in 1945) but is considered by New Age disciples to have been authored by the "Hierarchy of Ascended Masters," a pantheon of divine spirits. Seen as a major tool for world "transformation" and preparation to receive New Age teaching, the original English prayer has been translated into over fifty languages and is distributed chiefly by World Goodwill, a subsidiary of Lucis Trust, the custodian of Bailey's writings and a prominent nongovernmental organization member at the United Nations. Promoters promise "transforming life changes" to all who recite the invocation, even if they do not understand its meaning. The esoteric wording is ambiguous enough to be adapted to any religious belief, but to receive the benefits, it must be faithfully recited with no changes whatsoever.

This restriction springs from the New Age belief that the invocation is a divine formula that releases spiritual power when recited, independent of conscious intent. According to this view, the masses being encouraged to utter the invocation without comprehension are generating occultic energy, to be harnessed by the "Masters" for establishing their divine rule on earth. To initiates, the invocation is not left to ambiguity but is interpreted in at least three specific ways, depending on one's spiritual development. In contrast, the uninitiated are allowed to interpret it as they will, since all "true" meaning is beyond their understanding. This deception, Bailey wrote, "is for them, entirely good and helpful" (Bailey 1972, 165; as dictated by her Tibetan master, Djwahl Kuhl).

Among the decoded messages are two lines that directly concern the Jews: "Let the Plan of Love and Light work out. And may it seal the door where evil dwells." This Plan, accepted as authored by the Hierarchy, places high priority on removing all Jewish presence and influence from human consciousness, a goal to be achieved by eliminating Judaism. The strength and longevity of this Jewish influence is attributed to a negative occultic energy that has its source in "the Dark Force," a repository of cosmic Evil. To "seal the door" where this evil "dwells" refers to neutralizing the human "tools" of that Force who have enabled it to enter human consciousness. Bailey conclusively identified these human agents by citing their chief offense against humanity: plunging the world into monotheism. She was confident that this "door where evil dwells" would eventually be sealed "through the sheer weight of public opinion and through right human desire. Nothing can possibly stop it" (Lucis Trust 1997–2004).

—*Hannah Newman*

See also Bailey, Alice A.; Jewish Force; "The Plan" of the Hierarchy

References

Bailey, Alice A. and Djwahl Kuhl. *Discipleship in the New Age II: Teaching on Meditation, Part VIII* (New York: Lucis Publishing, 1972; orig. 1955).

Lucis Trust. *The Use and Significance of the Great Invocation*. 1997–2004. http://www.lucistrust.org/invocation/giman.shtml. (Accessed February 25, 2005).

Iranian Revolution

On January 16, 1979, Shah Mohammed Reza Pahlavi fled Iran after more than three months of crippling strikes and mass demonstrations against his rule. This was the culmination of years of widespread popular discontent and violent agitation by the Shi'ite religious establishment inspired by the exiled Ayatollah Khomeini. On February 1, Khomeini returned to Tehran to a welcome by millions, and ten days later, he successfully led a rebellion that brought down the interim government and the last vestiges of the Pahlavi establishment. A reign of terror soon broke out, with summary trials of former officials before revolutionary tribunals followed immediately by executions. Among the 600 people executed over the first six months of the revolution were a number of Jews, including Habib Elghanian, the former head of the Anjoman Kalimian, the umbrella organization of Iranian Jewry. Although Jews were not singled out as a group for retribution in the way that the Bahá'is were, several hundred Jews were jailed during this period, and the community was thoroughly demoralized. Most Jews were dismissed from their positions in the public sector, including government offices and the universities. Under the shah's secular, modernizing, but despotic regime, Jews and other non-Muslim minorities had prospered, and wealthy individuals enjoyed close relations with the governing elite. As far back as the 1960s, Khomeini had railed against the shah for giving high offices to Bahá'is, whom he accused of being Zionist agents, and for having relations with Israel and thus giving the Sunni Arabs the impression that "we Shi'ites are really Jews."

With the establishment of the Islamic Republic in April 1979, Jews together with Christians and Zoroastrians were recognized as tolerated minorities (*dhimmi*s), with complete freedom of religion. The new constitution stated that the government and all Muslims were obligated "to deal with non-Muslims on the basis of justice and goodwill," with the qualification that "this applies only to those who are not anti-Islamic and have not conspired against Iran." This last clause was sufficiently vague to be used to harass Jews who had families or other ties in Israel, and as late as 2000, Jews were being tried on such charges. The sentencing in Shiraz that year of ten Jews to prison terms ranging from two to eight years on such trumped-up charges led to an international outcry that resulted in all being released on clemency within two years.

Jews were by no means the only ones terrorized by the revolutionary committees, the Republican Guards, and the various paramilitary groups that ran rampant during the Islamic Revolution. Once the Islamic Republic was established, Jews were allowed a parliamentary representative like the other dhimmi communities. Like all non-Muslims, their communal institutions were subject to close government scrutiny and, in the case of schools, interference and control. Unlike Muslims, Jews traveling abroad usually had to leave some family members behind, and they were not allowed multiple exit permits. Official anti-Zionist rhetoric frequently blurred, as so often in the Muslim world, into anti-Jewish invective, which has left the community in a state of perpetual anxiety.

—*Norman A. Stillman*

See also Anti-Zionism; Islam and the Jews; Islamic Fundamentalism; Khomeini, Ayatollah

References
Abrahamian, Ervand. *Khomeinism: Essays on the Islamic Republic* (Berkeley and Los Angeles: University of California Press, 1993).
Bakhash, Shaul. *The Reign of the Ayatollahs: Iran and the Islamic Revolution* (New York: Basic Books, 1984).
Stillman, Norman A. "Fading Shadows of the Past: Jews in the Islamic World." In *Survey of Jewish Affairs, 1989.* Edited by William Frankel (Oxford: Institute for Jewish Affairs and Basil Blackwell, 1989), 157–170.

Iron Guard

Founded in 1927 by Corneliu Zelea Codreanu under the name Legion of the Archangel Michael, the Iron Guard was a Romanian fascist organization. The 16 percent of the vote it received in the parliamentary elections of December 1937 made it the country's third-largest party. Mounting political conflicts, however, led King Carol II to assume dictatorial power in February 1938, after which the guard was systematically pursued and its leader murdered. Territorial losses in the summer of 1940 and the unwarranted confidence in broad German support prompted the guard to make a new beginning. The National Legionnaire State, declared on September 14, 1940, divided governmental functions between the military under Ion Antonescu and the legion under its new leader, Horia Sima, but neither side was willing to cooperate. In January 1941, the legion attempted a coup d'état. With Hitler's approval—he was preparing to invade the Soviet Union and required the services of the Romanian army—the legion was smashed once and for all.

The Legion of the Archangel Michael was a phenomenon of the era of European fascism, but it also took shape around specific structural fault lines in Romania between 1918 and 1939. Among these were the country's precipitous democratization and the difficult integration of territories that had recently been under foreign domination. Coexistence with a variety of conspicuously differing ethnic groups, including a large and poorly integrated Jewish minority (4.5 percent of the population), was a source of increasing tension after World War I. A precarious international position, a surplus of university-educated young men, and an agricultural crisis worked together to destablize Romanian social and political life.

The Guardian of National Consciousness, a group founded in Iassy between 1919 and 1920, combining nationalism, socialism, and secularized Christianity with paramilitary shock-troop tactics, was one of the legion's precursors. Another was the antisemitic student movement of the 1920s. The legion built on traditional Romanian nationalism, transforming it after the war into a specifically Romanian form of fascism. Its hallmarks were a version of Orthodox Christianity suited to its politics and an emphasis on peasant-agrarian values and symbols. Seizing on many Romanians' reservations concerning the urban lifestyle of Jews as well as their linguistic-cultural dissimilarity, legionnaire antisemitism constructed a politically and religiously structured message of abhorrence for "foreigners" and "traitors." The acts of violence that emanated from this generalized hatred were at first aimed against middle-class political figures who resisted the guard and against "traitors" from within its own ranks. Later, many Jews fell victim to the excesses of legionnaires.

In 1930, after Codreanu's "conquest" of Bessarabia failed, he embraced the strategy of legality. The tactical reorientation led to the first sizable increase in membership—6,000 by the end of 1930, 28,000 by December 1933, and approximately 270,000 by late 1937. The legion benefited from the political turmoil caused by the sudden return of King Carol from exile. It exploited the dislocations caused by the Great Depression and the grievances engendered by a policy of forced industrialization (in 1934). Its core constituency came from socially ambitious and youthful elements of the middle classes who had been denied what they regarded as their appropriate places in state employment. The "dispossessed" rebeled against the "older generation," flaunting their fascist activism. Their protest against social inequities appealed to ever broader sections of the population, especially as the larger parties failed to live up to expectations. The legion developed into a party of general protest. But its propensity for violence and negatively defined aims militated against the retention of voters and members. When King Carol's dictatorship began active repression of the legion, it turned from a mass movement into a collection of terroristic cells.

—*Armin Heinen*

See also Antonescu, Ion; Codreanu, Corneliu Zelea; Romania; Romania, Holocaust in; Szalasi, Ferenc

References

Heinen, Armin. *Die Legion "Erzengel Michael" in Rumänien: Soziale Bewegung und politische Organisation—Ein Beitrag zum Problem des internationalen Faschismus* (Munich, Germany: Oldenbourg, 1986).

Livezeanu, Irina. *Cultural Politics in Greater Romania: Regionalism, Nation Building and Ethnic Struggle, 1918–1930* (Ithaca, NY: Cornell University Press, 1995).

Irving, David (1938–)

Unlike other authors whose primary interest is the attempt to distort or deny the Holocaust, the British author David Irving came to the question of the Final Solution by an indirect path, as part of his revisionist writing on World War II, which he began publishing in the 1960s. He argued against postwar historiography's portrayal of Germany, in general, and Hitler's demonic image, in particular. However, until the late 1980s, Irving refrained from explicitly denying the extermination of the Jews. His involvement in the discussion of the Final Solution began only at the end of the 1970s, after he had published *Hitler's War,* his most successful book, in which he depicted Hitler as a realistic and fair-minded leader. Irving claimed in this work that Hitler never gave any orders to exterminate the Jews. He further maintained that the genocide of European Jewry began as a consequence of local decisions, which received the support of SS supreme commanders Reinhard Heydrich and, eventually, Heinrich Himmler, without Hitler's approval or even knowledge.

In response, historians such as Gerald Fleming and Martin Broszat demonstrated that Irving had omitted important evidence and that he had misused, manipulated, and even altered documents to support his theory. For some leading Holocaust deniers, including Robert Faurisson, however, Irving did not go far enough because he did not forthrightly deny the Holocaust. Nevertheless, Irving's attitude toward Hitler as a "fair-minded" leader, as well as his "balanced" approach toward the role of Germany in the outbreak of World War II, made him popular among right-wing extremists and neo-Nazis, particularly in Germany. It may be assumed that Irving owed his unique status among wide circles on the extreme Right to his evident success as a writer. His books were put out by reputable publishers; *Hitler's War* gave him worldwide publicity and a degree of legitimacy. In contrast to the claims of fringe neo-Nazi and Holocaust denial writers, the thesis put forward by Irving, although widely criticized, became part of mainstream historians' debate on the genesis of the Final Solution. Moreover, even some of his strongest critics, such as Martin Broszat, conceded that he had managed to find several remarkable and hitherto unknown documents on the National Socialist period.

Until 1988, Irving avoided lending his explicit support to the deniers of the Holocaust. The event that caused him to cross that line was the publication of the *Leuchter Report,* which "scientifically proved" that the facilities in Auschwitz, Birkenau, and Majdanek were incapable of mass

Professor Deborah Lipstadt (left) is congratulated by Holocaust survivor Martin Hecht as she leaves the High Court in central London, April 11, 2000. British historian David Irving lost his libel action against Lipstadt and her publishers, Penguin Books. (Reuters/Corbis)

annihilation. Irving readily accepted this bogus evidence because Holocaust denial, after all, fit well with his general view of World War II. He could now "explain" his claim in *Hitler's War:* Hitler had no knowledge of the Final Solution because there was no planned, systematic operation to exterminate European Jewry. In October 1992, Irving chose to present his thesis at the eleventh conference of the Institute for Historical Review. While denying the existence of homicidal gas chambers, he conceded that there was sufficient evidence to prove the mass murder of Jews by firing squads in the German-occupied territories of the Soviet Union. These killings, he continued to claim, were carried out without Hitler's knowledge.

During the 1980s and the first half of the 1990s, more than any of the revisionists or deniers, Irving toured the world to promote his ideas. Time and again, he succeeded in gaining media attention. In response, Jewish antidefamation organizations and antifascist groups conducted a legal and public counterattack to impede Irving's lecture tours, considerably damaging his ability to sell books and promote his theories. Irving, no longer able to publish with the respected Macmillan or Viking Press, was reduced to working with small, unknown publishing houses associated with the extreme Right. In an attempt to end this obstruction, imposed on him by what he branded a "world Jewish conspiracy," he sued the American Jewish historian Deborah Lipstadt for discrediting him as a historian. After a trial in which Irving appeared as his own counsel and was confronted by the expert testimony of several well-known historians, High Court Judge Charles Gray ruled against Irving in April 2000, determining that he was indeed a sham historian who misrepresented and manipulated historical evidence for his own ideological reasons and that he was an active Holocaust denier, an antisemite, and a racist. (See "Irving vs. Lipstadt" at http://www.hdot.org/ieindex.html).

This verdict ended a protracted process during which Irving's ideological convictions drew him step by step toward the fringes of the extreme Right.

—Roni Stauber

See also Faurisson, Robert; Himmler, Heinrich; Holocaust; Holocaust Denial, Negationism, and Revisionism; Institute for Historical Review; *Leuchter Report;* Neo-Nazism, German

References

Evans, Richard J. *Telling Lies about Hitler: The Holocaust, History and the David Irving Trial* (London: Verso Books, 2002).

Lipstadt, Deborah E. *Denying the Holocaust: The Growing Assault on Truth and Memory.* Repr. ed. (New York: Plume, 1994).

Stauber, Roni. "From Revisionism to Holocaust Denial—David Irving as a Case Study." *Policy Study,* no. 19 (Jerusalem: Institute of the World Jewish Congress, 2000); also available at http://www2.h-net.msu.edu/~antis/papers/stauber/stauber.print.html. (Accessed on July 14, 2003.)

Islam and the Jews

Islam is a religion with a corpus of doctrines, beliefs, and practices that evolved over 1,400 years and has been subject to widely varying manifestations and interpretations. It is also a body politic, united at its beginning but more divided over time. It is, as well, a civilization that despite local and regional differences has significant elements of unity amid the variety. A historical survey of Islamic attitudes toward and treatment of Jews must therefore take into account this tripartite nature of what the term *Islam* comprises. As in the case of Christianity, the relationship between Judaism and Islam goes back to the very founding of the new faith. Jews figured into the Muslims' theological worldview, and Jews lived as a subject population under Muslim rule, sometimes under better, sometimes under worse conditions.

A number of fundamental notions in Islam about Jews and Judaism have their origins in the Koran, just as certain basic attitudes are grounded in the New Testament in Christianity. But because Islam did not begin as a sect within Judaism or claim to be *verus Israel* (the true Israel), as did Christianity, Muslim Scripture and later theological writings (with the exception of the *Sira,* the canonical biography of the Prophet Mohammed) do not exhibit anything comparable to the overwhelming preoccupation with the Jews that one finds in the New Testament, patristic literature, and later Christian theological writings.

Despite the traditions that Mohammed had met Jews prior to his theophany, there is no specific mention of *Yahud* (Jews) or Christians either in the koranic verses dating from the Meccan period (ca. 610–622). However, there are numerous references to the Children of Israel, who are mentioned as the recipients of earlier divine revelation. Moses is the archetypical prophet, and the Israelites are depicted as recipients of God's favor. Though most of the references are to the biblical Children of Israel, a few clearly are to contemporary Jews (for example, Suras 26:197 and 17:101), who are invoked as witnesses who can corroborate Mohammed's message. In the koranic verses from the Medinese period (622–632), the term *Jews* and phrase *those who are Jewish* appear juxtaposed to the term *Children of Israel* and reflect a radical change in the Arabian prophet's attitude as a result of the contradictions, mockery, and rejection he encountered from the Jewish scholars in Medina. Whereas the term *Children of Israel* appears throughout the Koran in both positive and negative contexts, the designation *Jews* is most frequently negative. Jews are associated with strife. They alone believe that they are loved by God and will attain salvation. They pervert words and blaspheme. They are usurers and corrupters. They have tampered with the texts of the Scriptures. They are the Muslims' worst enemies and, along with the pagans, are untrustworthy and ought not to be taken as friends. They are fated for a painful doom.

These negative depictions of Jews were expanded and amplified in the early Islamic hagiographic literature on the life of Mohammed and his companions and in works of koranic exegesis. In these texts, the conflict with the Jews of Medina takes on epic proportions, and the Jews appear as villainous caricatures—malicious, deceitful, but totally lacking in resolve. Though wicked and treacherous, they never appear as terribly effectual. They have none of the demonic qualities attributed to them in medieval Christian literature. Their ignominy stands in stark contrast to Muslim heroism and conforms to the koranic image of "wretchedness and baseness stamped upon them" (Sura 2:61). In the canon of statements and practices attributed to Mohammed, known as the Hadith, Jews are most frequently mentioned in traditions that emphasize the differences between Muslims and non-Muslims or that express disapproval of non-Muslim practices. In the small proportion of traditions where Jews are mentioned in a positive or neutral light, the term *Children of Israel* is more likely to be used. Because of the more negative connotation of the word *Jews* as opposed to *Children of Israel,* the latter tended to become the polite usage in Arabic when referring to Jews (in a semantic parallel to early modern French usage of *israélite* as a more polite term for *juif*).

A number of legal and social factors mitigated the potentially baneful force of these anti-Jewish stereotypes. Primary among these was that despite Mohammed's evolving hostility toward Jews and Christians, he never questioned the basic validity of their religion. They were only to be fought against until they submitted to Muslim rule as humble tribute bearers in accordance with the clear koranic injunction of Sura 9:29. As long as they accepted their status, they were not only to be tolerated, they were also to be entitled to the protection of the *Umma,* the Muslim commonwealth. Their legal status was that of *dhimmis* (protected persons). The *jizya* tribute, which became a poll tax in the caliphal empire, was considered the payment for this protection. The second factor that mitigated the harmful effects of anti-Jewish prejudices was that Islamic law prescribed one and the same legal role for Jews, Christians, and Zoroastrians in the Muslim state. That the Jews shared their inferior status with these far more numerous and hence more conspicuous religious communities diffused some of the anti-Jewish sentiments within a broader anti-dhimmi context.

The terms of this inferior status were summa-rized in a theoretical treaty between the dhimmis and Muslims known as the Pact of Umar, attributed to the second caliph Umar I (r. 634–644) but probably redacted under Umar II (r. 717–720). Many of its provisions and restrictions were only elaborated over the centuries. In return for their lives and property, freedom of economic endeavor, and the right to worship discreetly, dhimmis had to pay the jizya and property tax. They were to conduct themselves with the demeanor of humble subjects, never to carry arms, strike a Muslim, ride horses, or use normal saddles on their mounts. They were not to hold public religious processions, pray too loudly, or proselytize. They had to wear distinguishing clothing, which eventually led to special badges, specifically dyed outer garments, and a host of other sartorial regulations; these rules could dictate sleeve length, size, and type of headgear or footwear. In other words, they were to be permanent aliens within the Islamic polity. Many of these restrictions and their highly ramified refinements were probably inspired by the discriminatory legislation against Jews that was already in force in the Byzantine provinces conquered by the Muslims. The legal and social disabilities of the Jews and other tolerated non-Muslims were not uniformly enforced in all places and all times. During periods of economic prosperity and political and social stability, such as from the ninth to the twelfth centuries and the late fifteenth to seventeenth centuries, the interpretation and application of the system tended to be more liberal. Conversely, in times of stress, the discriminatory laws tended to be harsher and more restrictive as was particularly true in late medieval and early modern times in areas such as northwest Africa and Yemen, where the indigenous Christian population had disappeared and Jews were the only remaining dhimmis. Jews in these lands became increasingly confined to ghettolike quarters, such as the *mellah* in Morocco, the *hara* in Tunisia, and *qa'a* in Yemen. They also became subject to onerous and humiliating corvée labor and general social opprobrium. Even in lands where there was still a native Christian presence, Jews suffered from the growing animus toward non-Muslims. Sometime during the thirteenth or fourteenth century, a humiliating Jews' oath was introduced in Mamluke Egypt and Syria. The degrading, even ludicrous text in tone and intent is reminiscent of the notorious oath *More Judaico* in Europe.

Throughout the Middle Ages, the majority of the world's Jews lived in the Islamic world, and outbreaks of violence against them were relatively rare. Such violence often occurred when a Jew was perceived to have egregiously transgressed the boundaries of proper conduct by rising too high in the bureaucracy. The Zirid Jewish vizier Jehoseph Ibn Naghrela was killed by a mob in Grenada in 1066, and the entire Jewish community was sacked. A similar fate befell the vizier Harun Ibn Batash and the Jews of Merinid Fez in 1464. Anti-Jewish rioting only became a more frequent phenomenon in the twentieth century in the Arab parts of the Muslim world, with the anti-Jewish sentiments generated by Zionism and European colonialism. Forced conversions and mass exiles were even more rare than pogroms throughout Islamic history. This situation was in keeping with the clear koranic injunction that "there is no compulsion with regard to religion" (Sura 2:256). The few notable exceptions took place primarily under heterodox Muslim rule, for example, under the Almohades in North Africa and Spain during the twelfth and thirteenth centuries, in Shi'ite Yemen during the twelfth century, and in the Shi'ite holy city of Mashhad, Persia, in the nineteenth century.

In the twentieth and early twenty-first century, militant Islamist groups such as the Muslim Brotherhood, al-Jama'a al-Islamiyya, Hamas, and most recently al-Qa'ida have culled the most hostile pronouncement against Jews from Muslim traditional sources and have given them a centrality in their own doctrines and teachings. Sometimes these traditional texts have been joined with antisemitic canards, such as the Jewish conspiracy to dominate the world and the blood libel, borrowed from the European repertoire to inspire a holy war, not just against Israel, but against the West.

—*Norman A. Stillman*

See also Arab Antisemitic Literature; Ghetto; Hamas; Islamic Diaspora; Islamic Fundamentalism; Mohammed; Muslim Brotherhood; Usury; Zionism

References

Goitein, S. D. *Jews and Arabs: Their Contacts through the Ages.* 3rd rev. ed. (New York: Schocken, 1974).

Lewis, Bernard. *The Jews of Islam* (Princeton, NJ: Princeton University Press, 1984).

Stillman, Norman A. *The Jews of Arab Lands: A History and Source Book* (Philadelphia: Jewish Publication Society, 1979).

Islamic Diaspora

For most of the past 1,400 years, no significant numbers of Muslims lived outside the *Dar al-Islam* (the lands under Islamic dominion). However, during the latter half of the twentieth century and continuing into the twenty-first, large numbers of Muslims have migrated to Western Europe and the Americas in search of a better life. Antisemitism has made major inroads in many of these diaspora communities even as it has in the Islamic heartlands, and in Europe in particular, Islamic fundamentalist preachers and some intellectuals have engaged in antisemitic agitation, and Muslim youth appear to have become the prime perpetrators of violence against Jewish property and persons. Arab satellite television stations and Islamist websites and publications have conflated anti-Zionism and anti-Americanism with antisemitism. Though far less ubiquitous and massive, Muslim student groups and organizations have used blatant anti-Jewish rhetoric publicly and disseminated Jew-baiting propaganda even in the United States and Canada.

In Europe, more than 15 million Muslim immigrants and their descendants have provided a necessary pool of unskilled labor to do the menial work that Europeans no longer wish to perform. They tend to live in urban slums and the large public housing projects on the outskirts of cities. Throughout Western Europe, the Muslim population forms an underclass that is poorly assimilated and often highly alienated from the native majority. In France, Muslim immigrants who mainly come from the former French colonies in North and West Africa comprise between 8 and 10 percent of the total metropolitan population. Spain, Belgium, and the Netherlands also have large North African populations; in

Germany, the majority of Muslims are of Turkish extraction. In all of these countries and in the rest of Western Europe, there are also considerable numbers of university students from Arab countries.

Until the beginning of the twenty-first century, most antisemitic propaganda and activity in Europe came from the indigenous extreme Right—skinheads, neo-Nazis, Le Pen's National Front, and other such groups. Following the outbreak of the second intifada in the Palestinian territories in September 2000, there was a precipitous rise in antisemitic threats and violence in Western Europe. The French Ministry of the Interior recorded only 60 threats and 9 incidents for all of 1999, but it recorded 603 threats and 116 acts of violence in 2000, most occurring in the last months of that year, and these statistics are considerably lower than those of Jewish and outside monitoring organizations. According to the Stephen Roth Institute for the Study of Contemporary Anti-Semitism and Racism, Germany had 1,378 incidents in 2000 and early 2001 and the United Kingdom 405. The American Lawyers Committee for Human Rights noted that in the two years following September 11, 2001, approximately 2,000 antisemitic incidents occurred in Belgium. On December 5, 2001, Chief Rabbi Albert Gigi was assaulted in Brussels by a group of Arabic-speaking youths. In January 2003, a reform rabbi and peace activist, Gabriel Farhi, was stabbed at his synagogue in Paris by a masked youth who shouted "*Allahu akbar.*" Arson against synagogues, Jewish schools, and property became particularly widespread in France during the years 2000 through 2003.

Muslim youth in Europe have much greater access to the Internet than their coreligionists in the Islamic world. In addition to the many right-wing websites, there are numerous Islamist sites propagating antisemitic material, including *The Protocols of the Elders of Zion* and works of Holocaust denial. Islamist sites frequently link with antiglobalist and anti-American extreme left-wing sites and (since 2000) the European extreme Right. Among the eighty-two racist and antisemitic websites originating in Belgium, for example, one that belongs to the Arabian-European League, headed by Dyab Abou Jahjah, was cited in a complaint to the European Union (EU) Center for Equal Opportunity and Combating Racism in June 2003. The radical Islamist Hizb ut-Tahrir (Party of Liberation) maintains web pages in several European languages. It brands Jews as "a slanderous people" and incites Muslims to "kill them wherever you find them."

The widespread sympathy for the Palestinian cause and a growing hostility toward Israel among members of the European intellectual and governing elites have provided fuel to the antisemitic tendencies in the Islamic diaspora. Anti-Israel political demonstrations frequently include blatantly antisemitic placards and catcalls. Furthermore, the stubborn refusal of European governments to recognize, condemn, and take strong action against the problem during the first three years of the intifada exacerbated the phenomenon. The Socialist government of Lionel Jospin in France, for example, continually dismissed the problem of violence against Jewish persons and property as one of generalized delinquency. After the victory of the Center-Right government in the spring of 2002, the new minister of the interior, Nicholas Sarkozy, confronted the problem forthrightly and cracked down on it. A few progressive Muslim leaders, such as Soheib Bencheikh, the Mufti of Marseilles, have strongly condemned both Islamic fundamentalism and antisemitism, but their voices are in the minority. In 2003, the leaders of the EU noted the problem and issued an official statement of "deep concern." However, at the same time, the EU tried to suppress a report that it had itself commissioned because it showed that Muslims and pro-Palestinian groups were strongly linked to the current wave of European antisemitism—politically, a highly sensitive contention.

Although less numerous, frequently less vocal in public, and, with a few notable exceptions, less violent than their coreligionists in Europe, there is a sizable Islamic diaspora population in the United States and Canada, with estimates ranging from as low as 1.8 to as high as 7 million people. As in Europe, antisemitism is propagated in the North American Islamic diaspora by fundamentalist preachers, often with a Wahhabi or Muslim Brotherhood background. Islamist publications also propagate anti-Jewish canards. For example, Sheikh Abdessalam Yassine's book *Winning the World for Islam,* which contains a lengthy diatribe against the international Jewish conspiracy, is published in English by an Islamic fundamentalist printing house in Iowa. A variety of groups, some clandestine, such as the Muslim Brotherhood, and some operating openly, such as Muslim and Arab student associations on university campuses, are also propagators of antisemitism. Islamic student groups at anti-Israel demonstrations at the University of California–Berkeley and University of California–San Diego disseminated flyers with maliciously fabricated quotations from the Talmud such as "A gentile girl who is three years old can be violated" and "When the Messiah comes, every Jew will have 2800 slaves." The Muslim Arab Youth Association (MAYA) distributes a pamphlet entitled *America's Greatest Enemy: The Jew!* and the book entitled *The Struggle for Existence between the Quran and the Talmud.*

Public anger aroused by the September 11 attacks on New York and Washington, D.C., have caused Islamist militants to mute antisemitic rhetoric in public except on a few college campuses where they have leftist and Third World activist allies.

—*Norman A. Stillman*

See also Anti-Zionism; Arab Antisemitic Literature; Hamas; Holocaust Denial, Negationism, and Revisionism; Islam and the Jews; Islamic Fundamentalism; Le Pen, Jean-Marie; Netherlands in the Twentieth Century; *Protocols of the Elders of Zion;* Talmud

References

Bergman, Werner, and Juliane Wetzel. "Manifestations of Anti-Semitism in the European Union." http://www.eurojewcong.org/press/Date%202003-11-25%20Id%202/rapport%20antisem.pdf.

Chesler, Phyllis. *The New Anti-Semitism: The Current Crisis and What We Must Do about It* (San Francisco: Jossey-Bass, 2003).

Emerson, Steven. *American Jihad: The Terrorists Living among Us* (New York: Free Press, 2002).

Taguieff, Pierre-André. *La nouvelle judéophobie* (Paris: Mille et une Nuits, 2002).

Union des Étudiants Juifs de France and SOS Racisme. *Les Antifeujs: Le Livre blanc des violences antisémites en France depuis septembre 2000* (Paris: Calmann-Lévy, 2002).

Islamic Fundamentalism

The term *Islamic fundamentalism* is popularly used in the West to denote a number of radical, militant, revivalist movements within the contemporary Muslim world. The groups are also referred to as *Islamists,* a loanword from French. The other French designation, *intégristes,* has not caught on in English. Although these movements represent both the Sunni (for example, Muslim Brotherhood, al-Qa'ida, al-Jama'a al-Islamiyya, Hamas) and Shi'ite (for example, Khomeinism and Hizbollah) branches of Islam and hold a wide variety of views and doctrines, they share a rejection of Western secularism and the utopian goal of establishing a society that is completely Islamic in culture and totally governed by Islamic law in its pure form, first in their own countries and eventually throughout the entire world. They also tend to see the world as a Manichaean dichotomy between good and evil. Virtually all contemporary Islamists also embrace a number of antisemitic beliefs among their principal tenets.

The most common antisemitic notion among the broad spectrum of Islamic fundamentalists is that of a universal Jewish conspiracy as depicted in the *Protocols of the Elders of Zion.* Ayatollah Khomeini wrote in his *The Trusteeship of the Jurisconsult* that the true aim of the Jews "is to establish a world Jewish government." Even a relatively moderate Islamist, such as Rached Ghannouchi, the leader of the Tunisian Nahda movement, argues that there are among Jews "good people" (namely, those opposed to Zionism) and that not all are "polytheists." Nevertheless, he claims that Zionists want to inherit both the *Umma* (Muslim community) and the West and dominate the entire world, replace Washington with Jerusalem as the center of power, and destroy all humanist principles underlying civilization. For Sheikh Abdessalam Yassine, leader of the Moroccan Jami 'at al- 'Adl wa 'l-Ihsan (Justice and Charity Group), who is also considered a relative moderate, Jews are the embodiment of evil and all that plagues the modern world. Zionism and Jewry are synonymous. Jewish Hollywood is an accomplice in the Zionist world conspiracy. Yassine's book *Winning the World for Islam* contains a lengthy antisemitic diatribe and is translated into several languages, including English and French. For the Muslim Brotherhood, Jewry is the first and most pernicious of the four great evils to be combated. The others are "the Crusade," or Christian imperialism, communism, and secularism. An article from the October 1980 children's supplement of the brotherhood's magazine *al-Da'wa* (The Call) quotes a supposed Jewish book (the *Protocols of the Elders of Zion*) in which it is written, "We Jews are the masters of the world, its corrupters, the fomenters of sedition, its executioners!" The article calls on young Muslims to "annihilate their existence." Osama Bin Laden, in his 1998 "Declaration of the World Islamic Front for Jihad against the Jews and Crusaders," always placed Jewry at the top of the list of enemies to be confronted by holy war.

What sets most Islamists apart from traditional Islam is their adoption of an antisemitic worldview in which the fantasies of the *Protocols* are justified by proof texts from the Koran and the Hadith. This view, its theological justifica-

tion, and indeed a great deal of the overall social and geopolitical analysis of Islamic fundamentalists owe much to widely disseminated writings of the Egyptian Sayyid Qutb, the philosopher of the Muslim Brotherhood, who was hanged by Gamal Abdel Nasser in 1966.

—*Norman A. Stillman*

See also Arab Antisemitic Literature; Hamas; Hollywood, Treatment of Antisemitism in; Islam and the Jews; Islamic Diaspora; Khomeini, Ayatollah; Muslim Brotherhood; Nasser, Gamal Abdel; *Protocols of the Elders of Zion;* Zionism

References

Abrahamian, Ervand. *Khomeinism: Essays on the Islamic Republic* (Berkeley and Los Angeles: University of California Press, 1993).

Choueiri, Youssef M. *Islamic Fundamentalism* (Boston: Twayne, 1990).

Kepel, Gilles. *Muslim Extremism in Egypt: The Prophet and Pharoah* (Berkeley and Los Angeles: University of California Press, 1986).

Nettler, Ronald L. *Past Trials and Present Tribulations: A Muslim Fundamentalist's View of the Jews* (Oxford: Pergamon Press, 1987).

J

J Stamp

In late September 1938, German authorities began stamping a *J* in the passports of all German Jews. The decision to employ the stamp, supplementing the name change required under Nazi law for all Jews, followed negotiations with the Swiss government. Use of the J Stamp can be traced back to 1910, when it occasionally appeared on Swiss federal visa applications for Jews seeking residence rights. A stamp in the shape of a Star of David was also in use around 1919. Recently, it has been shown that the Swiss canton of Vaud made use of an identifying J Stamp, independently of Swiss federal authorities, to identify German Jews on its territory as early as 1937. Thus far, no evidence has come to light that other cantons followed this practice. By early 1938, some Swiss documents used "Aryan" and "non-Aryan" as routine identifications.

With the Nazi takeover of Austria on March 12, 1938, a refugee crisis erupted all over Europe as thousands sought to escape persecution. Members of Switzerland's Federal Council (the country's executive body) were worried that they could not deal with numbers much beyond the 5,000 or so refugees they had received since 1933, and on the recommendation of Heinrich Rothmund, the chief of the Swiss Federal Police, they implemented a visa requirement for all Austrians on March 28, 1938. In the meantime, concern over the acceleration of the "Aryanization" process, as well as the new immigration restrictions imposed around Europe, prompted the July 1938 convening of the Evian Conference to discuss a response to the Nazi persecutions. The failure of the conference, combined with the increase in refugees entering Switzerland from that point on, prompted the Federal Council to pass a decree on August 19: refugees without visas were to be turned back, especially Jews or anyone suspected of being Jewish.

In addition, as Germans began replacing Austrian passports with their own in April 1938, the Swiss became anxious that their measures would be fruitless. Rothmund hoped that, barring a universal visa requirement, which he favored, there would be means to distinguish "non-Aryans" and allow visa requirements to be imposed. In August 1938, the Swiss legation in Berlin passed on the suggestion to German authorities and threatened to reintroduce visa requirements for all Germans (these had been lifted in 1926). In early September, the German Foreign Office proposed to identify Jews by underlining their first names in red ink, instead of the normal black ink used in other German passports. However, because the red might be covered with a black line, the alternative marking of a *J* approximately 2 centimeters high on the first page of the passport became the standard practice. Rothmund negotiated an agreement in Berlin on September 29, 1938. The principle of reciprocity also affected Swiss Jews traveling to Germany, although without a special marking in their passports. The Federal Council adopted the protocol by unpublished decree on October 4, 1938. In the meantime, some other countries, including Sweden, moved to require identifying marks on passports, and others passed legislation designed to slow the flow of Jewish refugees into their lands. When Paul Grüninger, chief of police for the canton of St. Gallen, resisted these measures and took action to let Jews in, he was subjected to legal reprisals.

In summary, although the Swiss requirement of a J Stamp fell in line with other nations' rejection of Jewish refugees, it was unique in that it actually affected a change in German administrative practices.

—*Guillaume de Syon*

See also Aryanization; Evian Conference; Nazi Legal Measures against Jews; Switzerland; Yellow Star

References

Keller, Stefan. *Délit d'humanité: L'affaire Grüninger* (Lausanne, Switzerland: Editions d'en Bas, 1994).

Koller, Guido. "Der J-Stempel auf schweizerischen Formularen," *Schweizerische Zeitschrift für Geschichte* 49, no. 3 (1999): 371–374.

Unabhängige Expertenkommission Schweiz— Zweiter Weltkrieg. *Die Schweiz und die Flüchtlinge zur Zeit des Nationalsozialismus.* Vol. 17 (Zurich, Switzerland: Chronos, 2001).

Japan

Antisemitism in Japan combines Japan's centuries-old ambivalence toward foreigners with ideas about Jews imported from Europe. In the early nineteenth century, as Western nations began to impinge on the Japanese world, Japanese xenophobia was reformulated to deal with the threat. In 1825, the nativist thinker Seishisai Aizawa published his *New Theses,* arguing that Japan was in mortal danger of cultural subversion by adherents of the "occult religion" Christianity. Pointing to the fate of colonized Asian nations, Aizawa argued that Christians were out to destroy Japan, that trade and finance were among their weapons, and that teachings of brotherhood and charitable acts were mere tactics. Aizawa's ideas provided the groundwork for subsequent conspiracy theories about Jews.

Knowledge of Jews arrived in Japan through the medium of Western literature. In 1885, *The Merchant of Venice* became the first play by Shakespeare produced in Japan, and Shylock came to epitomize Jews in the Japanese imagination. *The Merchant of Venice* was used to teach Shakespeare in public schools throughout most of the twentieth century. The image of Jews as unscrupulous moneylenders was reinforced by Western dictionaries and encyclopedias that contained derogatory definitions of Jews as usurers and racial aliens.

The Bible was another major source of Japanese knowledge and imagery of Jews. The first modern translation of the New Testament appeared in 1880, and the reputation of Jews as obdurate, benighted, and diabolical spread with it.

Japanese Christians simultaneously became aware of Jews as God's original elect, however, and some of them, perhaps influenced by British Israelism, began to identify with Jews. Their motivation was to establish parity with Western Christianity and combat the cultural chauvinism of Western missionaries by claiming special access to Christianity's source. Yoshirō Saeki (1871–1965), a specialist in Nestorian Christianity at Tokyo University, and Zen'ichirō Oyabe (1867–1941), who studied at Howard University and received a doctorate from the Yale Divinity School, theorized that the Japanese were descendants of lost Israelite tribes who had landed in Japan in ancient times. In the late 1920s, under the pressure of increasing nationalism, Shōgun Sakai (1870–1939) modified this "common ancestry theory," arguing that the Japanese were the original Jews and that those foreigners who called themselves Jews were either their descendants or counterfeits.

The identification of Jews as conspirators against Japan came during the Siberian intervention (1918–1922), when as many as 72,000 Japanese troops were dispatched in an attempt to reverse the Russian Revolution. Japanese soldiers came into contact with the *Protocols of the Elders of Zion,* which they took back to Japan, using its depiction of a diabolical plot to explain the failure of their mission. The first complete translation of the *Protocols* was performed by Norihiro Yasue (1888–1950), who had been stationed in Siberia as a language officer and who became one of Japan's leading "Jewish experts" during World War II. The *Protocols'* theory of an international Jewish conspiracy to control the world was readily accepted in Japan, where suspicions of an "occult religious conspiracy" already circulated.

When Nazism arrived in Japan in the 1930s and Japan allied itself with Germany, antisemitism was transformed from a minority preoccupation to a respectable creed. During the war, the idea that the Jews were one of the threatening forces arrayed against Japan was widely accepted. The Foreign Ministry funded the antisemitic Association for International Politics and Economics, which conducted "scholarly" research on Jewish subjects, and accusations of pro-Jewish leanings were used by the government to persecute dissidents.

Even while this was going on, however, the Japanese allowed more than 20,000 Jewish refugees to find sanctuary in Shanghai, which Japan had occupied in 1937. Several thousand of these Jews arrived with visas issued, against government orders, by Chiune Sugihara, acting Japanese consul in Kovno (Kaunas), Lithuania, from late 1939 to August 1940. The Japanese resisted pressure from their German allies to exterminate the Jews, and Jewish life flourished in Shanghai.

Immediately after the war, "Jewish experts" such as Koreshige Inuzuka, who had been responsible for the Jews in Shanghai from 1939 to 1942 and who had proposed settling Jews in Manchuria for the benefit of the Japanese Empire (the Fugu Plan), fell temporarily out of favor. Then, with the advent of the Cold War, the Occupation "reversed course," rehabilitating many of those nationalists whom it had formerly purged. Inuzuka reinvented himself as a "friend of the Jews," and as head of the Japan-Israel Association and other organizations, he worked to promote Japanese-Jewish relations.

The most significant event of the immediate postwar period was the 1952 publication of Anne Frank's *Diary of a Young Girl*. Along with *The Merchant of Venice* and the *Protocols of the Elders of Zion*, Anne Frank's *Diary* would define Jews for the Japanese. Anne Frank came to represent all the innocent victims of war, and the Japanese, who were beginning to regard themselves increasingly as the victims rather than as the perpetrators of the war, identified with the young author and the Jewish experience. Reading the *Diary* became a rite of passage for adolescent Japanese girls. The book became such a fixture that the first sanitary napkin designed specifically for Japanese women was named "Anne's Day" after a passage in the *Diary* where Anne describes her first menstrual period.

Japan established diplomatic relations with Israel in 1952, when the Occupation ended and Japan regained its sovereignty. Relations with Israel have never been interrupted, but after the 1973 Yom Kippur War and in the aftermath of that year's Arab oil embargo, Japan, which depends heavily on the Middle East for its oil, adopted a pro-Arab foreign policy and became critical of the Jewish state. This government stance coincided with and was bolstered by leftist politicians and intellectuals, who were ideologically anti-Zionist and sympathetic to the Palestinians. Tokyo University professor Yūzō Itagaki was the most prominent member of this group. Though most left-wing criticism of Israel was responsible, it occasionally took a violent form, as when three terrorists belonging to the Japanese Red Army attacked disembarking passengers in Lod Airport outside Tel Aviv on May 30, 1972, killing twenty-four and wounding seventy-six. In other cases, left-wing writers have taken positions indistinguishable from right-wing antisemites, such as the journalist Takashi Hirose, who argued that the 1989 crash in the Japanese stock market was caused by an international Jewish cabal.

The Left's denial of Jewish peoplehood and depiction of Israel as the artificial product of a global imperialist conspiracy helped lay the basis for the recrudescence of antisemitism in the 1980s. Masami Uno, a fundamentalist Christian minister, ignited a "Jewish book boom" in 1986 with two best-sellers, *If You Understand the Jews, You Will Understand the World* and *If You Understand the Jews, You Will Understand Japan*, which revived the canard that an international Jewish conspiracy controlled the world and was out to destroy Japan. Bookstores set up "Jewish corners" to accommodate the ensuing flood of books based on the *Protocols of the Elders of Zion*, including works by prominent academics and legislators. Revisionist views of the Asia-Pacific War encouraged by the conservative prime minister Yasuhiro Nakasone and the economic dissatisfaction of many Japanese who felt left out of Japan's economic boom were factors behind the trend.

Despite international outrage, antisemitic books continued to be published into the 1990s and were not without real-world effects. Although it garnered only 0.03 percent of the vote, the overtly antisemitic Global Restoration Party (Chikyū ishin tō) fielded candidates in the 1992 Upper House Diet election in Tokyo, Osaka-Kobe, and Gumma prefecture. In 1993, the League of National Socialists (Kokka Shakaishugisha Dōmei) posted thousands of xenophobic, swastika-emblazoned handbills around Tokyo each week, denouncing "diabolical Judaism" and calling for the expulsion of foreigners. Finally, in March 1995, the pseudo-Buddhist Aum Shinrikyō (Pure Truth) religious cult, which imagined itself under attack by Jews, Freemasons, and other conspirators, released sarin gas on the Tokyo subway, killing 12 and injuring more than 5,000 in an effort to precipitate Armageddon.

Since 1995, antisemitism has gradually receded from public view. The most significant reason for this was the disrepute into which conspiracy theories fell following the Aum terrorist attack. The activism of American Jewish organizations such as the American Jewish Committee's Pacific Rim Institute and the Simon Wiesenthal Center, which worked with Japanese government officials and publishers to discourage antisemitic publishing, has also been important. Particularly effective and controversial was the Wiesenthal Center's call for an advertising boycott of *Marco Polo,* a glossy men's magazine that had published a Holocaust-denying article in January 1995. The action brought about the magazine's closure and the public humiliation of its publisher. Finally, the continuing decline of left-wing political influence has led to a marginalization of ideological anti-Zionism. Whether antisemitism will remain dormant in the future as Japan struggles with a declining population and increasing numbers of immigrants remains to be seen.

—*David G. Goodman*

See also Anti-Zionism; Freemasonry; Fugu Plan; Gospels; Judeo-Bolshevism; Nazi Research on the Jewish Question; Philosemitism; *Protocols of the Elders of Zion;* Shylock; Usury

References
Goodman, David G., and Masanori Miyazawa. *Jews in the Japanese Mind: The History and Uses of a Cultural Stereotype.* Expanded ed. (Lanham, MD: Lexington Books, 2000).

Jedwabne

A town of some 2,000 people in northeastern Poland, Jedwabne was occupied by Soviet forces in 1939. During the Soviet occupation, a unit of the Polish underground operating in the forest near Jedwabne was betrayed, and 250 people were arrested or killed in the subsequent shootout. The Polish townspeople accused the town's 1,600 Jews of pro-Soviet sympathies and erroneously blamed them for the betrayal. When German troops occupied the town on June 27, 1941, they were greeted as liberators by some of the townspeople, and there were spontaneous attacks on the Jews. On July 9, a small German police detachment arrived and met with the mayor and town council; it was agreed that the townspeople would be given a free hand to take revenge on the Jews. The following day started with scattered acts of random violence, after which town councillors, accompanied by German police, went from house to house to recruit townspeople. The Jews were then driven from their homes and assembled in the marketplace, where they were surrounded by a Polish crowd. A group of Jewish men were forced to break up a statue of Lenin and carry the pieces, in a procession with the town rabbi at its head, to a barn on the outskirts of the town. There, they were forced to dig a trench and bury the statue, after which they were killed. The remaining Jews were then also herded into the barn and shut inside; the barn was doused with gasoline and set afire. Apart from a handful of Jews who had managed to escape and find hiding places with Polish families, all the Jews died in the fire. According to Polish eyewitnesses, German participation in the events at the marketplace and barn was limited to taking pictures.

Similar occurrences took place in Radziłów, Wizna, and several other towns in the Jedwabne area. These events were probably part of the Germans' "self-cleaning action," aimed at encouraging east European populations to carry out pogroms. Most remained unresponsive to German pressure, however.

Twenty-two perpetrators were tried by the Polish Communist authorities in 1949 and one more in 1953. Twelve were convicted. One received a death sentence, later commuted; the longest term actually served was seven years. Subsequently, the massacre was officially ascribed to the Germans.

The matter was reopened by the publication of Jan T. Gross's book *Sasiedzi* (Neighbors) in 2000. The Polish Institute of National Memory (IPN) undertook an investigation, in the face of

Polish President Aleksander Kwaśniewski lays a wreath by the monument in Jedwabne, Poland, July 10, 2001. Kwaśniewski apologized for the massacre of hundreds of Jews by their neighbors sixty years ago. (Reuters/Corbis)

the raging controversy occasioned by the book. Subsequently, the president of Poland, Aleksander Kwaśniewski, officially accepted responsibility on behalf of his nation, and the primate of Poland, Cardinal Józef Glemp, publicly apologized on behalf of Catholics. However, he accompanied his remarks with the hope that the Jews would also "get around to apologizing" for their alleged role in imposing communism in Poland. A ceremony was held in Jedwabne on July 10, 2001, the sixtieth anniversary of the massacre, attended by Kwaśniewski but not by any representative of the church and boycotted by the townspeople under the leadership of the parish priest. A new plaque was dedicated at the site to replace the old one, which had blamed the Germans but, as a response to political pressure, did not identify the perpetrators. The IPN's final report appeared in November 2002. It substantially bore out Gross's allegations.

—*Steven Paulsson*

See also Judeo-Bolshevism; Poland; Poland since 1989; Stalinization of Eastern Europe
References
Brand, William, ed. *Thou Shalt Not Kill: Poles on Jedwabne* (Warsaw: Towarzystwo "Więź," 2001).
Gross, Jan T. *Neighbors: The Destruction of the Jewish Community in Jedwabne, Poland* (Princeton, NJ: Princeton University Press, 2001).
Machcewicz, Paweł, and Krzysztof Persak, eds. *Wokół Jedwabnego* (Around Jedwabne). 2 vols. (Warsaw: IPN, 2002).

Jehovah's Witnesses

A millenarian Christian community known for its ubiquitous door-to-door ministry, Jehovah's Witnesses called themselves Bible Students until 1931. The religion traces its modern roots to a Bible study group established in 1870 in Allegheny, Pennsylvania. The group, led by Charles Taze Russell (1852–1916), sought a restoration of original Christian belief and practice and held for the inerrancy of Scripture. In 1879, Russell founded the journal *Zion's Watch Tower and Herald of Christ's Presence* (now *The Watchtower Announcing Jehovah's Kingdom*), which set forth the developing beliefs of the Bible Students and, later, Jehovah's Witnesses. The journal challenged established churches on such doctrines as the Trinity, clergy-laity divisions, hellfire, and Christian involvement in politics and war.

According to Witness doctrine, Jehovah God established a series of covenants, each serving a role in the progressive outworking of divine purposes. Witness doctrine is supersessionist in that it maintains that God ordained a temporary period of Jewish chosenness, after which the opportunity was opened to people of all nations to obtain redemption through the Messiah, or Christ, Jesus. The Witnesses accept as historical the biblical accounts of the death of Jesus and of the first-century tension between Christians and Jews. Yet the Witnesses view certain members of the religious leadership, rather than Jews in general, as having been responsible for pressuring the Romans to execute Jesus. Thus, the Witnesses have long repudiated the notion of a transgenerational collective guilt of the Jewish people. Moreover, Witness writings explicitly reject the myths of ritual murder, blood libel, host desecration, and the *Protocols of the Elders of Zion.*

Discussions of antisemitism and the persecution of Jews figured heavily in the *Watch Tower's* expositions on Bible chronology and end-time prophecies. In 1879, the *Watch Tower* stated that "the return of the Jews to Palestine" could be expected during the "Day of the Lord." It asserted that first, Jews would experience unprecedented persecution, which would drive them to Palestine. The *Watch Tower* denounced antisemitism and saw the Zionist movement as the fulfillment of restoration prophecies. The political character of the Zionist movement notwithstanding, the Bible Students expected a religious revival among repatriated Jews and a subsequent return to divine favor. The Bible Students followed social and agricultural developments in Palestine with intense interest until the late 1920s, when restoration prophecies were reinterpreted as applying to "spiritual Israel," or chosen Christians. Thereafter, the *Watch Tower* accorded no prophetic role to modern Jewry. Neither did it attribute biblical significance to the founding of the state of Israel.

During World War I, the Bible Students' sharp criticism of the nations' participation in war and of clergy involvement therein brought severe repercussions, including incarceration and governmental bans. In the interwar period, the Bible Students adopted the name Jehovah's Witnesses and further distanced themselves organizationally and theologically from mainstream churches and politics. Some critics accused the Witnesses of being supported by a Jewish-Bolshevik conspiracy, a charge denied in Witness literature.

In Germany, the Nazi regime used similar allegations to justify brutal suppression of the Witnesses, even vilifying them in the notorious *Der Stürmer* newspaper. In June 1933, the Witnesses published a vigorous rebuttal in a document that some have interpreted as antisemitic in tone. Yet despite the doctrinal shift de-emphasizing the role of natural Israel in prophecy, Witness literature at that time continually exposed and denounced Nazi atrocities against the Jews. The Witnesses resisted Nazi pressure to cease using the name Jehovah and other Hebraic terms. They individually and collectively refused to share in Nazi violence against Jews and other victims. They also refused to bear arms for Germany. Consequently, Witnesses in Europe suffered relentless persecution; thousands went to Nazi camps and prisons, and more than 2,000 died.

Witnesses view Nazi persecution as one episode in a long history of oppression of true Christians by religious and political elements. The Witnesses consider the Holocaust to have been a satanic attack against the Jews and evidence of the blood guilt of apostate Christianity.

Up until the late 1920s, the *Watch Tower* asserted that Christians should not attempt to convert Jews to Christianity, since God's favor would be restored to them as Jews. In later periods, however, Witnesses have believed it their obligation to preach the Gospel among Jews and non-Jews alike. The Witnesses do not expect a mass conversion of Jews in the end-times, nor do they view the fulfillment of eschatological events as contingent on such conversion. Presently, they believe that Jews and non-Jews have equal opportunity to obtain divine favor.

—*Jolene Chu*

See also Gospels; Host Desecration; *Protocols of the Elders of Zion;* Ritual Murder (Medieval); Ritual Murder (Modern); *Stürmer, Der;* Supersessionism; Zionism

References

Chu, J., and J. N. Pellechi. "Jehovah's Witnesses and Jews: Diverse Paths, Parallel Journeys, Common Terminus." In *The Burdens of History: Post Holocaust Generations in Dialogue.* Edited by Sharon Leder and Milton Teichman (Merion Station, PA: Merion Westfield Press International, 2000).

Jesuit Order

Ignatius of Loyola (1491–1556) was the son of a well-respected Basque noble family. He sought glory and honor as a soldier. But after being severely wounded, he vowed to change his life and to dedicate himself to the service of God. In Paris in 1536, together with six friends, Ignatius sketched out a plan for the founding of a religious body, which later became the foundation for the Jesuit order. The friends pledged themselves to poverty and celibacy. Because of the war with the Turks, they could not make a pilgrimage to Jerusalem. Instead, they traveled to Rome in 1538, where they put themselves at the disposal of Pope Paul III and the cause of Catholic renewal. In a solemn ceremony on April 15, 1539, the new order was given the name Society of Jesus; papal confirmation came the following year.

Ignatius lived during a period of great turmoil within the church. He was convinced that reform had to proceed from within and that it had to be built on a deepened sense of piety. The Jesuit idea was new—not a turning away from but a dedication to the world, in order to win it for God. The Jesuit mission went out into the world to secure and strengthen the Catholic faith, to convert, instruct, and educate as well as to engage in scholarly and literary pursuits. Members were sent where their individual gifts could best be used.

Initially, the statutes of the Society of Jesus put no obstacles in the way of granting membership to Jewish converts or their descendants. Ignatius, personally, had no reservations about receiving converts, even quite recent ones, as long as they possessed the necessary aptitude. Among the first generation of Jesuits in Spain were several descendants of Jews, for example, the second general of the order, Diego Lainez, who, together with Francis Xavier, was one of the most important and learned of the founding members.

Under the immediate successors to Ignatius, the number of Jesuits of Jewish descent in Spain and Portugal grew to a level that prompted the Spanish kings and the Inquisition to urge the leaders of the order to change the admission requirements. The pressure of public opinion finally compelled them to prohibit the acceptance of *conversos,* or "New Christians," in 1592. The next year, at the fifth general assembly of the order in Rome, a statute was enacted that barred, for all time, the descendants of Jews from becoming members. The practical difficulties of implementing the rule led to a decision in the general assembly of 1608 that left the statute in place but stipulated that candidates from good Christian families would not have to provide proof of their non-Jewish ancestry beyond the fifth generation. The statute remained in force until the beginning of the twentieth century. It was significant especially for the Iberian Peninsula, where many Jews lived. A similar rule applied to those of Moorish ancestry. During the course of the seventeenth century, the generation of converso members died out. Thereafter, as the order grew and attracted members from among all nations and races, the exclusionary statute lost its significance. In 1923, the laws of the order were once again examined and confirmed. The evidence of a candidate's Christian ancestry now needed to go back only four generations and only in the male line.

Among the modern instances in which the Jesuit order has been accused of enmity toward the Jews, perhaps the most famous is the Dreyfus Affair that began in 1894, pitching France into a prolonged, many-sided crisis. The Jesuits, long the target of popular suspicion and literary accusations about their supposedly sinister schemes, took much of the blame for the sordid affair in both Jewish and non-Jewish circles. The Jewish writer and early Zionist Max Nordau declared that the whole trumped-up case had been the work of a Jesuit-inspired conspiracy. Republican opponents of the order were quick to point out that many of the highest-ranking officers of the French army had been schooled by Jesuits. Georges Clemenceau's newspaper, *L'Aurore*, hyperbolically described the whole affair as "nothing more than a Jesuit crime" (August 25, 1898). In the aftermath of the crisis, in which other elements of the church were more certainly implicated, the Third Republic punished its enemies and carried out a far-reaching separation of church and state. From 1899 to 1909, the order was abolished in France.

In the first two centuries of its existence, some found anti-Jewish tendencies in the Society of Jesus. After its abolition (1773–1814) was lifted, some accused it of being philosemitic. Point of view was crucial in the formation of these judgments. For example, French opponents accused the Italian Jesuit newspaper *Civiltà Cattolica* of being antisemitic. (During the Dreyfus Affair, its articles were undeniably so.) Kaiser Wilhelm II confided to Otto von Bismarck, by contrast, that "Jews and Jesuits always stick together." Many anti-Jesuit pamphlets contained the assertion that the order was nothing more than a gathering place for the offspring of rich Jews. Only after the Holocaust did this kind of calumny cease.

The question of whether the Jesuit order is philo- or antisemitic continues to be debated. As recently as the 1970s, reputable sources maintained that only since 1946 had it become possible for baptized Jews to become Jesuits. In fact, the sons of Jewish parents who had converted to Christianity could always become members, although they had to make a special application to do so. These requests were not simply rejected out of hand. Otherwise, the Jesuit fathers with Jewish names would not have had to flee the German provinces of the order after the Nazis came to power.

—Rita Haub
Richard S. Levy, translation

See also Barruel, Augustin; *Civiltà Cattolica;* Dreyfus Affair; Freemasonry; Judeo-Bolshevism; *Kulturkampf;* Nordau, Max; State-within-a-State; Ultramontanism; Vatican Council, First

References
Hartmann, Peter C. *Die Jesuiten* (Munich, Germany: C. H. Beck, 2001).
Kiechle, Stefan, and Clemens Maass. *Der Jesuitenorden heute* (Mainz, Germany: Matthias-Grünewald, 2000).
O'Malley, John. W. *The First Jesuits* (Cambridge, MA: Harvard University Press, 1993).

Jew Bill (1753)

From the Jewish resettlement in England during the reign of Oliver Cromwell (1649–1658) until the controversy surrounding the Jewish Naturalization Act of 1753, the legal status of England's 8,000 Jews remained imprecise. Restrictions and disabilities in certain areas coexisted with a relatively tolerant atmosphere that allowed the Jewish population to grow and develop its own cultural, economic, and religious interests. Yet the range of commercial disabilities weighed heavily, especially on foreign-born Sephardic Jews of the merchant class, who could be exempted only by means of a private parliamentary act of naturalization. Professing Jews could not even pursue this avenue because they were obligated to take the sacrament, a measure designed in 1609 to curtail the influence of non-Anglicans. Eventually, Joseph Salvador, a distinguished member of the Sephardi community, addressed the Duke of Newcastle in 1753 with a request to free Jews from the obligation of the sacrament before a private act of naturalization. Newcastle and his brother, the Whig prime minister Henry Pelham, were favorably inclined, feeling a sense of gratitude to the Sephardic elite for their political and economic support. Confidently, they backed a bill that was presented to Parliament in April 1753; it rapidly passed the House of Lords and House of Commons by the end of May, although a measure of opposition in the second and third readings in the Commons warned of future difficulty.

A spirited public controversy erupted, lasting several months and spawning an unprecedented outpouring of pamphlets, petitions, coarse visual material, newspaper columns, and songs (see entry on Caricature, Anti-Jewish [Early]). Merchants, church officials, and country lords mounted a concerted attack that spread fear of the consequences of improving the status of Jews. In particular, they warned against Jewish economic penetration and the corruption of the Anglican Church and English society. Judaism was slandered. With the assistance of parliamentary figures, talented hack writers, accomplished caricaturists, and sophisticated church officials, the opponents succeeded in magnifying the bill's potential harm and in reviving hostile images of the Jews. Anticipating a backlash in the upcoming national election, supporters of the bill backed off. Newcastle brought the proposal for the repeal to the House of Lords in November. The law was repealed, and the public outcry subsided.

Historians have differed on the meaning of the anti-Jewish outcry. Thomas Perry has argued for its contextualization within English politics of the eighteenth century, viewing it as an appendix to the perennial disputes over naturalization and immigration. In his estimation, the anti-Jewish atmosphere was a passing phase, the outgrowth of propaganda and a deflection of pent-up opposition to Whig leadership. In contrast, several other historians accord the anti-Jewish arguments greater importance, not only as revivals of medieval anti-Jewish slurs but also, especially in the anti-Jewish propagandistic visualizations, a turn toward modern "racial" stereotyping of Jews. The drama of 1753 postponed for generations any further attempts to modify Jewish legal status.

—*Richard I. Cohen*

See also Caricature, Anti-Jewish (Early); Emancipation; Hogarth, William
References
Endelman, Todd M. *The Jews of Georgian England, 1714–1830: Tradition and Change in a Liberal Society* (Philadelphia: Jewish Publication Society of America, 1979).
Felsenstein, Frank. *Anti-Semitic Stereotypes: A Paradigm of Otherness in English Popular Culture,* 1666–1830 (Baltimore, MD: Johns Hopkins University Press, 1995).
Perry, Thomas W. *Public Opinion, Propaganda, and Politics in Eighteenth-Century England: A Study of the Jewish Bill of 1753* (Cambridge, MA: Harvard University Press, 1962).

Jew Census (1916)

In November 1916, the Prussian War Ministry, which had operational control over all German armed forces, conducted a census to determine how many Jews served in frontline units. Every military bureaucracy kept records concerning religious affiliation, but the Jew Census was an antisemitically inspired initiative designed to reveal that Jews were cowards because they managed to avoid dangerous military duty. Historians are unsure about the exact origins of the census, but the War Ministry's ordering of the count came after antisemitic Reichstag deputies and a senior government official demanded that the military verify whether Jews were fighting and dying in the same numbers as Christians.

The official directive for the Jew Census came from War Minister Wild von Hohenborn on October 11, 1916, although the details were handled by an outspokenly antisemitic officer, Col. Ernst von Wrisberg. The Hohenborn directive stated that the census would address accusations from various sources that Jews were disproportionately excused from military service and poorly represented at the front. Hohenborn ordered every command along with occupation authority to submit a report for inspection, making clear that each should include the total number of officers, noncommissioned officers, and troops in each unit; he wanted to know how many of them were Jews and how many Jews had been awarded Iron Crosses of the first or second class. Jewish groups in Germany reacted with outrage at the impugning of their patriotism. Author Ernst Simon wrote that the census turned the "dream of community" into "fantastic disappointment." "Now we are labeled. Now we have been made into second-class citizens," a Jewish soldier wrote home (Zechlin 1969, 532–533). Wrisberg went before the Reichstag to insist that the census had nothing to do with antisemitism. Field Marshall Paul von Hindenburg urged Jews to embrace the census as an opportunity to prove themselves and defeat false suspicions. It never occurred to Hindenburg to view the military as having legitimized these very suspicions. Jews, meanwhile, did not fail to notice that they had to account for their service when other Germans did not.

Even after von Hohenborn was replaced as war minister, the Jew Census remained a high priority. The official results were never published, fueling suspicion among both antisemites and Jews alike. The final report included statistics, but none of the categories revealed anything significant. Most scholars agree that approximately 100,000 Jews served during World War I, 80,000 of whom served at the front. These numbers, along with the statistics on casualties and decorations, approximate those of the general population. The legacy of the Jew Census lived on after the war because both antisemites and German Jews used wildly divergent statistics to undermine each other's claims. Although only dimly understood at the time, the Jew Census signaled the beginning of a new, more radical wave of antisemitism that was to poison the political life of the Weimar Republic.

—Brian Crim

See also Central Association of German Citizens of Jewish Faith; League against Antisemitism; Ludendorff, Erich; Roth, Alfred; Weimar

References
Angress, Werner T. "The German Army's 'Judenzählung' of 1916—Genesis—Consequences—Significance," *Leo Baeck Institute Year Book* 23 (1978): 117–138.

Zechlin, Egmont. *Die Deutsche Politik und die Juden im Ersten Weltkrieg* (Göttingen, Germany: Vandenhoeck and Ruprecht, 1969).

Jew of Malta, The

This tragedy by Christopher Marlowe (1564–1593) was written around 1589 and first published in 1633. Its protagonist was the most popular stage Jew before Shylock. The play is introduced by Machiavel, a diabolical figure that appeared here for the first time in London theaters. This misleading but very popular caricature of the political philosopher Niccolo Machiavelli originated from mostly French pamphlets, which denounced him for propagating atheism and advocating the use of all conceivable means to obtain power or to acquire riches. Machiavel introduces the Jew Barabas, a merchant and usurer of immense wealth, as his most faithful follower.

At the beginning of the play, the Christian governor Ferneze confiscates Barabas's estates in order to pay tribute to the Turks and has his house converted into a nunnery. The rest of the play consists of a series of episodes exhibiting the Jew's Machiavellian ruthlessness and malicious cunning as he takes his revenge by inciting murders and poisoning various people, among them his daughter and a whole convent of nuns. After siding with the Turks and being instrumental in their conquest of Malta, he is appointed governor. Changing sides again, he sets an ingenious trap to kill the Turkish leader. When Ferneze springs the trap, however, Barabas himself falls into a cauldron of boiling oil, crying out in vain for Christian mercy and cursing Christian and Turk alike.

The world of this tragedy is wholly materialistic; Christians and Turks are just as covetous for gold as the Jew. No figure gains tragic stature or arouses compassion, for even the most atrocious events are presented as ludicrous and grotesque. In creating the protagonist, Marlowe used popular prejudices about Jews and combined them with Machiavellian malice.

Barabas belongs to the series of almost superhuman figures that Marlowe devised for the London stage with extraordinary success: the shepherd Tamburlaine conquering all Asia, Dr. Faustus selling his soul to the devil for absolute knowledge and control over nature, Barabas relentlessly pursuing his revenge on the world. As "overreachers" driven by indomitable ambition, they rebel against a divinely imposed world order, thus adumbrating a new era of boundless individualism, reckless enterprise, and uninhibited capitalism. From all that is known about Marlowe, he does not seem to have written this play out of any particular hatred against Jews. His contemporaries thought him an atheist who denied the divinity of Christ. He is reported to have said that Christ better deserved to die than Barabas and that the Jews made a good choice in crucifying him. When the government eventually investigated these allegations, Marlowe was already dead, the victim of a quarrel in a tavern.

A crude combination of scenes from this play and from *The Merchant of Venice* was performed in German by English comedians in German and Austrian towns and courts throughout the seventeenth century. Modern criticism has tended to evaluate the play as a farce rather than a tragedy. To literary historians, its Machiavellian protagonist has been of interest mainly for its influence on Shakespeare and other dramatists.

—*Wolfgang Weiss*

See also Caricature, Anti-Jewish (Early); English Literature from Chaucer to Wells; Misanthropy; Shakespeare, William; Shylock; Usury

References

Grantley, D., and P. Roberts, eds. *Christopher Marlowe and Renaissance Culture* (Aldershot, UK, and Brookfield, VT: Scolar Press, 1996).

Lunney, R. *Marlowe and the Popular Tradition: Innovation in the English Drama before 1595* (Manchester, UK: Manchester University Press, 2002).

Thomas, V., and W. Tydeman, eds. *Christopher Marlowe: The Plays and Their Sources* (London: Routledge, 1994).

Jewish Anti-Fascist Committee

After the German invasion of the USSR in June 1941, Henryk Erlich and Wiktor Alter, two prominent Jewish socialists who had been arrested in 1939, were approached while still in prison by Lavrenti Beria, head of the Soviet secret police (Narodnyi Komissariat Vnutrennikh Del, or NKVD). He suggested that they initiate an international anti-Fascist movement to garner support from "world Jewry" on behalf of the Soviet war effort. Their initial attempts, undertaken with great enthusiasm, failed to elicit the desired response. The two men were promptly rearrested; Erlich committed suicide in 1942, and Alter was shot in the following year.

However, the idea of tapping into Jewish money and exploiting the Jews' natural hostility toward the Nazis was soon revived. In the spring of 1942, the Soviet authorities approved the creation of a Jewish Anti-Fascist Committee (JAC), closely supervised from the outset by the organs of state security. JAC aimed to help the war effort by collecting funds for the Red Army, especially from among American Jews. The committee was allowed to publish a Yiddish newspaper, *Eynikkeyt* (Unity), and Solomon Mikhoels, the president of JAC, and the poet Itsik Fefer were allowed to travel to the United States and Great Britain in order to solicit help from the Jewish communities there, which they evidently did with considerable success. To aid in these activities, the committee commissioned the best-known Soviet Jewish war correspondents, Ilya Ehrenburg and Vasily Grossman, to collect material to be published on the Nazi murder of Jews on Soviet territory. Abbreviated versions of this so-called *Black Book* were published in the West during the war. But whether from innate anti-semitism or from a concern that the Soviet cause would be tainted by being too narrowly identified with that of the Jews, the regime never allowed publication of the *Black Book* inside the USSR. Nor did Soviet domestic propaganda ever mention the targeting of Jews for genocide or acknowledge their extraordinary suffering.

Once Nazi Germany was defeated, the Soviet regime had no further use for JAC. Indeed, it seemed positively dangerous that a semiautonomous organization with Western contacts might agitate in defense of particular Jewish interests, call attention to the existence of the Final Solution, or make public the existence of ongoing Soviet antisemitism. In fact, Stalin's last years were a period of state-sponsored antisemitism. Jews, branded "cosmopolitans" and suspected of secret loyalties to the new state of Israel, became the targets of an explicit and menacing antisemitic campaign, no doubt a consequence of Stalin's ever increasing prejudice. The leaders of the defunct JAC, together with many other prominent Jews and non-Jews, fell victim to a new series of purges.

—*Peter Kenez*

See also Anti-Zionism in the USSR; Doctors' Plot; Purges, Soviet; Stalin, Joseph; USSR

References

Ehrenburg, Ilya, and Vasily Grossman. *The Complete Black Book of Russian Jewry* (New Brunswick, NJ: Transaction, 2002).

Rubinstein, Joshua, and Vladimir Naumov, eds.

Stalin's Secret Pogrom: The Postwar Inquisition of the Jewish Anti-Fascist Committee (New Haven, CT: Yale University Press, 2001).

Jewish Council (Budapest, 1944)

When the Germans occupied Hungary in March 1944, Hungarian authorities immediately ordered Jewish leaders to obey all German instructions. To ensure total compliance, the occupiers took 3,000 Jews hostage, imposed strict censorship, and banned Jews from traveling. In keeping with the Nazi policy of involving prominent Jews in their community's liquidation, the SS ordered an elderly, respected Jewish leader, Samuel Stern, to head the Budapest Jewish Council (Zsido Tanacs, [JC]) and made that body responsible for conveying German orders to Hungary's Jews and then seeing that they were obeyed.

The realities of occupation left Hungarian Jewry totally isolated and bereft of allies; in particular, the virtual withdrawal of the powerful head of state, Adm. Miklós Horthy, from public affairs undid Hungarian Jewry's carefully developed relationship with the highest levels of government. Overnight, the JC was saddled with ministering to an entrapped, traumatized, largely impoverished, divided, and totally defenseless community of 750,000.

Despite SS assurances to the contrary, the deportation of Jews to Auschwitz commenced on May 15, 1944, and by July 7, when Horthy banned further deportations, approximately 450,000 provincial Jews had been sent to the death camp. During this period of German hegemony, the JC had the resolve but lacked the allies, influence, and opportunity to oppose the Final Solution in a meaningful manner. Horthy's emergence from political hibernation, however, renewed the de facto JC-Horthy symbiosis. Until Horthy's overthrow on October 15, 1944, JC initiatives and Horthy's authority combined to protect Hungary's remaining Jews. In particular, the JC contributed substantially to the official note of late August that notified Germany of Hungary's new policy henceforth to safeguard its Jewish citizens.

Although formally rejecting "illegal" procedures, mindful of the 3,000 Jewish hostages, the JC engaged selectively in covert, unauthorized activities. The zenith of such resistance was Samuel Stern's secret agreement with the Hungarian Independence Front to arm some 25,000 Jewish Labor Service conscripts in order to help defend Horthy's proposed armistice with the USSR. This virtually unknown attempt at mass Jewish armed resistance was unique in the Holocaust.

Horthy's overthrow inaugurated the brutal reign of Ferenc Szalasi, reducing the JC to little more than the issuing of appeals to conscience. Simultaneously, however, it strove to ameliorate the Jews' increasingly desperate situation by establishing public kitchens, collaborating with the few neutral diplomats remaining in Budapest, and secretly falsifying documents.

For decades after the war, assessments of the Jewish Council remained frozen in two damning judgments: first, that the JC was composed of servile collaborationists whose fixation on self-preservation ensured the success of the Final Solution in Hungary, and second, that the JC consisted of elderly, frightened, conservative, wealthy men of limited vision who, despite good intentions, proved tragically ineffective against German might when combined with Hungary's wholesale collaboration. Recent research clearly indicates that the JC, especially from July 7 to October 15, often displayed courage, dedication, vision, and political skill—on occasion of a very high order—in evading and sometimes even confounding the Nazis. A fairer judgment of its service in these darkest of times would be that despite unprecedented handicaps, the JC played a principal part in saving those Hungarian Jews whom it was possible to save. At liberation, Budapest contained 120,000 Jewish survivors, more than any other city occupied by German forces.

—*Tom Kramer*

See also "Blood for Trucks"; Eichmann, Adolf; Holocaust; Horthy, Miklós; Hungary; Hungary, Holocaust in; Kallay, Miklós; Szalasi, Ferenc

References

Braham, Randolph L. *The Politics of Genocide: The Holocaust in Hungary.* 2 vols. (New York: Columbia University Press, 1994).

Kramer, T. D. *From Emancipation to Catastrophe: The Rise and Holocaust of Hungarian Jewry* (Lanham, MD: University Press of America, 2000).

Jewish Force

The Jewish Force is an esoteric New Age term referring to a negative cosmic energy wielded by the Jewish people, discussed at length by occultist Alice Bailey in her landmark treatise *Externalisation of the Hierarchy* (1957). She presented the concept as part of the "Ancient Wisdom," divine teaching transmitted from the "Ascended Masters"—the hierarchy of disembodied spiritual guides revered in New Age religion.

Acting in opposition to the three positive Energies emanating from the "Logos," a trinity of deities operating through Will, Love, and Wisdom, the Jewish Force is a parallel energy of roughly the same magnitude. With typical ambiguity, Bailey identified this force as (1) a "thought form" invented by the Jewish mind that operates through magic and money (or alternately, through emotion); (2) an emanation characterized by materialism, radiating out from the "Dark Forces" or "Black Lodge," repositories of cosmic Evil; and (3) a personal manifestation similar to the "Ascended Masters," who, like them, has transmitted teachings to humanity, namely, the God of the Jews.

The Jewish Force influences the Jews and others toward materialism and separatism, increasing world tensions. It is itself a "separated world center of energy" as well, which Bailey predicted would be of temporary duration in the cosmic scheme of things. Her repeated reference to separateness stresses the evil nature of the Jewish Force, since "separatism" is a sin in New Age teaching. The Jewish people are the "world center," or the humanly channeled manifestation of a spiritual energy, for the Jewish Force. Bailey concluded that the Jewish Force would eventually be conquered by the Hosts of Light, reversing their defeat sustained in an earlier age. But the tide can be turned only after the disappearance of the Jews, who have been "feeding" this force through their loyalty to Jewish identity. Elsewhere, she asserted that the Jewish people cannot be expected to disappear until the Jewish Force itself is eliminated, implying a belief that it is not the Jews who keep their God alive but the opposite. Humanity's final liberation from the Jewish Force is to be achieved through cosmic warfare waged by the Logos against their divine Opponent. Enlightened humanity can aid in the struggle by erasing the negative "thought form" from human consciousness. One such human effort is collective recital of "the Great Invocation."

—*Hannah Newman*

See also Bailey, Alice A.; Invocation, The Great; New Age

"Jewish" Press

Antisemites have long maintained that the Jews rule the newspaper and publishing industries. Consequently, they are in a position to direct public opinion according to their own agenda, and that is why public opinion is *not* the opinion of the people. In fact, the people are manipulated and misled into serving the interests of the Jews. The Jews pursue two major objectives by this means. First, they subvert a people's essential national character, its sense of right and wrong, and its traditions, religion, and consciousness of self. Domination of the press by the Jews subjects "the German spirit," "French civilization," and so forth to permanent attack while simultaneously denying them the possibility of self-articulation. Second, it renders impossible the "objective" reporting of Jewish scheming. Jews are, by the same means, able to keep information about their interests, plans, and conspiring out of the news. Thus, control of the press bestows on the Jews an extraordinarily important strategic advantage, not the least because it seals off the nation from the antisemites who would otherwise "enlighten" it about the enemy.

From the nineteenth century to the present day, the stereotype of the "Jewish" press has become extremely widespread. Klemens Felden's study of representative antisemitic writings between 1850 and 1895 demonstrates that fully 80 percent of them employed the stereotype. What began in the nineteenth continued into the twentieth century. Scarcely a prominent antisemite is to be found—be it Heinrich von Treitschke, Édouard Drumont, Adolf Hitler, or any number of Holocaust deniers—who has refrained from making the so-called Jewish press a significant part of the indictment against Jews. During the Third Reich, newspapers and publishing houses deemed Jewish were swiftly "Aryanized."

The concept of the "Jewish" press is often re-marked on in the scholarly literature but rarely systematically analyzed. The frequently advanced explanation for the prejudice—that overrepre-sentation of Jewish publishers, journalists, and authors was its root cause—is, generally speaking, wrongheaded. It purports to deduce antisemitic prejudices from the objective peculiarities of the Jewish group. Thus, prejudice appears to be a re-sponse to real, although perhaps exaggerated, conditions. This genre of elucidation comes close to legitimizing antisemitism instead of subjecting it to careful analysis. Aside from its theoretical shortcomings, such an explanation cannot make clear why the prejudiced notion of the "Jewish" press has existed in times and places when and where the presupposed overrepresentation of Jews has not existed. Jacob Toury, for example, has shown this to be the case in Germany be-tween 1815 until 1871. The same could be demonstrated for Austria.

The theory of overrepresentation becomes wholly untenable when one analyzes the texts that utilize the stereotype. What exactly is meant by the term *Jewish press?* Most who have em-ployed it certainly have not been concerned with periodicals dealing with Jewish religious, com-munal, or cultural affairs—the actual Jewish press. Antisemites decrying the Jewish press do not name names, or they list the same few names repeatedly. In Germany, the most familiar exam-ples were the newspapers *Frankfurter Zeitung, Vossische Zeitung,* and *Berliner Tageblatt* and the publishing houses of Ullstein and Mosse. But in the imperial era, Theodor Fritsch's *Handbook of the Jewish Question* averred there were 3,353 Jew-ish newspapers. In 1920, Hitler spoke of 19,000. Obviously, such inflated numbers went well be-yond the newspapers that were owned by Jews or on which Jews performed leading functions. The reason for this was that the antisemites aimed their attacks against the entire press that was nei-ther antisemitic nor *völkisch* (racist-nationalist), in other words, primarily the liberal and socialist newspapers, which either ignored antisemitic ag-itation or heaped scorn on it. In this way, a ready explanation could be found for the inability of the antisemitic press to mold public opinion, even though it was the "true embodiment" of

that opinion. These wildly expanded parameters of the Jewish press were effortlessly arrived at by antisemites who found it axiomatic that both lib-eralism and socialism were Jewish inventions.

Such thinking processes help to explain why the stereotype was and is so widespread. It was im-portant for antisemitic writers to explain their struggle for the public mind in antisemitic terms. Their logic might well have been expressed with the following rule of thumb: "Either you are for 'our people,' or against it. Those against are 'ene-mies of the people,' *ergo* Jews or the dupes of Jews." For this old formula to gather strength, however, something more decisive was needed. Next to money, the daily mass-circulation news-paper had become during the course of the nine-teenth century the quintessential medium defining bourgeois, capitalist society. It constituted a new sort of public sphere and then monopolized it. In antisemitic texts, the symbolic power of money and the press often appeared in tandem: "Jews dominate Germany's stock market and press," Treitschke complained in 1879 (in Levy 1991, 70). A century later, the controversy that erupted over Kurt Waldheim's Nazi past (during his cam-paign for the Austrian presidency) could be ex-plained away by some people with the claim that Jews ruled American politics through "money and headlines." Between these two instances, Hitler declared that the battle against the Jewish press was bound to "reveal the entire spirit of materialism," in order that once again "the common good" could stand above "naked egoism."

For antisemites, the Jewish embodiment of money and the press operated as a perfect exam-ple of modern society. Newspapers mediated in-formation. Money mediated universal acts of ex-change in a capitalist economic system. Both media epitomize what is distinctive about mod-ern society. Using these media gives rise to the modern experience: society is impersonally con-stituted. The newspaper symbolized the "new tempo of the era. . . . He who was intent upon rootedness and duration damned the newspaper as evil, the enemy of all true culture" (Mosse 1975, 212). Antisemites pitted against this enemy an imaginary "Community of the Race" in which individuals and interests were not ne-gotiated through the Jew-dominated media but rather directly expressed, understood, and valued because they were expressions of common descent, history, customs, convictions, and feelings. Therefore, the battle against the Jewish press became part of a campaign against materialistic, modern, pluralist society itself. Its countermodel was a "traditional" community that never, in fact, existed, the modern invention of antimodernists.

—*Klaus Holz*

Richard S. Levy, translation

See also **Antisemitic Correspondence;** Aryanization; Drumont, Édouard; Fritsch, Theodor; *Handbook of the Jewish Question;* Hitler, Adolf; Holocaust Denial, Negationism, and Revisionism; Marr, Wilhelm; Nazi Cultural Antisemitism; Nazi Legal Measures against Jews; Stoecker, Adolf; Treitschke, Heinrich von; Waldheim Affair

References
Cobet, Christoph. *Der Wortschatz des Antisemitismus in der Bismarckzeit* (Munich, Germany: W. Fink, 1973).

Fritsch, Theodor. *Der jüdische Zeitungs-Polyp* (Leipzig, Germany: Hammer, 1923).

Holz, Klaus. *Nationaler Antisemitismus: Wissenssoziologie einer Weltanschauung* (Hamburg, Germany: Hamburger Edition, 2001).

Levy, Richard S., ed. *Antisemitism in the Modern World: An Anthology of Texts* (Lexington, MA: D. C. Heath, 1991).

Mosse, George. *The Nationalization of the Masses* (New York: New American Library, 1975).

Jewish Question

In a very general sense, a Jewish question existed in Christian Europe since at least the Middle Ages. In modern times, the specific phrase *the* Jewish Question has been used in a general, often imprecise way. However, beginning in the mid-eighteenth century, something more specific and historically unique was increasingly meant by it: should Jews be granted civil equality, repealing the often humiliating special laws under which they lived? This more precise question had, at the same time, wide-ranging implications, principal among them the issue of how much Jews, once emancipated from discriminatory laws, could be expected to blend into the peoples of Europe, participating with equal rights and dignity in the society and culture of the new and old nation-states of the nineteenth century.

The Jewish Question may be placed in the company of a number of widely debated issues, such as the Woman Question or the Social Question, that emerged in response to modern times. Indeed, the Social Question and the Jewish Question overlapped, in that the perceived threat of exploitation and corruption by Jews of non-Jews in an emerging "free" or capitalist economy became a key theme of the Jewish Question. The growing confidence in the progress of enlightenment and toleration meant that many contemporaries believed these questions had rational answers and political solutions.

It soon became evident, however, that solutions to the Jewish Question would be long in coming. By the early twentieth century, the noted British author and editor of the *Times* of London, Henry Wickham Steed, expressed a widespread sentiment in terming the Jewish Question "one of the greatest problems in the world." He believed that no one "can be considered mature until he has striven to face it squarely on its merits" (Lindemann 1997, ix). That many Jews regarded Steed's own conclusions to be hostile at the same time that many non-Jews accused him of being pro-Jewish suggests the extent to which discussions of the Jewish Question frequently resembled a dialogue of the deaf.

The bewildering complexities and ostensibly irreconcilable aspects of the Jewish Question were many. Jewish self-definition over centuries and millennia as "a people apart" ran counter to the ideals of citizenship in a modern state. If the identity of Europe's Jews was linked to their claims to be the descendants of the ancient Israelites or if their intricate laws and customs were to be considered an essential part of their religion, how could they embrace the laws and cultural identities of other peoples without abandoning that religion? Even more, if Jews thought of themselves as chosen by God for a special destiny and commanded by Him to remain separate from other nations (*goyim*), how could they entertain notions of equality within those nations?

Christian self-definition, similarly, involved deep-rooted attitudes toward Jews that made equality with them seemingly inconceivable: Jews were non-European "outsiders," wandering under a divine punishment and ineradicably different in nature (or "race"). Even liberal non-Jews typically regarded Jews as deceitful, fanatically separatist, and physically degenerate. For such liberals, the Jewish Question had to do, first of all, with how to "improve" or "civilize" them, so that they might eventually become responsible and useful members of a modern state and society. Although many on the Left favored religious toleration and expressed sympathy for Jews as victims of Christian oppression in the past, very few were interested in tolerating the Jews in their present condition. On both the Right and the Left, non-Jews expressed concerns that a "rise" of the Jews (especially as capitalists), without a fundamental reform on their part, would lead to destructive results in society as a whole.

In a remarkable outpouring of books, pamphlets, and other pronouncements, a wide array of solutions to the Jewish Question were proposed, ranging from assimilation, which usually implied an eventual disappearance of a separate Jewish identity, to various Jewish nationalist positions toward the end of the century, including Zionism, which looked to a physical separation of Jews from non-Jews. What came to be called antisemitism by the 1880s represented another solution, demanding the de-emancipation of the Jews and, in some instances, their segregation from non-Jews. Of course, from the beginning, strict traditionalists, whether Christian or Jewish, questioned the wisdom or feasibility of changing the premodern legal and social isolation of the Jews.

In very broad national and geographic terms, two contrasting approaches to the Jewish Question emerged, the French and the Russian. (A third might be distinguished in the United States, where the Jewish Question did not arise, in the most limited sense of the term, because the nation's founding constitution already granted Jews civil equality.) The French approach most directly reflected the sweeping egalitarianism of the Enlightenment. In late 1791, after nearly two years of acrimonious debates in the revolutionary National Assembly, civil equality was granted to France's approximately 40,000 Jews, roughly 0.2 percent of the total population. In the immediately following years, France's revolutionary armies conquered large areas of central and southern Europe, emancipating Jews as they went.

In 1806, the Emperor Napoleon, responding to complaints that Jews were not, in fact, reforming, obtained from the specially convoked Assembly of Jewish Notables a formal affirmation that French Jews were committed to embracing modern citizenship, as well as French nationality. In so doing, the assembly ignored or radically reinterpreted a significant part of the beliefs and practices that had long been part of the identity of Europe's Jews. A highly centralized state linked to the ideal of "integral nationalism" meant that French language and culture were to be adopted by all citizens, with little or no recognition of what would later be termed *hyphenated* or *multicultural* identities for "minorities" in France.

The situation of Jews in the backward and despotic Russian Empire was fundamentally different and far more complex, in part because of the vast territories ruled by the tsars; the empire's heterogeneous population; and the large, rapidly growing numbers of Jews there, who numbered approximately 1.5 million at the beginning of the century and 5 million by its end. Constituting the overwhelming majority of the Jews in Europe, the Jews of the Russian Empire were also known to be the poorest and most "uncivilized" of any country. Feelings of national identity were less developed than in the West, for both non-Jews and Jews, and Russia's leaders felt threatened by and remained deeply suspicious of western European models. Offering all Russian subjects civil rights on the French model was, to say the least, not even considered. However, as the nineteenth century progressed, especially during the reign of the reforming Tsar Alexander II (1855–1881), tsarist officials discussed the pros and cons of offering favored segments of the Jewish population greater legal equality, particularly those few who learned Russian and acquired a modern education, rendering them useful to the state. But there was much uncertainty, inefficiency, and hypocrisy in tsarist policy; it lurched over the course of the century from relatively benevolent efforts to "improve" the Jews to increasingly impatient and malevolent efforts to combat what officials perceived as the stubborn resistance to Russification by the overwhelming majority of the Jewish population, as well as the Jews' destructive competition and corruption of the Christian population, especially the peasantry. By the last decades of the nineteenth century, Jews began to emigrate from Russia by the hundreds of thousands and ultimately millions. This mass exodus was a reaction to economic hardship as well as popular violence and legal harassment, but clearly, both tsarist leaders and a growing part of Russia's Jewish population concluded that a humane and reasonable solution to the Jewish Question was no longer feasible.

In the neighboring Habsburg Empire, another multinational realm and second only to tsarist Russia in the number and proportion of Jews within its borders, long discussions of the Jewish Question finally led to the granting of civil equality in 1867. At the same time, there was little pressure on Jews by Habsburg authorities to cast off, on the French model, the national element of their Jewish identity. However, significant numbers of Jews in the Habsburg Empire enthusiastically embraced the language and culture, especially the high culture, of the Germans and Magyars. Similarly, Jewish relations with the Habsburg authorities were notably more harmonious than was the case in Russia. Still, a Jewish Question remained, in that hostility toward Jews in the form of political antisemitism grew into a major issue, as the election of the antisemitic Karl Lueger as mayor of Vienna (from 1897 to 1910) demonstrated. It was not accidental that Theodor Herzl, the founder of modern Zionism, grew up in Budapest and made his career as a journalist in Vienna.

The French model was particularly problematic for Germans, in that, especially after the French Revolution, they tended to define themselves in opposition to the French. The divided German states in the early nineteenth century dealt variously with the Jewish Question but generally preferred a cautious and an incremental approach in regard to civil equality for Jews. At the same time and somewhat paradoxically, the culture and intellectual life of this "philosophical people" gave evidence of a spectacularly productive blending or symbiosis with Jews, in the sense that modern Jewish genius blossomed in German-speaking lands, including much of the Habsburg Empire, as nowhere else. Similarly, the Jewish Question—*Die Judenfrage*—was perhaps most influentially and penetratingly explored by German-language thinkers, Jewish and gentile, in the late eighteenth and early nineteenth centuries; nearly all major German thinkers composed reflections on the issue. Full civil equality for German Jews came with the formation of the German Reich in 1871, but in that reich, as in the Habsburg Empire, popular hostility in the form of modern political antisemitism soon arose to challenge the granting of civil equality to the Jews and to spread alarm about what they perceived as rising Jewish power economically, socially, culturally, and politically.

In general, the initial optimism in western and central Europe about eventually solving the Jewish Question gave way, by the mid-1870s, to a growing pessimism, paralleling skepticism about Enlightened ideals. Such was true even in France, where, at the turn of the century, the hatred that erupted against Jews during the Dreyfus Affair sent shock waves throughout Europe. Even deeper gloom about the likelihood of a rational and humane solution to the Jewish Question emerged after the catastrophic decade of war and revolution between 1914 and 1924. There were, to be sure, some briefly hopeful stretches following the end of the war, with the convening of the Paris Peace Conference in 1919. For a few years, the Weimar Republic seemed to offer hope, but it soon collapsed, and the Nazis came to power. The fall of the tsars and the civil equality granted Jews in the Soviet Union, again, at first seemed to promise a resolution of the Jewish Question, but in practice, communism turned out to be anything but rational or humane for Jews or any of those living under its rule. Moreover, the antisemitic specter of Judeo-Bolshevism and Marxist world revolution, awakened by the birth of the Soviet regime, further aggravated fantasies of Jewish conspiracies and plans to rule the world.

After World War II and the Holocaust, the specific term *the Jewish Question* came to have a dated feel, in part, no doubt, because Jews had achieved formal civil equality in all of Europe. Similarly, the more elusive issues of Jewish social and cultural adaptation became somewhat less divisive because of a growing tolerance of the concept of Jewish separateness, related to a more sympathetic understanding of Jewish religious tradition. A Jewish state was created in 1948, with its own claims to a solution of the Jewish Question, and in the United States, Jews prospered and felt at home as never before in history—a particularly significant development because of the power of the United States and because it replaced Russia as the country with the largest population of Jews in the world.

Insofar as the Jewish Question retained an urgency in the second half of the twentieth century, it was often reformulated in terms of the persistence of antisemitism and of hostile attitudes toward the state of Israel (the two often being linked). Also subtly linked to earlier discussions of the Jewish Question was a rising alarm, especially by the last decades of the century, that "too friendly" environments, the American in first place, were leading to the disappearance of Jews through voluntary assimilation into surrounding gentile societies. The various partial solutions to the Jewish Question after World War II were all deeply diminished by the trauma of the Nazi Final Solution and, until the collapse of the Soviet Union and its satellites, by the continued, if more covert, persecution of Jews on the other side of the Iron Curtain. Another area of rising concern by the end of the century was the extent to which the antisemitic reaction to the Jewish Question in Europe had been taken up by the Arab and Muslim world.

—*Albert S. Lindemann*

See also Alsace; Austria; Dohm, Christian Wilhelm von; Emancipation; France; Herzl, Theodor; Hungary; Infamous Decree; Islam and the Jews; *Jewish Question, The;* Judeo-Bolshevism; Lueger, Karl; Marx, Karl; May Laws; Pale of Settlement; Philosemitism; Pogroms; USSR; Wandering Jew; Zionism

References

Auerbach, Rena R., ed. *The "Jewish Question" in German Speaking Countries, 1848–1914: A Bibliography* (New York: Garland, 1994).

Bein, Alex. *The Jewish Question: Biography of a World Problem* (Rutherford, NJ: Fairleigh Dickinson University Press, 1990).

Erspamer, Peter R. *The Elusiveness of Tolerance: The "Jewish Question" from Lessing to the Napoleonic Wars* (Chapel Hill: University of North Carolina Press, 1997).

Klier, John D. *Imperial Russia's Jewish Question, 1855–1881* (Cambridge: Cambridge University Press, 1995).

Lindemann, Albert S. *Esau's Tears: Modern Anti-Semitism and the Rise of the Jews* (Cambridge: Cambridge University Press, 1997).

Ungvári, Tamás. *The "Jewish Question" in Europe: The Case of Hungary* (Boulder, CO: Atlantic Research and Publications, 2000).

Jewish Question, The (1843)

In response to the public controversy concerning the legal status of Prussian Jewry, Bruno Bauer first published *The Jewish Question* (*Die Judenfrage*) in the leading Young Hegelian periodical *Deutsche Jahrbücher für Wissenschaft und Kunst* (German Yearbook for Scholarship and Art) in November 1842. He then added a seventh section before publishing the essay separately early in 1843.

Bauer claimed that the entire issue of Jewish emancipation had been wrongly understood. Jews, as Jews, were not capable of being emancipated, nor was a Christian state capable of emancipating either Jews or Christians. By appealing to the Christian state for equality, the Jews were in effect legitimizing it and thus subverting the cause of general emancipation. To facilitate *genuine* emancipation, the state and the individual alike would have to forgo their religious orientation. Ultimately, both would need to avow an active atheism. This "conflation of right and morality" that turned "a legal act into an act of conscience" was to form one of the main points of departure for the critique subsequently directed against *The Jewish Question,* most famously by Karl Marx (Moggach 2003, 148).

Although it is true that Bauer's vision was predicated on the demise of both Judaism and Christianity, he nevertheless portrayed Christianity as an advance over Judaism. Christianity had radicalized the implications of Judaism and thus predisposed its adherents toward emancipation. Even the forms of prejudice Christians still maintained were preferable to those he attributed to the Jews. Bauer denounced the shortcomings of the Jews in far greater detail and with inordinately more bile and passion than he mustered for any of his critical remarks on Christianity.

Bauer's contentions were not derived from

empirical evidence but reflected a philosophical deduction that demonstrated rather dramatically the use to which a reductionist reading of the Hegelian notion of Judaism's obsolescence could be put. By its very existence, postbiblical Jewry had set itself not only against the course of historical development, Bauer argued, but also against any potential for perfection that might have inhered in biblical Judaism. Jewry was not even capable of providing a comprehensive account of its own essence because in order to do so, it would have to perceive of itself as the precursor of Christianity. Bauer's adherence to Hegelian thought was clearly only perfunctory and self-serving at this point in his intellectual development. He conceded, for instance, that Judaism, too, had once represented a truth, only to add the dismissive remark, "But how many truths has history come up with since!" (Bauer, *Judenfrage*, 81). The Hegelian notion of historical Judaism as a partial representation of truth valid in its own time was utterly overdetermined by Bauer's fixation on its obsolescence.

Perhaps the most portentous notion Bauer developed in *The Jewish Question* was that of an insurmountable chasm between the (chimerical) Jewish nationality and all other (real) nations. This conception would seem to prefigure the way in which modern antisemitism tends to treat Jewry—not as another nation but as the negation of the national principle itself. Yet *The Jewish Question* was by no means Bauer's most crucial contribution to the emergence of modern antisemitism. His later, thoroughly post-Hegelian, and overtly antisemitic pronouncements would play a far more influential and innovative role.

—*Lars Fischer*

See also Bauer, Bruno; Christian State; Emancipation; Jewish Question; *Judaism as an Alien Phenomenon;* Marx, Karl; Young Hegelians

References

Leopold, David. "The Hegelian Antisemitism of Bruno Bauer," *History of European Ideas* 25 (1999): 179–206.

Moggach, Douglas. *The Philosophy and Politics of Bruno Bauer* (Cambridge: Cambridge University Press, 2003).

Rotenstreich, Nathan. "For and Against Emancipation: The Bruno Bauer Controversy," *Leo Baeck Institute Year Book* 4 (1959): 3–36.

Jewish Question as a Racial, Moral, and Cultural Problem, The

Eugen Dühring published *The Jewish Question as a Racial, Moral, and Cultural Problem* (*Die Judenfrage als Rassen-, Sitten- und Kulturfrage*) in November 1880, not in 1881 as the title page falsely stated. The timing was not incidental. The market for antisemitic literature in and beyond Berlin had been greatly enlarged by the interventions of Heinrich von Treitschke and Court Chaplain Adolf Stoecker during the so-called Berlin antisemitism controversy already under way when Dühring entered the fray. The stated purpose of Dühring's own intervention, which appeared in multiple revised editions (1881, 1886, 1892, 1901, 1930), was to demonstrate what he understood to be the proven harmfulness and intolerability of the Jewish race.

Dühring asserted that all the deeds of the Jews revealed a "primordial, tribally inherited evil" (1886, foreword and elsewhere). "In service to their deity," they "murder individuals of the better races." Mixing in their Jewish blood through marriage, they "make worse and spoil" other peoples (1880, 141). He demanded repeatedly that "modern nations of better racial character" take "drastic measures" to rescue themselves from the Jews (later, he preferred the term *Hebrews*). He wanted Jews who had converted to Christianity to be treated exactly like those who had not. Dühring thus distinguished himself from "Christian" antisemites who held out some hope that the negative traits of Jewry could be cured through baptism. In the Nazi era, he was celebrated in the late Theodor Fritsch's journal as the "German father of racial thinking" (*Hammer* 1937, 36).

In fact, the Nazis' praise was not misplaced, for the biological vocabulary militant antisemites came to favor was already present in Dühring's work. In every successive edition of *The Jewish Question* the author outdid himself in the use of similes and metaphors designed to dehumanize Jews: they were, for example, described as beasts of prey, snakes, vermin, parasites, and poisonous growths. Joseph Goebbels followed his lead, comparing Jews to the potato blight; Heinrich Himmler thought ridding Germany of the "lice" (Jews) would constitute a sanitation measure. Dühring reinforced the rejection of Jews with constant assurances that all their characteristics were racially inherited and therefore immutable.

In general, he proceeded by converting his assertions into unquestionable facts. Thus, he identified being human with being "Aryan," drawing the further conclusion that "the better sort of humankind has . . . the right to eradicate the racially harmful" (Dühring, *Personalist und Emancipator,* 282; and elsewhere). He arrived at this sort of extremism gradually and relatively late in life. Although always inclined to "the language of hardness," he at first suggested more moderate-sounding "practical solutions" to the Jewish Question—for example, a legal declaration stating that "no person of Jewish descent may practice public instruction" (1880, 140ff). Neither should they be allowed to serve as judges or in civil administration. Year by year, however, he advanced to more radical solutions to the Jewish Question. Limiting measures, such as internment, population reduction, and segregation, eventually gave way to demands for expulsion and then for extermination and annihilation (*ausrotten und vernichten*).

Dühring never employed the term *Final Solution,* but he demanded repeatedly that the "world be relieved in a fundamental way from the Jewish essence" and that the Jewish Question be "conclusively solved," even if this required the use of weapons (1901, 134ff).

—*Birgitta Mogge-Stubbe*
Richard S. Levy, translation

See also Dühring, Eugen; Jewish Question; National Socialist German Workers' Party; Stoecker, Adolf; Treitschke, Heinrich von

References

Cobet, Christoph. *Der Wortschatz des Antisemitismus in der Bismarckzeit* (Munich, Germany: Fink, 1973).

Jakubowski, Jeanette. "Eugen Dühring: Antisemit, Antifeminist und Rassist." In *Historische Rassismusforschung. Ideologen—Täter—Opfer.* Edited by Barbara Dancwortt, Thorsten Querg, Claudia Schöningh, Wolfgang Wippermann (Hamburg, Germany: Argument, 1995).

Jews and the German State, The (1861)

One of the few overtly antisemitic works of the 1860s, *The Jews and the German State* (*Die Juden und der deutsche Staat*) by H. Naudh went through twelve constantly revised editions by 1892. Theodor Fritsch's Hammer press issued this "classic" of antisemitism for the last time in 1920. H. Naudh was the pseudonym for a shadowy Berlin writer named Johannes Nordmann, who also contributed pamphlets and essays to Wilhelm Marr's *Deutsche Wacht* (German Watch) and Fritsch's *Antisemitic Correspondence.* Fritsch questioned Naudh/Nordmann's authorship of the book, alleging that he received extensive help in both content and style from Lothar Bucher, Otto von Bismarck's collaborator, and Hermann Wagener, a high-ranking member of the Prussian Conservative Party and former editor of its newspaper, the *Kreuzzeitung.* If true, the work would gain historical significance as evidence of the existence of antisemitic views among individuals close to the levers of power in Prussia.

The Jews and the German State took an unequivocal stand against Jewish emancipation, even before it became law (between 1869 and 1871). Jews, according to Naudh, had no right to rule over Germans and should be excluded from holding public office. He built his case on the Talmud and the Bible, asserting that they constituted a theocratic political constitution in which civil law and religious law were one and the same (Naudh 1920, 12). The German state, he warned, "may not ignore the moral content of an alien, peculiar religion, nor can it overlook the existence of a foreign race that embodies dogmas that endanger the commonwealth" (6). Jewish law rendered "all other peoples the objects of their robbery and exploitation" (29), he said, and "in the hands of the Jews every question becomes a money-question" (43). Naudh doubted that assimilation was possible because "no nation clung to its peculiarities as stubbornly as the Jews" (27). They constituted a state-within-a-state. "For the time being," he conceded grudgingly, Jews would have to be tolerated in the private sphere (20).

Going beyond his scriptural interpretation of Judaism, Naudh also argued on the basis of racial theory, history, anthropology, and "physiognomy" to make his case that Jews were objectionable due to their physical characteristics. Like Marr and many others, he subscribed to the notion that Jews were incapable of physical labor. The well-established stereotype of the dangerously beautiful Jewess also appeared in his musings. Germans and Jews represented opposite, antagonistic poles. Germans belonged to the noblest branch of the Indo-Germans, whereas Jews, even among their Semitic brothers, were regarded as the "ignoblest offspring of the family" (28). Not surprisingly, Naudh was a champion of the "Aryan Christ" (42).

The conclusions drawn in the book were not immediately consequential in the 1860s, but many of the conceptions presented there inspired the development of antisemitic politics later in the century. Naudh claimed that the state was an expression of a national personality (*Volkspersönlichkeit*) and that national feeling formed the basis of *Volk* (people) and state. States without a uniform nationality base inevitably had to perish. Jews living in Germany did not belong to the German state; they were "only German-speaking Jews, not Jewish Germans" (20–25). In 1861, before German unification, Naudh prophesied that a German state whose institutions and administration allowed Jews to "nest" within them "would go to ruin like a house beset by fungus" (8). The foreword to the 1878 edition confirmed that his fears had now been realized: "the Jewish Reich of the German nation" had come into being with remarkable speed, and the decline of the Germans could be dated from that time forth (10).

—*Matthias Brosch*
Richard S. Levy, translation

See also *Antisemitic Correspondence;* Antisemitic Political Parties; Fritsch, Theodor; *Judaism as an Alien Phenomenon;* Marr, Wilhelm; State-within-a-State; Wagener, Hermann

References
Naudh, H. [Johannes Nordmann]. *Die Juden und der deutsche Staat.* 13th rev. ed. (Leipzig, Germany: Hammer Verlag, 1920).

Jews' Beech, The (1842)

The critical controversy surrounding *The Jew's Beech* (*Die Judenbuche*), a canonical novella by Annette von Droste-Hülshoff, Germany's foremost woman author of the classical period, has a great deal to do with the expectations brought to the work. If one rigorously observes historical context, then one must concede that even the most pronounced anti-Jewish bigotry (expressed by a leading character, Margreth) seems relatively muted compared to the antisemitic rhetoric of the day. Yet its canonical status means that this story has been specially selected from its many contemporaries—that is, explicitly dehistoricized—for its supposed power to edify and convey the transcendent values of German *Kultur*. Particularly in the post–World War II period, critics have turned to this novella as a beacon of moral guidance for its alleged font of Judeo-Christian values. This task considerably overtaxes the novella and has called forth fundamental reassessments.

The Jews' Beech retells the story of an actual murder of a Jew, and due, in part, to the author's reliance on a historical chronicle of that event, it has been ascribed to the realist tradition. Yet it is clearly a Christian morality tale in its broader ambition (if not its final execution), and this design explains the author's numerous additions and alterations to her source material, including a parallel plot in which the failure of superstitious Christians to rise to their religious calling is coded as "Jewish." The plot traces the troubled career of a young shepherd boy named Friedrich, who borrows money from the Jew Aaron to buy an expensive silver watch. When Friedrich cannot repay the loan—he is publicly humiliated at a village wedding—there is a violent altercation, and Aaron is later found dead. Friedrich and his look-alike bastard cousin, John Nobody (Johannes Niemand), take flight that evening. They are not seen again until a quarter century later when, after sundry misadventures, including years in Turkish slavery, one of them—we do not know which—returns to the village as an old man. Within a year, he is found hanging in the beech tree, which the Jewish community had bought from the Squire and inscribed with a retributive "Hebrew charm" (Brown 1978) to commemorate the theretofore unresolved murder of Aaron. On the basis of dubious evidence, the Squire proclaims the decomposing corpse to be that of Friedrich, prompting many readers to affirm the mysterious efficacy of the Jew's beech tree in obtaining justice for the wronged Jew. For not a few critics, this bespeaks a deep moral order within a seemingly chaotic universe.

In defense of the novella, Droste-Hülshoff's best-known work in an oeuvre that comprises mainly poetry, critics have pointed out that the depiction of the Jewish community is actually respectful, that the social position and characterization of specific Jewish figures (Aaron, Aaron's wife, the generic "Lumpenmoises" and "Wucherjoel") are historically accurate or nearly so, and that even Margreth's antisemitic outburst might be viewed as something the author wished to critique rather than endorse. Although the first two points may be true and the third is at least debatable, all of this misses the fundamental anti-Judaic polemic that structures this tale. If Droste-Hülshoff failed to endorse crass antisemitism à la Margreth, she made the Jews the easy villains and thereby enabled her Christian target audience to overlook its own "Jewish" vices. Throughout the novella, Christians are taught to recognize their shortcomings by means of negative Jewish exemplars that are then applied to Christians. When Aaron interrupts the Christian wedding to demand repayment, we witness the incursion of the material into the spiritual. Shortly thereafter, the narrator exposes the wedding itself—a mismatched union of a beautiful young girl with a wealthy older man—to be little more than a matter of business (*ein Geschäft*). Similarly, the injustice of unbridled timber poaching practiced under the cover of night by the infamous blue shirts (*Blaukittel*) is explained by linking it with the better-known "Jewish" practice of usury. It may be tempting to see in this indictment of Christians *as Jews* a conciliatory dissolution of distinctions, but that would be mistaken. Droste-Hülshoff's thoroughgoing critique of modernity, secular rationalism, and legalism as "Judaized" and therefore inferior to Christian inwardness depended very much on upholding the religious dichotomy. What perhaps rescues this extraordinary novella from the precincts of predictable religious didactic literature is the crisis of faith reflected in the final suicide, where the unidentified returnee misconstrues (or cannot accept) Christ's sacrifice and therefore kills himself. Here, the conservative Catholic author shifted from her overriding suggestion that there was something wrong with Christians—namely, their residual and atavistic "Jewish" behavior—to the brief but profound consideration that there was something inherently amiss within Christianity itself (Donahue 1999).

The recent interest in recovering and celebrating literary "foremothers" has prevented some critics from admitting this darker side to the tale and to the author herself. Droste-Hülshoff was a garden-variety antisemite, who once said of the radical Young German author and journalist Heinrich Laube, "If he's not a Jew, then he deserves to be one" (Letter to Luise Bornstedt, February 2, 1839, cited in Donahue 1999, 44). (He was not, in fact, a Jew.) But for Droste-Hülshoff, the term *Jew* designated that which needed to be redeemed or at least overcome—a notion repeatedly conveyed in her most celebrated work.

—*William Collins Donahue*

See also Arndt, Ernst Moritz; Bauer, Bruno; Heine, Heinrich; *Jewish Question, The;* Riehl, Wilhelm Heinrich; Young Germany
References
Brown, Jane K. "The Real Mystery in Droste-Hülshoff's *Die Judenbuche*," *Modern Language Review* 73 (1978): 835–846.
Donahue, William Collins. "'Ist er kein Jude, so verdiente er einer zu sein': Droste-Hülshoff's *Die Judenbuche* and Religious Anti-Semitism," *German Quarterly* 72 (1999): 44–73.

Jud Süss (Joseph ben Issachar Süsskind Oppenheimer), (1692–1738)

The personality and career of Joseph ben Issachar Süsskind Oppenheimer, known as Jud Süss, received a great deal of attention from eighteenth-century contemporaries and a variety of twentieth-century polemicists, historians, and antisemites. Süss became an influential court factor and financial adviser to Duke Karl Alexander of Württemberg. Appointed state counselor in 1732, he directed financial affairs and implemented a series of policies to develop the treasury, create significant economic monopolies, and increase the duke's power and revenues. In these activities, he appears to have imitated the practices of his non-Jewish noble contemporaries, and he is generally portrayed as having

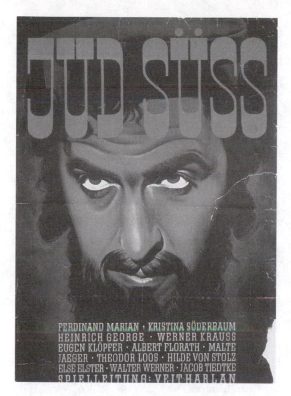

Poster advertisement for German motion picture, showing head of bearded Jewish man. (Corbis)

strayed far from Jewish observance, unsuccessfully attempting to obtain noble status. His personal life, as distinct from his professional life, has also traditionally been presented in a rather negative light. With the sudden death of his benefactor in March 1737, Süss was arrested, charged with treason and embezzlement. His property was confiscated, and he was sentenced to death. Offered the opportunity to convert and save his life, he instead opted to return to formal Jewish observance and piety, a move for which he has been positively remembered by some historians. He was beheaded in a public spectacle.

On the one hand, the personal activities of Süss need to be separated from his status as a Jew. Süss succeeded in amassing power and wealth and at the same time alienated many people because of his reputed extravagance and harsh policies. On the other hand, his visible position combined with his Jewishness to foster and exacerbate anti-Jewish sentiment. Duke Karl Alexander's Protestant opponents in the Landtag (state par-

liament) accused Süss of having a lust for power and pursuing deliberately anti-Christian policies.

Portrayed as a villain by most of his contemporaries, Süss also found some more favorable or at least ambivalent treatment in his own day. This "for and against" interpretation of the man persisted into the twentieth century. In 1925, Lion Feuchtwanger published a historical novel about Süss that became a best-seller in the 1930s, with some 200,000 German copies and translation into more than fifteen languages. Feuchtwanger used Süss's story to address some of his own concerns and as a means to combat the antisemitism of Weimar Germany. Nazi propaganda, predictably, made far different use of the man's life and personality. *Jud Süss,* the inflammatory film by Veit Harlan (in 1940), was one of only a few overtly antisemitic films released by the Nazis. In it, a wholly loathsome Süss is portrayed not only as an abuser of power and exploiter of honest Germans but also as a sexual predator. As with many figures in Jewish history, Jud Süss has had a long and complicated part in the chronicles of antisemitism.

—*Dean Phillip Bell*

See also Court Jews; Film Propaganda, Nazi; Weimar

References

Meyer, Michael A., Michael Brenner, Mordechai Breuer, and Michael Graetz, eds. *German-Jewish History in Modern Times* 4 vols., especially vol. 1, *Tradition and Enlightenment: 1600–1780.* (New York: Columbia University Press, 1996).
Israel, Jonathan. *European Jewry in the Age of Mercantilism: 1550–1750.* (Oxford and London: Clarendon Press, 1998).
Stern, Selma. *Jud Süss* (Munich, Germany: G. Müller, 1973; orig. 1929).

Judaism as an Alien Phenomenon (1862–1863)

Judaism as an Alien Phenomenon (*Das Judenthum in der Fremde*), an extended essay by Bruno Bauer (1809–1882), first appeared in the Prussian Christian conservative lexicon edited by Hermann Wagener, an outspoken opponent of Jewish emancipation. In its enunciation of all the major anti-Jewish tropes, *Judaism as an Alien Phenomenon* (republished as a pamphlet in

1863) is a seminal work, with much greater influence on the politicalization of antisemitism in Germany than Bauer's better-known essay *The Jewish Question* (1843).

Bauer was an accomplished and prolific biblical scholar, historian, theologian, and philosopher. In this piece, he treated the history, religion, and character of the Jews in a magisterial but thoroughly jaundiced way. The destruction of the First Temple in 70 CE, for example, was described as nothing more than a justifiable act of defense on the part of Rome; medieval Jews were said to concentrate in commerce not because they were excluded from honest forms of livelihood but out of "physiological" necessity. Bauer contended that Jews did not even truly fathom the meaning of their own Talmud and what he considered its unfailingly vengeful nature because they were enthralled with the superstitious veneration of apocryphal rabbinic names (Bauer, *Judenfrage,* 12). As in his 1843 essay that provoked Karl Marx, Bauer still insisted in the 1860s that Judaism was a dead religion that rendered its tribal adherents incapable of creative labor in the arts or sciences and drove a wedge between them and the "general flow of life." The notable difference between this essay and the earlier one was that it reduced every despicable feature in the history of the Jews to an unalterable set of malevolent racial characteristics.

How, then, did Bauer account for the contributions of modern Jews to European culture and politics? Restless and uncertain by nature, inherently dissatisfied with the status quo, Jews mastered only the outward signs of culture, he argued; their cultural products were derivative and worthless (629). Embittered and filled with rancor (*Groll*), they latched onto political movements not out of any idealism but to enrich themselves, dominate others, and move toward world domination (Bauer 1862, 614). He explained their participation in the revolutions of 1848 as a racially conditioned love of anarchy and the shameless "hot pursuit of high offices of state" (667). All this—and the Jewish Question in general—was made possible by the naïveté, weakness, and intellectual laziness of Christians: parasites only thrived on a weak host (623, 629, 666). These themes and many others were picked up by admiring antisemitic ideologues, especially Wilhelm Marr and Eugen Dühring.

Strangely, Bauer's essay offered no political solution to the problem of the Jews. In 1862, before Jews had achieved full emancipation in most of central and eastern Europe, he thought that they could not possibly hold on to whatever advantages they currently enjoyed. The "specter of Jewish domination" would inevitably awaken the threatened Christian peoples from their slumbers. Jews always miscalculated, always failed to realize that their arrogance and greed would drive their hosts to crush their impertinence. Their history was full of such reversals, and another, Bauer confidently predicted, was in the offing (619, 670–671).

—*Richard S. Levy*

See also Bauer, Bruno; Dühring, Eugen; Emancipation; *Jewish Question, The;* Marr, Wilhelm; Marx, Karl; Talmud; Wagener, Hermann; Young Hegelians

References

Bauer, Bruno. "Das Judenthum in der Fremde." In *Neues Conversations-Lexikon. Staats- und Gesellschafts-Lexikon.* Edited by Hermann Wagener (Berlin, 1862): 10: 614-692.

Moggach, Douglas. *The Philosophy and Politics of Bruno Bauer* (Cambridge: Cambridge University Press, 2003).

Judaism in Music (1850, 1869)

Judaism in Music, an essay by German composer Richard Wagner (1813–1883), first appeared in the *Neue Zeitschrift für Musik* (New Journal for Music) in 1850 under the pseudonym K. Freigedank ("free thinking"). It was reissued in 1869 with the author's real name and came out thereafter in several new editions. It was also translated into French (in 1850), Italian (in 1897), and English (in 1898). The essay started out as an attack on the unnamed composer Giacomo Meyerbeer and grew into a diatribe against the alleged destructiveness of all Jewish influence in contemporary European culture. Wagner at first chose to exclude the piece from an edition of his collected writings but later included it.

The ideas in this essay were largely in line with other contemporary reactions against Jewish emancipation that exaggerated the supposed threats to German culture posed by Jews' successes in the arts. Wagner argued that "the Jew" had been held back from contributing to true German art because of his language and cultural background but in recent times had managed to influence European culture, owing to the latter's inherent weakening. Despite the poisonous tone of much of the essay, Wagner did not, in the end, suggest that the Jew be excluded from a thriving German cultural life, and he even proposed that the Jew could overcome his cultural inferiority, albeit not through religious conversion alone but through total assimilation and denial of self. He used the term *Untergang* (going under) to describe this process, a term that unfortunately took on more violent implications in later twentieth-century interpretations of the text.

What distinguished this essay from others of its time, however, was the ambitious and elaborate exploration of supposed Jewish traits, some of which could be tied to physical characteristics. Presuming that Germans harbored a "natural revulsion" toward the Jews, Wagner referred to the Jews' "unpleasantly foreign" physical appearance and launched into a lengthy examination of Jewish speech, claiming that Jews could never acquire fluency in modern European languages. He detailed the "repulsiveness" of Jewish speech tones and claimed that Jews were unable to engage in meaningful dialogue or express deep emotions. Jews, in Wagner's view, nevertheless managed to dominate the musical world, and he attributed their success to the relative ease by which musical style can be imitated, leaving it vulnerable to Jewish appropriation. He argued that such Jewish "imitations" were doomed to failure, however, since Jews could only draw on sterile and outmoded synagogue chants for inspiration. He claimed to identify such emotional emptiness and superficiality in the works of Felix Mendelssohn and the unnamed Meyerbeer.

Wagner's views never quite crossed over into identifying the Jews as a distinct race, and he endorsed a process of redemption by which Jews such as Ludwig Börne had supposedly freed themselves from their burdensome legacy. Nevertheless, the explicit descriptions of Jewish traits that could be linked to physical characteristics,

the ambiguity of the term *Untergang* as the solution to the Jewish "problem," the evocation of biological metaphors—he referred to Jewish-dominated German music as a "worm-infested corpse"—and the violent recommendation for "the forceful ejection of this destructive foreign element" that he put forth but immediately rejected as impracticable in the preface to the 1869 reissue all served as fodder for later arguments promoting racial antisemitism and, ultimately, the extermination of European Jewry.

—*Pamela M. Potter*

See also Emancipation; Marr, Wilhelm; Masculinity; Musicology and National Socialism; *Verjudung*; Wagner, Richard

References

Fischer, Jens Malte. *Richard Wagner's "Das Judentum in der Musik": Eine kritische Dokumentation als Beitrag zur Geschichte des Antisemitismus* (Frankfurt am Main, Germany: Insel Verlag, 2000).

Katz, Jacob. *The Darker Side of Genius: Richard Wagner's Anti-Semitism* (Hanover, NH and London: Brandeis University Press, 1986).

Wagner, Richard. "Judaism in Music." In *Richard Wagner—Stories and Essays*. Edited by Charles Osborne (London: Owen, 1973), 23–39.

Judensau

The *Judensau* (Jew's pig) was an image that depicted Jews as offspring feeding from the teats of a sow. Originating in thirteenth-century Germany, it was confined almost exclusively to German-speaking lands for the next six centuries. In its origins, it was intended as a Christian allegory representing supposed Jewish gluttony (*gula*) or carnality. The literary origin is unknown, but John Chrysostom, in his infamous homilies, referred to Jews as gluttonous hogs. Over the course of the centuries, however, Judensau images intensified in their obscenity and antisemitic impact. Jews (sometimes identifiable as rabbis) were depicted holding up the sow's tail while another Jew (also occasionally identifiable as a rabbi) consumed her excrement. Often, the devil was represented, with Semitic features emphasized, superintending the proceedings with evident delight. Occasionally, this disgusting negative stereotyping was associated with another revolting image: a dead baby (frequently Simon

The *Judensau*, or Jew's Pig. This mid-fifteenth-century woodcut, portraying an image that was popular for centuries, depicts Jews sucking the teats of a monstrous pig and even licking its posterior. (The Art Archive)

of Trent [d. 1475]) with multiple puncture wounds from needles or daggers used to victimize the infant in a "ritual murder," the practice by which Jews were alleged to murder the children of gentiles in order to use their blood in unleavened bread. Such images were widely disseminated. The Judensau was represented not only on woodcuts, broadsheets, and playing cards but also on the walls of several German cathedrals and churches, including one in Wittenberg. It was there that Martin Luther dwelled bizarrely, in one of his two infamous anti-Jewish tracts, on the pig as the taproot of Jewish capacity and intelligence. Shortly thereafter, the Judensau was to be seen on the Sachsenhauser Bridge (with the corpse of a dead baby, the victim of a ritual murder) in Frankfurt am Main. Beneath the images was a caption that read: "On Maundy Thursday in the year 1475, the little child Simon [of Trent] was murdered by the Jews." J. W. Goethe, a native son of the city, remarked that what made these images astonishing was not that they were produced by private hostility but that they were "erected as a public monument."

The increasing and foul abusiveness of the iconography and its widespread dissemination and representation on ecclesiastical and secular buildings reflected the worsening of anti-Jewish attitudes in late medieval Europe, especially in the lands of the Holy Roman Empire. It also reflected the growing tendency to dehumanize Jews iconographically. Finally, one of the cruelest ironies of the image is that it depicted Jews feeding from and in some cases worshiping an animal that had always been, for them, an object of revulsion and religious prohibition.

—*Kevin Madigan*

See also Caricature, Anti-Jewish (Early); Chrysostom, John; Iconography, Christian; Luther, Martin; Pork; Ritual Murder (Medieval); Simon of Trent
References
Fabre-Vassas, Claudine. *The Singular Beast: Jews, Christians, and the Pig.* Translated by Carol Volk (New York: Columbia University Press, 1997).

Shachar, Isaiah. *The "Judensau": A Medieval Anti-Jewish Motif and Its History* (London: Warburg Institute, 1974).

Judeo-Bolshevism

The Russian Revolution of 1917 gave birth to the myth of "Jewish Bolshevism." Since then, the notion of Judeo-Bolshevism has radiated worldwide, becoming a handy tool with which to defame the Soviet system and Jews generally. The origins of the myth and its drawing power can be accounted for by the terrorism of the early days of the Soviet regime, dramatically and visibly exercised by Bolsheviks of Jewish descent—a phenomenon explainable as a result of discrimination against Jews under the tsarist autocracy but easily exploitable by antisemites. A full twenty years before the revolution, Theodor Herzl, among others, noted with regret that universal socialism acted as a lure for east European Jewish intellectuals, who often saw it as the only cure for antisemitism. That the "assimilated Reds" who exercised power in the early days of the revolution were, in Isaac Deutscher's apt description, actually "non-Jewish Jews" made little difference. To antisemites in particular, Soviet Russia could be portrayed convincingly as "Soviet Judea."

In fact, the prominence of Jewish Communists in the Third International (Comintern) and in the Cheka, the Soviet secret political police, obscured the fact that the Jewish presence was far greater in the quickly outlawed Social Revolutionary Party and in the Menshevik faction than among the Bolsheviks. But the visibility of the so-called assimilated Reds deflected attention from the reality that the great majority of bourgeois and observant Jews regarded the totalitarian Bolsheviks as a danger to their continued existence. An Odessa rabbi pronounced the anathema on Leon Trotsky and other Jewish Bolsheviks, and in Moscow, a rabbi gloomily observed, "The Trotskys make the revolutions, but the Bronsteins pay for it." (Trotsky, Vladimir Lenin's most famous "Jewish" partner, was born Lev Davidovich Bronstein.) Thanks to Jacob Sverdlov, the first president of the Soviet state, and Yakov Yurovsky, the local leader of the Cheka who personally shot Tsar Nicholas II, two Jews could be held responsible for executing the royal family. This fact had nearly the same dire consequences for the myth of Jewish Bolshevism as the fact that the Association of Militant Atheists was led first by Trotsky and then by Emelian Jaroslavski, both of Jewish descent.

Acts of anti-Christian persecution readily persuaded Christian antisemites to overlook the Bolshevik suppression of Judaism (together with its sacred language), as well as Islam. However, the advancement of Russian Jewish secular culture in the pre-Stalinist years of the Soviet state, the acceptance of the Yiddish language in law courts, and the fostering of Yiddish newspapers, publishing houses, and theaters all made it easy to denounce the Soviet regime as a "Jewish Power" (*zydovskaja vlast*).

The export of communism from the USSR reinforced the myth. To the chagrin of Jewish liberals and the Orthodox, a number of Jewish-born revolutionaries operated in the West as Bolshevik agents or fellow travelers. The communist parties they helped establish as constituent elements of the Comintern were covertly financed by Moscow. Such circumstances made it credible in the bourgeois Christian world to speak with contempt and fear of "Judeo-Bolshevism," a shorthand way of insinuating that Bolshevism was an intrinsic expression of the Jewish character. Even the occasional Jewish observer, then and now, claimed to see an "element of truth" in the formula. After 1917, a few Jewish revolutionaries, in the throes of euphoria, boasted that socialism and communism were "Jewish" products. Such loose talk and semitruths made it easy for antisemites to construct conspiracy theories and then disseminate them successfully.

According to Norman Cohn, the myth of a Jewish-communist conspiracy has become even more potent than the myth of a Jewish-Masonic conspiracy. Because the equation of Jews and communists assumed the strength of dogma in the thinking of Adolf Hitler, it has been argued that it is essential to follow the track of the myth of Judeo-Bolshevism in order to comprehend the genocide of the Jews. But it is important to remember that the notion of Judeo-Bolshevism was not the sole possession of racist antisemites. For example, the Jesuit Gustav Gundlach, writ-

This poster titled "The Eternal Jew" in faux Hebrew lettering advertised a great political exhibit in Munich (1937), designed "to strike the first blow against "Judeo-Bolshevism." Note the Russian whip (knout) and the Soviet Union tucked under the arm of the distinctly eastern European Jew. (Topham /The Image Works)

by Russian Jewish agents, sent by Moscow because they were experts in fomenting civil war. For Hitler, the fact that the Munich and Budapest soviet republics of 1919 were led by Eugene Leviné and Bela Kun, with the aid of numerous Jewish commissars, justified the claims he made about the "transitory Jew-dictatorship" in *Mein Kampf.* Before the fall of Bela Kun, which provoked a pogrom in Hungary, his government was denigrated worldwide as a "Jew-republic." Hilaire Belloc, writing in his antisemitic *The Jews* (1922), attributed Hungary's Bolshevik episode to the revolutionary leader "Cohen." In her *Secret Societies and Subversive Movements* (1924), the conspiracy expert Nesta Webster, like Belloc, distanced herself from the idea of "arcanely organized schemes," preferring to base her theory of a Jewish world plot on the primitively simple but nonetheless effective equation "Jew = Communist."

In the realm of elaborate conspiracies, the *Protocols of the Elders of Zion,* fabricated in Russia at the turn of the twentieth century, assumed major importance. The work described a sinister plot revolving around a shadowy group of Masonically organized Jews seeking, through the most demonic machinations, to achieve world domination. It was not the original edition but rather the later (post-1919) revised and often augmented versions, appearing in many languages, that had the most profound and global effects. In the world according to the *Protocols,* Trotsky and Kun could be denounced as agents of the conspiracy, "proof" that the elders of Zion actually existed.

Henry Ford's ghostwritten *The International Jew,* also translated into many languages, did not wholly subscribe to the manufactured elders. But the intricacies of the conspiracy were less important for the Freemason Ford—and for prominent Nazis, as well—than the simple equation theory. Thus, Ford branded "the Jews" as "world-Bolsheviks," who were "in overwhelming measure the instigators of the German Revolution" of 1918. He designated Bela Kun as the "Senior Red" and detected the "pan-Jewish stamp upon Red Russia." In his reworking of the *Protocols,* Alfred Rosenberg, Hitler's Baltic German Bolshevism expert, denounced "Jewish Soviet bosses"

ing in the *Lexikon for Theology and Church* in 1930, distinguished between two varieties of antisemitism in Christian circles: an "allowable, politically objective" antisemitism and an "impermissible, un-Christian, racist-nationalist" variety. This line of argument could be found among Protestants, too, and it was also the view of the Hungarian Jesuit Bela Bangha, expressed in an essay on Catholicism and Judaism in 1934. He, as a Christian, rejected the "so-called racist antisemitic view" but at the same time voiced the conviction that the workings of Marx, Trotsky, and Bela Kun, the Hungarian revolutionary, had to "be credited to the account of Jewry!" (in Rogalla von Bieberstein 2002, 265).

This fatal attribution of collective guilt entrenched itself among the Nazis all the more firmly because of attempted communist uprisings in Germany and Austria between 1919 and 1923. At least in part, these events were managed and their "Jew-Terror," holding them responsible for millions of Russian dead. The prominence and radicalism of Jewish revolutionaries in Russia and the West translated into an extraordinarily poisonous, murderous, and *new* kind of antisemitism; this was the judgment of many contemporaries, including middle-class Jewish observers. A *völkisch* (racist-nationalist) leaflet that emerged directly out of the revolutionary turmoil of 1919 in Munich expressed this view, with typical brutality: "Bolshevism is the doing of the Jews [*Judensache*]. There could be no Bolshevism without Jews"(a similar message is reproduced in facsimile in Rogalla von Bieberstein 2002, plate VII).

Another book of the same period and milieu, little known today, was Georg Schott's *Volksbuch vom Hitler* (Hitler Primer [1924]). Therein, the talk was of a "Jewish-Marxist revolution." Theodor Fritsch's *Handbook of the Jewish Question* provided the axiomatic definition of Bolshevism—a "Jewish movement." Substantiation for these views was supplied by Henry Ford as well as the so-called Elders of Zion. Schott quoted from Hitler's statement at his trial for treason in 1924, in which he spoke of Germany's future and the "annihilation of Marxism" and went on to speculate in macabre fashion about what a "final solution [*endgültige Lösung*] of the Jewish Question" might look like. In the 1933 reissue of the book, Schott reiterated his 1924 comment that many people imagined such a solution would involve a "Jew-pogrom of enormous scope."

Hitler's dogmatic belief in Judeo-Bolshevism is often undervalued as a motive for his demonic and pathological Jew-hatred. It ought not be, for it helped legitimate an unprecedented genocide. Nazi antisemitism drew from two polluted wellsprings—an inherited racist, radicalized Jew-hatred and a fanatical antagonism toward Marxism and Bolshevism. When these two came together, they engendered a murderous dynamism.

In the West, the myth of Judeo-Bolshevism gradually lost some of its intensity after 1917. For the National Socialists, however, thanks to the Stalinist terror, it retained its vitality long enough to be put in service as a pretext for the war of conquest in the East. Although the Nazis registered their approval of Stalin's show trials of the 1930s as "Jew-Purges," the war against the Soviet Union in 1941 was nevertheless still a "crusade" against Jewish Bolshevism. Thanks to the firmly ingrained and well-developed myth, the regime's war propaganda could, with some degree of success, make a quasi-moralistic appeal to middle-class and religious elements in and beyond Germany.

—*Johannes Rogalla von Bieberstein*
Richard S. Levy, translation

See also Belloc, Hilaire; *Dearborn Independent* and *The International Jew;* Ford, Henry; Freemasonry; *Handbook of the Jewish Question;* Hitler, Adolf; Hungary; Jesuit Order; *Protocols of the Elders of Zion;* Purges, Soviet; Rosenberg, Alfred; USSR; Webster, Nesta

References
Gerrits, André. "Antisemitism and Anti-Communism: The Myth of 'Judeo-Communism' in Eastern Europe," *East European Affairs* 25 (1995): 49–72.
Meyer zu Uptrup, Wolfram. *Kampf gegen die "jüdische Weltverschwörung": Propaganda und Antisemitismus der Nationalsozialisten 1919 bis 1945* (Berlin: Metropol, 2003).
Muller, Jerry Z. "Communism, Anti-Semitism and the Jews," *Commentary* 86 (August 1988): 28–39.
Rogalla von Bieberstein, Johannes. *"Jüdischer Bolschewismus": Mythos und Realität* (Dresden, Germany: Edition Antaios, 2002).

Jung, Carl Gustav (1875–1961)

Carl Gustav Jung was a Swiss psychiatrist and the founder of analytical psychology. From 1907 through 1912, Jung maintained close professional and personal ties to Sigmund Freud, the founder of psychoanalysis. Accusations of anti-Jewish prejudice on Jung's part first surfaced shortly after his break with Freud in 1913. The bitterness of their final rupture deeply wounded both men and continued to fuel their professional rivalry for many years. Freud himself appears to have been among the first to accuse Jung of prejudice against Jews.

Although Freud's motives may be questioned, the criticism surrounding Jung's conduct in the 1930s cannot be so easily dismissed. Of particular concern are Jung's comments on racial psychology and his conduct as president of the General Medical Society for Psychotherapy.

Jung's theories elaborating a collective unconscious with a racial component first appeared in the period following his break with Freud. In *The Role of the Unconscious,* completed in 1918, he discussed the psychological differences between Christians and Jews. Even though Jung's racial psychology predated the emergence of National Socialism, the congruence of his ideas with Nazi racial ideology won him the admiration of many in the movement. When Nazism triumphed in Germany—and given the heavy Jewish presence in modern psychotherapy—opportunities for Jung's personal advancement naturally presented themselves.

In June 1933, five months after Hitler assumed power, Jung was elected president of the International General Medical Society for Psychotherapy, an organization founded in Germany to promote psychotherapy as a profession. With its largely German membership, the young society faced the loss of intellectual independence and indeed the possibility of extinction at the hands of the Nazis. Jung's predecessor, Ernst Kretschmer, had resigned as president rather than endure the forced alignment of the organization with the National Socialist political agenda. Evidence suggests that the society's membership viewed Jung as a more viable candidate because the Nazis would find his theories more acceptable; thus, the organization might escape further political interference.

For his part, Jung did not fail to see the threat to the nascent profession posed by the Nazi regime, and he therefore sought to limit German power within the organization. His strategy was to reconstitute the society as an international umbrella organization encompassing separate and largely autonomous national groups, the largest and most influential of which was the German. From the start, Jung adopted a moderate stance vis-à-vis the German branch, seeking cooperation with its powerful and politically connected leader, Matthias Göring (a cousin of Hermann Göring). Although Jung's actions may be defended as necessary for the survival of the organization, his cooperation allowed the German group to function as an ideological arm of the regime while maintaining its international connections and credentials.

Perhaps most controversial in assessing Jung's attitude toward antisemitism was his role as editor of the society's official journal, the *Zentralblatt für Psychotherapie* (Psychotherapy Bulletin). The December 1933 issue, the first under his stewardship, stated his position on politics and methodological diversity. Though vowing to remain impartial, Jung acknowledged that his policy would distinguish between Germanic and Jewish psychological theories. He further declared that such differentiation could only prove beneficial to the profession. It has been argued by Jung's defenders that such a statement was merely pragmatic, but it signaled an ominous shift in editorial direction that grew more pronounced in later issues. To make matters worse, Jung's essay appeared alongside a call by Matthias Göring for the psychotherapists to support the Nazi agenda.

Jung's conduct provoked an international furor. Responding to his critics in 1934 and throughout the remainder of his life, he denied that he had ever made value judgments about Jews and pointed out that his conception of racial psychology predated Nazi ideology by many years. Thus, he argued, he had not attempted to curry favor with the regime, as his detractors maintained. Noting the common threat of persecution faced by all psychotherapists, he insisted on the importance of his actions to the survival of the profession.

Jung's defense of his actions strikes many as disingenuous. It is impossible to know with certainty what his true intentions may have been, but his conduct betrayed a disturbing lack of moral awareness and a degree of professional opportunism. But did this constitute antisemitism? Jung, it should be said, was no mere pawn of the Nazis. His growing and open criticism of the regime diminished his influence within the organization and led to his withdrawal from participation in 1940. His departure cleared the way for the German branch to seize control of the organization, turning it into a blatant tool of Nazi ideology.

—*Laura Higgins*

See also Freud, Sigmund; Psychoanalysis
References
Cocks, Geoffrey. *Psychotherapy in the Third Reich: The Göring Institute* (New York: G. P. Putnam's Sons, 1985).

———. "The Nazis and C. G. Jung." In *Lingering Shadows: Jungians, Freudians, and Anti-Semitism*. Edited by Aryeh Maidenbaum and Stephen A. Martin (Boston and London: Shambhala Publications, 1991), 157–165.

Grossman, S. "C. G. Jung and National Socialism," *Journal of European Studies* 9 (1979): 231–259.

Justinian Code (*Corpus Iuris Civilis*)

Justinian I, Roman emperor in the East from 527 to 565, was devoted to the church. The first book of his Justinian Code (*Corpus Iuris Civilis*) appeared in 534 and was dedicated to problems arising from religions. Most of the statutes hostile to Jews and their religion are found in two chapters of the first book: "On the Jews and Caelicolae" (1.9) and "That neither Heretic, Pagan, nor Jew May Own or Circumcise a Christian Slave" (1.10). After the publication of the code, Justinian took up the subject of the Jews again in his *Novellae* (New Constitutions), especially in N. 45 (537) and N. 146 (553).

In his Digest 48.8.11, circumcision was allowed only for Jews by birth but prohibited for proselytes and slaves. Judaism ceased to be a permitted religion, although some Jewish practices were still allowed. The purpose of this and other legislation was to induce Jews to convert to Christianity and to show Christians the superiority of the church over the synagogue. Meanwhile, conversion to Judaism was punishable by death and confiscation of the offender's goods (Code 1.7.1, 1.7.5, 1.9.12). Jews who stoned Jewish converts to Christianity were condemned to be burned alive (C. 1.9.3), and Jewish law could not be applied in matters of matrimony (C. 1.9.7). The Constitution in Codex 1.9.8 established that

Jews, who live under the Roman common law, shall address in the usual way the courts in those cases which concern their superstition as well as those that concern courts, laws and rights and all of them shall accuse and defend themselves under the Roman laws. Indeed, if some of them shall deem it necessary to litigate before the Jews in a common agreement in the manner of arbitration and in civil matters only, they shall not be prohibited by public law from accepting their verdict. The governors shall even execute their sentences as if arbiters were appointed through a judge's award.

This precept meant that it was no longer an obligation to settle religious issues judicially. At the same time, however, the parties to a dispute were permitted to turn to rabbinical courts, should they mutually agree to do so. Jews were excluded from holding administrative and honorary offices as well as from municipal dignities and legal practice (C. 1.9.19, 1.9.18, 1.4.5 pr., 2.6.8). Justinian also altered the date of Passover so that it did not fall before the Catholic Easter (Procopius, *Historia arcana*, 128, 16–18).

Of special importance was the emperor's *Novella* 146, *De Hebraeis* (On the Hebrews) dating from 553, in which the Jewish service in the synagogue came under state regulation. For example, the Bible could still be read in any language, provided it was understandable to the listeners, but the emperor recommended the Septuagint (preferred by the church). For the first time, an attempt to proscribe the study of the Talmud became a matter of law; Justinian forbade the reading of the Mishnah, or the Oral Law in general, which he considered a human invention that distorted the Scriptures. Rabbis were thenceforth forbidden to punish unobservant Jews. Thus, *De Hebraeis* clearly signified a further restriction of the legal autonomy in purely religious matters that Jews had once enjoyed.

The change in terminology from the pagan to the Christian period is also much in evidence elsewhere in the Justinian Code. During the pagan era, the customary formula describing the Jewish religion was "the national laws, customs and beliefs of the Jewish people." Derogatory Christian formulations, now fully embraced by the law, referred to Jews and Judaism as "superstitious beliefs, law and worship," "the evil sect whose contact defiles," "enemies of Roman laws," and "the evil of mankind." The dogmatic position of the church was now anchored in Justinian's legislation. It combined a modicum of toleration for some aspects of Jewish worship with a large measure of persecution. The *Corpus Iuris Civilis,* the legacy of the Roman Empire, established the basic framework of Jewish status in the Middle Ages.

—*Alfredo Mordechai Rabello*

See also Circumcision; Constantine, Emperor; Gregory the Great, Pope; Roman Empire; Theodosian Code

References

Rabello, A. M. "The Legal Condition of the Jews in the Roman Empire." In *Aufstieg und Niedergang der Römischen Welt* (Berlin: Walter de Gruyter, 1980), 13: 662 ff.

———. *Giustiniano, Ebrei e Samaritani alla luce delle fonti storico-letterarie, ecclesiastice e giuridiche.* 2 vols. (Milan, Italy: Giuffré, 1987–1988).

———. *The Jews in the Roman Empire: Legal Problems, from Herod to Justinian.* Variorum Collected Studies Series (Aldershot, UK: Ashgate, 2000).

K

Kallay, Miklós (1887–1967)

The son of a long-established, landholding gentry family, Miklós Kallay was a close friend, trusted confidant, and ideological confrere of his political patron, Adm. Miklós Horthy, regent of Hungary. Kallay was a dedicated patriot and a staunch anticommunist whose political career was noted initially for its pragmatism, especially with regard to his policies toward Germany.

Appointed prime minister by Horthy in March 1942, at the peak of Germany's military fortunes, Kallay at first maintained his predecessors' prowar policy. But the destruction of Hungary's army in the USSR (in January 1943) and Germany's great debacle at Stalingrad (in February 1943) led Kallay, with Horthy's support, gradually to extricate Hungary from the Axis alliance.

The Kallay-Horthy compact's prime objective was to keep Hungary free from both Nazi and Soviet domination. As Germany's military position deteriorated, Kallay's emissaries in neutral countries initiated secret negotiations with the West. In September 1943, a confidential provisional armistice was signed with Great Britain. Hungarian units remained detached from frontline duty in the USSR. Apart from neutral countries, Hungary remained the only European state free of German forces. By year's end, Hungary had become a de facto nonbelligerent.

Despite intense local antagonism, Kallay also confronted pro-Nazi influence in domestic politics. He allowed the Left greater room to maneuver; in December 1943, fifteen officers (including three generals) considered responsible for civilian atrocities in occupied Yugoslavia were brought to justice—the first war crimes trial of World War II. Pressure on the Jewish community was eased, and in spite of Germany's dogged insistence, Kallay refused to implement the Final Solution in Hungary.

During Kallay's premiership, Hungarian Jewish citizens retained freedom of domicile and movement and remained free of the yellow star, the terror of arbitrary arrest, and summary deportation; Jews also sat in the upper house of parliament and continued to be able to support themselves, within the legal restrictions imposed on them. Ironically and perhaps tragically, Miklós Kallay was so successful in maintaining Hungarian independence and safeguarding the country's Jews that Hungarian Jewry fell into the trap of considering itself secure in an island sanctuary, isolated and insulated from the fate of other Jews under Nazi rule or influence.

Considering the pressures under which the prime minister operated, there were most probably unavoidable negative aspects to his premiership. As a cover for his overall anti-Nazi strategy, Kallay considered it essential to make strictly limited concessions to the rampant ultra-Right. Unfortunately for Hungarian Jewry, his concessions—including financially discriminatory legislation and tolerance of virulent Judeophobia—reinforced preexisting populist opinion as to the legitimacy of anti-Jewish propaganda, which further heightened expectations regarding the need to solve the so-called Jewish Problem. With the German occupation of Hungary in March 1944, Kallay's government was replaced by a militantly collaborationist, pro-Nazi regime. On the brink of defeat by the Allies, Hitler's war against the Jews—the only war he was still capable of winning—had marched into Hungary.

—*Tom Kramer*

See also Horthy, Miklós; Hungary; Hungary, Holocaust in; Judeo-Bolshevism; Szalasi, Ferenc

References

Braham, Randolph L. *The Politics of Genocide: The Holocaust in Hungary.* 2 vols. (New York: Columbia University Press, 1994).

Kramer, T. D. *From Emancipation to Catastrophe: The Rise and Holocaust of Hungarian Jewry* (Lanham, MD: University Press of America, 2000).

Sakmyster, Thomas. *Hungary's Admiral on Horseback: Miklos Horthy, 1918–44* (New York: Columbia University Press, 1994).

Kant, Immanuel (1724–1804)

Historians Jacob Katz and Paul Lawrence Rose have argued that Immanuel Kant was a fervent antisemite. Kant's contemporaries would probably have been astounded by this claim, for he was a man who regarded Moses Mendelssohn as one of his closest intellectual friends, had a number of Jewish students (with whom he maintained lifelong friendships), opposed linking citizenship to religion, and responded warmly to a group of Jewish disciples attempting to reform Judaism by embracing the moral teachings of the Gospel—stripped of Christian theological doctrines—along with the Torah.

Philosopher Immanuel Kant. There is some reason to suspect that when Kant engaged in anti-Jewish rhetoric he was trying to divert attention from the Judaic strains in his own thought. (Library of Congress)

Kant did, however, make some antisemitic remarks in his correspondence, notably when, addressing Solomon Maimon's response to his work, he wrote that "Jews always like to gain an air of importance for themselves at someone else's expense." He also characterized Jews in his *Anthropology* as a "merchant people" whose main principle was to get the better of others in business; he described Judaism in his *Religion within the Limits of Reason Alone* as a law rather than a religion; and he expressed his approval of the reformed Judaism mentioned earlier, by saying, in his *Conflict of the Faculties,* that it would lead to "the euthanasia of Judaism."

So, was Kant an antisemite or not? His remarks alone cannot tell us much. Casually contemptuous remarks about Jews and Judaism were part of the conversation of practically everyone at that time. Even Gotthold Ephraim Lessing (1729–1781), the greatest philosemite of the eighteenth century, wrote in his "Education of the Human Race" that the rabbis promoted "a petty, crooked, hairsplitting understanding" of texts and imparted a corresponding character to

the Jewish people (section 51). Moreover, for all that Kant welcomed the movement to include the Gospels within Judaism, he did not advocate the conversion of Jews to Christianity proper, and indeed, he called it an advantage of this movement that it "would leave the Jews a distinctive faith" (Kant 1992, 95). The remark about the euthanasia of Judaism, horrifying as it is in the light of later German history, did not give any approval to the euthanasia of Jews as *people.* Rather, Kant looked forward—explicitly and in that very passage—to a euthanasia of all specific religious faiths, including all Christian ones, in favor of a universal moral religion that would substitute good works for rituals and doctrines.

Finally, there is, if anything, a Judaic rather than an antisemitic cast to Kant's thought as a whole. Four important themes run through his philosophy:

1. Neither God's existence nor anything about God's nature can be an object of knowledge.

2. The basis of morality is adherence to a law, not any kind of sentiment, including love.
3. Religion can be approved of rationally only to the degree it sees moral action as the service of God: neither faith in a theory about God's nature nor rituals of any kind can possibly be essential to religion.
4. Human beings are fully capable of being good on their own. "Original sin," insofar as one wants to retain that notion, must be understood simply as the strong temptation within us to violate the moral law, not as a blemish that our free will can never overcome.

These beliefs cohere much better with Jewish rather than Christian views. Maimonides (1135–1204) had already articulated the first of Kant's themes, and this theme along with the third deprive us of any reason to believe in doctrines such as the Incarnation and the Trinity, without which Christianity ceases to be interestingly distinct from Judaism. The second and fourth themes represent views of morality that Jews had long maintained *against* Christian beliefs.

There is, therefore, some reason to suspect that when Kant engaged in anti-Jewish rhetoric, he was trying to divert attention from the Judaic strains in his own thought. In any case, it is easy to see why Kant was so attractive to such modern Jewish philosophers as Samson Raphael Hirsch, Hermann Cohen, and Martin Buber. Kant was for them what Aristotle was for Maimonides—far and away the most important influence on their thought. This attraction of Jews to Kant does not by itself dispel the attribution of antisemitism. But together with the fact that Kant maintained friendly and respectful relations with many Jews he knew, it should lead us to treat that attribution with some skepticism.

—*Samuel Fleischacker*

See also Dohm, Christian Wilhelm von; Emancipation; Fichte, J. G.; Hegel, G. W. F.; Herder, J. G.; Lavater, Johann Kaspar; Michaelis, Johann David; Philosemitism; State-within-a-State

References

Kant, Immanuel. *Conflict of the Faculties.* Translated by Mary J. Gregor (Lincoln: University of Nebraska Press, 1992).
Katz, Jacob. *From Prejudice to Destruction* (Cambridge, MA: Harvard University Press, 1980).
Low, Alfred D. *Jews in the Eyes of the Germans* (Philadelphia: Institute for the Study of Human Issues, 1979).
Rose, Paul Lawrence. *Revolutionary Anti-Semitism in Germany* (Princeton, NJ: Princeton University Press, 1990).

Khomeini, Ayatollah (1902–1989)

Ayatollah Ruhollah Musavi Khomeini was the founder and supreme spiritual guide of the Islamic Republic of Iran from 1979 until his death a decade later. His success in toppling the secularist pro-Western and pro-Israeli Pahlavi Shah was arguably the single most important inspiration for militant Islamist movements in the last two decades of the twentieth century. Though he was a cleric of the minority Shi'ite sect of Islam, many of the principal themes of his message resonated among fundamentalist Sunni Muslims as well. The ayotallah's regime also made use of Iran's oil wealth to subsidize Islamic revivalist and revolutionary movements throughout the world.

As with other contemporary theoreticians of Islamic revivalism, there was an antisemitic strain in Khomeini's thought, despite claims by both the ayatollah and his followers that he was only anti-Zionist and not antisemitic. In his writings, the words *Jew, Zionist,* and *Israeli* were often used interchangeably. In his book *Vilayat-i Faqih: Hokumat-i Islami* (The Trusteeship of the Jurisconsult: Islamic Governance), he reiterated the traditional Muslim legal position that *dhimmis* (members of the koranically recognized religions, which include Jews) were entitled to protection if they paid the *jizya* (poll tax) and accepted Islamic suzerainty, but he also specifically singled out the Jews as both historical and contemporary enemies of Islam. In the book's foreword, he stated: "The Islamic movement was afflicted by Jews from its very beginnings, when they began their hostile activity by distorting the reputation of Islam, and by defaming and maligning it. This has continued to the present day." Classical tropes of European antisemitism were also absorbed into Khomeini's thought. He described Jews as predatory exploiters who had spread throughout Iran and had gained control of its markets. Khomeini viewed the Arab-Israeli conflict as a war of all Muslims together against the Jews and their leaders. His book *Tujah Isra'il* (Confronting Israel), published in Arabic in 1977, made no distinction between Jews and Israelis. In an act rich with symbolism, Yasir Arafat, the first foreign leader to visit the newly established Islamic Republic of Iran, was publicly embraced by the ayatollah, and the Palestinian Liberation Organization was given the former Israeli diplomatic headquarters in Tehran.

In the wake of the revolution establishing the Islamic Republic, there was a bipolarity in the attitude toward and treatment of Iranian Jews that reflected the ayatollah's own schizophrenic views on the subject. Bahá'is, whose religion is not recognized by Islam, were persecuted as Zionist henchmen or as crypto-Jews. A number of Jewish communal leaders were arrested in 1979, and ten, including Habib Elghanian (the former president of the Anjoman Kalimian, the national association of Iranian Jewry), were executed on charges ranging from treason, drug trafficking, and "connections with Israel" to "corruption on earth" and "warring against God" (the latter two being koranic formulations). Several hundred more Jews were imprisoned. The community as a whole, however, was not subject to outright persecution, and institutions such as synagogues, Jewish schools, and the Anjoman Kalimian continued to function, although in a state of constant fear and under close government scrutiny. The cognitive dissonance between Khomeini's assurances that dhimmis were entitled to full rights and protection and that they need not fear for the future and the relentless demonization of Israel, Zionists, and Jews by the ayatollah and the Iranian leadership resulted in the flight of more than three-fourths of Iran's 80,000 Jews.

—*Norman A. Stillman*

See also Arafat, Yasir; Iranian Revolution; Islam and the Jews; Islamic Fundamentalism

References
Abrahamian, Ervand. *Khomeinism: Essays on the Islamic Republic* (Berkeley and Los Angeles: University of California Press, 1993).
Algar, Hamid, ed. and trans. *Islam and Revolution:*

Writings and Declarations of Imam Khomeini (Berkeley, CA: Mizan Press, 1981).
Lewis, Bernard. *Semites and Anti-Semites: An Inquiry into Conflict and Prejudice* (New York and London: W. W. Norton, 1986).
Stillman, Norman A. "Fading Shadows of the Past: Jews in the Islamic World." In *Survey of Jewish Affairs, 1989.* Edited by William Frankel (Oxford: Institute for Jewish Affairs and Basil Blackwell, 1989), 157–170.

Kielce Pogrom (1946)

On July 4, 1946, the deadliest pogrom of the post–World War II era took place in the provincial capital of Kielce District in southeastern Poland. At the beginning of the war, the town of Kielce had a population of 28,000 Jews. Only 400 of them survived the Holocaust or returned there by 1946. In the space of a few hours on July 4, 36 Jews, most of them living in a single house on Planty Street in the center of town, were shot or beaten to death by townspeople, militiamen, police, and workers from nearby factories. The overall number of victims may have been as high as 42.

The reasons for the carnage are, half a century later, still a matter of serious disagreement. Many key pieces of evidence have been lost or purposely destroyed, although important new sources of information have become available since the fall of the Communist regime in 1989. Among the many hypotheses proposed to account for events in Kielce, the most credible are antisemitism and provocation on the part of the authorities. The events contained many elements of provocation by default—for example, the passive attitude of local law enforcement and special forces, especially the head of the Security Agency (Urzad Bezpieczenstwa). This official passivity, combined with a mood of antisemitism that was strongly present in the Kielce region before and after the war, may have given the green light to rioters. Moreover, the Kielce violence was not an isolated event in postwar Poland. Other physical attacks and some deaths took place in the months after the end of the war.

The immediate cause of the pogrom was also deeply rooted in antisemitism, as well as in actions undertaken by the militia and regular soldiers. The disappearance and reappearance of a nine-year-old boy who, probably to avoid punishment, told his parents of being taken to a cellar by a mysterious gentleman immediately stirred up familiar legends of Jewish ritual murder among the adults. The rumors of the "kidnapping" and allegations of other missing children flew about the town, spread with the help of militia patrols and townspeople.

The pogrom began in the late morning after soldiers and the police entered the house on Planty Street. Jews were ordered to surrender their weapons. When some of them apparently did not comply, the killing began, spreading beyond the original site into the rest of the town. The events in Kielce accelerated the emigration of the remnant of Polish Jewry; the number of departures in the months immediately following the pogrom rose manifestly. Jews no longer felt safe in Poland.

The Kielce pogrom also had weighty effects within Polish society and government. Major political powers felt called on to speak out. Once order was restored, government authorities hastily put many of the perpetrators on trial; in the first show trial, full of irregularities, nine defendants received death sentences. The Communists, in an attempt to solidify their growing power in Poland, tried to use the incidents in Kielce to discredit the anti-Communist opposition—by having the world see their enemies as barbaric pogromists. Members of the opposition, meanwhile, accused the Communists of actually inspiring the pogrom to divert international attention from a recent national referendum, the results of which they had undoubtedly faked in their own favor. The independent examination of the pogrom, demanded by the opposition, was subverted by government censorship and police agencies. Within the still influential Catholic Church, many positions taken with regard to the pogrom: unanimous condemnation of the violence; contextualization of the Kielce events in the political situation of postwar Poland; and authentication of the "ritual cause," the kidnapping of children by the Jews. After 1989, a special historical commission was set up to investigate the happenings; it has yet to clarify all the circumstances surrounding the Kielce pogrom.

—*Bożena Szaynok*

See also Hlond, August; Jedwabne; Judeo-Bolshevism; Poland; Purge of 1968; Ritual Murder (Modern)

References

Engel, D. "Patterns of Anti-Jewish Violence in Poland, 1944–1946," *Yad Vashem Studies* 26 (1998): 43–85.

Szaynok, Bozena. *The Pogrom of Jews in Kielce, July 4, 1946.* (Warsaw: Bellona Publishing, 1992).

Kishinev Pogrom (1903)

An anti-Jewish riot, or pogrom, occurred in the Russian city of Kishinev, in Bessarabia Province (present-day Chisinau, Moldova), between April 6 and 8, 1903 (April 19 to 21 on the Western calendar). A total of 51 persons perished during the violence, 49 of whom were Jews. Approximately 500 were injured, and 700 homes and 600 businesses were vandalized. Damages were estimated at 2 million rubles. The pogrom acquired worldwide notoriety as a symbol of Russian mistreatment of the Jewish population. It engendered political action among Russian Jews and inspired classic literary works. The Kishinev events also spawned several enduring myths.

The pogrom began on the Russian Orthodox Easter. A climate of ill will had been created in the city by a blood libel (ritual murder accusation) in the nearby town of Dubossary and the virulently antisemitic reporting of the local paper, *Bessarabets,* edited by Pavolaki Krushevan. Although Kishinev was a provincial capital and a garrison town, the local civilian and military authorities failed to act in timely fashion or to coordinate their efforts. (The governor, R. S. von Raaben, was made the scapegoat for these failures and dismissed from office.)

The principal myth surrounding the events at Kishinev was the belief that the pogrom was planned or at least tolerated by the Russian authorities, at either the local or national level. The involvement of national authorities seemed to be confirmed when the the *Times* of London published a dispatch said to have been sent to von Raaben by V. K. Pleve, the minister of internal affairs. The dispatch was dated twelve days before the events, and it appeared to confirm that the authorities were expecting a pogrom and that they were instructing the local authorities not to undertake energetic measures to suppress it. In fact, the Pleve Dispatch was probably a forgery, although it apparently reflected official disdain for the safety of the Jews. The second myth surrounding Kishinev was the extreme violence that characterized the pogrom, including mutilations, decapitation, and mass rapes, and the extreme passivity of the Jewish population in the face of it. Although most deaths were the result of beatings, the lurid description of the accompanying atrocities were greatly exaggerated. Moreover, the Jews mounted efforts at self-defense.

The Kishinev pogrom did much to discredit Russia in the eyes of the outside world. Within Russia, it proved a valuable mobilizing tool for political activists of all persuasions. Liberal critics of the regime, such as S. M. Dubnow, helped to organize a collective letter to Jewish communities, urging Jews to discover self-respect and undertake self-help and self-defense. The Social Democratic Jewish Workers' Bund also advocated self-defense and claimed credit when Jews offered armed resistance to a pogrom in Gomel (Homel), in Mogilev Province. later that summer.

The Hebrew poet Khaim Nakhman Bialik composed two poems devoted to Kishinev. The first, "On the Slaughter," could be viewed as a bitter appeal for vengeance: "Fit Revenge for the spilt blood of a child / The devil has not yet compiled." The second, "The City of Slaughter," became a classic of modern Hebrew literature. The poem invoked the image of a powerless Jewish God and, on a superficial level, appeared to condemn the cowardly lack of resistance to the pogrom on the part of Kishinev Jews: "Crushed in their shame, they saw it all / They did not stir or move." Others interpreted the poem as an ardent call for Jews to discover their national self-worth. The pogrom also inspired a celebrated piece of journalism, "House No. 13," by the Russian writer Vladimir Korolenko.

—*John D. Klier*

See also Krushevan, Pavolaki; Pogroms; *Protocols of the Elders of Zion;* Ritual Murder (Modern); Russia, Revolution of 1905

References

Judge, Edward H. *Easter in Kishinev: Anatomy of a Pogrom.* (New York: New York University Press, 1992).

Klier, John D., and Shlomo Lambroza, eds. *Pogroms: Anti-Jewish Violence in Modern Russian History* (Cambridge: Cambridge University Press, 1992).

Kladderadatsch

The illustrated satirical-political weekly *Kladderadatsch* (meaning "loud noise" or "explosion" in north German dialect) was founded in Berlin during the 1848 revolution and made its mark by fully and caustically supporting its liberal, democratic, and national aims. It was begun by David Kalisch, a Jewish tradesman by profession who became acquainted with Karl Marx, Heinrich Heine, and other German emigrants in Paris. He made a name for himself with humorous, rhymed parodies and satires (known as *Posse*), often in the local Berlin dialect. These skits were performed on the vaudeville stage and often sported unmistakably Jewish figures, such as bankers or *Ostjuden* (eastern European Jews), who frequently spoke in corrupt, Yiddish-tinged German while commenting on current political, social, and cultural affairs. As of 1849, Kalisch shared the editorship of the *Kladderadatsch* with Ernst Dohm, a former student of Protestant theology; Rudolf Löwenstein, who was also Jewish, was a frequent contributor; the house graphic artist was Wilhelm Scholz, and the publisher was the Catholic Albert Hofmann. The first three, all of whom came from Breslau as young men, were commonly known as "the wise men" of the *Kladderadatsch.*

Even though Kalisch and Löwenstein later converted, the three wise men were often identified as Jews, an identification that was not detrimental at the time. *Judenwitze* (Jewish jokes) and Jewish stock figures, such as the banker "Zwickauer" who spoke a mixture of Yiddish and German, continued to be mainstays of the fare offered by the *Kladderadatsch* during the first and most successful generation of its existence. Subscriptions rose from between 2,000 and 3,000 in 1849 to approximately 20,000 in 1852; subscribers numbered 36,500 in 1861 and 40,000 in January 1870, representing a larger circulation than the leading dailies of that time and equaling that of its competitor, the *Fliegende Blätter*. The number of subscribers held steady through the 1870s but began declining by the mid-1880s when editorial policies underwent significant changes.

An 1863 observer noted that:

Kladderadatsch is clearly the most widely read of German papers, but has simultaneously the most corrupting influence, because it drags down into the mud even the most noble subjects due to its characteristically caustic Jewish jokes. The paper is proud of attacking each and every single authority in the state; it swarms full of insults, all under the guise of making jokes. . . . The owner of the paper, Hofmann, has attained unimaginable wealth thanks to such measures, and attainment of wealth is the only object of his efforts, even when he cursorily participates in furthering a Jewish-democratic movement. This is attended to in an excellent manner by the three primary contributors of the paper, all of whom are Jews. (in Schulz 1975, 215; translated by the author)

In the late 1870s, the *Kladderadatsch* commented on the rise of Court Chaplain Adolf Stoecker's antisemitic agitation and on Heinrich von Treitschke's fulminations in its characteristically mordant style, poking fun at both. But editorial policies, particularly vis-à-vis antisemitism, soon changed, registering the effects of Otto von Bismarck's abandonment of his liberal allies in the Reichstag and his turn toward conservative politics. The journal became decidedly antisemitic only after its founders and mainstays had passed away, retired, or been replaced by a new generation of contributors.

This explicit support of antisemitic causes may well have contributed to the decline of the *Kladderadatsch,* which slowly but surely lost its influence as well as its readership. During the Weimar era and in the Third Reich, circulation dwindled to approximately 10,000. Revealingly, the *Kladderadatsch* lost ground to two rival Berlin satirical weeklies, both of which continued in the footsteps of the best traditions of the original *Kladderadatsch. Berliner Wespen* and *Ulk* employed talented and well-integrated Jewish humorists, capable of dispensing "Jewish" jokes to an appreciative German audience—once the hallmark of the *Kladderadatsch.*

—*Henry Wassermann*

See also *Angriff, Der;* Caricature, Anti-Jewish (Modern); *Fliegende Blätter; Gartenlaube, Die;* Heine, Heinrich; *Simplicissimus;* Stoecker, Adolf; *Stürmer, Der;* Treitschke, Heinrich von
References
Allen, Ann Taylor. *Satire and Society in Wilhelmine Germany: "Kladderadatsch" and "Simplicissimus," 1890–1914* (Lexington: University of Kentucky Press, 1984).
Schulz, Klaus. *"Kladderadatsch": Ein bürgerliches Witzblatt von der Märzrevolution bis zum Nationalsozialismus, 1848–1944* (Bochum, Germany: Brockmeyer, 1975).

Kolbe, Maksymilian (1894–1941)

A Franciscan friar, Maksymilian Kolbe earned a Ph.D. from the Gregorian University in Rome in 1915. With some other young friars, he founded the society of the Knights of the Immaculate in 1917, and he received a degree in theology in 1919. He returned to Poland after independence and founded a proselytizing monthly newspaper, the *Knight of the Immaculate,* which ultimately reached a circulation of 750,000. In 1927, he established the monastery and publishing house of Niepokalanów, near Warsaw. Between 1930 and 1936, he served as a missionary in Japan, founding a branch of his order in Nagasaki and a Japanese edition of his newspaper.

The *Mały Dziennik* (Little Daily) began publishing in 1935, in Kolbe's absence; the inexpensive paper soon became the largest-selling daily in Poland. By 1939, Niepokalanów had become the world's largest Catholic monastery, housing 700 friars and novices, and it operated a short-wave radio station in addition to its extensive publishing concern. When the war broke out, these operations were shut down, and the friars turned to social work. Kolbe was imprisoned by the Nazis and released in 1939, then arrested again in 1941 and sent to Auschwitz. There, he offered himself in place of a married prisoner who was to be executed as a hostage, and he died in the camp's punishment barracks. He was canonized in 1982.

The Niepokalanów newspapers conformed to

the usual Catholic views of the time, sometimes publishing extremely antisemitic articles. Although Kolbe's defenders claim that he did not exercise editorial control and did not share these opinions, a recently published selection of his writings attributes some of the articles to him. In one of them, he described the Jews as the hidden force behind Freemasonry, which he called "the army of the Antichrist."

—*Steven Paulsson*

See also Antichrist; Freemasonry; Poland
References
Modras, Ronald. *The Catholic Church and Anti-Semitism: Poland, 1933–1939* (Chur, Switzerland: Harwood Academic Publishers, 1994).

Konitz Ritual Murder (1900)

On March 11, 1900, in the town of Konitz in West Prussia, a vicious murder of an eighteen-year-old boy occurred, letting loose a storm of accusations that the local Jews had committed a ritual murder of a Christian. Hostile feelings gathered force in the following months, culminating in the largest outbreak of antisemitic violence in Wilhelmine Germany.

Despite the brutality of the crime (the body had been cut to pieces and its parts distributed around town), the killer was never found. But as the parts seemed expertly cut, local people as well as the Berlin police suspected a trained butcher. Two butchers lived near the supposed scene of the crime: Gustav Hoffmann, a Christian, and Adolph Lewy, a Jew. The Berlin police suspected Hoffmann, whereas most of the townspeople presumed the perpetrator was Lewy. When police interrogated Hoffmann, violence broke out.

The violence was based on popular belief in the blood libel—that Jews kill Christians (preferably boys) around Passover, drain them of their blood, and use the blood in the baking of matzah. A tenacious tale, the blood libel had its Christian origins in the High Middle Ages; subsequently embellished by centuries of antisemitic writings, it still held people in its grip in the year 1900. In Konitz, the editor of a Berlin antisemitic newspaper, the *Staatsbürgerzeitung*, further fanned local superstitions and helped the Christian butcher write his accusation of the Jewish butcher. This accusation drew on the rumor and gossip of the streets, as Christian neighbor denounced Jewish neighbor for murderous complicity in an alleged Jewish plot. The town—comprising roughly 10,000 inhabitants, mostly German-speaking, half Protestant, half Catholic, with approximately 300 Jews—became polarized. Violence ensued; it involved rock throwing, beating the houses of Jews with sticks, and the shouting of "Jews out" and "Beat the Jews to death." In Konitz and the towns around it, some thirty antisemitic riots occurred, culminating in the ransacking of the synagogue in Konitz and an attempt to burn it down. Although these riots only involved isolated cases of physical abuse of Jews, they were not quelled until early June, when the Prussian army marched into town to restore order. As this occurred, people in Konitz and the surrounding towns denounced the army as a "Jewish defense force."

Bright moments did exist in what seemed like the recrudescence of medieval darkness. Many, though not all, of the Berlin inspectors dismissed the ritual murder tale as ludicrous, and many, but again not all, of the Prussian officials sought to uphold law and order and protect the Jews. In addition, some local citizens stood up against the contagion of rumor and denunciation. Finally, although the killer was never found, the authorities tried a number of people for perjury, including early accusers of Adolph Lewy.

The Konitz case was the last major outbreak of the ritual murder accusation in Germany before the advent of Nazism. It therefore serves as a turn-of-the-century barometer for antisemitic beliefs and their potential for turning Christian citizens against their Jewish neighbors.

—*Helmut Walser Smith*

See also Antisemitic Correspondence; Antisemitic Political Parties; Polná Ritual Murder; Ritual Murder (Medieval); Ritual Murder (Modern); Xanten Ritual Murder
References
Smith, Helmut Walser. *The Butcher's Tale: Murder and Anti-Semitism in a German Town* (New York: W. W. Norton, 2002).

Kosher Slaughtering

Debates about how to kill livestock were widespread in late nineteenth-century Europe and

North America. Animal protectionists—the main initiators of these debates—demanded that butchers be better trained, that preparations and killing techniques be improved, and most important, that all livestock be stunned before slaughter (either with a hammer or a shooting mask). One particularly controversial issue was the practice of *shehitah* because it prohibited such stunning procedures.

The term *shehitah* refers to the traditional Jewish method of slaughtering animals in order to render them kosher. The practice of shehitah had been implemented in ancient times to guarantee the bloodlessness of meat and to protect animals from unnecessary suffering. Closely regulated by the laws of the Talmud and Shulcan Aruch, shehitah requires special preparations (a benediction), tools (the *halat* knife), procedures (cutting and bleeding), and an expert butcher (the *Shohet*). The most important aspect of this procedure was the complete drainage of blood, which, according to ritual, could only be accomplished if the animal's muscle functions and vital organs were intact. This, in turn, required that the animal not be stunned. Although many animal protectionists considered this practice inhumane, Jewish officials argued that it was no crueler than other forms of butchering and that it was, moreover, a religious rite.

Debates about the humanity of shehitah occurred in Switzerland (the first country to make stunning mandatory, in 1854), England, France, the United States, and many other nations, but they were most pronounced in late nineteenth-century Germany, where they coincided not only with the political emancipation of Jews but also with the rise of political antisemitism. It is difficult to assess to what extent antisemitic sentiments played a role in the arguments of animal protectionists, but the controversy clearly took on antisemitic overtones in Germany once it entered the Reichstag in the mid-1880s. For the antisemitic Reichstag deputies Otto Böckel and later Max Liebermann von Sonnenberg, shehitah provided a perfect pretext for expressing their anti-Jewish sentiments while hiding behind an alleged concern for the humane treatment of animals. Claiming that shehitah was a cruel and uncivilized practice, the antisemites in the Reichstag demanded that Jews abandon this practice if they wanted to be part of German society. Most other politicians, especially the Catholic Center Party leader Ludwig Windthorst and the Social Democrat Wilhelm Liebknecht, rejected these arguments, insisting that religious freedom had to be guaranteed because it was one of the principal rights of German citizens, including Jews. The increasingly antisemitic nature of these debates became obvious in the 1890s when the antisemites repeatedly attempted to put the issue on the Reichstag agenda, only to have their efforts immediately rejected by the majority. Similar proposals in the state parliaments of Baden and Bavaria also went down to defeat. The only exception was in the Kingdom of Saxony, where a law that made the stunning of all livestock mandatory remained in effect from 1892 until 1910, when it was repealed.

By 1900, the debate about shehitah had all but disappeared from the official political arena, yet it continued in some radicalized animal protection organizations and scientific publications. During the Weimar Republic, the issue remerged wherever the Nazi Party gained sufficient political clout. Shortly after rising to power in 1933, the Nazis passed a new slaughter law that effectively outlawed the practice of shehitah. Similar laws were passed in Norway (in 1929), Poland (in 1936), Sweden (in 1937), Hungary and Italy (in 1938).

—*Dorothee Brantz*

See also Böckel, Otto; Center Party; Dietary Laws; *Kulturkampf;* Lieberman von Sonnenberg, Max; National Socialist German Workers' Party; Nazi Legal Measures against Jews; Nazi Party Program; Social Democratic Party; Weimar

References

Berman, Jeremiah. *Shehitah: A Study in the Cultural and Social Life of the Jewish People* (New York: Bloch Publishing, 1941).

Brantz, Dorothee. "Stunning Bodies: Animal Slaughter, Judaism, and the Meaning of Humanity in Imperial Germany," *Central European History* 35, no. 2 (2002): 167–194.

Kralik, Richard von (1852–1934)

Richard von Kralik, prolific writer, polemicist, and implacable, if subtle, antisemite, settled in

Vienna in the early 1870s. The son of an affluent Bohemian crystalware manufacturer, Kralik was independently wealthy for most of his life. Even as his fortunes declined, he continued to write and to conduct his cultural crusades through radically changing circumstances. Indefatigable, he was writing until a few days before his death.

Having established himself in one of Vienna's most fashionable districts by the 1890s, Kralik held forth as a guru of cultural conservatism and the main attraction of what was perhaps the capital's last literary salon. His followers, who for a time consisted of some of Vienna's high society, continued to perform his plays and readings for more than forty years after his death.

A muddled racialist rather than a racial essentialist, Kralik became most strident in his antisemitic polemics following World War I. The Oberammergau Passion Play, which he attended in the early 1880s, may have stimulated his brand of antisemitism, which was energized by his religiosity. The dramatization of Christ's betrayers embodied what Kralik deemed "essentially Jewish traits" and would, in any case, have appealed to his warped romanticism. During the political upheavals in 1919, Kralik blamed the Jews for the revolutions in eastern Europe and for much of the general decay of European civilization. As a remedy, he sought to reopen "the traditional wells of European culture" through a synthesis of Germanic paganism, Greco-Roman literature and architecture, and religiously inspired Christian arts. Kralik was viewed by his followers as a bulwark against modern evils: naturalism in drama and literature, abstraction in art, and anarchy in politics. During the 1920s and 1930s, he received prestigious awards and honors from the Viennese Social Democratic municipality and national republican leadership—ironically, because Kralik was both antirepublican and antisocialist.

Apart from his condemnation of the "Jewish-inspired" decay of European culture and politics, Kralik was also highly critical of postwar politics in general. He loathed Woodrow Wilson ("Professor Wilson") as the personification of Western democracy and the source of Austria's problems. Though he respected Benito Mussolini for restoring "order" in Italy, he ridiculed Hitler as a mis-guided upstart who had left his homeland to stake out a career in Germany (even though Kralik himself was an émigré from Bohemia). Following the annexation of Austria in 1938, he was posthumously hailed as a prophet of the new German Reich.

As a déclassé member of the late Austrian imperial and then republican cultural elite, Richard von Kralik embodied the complex hatreds and frustrations of many like himself who blamed traditional scapegoats for unprecedented problems that they but dimly understood.

—*Richard S. Geehr*

See also Austria; Bettauer, Hugo; Judeo-Bolshevism; Oberammergau Passion Play
References
Geehr, Richard S. *The Aesthetics of Horror: The Life and Thought of Richard von Kralik* (Leiden, the Netherlands: Brill, 2003).

Kraus, Karl (1874–1936)

Born a generation after Sigmund Freud, Karl Kraus was perhaps best known in Vienna during the years leading up to World War I. He is remembered for his unrelentingly bitter and barbed criticism of the fin-de-siècle bourgeois culture during Vienna's twilight years. Kraus's first pamphlet, *Die demolierte Literatur* (Literature Demolished [1897]), written after Vienna's famous literati coffeehouse Café Griensteidl was torn down, owed its success to his bold lampooning of lionized authors such as Arthur Schnitzler, Hugo von Hofmannsthal, and Hermann Bahr.

Kraus's position vis-à-vis Vienna's bourgeois culture was as complex as his own sense of Jewishness. Brought up in the Jewish faith, he formally renounced his connection to Judaism in 1899. But the year before taking this step, his pamphlet *Eine Krone für Zion* (A Crown for Zion) had already bitterly attacked Thedor Herzl and the Zionist program and clearly embraced assimilation. His personal solution to the identity dilemma experienced by a great many in Vienna's acutely fractionalized Jewish population was to shed Jewishness in favor of universalist humanistic ideals. His goal as a moralist and as a satirist was to transcend racial and social barriers and to present his world as an ethical unity. But the break was never clean or total. Kraus's conflicted and vehement repudiation of his Jewish identity surfaced in many of the satirical writings and polemics he published in his influential journal *Die Fackel* (The Torch). In 1912, he took the next step, formalizing his connection to Vienna's dominant culture by freely (but privately) accepting baptism and entering the Catholic faith. He remained in the church until 1923, when he renounced his religion once again. In Vienna, the pressure on Jews to convert was very intense. Many, particularly those connected to the city's upper bourgeoisie, bowed to the pressure in order to further their careers. Gustav Mahler would probably have never become the director of the Vienna Opera or the Hamburg Opera had he not accepted baptism.

Kraus's conversion has been seen by some as an attempt to overcome the overt antisemitic realities of his day; others saw it as an eventually unsatisfying attempt to achieve personal redemption. Most commonly, Kraus is numbered among the "self-hating" Jews. Categorizing him in this way is problematic, however. His hatred was not so much directed at Judaism per se but rather at the overwhelming presence of Jewish individuals in the commercial and financial spheres of Vienna, especially in the world of journalism. Kraus abhorred the blatant commercialization of all aspects of modern life and reveled in publicly ridiculing individuals he saw as crass exploiters of human affairs. Prominent Jewish entrepreneurs often took the brunt of these venomous attacks, which made abundant use of antisemitic clichés and hateful stereotypes. From 1899 to 1936, Kraus was able to draw from the deep well of his anger to fill the pages of *Die Fackel.*

—*Istvan Varkonyi*

See also Austria; Herzl, Theodor; Schnitzler, Arthur; Self-Hatred, Jewish; Zionism
References
Fischer, Jens Malte. *Fin de Siècle: Kommentar zu einer Epoche* (Munich, Germany: Winkler Verlag, 1978).
Timms, Edward. *Karl Kraus: Apocalyptic Satirist* (New Haven, CT: Yale University Press, 1986).

Krushevan, Pavolaki (1860–1909)

The antisemitic writer, journalist, and parliamentarian Pavolaki Krushevan was born in the Russian province of Bessarabia (present-day Moldova), where he made an early career as a novelist and contributor to periodicals of a liberal orientation. In 1896, he founded the daily newspaper *Bessarabets* (The Bessarabian) in the provincial capital of Kishinev (present-day Chisinau). Krushevan soon dropped the paper's initial liberal editorial outlook, turning to the advocacy of crude, reactionary politics and making antisemitism a principal ingredient of the paper's journalism. Krushevan blamed Jews for all the ills, economic and social, of the region. In early 1903, the paper carried extensive and provocative articles about a blood libel (the claim that the Jews kidnapped and murdered Christian children to use their blood for ritual purposes) in the nearby town of Dubossary. Krushevan and *Bessarabets* were widely blamed for creating the climate of interethnic hostility that led to the notorious Kishinev pogrom in April 1903. In retaliation, a young Zionist, Pinkas Dashevskii, attacked Krushevan on a St. Petersburg street in June 1903, lightly wounding him. After a sensational trial, Dashevskii was sentenced to five years at hard labor (but amnestied in 1906).

Krushevan lost control of *Bessarabets* in 1906, but he published other newspapers—*Drug* (Friend), in Kishinev between 1905 and 1914, and *Znamia* (The Banner) in St. Petersburg. The latter newspaper published the first Russian version of the notorious antisemitic forgery known as the *Protocols of the Elders of Zion,* in 1903.

Krushevan was among the founders of a militantly antisemitic political party, the Union of the Russian People, and was elected to the Russian parliament, the Second State Duma, on its electoral list in 1907. He had a brief and undistinguished parliamentary career but remained an antisemitic agitator until his death in 1909.

—*John D. Klier*

See also Black Hundreds; Kishinev Pogrom; *Protocols of the Elders of Zion;* Ritual Murder (Modern); Russia, Imperial; Zionism
References
Cohn, Norman. *Warrant for Genocide: The Myth of the Jewish World Conspiracy and the "Protocols of the Elders of Zion."* New ed. (London: Serif, 2001).

Judge, Edward H. *Easter in Kishinev: Anatomy of a Pogrom* (New York: New York University Press, 1992).

Ku Klux Klan (1915–1941)

Our usual images of the Ku Klux Klan (KKK) involve terrorist night riders in the post–Civil War South or the hooded figures of hate who tried to stop the modern civil rights movement during the 1950s and 1960s. By sheer numbers, however, the largest Klan in U.S. history thrived during the Roaring Twenties.

This "second Klan" was immensely powerful—and in places with which it is not typically associated. Klan members took over the legislatures or governorships of states with low minority populations, such as Indiana, Colorado, and Oregon. Overall, an estimated 2 million Klansmen—and thousands of Klanswomen—put on white hoods and set crosses ablaze.

The fiery rebirth of the second Klan occurred in 1915 at Stone Mountain, Georgia, outside of Atlanta, following the opening of D. W. Griffith's *Birth of a Nation*. The virulently antiradical political environment in the years after World War I nurtured its rapid growth. Part fraternal lodge, part political organization, the Klan reached its peak in most states during the early 1920s. By the end of the decade, its influence had radically declined, in part, because of strong opposition but also and especially because of internal feuds and the exposure of considerable corruption.

The second Klan differed from its predecessor and successor both in its mass popularity and in its methods and goals. At times, the second Klan engaged in racist terrorism. Yet violence of this sort was relatively infrequent; commercial boycotts of Catholics and "non-Aryans" were more common than lynchings. Indeed, this Klan saw itself—and operated during this conservative decade—as a mainstream urban political movement. Prohibition, the suppression of vice, the inculcation of a hyperpatriotism, and the enforcement of other white Protestant moral "values" were its primary purposes.

KKK members specifically targeted bootleggers and adulterers, but they also and more generally saw immigrants, Catholics, blacks, and Jews as enemies. Especially in the North and West, anti-Catholic sentiment was one of the chief mobilizing forces of the organization. Antisemitism, however, was never far from the surface. Klan members regarded Jews as too cosmopolitan to be patriotic and too cohesive to be public-spirited. Jews were deemed responsible both for bolshevism and the worst excesses of international banking. They were "vermin," "scum," and bent on "world domination" (Maclean 1994, 135).

The banality of the Klan's antisemitism did not make it any less powerful, however. In conjunction with the rise of other forces of hate during the period, such as Henry Ford and his *Dearborn Independent,* the Klan helped make the 1920s one of the most antisemitic decades in U.S. history. In the end, though, the organization's excesses also helped to discredit Jew-hating. Since its demise, no American organization as popular as the Klan has adopted antisemitism as a core value.

—*Robert D. Johnston*

See also Banker, Jewish; *Dearborn Independent* and *The International Jew;* Duke, David; Judeo-Bolshevism; Militia Movement; United States; White Power Movement

References
Blee, Kathleen M. *Women of the Klan: Gender and Racism in the 1920s* (Berkeley: University of California Press, 1991).
Jackson, Kenneth T. *The Ku Klux Klan in the City, 1915–1930* (New York: Oxford University Press, 1967).
Maclean, Nancy. *Behind the Mask of Chivalry: The Making of the Second Ku Klux Klan* (New York: Oxford University Press, 1994).

Kulturkampf

The *Kulturkampf* (struggle for civilization) is the name commonly given to a series of repressive measures that Prussia, as well as other German states, directed against the Catholic Church in the 1860s and 1870s. When the church resisted these measures, bishops, priests, and Catholic politicians were interned. In a narrow sense, the Kulturkampf was a political struggle between church and state. From a wider perspective, it involved a conflict between German liberals, the most enthusiastic supporters of the repressive measures, and Ultramontane Catholicism, predicated on the antimodern postulates of the First Vatican Council. In this wider sense, the Kulturkampf was also a European phenomenon.

Within the political culture of German Catholicism, the Kulturkampf represented an early high-water mark of Catholic antisemitism, as many Catholic leaders accused liberal Jews of supporting Kulturkampf legislation. The accusation, however, was largely misplaced. Although some Jews supported the repressive measures, most did not, including prominent Jewish delegates to the Reichstag. The more general association of Jews with liberalism also aroused Catholic ire. In pamphlets and popular newspapers and during elections, Catholics rarely tired of depicting Jews as urban liberals, rapacious capitalists, and enemies of Christianity. If these sentiments rarely shaded into racial antisemitism in the Kulturkampf era, they were nevertheless harsh enough.

During the Kulturkampf, prominent Catholic politicians—Ludwig Windthorst, the leader of the Catholic Center Party, foremost among them—attempted to quiet the simmering antisemitism among their constituents. On the floor of the Reichstag and in the corridors of power, Windthorst was largely successful. But within the popular culture of Catholicism, antisemitism ran deep and was nurtured by the perception of Jewish responsibility for the Kulturkampf. Moreover, this antisemitism did not dissipate after the Kulturkampf came to a close in 1878, when Otto von Bismarck and Pope Leo XIII were able to reach a diplomatic accord. Instead, antisemitism lingered and rendered Catholics vulnerable to an unfettered populist politics, with starker antisemitic tones, in the years that followed. This was true in the Rhineland, where the Xanten ritual murder case of 1891 and 1892 was nourished by antisemitic agitators; it was also true in Bavaria in the 1890s, where peasant parties, less shy about their antipathies toward Jews, mounted serious challenges.

The situation can be attributed, in part, to the deep wells of popular piety, partly in the wide field of Catholic politics in Europe. The Kulturkampf, in the sense of a conflict between liberalism and Ultramontanism, was waged across Europe, and in the 1870s, other Catholic leaders, notably in France and Austria, also resorted to antisemitic politics. Insofar as German Catholics were part of this wider struggle, their antisemitism, a reflex of their still deeper antiliberalism, became an important part of their political identity. But unlike Catholics in France and Austria, Catholics in imperial Germany, like Jews, remained a vulnerable minority. Their political leaders therefore urged circumspection at a time when antisemitism ran full gallop elsewhere.

—*Helmut Walser Smith*

See also Boniface Society for Catholic Germany; Center Party; Memminger, Anton; Papacy, Modern; Ratzinger, Georg; Ritual Murder (Modern); Ultramontanism; Vatican Council, First; Xanten Ritual Murder

References

Blaschke, Olaf. *Katholizismus und Antisemitismus im Deutschen Kaiserreich* (Göttingen, Germany: Vandenhoeck and Ruprecht, 1997). Mazura, Uwe. *Zentrumspartei und Judenfrage, 1870–1933: Verfassungsstaat und Minderheitenschutz* (Mainz, Germany: Matthias-Gruenewald, 1994).